PILGRIMAGE FOR PEACE

UN Photo 169681 / J. Isaac. March 1987

PILGRIMAGE FOR PEACE

A Secretary-General's Memoir

Javier Pérez de Cuéllar

St. Martin's Press
New York

Portions of chapter 1, "Thoughts Still on My Mind," originally appeared in "Reflecting on the Past and Contemplating the Future," by Javier Pérez de Cuéllar, in *Global Governance: A Review of Multilateralism and International Organizations,* volume 1, no. 2. Copyright © 1997 by Lynne Reiner Publishers, Inc. Reprinted with permission of the publisher.

ISBN 0-312-16486-6

Library of Congress Cataloging-in-Publication Data
Pérez de Cuéllar, Javier, 1920-
 Pilgrimage for peace : a secretary-general's memoir / by Javier
 Perez de Cuéllar.
  p. cm.
 Includes bibliographical references and index.
 ISBN 0-312-16486-6 (alk. paper)
 1. Pérez de Cuéllar, Javier, 1920- . 2. United Nations—
Biography. 3. Statesmen—Peru—Biography. I. Title.
D839.7.P47A3 1997
929.82'8'092—dc21
 [B]   97-9798
                                                         CIP

Design by Acme Art, Inc.
First edition: September 1997
10 9 8 7 6 5 4 3 2 1

For Marcela

Loving companion along the way

CONTENTS

LIST OF MAPS

All maps reproduced by permission of the United Nations.

FOREWORD

These memoirs provide a personal account of events with which the United Nations was concerned during the ten years, from 1982 to 1992, that I served as United Nations Secretary-General. They are not intended to be a comprehensive history of all that was done by the United Nations during those years. That is the subject matter of many other books. I have concentrated on those developments in which I had the largest personal involvement. For this reason much is described in terms of the role that I played.

I would not wish this to obscure the contribution made by the members of my staff. My actions, the decisions I reached, reflected the advice and hard work of Secretariat personnel, especially the members of my immediate office and the heads of the various departments, and of the United Nations Children's Fund (UNICEF), the United Nations Development Program (UNDP), the United Nations Population Fund (UNFPA) and other functional programs that are so important to the enhancement of human security. They were directly engaged on my behalf in mediation and conflict management and in the provision of humanitarian and economic assistance in every country and region in which the United Nations was involved. As my chef de cabinet, Virendra Dyal kept the events and personalities of these years in remarkable order and unfailingly saw to it that the full resources of the United Nations were available as needed in meeting the wide-ranging tasks that world conditions imposed on the Organization.

The United Nations Secretariat frequently has been maligned as incompetent, overpaid, lazy and even corrupt. None of this is true. The Secretariat is composed of gifted and committed people—sometimes overqualified for the work they are assigned—who for the most part work hard in pursuit of the goals of the United Nations Charter and in fulfillment of the tasks laid down by Member States. In the past some staff members retained an overly close connection with their national governments. Some governments, in turn, were not reluctant to place pressure on me and on my staff in pursuit of their national interests. But with few exceptions, Secretariat personnel retained the impartiality that is the duty of an international civil servant.

Coming from more than 150 countries, staff members represent highly disparate work cultures and management styles. A very few, as in any bureaucracy, followed a personal culture of minimum work and maximum privilege. On the whole, however, the remarkable thing is how well this widely diverse staff functions within the framework of bureaucratic procedures that follow largely American models. To my knowledge, no international crisis has been the result of Secretariat incompetence. The staff, which has never been large and which was reduced in the aggregate by some 17 percent during my tenure, never failed to meet the demands that were placed upon them, and some of these demands were new and onerous. As a group, the Secretariat has my admiration and gratitude.

For exceptional assistance in the preparation of this book, I am deeply indebted to James Sutterlin. Having worked closely with me in the United Nations, in the most constructive way, Jim was able to put my thoughts and experiences into words and find ways of bringing into understandable context the vast range of actions in which I was involved. Without his work, this book, the drafting of which was largely in his hands, would not have been possible.

I am grateful, also, to Alvara de Soto, Hedi Annabi, Giandomenico Picco, Issa Diallo, Hisham Omayad, Benon Sevan, Francesc Vendrell, Jean-Claude Aimé and Lisa Buttenheim, who helped me to recall people and events and the context in which they figured and who reviewed with helpfully critical attention the portions of the manuscript covering subjects with which they were familiar. Issa Diallo had prepared his own account of developments in Africa, which he generously made available for my use. I wish also to thank Miklos Pinther, chief of the Cartographic section, Department of Public Information, United Nations, for his generous assistance with the maps.

Given the fallibility of memory, a book of this nature requires extensive documentary research. Jean Krasno, Rafael Bonoan and Ann Gilbert went through the thousands of documents in my personal and official files, identified the important ones and put them in substantive and sequential order. Rafael Bonoan sketched out a first draft of the chapter on Afghanistan. Liisa Fagerlund, the Chief of the UN Archives Section, and her staff were unfailingly cooperative in making available all the archival resources of the United Nations. Jennifer Thomas willingly helped to find material that remains in the files of the Secretary-General's Office. Sheila Klein put the manuscript of this book into final form with incomparable skill and patience. Finally I wish to express my appreciation to Yale University under whose auspices this book was written. The unfailing support and the hospitable and scholarly environment afforded by International Security Studies and UN Studies at Yale, where Jim Sutterlin is a Distinguished Fellow, was invaluable throughout the duration of time that these memoirs were in preparation.

REMINISCENCES AND REFLECTIONS

In recalling for the purposes of these memoirs the events of my ten years as Secretary-General, I was brought inevitably to reflect on the nature and the record of the organization that I served and on experiences that color even now my memories of things past. In these first chapters I am recording these random reflections and reminiscences, along with a few details of my earlier life, as an introduction to the more structured description of conflicts and crises that follows. With this background, the reader may better judge the role that the United Nations and its members and the Secretary-General have played in world affairs during the memorable decade of the 1980s and even before.

ONE

THOUGHTS STILL
ON MY MIND

THE YEARS SINCE THE FOUNDING OF THE UNITED NATIONS have been years of fundamental enlargement of human expectations, a development that was encouraged by the principles and purposes enunciated in the United Nations Charter. Self-determination met the desire of hundreds of millions of people for independence and an opportunity to be free. Cooperation in solving economic, social and humanitarian problems led, for the first time in human history, to the production of enough food to feed the world's inhabitants, if not, unfortunately, the means to get it to the millions of people in need. Advances in medicine answered the hopes for healthier births and longer lives while sociologists, scientists, economists and doctors have together produced the means to stabilize the vast increase in the number of persons born with the legitimate expectation to share in the world's bounty. For the first time since writing was invented, the majority of human beings can read and write. The hopes of women for equal status in society as promised in the UN Charter are slowly being met albeit with setbacks along the way.

Developments such as these, if seen in the perspective of the half century of the United Nation's existence or even of the decade when I was Secretary-General, show clearly that this has been a time of unparalleled human advancement, something often obscured by the perils that have accompanied it. Yet human expectations exceed what has been accomplished, and understandably so. Most of humanity still lives in poverty. Millions of people are driven from their homes by forces over which they have no control. Devastating diseases remain unconquered, and human excesses threaten the environment on which all depend. In an era of instantaneous communication and global transparency, people even in the most remote countries know that these conditions can be improved. There will be conflict in the world until human aspirations, spurred by the demonstrated potential of ever-improving technology, are met in far fuller measure than is now the case. In thinking of the tasks that face the United Nations in the next years, this reality must be faced.

Despite its sometimes image of stodginess, the United Nations has been the groundbreaker and mobilizer in movements for the control of nuclear and chemical weapons, protection of the environment, population planning and sustainable development. The extent to which the UN-defined universal norms bring closer to realization a just and equitable world is hard to quantify. But I am certain that they have had a constructive effect. Who can deny that the instruments on human rights developed in and promoted by the United Nations have inspired broader respect for, and understanding of, human rights? There is much that is controversial about the United Nation's record of promoting economic and social development, but it is incontestible that the development assistance provided by UN functional agencies has brought progress in human well-being. The vast humanitarian assistance, the improvements in health care, the support for millions of refugees are all examples of UN achievements that have made a difference in the lives (and the life expectancy) of millions of people. As I have thought of my years in office, now free from the distorting influence of daily crises, it has become clear to me that these have been signal contributions to a better world. I say this even while knowing full well that the performance of the United Nations in some of these areas has left much to be desired.

THE UNITED NATIONS AND ECONOMIC DEVELOPMENT

Coming from the Third World, I was especially unhappy during my ten years as Secretary-General with the failure of the United Nations to work as a system more effectively for economic and social development within the framework of commonly agreed goals. I was disappointed that the United Nations could not bring more constructive dialogue between developed and developing countries. This was primarily because the North and the South hold conflicting views on the most effective means to achieve development. The developed countries resisted any approach that called for a mass transfer of resources without assured control over their utilization. The developing countries tended to seek progress through grandiose plans rather than pragmatic incremental steps. This was well illustrated by the call for a new international economic order. I was genuinely sympathetic with the objective of this plan, which was essentially to increase the levels of multilateral assistance and give Third World countries greater control over its flow. But I saw it as unrealistic and overly ambitious. The wealthy countries were clearly not prepared to accept such a broad, seemingly open-ended concept. Nevertheless, endless debate was devoted to this chimera, with the sole result of increasing distrust between North and South.

It can be persuasively argued that, over the years, there has been inadequate leadership on the part of the Secretary-General and the UN Secretariat in placing the United Nations in the forefront of economic thinking. I would not contest this. Neither I nor any of my predecessors was a trained economist. Moreover, the political and administrative demands on the Secretary-General have always come first. As a result, the Secretary-General is heavily dependent on his senior economic advisors to carry the main weight in the economic field. With rare exceptions, they have not had the recognized intellectual authority needed to provide leadership within the UN system or among UN members.

There are also structural weaknesses in the economic field within the UN system. Among its agencies, the World Bank and the International Monetary Fund (IMF) have by far the greatest resources to contribute to global development. They operate as independent institutions, originating and implementing many effective programs. However, in my time these programs were not formulated within the framework of a common strategy in coordination with other parts of the UN system or with the Secretary-General. At times the financial institutions worked at cross-purposes with other UN offices even as they have pursued the common objective of improving present conditions and future prospects within a given country.

The Economic and Social Council (ECOSOC) has never had the authority or the capability to formulate global economic and social policies, nor has it coordinated the activities of the specialized UN agencies such as the World Bank and the International Monetary Fund as foreseen in the Charter. Most of the many recommendations for reform of ECOSOC have come to naught. In my annual report to the General Assembly in 1987, I suggested that it be transformed into a ministerial-level body as a means of enhancing its effectiveness. This recommendation was eventually realized in part. ECOSOC decided to hold a high-level "segment" devoted to a specific subject as part of its annual sessions. The results have not been impressive. I have come to the conclusion that ECOSOC is so redolent of failure as to compromise any prospect of greater effectiveness. The best course would be to start afresh with a new organization having a narrower focus and greater authority.

I found the Administrative Committee on Coordination (ACC), which includes the heads of all the specialized agencies and functional offices in the UN system, hardly more satisfactory than ECOSOC as an instrument for the coordination of system-wide programs, although it is intended to meet, in part, this need. While the Secretary-General serves as chair of this body, the heads of the specialized agencies are not subject to his supervision. They are in no way dependent on the Secretary-General—neither for their selection (or their dismissal) nor for their budgets. It was my custom to open each session with an overview of the international situation in the hope that this would lead to a free discussion of how the various parts of the UN system could work together to alleviate the problems confronting the world community. Such discussion seldom occurred. Generally my presentation was received in respectful silence. Discussion became lively only when purely administrative questions, such as salary levels and the varying conditions for retirement among the agencies, were raised. When planning began for the United Nations, President Franklin D. Roosevelt first suggested that the head of the organization be called "moderator." I often felt, and still do, that this would have been a good innovation. The Secretary-General would be in a stronger position to bring greater coordination among the many agencies and programs of the UN system if he could exercise the authority of moderator vis-à-vis their chiefs.

I must emphasize that such problems as these, which often seemed to me more frustrating than the repeated political crises that I faced, did not prevent the United Nations from making the notable contributions to human well-being that I have listed. What is most remarkable is that these contributions were achieved in a time of political tension and spiraling armaments and despite fundamental disagreements among member states regarding approaches to development and, during most of my tenure, the interpretation of human rights.

THE IMPORTANCE OF NONGOVERNMENTAL ORGANIZATIONS

The experience of these years of economic and social crises in Africa and elsewhere gave me a new appreciation of the crucial importance of nongovernmental organizations (NGOs). Frequently, NGOs were already engaged in providing varied forms of humanitarian aid before assistance of governments and intergovernmental organizations was forthcoming. Organizations such as *Médicins sans Frontière,* Care International, Caritas, Catholic Relief Services, the International Committee of the Red Cross (ICRC), OXFAM and Save the Children, to name only a few, were on the spot, usually with a good knowledge of local conditions and enjoying enviable flexibility of operations and extremely dedicated staffs.

These NGOs have to be seen as partners of the United Nations. I created an interdepartmental committee in the Secretariat in 1983 to maintain close ties with the nongovernmental community and gave instructions that my door should always be open to NGO representatives. I met regularly with the secretary-general of Amnesty International and the president of the ICRC. Before each trip abroad I was briefed confidentially by Amnesty International on individual cases of human rights abuse on which I might usefully intervene. It was my practice to take along a list of such cases on my travels. I would then find occasion to speak in strict privacy with the head of state in the country concerned and ask that he do whatever he could to rectify the abuse. I often found this possible as I walked by a president's side on the way to a ceremonial occasion, or sometimes during an official dinner, hopefully without spoiling my host's appetite. While I kept no records, I estimate that there was a favorable outcome in 90 percent of those cases. I called this my "discretion diplomacy." It was a small but significant indication of the benefit that can accrue to the people of the world from close cooperation between nongovernmental organizations and the United Nations.

COLD WAR FALLOUT

The Cold War slowed the vast changes in the human condition that have marked the post–World War II years, especially by encouraging a huge and unproductive investment of resources in arms; but it could not prevent them. It did, however, cause an ossification of political relationships. When I assumed the post of Secretary-General in 1982, the Security Council had long been largely immobilized. My predecessors and I assumed the lead in trying to resolve conflicts because there was otherwise a vacuum. In rare cases in which U.S.-Soviet rivalry was not a factor, such as the Falklands crisis, I could and did move independently to seek a peaceful solution. Even where this rivalry was a factor, as in Afghanistan, I was able, acting independently from the Security Council (where a Soviet veto had frozen any movement), to facilitate an agreement that brought the withdrawal of the Soviet troops. However, the withdrawal was basically dependent on agreement between the Soviet Union and the United States, and that happened only when the Cold War thawed.

The malevolent influence of the Cold War extended into the Secretariat. Certain influential members of the U.S. Congress, frequently inspired by the neo-conservative Heritage Foundation, acted as if UN Headquarters served mainly as an outpost for the KGB. At the insistence of Congress, the U.S. government imposed severe restrictions on the travel of Secretariat members who were Soviet Bloc nationals. I felt compelled to take serious issue with Washington on this action as it contravened the Headquarters Agreement between the United Nations and the U.S. government. However, I was unable to persuade the United States to withdraw the restrictions.

The Soviet Union, it must be added, provided an unhappy catalyst for some U.S. actions. While I had no way of knowing which Soviet staff members were from the KGB, it was quite apparent that a number of them did not devote all of their time to Secretariat duties. Even worse, the Soviet Union, like all the other then-Communist countries except Poland, required that its nationals in the Secretariat, all of whom were on temporary assignment from Moscow, turn over a substantial portion of their dollar salaries to the Soviet government, thus lending a certain credibility to Washington's claim that American taxpayers were paying for Soviet spies. As long as the Cold War continued, Soviet staff members, whether KGB or not, owed their first loyalty to Moscow rather than to the United Nations. It was expected that any information they obtained would be reported to the Soviet Mission. As a result, and to their understandable frustration, the Soviet nationals in my office were excluded from sensitive functions.

DEALING WITH WASHINGTON

The United States is by any measure the most important member of the United Nations. To a significant extent, the effectiveness of the Organization depends on American leadership and support. For this reason, the critical attitude of the U.S. government and a portion of the U.S. media toward the United Nations during the first years of my tenure was profoundly disturbing. In January 1982, only a few weeks after I became Secretary-General, the U.S. Permanent Representative to the United Nations, Jeane Kirkpatrick, gave a speech at the Council on Foreign Relations in New York structured on four points:

- The United Nations is an important body, worthy of our attention.
- The United Nations is not at all the institution its American founders hoped for.
- The United Nations does not reflect or represent the world in the way representative bodies usually do.
- The great question for the United States and other countries committed to national independence, self-determination and democracy is whether the United Nations can be made a more effective, problem-solving tool that will help to resolve differences rather than exacerbate them.

Mrs. Kirkpatrick then proceeded to answer this question in the negative. The UN process, she said, "breeds polarization."

Such statements by Mrs. Kirkpatrick, of which there were many, were influential in defining the American attitude toward the United Nations during the administration of President Ronald Reagan. This attitude found expression in an ideological distrust of the United Nations as an organization where democracies faced a hostile majority of communist and other dictatorial regimes. In this view, the greater authority the United Nations had, the greater the influence of these undemocratic forces would be in the world. U.S. entanglement in the multilateralism represented by the United Nations would limit American freedom of action and compromise its capacity to defend democracy.

The State Department was required to keep count of the votes in the General Assembly to show which states voted against the U.S. position. These figures confirmed that, in well over half of the votes recorded, a majority in the General Assembly was against the U.S. position. The statistical basis of the State Department's figures was faulty, however, since many resolutions are adopted by the General Assembly by consensus or without a vote. State Department calculations did not take this fact into account. When the Secretariat analyzed the voting record of the General Assembly, including resolutions that were adopted by consensus or without a vote, quite a different picture emerged. On more than half the resolutions, a majority voted with the United States. The Secretariat figures were released to the press. Entirely fortuitously, they were reported prominently in the *Washington Post* on the day Ambassador Kirkpatrick was making a speech concerning the hostile majority in the United Nations. The U.S. side sent word to the Secretariat that publication of the statistics was inappropriate and that the methodology used to obtain them was fallacious.

Such vote counts, no matter how they came out, were hardly meaningful since a country with the power of the United States, having permanent membership in the Security Council, can never be truly isolated or deprived of influence by votes in the General Assembly. The real problem was that the United States was in the minority fairly consistently on three high-profile, recurrent issues: the Middle East; the UN budget, which a number of senators and congressmen contended was out of control; and South Africa. If a General Assembly resolution was highly critical of Israel, the United States and Israel sometimes cast the only opposing votes. The assembly also adopted, by strong majorities, resolutions condemning the U.S. military invasions of Grenada and Panama.

Thus the United Nations could be portrayed by neo-conservatives with considerable influence during the Reagan Administration as a haven for Communist spies, as an institution inherently inimical to American interests and as a profligate organization, badly administered, whose budget was decided by a majority that contributed very little to cover it. I came reluctantly to the conclusion that these forces were aiming at U.S. withdrawal from the United Nations and that there were some within the government who shared this objective.

Given the pivotal U.S. role in the organization, I considered it of the highest importance to counter this attitude and to maintain a positive and constructive relationship with the United States government. There was no subject to which I devoted greater attention or that caused me greater concern during my first term as Secretary-General. In speaking with President Reagan and with Secretary of State Alexander Haig during my first official visit to

Washington in January 1983, I urged that the United States use the United Nations to the fullest effect. I suggested that as an independent Secretary-General, my good offices could serve to prevent conflicts from breaking out and leading to acrimonious debates in the Security Council.

Secretary Haig said the United States did not want to "just go along" with others. It would speak its position clearly when it felt there was a need to do so. Haig thought a "cease-fire" in UN resolutions was desirable. Moreover, the United States was "upset" by the politization in the functional bodies of the United Nations. Nonetheless, the United States remained supportive of the UN system. Its disagreements with the "majority," he said, were because the latter were, on occasion, eroding the system.

Washington's criticism of the United Nations took its most virulent form in the withholding of substantial portions of the assessed U.S. contribution to the regular UN budget and, subsequently, to the peacekeeping account as well. The United States, like all other members, is bound under the Charter to pay its share, as apportioned by the General Assembly, of regular UN expenses. The U.S. assessment was then 25 percent (slightly more for peacekeeping). The United Nations thus is financially heavily (too heavily, I think) dependent on the United States. Due to the U.S. withholdings by the end of 1986 the United Nations was literally on the brink of bankruptcy despite economies that I had introduced that saved approximately $30 million annually. This financial problem was to plague me for the rest of my tenure as Secretary-General. What troubled me most was the potentially weakening effect disregard for a Charter obligation by the country most responsible for drafting the Charter could have on the United Nations. In 1988, when the U.S. debt had reached almost $500 million, I expressed my concern to President Reagan in blunt terms. I stated that the legal obligation of the United States to pay its assessed contribution derives from an international treaty between the United States and the United Nations. I then posed the question: "Will it be said that one legacy of the Reagan Administration will be the destruction of that which Roosevelt started?" The President replied that he was sympathetic and turned the conversation to other subjects.

This was not my first conversation with President Reagan on the United Nations' financial problem. During a meeting in the Oval Office in March of 1986, after the President had greeted me with a genial but unexpected "¿Como está?" he introduced the subject by warning that the United Nations should not get into the same financial condition as the United States. I noted that that depended heavily on the United States and explained the situation as it then existed in some detail. The President responded that, in his opinion, the same system should be followed in the United Nations as in a country club. "If dues are not paid, the member loses his privileges." Ambassador Vernon Walters, who was then the U.S. Permanent Representative to the United Nations, explained that was precisely the system followed in the General Assembly. A Member State that fell more than two years in arrears could lose its voting privileges.

At the end of this meeting, when the conversation turned again to the United Nation's financial problems, President Reagan said that it reminded him of a story. As I might know, he said, he had spent some time in Hollywood. The story was of an underemployed actor and his agent. The actor wished to acquire a certain very beautiful home and asked the agent to look into the possibilities of buying it. After a short time, the agent returned and said that he had both good news and bad news. The good news was that the house was available and that the asking price was only $500,000, which was a bargain. The actor, in high spirits, said that was great and asked what the bad news was. The bad news, the agent replied, was that the owners were demanding $500 as a down payment.

After that, as he graciously walked me to my car, the President told me privately that he would talk to friends on Capitol Hill and see to it that the United Nations received its due. Unfortunately, this did not occur.

President Reagan addressed the General Assembly more frequently than any of his predecessors. He repeatedly expressed American support for the United Nations, as did his Secretary of State, George Shultz. I don't believe that either had an ideological prejudice against it. Neither, however, were they inclined to do battle with those in Congress and in the administration who were hostile to the Organization. I referred to this situation when I wrote in my 1986 Annual Report to the General Assembly that there was the need "for a more vigorous and determined defense of the Organization by those who believe . . . that the safety net which the United Nations constitutes for the world's security should not be allowed to become tattered. The United Nations needs its champions; they must speak more boldly and knowledgeably."

I gained the impression that Secretary Shultz found it tactically useful to remain aloof from controversies in Washington over the United Nations in order to maintain his freedom of action in other areas he considered more important. He appointed Alan Keyes, who as a deputy to Ambassador Kirkpatrick had been outspoken in his criticism of the United Nations, as assistant secretary of state in charge of international organizations and, for a long time, let Mr. Keyes have free rein in his highly vocal and tendentious management of United Nations affairs. When John Whitehead was appointed deputy secretary of state, Secretary Shultz gave him a special mandate to follow UN affairs. With Whitehead's arrival, the situation in the State Department, at least, changed for the better. Whitehead, while critical at times of UN administrative and budgetary practices, was always ready to listen to the United Nation's problems and to do what he could to alleviate them. I found in him the responsive dialogue partner that had been missing in Washington until then. After Whitehead took office, Secretary Shultz confirmed in a letter to me that the United States recognized that it was under a legal obligation to pay its assessed contribution to the regular budget. For his fairmindedness toward the United Nations, John Whitehead quickly became the butt of sharp attacks from the Heritage Foundation (of whose board of directors he had once been a member) and was publicly accused by Alan Keyes of racial discrimination.

I must emphasize that it was possible to work constructively with George Shultz and with his successor, Jim Baker, on the various political problems that we faced while I was Secretary-General. Even when attacks on the United Nations were most intense in Washington, the Secretary of State and the President treated me with respect and consideration. While Shultz never welcomed UN participation in the search for a Middle East settlement and was long reluctant to see UN involvement in the Central American peace process, he freely and generously acknowledge the value of the United Nations in ending the Iran-Iraq war, in facilitating Namibia's transition to independence and in gaining the withdrawal of Soviet forces from Afghanistan. By the end of the Reagan Administration, cooperation between the United States and the United Nations had grown much closer, as if in preparation for the new flowering of the relationship when President George Bush turned to the United Nations as the legitimizing institution for repelling Iraqi aggression against Kuwait and, along with Mikhail Gorbachev, saw the United Nations as central to a new world order. Unfortunately, the more positive U.S. attitude toward the United Nations did not lead to the elimination of American financial arrears. At a meeting in June 1990 covering important substantive issues, President Bush began by saying "I want to tell you of the great embarrassment I feel about the money the United States owes to the United Nations. . . . Great nations, like great men, should keep their word." The President underscored his recognition that the nonpayment by the United States put me, "a friend of long standing," in an extremely difficult position. He welcomed my intention at the time to talk with members of Congress on the problem and said, "The harder you can come down on the need for the United States to keep its commitment, the better."

Despite my direct approaches to senators and congressmen and repeated appeals to the administration, this problem remained unresolved throughout my tenure and was to become even greater for my successor. It remains for me a matter of great regret that I had to devote precious time in almost every conversation I had with Presidents Reagan and Bush to dunning the United States to pay its bills.

FIVE YEARS OF STAGNATION

Politically, the ten years between 1982 and 1992 can be divided into two segments that correspond almost exactly with my two terms as Secretary-

General. The first five years were dominated by the Cold War, which seemed to congeal international relations into a kind of slow-moving glacier that challenged any redirection. The Security Council was largely frozen in its grip. The first thing that I did after being elected Secretary-General was to try to identify in my mind the conflicts and points of tension and to assess the global economic and social situation that I would be concerned with. Looking back, I wonder that I did not find my list more daunting than I did. Most alarming was the situation in East Asia and the Middle East. Iraq and Iran were in the midst of a cruel war that was, in part, a response to the threat perceived by other Islamic countries to the triumph of an evangelical fundamentalist regime in Tehran. A de facto state of war, centered in Lebanon, existed between Israel and the Palestine Liberation Organization (PLO). The Soviet Union was in uncomfortable occupation of Afghanistan. Relations between the Soviet Union and the United States were at a nadir. The African continent was suffering the cruelty of racial oppression in South Africa and lay broadly under the threat of widening postcolonial conflict. Peace in Central America was the victim of social strife and insurgency. Negative growth had set in in South America. In the poorest countries, development was faltering and debts were rising. And casting its ominous shadow over all was the mounting arsenal of nuclear weapons, bearing in them the threat to humanity's very survival.

In September 1982, I began my first Annual Report to the General Assembly with the statement that the past year had seen an alarming succession of international crises as well as stalemates on a number of fundamental international issues. The Security Council seemed powerless to ensure that its decisions were respected. The measures for collective security that were provided in the Charter could not be applied in the divided international community. We were, I warned, "perilously near to a new international anarchy." In retrospect, I have to say that this last phrase, which attracted quite a few headlines, was an overstatement. It ignored the fact that outside the political arena developments were under way that could contribute in the longer term to a more stable world. Governments were beginning to face the need for population planning. The struggle to protect the global environment, which symbolically had begun with the United Nations Conference on the Human Environment in 1972, was gaining momentum. The development institutions of the UN system were beginning to concentrate their efforts on the elimination of poverty.

The beneficial effects that could be expected from these developments in the long term, however, could not lift the pall of immobility that blanketed East-West relations, nor could they alter the fact that the United Nations was not being used for the purpose for which it was created—the resolution of conflict and the maintenance of international security. There was a certain stability in international relations that was imposed by the two superpowers. But it was a fragile and retrogressive stability built on fear and cemented with arms. The time was perilous and wasteful in terms of the world's resources and of the United Nations' potential as an instrument for peace. Those years, in which the world was held politically ransom to the Cold War, should never be looked back on with nostalgia.

As I prepared what I intended to be my last Annual Report in the late summer of 1986, I could not point to a single conflict that had been resolved during the previous five years as a result of the United Nation's efforts. The Security Council remained in a state of stasis. The financial problem of the United Nations had reached a truly critical stage. These were the circumstances that prevailed when I was urged—perhaps pressured would be a more accurate word—by the five Permanent Members of the Security Council to accept a second term in office. When first elected I had said that I would not run for a second term. I did not. I am strongly convinced that a person should never campaign for the position of Secretary-General, because with campaigning come obligations that have to be fulfilled if the campaign is successful. I was not eager to accept a second term, and my wife urged against it in part because I had just undergone triple bypass heart surgery. The surgery had been a complete success, however, and my doctors assured me that my health was good. My health was not an issue one way or the other in my decision to accept a second term.

I suppose, subliminally at least, I was motivated by a desire to accomplish more for world peace than had been possible during my first five-year term. The rational basis of my decision, however, was threefold. First, the reality was inescapable that the United Nations was in a parlous condition, threatened with bankruptcy and facing the certain necessity of severe financial restrictions and staff reductions. It seemed to me disloyal to the Organization not to stay the course and try to bring it to safety. Further, the support extended by the Permanent Members was proof to me that I enjoyed the respect and trust of their capitals even if the United Nations as an organization did not. Most important, there was evidence of a widening constituency of basically pragmatic govern- ments with a clear grasp of the economic and social requirements of a world in which the destinies of all countries were becoming ever more linked. The ideological constraints on more productive relations between the North and the South were loosening. Looking ahead, the emerging characteristics of the future world society strongly suggested the increasing need for effectively structured multilateral cooperation—in other words, for an improved United Nations. This was the strongest motivating factor in my decision to agree to a second term.

A NEW ERA

In 1977 a period began marked by dramatic and profound change, unparalleled in history in their swiftness. The catalytic figure in this transformation of societies and nations was without doubt Mikhail Gorbachev, one of the most impressive leaders I have had the opportunity to deal with. The changes, however, went beyond what any man alone could inspire. Underlying and, in a sense, defining this new era were those human aspirations for freedom and economic progress that in a time of enormous technological innovation were stimulated by the decline of colonialism, by an extraordinary growth in travel—consider only the effect of travel *within* the Communist bloc—and, most of all, by the new global transparency that technology and travel brought with them.

The beginning of this new era was marked by an increased commonality of interests among governments, even those with conflicting ideologies and different economic systems. Common interests became evident in achieving sustainable economic development, preserving a hospitable global environment, eliminating the most egregious infringements of human rights, controlling diseases such as AIDS that respect no national borders and, by no means least, avoiding nuclear destruction. It was this last named, after all, that brought the most opposite of political statesmen, Ronald Reagan and Mikhail Gorbachev, together. These widely shared interests underlay such diverse developments as the loosening of centrally controlled markets, the growth of civic human rights movements in Eastern Europe and the growing pressure against apartheid in South Africa.

I have mentioned that in my first Annual Report to the General Assembly, I warned that the world was near to a new international anarchy. Five years later, in my 1987 report, I found that there was a nascent solidarity among nations in addressing serious problems with global implications. It was as if "the sails of the small ship in which all the people of the earth are gathered, had caught again, in the midst of a perilous sea, a light but favorable wind." If the first was something of an exaggeration, the second turned out, in its prescience, to be a distinct understatement.

While the Cold War came to a symbolic end with the destruction of the Berlin Wall, its decline was first marked in the United Nations by a very cautious new willingness on the part of the United States and the Soviet Union to work together in the Security Council to bring long-standing regional conflicts to an end. This bore fortunate fruit and brought leaders in many capitals, including Washington, to appreciate more fully the value of the United Nations as an essential instrument in conflict resolution. There were remarkable achievements: the end of the war between Iran and Iraq; independence for Namibia; the withdrawal of the Soviet army from Afghanistan; the restoration of an independent Cambodia; the peace process in Central America; and—of a very different nature—the defeat of Iraqi aggression in Kuwait.

The cooperation of the Permanent Members of the Security Council, especially the United States and the Union of Soviet Socialist Republics, was an essential element in resolving all of these crises. It would have been self-defeating hubris to assume that the United Nations or the Secretary-General could independently bring peace in any one of these cases. It was necessary, as it will continue to be, to mobilize the constructive efforts of the Permanent Members of the Security Council, influential regional powers and, in some cases, regional organizations to work in cooperation with the United Nations in bringing a solution. But the United Nations' contribution in each of the cases was central and indispensable.

As I observed the performance of the Security Council during the Gulf War and subsequently in Somalia (largely as an outsider), I perceived that powerful as the Council may seem when the Permanent Members are in agreement, its decisions, to be fully effective, must be perceived by the wider UN membership as justified by the circumstances and objectives. The power at the disposal of the Security Council is the power inherent in the solidarity of nations opposed to the transgression of the United Nations Charter. It is, first and foremost, the power of the principles that the Charter represents. Objective circumstances have not permitted the Council to enforce these principles consistently. To try to do so when the prospects of success are dubious risks the Council's credibility. Yet to apply the principles only when success is assured also can jeopardize the Council's credibility and prestige. My conclusion is that it is better to risk failure than to stand idly by in the face of serious threat to human security. I readily admit that this conclusion is reached more easily in the abstract than in reference to specific conflict situations, more easily stated out of office than in.

THE CHALLENGE OF A CHANGED WORLD ORDER

In one sense the United Nations was well prepared for the end of the Cold War: Its Charter had been written in the presumption of harmony among the major powers. During the last years of my second mandate the representatives of the five Permanent Members of the Security Council adopted the habit of joint consultations with an enthusiasm born of the realization of the power they could exert when acting together. (It also, I suspect, confirmed to all Five that they should never give up the special status of Permanent Member.) As an organization, however, the United Nations was not adequately prepared to implement efficiently Council decisions involving the use of force in internal conflicts. The United Nations lacked:

- Adequate funding, managerial staff and command and control procedures for peace-enforcement operations.
- Guidelines (or precedents) for ending societal disruption and conflict within states.
- Appropriately trained troops in sufficient numbers and with the

necessary equipment to meet the greatly expanded need for peacekeeping and enforcement measures.

- An efficient system for coordinating and integrating the work of the various functional offices and agencies involved in promoting human security where it has been endangered by civil strife or humanitarian crises.

As I considered the action to be taken by the United Nations in the various internal conflicts that arose as the Cold War ended, I felt restricted by the knowledge of these weaknesses. As a graduate in international law, I was schooled in the long-sacred principle of nonintervention in the domestic affairs of states and the sanctity of state sovereignty. I brought these principles, which are an integral part of the United Nations Charter, with me as Secretary-General. The instances faced by the United Nations of civil conflict accompanied by, or stemming from, massive abuse of human rights or humanitarian crises required that these principles be rethought. I did not find this process easy nor am I confident today that the right solution has been found in all cases. It cannot be contested that the first and principal purpose of the United Nations is the maintenance of peace and international security. The Organization is committed both to the sovereignty of states and to the protection of human rights. If peace is now and in the future threatened as much or more by internal strife as by international conflict, then surely the United Nations, in pursuit of its first purpose, must be concerned with internal, civil violence, including the serious infringement of human rights. I have no doubt that a major challenge for the United Nations well into the future will be to find the right balance between respecting, or perhaps redefining, sovereignty and maintaining peace and the security of humankind. I do not believe that the principle of nonintervention in matters that are within the domestic jurisdiction of states can be regarded as a protective barrier behind which human rights can be systematically violated with impunity. The principle of respect for sovereignty would only be weakened if it were to carry the implication that sovereignty in this day and age includes the right of mass slaughter or the launching of systematic campaigns of decimation or forced exodus of civilian populations. The dilemma is that while violations of human rights unquestionably imperil peace, disregard for the sovereignty of states could spell international chaos.

As the great global confrontation between East and West—between communism and democracy—diminished, the problems that must be dealt with in the new era emerged with sometimes daunting clarity. These are the problems inherent in the triangular relationship among development, freedom (democracy) and peace. The three are interdependent. If the United Nations is to lead in the pursuit of peace, it also must be able to promote the growth of democratic societies and encourage the development of economic well-being on which both democratic governance and peace ultimately depend. At the end of my second term as Secretary-General, this is what I saw as the major challenge facing national governments and the United Nations.

TWO

FROM LIMA
INTO THE WORLD

BECAUSE THIS BOOK PROVIDES AN ACCOUNT OF CRISES AND CONFLICTS in the far reaches of the world from my perspective as the Secretary-General of the United Nations, it is no more than fair to provide at the beginning a brief account of how I came to occupy this unique and often misunderstood position. Some familiarity with this background will help the reader to understand the approach that I took to the events of those tumultuous years and to assess the influences at play on my judgment. I start, then, by telling you who I am.

In the old city of Lima, when I was young, there were many shops selling imported goods from faraway lands. Each shop flew the flag of a particular country. With my cousin I would go there and we would count the flags from this country and that. It seemed to me that the flags of all the countries of the world were there except that of the United States of America. For that great country the flag of the Grace Company had to suffice. My cousin and I made of it a kind of game. He favored China and I favored France, and we would see which of the two had the more flags flying.

I always lost. There were many more Chinese merchants in Lima than French. These flags that brightened the old streets of the capital—the only city I had seen—had for me the attraction of an unknown world, an attraction that before too many years had passed would bring me far from the Peru in which I was raised. I cannot say why at that early age, with hardly any knowledge of where France lay on the globe, I felt a particular attraction to the tricolor of that country. It was the beginning of an affinity to French culture that has endured all my life. Perhaps in an earlier existence I was a Frenchman—a musician or an artist, I like to think. But in this life my origins were very different.

I was raised with relatives in a family in which there were three children, two cousins and myself, all very close in age. I felt completely at home in this close-knit household, although neither my father nor my mother was part of it. I never knew the loneliness of an only child. The customs of my family were European. One of our ancestors was an architect who had come from Spain in the sixteenth century to help build the fortifications of Lima. He was the first seed of our Peruvian family tree. Other members of the family had come more recently from Spain. We were a *rentier* family, comfortable but not rich and, naturally, conservative. When, in the school run by Spanish priests that I attended, there were political debates, I always pled the conservative cause. But I do not recall being deeply concerned with Peruvian politics.

I had, in fact, little contact with Peruvian life outside the limited circle of similar bourgeois families and of my schoolmates in the Spanish catholic school. Yet I very much loved my city. When I was 10 or 12 years old I dreamed of one day becoming mayor of Lima. As I grew older what interested me was the history and culture of Peru and, most of all, the world beyond. I collected foreign coins and stamps, learning from the latter the names of the British and French colonies, which at that time were still extensive. We acquired for the household a large and impressive radio, a Grundig, and I listened for hours to all the foreign stations I could find. I still vividly recall hearing Adolf Hitler, whose harangues came through with surprising clarity, perhaps because the Grundig was well attuned to German wavelengths. I could not understand the words but I sensed even then their import of hatred and intolerance that were for me repellent.

I was interested in foreign languages as well, but there my experience was mixed. Oddly, at my Spanish Catholic school English was taught by a Pole whose familiarity with correct English pronunciation was faint at best. I have always, perhaps unfairly, attributed to this good gentleman my own long-standing problems with English. For French, one of my cousins had a private French tutor. I would sit in, uninvited, on her lessons, and when my cousin was attracted to other pursuits I inherited "mam'selle" and made a good beginning in what would be my second language. "Mam'selle" was from Alsace and while her French was excellent, her temperament was distinctly German. When I spoke to her of the German broadcasts we had heated exchanges—in French—as to the merits of Hitler and his Nazi policies.

There was music too in this family house in Lima, a player piano, in Spanish we called it *pianola,* with rolls of Beethoven, Schubert and Chopin that I would play many times over, pumping energetically with my feet at what I hoped was the appropriate tempo. Since then I have always been surrounded with music. In New York I kept three classical music stations on automatic dial and, not infrequently, as I listened to music and pondered in the late evening the intricacies of problems that faced me, I heard, by chance, those melodies still familiar from the *pianola*. So much of what we are in maturity springs from such experiences of youth.

At the university in Lima I studied in two faculties, law and literature, for both of which I have retained throughout my life a strong attachment. When I was barely 20 and still at the university, I wanted to gain some independence so I obtained a job under a student intern program as a clerk in the Peruvian Foreign Ministry. Thus I entered, really unknowingly, the career path that took me eventually to the United Nations. Some of my relatives insist that even as a very young boy, I was the mediator in family quarrels. I suspect this is largely apocryphal, but it is true that it was never my bent to impose my views on others.

During my university years and before, I was a good student in most of my subjects (Latin being the notable exception) but not quite at the top of the class. It has never, I must say, been in my character to be totally immersed in one particular subject. I have always distanced myself from obsession. Detachment is not usually a quality that impels a student to the top of the class, but I would claim it as an advantage as Secretary-General. To be able, like a good chess player, to stand back and see a problem in perspective, to be able to move unencumbered from one issue to another, are certainly desirable qualities for any responsible international civil servant.

A FIRST TASTE OF THE UNITED NATIONS

In my life I have been the frequent beneficiary of good fortune, most importantly to have served as Secretary-General of the United Nations at a time of fortunate change in the relations of nations and in the governance of many. But good fortune began much earlier. Immediately upon completion of my law studies in 1944, at the age of 24, I entered the career diplomatic service as third secretary. A friend of the family was then the deputy foreign minister of Peru, and as I was fluent in French, he arranged that my first diplomatic assignment would be Paris, a prize he had intentionally withheld until I obtained my law degree. World War II was still under way. It was necessary to travel first to New York and wait there many weeks for a Portuguese ship to take me from Philadelphia to Europe, to a Paris still darkened by war. There, finally, I saw in its rightful place the tricolor, so well remembered from the old streets of Lima, flying once again in all its pride.

Scarcely a year after my arrival in Paris, in late 1945 I received instructions to join the Peruvian delegation to the Preparatory Commission of the United Nations, which was then meeting in London to plan the structure of the new world organization. I was almost 26 years old and exhilarated both at the prospect of serving in another of the world's great capitals and of being present at the formative stage of a new organization whose purpose was to preserve world peace. This was my first contact with the United Nations, which had been founded only a few months earlier in San Francisco with a Charter—still largely unchanged until today—that rested squarely on the principles of democracy: freedom, equality, respect for human rights and the rule of law.

In the aftermath of war, there was in London a sense of renewal, of a fresh beginning. I sensed the spirit of hope that pervaded the Commission meetings. Many distinguished world leaders were there as participants working to create a multilateral instrument for peace, conscious of, but undaunted by, the failure of its predecessor, the League of Nations. I was then, as I have always been, a close observer of events and people, even if I sometimes give the impression of one whose mind is elsewhere. My memory is crowded still with the experiences of those days in London, memories in which the trivial is mixed with the significant developments that even now shape the structure and procedures of the United Nations. I remember my surprise at seeing Eleanor Roosevelt, the former First Lady of the United States, casually reading the *New York Times* in the front row of an assembly. I was, obviously, not yet inured to the occasional *langueurs* of even the most important international conferences, nor could I foresee that years later as I sat on the high podium of the General Assembly, I would sometimes be occupied with memoranda and telegrams while below me a national representative spoke. I also recall the lively—even scheming—competition among countries for positions in the various bodies of the new organization. I was astonished at the intrigues of countries that were vying with Peru for membership on the Economic and Social Council, which was limited to 18 states. This kind of "diplomacy" was a new world for me. I followed the decisions on the organization of the Secretariat, on the procedures that would govern how matters of peace and war would be handled in the new organization. I observed too the appointment of Trygve Lie as the first Secretary-General and the interplay of national interests that influenced the process.

It would be pure romanticism to suggest that there in London I had any premonition, or even idle dream, that I might someday fill the same unique position. The reality is that I never thought of becoming Secretary-General and even at the hour of appointment was still surprised that this honor and challenge had come to me. When the work of the Preparatory Commission ended, I returned to my duties in Paris. It would be many years before I again had direct involvement in the United Nations.

STAGES TOWARD AN UNEXPECTED GOAL

My career took me to positions of increasing seniority in London, La Paz and Rio de Janeiro and in the Foreign Ministry in Lima, where I served as head of the Legal, Administration and Political departments as well as chief of protocol (not, I should add, all at the same time). In 1962, I was given my first ambassadorial post, Switzerland. After two years there I returned to Lima to become deputy foreign minister, a post which in Peru is always filled by a career diplomat. Two years later, in 1968, there was a coup d'état. As I was considered too closely associated with the previous regime, I was again sent to the field but this time with a certain amount of drama. The new government decided to establish diplomatic relations with the Soviet Union, a country with which Peru had never had permanent relations even in the time of the czars. This was a major event, and when I was chosen to be Peru's first ambassador I received a great deal of publicity, becoming for the first time something of a public figure in my own country. I arrived in Moscow in the midst of the stultifying atmosphere of the Brezhnev era. Nevertheless I sought to extend the friendship and goodwill of my country independently of ideological considerations. Apparently this made a lasting impression on the Soviet leadership, since as UN Secretary-General I was always warmly received by Soviet leaders, even when the topic to be discussed, such as Afghanistan, might not have been of their choosing.

While in Moscow I discovered the extraordinary warmth of the Russian people. As has been true wherever I have served, I sought pleasure and release in the aesthetic side of life, and I discovered that there was a vibrant artistic community just below the gray surface of conformity. The work of many artists who were prohibited from exhibiting was exciting. I purchased several of these "forbidden" paintings. Later in New York I hung a Post-Impressionist one, in which fresh flowers symbolizing truth are juxtaposed with a sullied portrayal of the youth organization (Konsomol) edition of *Pravda,* in a prominent place in the library of my residence. In the days before Gorbachev, the painting was always removed temporarily if Soviet guests were expected. Once Andrei Gromyko came to the residence for a meeting and I realized that the painting remained very obviously in place. I was careful to steer the foreign minister to another room, keeping him well shielded from the offensive sight.

I had been in Moscow some two years when I received a call from Lima to the effect that the government felt something more should be made of the Peruvian presence in the United Nations and I was the man to do it. I was to go to New York as the Permanent Representative of Peru. My first reaction was hesitant. Apart from those long-ago days in London, I had no experience with the United Nations. I had always been primarily concerned with bilateral political relations. I had passed through New York many times over the years but never visited the great glass house on First Avenue. But I accepted, of course, and was soon totally absorbed in the life of the United Nations.

That life is quite apart from the life of New York City. It is a world unto itself, a world of numbing meetings interspersed with far-off crises, a world where the truly significant is sometimes lost in the flood of words and paper, a world populated by talented and cosmopolitan people capable of major achievements and also of jealousy and intrigue intensified at times by national or regional rivalries. It took me a good while to understand the intricacies of UN operations and to appreciate the Organization's potential, which is by no means constant, dependent, as it is, on the attitudes of its members and on their relations with each other. To me it became quickly apparent that the Organization was of greatest value to the smaller countries. In the UN framework they could maintain contact with countries with which they had no bilateral representation. Their influence, when combined with that of other countries, would afford them an influence they could not hope to have alone. Especially for countries that have emerged from colonialism, UN membership is a necessary symbol of legitimacy; as such, it affords them not only a sense of "belonging" but also a sense, albeit fragile, of security.

While Permanent Representative I served twice as President of the Security Council. I looked forward to this experience with much excitement. The Council, after all, has the responsibility to deal with conflict and threats to the peace wherever they erupt. According to the Charter, the Council must be able to function continuously, which means that members should be available to deal with emergencies that may arise at any time, day or night. My first term as President was a disappointment. Nothing happened. No sudden crisis erupted that would require the Council to act under the skillful leadership of the President. My second term as Council President was better from that point of view but worse, I fear, for the world. There was a coup against President Makarios in Cyprus and a strong Turkish force landed on the island. This was my introduction to the Cyprus problem with which I was to be concerned—not without considerable frustration—for the next 17 years.

Dr. Kurt Waldheim was at that time Secretary-General. I found him to be an intelligent and conscientious man who worked extremely hard, if often in vain, to solve the various crises that arose. Others, I know, viewed him differently, but he always treated me with the greatest courtesy. Often he would ask me to come in at the close of the day for a quiet discussion of current problems. During 1975, because of my recent divorce and remarriage, I was contemplating retiring from the Peruvian diplomatic service. Exactly at this time, Dr. Waldheim asked if I would accept the position of Executive Director of the United Nations Environment Programme, replacing Maurice Strong. Feeling that I had inadequate experience in the environment field, I declined. A little later the Secretary-General approached me again, this time to become the Special Representative for Cyprus. Recalling that I had dealt with the Cyprus problem as President of the Security Council, Waldheim insisted I would be perfect for the job. Even while sensing that something more than perfection was required to bring agreement between the Greek and Turkish communities, I accepted and thus became for the first time an international civil servant on secondment from the Peruvian government.

I remained in Cyprus for almost two years (an experience I describe in some detail in chapter 9) and was then recalled by my government to serve as ambassador to Venezuela. I had been there hardly more than a year when Kurt Waldheim called to ask that I return to the United Nations to become one of the two Under-Secretaries-General for Special Political Affairs. My service in Caracas was pleasant and rewarding, and I was not eager to leave. But my foreign minister, after consulting the President of Peru, strongly advised that I take the New York position, since it was important and it would be good to have it filled by a Peruvian. So with considerable regret I left Caracas in 1979 and assumed this post in the Secretariat. I began then to see, more clearly than had been possible from Cyprus, how the United Nations functions from the inside. The Organization is unique in many ways, not least in its staff, consisting then of persons from some 150 countries, many of which have widely differing bureaucratic cultures. Its complexities are not to be understood overnight. Later, when I found myself in the Secretary-General's chair, I was extremely grateful to have had this experience.

In 1981 I resigned from my position in the Secretariat and, at the request of my government, returned to Lima to become ambassador to Brazil, one of the most important diplomatic posts for Peru. Although the appointment was publicly announced, domestic politics intervened. At that time ambassadorial appointments in Peru, as in the United States, required Senate approval. Because of the personally motivated manipulations of one or two senators, my appointment received only plurality support and not the required majority. Thus, when word reached Lima that my name was being mentioned in the race for Secretary-General, I was in a somewhat awkward position. I should make clear that I had no party affiliation, but my political orientation was liberal—a far cry from my boyhood leanings. (Much later, when I ran for the presidency of Peru, I headed a diverse coalition but was clearly identified as the liberal candidate.)

APPOINTMENT AS UN SECRETARY-GENERAL

There were two major contenders for the five-year term of Secretary-General that would begin on January 1, 1982. One was Kurt Waldheim, who was ardently seeking a third term. The other was Salim Salim, the foreign minister of Tanzania and former Tanzanian Permanent Representative to the United Nations who, to the considerable discomfiture of the United States, had literally jumped with joy in the General Assembly when the People's Republic of China was recognized as the legitimate representative of China. George Bush was at the time U.S. Permanent Representative, and we had become personal friends. He approached me to ask that Peru vote against the People's Republic. I told him that I could not, first because I had firm instructions from Lima, and second because I felt personally that the People's Republic should be admitted. It is ironic that Bush, having vigorously campaigned—no doubt under instructions—against the acceptance of the People's Republic in the United Nations, was named U.S. ambassador to Beijing not too long thereafter.

The selection process for a Secretary-General begins in the Security Council, which is expected to recommend a candidate to the General Assembly for appointment. The selection is subject to the veto of any one of the five Permanent Members of the Council: China, France, the United Kingdom, the Soviet Union (now Russia) and the United States. In repeated votes in the Council, Dr. Waldheim and Minister Salim were consistently vetoed. The ballots were secret but it was generally assumed that Waldheim was being vetoed by China, which was determined that there should be a new Secretary-General from the Third World, and that Salim was being vetoed by the United States. There was a total impasse.

I do not know which country or countries put my name into circulation. I do know it was not initially Peru. However, when it became known that my name had been seriously mentioned, the Peruvian government—perhaps, among other reasons, still feeling embarrassed over the failure of the Senate to act on my nomination as ambassador to Brazil—decided that my candidacy should be strongly supported. A Peruvian Secretary-General would bring great prestige to Peru. A prominent Peruvian diplomat (and close relative of the President), Ambassador Celso Pastor de la Torre, was dispatched to New York to lead the effort. For my part, I made a firm decision not to mount a personal campaign. This reflected my long held view that a candidate for the Secretary-General post should make no promises or commitments or become indebted to a particular country or group of countries that could later prejudice his or her independence of judgment and action. This, I strongly believe, is the first requirement of a successful incumbency.

My government and many of my friends found my attitude frustrating. Ambassador Pastor, who organized a most skillful campaign, called repeatedly to urge that I come to New York from my home in Peru and talk personally with the various Permanent Representatives whose votes would be crucial. I refused.

In December, the Permanent Representative of Uganda, Olara Otunnu, assumed the presidency of the Council. Time was becoming very short since the General Assembly was scheduled to adjourn in less than three weeks. Under the circumstances, Ambassador Otunnu suggested that Secretary-General Waldheim and Minister Salim "stand aside" for a while without withdrawing from the race to see if a successful candidate might emerge. Many hopeful candidates did rush to the fore. Otunnu then organized, with noteworthy ingenuity, a secret straw poll of the 15 Council members, giving the five "veto" powers blue ballots and the others white ballots. In this way it was possible to determine not only which of the candidates had the strongest numerical support but also which, if any, would not be vetoed. While in this process I did not receive the largest number of ballots; of all the candidates, I alone received no negative blue ballot.

Once this was clear, a further vote was taken in which the Security Council decided by a vote of 14 to 1 to recommend that the General Assembly appoint me as Secretary-General, which the assembly did forthwith by consensus. I later learned that the one negative vote in the Security Council was cast by Tunisia. The Tunisian ambassador's instructions from his government, which, surprisingly, was totally committed to Kurt Waldheim, left him no choice.

I had gone with my wife to a rather isolated resort not far from Lima in the days before the Security Council action and was largely unaware of developments in New York, although a Peruvian colleague in the Secretariat, Emilio de Olivares, had called and said, in effect, "Javier, this is for real." On returning to Lima, I received the first word of the council's vote from the wife of the Spanish ambassador in New York, who gave me the news on behalf of her husband, Jaime de Pines, a Security Council member. Kurt Waldheim called shortly thereafter to congratulate me and say that I was the only candidate in whose election he could take genuine satisfaction as his replacement. My appointment was greeted with widespread relief, due, I suspect, as much to collective exhaustion after the long and tortuous selection process and a desire to adjourn for Christmas as to anything else. I was not considered by most an exciting choice for the job.

Barely two weeks were left for me to prepare to move to New York and undertake a unique position in which success must derive not from power but from persuasion and patience, from impartiality and discretion and from the capacity to judge accurately the character of individuals and the significance of events. I did not lack confidence in assuming the post of Secretary-General— my whole career had, in a sense, prepared me for it—but I was not certain, even after my years in the United Nations, that I had full mastery of the multilateral relationships that dominate the Organization. I knew too that UN management required a firm and skillful hand, and this was the area in which my experience had been most limited.

I had not thought of myself as a Latin American candidate for the Secretary-Generalship because I do not believe that the Secretary-General of the United Nations should represent any one region more than another. His mandate is global. I was very conscious, however, that I was a man of the Third World who would be assuming the post after the ten-year tenure of a Secretary-General from the developed world. It was my ambition to stimulate sustained North-South negotiations on development, independent of the grandiose and essentially unproductive framework of a new international economic order. I believed then, as I believe now, that North-South economic negotiations, if directed toward concrete problems, can be productive and are of fundamental importance for the maintenance of international peace and security.

So I went to New York with good heart and strong purpose, sensing that much could be accomplished yet knowing too that, in its history, the United Nations had given as much evidence of limitations as proof of potential in building a peaceful world.

I took the oath of office, swearing my loyalty to the United Nations and the principles defined in its Charter, on the first day of 1982. I was profoundly aware that although chosen by election, my mandate was, and would remain, radically different from that of an elected politician. For, once in office, the Secretary-General must maintain his independence from those who elected him. Therein lies a paradox: The Secretary-General is the servant of an organization of governments in which, if he is to serve them well, he dares not be their captive. As soon as I took the oath, I knew I must be totally impartial in dealing with any matter in which the interests of some or all of those who elected me were, in my view, contrary to the principles of the Charter. If there were to be conflicts between member governments, as there frequently would be, I would need to hold myself at the very center of the scales of judgment. The Secretary-General must be mediator and standardbearer, moderator and guide, conciliator and arbiter, impartial in all. During the following ten years I was called upon to fill all these roles.

There were times of disappointment—in leaders and governments—times when, in the search for peace, I felt like the man in the ancient myth condemned to roll a stone constantly uphill yet never reach the top. At the end of my first five-year term I did not have a sense of accomplishment. Rather, the realization that so much still needed to be done in the interest of peace persuaded me to accept the second five-year term for which I was chosen unanimously both by the Security Council and the General Assembly. I shall be ever grateful for this second chance, for in the next five years more progress was made than I could have imagined possible. Through an extraordinary combination of developments, the United Nations progressed from an organization widely seen as marginal in questions of war and peace to one on which the world increasingly depends for security. I hope to convey in these pages some understanding of the work done by this Organization and of a Secretary-General in action during a time of seminal change. In describing the courses I personally followed in dealing with conflicts and crises, I have no desire to bring glory on myself or opprobrium on others. It is the United Nations and the ideals on which it is founded that constitute the vital element in an emerging world structure of peace. If, in the chapters that follow, it can be seen that, in whatever I have contributed, I have acted with impartiality and fairness in consonance with the principles of the Charter, then I shall be content. The long journey from Lima will have been worthwhile. The journey could almost certainly have lasted longer. Several members of the Security Council asked that I remain at least two more years. President Bush repeatedly urged that I accept a third term. I declined not because I was tired of shouldering the burden but because I was convinced that, in the words of the Bible, for everything there is a season. The season of maximum accomplishment for a Secretary-General is no longer than ten years. After that, no matter how good the record—and I regard mine with satisfaction—the stimulus of a new voice and of a fresh perspective is needed. This must be recognized to do justice to the importance of the position of the Secretary-General in the pursuit of peace and justice in the world.

THE MIDDLE EAST AND BEYOND

Since shortly after its establishment, the United Nations has been intimately involved in the history of the Middle East—in its enduring conflicts and its occasional peace. From the beginning of my term as Secretary-General, I felt that developments in this area, more than in any other, could threaten world peace because the main opponents there were closely linked to the United States or the Soviet Union without being under the full control of either. I was also convinced that if there was to be peace, the people of this region could make a unique contribution to human well-being because of the resources, skills and historical heritage with which they were endowed. I saw both hope and despair in the evident destructiveness and danger of the continuing strife—hope that the

very intensity of the repeated crises would bring recognition of the necessity of

solution; despair in the reality that this did not happen, in the shortsightedness

of leaders, in the perpetuity of hatred and distrust; despair in the very

intractability of some of the problems. Despair, I must admit, tended to triumph

over hope. But despair, like optimism, is an emotion in which a Secretary-

General should not indulge.

THREE

THE BATTLE
FOR LEBANON

THE LEBANESE ARE TRUE DESCENDANTS OF THE PHOENICIANS—cultured, cosmo-politan and shrewd. Their country had long offered a model of how people of differing religious faiths and group loyalties can live together in peace and mutual respect. But in the 1970s the internal harmony, long under strain as a result of the massive influx of Palestinian refugees, was shattered by civil war—a conflict in which external forces were as important as domestic tensions between and within the Moslem and Christian communities.

In the south the Palestine Liberation Organization (PLO) gained such wide control that it, rather than the government in Beirut, exercised de facto control in the area, using it as a launching pad for terrorist attacks against Israel, prompting, inevitably, retaliatory Israeli raids. When, in 1978, the PLO carried out a commando raid in the vicinity of Tel Aviv, Israel reacted by sending a military force that occupied all of Lebanon south of the Litani River except for the city of Tyre.

On March 19 the UN Security Council adopted Resolution 425, calling for strict respect for the territorial integrity, sovereignty and political independence of Lebanon and for the immediate withdrawal of Israeli troops. It also decided to establish, as strongly urged by the United States, a UN interim force for southern Lebanon "for the purpose of confirming the withdrawal of Israeli forces, restoring international peace and security and assisting the government of Lebanon in ensuring the return of its effective authority in the area." Secretary-General Kurt Waldheim submitted forthwith a plan of action, document S/12611, according to which the United Nations Interim Force in Lebanon (UNIFIL) would be established to carry out the assigned functions in an "area of operations" that would be defined by the nature of its tasks. The area was to include all the territory between the Litani River and the Israeli border.

The Israeli forces gradually completed their withdrawal in June 1978 but a Christian militia, supported by Israel (termed "de facto forces" by the United Nations) denied UNIFIL entry to a narrow strip north of the Israel border. Thus UNIFIL was unable to incorporate the most sensitive area for infiltration into its area of operation. UNIFIL's mission was also greatly complicated by the presence in southern Lebanon of "armed elements," the euphemism the United Nations used for the armed Fatah contingents of the PLO. UNIFIL was to become a major pawn in the catastrophe that would strike Lebanon shortly after I became Secretary-General.

Although a cease-fire that had been negotiated among the various forces the preceding summer was still in force in Lebanon in the early months of 1982, warnings of renewed crisis were apparent. There were terrorist incidents in Israel and in April that country launched a series of air strikes near Beirut. In April, Israel was scheduled to complete its withdrawal from the Sinai in accordance with the Camp David Agreement. The assumption was widely held that having secured its southern border through the peace treaty with Egypt, Israel would move next to secure its northern border from the threat of PLO incursions and seek a peace agreement with Lebanon.

The Lebanese Permanent Representative to the United Nations at the time was a diplomat of notable erudition and sophistication, a man who I came to feel was the last of his breed. His name was Ghassan Tueni. In February 1982 he gave a remarkably prescient speech at Harvard University, which he began by stating that "it is a strange feeling to be the Ambassador of a country which, everybody tells you, is going to be invaded tomorrow." Nearing the end, he said, "The details, and variants, of the all-too-publicized scenario are well-known: Operation Litani II, we are told, will be much more important than the March 1978 Operation Litani, both in scope and consequences. Geographically, it should go as far as Beirut. Militarily, it will use land, air and sea forces, and will unfold in a manner designed to destroy completely the PLO structures, armaments and bases. Politically, it should suck the Syrians into being involved, drive both the Syrians and the PLO out of Lebanon and open the way for a total reconsideration and redrawing of the map."

On June 2, Philip Habib, the Special U.S. Envoy for the Middle East, called on me prior to undertaking an extensive trip to the area. His mission, he told me, would relate principally "to the future of Lebanon." I would have repeated occasions to meet with Habib during the Lebanese crisis. He was a man of obviously quick intelligence, self-assured and a little brusque in manner, but straightforward and candid. To me it was especially interesting that this man, the son of Lebanese immigrants, should have such an important role in the formulation and implementation of American policy in the Middle East. His ancestry was no doubt an advantage in dealing with the quarrelsome Lebanese leaders, although I did not find that it gave him particular insight into what they would do. On this occasion Habib said that stabilization of the situation in Lebanon was beyond the power of the United States alone. Therefore, the United States wished to enlist the support of as many of the other states in the region as possible. The Egyptian deputy foreign minister, Boutros Boutros-Ghali, had advised that the Soviet Union should be brought into the picture. At this stage, however, the United States wished to involve only "positive groups." In the course of our conversation, and during an earlier one with UN Under-Secretary-General Brian Urquhart, Habib said that there was a "hawkish" group within the Israeli cabinet and armed forces that wished to "clear out the PLO." The group had been restrained, so far, by strong U.S. pressure and by the prospect of an unacceptable number of casualties.

On the following day, the Israeli ambassador in London was attacked and seriously wounded, an event for which the PLO took credit. This was what the hawkish group in Israel had been waiting for. I immediately issued a statement condemning the attempted assassination. I also telephoned the Israeli ambassador in New York to express my personal revulsion at the act. I took the occasion to state my hope that the Israeli air attacks on Beirut would cease. The attacks continued, however. On June 4, Ambassador Tueni informed the Security Council that there had been no less than nine successive bombing raids on Beirut and that Israeli forces had begun to shell an area in south Lebanon. UNIFIL confirmed that there were heavy exchanges of fire between PLO positions in the south and the Israel Defense Force (IDF) and the associated Christian militias.

Brian Urquhart urgently contacted Morris Draper, Philip Habib's deputy in the State Department, on the situation. Draper told him that if PLO fire on Israeli settlements in northern Galilee continued, it was inevitable that the hawk faction led by Ariel Sharon would overcome the moderates in the Israeli cabinet and a major military operation in Lebanon would be launched. Urquhart passed this assessment on to Hassan Rahman, a member of the PLO Observer Mission, as Draper had requested him to do and suggested that Rahman inform PLO Chairman Arafat. Urquhart stressed that the only hope of preventing a military operation would be the cessation of PLO fire into Israel, although in view of the Israeli raids "we fully understood how difficult it would be for Arafat to order a unilateral cessation of firing."

THE SECOND ISRAELI INVASION

On June 5, I made a public appeal for a cease-fire. At the time, a summit meeting of the Group of Seven was taking place in Versailles. I sent an urgent message to President Mitterrand asking for his support and that of the other Western leaders for my efforts "to restore peace in a region where the unleashing of violence could have incalculable consequences for the entire world." Also on June 5, the Security Council, taking note of a report I provided on the continuing hostilities, adopted Resolution 508 calling upon all parties to the conflict to cease immediately and simultaneously all military activities within Lebanon and across the Lebanese-Israeli border by 6:00 A.M. on June 6. Instead, on that very day, Israeli forces crossed into Lebanon in strength in an action that the Israeli Government designated "Peace for Galilee."

The Security Council promptly and unanimously adopted a further resolution, 509, this time demanding that Israel withdraw all its military forces forthwith and unconditionally to the internationally recognized boundaries of Lebanon. It also demanded that the parties observe the cease-fire that the Council had already called for and that they communicate their acceptance of the new resolution to the Secretary-General within 24 hours.

Lebanon replied that "despite the present Israeli aggression," it had not become a party to the hostilities. It could only regret that the Security Council had not provided stronger means to implement its resolution. Yassir Arafat replied that "the Lebanese Palestinian Joint Command has decided to agree . . . to Security Council resolution 509." The Israeli reply stated:

- The "Peace for Galilee" operation was ordered because of the intolerable situation created by the presence in Lebanon of a large number of terrorists operating from that country, equipped with modern, long-range weaponry, threatening the lives of the civilian population of Galilee.
- Any withdrawal prior to the conclusion of concrete arrangements which would permanently and reliably preclude hostile action against Israel's citizens is inconceivable.
- Self-defense is one of the fundamental rights of sovereign states.
- The government of Israel reiterates that "Israel continues to aspire to the signing of a peace treaty with independent Lebanon, its territorial integrity preserved."[1]

The UNIFIL area of deployment was directly in the path of the advancing Israeli forces. The Israeli military command informed the UNIFIL commander, Lieutenant General William Callaghan from Ireland, of the impending invasion 90 minutes before the operation began. General Callaghan replied that his forces would block roads and all possible passages through their area of operation to hamper the Israeli advance. This the UNIFIL forces did, delaying, at least in one location, for several hours the advance of an Israeli armored unit. UNIFIL's mandate, size and equipment was that of a peace-keeping force, however. Its main strength was symbolic, and in this case the symbolic had no effect. The IDF moved inexorably northward; while it did not attempt to displace UNIFIL, it assumed wide authority in its area of operation and in other areas that it occupied.

Farouk Kaddoumi, head of the PLO Political Department, complained bitterly to me the next day that, according to his information, UNIFIL had been instructed to let the Israelis go through. He quoted Israeli Chief of Staff Rafael Eitan as having said that General Callaghan had agreed to this. Kaddoumi said that he would have expected UNIFIL to stop the advancing army by blocking roads and other methods of communication. Brian Urquhart, who was with me and who had been keeping in close touch with UNIFIL, said that was exactly what the UN troops had sought to do. They were, however, in no way able to stop a large, heavily armored Israeli force. The PLO fighting forces themselves, Urquhart noted, had been unable to stop the Israelis. I rejected any intimation that UNIFIL soldiers had not performed properly. All subsequent evidence confirmed that they had conducted themselves bravely and honorably under grave threat.

Even prior to the massive Israeli invasion in June, the situation in Lebanon was extremely unhappy from almost every point of view. In Beirut political stability was fragile and government authority was tenuous, at best. Security was heavily dependent on the Syrian army, which had entered Lebanon as a peacekeeping force of the Arab League but, in fact, controlled a large portion of Lebanese territory. In the south, the contest between the PLO and Israel held the inhabitants in terror. It was hardly imaginable that the situation could become worse. The Israeli invasion that began on June 6 had set in motion a chain of events that were truly disastrous for Lebanon and, I believe, also for Israel.

I was continuously involved and personally determined, from a humanitarian as well as political point of view, to do everything possible to end the horror. I met at one time or another with all the protagonists and came to know some extremely well. I was appalled by the dubious judgment that was widely shared among them and shocked by actions that showed a disregard for human life and amounted, in some instances, to blatant villainy.

In making such a harsh judgment, I am not unmindful of the legitimate concern of the Israeli Government to protect its citizens from PLO attacks or to gain peace with another of its neighbors. Nor can I blame the PLO for its efforts to bring some satisfaction to the sorely treated Palestinian people. Honorable objectives, however, can be shamed if they are pursued by shameful means. This was the case in Lebanon, and by no means only by Israel and the PLO. Lebanese factional leaders and Syria deserve a fair share of blame with still enough left over for Iran, Iraq and Libya.

As the multifaceted conflict unfolded, the question arose repeatedly as to how, or if, UNIFIL or other UN military personnel could be used to stabilize the situation, protect Lebanese civilians and Palestinian refugees caught in the repeated battles and monitor a potential settlement. UNIFIL's position was awkward, to say the least, in the wake of the Israeli invasion. The force consisted of 7,000 men. It had served, in the absence of Lebanese authority, to restore a remarkable degree of security and stability in its area of deployment. Conditions there were in marked contrast with those in most of the rest of Lebanon. Now the IDF was occupying the area along with the so-called de facto forces of Major Saad Haddad. Units of the Lebanese army had been stationed with UNIFIL to provide at least the semblance of an official Lebanese presence. Sixty-five of these Lebanese soldiers who were serving under operational control of UNIFIL were seized by the Israelis and turned over to Major Haddad. Other Lebanese soldiers in the UNIFIL area were also harassed and eventually decamped.

The question quickly arose as to what the UNIFIL's mission could be if Israel occupied the territory. UNIFIL's mandate had seemingly lost its relevance, at least temporarily, and, anyway, it was due to expire on June 19. I sent instructions to General Callaghan that, for the present, he should maintain UNIFIL's position and render all possible humanitarian assistance to the local inhabitants. But I would need to make a strong recommendation to the Council if the mandate was to be extended beyond the expiration date.

On June 9, Vice President George Bush came to see me in New York, accompanied by UN Ambassador Jeane Kirkpatrick. When I told him that according to the latest reports I had received, a large air battle between Israeli and Syrian planes was taking place over the Bekaa Valley, he commented that Israel's professed intention had been to secure the southern part of Lebanon and then withdraw. Mrs. Kirkpatrick confirmed that the United States had been assured that Israel would not attack Syrian positions. I mentioned the difficult position in which UNIFIL found itself. Ambassador Kirkpatrick raised the possibility of expanding UNIFIL's "zone" both to the north to include the PLO strongholds and to the south to encompass the area now controlled by Major Haddad and his Christian militia. This was an idea that was to come up repeatedly during the next months. I pointed out that it would require the approval of the Security Council, which I thought would be difficult to obtain since expansion to the north could be seen as protecting Israel's military gains. Bush expressed the hope that one positive result of the tragic situation would be the removal of Major Haddad's forces from their enclave.

Very shortly after this conversation Ambassador Kirkpatrick sent me an aide-mémoire stating that the United States was in full sympathy with my concerns about the safety and integrity of UNIFIL. The United States felt that UNIFIL had played "a critical and gallant" role. At this juncture the United States considered it extremely important that UNIFIL's integrity and presence be maintained. Almost simultaneously the Soviet Union issued a statement condemning the Israeli action in the strongest terms and demanding that the Security Council take immediate steps to halt the Israeli aggression. This statement made no mention of UNIFIL.

While the IDF presence in the UNIFIL area of operation had thinned out after the initial invasion, Israeli soldiers remained and sought to impose the permanent presence of the de facto Haddad militia, which UNIFIL was instructed to resist. As a result, there were continuing confrontations. A number of important troop-contributing states were unhappy with a situation in which their soldiers were at risk in a UN peacekeeping operation that appeared to have lost its purpose. Even Brian Urquhart, who as the Under-Secretary-General in charge of peacekeeping operations gave strong and sage leadership to UN peace-keeping undertakings, was of two minds. In the end, however, his advice was unequivocal. UNIFIL could still have a role to play in the restoration of peace in Lebanon. It could, at the very least, provide humanitarian assistance and some protection to those in southern Lebanon who had been deprived of home and subsistence by the war. Of equal or even greater importance in my mind was the stark fact that if UNIFIL was withdrawn, southern Lebanon would be turned over completely to Israel. There would be no authority in the area other than Israel's surrogate, Major Haddad.

On June 17, two days before the mandate would expire, I was invited to lunch by President Ronald Reagan in his Waldorf Towers suite. The President had come to New York to address a special session of the General Assembly on disarmament. I had spoken to him several times by phone in connection with the Falklands/Malvinas crisis (Chapter 15), but this was our first personal encounter. As in all subsequent meetings, I found the President courteous, affable and attentive. During the lunch he received a telephone call from Bashir Gemayel, the putative president of Lebanon. I do not know why he called, but during the conversation President Reagan told him that I was there and Gemayel then asked to speak to me as well. Although I do not remember what he had to say, I do remember very well that on the way back to my seat from the phone, I noticed behind the flower arrangement on the table the two- by four-inch briefing cards that President Reagan was using in talking with me. This was my first realization that he relied on such cards for all substantive exchanges.

President Reagan's limited knowledge of subjects under discussion was, I must admit, disconcerting. But I found it a virtue that he did not pretend to know more than he did. He never lectured. When I told him why I thought the UNIFIL mandate should be extended, placing emphasis on the humanitarian assistance the UN troops could provide during this period of violence and dislocation, he agreed. He supported the retention of UNIFIL from then on. It was as simple as that. With firm American support and a specific request from the Lebanese government, the UNIFIL mandate was extended, as it would be again and again up until the present day. The major question would be not so much its existence as its function. How could UNIFIL be best used to restore stability in southern Lebanon, afford protection to Lebanese living there and elsewhere, including Beirut, and ensure the full withdrawal of Israeli forces?

As the Israeli invasion engulfed Beirut and repeated cease-fire agreements were ignored, I addressed a letter to Israeli Prime Minister Menachem Begin on June 24 urging that he do everything in his power to bring about an end to the hostilities. At the same time, I sent letters to Yassir Arafat, President Hafez Al-Assad of Syria and President Reagan informing them of my letter to Begin and urging that each do whatever possible to bring about an effective cease-fire as soon as possible. In the letter to President Reagan I recalled that the United Nations had military observers in the Middle East who would be immediately available to assist in implementing a cease-fire if one could be brought about.

The Security Council at this point was regrettably passive. Egypt and France circulated a draft resolution, but the Lebanese government itself made no move to call the Council into session. The PLO proposed that UNIFIL should be deployed in Beirut but this was strongly opposed by Israel and stood no chance of U.S. concurrence. Council members appeared traumatized by the problem of getting agreement on a meaningful resolution text and by the likely ineffectiveness of any action they might take. Finally, on August 1, 1982, the Council adopted Resolution 516, which again demanded a cease-fire and authorized the Secretary-General, on the request of the Lebanese government, to deploy UN observers to monitor the situation in and around Beirut. Lebanon immediately made such a request. I then instructed the Chief of Staff of the UN Truce Supervision Organization in Jerusalem (UNTSO), Lieutenant General Emmanuel A. Erskine, to make arrangements with the parties concerned. The Lebanese government and Chairman Arafat both communicated their readiness to comply with the Council resolution and to cooperate with the UN observers. In the absence of any response from Israel, I ordered a small UN Observer Group to proceed to the vicinity of Beirut and to make such observations as were possible without the cooperation of the Israeli forces. The group took up positions in areas still under the control of the Lebanese government and began to report on developments in the city. They could not get to the center of Beirut, however, since they were unable to pass through Israeli lines.

In the early days of August, the United States on its own without UN assistance, negotiated an understanding with the PLO on the withdrawal of PLO fighters from the Beirut area, where they were, by then, concentrated. The Israelis viewed this as a major victory, which justified their "Peace for Galilee" operation. It was patently a welcome development for the newly elected but not yet installed Christian president of Lebanon, Bashir Gemayel. Gemayel was reportedly prepared to sign a peace treaty with Israel, thus bringing to fruition another objective of Israeli policy. Israel would have peace on both its southern and northern borders.

Neither Israel nor the Lebanese government was willing to rely on the United Nations to monitor the PLO withdrawal. The task was given instead to a multinational force consisting of French, Italian, U.K. and U.S. troops, organized totally independently from the United Nations. On August 16, the heads of the French and Italian missions in New York called on me separately and informed me of their governments' decisions to participate in the multinational force. Each indicated that his government would have preferred that this task be carried out by a UN peacekeeping force, but this was not possible because of the opposition of one of the parties. Each government had insisted, however, that UN observers should play a role in the withdrawal process. Four days later I received a letter from President Reagan stating that "As you know, the government of the Republic of Lebanon has requested the deployment of a multinational force in Beirut to assist the Lebanese armed forces as they carry out the orderly and safe departure of Palestinian personnel now in Beirut." The United States, he said, had agreed to deploy a force of about 800 personnel to Beirut for a period not to exceed 30 days. "It is my firm intention and belief," he stated, "that these troops will not be involved in hostilities during the course of this operation." The U.S. force, he wrote, would work closely with the UN observer group stationed in the Beirut area.

While I doubted that peace could be restored in Lebanon or elsewhere in the Middle East through the force of Israeli arms, I recognized that the departure of the PLO fighters could bring the destruction that was going on in Beirut to an end and was key to the withdrawal of Israeli troops from Lebanon. I therefore sent a message to the Prime Minister of Lebanon expressing my deep gratification on the successful conclusion of an agreement aimed at bringing to an end the tragic situation in Beirut. The UN Observer Group in Beirut was still limited to ten persons; while it gained freedom to circulate throughout Beirut and report on the departure of the PLO forces, its role in the operation was marginal at best.

On August 23 Bashir Gemayel was installed as President of Lebanon, declaring in an inaugural statement that he was "the President of all Lebanon." Three weeks later, on September 14, he was assassinated, and the Israeli army moved back into West Beirut. On the afternoon of September 17, units of the Christian militia, which Gemayel had headed, entered the Sabra and Shatila refugee camps in the southern suburbs of Beirut and massacred a large number of Palestinian refugees. The UN Observer Group had access to the area and saw the devastation. It noted the failure of Israeli forces present in the area to take any preventive action and reported this through channels to UN Headquarters.

On September 19, the Security Council, in Resolution 521, condemned the massacre and authorized an increase in the UN Observer Force from 10 to 50. It also requested that I initiate urgent consultations on additional steps that the Council might take, including the possible deployment of UN forces. The next day I was able to inform the Council that additional observers were on their way to Beirut and that 2,000 men from UNIFIL could be sent to Beirut if required.[2]

I also wrote to Secretary of State George Shultz and told him that the Lebanese government had declared it would agree to any form of additional assistance that could be provided expeditiously. In my view, the most practical form of such assistance would be two to three battalions redeployed to Beirut from UNIFIL. This could be done very quickly, but only if Israel was prepared to cooperate, since the units would have to go through Israeli-controlled territory. I requested the urgent support of the United States in persuading the Israeli government to reverse its policy regarding the redeployment of UNIFIL in areas other than the one in which it was now stationed.

The United States was either unable or unwilling to do this. The Council, primarily because the United States did not concur, did not authorize the redeployment of UNIFIL units to Beirut. Instead, on September 24, the multinational force returned to Beirut, where internecine strife had resumed in full fury. This proved to be an invitation to yet further tragedy. Only a few days later, on September 29, I met with Secretary Shultz, who was in New York for the General Assembly, and asked how he saw the future of UNIFIL, given the existence of the multinational force. The Secretary responded that it was extremely important that the UNIFIL mandate be extended. Israel would withdraw from Lebanon only if it was confident in arrangements regarding its northern border. In this context, UNIFIL had a potentially extremely important role to play. I asked how the United States foresaw the strengthening of UNIFIL, "by adding to its size or its muscle?" The secretary thought that it would be best to leave UNIFIL terms of reference as they stood.

I cannot say with any certainty that 2,000 UN peacekeeping troops could have stabilized the situation in Beirut after Israel occupied a sizable portion of the city. Even if the Israelis had withdrawn their objections, I am not confident that Security Council members would have agreed to maintain a UN peacekeeping force in Beirut if it appeared that the force was protecting a Lebanese government that was prepared to sign a peace treaty with Israel. Thus I cannot assert that the United Nations could have succeeded where the Western powers failed. I can say, however, what I felt at the time: that the deployment of the multinational force with the evident purpose of protecting the government in power was misguided. Brian Urquhart, with his long experience in peacekeeping, stated openly that impartiality is the absolute requisite of a peacekeeping force; without it the multinational force was in for trouble. The harrowing experience of the Americans and the French contingents in the force and its subsequent withdrawal was proof, if proof was needed, of this cardinal rule—a rule that the United Nations itself would fail to follow a decade later in Mogadishu, Somalia, also with unfortunate results.

PROBLEMS IN THE SOUTH

While world attention was focused mainly on developments in Beirut, the situation in southern Lebanon under Israeli occupation was also highly unsatisfactory. The invasion and the fighting with PLO forces had caused widespread dislocation and destruction. Both Lebanese and Palestinians were left homeless. The Palestinians fled—or were driven—to the large camp areas. Palestinian schools, which had been run by the United Nations Relief and Works Agency for Palestine Refugees (UNRWA), ceased to function. Initially the Israeli forces refused to allow UNIFIL or UNRWA to bring assistance to the refugee camps, claiming that Israel was providing totally for all the needs of the population. Although Israeli restrictions on relief deliveries gradually were relaxed, sporadic interference continued. The Israelis carried out frequent actions intended to eliminate all residual PLO military or terrorist capacity. Inevitably, many innocent Lebanese and Palestinians were injured.

Various governments addressed complaints to me and to the President of the Security Council about the Israeli actions. Yassir Arafat sent repeated messages reporting Israeli attacks on refugee camps and against Palestinians who were being held captive in Ansar prison in the southern border zone. The Commissioner-General of UNRWA, Olof Rydbek, confirmed to me that the Palestinian population in the south was terrified by the possibility of another massacre and was pleading for greater UN protection.

I raised this disturbing situation with Israeli Foreign Minister Yitzhak Shamir on September 30, 1982, during the regular session of the General Assembly. It was my first personal encounter with him. Because of the deep respect that I have always held for the State of Israel, I sought to avoid any appearance of hostility. Indeed, my deepest feeling at the time was not one of hostility at all but rather bewilderment and despair that a democratic government with highly intelligent and rational leaders could have undertaken such a misguided action as extending the Peace for Galilee operation to Beirut. Not then nor in subsequent meetings, did Mr. Shamir, make my task an easy one. He impressed me as doctrinaire, without the innate courtesy of Menachem Begin.

In response to my comments, Minister Shamir contended that Operation Peace for Galilee was directed solely against the PLO. He stated that rarely, if ever, in modern history had an army hazarded so much as did the Israel Defense Force in an attempt to minimize casualties among the civilian population. The

Israeli Permanent Representative, Yehuda Blum, who was with the foreign minister, said that the PLO had deliberately established its emplacements within refugee camps, villages and civilian neighborhoods, using the civilian population in an attempt to shield itself. Mr. Shamir was ambivalent on the desirability of retaining UNIFIL.

I had no difficulty in accepting that the Israeli army had sought to avoid civilian casualties. UNIFIL had observed this. What I missed on Shamir's part was any sense of sorrow or regret over the tragedies that had occurred as the result—even if unintended—of Israeli actions.

UNIFIL'S ROLE IN A CEASE-FIRE

With the return of the multinational force to Beirut following the Sabra and Shatila massacres, the Israel Defense Force withdrew from the city to a line south of the airport. In the brief period of relative calm that ensued, the United States encouraged Israel and Lebanon to begin talks on an agreement to regularize the situation in Lebanon. During a meeting in Washington in mid-January 1983, Secretary Shultz told me that the talks were moving forward. The United States would be putting pressure on the Israelis to withdraw. The secretary added, however, that "Israel will not leave unless Syria and the PLO are committed to withdraw." He thought that a future mission for UNIFIL might emerge from the negotiations. "We would then come back to the UN," he said. "There's no point in fussing now."

In mid-March Ambassador Morris Draper informed Brian Urquhart about conversations that had taken place in Washington among President Reagan, Secretary Shultz, Foreign Minister Shamir and Foreign Minister Elie Salem of Lebanon. He said that the security arrangements suggested by Israel, including an Israeli presence in southern Lebanon, had been too far-reaching and had been declared unacceptable by President Reagan and Secretary of State Shultz. The President, in particular, was very firm on this point. The United States had pressed very hard for UNIFIL to play a supporting role in south Lebanon.

On May 17, 1983, Israel and Lebanon signed the Agreement on the Withdrawal of Troops from Lebanon. On that same day I met with Secretary Shultz in Washington. He had played a personal and direct role, involving intensive shuttle diplomacy among the various capitals concerned in the Middle East, to get the two countries to sign. I congratulated him on his achievement and stated that I remained at the disposal of the parties and hoped to be informed of any way I might help.

The secretary replied that under the agreement, the United Nations would have an important role to play. It would be responsible for surveillance and observation around the refugee camps and in other key areas, such as highways and ports, where heavy movement was likely. A unit of UNIFIL would be bivouacked in the Sidon area and could send observation teams to Sidon and Tyre. Lebanon would be solely responsible for camp security, UNIFIL would not be asked to assume this responsibility.

I said that the functions of UNIFIL as described by Secretary Shultz would amount to a weakening of its presently mandated responsibilities. If it was to be active only at the request of the Lebanese government, it might find itself performing an autopsy on a tragedy that had already occurred. If, however, the United Nations were given the responsibility of protecting the Palestinian camps, it might be able to play a useful role. I expressed doubt as to the willingness of the Security Council to go along with the functions of UNIFIL as described by the secretary. Shultz insisted that Lebanon must have the police function for the camps. UNIFIL's role, in his opinion, should be that "of an impartial and international conscience watching the Lebanese exercise protection of Palestinians."

The agreement between Israel and Lebanon amounted to a peace treaty in everything but name. Under the agreement, all of Lebanon south of the Awali River (encompassing the entire UNIFIL area of operation) was designated a joint Israeli-Lebanese security zone. The government of Lebanon might request the Security Council to authorize the stationing of "one unit" of UNIFIL in the Sidon area for the purposes described to me by Secretary Shultz. The agreement made no mention of stationing units in areas of heavy movement. Implementation of the agreement was dependent on the withdrawal of all other foreign forces—that is, Syrian and PLO.

I found it difficult to understand how a realistic and experienced person such as George Shultz could have worked so hard to obtain this agreement and could place such faith in it. Having worked successfully with the Saudi leadership as a corporate executive and seen the resources that Saudi Arabia controlled, perhaps he placed unrealistic confidence on the influence that the Saudis could, and would, exercise on Syria and the PLO. Implementation of the Agreement was dependent on the latter two and on the Security Council—none of which had participated in the negotiations or concurred in the results. The American objectives were certainly constructive: to obtain Israeli withdrawal, restore the sovereign independence of Lebanon and bring peace between Israel and a second Arab country. I was more than ready to do whatever I could to see these objectives realized; but I considered this agreement badly conceived for the purpose.

A few days later I spoke in New York with the Syrian Permanent Representative to the United Nations, Dia-Allah El-Fattal, and asked if, in the Syrian view, there was any way that I could be of assistance in this complicated situation. The ambassador said he knew that the United Nations had not been a participant in the Israeli-Lebanese negotiations. The agreement required a change in the mandate of UNIFIL, which would be difficult to obtain. Moreover, the agreement was, and would remain, unacceptable to Damascus. Syria had never said that it would not withdraw its forces from Lebanon, but, he stressed, "it could not, for the sake of Lebanon, leave that country under Israeli hegemony." The Soviet ambassador, Oleg Troyanovsky, came to see me to say that the Soviet Union might well oppose *any* continuation of UNIFIL. The Soviet Union would not be able to accept any Security Council resolution that implied support for, or appeared to condone, the May 17 agreement between Israel and Lebanon. The Lebanese foreign minister, Elie Salem, told me at a July 15 meeting that Assad's objectives were "in that order, his own security, the control of Lebanon and the PLO, considerable economic aid (perhaps as high as $40 billion), the return of the Golan Heights and, finally, an agreement with Lebanon on economic cooperation." Mr. Salem was convinced that President Assad would not withdraw his 50,000 troops from Lebanon for a lesser price. Perhaps this was Mr. Salem's way of saying that the situation was hopeless.

The Israelis, facing mounting casualties inflicted by Lebanese Moslem guerrilla groups and increasing domestic dissatisfaction began in September 1983 what would become a unilateral withdrawal, by redeploying their forces from the environs of Beirut to south of the Alawi River. Bitter fighting broke out in the evacuated area and in Beirut between Christians and Druse, between the Lebanese Army and the Shi'ites, and finally between the Christians and the Shi'ites. The Druse were supported by Syria with the evident aim of destroying the agreement between Lebanon and Israel. I issued an appeal for support of efforts under way for a cease-fire and the restoration of national unity. Unfortunately, it had no discernible effect. The multinational force came under fire, and both the Americans and the French suffered casualties.

Under these circumstances, the Lebanese President, Amin Gemayel, sent Ghassan Tueni back to the United Nations to explore the possibility of the deployment of a UN peacekeeping force in the area of combat. Tueni explained to Brian Urquhart that the Lebanese government did not, itself, wish to bring a complaint against Syria in the Security Council; rather, it hoped that a "third party"—presumably me—might raise the matter. Urquhart pointed out that such an action by the Secretary-General would be extremely difficult in what was an internal civil war situation. Any decision to deploy a peacekeeping contingent would, in any event, be up to the Security Council and that would depend on agreement between the United States and the Soviet Union. Some days later Ambassador Roger Kirk of the U.S. State Department called Brian Urquhart to inquire whether, in the event of a cease-fire in and around Beirut, UN observers would be available to monitor it. Urquhart explained that this too would depend on a decision of the Security Council. It was apparent that agreement did not exist in the Council between the United States and the Soviet Union. The key to any solution, he suggested, lay in discussions between those two countries.

In late September 1983, a cease-fire was achieved among the Lebanese parties that provided for "neutral" observers. As I felt that this was a role that the United Nations could usefully fill, I telephoned President Assad of Syria—his country had been instrumental in bringing the cease-fire about—to offer our assistance. Mr. Assad is not a person one gets to know very well even after repeated meetings, and at this time I hardly knew him. A telephone conversation was bound to be difficult since we had no common language. Nonetheless, I considered personal contact essential since President Assad would have the major influence on how the cease-fire was implemented. After congratulating him on the contribution to peace that his government had made, I told him that, with the agreement of the Security Council, the UNTSO observers already present in part of Beirut could monitor the cease-fire.

Despite the language problem, there could be no misunderstanding that this was not what President Assad had in mind. While he disavowed direct knowledge of the discussions between the Lebanese parties on the subject, he knew "full well" that the agreement provided that the observers would come from countries whose neutrality was accepted by the parties. There would be direct contact with these states to obtain their assistance. He said that I would surely appreciate the reason for insisting on this, given the negative role the multinational force had played, in that it had come as a neutral force and ended up fighting on the side of one party against another. I pointed out that the United Nations had nothing whatever to do with the multinational force. President Assad said this was completely clear to him, he had only referred to that force because the question of observers had been raised. While he said he was willing to hear any further opinions on the topic, it was quite clear that his mind was set against UN monitors. President Gemayel called me the very next day to say that, in his interpretation, "neutral" meant UN observers.

In discussing the Lebanese situation with me on September 30, Prime Minister Margaret Thatcher said she failed to understand how a cease-fire could have been signed without specific agreement on who the observers were to be. She was convinced that observers would have to come from the United Nations since an observer group needed an international authority to report to and someone to pay for its services. The problem, as she saw it, was how to bring influence to bear on Syria. She had raised the issue with Prime Minister Indira Ghandi of India, "who had for once denied having any influence to exert." Mrs. Thatcher thought that Syria's real objective was to see the multinational force depart without another force taking its place. I believe that, as was so often the case, Mrs. Thatcher was right. No observers ever materialized to monitor the cease-fire.

The Security Council took no action. Syria continued to object to any UN involvement in monitoring the cease-fire, and the Soviet Union made clear that it would veto any action that would institute monitors. In an ironic, and I think tragic, way the situation was the mirror image of that which had prevailed earlier, when Israel occupied Beirut. Then the Israelis objected to the deployment of a UN peacekeeping force in the city, and the United States, in supporting Israel, blocked such a move. Now it was the Soviet Union that blocked the deployment of UN observers to monitor a cease-fire in accordance with the wishes of Syria.

Without effective monitoring, the fragile cease-fire soon collapsed, and American attempts to broker a new one were to no avail. Attacks on the multinational force increased. The French and the Americans hit back, the French by bombing Moslem installations from the air and the Americans by bombarding them from offshore warships. The Americans were determined to preserve the Gemayel government and with it the agreement signed by Israel and Lebanon, which Lebanon had not yet ratified. Then, on October 23, 1983, a truck carrying high explosives rammed into a barracks at the Beirut airport where the U.S. Marine contingent of the multinational force was sleeping, killing 241 marines. A simultaneous attack on a French barracks killed a number of French troops. These events marked the beginning of the end of the multinational force.

THE PLO DEPARTS

While the battle was raging between the various Lebanese factions around Beirut, a serious revolt against Arafat's leadership developed within the Al Fatah (the military arm of the PLO) located in the Bekaa Valley. The bitter armed conflict between the group led by Colonel Saed Abu Musa against forces loyal to Arafat spread to the northern port city of Tripoli, where the civilian population, engulfed in the deadly crossfire, suffered many casualties. The Abu Musa forces were clearly supported by Syria and reportedly by Libya, although the Libyan Permanent Representative to the United Nations made a special demarche to me to deny his country's involvement. The ambassador said that if there were Libyans fighting in Lebanon, they were under Syrian command with the exclusive objective of helping Syria.

I received a letter from Yassir Arafat asking for my assistance in bringing the fighting to an end. He expressed a willingness to negotiate a conciliation with the Abu Musa group. After calling urgently for a cease-fire, I met with the Syrian ambassador and asked if his country could use its influence to end the fighting between the PLO factions. On November 10 the Syrian ambassador returned with a stiffly worded memorandum from his government maintaining that Syria had pursued lengthy efforts with the parties to avoid the kind of dispute that had arisen. The fault was entirely Arafat's who had rejected his comrades' call for "democratic negotiations."

During this conversation I passed on to the Syrian representative the following message that had been given to a UN military officer in the field by a senior Israeli Foreign Ministry official:

- Israel had no intention of staying in Lebanon and would leave when it felt reasonably assured of not being attacked from Lebanese soil.
- Israel recognized Syria's special interest in and need for special relations with Lebanon. Israel also recognized that Lebanon is basically an Arab country.
- Israel would not tolerate "terrorist" bombing attacks on its forces and would retaliate if they continued. Israel expected Syria to prevent "terrorist" forces from operating from Lebanon into Israel.
- Israel felt that at least a tacit understanding should be reached with Syria regarding respective limits in Lebanon and referred to the "red line" understanding of 1976.

I never knew whether Syria responded to this message.

With the assistance of Saudi and Syrian mediation, an agreement was reached to stop the PLO internecine fighting. The agreement provided for the evacuation from Tripoli of the PLO fighters loyal to Arafat. Arafat himself had gone to Tripoli from his base in Tunis in order to rally his forces. Instead of victory, however, he was forced for the second time—first by the Israelis and now, in effect, by the Syrians—to lead his troops out of Lebanon into quasi-exile.

The arrangements for the evacuation provided that five Greek ships would sail to Tripoli and pick up the PLO forces, including Yassir Arafat. Arafat transmitted a request to me that the ships be allowed to fly the UN flag as a security measure, primarily against possible Israeli attack. This posed a serious question since there was no precedent for such action. The UN flag had been flown only on ships engaged in UN operations or, in several cases, as a symbolic show of support for the United Nations. The United Nations had not been party to the negotiations in Tripoli or to the evacuation arrangements of the PLO forces.

It seemed to me that, on purely humanitarian grounds, the United Nations should do whatever it could to facilitate the resolution of a situation that had already cost the lives of many innocent Lebanese and caused great destruction to Lebanese property. I was therefore inclined to grant the request. As I was certain the Security Council would be unable to reach quick agreement on a resolution that would authorize the use of the UN flag, I decided simply to inform the Council of the situation and request their "understanding" of the action I was taking.

I first telephoned President Gemayel on December 2, since technically the Lebanese would be responsible for the evacuation, and said I would like to have his authorization to respond favorably to Arafat's request. The President, whose lack of political experience was compensated by a very Lebanese entrepreneurial shrewdness, responded that "any withdrawal of foreign troops from his country should be carried out under the authority, and in the presence, of the Lebanese army." I took this as a tacit indication that he would not object to the use of the UN flag.

In my subsequent statement to the Council on December 3, I said it was my understanding that 3,000 armed elements and possibly an additional 1,000 militia, carrying personal weapons only, would be transported from Tripoli by sea. Their probable destinations would be Tunis and the Yemen Arab Republic. On December 8, the Greek Permanent Representative to the United Nations informed me by letter that four Greek ferryboats would leave Greece on that date and requested permission that the UN flag be hoisted "as soon as the ships enter the dangerous zone and not after their arrival in the port of Tripoli." I replied that I had decided to authorize use of the UN flag and that the statement that I had made on the subject to the Security Council had the Council's support.

On the same day, I received a message from Yitzhak Shamir, who had replaced Menachem Begin as Prime Minister of Israel, referring to the explosion of a bus two days earlier in Jerusalem for which the PLO had claimed responsibility. Four persons were killed and 43 wounded. The Prime Minister requested that "in light of this horrendous crime perpetrated by the PLO terrorists . . . I cancel the arrangements that have been made to give them safe conduct under the United Nations flag." While I found the bus attack reprehensible, I did not feel that it was a reason to cancel an arrangement that would help to stop even greater suffering by innocent people in Lebanon.

The evacuation was completed without incident and peace was restored at least in Tripoli. The Israeli Mission issued a press release, however, characterizing the operation as "grotesque," and the Israeli ambassador sent me a letter stating "These developments must be viewed as a dangerous precedent by all those committed to combatting terrorism."[3] I found the Israeli complaint ironic. A major purpose of their invasion of Lebanon was to expel the PLO fighters. With the evacuation from Tripoli, this objective was largely accomplished and, remarkably, through the actions of Syria, Israel's bitter enemy. The two governments were joined in at least one thing, their shared hostility toward Yassir Arafat.

THE FIGHTING CONTINUES

The expulsion of the PLO armed forces did not bring peace to Lebanon. The situation in Beirut became ever more chaotic as the fighting between Christian militia and the various Moslem groups grew fiercer, entailing, eventually, combat between factions within the Christian camp and between Druze and Shi'ite on the Moslem side. In the area still occupied by the Israelis, attacks by Moslem resistance forces became widespread. Syria exercised strong influence on the course of the conflict through the presence of its army. Syrian objectives, as far as I could see, were fourfold: (1) to maintain a position in Lebanon that would permit it to exert strong influence on the country over the long term; (2) to bring about the withdrawal of Israeli forces; (3) to get rid of Yassir Arafat and his supporters; and (4) to destroy the May 17, 1983, agreement between Lebanon and Israel.

I felt strongly that the United Nations should do everything possible to end the disaster that had befallen Lebanon, one of the original members of the Organization. At the beginning of 1984, I wrote of my concerns to the U.S. Secretary of State. I suggested the desirability of developing an agreed international approach that would encompass a timeframe for the withdrawal of all foreign forces, the use of UN peacekeeping and observer forces to facilitate the withdrawal and a substantial increase in the number of UN military observers in and around Beirut. I expressed the hope that there might be high-level discussions on the matter between the United States and the Soviet Union, followed by consultations with other members of the Security Council and with the parties concerned. Ambassador Kirkpatrick delivered the letter personally to the Secretary on my behalf.

Secretary Shultz's response was noncommittal. In speaking to Ambassador Kirkpatrick, he referred repeatedly to the role foreseen for UNIFIL in the Lebanon/Israel agreement in relation to the Palestine refugee camps. He was now convinced, however, that any change in the mandate of UNIFIL would be vetoed by the Soviet Union. It would therefore be advisable to wait "for more favorable circumstances" to seek a broadening of UNIFIL's mandate. In a written reply to me on January 22, the secretary stated that it was too early to know whether alternative arrangements by the United Nations would be necessary or possible to aid the Government of Lebanon after the multinational force was withdrawn. But he thought that it was "the growing strength and confidence of the Government of Lebanon which provides the most effective means of supplanting the role of the MNF." Oddly, three days earlier, President Reagan had addressed a letter to two Democratic congressmen in which he spoke of "an expanded or different UN role in Lebanon" as preferable to broadening the participation in the multinational force and said that the United States had had initial talks with the Secretariat on this issue. On January 6, Prime Minister Thatcher sent me a personal message, through Sir John Thomson, in which she said that the British government had repeatedly made clear its wish to see a greater involvement of UN peacekeeping in Lebanon and that she was "much encouraged by my continuing advocacy of such a course."

On February 8, the United States Permanent Mission delivered a paper to my office outlining a revised U.S. policy toward Lebanon. President Reagan had decided, at President Gemayel's request, "to redistribute U.S. political and military resources in Lebanon." U.S. military efforts would henceforth be concentrated on providing training and equipment for the Lebanese army. The U.S. marine contingent of the multinational force would be redeployed from the Beirut airport, where they had been providing security, to ships offshore. No mention was made of any arrangements to replace the marines or the rest of the multinational force, which was bound to follow the U.S. example, in providing security in the strife-torn capital. I telephoned Secretary Shultz on February 10 to express the most serious concern for what lay ahead unless some such arrangements were made. The secretary asked if UN forces could move to Beirut immediately. I explained that certain requirements had to be met: There had to be a specific request from the Lebanese government, action by the Security Council to authorize such a move, the assurance of cooperation of all the parties concerned and clear terms of reference. The members of the Security Council would have to work together and exert influence where they could if these requirements were to be met. Shultz said that he understood and he thought there were signs of positive change in the Soviet and Syrian attitudes toward deployment of a UN force.

This seemed to be confirmed when, three days later, on February 13, the Soviet Deputy Permanent Representative, Richard Ovinikov, informed me that the Soviet Union was ready to consider the establishment of a UN peacekeeping force in Beirut provided that all multinational forces and the naval forces of all multinational contingents be withdrawn from Lebanese waters and that these forces would not interfere again in Lebanese affairs.

I asked Ambassador Ovinikov what he thought the Syrian position might be. He replied that it probably was surprisingly close to that of the Soviet Union. In this understandable assumption he was wrong. After extensive bilateral consultations among Security Council members, including the Soviet Union, a resolution originally drafted by the French, calling for the immediate deployment of a UN force to the Beirut area to monitor the cease-fire[4] and to help protect the civilian population, including the Palestinian refugees, was tabled in the Security Council. The resolution did not specifically call for the withdrawal of the multinational force or accompanying of ships from Lebanese waters, but it did request Member States to refrain from any military action that might jeopardize the reestablishment of peace and security in Lebanon and to facilitate the task of the UN force. The import of the wording was clear. Nonetheless, the Soviet Union vetoed the resolution in support of the continuing Syrian position that the problems in the Beirut area were internal ones, in which the United Nations should not be involved.

Following this disheartening vote I appealed to the Council "to continue to consider the situation in Lebanon with the intent to find ways in the near future for the UN to expand its role in Lebanon for the benefit not only of Lebanon but also for the cause of international peace and security."

THE CONFLICT IN SOUTHERN LEBANON

Developments in southern Lebanon followed a course similar in its frustrations to the situation in Beirut but quite different in its parameters. In May 1984, Israel announced its intention to withdraw its military forces from Lebanon without repeating its earlier requirement that Syria also withdraw its troops. The withdrawal would be dependent, however, on the completion of satisfactory arrangements to provide security for the northern part of Israel. Such arrangements would have to be worked out with the Lebanese government, with the cooperation of Syria. Israel's view of UNIFIL had meanwhile become more positive, and it foresaw UNIFIL moving into the areas evacuated by the Israel Defense Force. In the early fall, the Shamir government in Jerusalem was replaced by a coalition of Labor and Likud in which the Prime Minister's post would alternate between the two parties. Shimon Peres became Prime Minister. With this change the prospects of Israeli withdrawal from Lebanon seemed markedly improved since I knew from earlier meetings that Peres wished strongly to see the Lebanese adventure ended.

I met with Peres in New York in October. I found him then, as I always did in the future, to be a man of imagination and high intelligence, profoundly dedicated to the security of his country but undoctrinaire—even something of a schemer—in his attitude. We joked about the similarity of our names and decided that since our ancestors were both from Spain, there was perhaps a distant relationship and a trace of Jewish blood in Pérez de Cuéllar, something that I doubted but of which I would not be ashamed. Peres told me that he was still trying to find ways to bring an end to Israel's involvement in Lebanon. His country's desire to pull out was genuine but its forces would remain there unless three basic conditions were met:

- Syria would commit not to move its forces southward beyond their present deployment.
- Syria would prevent infiltration across Syrian lines.
- UNIFIL would replace the Israel Defense Force in the areas it evacuated.

The Prime Minister hoped that the United Nations could help this process along in a quiet way. Members of my staff were told by Syrian representatives that

Syria, too, favored a wider role in the south for UNIFIL to help restore the authority of the Lebanese government. Progress was blocked, however, because the Lebanese government, which had abrogated the May 17 agreement between it and Israel, now refused to hold direct talks with Israel. I have no doubt that this position was prompted by Syria, which did not wish to see any Lebanese action that could be construed as renewed recognition of Israel. Brian Urquhart traveled to Lebanon, Syria and Israel to explore the possibility of resolving the impasse by holding UN-sponsored talks between the Israeli and Lebanese military. Lebanon was initially hesitant but eventually all parties agreed. On October 31, I informed the president of the Security Council that I was convoking a conference of military representatives of Lebanon and Israel to discuss military aspects relating to the withdrawal of Israeli forces and security arrangements in southern Lebanon.

The talks began at Naqoura on November 5 with much hope invested in them, even though hope in Lebanon was an evanescent commodity. They ended on January 24, 1985, a complete failure. The essential problem was that while Israel recognized the sovereignty of Lebanon over all of southern Lebanon and reiterated its commitment to withdraw all its forces from Lebanese territory, it refused to define how security would be maintained in the area north of the Israeli border. While it favored the extension of UNIFIL's mandate to the north of the UNIFIL area of operations, it would not commit itself to the replacement of the IDF by UNIFIL in the border area.

In the midst of the talks, on January 15, the Israeli cabinet adopted a unilateral plan for the withdrawal of its forces in three stages. In the first stage, the Israeli forces would withdraw from the Sidon area. The conditions of the second and third stages covering the remainder of the occupied zone would be decided later based on the success of the first stage. The Lebanese, who had been unwilling to agree to the deployment of UNIFIL to the north without commitment that it could deploy south to the international border with Israel, demanded a timetable and plan for the complete withdrawal of Israeli forces. It would discuss with the United Nations the latter's role in the occupied zone after receipt of such a plan. The two positions were irreconcilable. Shortly after the collapse of the talks, the Israeli cabinet approved a proposal put forward by Defense Minister Yitzak Rabin to establish a security zone in southern Lebanon along the border with Israel. Security in the zone would be maintained by the South Lebanon Army, which was entirely responsible to, and financed by, Israel. In June 1985, Israel announced that its withdrawal from Lebanon had been completed. In fact, however, Israeli soldiers continued to man positions in the border security zone along with South Lebanon Army troops. Israeli personnel circulated freely across the border.

Rabin was the strongest proponent of retaining the security zone under Israeli control. Knowing that he held a harder position on this than Prime Minister

Peres or the Israeli military, I spoke to him directly at a relatively early stage of the Naqoura talks. He was simply not prepared to depend on UNIFIL to protect Israel from infiltration or bombardment from Lebanese territory. He maintained that UNIFIL was a weak arrangement because unlike the UN Disengagement Observer Force deployed between Syria and Israel (UNDOF), it was not based on an agreement between the two governments. I argued that UNIFIL had been quite effective in preventing infiltration through its area of operation. Few, if any, attacks on Israel had originated there. Empowerment of the South Lebanon Army, and continued presence of Israeli military in southern Lebanon, was bound to lead to prolonged conflict with Lebanese resistance groups and would never be acceptable to any Lebanese government. But the Israeli position did not change then or later. UNIFIL has never been able to extend its deployment to the border, as had been the intention when it was first formed in 1978.

I fully understood Israeli concern for the security of its northern border area; Israeli settlements there were obviously vulnerable to cross-border attacks. Yet, I remain convinced that the Israeli policy was counterproductive. Israel's retention of the security zone provided a rallying point for extremist Moslem elements in Lebanon who had by now replaced the PLO in mounting attacks against Israel. Eventually, in 1993, Israel would again find it necessary to cross the border in force to counter the threat posed by these extremist elements. The security zone did not prevent this threat from persisting and even growing. UNIFIL could not have prevented the growth of fundamentalist power in southern Lebanon. I am convinced, however, that it could have afforded Israel greater security than the maintenance on Lebanese territory of a mercenary force loyal to a foreign power.

RENEWED CIVIL WAR

When Israel withdrew its troops from most of occupied Lebanon, the government in Beirut was able to send units of the Lebanese Army to the south to protect Palestine refugee camps and to establish a tenuous presence north of the UNIFIL area of operation. The government of President Amin Gemayel was itself weak, however, and largely dependent on Syria for such authority as it was able to wield. When Gemayel's term of office expired, he chose to appoint as his successor the Lebanese chief of staff, General Michel Aoun, an action contrary to constitutional procedures, which required that the president be elected by the parliament. Again civil war broke out, this time even more destructively than before, in the face of a political situation so chaotic that it defies description. General Aoun, who assumed the presidency with the avowed intention of ridding Lebanon of all foreign forces—meaning the Syrians in particular—was not recognized by the prime minister, El-Hoss, whom Syria supported. France took the lead in efforts to bring the crisis to an end, proposing that 1,200 to 1,300 UNIFIL troops be sent to Beirut for deployment around the building where the parliamentary election of a new president was to take place and to escort each of the 70-odd deputies to and from the building.

In this instance I had grave reservations about sending UN troops to Beirut. They would be subjected to great danger in the midst of a continuing conflict that they could not hope to control. I felt that it was an Arab responsibility to save a fellow Arab state from total destruction. Therefore, I welcomed the decision of the Arab League to appoint a ministerial committee to seek a solution to the crisis. The Security Council, at my instigation, expressed full support for the efforts of the committee and, in document S/20554 of March 31, 1989, called—once again—for an immediate cease-fire. The ministerial committee, under the chairmanship of Sheik Sabah Al-Ahmad Al-Sabah, the foreign minister of Kuwait, developed a three-pronged plan for an immediate and definitive cease-fire; a lifting of the blockades imposed by the various parties on ports, airports, roads and the crossing points between East and West Beirut; and the deployment of a 312-man Arab observer force on the demarcation lines. I met in Geneva with Sheik Al-Sabah at the end of April and congratulated him on the action taken by the Arab League to bring peace to Lebanon. He said that unfortunately they still had a long way to go before reaching this goal. The Lebanese prime minister had accepted the League plan and expressed his willingness to cooperate. General Aoun had been less forthcoming. The situation was made more difficult because of foreign intervention. The Syrians made promises to observe the cease-fire that they did not keep. Minister Al-Sabah told me that he had spoken directly with Syrian Vice-President Abdel Halim Khaddam, but the conversation had led to nothing.

The difficulties to which the minister referred were very real. Iraq was providing support for General Aoun, presumably to counter Syrian support for the various Moslem groups. In the next weeks shelling intensified around Beirut. Arab efforts to consolidate a new cease-fire failed. It also turned out that given the dangers entailed in deployment in Beirut, few Arab states were prepared to provide observers for the projected observer force. On August 1 the Tripartite High Committee of the League of Arab States, consisting of Algeria, Morocco and Saudi Arabia, announced that its efforts in Lebanon had failed. Given the impasse, it did not see the utility of attempting further action.

THE CIVIL WAR ENDS

In the midst of an ever-worsening situation that threatened the very existence of the State of Lebanon, a vacuum had developed in efforts to end the crisis. I felt deeply that the United Nations must do something to end the carnage and destruction. The full weight of the Security Council must be brought to bear, especially that of the five Permanent Members. In the circumstances I decided that I should use the authority given to the Secretary-General in Article 99 of the UN Charter to bring the crisis to the attention of the Council. I resorted to this procedure only two other times in the ten years of my tenure as Secretary-General. First, however, I needed to consult with the five permanent members.

I met with the five ambassadors on August 11. Using more dramatic language than is my usual wont, I said that with the failure of the Arab League initiative, the last vestige of hope for the Lebanese people had evaporated. Violence, hostage-taking and worse had escalated to an unprecedented and horrifying degree. An effective cease-fire was imperative but I doubted whether an appeal by myself or by the Council would, without the strong support of the Permanent Members, be sufficient to achieve it. I suggested that it would be ideal if ways could be found to give new life to the Tripartite Committee, since Lebanon remained inherently an Arab problem. Should this fail, the international community had no alternative but to act collectively to end this crisis. At this critical point I was considering using my authority under Article 99 to bring this matter before the Council, I said, and asked for the ambassadors' views.

All expressed agreement with my assessment and indicated that their governments would support whatever action I decided to take. The French ambassador, Pierre-Louis Blanc, was the most outspoken. He had just learned that two shells had fallen on the French Embassy in Beirut and said that France was making a démarche in Damascus asking the Syrians to stop shelling Beirut. The British ambassador, Sir Crispin Tickell, was the most candid. He regretted that he had nothing original to say other than that his government felt impotent, as others did, and saw Lebanon as a battlefield between two parties, one of whom was not present in the area. I was not sure which two parties he had in mind. More than two had muddied the Lebanon waters.

On August 15, acting under Article 99 of the Charter, I asked that the Security Council be convened urgently "in order to contribute to a peaceful solution of the problem."[5] The Council met at midnight that same day and agreed on a presidential statement calling on all the parties to observe a total and immediate cease-fire, to open the lines of communication and to lift all sieges. The Council also invited the Secretary-General to pursue all appropriate contacts, in liaison with the Tripartite Committee, in order to ensure observance of the cease-fire.[6]

The members of the Tripartite Committee did not respond to the Security Council's call or to my urgings until Syrian President Asad, after a meeting with Algerian President Chadli Bendjedid, withdrew his objections to the Committee's endeavors. Meanwhile, as a result of the action taken by the Security Council and pressure exerted by the five Permanent Members, the cease-fire became effective enough to encourage the Tripartite Committee to resume its efforts. The Committee proposed a new plan that again foresaw a comprehensive cease-fire throughout Lebanon, the creation of a Lebanese Security Committee to oversee implementation of the cease-fire and the lifting of the port blockades. The Lebanese parliament was to meet on September 30, 1989, to prepare a National Reconciliation Charter. While Shi'ite and Druze leaders initially rejected the tripartite plan, both Prime Minister El Hoss and General Aoun accepted it. Of critical importance, this time it was welcomed by Syria.

Subsequently, members of the Lebanese parliament met under the auspices of the Tripartite Committee in Taif, a resort in Saudi Arabia, and reached agreement on a process of peace and national reconciliation. The agreement was enthusiastically welcomed in the United Nations. The five Permanent Members of the Security Council issued a joint statement expressing their determination to support the restoration of Lebanon's sovereignty over the whole of its territory. The French foreign minister stressed the "exceptional, even unprecedented character" of the statement of the Five, which had been adopted "at the request of France." It was certainly significant evidence of the new willingness of the five Permanent Members to work together in the interests of regional peace and of the thawing of the Cold War.

The Taif agreement was fundamentally flawed. Although it set a timetable for the withdrawal of Syrian forces, it also legitimized their presence in Lebanon. In 1997 they are still there, just as Israeli troops continue to circulate freely in the security zone in the south. The Lebanese government was unable to reassert its authority in the Bekaa, where the Syrian army was in control. North of the security zone and the UNIFIL area of operation Shi'ite groups, especially the fundamentalist Hizbollah, resisted control from Beirut. Nonetheless, the agreement did bring the civil war to an end. The government in Beirut became stable enough for reconstruction of the country to begin.

The cost of the Lebanese conflict in lives and property and in suffering remains incalculable. The Lebanese people were the victims of external intervention and invasion, of a conflict that their unwelcome guests, the Palestinians, brought with them and of the ambitions and jealousies of sectarian leaders who put their own interests above those of the country. These same factors severely limited what the United Nations could do to bring about peace. Aside from the important action taken by the Security Council, especially its Permanent Members, to encourage and support the work of the Tripartite Committee, the United Nations played only a marginal part in ending the civil war. It was prevented from deploying peacekeeping forces to alleviate the long-lasting conflict around Beirut. But the level of security in the area where UNIFIL was deployed was far greater than in any other part of Lebanon. The United Nations Relief and Works Agency for Palestinian refugees was active throughout the conflict in assisting and protecting Palestinians in spite of the sometimes uncooperative attitude of the IDF. At my request, various UN agencies combined efforts to bring economic assistance for the reconstruction of Lebanon, assistance that was of necessity modest since contributions from the international community were small. In all of these activities, the United Nations preserved its impartiality among the many elements, internal and external, that were involved in the struggle; a very considerable achievement in the circumstances.

The Lebanese people were not alone in benefitting from the United Nations' presence. Israel, while late in acknowledging it, also gained security from the deployment of UNIFIL. Infiltration into Israel through the UNIFIL area was largely stopped. The area was kept free of weapons that could target northern Israel.

Yet, in the Lebanese war, there were mostly losers. First among these were the Lebanese people. Just below them I would put Israel and Yassir Arafat's PLO. The massacres committed by the Christian Lebanese militia in the Sabra and Shatila camps, which the Israel Defense Force did not move to prevent, ravaged the high esteem in which Israel was widely held as a humanitarian state. The vaunted reputation of the defense force and the morale of its soldiers were harmed by the persistent resistance of various Lebanese Moslem groups. The unity of the Israeli population was shaken by the evident failure of Operation Peace for Galilee. Israeli Prime Minister Begin became a virtual recluse, presumably from a sense of responsibility for the tragic miscalculations of the Lebanese adventure.

Yassir Arafat also lost. The PLO lost its last front-line position in the battle with Israel to regain a Palestinian homeland. Its coherence was shattered by mutiny. In the days to come, the *intifada* movement on the West Bank and in Gaza would become a more effective actor than the PLO. While Arafat was to survive as the leader of the Palestinian people, the image of him leading his troops into exile, which was broadcast throughout the Arab world, was for a time, at least, that of a man of declining charisma and dubious authority.

Only Syria came close to achieving its goals in the battle for Lebanon.

Ironically, though, the losses suffered by Israel and the PLO in Lebanon may well have contributed to the understanding that was later, in 1993, to be reached between them—to the patent discomfiture of President Assad. In Lebanon both learned that peace in the struggle between Israel and the Palestinians, which is central to the entire Middle East conflict, could not be achieved only on one side's terms. Out of the tragedy of the Lebanese war grew recognition of the ultimate necessity of compromise.

FOUR

WORKING FOR A MIDDLE EAST PEACE SETTLEMENT

THE DISASTER THAT AFFLICTED LEBANON—the foreign invasion, the civil war, the flood of refugees—had to be seen as an acute outbreak of the disease that infected the entire Middle East. While it was essential to treat the outbreak and alleviate the effects, it was obvious that the disease itself could not be cured in Lebanon. The danger existed that the very urgency of the Lebanese conflict would divert attention from the necessity of working on the fundamental problem of a Middle East settlement. There was a palpable necessity to get to the root of the problem. This was a point of clear agreement in my earliest contacts, as Secretary-General, with the American and Soviet governments. I recall George Shultz saying in one of our first meetings that the peace process should go forward without waiting for a full resolution of the Lebanese situation. Now, he said, was the time for people to come to the negotiating table and start talking.

Initiatives aimed at a Middle East settlement were not lacking. Early in 1982, Arab countries, together with the Palestine Liberation Organization, agreed on the "Fez plan," which foresaw Israeli withdrawal from all occupied territories, the dismantling of Israeli settlements, brief transitional administration of the West Bank and Gaza by the United Nations and the establishment of an independent Palestinian state with Jerusalem as its capital. On September 1, 1982, the very day on which the PLO fighters were evacuated from Beirut, President Reagan announced a major American plan. The President reiterated America's commitment to the security of all states in the area, called for Israeli withdrawal in return for peace in accordance with Security Council Resolution 242 and proposed that the Palestinians in the West Bank and Gaza be given the possibility of self-government in association with Jordan. The status of the Israeli settlements, and of Jerusalem, would be determined through negotiations among the parties. The United States would not support extraterritorial status for the settlements, but neither would it support efforts to deny Jews the opportunity to live in the West Bank and Gaza "under the duly constituted governmental authority there, as Arabs live in Israel."[1]

In a letter addressed to me the day after the President's statement, Secretary Shultz emphasized that the U.S. Administration sought a real settlements freeze and favored participation by Palestinian inhabitants of East Jerusalem in the election for the West Bank/Gaza authority. It would oppose dismantlement of the existing settlements. The Secretary said that the United States had been planning a significant effort on behalf of the peace process before the war in Lebanon intervened. The conflict only accentuated the urgent need to press forward. Secretary Shultz wrote that the President wanted me to know "that he is personally committed to the course on which he is now embarked. He intends to stand by the positions . . . whatever the reaction from other quarters."[2] The American plan clearly foresaw direct negotiations among the parties.

While Resolutions 242 and 338, adopted by the Security Council in connection with the Arab-Israeli wars of 1967 and 1973 respectively, were generally seen as central to any solution of the Middle East problem, the United Nations had not been active in the search for peace in the Middle East since 1973, when the efforts of Ambassador Gunnar Jarring, as Special Representative of the Secretary-General, came to an effective end. The United Nations had no role in the Camp David Accords. (A UN peacekeeping operation was envisaged for the Sinai but was opposed by the Arab countries and the Soviet Union.) In light of the increasing danger posed by the unresolved problem of the Middle East, I felt the United Nations had a responsibility to reactivate its work for a comprehensive settlement for the region. I never believed that the United Nations or I personally should compete with the United States or others who were pursuing the same goal. Rather, it seemed to me that the United Nations could offer a number of advantages in a negotiation process—either in support of other approaches or in a UN-led effort.

The main problem with the American approach, as I saw it, was that it excluded the PLO and the Soviet Union from participating in negotiations on a settlement, whereas both were bound to be important players. Moreover, success of the plan depended on direct negotiations between Israel and the Arab parties without any protective umbrella to shield the Arabs from accusations of premature recognition of Israel. The Soviet Union, meanwhile, began to promote the idea of a vaguely defined international conference to negotiate a

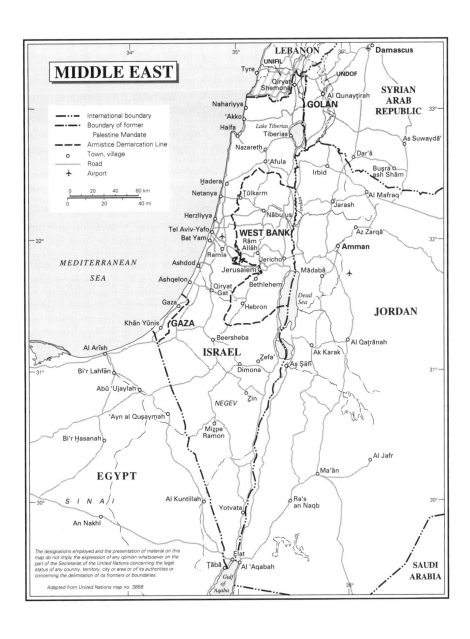

MIDDLE EAST

International boundary
Boundary of former
Palestine Mandate
Armistice Demarcation Line
o   Town, village
Road
✈   Airport

| 0 | 20 | 40 | 60 km |
| 0 | 20 | | 40 mi |

LEBANON

Damascus

UNIFIL

Tyre

Qiryat
Shemona

UNDOF

Al Qunayṭirah

Nahariyya

GOLAN

SYRIAN
ARAB
REPUBLIC

'Akko

Haifa

Lake Tiberias

Tiberias

As Suwaydā'

Nazareth

'Afula

Dar'ā

Irbid

Buṣrá
ash Shām

Ḥadera

Netanya

Ṭūlkarm

Al Mafraq

Jarash

Herzliyya

Nābulus

Az Zarqā'

Tel Aviv-Yafo

WEST BANK

Bat Yam

Rām
Allāh

Amman

Ramla

Jericho

MEDITERRANEAN

Ashdod

Jerusalem

Mādabā

SEA

Ashqelon

Bethlehem

Qiryat
Gat

*Dead
Sea*

Gaza

Hebron

JORDAN

Khān Yūnis

GAZA

Beersheba

Al Qaṭrānah

Al Arīsh

ISRAEL

Zefa'

Ak Karak

Bi'r Lahfān

Dimona

Aṣ Ṣāfī

Abū 'Ujaylah

NEGEV

Zin

'Ayn al Quṣaymah

Miẓpe
Ramon

Bi'r Ḥasanah

Al Jafr

Ma'ān

EGYPT

S I N A I

Al Kuntillah

Yotvata

Ra's
an Naqb

An Nakhl

Elat

Ṭābā

Al 'Aqabah

*Gulf
of
Aqaba*

SAUDI
ARABIA

The designations employed and the presentation of material on this
map do not imply the expression of any opinion whatsoever on the
part of the Secretariat of the United Nations concerning the legal
status of any country, territory, city or area or of its authorities or
concerning the delimitation of its frontiers or boundaries.

Adapted from United Nations map no. 3858

Middle East peace agreement. I would spend a good many years seeking to gain support for the international conference idea because the General Assembly adopted resolutions that called on me to do so. Yet I did so with little belief that such a conference could succeed. The resolutions specifically foresaw that the PLO would have the right to participate in the conference on an equal footing with all other parties; at the time, this was clearly unrealistic.

I felt that the Security Council offered a forum for negotiations that could minimize the problems inherent in both the American plan and the international conference approach. Because of its Observer status at the United Nations, the PLO already had the right to participate, when invited, in Security Council deliberations. PLO participation would therefore not need to be raised as a new issue; nor would PLO participation constitute any change in its status. Soviet participation would be automatic but within a framework where the United States (and, vicariously, Israel) enjoyed the safeguard of the veto. Furthermore, the Council was of a manageable size for negotiations and the five Permanent Members constituted a core group among whom positions could be developed and eventually pushed with the power and influence that these five countries enjoyed. (This last consideration became especially important in my mind after it was proven in 1987, in the context of the Iran-Iraq war, that the Permanent Members were able to cooperate effectively in bringing a regional conflict to an end.)

When I visited Moscow in the fall of 1982, I pursued this subject with President Brezhnev and Foreign Minister Gromyko. Brezhnev reiterated mechanically the Soviet call for an international conference but showed more spirit in insisting that the United Nations, and the Secretary-General personally, were expected to contribute to the achievement of the legitimate rights of the Palestinian people. I noted that Brezhnev referred to the "legitimate rights" of the Palestinian people, the terminology preferred by the Americans, rather than the "inalienable rights," the wording used by the PLO and the Arab countries. (Less than two years later, when I attended Brezhnev's funeral, his successor, Konstantin Chernenko, spoke from the same brief, and with similar lassitude, on the Middle East.)

When I spoke with Gromyko during the 1982 visit, he said that the Soviet Union sympathized with the idea that the United Nations should play a more active role in the Middle East problem, but discussions in the Security Council "where ideas could be vetoed by any Kirkpatrick" were not always congenial to a solution. As for the Reagan plan, it was, in the foreign minister's view, evidently couched in Israeli terms. It provided for neither a Palestinian state nor Israeli withdrawal from occupied Arab land, both of which were essential to a Middle East settlement.

Thus, by the end of 1982, three approaches to negotiations on a Middle East settlement were in play: direct negotiations between Israel and the other parties without PLO participation; an international conference in which the PLO would participate; and development of a peace agreement through discussions in the Security Council.

On December 13, 1983, the General Assembly adopted Resolution 38/56C endorsing the call for an International Peace Conference on the Middle East, for which it listed extensive guidelines, none of which had any chance of acceptance by Israel. The resolution requested me, in consultation with the Security Council, "to undertake preparatory measures to convene the conference." I believed that there would be no sense in proceeding with preparatory measures until there was agreement on who should attend the conference. The best course was to put this question to the test. I therefore sent a letter to the president of the Security Council stating that "bearing in mind the provisions of the General Assembly resolution," the following governments and authorities could be invited to participate in the conference: the 15 members of the Security Council, the governments directly involved in the conflict that were not members of the Security Council and the Palestine Liberation Organization.

I stated further that it would be my intention to address letters to the Permanent Representatives of these governments and to the Permanent Observer of the PLO, informing them of the list of participants as agreed in consultation with the Security Council and requesting their participation in the conference. If the members of the Security Council agreed with this plan of action, I would proceed accordingly. Of course, the members did not agree on this plan, since PLO participation was entirely unacceptable to the United States. Under the circumstances there could be no point in proceeding with other preparatory measures such as deciding on the time and venue and agenda. I wanted this point to be clearly demonstrated, given the obligations under which the General Assembly's resolution had placed me. Realizing that insistence on PLO participation could block the possibility of an international peace conference indefinitely, I considered going back to the Council with a revised attendance list that eliminated the PLO. I decided against this for three reasons. It was clear, first of all, that this formula would be unacceptable to other members of the Council, including the Soviet Union. Second, the General Assembly resolution under which I was acting specified that the PLO should be invited to attend the conference on an equal footing with other participants. Finally—and, for me, most important—I was convinced that no sound peace treaty for the Middle East could be achieved without the participation of the PLO in some form.

Israel's response to the General Assembly resolution was a categorical rejection of the idea of an international conference in any form. In a letter addressed to me on April 26, 1984, the Israeli Permanent Representative, Yehuda Blum, said that any serious attempt to advance the cause of peace in the Middle East "must be initiated through direct negotiations based on Security

Council Resolution 242." There was obviously a complete impasse on the idea of an international conference.

AN EXPLORATORY JOURNEY

None of the other proposals for resolution of the Middle East problem were faring any better. There was no end in sight either to the war between Iran and Iraq or to the Israeli and Syrian presence in Lebanon. There was serious discord among the Arab countries on various subjects, including Yassir Arafat's credibility as leader of the PLO. Given the dangers to peace inherent in these conditions, I decided to make an exploratory trip to the region, my first since becoming Secretary-General. From June 5 to June 13, 1984, I visited Egypt, Lebanon, Syria, Jordan and Israel in that order. In each country I had the opportunity to meet with the top leaders and to hear, firsthand, their concerns and their hopes. I had no mandate from the General Assembly or the Security Council for the trip, nor did I have any new proposals to put forward. My intent was to elicit the views of the regional leaders on the best negotiating framework for a comprehensive settlement, to discuss means of achieving Israeli withdrawal from Lebanon, and, generally, to evaluate how I might be of assistance in reducing tensions in the area. I wanted by my presence to make clear that the United Nations had a strong interest in the Middle East problem and could be an important factor in its alleviation. I thought also that it would be valuable for me to get to know the Middle East leaders better and for them to get to know me. At least this last purpose was well served.

In each country I found that there were particular preoccupations and, of course, a large disparity in attitude and personality among the various leaders. Yet I detected a distinctly pragmatic attitude in all five capitals. There was a general and, I found, genuine desire for peace. While bitterness, distrust and despair were evident, they were not expressed in rhetorical terms. In synthesizing my impressions at the end of the journey, what emerged most strongly as characteristic of the leaders at that time was realism, frustration and, among the Arabs, a lack of common strategy.

I found Egyptian President Hosni Mubarak to be a solid leader, determined to bring Egypt out of the isolation that had resulted from the Camp David Accords but, at the same time, anxious to retain a constructive relationship with Israel. The President did not strike me as a man of great imagination. He was following a path that had been laid out before him. In this he was steadfast. He was deeply concerned over the future of the Palestinians, especially in the West Bank. He was convinced that the Soviet Union as well as the United States would have to participate in any successful negotiating process. Like the other Arab leaders whom I met subsequently, President Mubarak favored a more prominent UN role in the Middle East peace process and saw potential value in my idea of using the Security Council as a forum in which the negotiating process could be started.

While in Cairo, I had two lengthy conversations with the minister of state in the Foreign Ministry, Boutros Boutros-Ghali, without suspecting in the least that he would one day be my successor. He was the de facto foreign minister, prevented by his Christian religion from occupying that post in the cabinet. Whereas President Mubarak gave the impression of stolidness, Boutros-Ghali struck me then and later as a man of cosmopolitan intellect whose mind ranged widely across the foreign policy spectrum. He exuded self-confidence and courtesy. He dwelt more on Africa than on the Middle East, expressing strong support for what he called the South-South dialogue. He thought a new strategy was needed in which African states could be united in the fight against apartheid. Egypt would take the lead in mapping out a new approach. Like President Mubarak, he expressed great concern about the situation of the Palestinians in the occupied territories. He thought that Israel was in the process of destroying the Palestinian structure there; making the Palestinians a *Lumpenproletariat* of Israel. Completion of this process would mark a point of no return. Egypt, he said, would not object to an international conference on the Middle East, but meanwhile, after the Israeli elections that were to be held that summer, Palestinian autonomy talks could be resumed.

I found the Syrian leadership more receptive than that of any of the other countries I visited to a role for the Security Council in a Middle East settlement. In speaking to President Assad, I said that while the tragedy of Lebanon was a matter of the utmost concern, the fundamental problem of the area was the Palestinian question. It was my impression that the Israeli government was not really interested in a solution since it was counting on eventual acceptance by the international community of faits accomplis. I felt that for this reason it was especially important to get some form of negotiations started. If an international conference was not possible, the Security Council might provide an alternative.

President Assad is not a man who is generous in his words. While I have described Mubarak as stolid, I would characterize Assad as impassive. He favored, in principle, an international conference but thought it was foolish to worry about its format until there was greater agreement on the idea. Washington's policy in the Middle East was simply Israeli policy. President Assad's main preoccupation was Lebanon; in this connection, he expressed pride in his country's role in bringing about a government of national unity, which had once been considered an impossibility. At the same time, some frustration was evident in the President's remarks about the political divisions in Beirut. He feared that if the present government failed, it would be the end of Lebanon as a unitary state. Syria was ready to cooperate with the United

Nations in southern Lebanon as long as UN policy was aimed at Israeli withdrawal. Syria would withdraw its troops from Lebanon once the Israeli troops were gone and the Lebanese government asked it to do so.

When I reached Lebanon I could well understand the Syrian concern about its future. Conditions in Beirut were appalling. The so-called government of national unity was so divided—and conditions in the city were so dangerous—that the cabinet could never meet. I had to fly by helicopter from the presidential residence located in Baabda, a suburb of East Beirut, to the office of Prime Minister Rashid Karami in West Beirut. The city was completely divided. So, too, were the views of President Gemayel and the prime minister, not to speak of Nabih Berri, the Shi'ite leader who held the post of Minister of the South. The Prime Minister contended that Lebanon was the victim of an international plot, and he expressed pride that his government had abrogated the May 17 agreement with Israel, which, of course, was the agreement that President Gemayel had signed. President Gemayel supported the idea of making south Lebanon into a zone of peace from which the PLO would be excluded but was completely opposed to the United Nations' providing a buffer between Syrian and Israeli forces, fearing that this would result in the partitioning of Lebanon. He devoted part of our conversation to the promotion of Lebanese staff members in the UN Secretariat, which under the surrounding circumstances struck me as hardly serious. Berri, whom I saw in West Beirut, said that the Shi'ite organization Amal could deploy between 12,000 to 15,000 troops to provide security in the South, contending that they could do a better job than the Israeli-supported South Lebanon Army. "The Israelis," he said, "have nothing to fear unless they want to turn Lebanon into a North Bank."

The most troubled leader whom I saw was King Hussein of Jordan. He expressed a sense of despair over developments in the Occupied Territories. He also was discouraged by Washington's attitude. In the King's view, Washington was trying to monopolize the political scene but remained reluctant to commit itself to real progress. He doubted that a Labor victory in Israel, should it occur, would bring much change in Israeli policy. Still, he believed that Shimon Peres could be an acceptable interlocutor. So much has been written about Hussein as the "little king" that his short stature came as no surprise to me. I was surprised, though, on this first meeting, and impressed in all subsequent meetings, by the utter seriousness of his demeanor. One senses that he bears the weight of the Middle East problem on his shoulders and that he finds it very heavy.

The Jordanian foreign minister, Tahar Masri, was forthright in stating that the Jordanians were prepared to speak with the Israelis directly but only in the framework of an international conference or a UN forum. The King and all his cabinet clearly were exasperated with Yassir Arafat.

The final stop on my trip was Israel, where I was treated with great respect. As always, the Israelis made a clear distinction between the United

Nations—which they distrusted—and the Secretary-General. I met with Prime Minister Shamir and David Kimche, director-general of the Foreign Ministry, as well as with the leader of the Labor party, Shimon Peres. The Israeli positions were well known to me, the only surprise was that neither the Prime Minister nor the director-general expressed objections to my idea of according a role to the Security Council in discussions on a Middle East peace settlement. The Prime Minister was forceful, however, in his opposition to an international conference; he contended it would be bound to be transformed into a propaganda exercise against Israel.

In talking with Shimon Peres, I explained that I hoped that my trip to the Middle East might help to start a negotiating process. I felt that the present situation could explode at any moment. Peres shared the same view. He thought the problem of negotiations was a structural one. All of the problems could not be tackled at one time. It would be foolish, he thought, to bring moderates and extremists around the same table. The first thing to accomplish, in his view, was the withdrawal of all foreign forces from Lebanon. His party did not feel that a broader peace process had any chance of success under existing circumstances. After resolving the situation in Lebanon, the next step would be to start negotiations with Jordan. He did not think that Arafat, "who for 16 years had not been able to make up his mind," would be a valid interlocutor.

On my return from these visits to the five Middle Eastern capitals, I went to Washington, where I had the opportunity for an extensive review of the international situation with George Shultz. I told the secretary that I had sensed a widespread anxiety during my trip, especially in Egypt and Jordan. Shultz appeared somewhat displeased by this remark and asked "Anxiety about what?" I said that there was anxiety because of the stalemate in negotiations. The Arabs were concerned that as long as a diplomatic vacuum persisted, Israel would continue to consolidate its position in the occupied territories. I had found in all five countries a desire to find peaceful solutions to the problems. There had been a notable lack of rhetoric. The Arab governments were, of course, in favor of an international conference, but they had also seen merit in my concept of using the Security Council as an instrument for a gradual beginning of negotiations. Even the Israelis, despite their general distrust of the United Nations, had not opposed the idea.

Secretary Shultz interjected that it should be clear that the United States could not participate in what I had referred to as an international conference. He did not wish to seem "more Israeli than the Israelis," but the United States had very firm commitments on which it could not renege. He asked, rather testily, that I not place the United States in the same category in which I had placed Israel—that is, acquiescing by silence. Throughout the discussion I had the impression that Secretary Shultz had been traumatized by the failure of the May 17 agreement between Lebanon and Israel, an agreement to which he had devoted so much time and energy. He compared the situation in Lebanon to a shifting bonfire, beyond the control of the Lebanese government. In the circumstances, no one could expect Israel to withdraw completely. He was convinced that most of those who had opposed the May 17 agreement had not read it—except for the Syrians.

In July I was again in Moscow. In a long conversation with Foreign Minister Gromyko, I reviewed the impressions I had gained from my Middle East visit. The subject of the Middle East and an international conference prompted Mr. Gromyko to recall the League of Nations ("in which the Secretary-General spoke with the same voice as the British and French who controlled the organization"); Dunbarton Oaks ("where Stettinius, Halifax and he had sat around the same table planning the future world organization—no thought then of excluding the USSR"); and, as always in every conversation I had with Mr. Gromyko on the Middle East, his vote in 1947 in favor of the establishment of Israel. The Soviet Union still favored the existence of Israel. However, the Minister continued (and it was a large "however"), the United Nations should be more active in defending the interests of the Arabs. I was justified in "stirring the pot" in the right direction. Israel was the aggressor and should be kept under constant pressure. Mr. Gromyko continued to feel that the international conference on the Middle East "was the right answer." He was doubtful about initiating a new negotiating process in the Security Council since he feared it would entail further concessions to Israel.

I found Andrei Gromyko's perception that I was "stirring the pot" quite on target; that was precisely what I sought to do during the long years of stalemate on the Middle East problem. Whether this "stirring" took place in the framework of an international conference or the Security Council or through bilateral negotiations did not seem to me of intrinsic importance. I was by no means alone. George Shultz pursued the Reagan Plan with vigor but ran into repeated obstacles. By 1985 the Americans had accepted the concept of an international conference as providing an umbrella—and nothing more—for bilateral negotiations between the parties. This effort faltered by the spring of 1986 as a result of, among other things, differences on the participation of the Soviet Union, a split in the Israeli Government on accepting the plan, waffling on the part of the PLO on acceptance of Security Council Resolutions 242 and 338 and, finally, a break between King Hussein and Yassir Arafat, which caused the King to wash his hands publicly of the whole enterprise.

DEFINING AN INTERNATIONAL CONFERENCE

In January 1987, the General Assembly, in Resolution 41/43D, again called for the urgent convocation of an International Peace Conference on the Middle East.

This time the assembly requested me not only to continue my efforts to convene a conference but also to organize a preparatory committee to include the Permanent Members of the Security Council. I quickly found that while the United States had accepted the concept of an international conference as an umbrella for the initiation of bilateral negotiations, it was not prepared to cooperate in the formation of a preparatory committee nor did it favor informal consultations among the five Permanent Members as had by then been initiated in connection with the war between Iran and Iraq. I was told by the U.S. Deputy Permanent Representative, Herbert Okun, that the Middle East situation had not "matured" enough for the Permanent Members to engage in joint consultations.

At this point, in late March 1987, the very articulate director-general of the Israeli Foreign Ministry, Avraham Tamir, outlined to me in clear and non-rhetorical language the position of the Israeli government on an international conference. Israel, he said, accepted the principle of an international conference but only as a framework for direct talks between the parties. Israel could not accept an international conference that would have the power to veto agreements reached between the parties. I, in turn, stated that I saw no contradiction between an international conference and bilateral negotiations. On the other hand, I failed to see how the preparations for the conference could be handled bilaterally among the parties when Israel had no diplomatic relations with the Soviet Union or with any of the parties to the conflict except Egypt. Some channel of communication would be necessary. In this the United Nations could be of help. I was undertaking consultations on "an" (not "the") international conference (even though the General Assembly resolution referred to "the" conference), but I was not a prisoner of this formula. I considered that if there was another option, it was my duty to pursue it.

In June 1987, I discussed the Middle East problem in a very wide-ranging conversation with General Secretary Gorbachev in Moscow. (Other aspects of the conversation are described in chapters 7 and 8.) Gorbachev contended that progress toward an international conference was impeded at the moment by U.S. and Israeli insistence on using the conference to cover their policies. The Soviet Union would not "recriminate," but it would also not just mark time. I said that I myself did not entirely understand the Israeli position. They did not want a plenary that could impose solutions or serve as an appeals body for the bilateral negotiations. But, as I had stated to the Israelis, there were some issues, such as security guarantees, that could only be handled multilaterally. I noted that the disunity among Syria, Jordan and the PLO was not helpful and that Syria, in particular, needed to take a more constructive attitude.

Gorbachev said that he had explained to these and other countries that reality should be accepted, with guarantees for the existence of all. But Israel must withdraw from the occupied territories. I said that one reality being used to delay the peace process was the lack of relations between the Soviet Union and Israel. I understood that the Soviet Union would be prepared to take a decision on this question once an international conference was a certitude. Gorbachev nodded but said only that there were contacts at the United Nations between the two countries. In a separate conversation, Foreign Minister Shevardnadze insisted that the Secretary-General and the Permanent Members, in the form of a preparatory committee, a working group or something else, should take charge of preparations for the international conference.

Less than a month later I discussed these same subjects with Shimon Peres in Geneva. Peres was extremely anxious to know whether Gorbachev had accepted that the international conference should not have the right to veto or to impose solutions. I said that he had and that the Soviet ambassador in New York had said the same. Gorbachev had made it clear that the Soviets wanted the Palestinians to play a role in the conference. He had not mentioned the PLO specifically, but Shevardnadze had. I told Peres that I had gained the strong impression in Moscow that the Soviets would accept any formula that would give the Soviet Union a role. Their overriding wish was to be included in the process. Peres said that public opinion in Israel was still strongly in favor of direct negotiations. The international conference proposal was therefore a heavy political burden for him. I commented that Israel held the key to progress. Peres responded that "he was looking for the keyhole."

Early in 1988, Secretary Shultz developed yet another plan for Middle East negotiations. In this case, Assistant Secretary Richard Murphy briefed me on the plan before Mr. Shultz left to visit the parties directly concerned. The unique feature of the American approach was that implementation of interim arrangements for self-government in the West Bank and Gaza would be "interlocked" with the opening of negotiations on an overall Middle East solution. When I asked about the current attitude of the Israeli government, Murphy conceded that Mr. Shamir was not yet ready to discuss trading territory for peace. It was also still unclear whether the PLO was prepared to accept Resolution 242 officially.

After visiting Moscow, Jerusalem, Damascus, Amman and Cairo, Secretary Shultz prepared a statement of understandings in the form of letters to the principal parties outlining the steps that he was convinced were necessary "to achieve the prompt opening of negotiations on a comprehensive peace."[3] The statement provided that "two weeks before the opening of negotiations, an international conference will be held. The Secretary-General of the United Nations will be asked to issue invitations to the parties involved in the Arab-Israeli conflict and the five Permanent Members of the Security Council. . . . The conference will not be able to impose solutions or veto agreements reached."

My concurrence in this arrangement was not sought, nor, as far as I know, were the Permanent Members, other than the Soviet Union, consulted. After learning of the plan, I told a group of Arab cabinet ministers who were in New York that I was not interested in playing the role of curtain-raiser at a purely symbolic international conference on the Middle East. The conference would have to deal with certain substantive issues, such as security guarantees. I told the ministers that it was ludicrous to think that bilateral negotiators could make decisions on behalf of the potential guarantors. Progress was difficult to envisage if the United States and Israel did not realize the necessity of dealing with some substantive matters multinationally. I later repeated these views to the Soviet Ambassador. In the end, it did not matter since, of all the parties, only Egypt agreed to the American plan.

When President Gorbachev visited UN Headquarters in December 1988, I had occasion to continue our earlier discussion on the Middle East. Gorbachev was much encouraged by the decision taken by the PLO under Arafat's leadership to accept the provisions of Resolution 242. He felt that the Middle East "was an old knot, but now was the time to untie it." The PLO had made a move, he said, but Israel had not responded. I urged once again that the five Permanent Members of the Security Council work together on the problem. President Gorbachev did not respond specifically to this thought but emphasized the importance of joint U.S./Soviet steps without which a settlement could not move forward. He was confident that Washington would move in the direction of an international conference. I suggested that the Soviet government should help Arafat to understand what further action on his part was needed. The Soviet President commented only that "today no one would accept pressure."

Prime Minister Shamir visited the United Nations in June and told me that Israel appreciated Secretary Shultz's efforts. "He comes and goes a lot. We wish him success. But . . . I am afraid that if one's efforts are directed along the lines of an international conference, one will not bring forward the prospect of real negotiations for peace." I told the Prime Minister that "in a sense, you are the oldest problem we have in this house and we want to solve you." The Prime Minister responded that his people did indeed have an ancient history. Throughout the lengthy conversation, Mr. Shamir's distrust of the United Nations was evident, although he expressed appreciation for UNDOF, the UN peacekeeping operation in the Golan Heights. I cautioned, in this regard, that UNDOF should not be considered a permanent fixture. The United Nations was not there to protect a status quo that was not legal. Mr. Shamir said he took my point.

NEW GOVERNMENTS IN ISRAEL AND THE UNITED STATES

In November 1988 elections were held in Israel; as a result, Shamir was able to form a Likud-led government. Moshe Arens became foreign minister. Both men had opposed Resolution 242, the Camp David Accords and any dealings with the PLO. I did not think their attitude was likely to change. While the PLO by then had formally accepted Resolution 242 and the United States had begun a dialogue with PLO representatives, the PLO also had proclaimed the founding of an independent Palestinian state. My expectation was confirmed when Mr. Shamir called on me in April 1989 for another lengthy and, on this occasion, generally good-natured conversation. The Prime Minister reiterated his opposition to any form of international conference on a Middle East settlement. He remarked that he knew the parties *said* such a conference could not impose a solution but in fact most of them *hoped* to do just that. While he repeated several times that his government held me personally in great respect, he made equally clear that Israel saw no role for the United Nations in the Middle East peace process. I must admit I saw no prospect for productive negotiations as long as the Likud government remained in power.

There was also a new administration in Washington. The Bush Administration, especially Jim Baker, the secretary of state, seemed to be taking a more realistic attitude toward the Middle East than its predecessor. There was no indication, however, that it would try to force Mr. Shamir to agree to an international conference. This was the subject of a very candid exchange during my first meeting with Secretary Baker, which took place in Washington on March 23, 1989. I told the secretary that I was under continuing pressure to pursue my consultations with members of the Security Council with regard to a Middle East solution. I stressed my by then well-known view that it was important for the Security Council to be seen as actively involved in the matter. This might even help to calm the *intifada.* It was not my intention to put forward specific proposals but rather to show through the discussions that the international community was concerned with the situation and that there was some movement.

Jim Baker replied rather sharply that "We *are* concerned and we believe we are pursuing a more productive path." The PLO and the United States, he said, were engaged in a dialogue. The United States had published a human rights report that was highly critical of Israel. The idea entertained by some Western European governments, however, that the United States could deliver Israel "on a platter" was totally unrealistic. What was necessary was to work on Israel and, concomitantly, on the PLO. The secretary felt that a UN effort could "preempt" the promise of the current U.S. approach. I said—and only a week earlier I had said more or less the same thing to Israeli Foreign Minister Arens— that the problem at present was that the current Israeli leadership said no to every practical proposal. Baker agreed that this was the case. He thought the Israelis knew they were losing in terms of public opinion. The United States was actively engaged in seeking a solution. "Believe me," he said, "we are not just sitting back and stonewalling on behalf of Israeli negativism."

This first meeting with Secretary Baker covered numerous other subjects and while the discussion on the Middle East was at times sharp in tone, I found the secretary to be innately courteous. He was fully informed and refreshingly straightforward. He struck me as pragmatic and self-confident but quite ready to listen to opposing views. He showed a quickness and suppleness of mind that went well beyond shrewdness.

I received a letter from the secretary following Shamir's April visit to Washington in which he gave more formal expression to his thinking on how to advance the Middle East peace process. His main point was that the key to progress in the region lay in developing a political process "of dialogue and negotiations involving both Israel and the Palestinians." The secretary felt that Shamir's proposal for elections for Palestinian representatives in the occupied territories to negotiate interim arrangements with Israel could prove productive. Prime Minister Shamir had stated that the elections could launch a "political negotiating process," terminology he had not used before. The United States felt that elections in the West Bank and Gaza could contribute to reduced tensions on the ground, creating a positive atmosphere that could set the stage for negotiations.

I could not share Jim Baker's optimism. I suspected that Washington was going along with Shamir's approach largely because there was no other way to maintain the appearance of some movement on the Middle East problem. The U.S. Permanent Representative, Tom Pickering (who had once been the U.S. ambassador to Israel), told me that the U.S. position on an international conference had not changed but the time was not ripe. The present challenge, as the United States saw it, was to bring Israelis and Palestinians together, to reduce tension on the ground and to lower the level of violence.

During a lengthy conversation in Geneva on April 20, 1989, Yassir Arafat, now the President of the newly proclaimed Palestinian state, told me he had received two messages relative to the Shamir peace plan from Yitzhak Rabin, who had remained defense minister in the Shamir government. The messages, which had been conveyed to Arafat discreetly in Tunis, had distanced Rabin from Shamir's proposal for elections in the occupied territories. In the second message, which was dated April 18, Rabin had put forward an alternative proposal. In essence, it repeated the Camp David formula but crystallized a little more what would ensue after the five-year transitional period of Palestinian autonomy. Rabin suggested that at that time he would be prepared to accept the independence of the Palestinian people. Rabin had requested a response before he undertook a planned visit to the United States in mid-May. Arafat said that he had sent an interim, noncommittal response but promised to bring the matter up at a meeting of the Palestinian leadership.

In July 1989, I again met with Arafat, this time at a summit meeting of the Organization of African Unity in Addis Ababa. When I mentioned that I expected to see Jim Baker soon in Paris during the conference on Cambodia, Arafat asked that I "tell Baker that if they want an election, we will accept it. But it will have to be conducted under a Namibia-like process: UN troops; UN supervision; deployment of UN forces."

I never felt that, as Secretary-General, I could support the idea of elections in the occupied territories for representatives to negotiate an interim arrangement for the territories with Israel. The Palestinian problem extended to all the Palestinians who were living as refugees in Lebanon and elsewhere. They would have to be represented in any negotiations between Palestinians and Israel. The General Assembly had determined the PLO to be the sole legitimate representative of the Palestinians, and I did not see how I could support a process that was clearly designed to circumvent the PLO. Beyond that, and more important, the idea had no chance of success. The PLO was bound to oppose it, which meant that few Palestinians would cooperate. I presumed that Jordan also would be against the concept. Secretary Baker wrote to me repeatedly describing U.S. efforts in support of the proposed elections in the occupied territories. In a letter of October 19 he specifically suggested that it would be helpful if I could voice support for the idea of dialogue to structure elections and negotiations and encourage the PLO "in this vein." I replied that of course I would try to be of help, but the Secretary would appreciate that, "as Secretary-General, it will always be necessary for me to stress the need for a comprehensive settlement based on Security Council Resolutions 242 and 338, and taking into account the legitimate rights of the Palestinian people."

KEEPING THE POT BOILING

Even under the unpromising circumstances at the beginning of 1989 I considered it my responsibility to continue to keep the pot boiling, as Mr. Gorbachev had said. Moreover, the General Assembly on December 15, 1988, had passed yet another resolution, 43/176, requesting me to facilitate the convening of the International Peace Conference on the Middle East. Accordingly I met individually with the five Permanent Members of the Security Council during April and posed the following three questions to each:

1. What role can the Permanent Members together with the Secretary-General play at this juncture, bearing in mind that the United States is opposed for the time being to the idea of the Five working as a group, and furthermore that the situation in the Occupied Territories continues to deteriorate?
2. Both the Soviets and the PLO have suggested the appointment by the United Nations of a Special Representative on the Palestine question. What is the position of the Five on this proposal?

3. One of the parties—Egypt—has suggested that the Five and the Secretary-General hold consultations with representatives of each of the parties. How practical is this proposal?

In answer to the first question, France, the United Kingdom and the Soviet Union were in favor of informal consultations among the Five and of the Five with the Secretary-General. The United States was opposed. Regarding question 2, the appointment of a Special Representative, the United States was opposed and the United Kingdom and France had reservations, both preferring that the Secretary-General retain direct responsibility for this matter. The Soviet Union favored the appointment. In answer to the third question, France favored consultations between the Five and the Secretary-General on the one hand and with each of the parties on the other. The United Kingdom and the United States were opposed. The Soviet Union did not answer the question directly but instead referred to the importance of the development of contacts by the Secretary-General with the parties. China did not respond to any of the questions.

Although I continued to meet periodically with the Permanent Members, the United States remained inalterably opposed to utilization of this forum as a means of proceeding to serious talks among the parties on a Middle East settlement. U.S. Ambassador Pickering was authorized to attend the meetings but only to listen to what was said. I repeatedly made clear that I was not trying to establish the Five or the Security Council as a mechanism to deal with the Middle East. In a July 1990 meeting with the U.S. Assistant Secretary of State for International Organizations, John Bolton, I noted that Yassir Arafat had indicated to me only a week earlier that he alone among his PLO colleagues understood that it would be advantageous to avoid further debate and resolutions in the Security Council on the occupied territories. I felt that occasional meetings of the Five could serve to support Arafat's moderate position and also would send a signal to the Palestinians that they were not forgotten. The Americans were not to be persuaded, however, and, in the end, my consultations with the Five on the Middle East came to nothing. The last meeting took place on the eve of the Iraqi invasion of Kuwait.

A NEW ISRAELI PEACE INITIATIVE

Meanwhile, the Israeli cabinet, in May 1989, approved Prime Minister Shamir's peace initiative, which foresaw negotiations between Israel and a Palestinian delegation on a transitional period of self-rule in Gaza and the West Bank. Egypt and Jordan were invited to participate if they chose. Not later than three years after the beginning of the transitional period, negotiations on a permanent solution would begin. Three things were ruled out: establishment of a Palestinian state; participation of the PLO; and "any change in the status of Judea, Samaria and Gaza other than in accordance with the basic guidelines of the [Israeli] Government." The United States gave strong support to this plan. Secretary Baker wrote to me on May 26 "to review where things stand." He described his recent talks in Moscow, where Soviet leaders had agreed that the elections proposal was worth studying although they renewed their call for consultations among outside parties on issues relating to an international conference. Baker had reiterated the U.S. view that a properly structured international conference could, at an appropriate time, launch negotiations on issues requiring multilateral treatment, but the appropriate time had not yet come. The first task now, the Secretary wrote to me, was to bring about meaningful political dialogue between Israel and the Palestinians—not a new idea on his part.

Five months later, during which no real progress had been made in arranging such a dialogue, Jim Baker wrote to me again on the subject. In a letter dated October 19, 1989, he said two key issues needed to be worked through: who will participate in the dialogue and what will be discussed? These were practically the same questions that I had addressed to the Permanent Members of the Security Council in the context of a possible international conference. Secretary Baker suggested that there were things I could do to make this process succeed. Public statements supporting the idea of the dialogue would be most helpful—something, it will be recalled, I had already said I could not do. Further, he wrote, "in your contacts, especially with the PLO, you should keep them focussed on what is available and possible now, and highlight the consequences of imposing conditions that will block a potentially historic process from beginning." Nothing was said about a UN role in the process.

Violence continued in the West Bank and Gaza. One bloody incident in which a demented Israeli gunned down eight Palestinian workers from Gaza was brought to the Security Council, which met in Geneva so that Arafat, who was denied entry to the United States, could make a statement. The United States vetoed a resolution calling for a Security Council mission to investigate conditions in the occupied territories, as Israel had made clear it would not permit such a mission entry. Having in mind the United Nations' responsibility to afford such protection as possible to the Palestinian inhabitants of Gaza and the West Bank and desiring also to show that even though the Security Council mission was blocked something could be done, I decided to send Jean-Claude Aimé to the area to assess the situation, as I had done earlier with Lebanon. Aimé reported that the voice of moderation in the occupied territories was in serious danger of being silenced by a younger generation who had known nothing but life under occupation. A deep frustration was evident throughout the territories, and there was intense resentment of the practice of arbitrary arrest and imprisonment. Foreign Minister Arens, with whom he met, had expressed willingness to review some Israeli practices in the territories, but on policy matters such as settlements he was not forthcoming.

In light of this report, and my conviction that the Israeli peace initiative, as formulated, could not succeed, I wrote President Bush on July 17 to express my grave concern over developments in the Middle East, especially over the affirmation in the policy guidelines of the new Shamir Government that settlement in all parts of *Eretz Israel* (which would include the West Bank) was the right of all Israelis and an integral part of the state's security. I feared that this policy would lead to further tension and violence. President Bush and Secretary Baker took a strong stand against the settlement of new Jewish immigrants from the Soviet Union in the West Bank, making the guarantee of large loans for immigrant housing conditional on Israeli commitment that the funds would not be used for such settlements. The Israeli government did not alter its policy guideline, however, and further settlements were established.

THE IMPACT OF THE GULF WAR

The Gulf War, which erupted just at this time, profoundly changed the political landscape in the Middle East. The stunning triumph of Operation Desert Storm in restoring the sovereignty of Kuwait was widely seen as opening an opportunity to achieve a comprehensive peace settlement in the Middle East. The United Sates moved quickly to take advantage of it. In a major speech before a joint session Congress on March 6, 1991, President Bush declared that the quest for solutions to the problems in Lebanon, in the Arab-Israeli dispute and in the Gulf must go forward with new vigor and determination. "A comprehensive peace," he said, "must be grounded in UN Security Council Resolutions 242 and 338 and the principle must be elaborated to provide for Israel's security and recognition of the legitimate Palestinian political rights. . . . The time has come to put an end to the Arab-Israeli conflict." Secretary Baker promptly traveled to the Middle East in an energetic effort to establish the basis for a negotiating process, something that the Israeli peace initiative had not provided.

I visited Washington in May, and at a White House lunch on May 9, President Bush asked Jim Baker to summarize where his efforts stood. The Secretary said that he was trying to arrange what the Israelis could refer to as a "regional meeting" and the Syrians could call an "international conference." The conference would have no veto power. Its purpose would be to bring the parties together in order to hold bilateral meetings. Israeli Foreign Minister David Levy had at first accepted the Syrian position that the conference should be "continuing" in nature, but Prime Minister Shamir had retracted this as a terrible mistake. Agreement had been reached among the parties on the terms of reference for the conference, namely, a comprehensive settlement based on

Resolutions 242 and 338, without the Israeli qualifier that it should be based on the Camp David formula or the Arab qualifier that Resolution 242 meant "land for peace."

Israel, Mr. Baker said, continued to resist any role whatsoever for the United Nations, while Syria was equally insistent that the conference should be held under UN auspices. The Secretary stressed that, in the U.S. view, there should be some UN involvement, at the very least an observer appointed by the Secretary-General. He had in mind something like the Mena House talks in Cairo in 1977, where the UN involvement was less formal than in the case of the Geneva Peace Conference in 1973, which had been held under UN auspices. I said that I did not think the United Nations should be present at an international conference "purely as a photo opportunity." The Secretary replied, "But you did this in 1977, you attended the Mena House meetings as an observer." I did not wish to have any unpleasantness with Jim Baker and said simply that I had not attended Mena House, that I was a different man. If the United Nations was involved, I believed it should play an active role. President Bush ended the discussion by saying that the important thing was to get the parties of the age-old conflict talking to each other.

THE MIDDLE EAST PEACE CONFERENCES

On October 19, 1991, I received a letter from Secretary Baker and the Soviet foreign minister, Boris Dmitriyevich Pankin, transmitting an invitation from President George Bush and President Mikhail Gorbachev to attend a peace conference to be convened in Madrid on October 30, 1991. The United Nations was "invited to send an observer, representing the Secretary-General." So the United Nation was to be present only for a photo opportunity. (It turned out to be hardly even that since the UN representative, Ambassador Edouard Brunner, was seated with other observers so far in the rear as to be out of camera range.)[4] Despite an acute sense of chagrin, I accepted immediately, stating what I fully recognized: The conference represented a historic opportunity to advance the prospects for genuine peace throughout the region. I extended my congratulations on this remarkable achievement.

The Madrid conference was intended to lead immediately to direct negotiations between Israel and the Arab parties, thus meeting Israel's basic demand. But the comprehensive settlement was to be sought on the basis of Resolutions 242 and 338, thus implying acceptance of the principle of land for peace, which the Shamir government had staunchly rejected. The conference would have no power to impose solutions or veto agreements, and it could be reconvened only with the consent of all the parties, something on which Israel had insisted. On the other hand, there was no prohibition against PLO participation in the Palestinian-Jordanian delegation (although recognized PLO officials did not participate). To have brought the parties together, especially the Israeli and Syrian governments, on this basis represented a signal diplomatic achievement for which President Bush and Secretary Baker merit great credit. Had the Gulf War not occurred, this conference almost certainly would not have been possible. I recognized that the United Nations could not have been the decisive factor in initiating negotiations at Madrid and in the agreements between Israel and the PLO and Israel and Jordan that followed. The influence that led the parties to these momentous decisions came from elsewhere: from the shift in power that resulted from the Gulf War; from the determination of the United States to bring the parties together when the window of opportunity arose; from the chastening experience of both Israel and the PLO in Lebanon; from the *intifada* and the resultant blemished image of Israel in the United States; from the collapse of the Soviet Union; and, not least, from the demise of the Shamir Government in Israel.

FIVE

THE DECISIVE ISSUE: THE PALESTINIANS

THE PLIGHT OF THE PALESTINIANS was distressing when I became Secretary-General in 1982 and it was destined to become worse during my years in office. I have already described the tragic events in Lebanon that directly involved the Palestinians resident there. Their situation also deteriorated on the West Bank, in Gaza and in East Jerusalem. The Palestine Liberation Organization had been recognized by the General Assembly as the sole legitimate representative of the Palestinian People before I became Secretary-General. Therefore, I felt it was incumbent on me to establish a constructive relationship with the PLO in the hope that such a relationship would serve the cause of reconciliation and peace in the Middle East. Very shortly after becoming Secretary-General, I sent a letter to PLO chairman Yassir Arafat stating that I wished him to know that I would do all I personally could to work for a just and comprehensive Middle East settlement. I was convinced, I wrote, that such a settlement must take fully into account the aspirations and legitimate rights of the Palestinian people. I expressed the hope that we would remain in close personal touch. This hope was more than fulfilled.

As I have mentioned, normally I am able to make an assessment of the character of a person with whom I am dealing quickly—perhaps not always accurately but, for me, at least, definitively. Yassir Arafat was one of the rare exceptions. I found him something of an enigma. I knew that he had maintained his leadership of the Palestinians under extremely challenging circumstances and that he must be capable of authorizing acts of terror for which the PLO was responsible. Yet he did not show the charisma or forceful personality one would expect from a strong and, when necessary, ruthless leader. From his language, it was evident that he was a man of intelligence and education. I was frequently struck by how fully and quickly he was informed on international developments. He was clearly the master of an impressive information system. In this he was a match for the Israelis. I do not believe that he ever acted out of ignorance. Nor, it seemed to me, did he act out of hatred. He acted rather on the basis of his calculation as to how at any given time the cause of Palestinian independence could best be served and how his leadership of the PLO and, with it, his influence in the Arab world could best be maintained. Ultimately I came to the conclusion that he was a calculator rather than a strategist. For most of the other major figures engaged in the Middle East game, the holy writ was Security Council Resolution 242, whether they were prepared to comply with it or not. But for Arafat, it was General Assembly Resolution 181, which had provided for the partition of Palestine into a Jewish and an Arab state, the latter being the state that was destined for the Palestinians.

In April 1982, just when Israel was withdrawing from the Sinai under the Camp David Accords, an unfortunate incident occurred in Jerusalem that caused consternation in the Arab world. A man, who later turned out to be a deranged non-Jewish tourist, set off an explosion inside the al-Haram mosque, one of the holiest Moslem shrines, causing extensive destruction. Israeli soldiers then entered the mosque area and, in the ensuing melee, shot a number of Arab civilians. This was the first of repeated incidents, many sparked by Arab terrorist attacks against Israelis, that marked the ever-deteriorating situation in the Occupied Territories during my tenure. Two policies of the Israeli Government, after it had come under the leadership of the right-wing Likud party, turned an unhappy and perilous situation in the occupied territories into a disastrous one with potentially fateful consequences for Israelis as well as Palestinians.

The first was the credo of a God-given Land of the Jews—*Eretz Israel*— that includes the West Bank of the Jordan River, which first Likud and then the Israeli government began to refer to as Judea and Samaria, the Jewish kingdoms that had existed in biblical times in the territory. The second policy was that of support for greatly expanded Jewish settlement in the Occupied Territories, especially the West Bank.

Previous Israeli governments had supported the establishment of a limited number of Jewish settlements for purposes of defense. But the Likud government encouraged so many settlements that they seemed to be colonizing the area—establishing a major Jewish presence in the territory as an irreversible fait accompli. The growing settlements, when combined with constant reference to Judea and Samaria as part of *Eretz Israel,* to which Likud gave a geographic rather than spiritual definition, inevitably led the Palestinians to assume that the Israeli government intended the permanent incorporation of the West Bank and

Gaza into Israel. The Foreign Policy Guidelines of the second Begin government, which took office in August 1981, clearly signaled this goal.[1]

My close advisors who were directly concerned with the Middle East— Brian Urquhart, Marrack Goulding, Jean-Claude Aimé, and Lisa Buttenheim— made frequent trips to the area to assess the situation. All brought back reports of a serious increase in tension and hostility in the occupied territories and, with the outbreak of the *intifada* in December 1987, of the danger of explosion. The PLO submitted a constant stream of complaints to the United Nations on violations of the human rights of the population by the Israeli authorities. In 1968 the General Assembly had established a Special Committee to Investigate Israeli Practices Affecting the Human Rights of the Population of the Occupied Territories, but Israel refused to cooperate with the Committee.[2]

The violence in the Occupied Territories had an unfortunate effect not only on the relationship between the United Nations and Israel; it also had prejudicial consequences for relations between the United Nations and its host country, the United States. The PLO had long been identified in the United States as a terrorist organization, and the increasing frequency of incidents in the Middle East stimulated action in Congress against the organization. On December 22, 1987, the U.S. Congress, despite the strong objections of the Department of State, adopted the Anti-Terrorism Act of 1987, which prohibited the PLO from establishing or maintaining an office within U.S. jurisdiction. On March 11 of the following year, Attorney General Edwin Meese III notified the head of the PLO Observer Mission that as of March 21, "maintaining the PLO Observer Mission to the United Nations in the United States will be unlawful." This action put the United Nations and the United States in direct confrontation.

In the legal opinion of the United Nations, members of the PLO mission were invitees to the United Nations because of the Observer status accorded the organization by the General Assembly. As such, under the Headquarters Agreement between the United States and the United Nations, the United States had a legal obligation to permit them to carry out their official functions at the United Nations. I had communicated the UN position to the U.S. Permanent Representative, Vernon Walters, while the congressional action was still under consideration. The State Department transmitted this same position to Congress with the objective of heading off the projected legislation. Ambassador Walters told me that "everybody in Washington agreed on this position except Mr. Meese." Walters had just sent a message to the State Department and the White House emphasizing that the United States would be severely criticized for the action even by its close allies, that the matter would be taken to the International Court of Justice and that the next General Assembly might not be held in New York. He assured me that the matter had been brought directly to the attention of President Reagan.

When it became apparent that Congress was determined to pass the legislation, I wrote officially to Ambassador Walters and asked him to confirm that even if the proposed legislation became law, the existing arrangements for the PLO Observer Mission would not be changed. I warned that without such assurance, a dispute between the United Nations and the United States concerning the interpretation and application of the Headquarters Agreement would exist and I would be obliged to enter into the dispute settlement procedure foreseen under the agreement. Nevertheless, the Attorney General proceeded to serve notice on the PLO Mission that it must cease operation.

An extraordinary series of legal actions followed that will no doubt find a prominent place in the record of legal precedents. The UN Secretariat sought to initiate preparatory measures with the legal advisor of the State Department, Judge Abraham Sofaer, for a dispute settlement procedure. After agreeing to this step, the State Department repeatedly delayed action, moving eventually to the position that the legislation providing for the closure of the PLO Mission overrode U.S. obligations under the Headquarters Agreement. This, it contended, applied also to application of the dispute settlement procedure. While the United States urged that the matter not be referred to the International Court of Justice, the General Assembly did just that. The United States denied the Court's jurisdiction and refused to participate in its hearings. Nonetheless, the Court ruled unanimously (with the participation of the American judge) that the United States was under an obligation to enter into arbitration for the settlement of the dispute between itself and the United Nations. The General Assembly, on May 13, 1988, adopted, by a recorded vote of 136 to 2 (the United States and Israel cast negative votes) with no abstentions, Resolution 42/232 urging the United States "to abide by its international legal obligations and to act consistently with the Advisory Opinion of the International Court of Justice." I wrote to the U.S. secretary of state to bring to his attention the International Court of Justice advisory opinion and the General Assembly resolution and expressed the hope that the U.S. Government would abide by its international legal obligations.

The definitive step in settling this issue was taken, ironically, and certainly with quite different intent, by the U.S. Department of Justice. Acting under the provisions of the new law, the attorney-general sought a court injunction (order) to empower him to apply the law against the PLO Mission. I had, until then, felt it advisable to avoid referring the matter to a domestic court, since the Secretariat held that the U.S. obligation stemmed from international legislation. However, the PLO decided to object to the injunction before the American court. I thought it best that the United Nations not become a party to the proceedings but appear before the judge as amicus curiae. In a separate action a group of distinguished Americans, some of whom were Jewish, filed a challenge to the constitutionality of the legislation before the same district court.

The two cases were heard together on June 8, 1988, before Judge Edmond Palmieri in the Federal District Court of the Southern District of New York. The United States was represented by the district attorney Rudolph Giuliani (later to become Mayor of New York City) and the PLO by former U.S. Attorney General Ramsey Clark. Judge Palmieri, who was 81 years old, was remarkably well prepared and directed the proceedings vigorously. The central issue in the case was whether the domestic legislation, enacted subsequent to the international treaty in question, overrode the treaty obligations. When invited to speak in the role of amicus curiae, Carl-August Fleischhauer, the highly competent legal counsel of the United Nations, said that

> . . . in any democratic country, the legislative branch of government has the power to prevent the executive branch from complying with international treaty obligations. Such legislative action does not, however, do away with the existence of these international obligations under international law . . . in many countries very stringent tests are required before it can be assumed that a piece of domestic legislation actually has the effect of overruling and blocking compliance with an international obligation. The United States Courts have developed such standards and criteria in a particularly impressive way. The present case calls for the judicious application of these standards.

The judge, after hearing the argumentations of Clark, who made a brilliant 30-minute presentation, and Giuliani, who argued that it was the clear intent of Congress to close the PLO Observer Mission, ruled against the government. His finding was that only where a treaty is irreconcilable with a subsequently enacted statute and Congress has shown a clear intent to supersede a treaty does the statute take precedence. The court held that the Anti-Terrorism Act did not alter U.S. obligations under the Headquarters Agreement because it failed to disclose the clear legislative intent necessary for the court to act in contravention of the Headquarters Agreement. Thus the Government was precluded from acting against the PLO Mission to the United Nations.

I was greatly pleased with the judge's findings both because they eliminated the need for the Secretariat to continue to do battle with the U.S. Government on behalf of the PLO and because they demonstrated again the fairness and independence of the American court system. I did not have the opportunity to meet Judge Palmieri, but I would like to have done so.

Unfortunately, the difficulties with the U.S. Government with regard to the PLO were not over. On July 31, 1988, King Hussein of Jordan, seeing the PLO move toward direct negotiations with Israel as an opportunity to distance himself from the Palestinian issue, cut Jordan's legal and administrative ties to the West Bank. This meant that Jordan would no longer pay the salaries, as it had until then, of approximately 30 percent of the Palestinian bureaucracy. The king's move caused the PLO great concern because of the financial loss suffered by the Palestinians and because of uncertainty as to how the Israelis would react. Chairman Arafat discussed the situation with me at length during a meeting in Geneva on August 27. He said that his major objective was to obtain safety and protection for the Palestinians in the Occupied Territories. He did not know exactly how to proceed in the wake of the Jordanian action, but he was thinking of the possible establishment of a regime in the territories under UN auspices or of making them into a UN mandate "like Namibia." He said the PLO was also studying steps to take to declare independence that would comply with General Assembly Resolution 181. After independence was declared, the PLO would establish a government-in-exile.

I assured the chairman that the United Nations was prepared to increase the assistance provided by the UN Relief and Works Agency for Palestinian Refugees (UNRWA). The Security Council had just issued a statement condemning Israel's expulsion of civilians from the occupied territories as a violation of the Fourth Geneva convention and requested the High Contracting Parties to ensure respect for the Convention. I thought I could use the Security Council statement as a tool to do more for the Palestinians. As to the establishment of an independent Palestinian state, I told the chairman that personally I would very much welcome it because of my affection for his people. My room for action, however, was very limited since everything would depend on the reaction of the members of the Security Council and of the General Assembly.

It was clear from Arafat's remarks that the Jordanian action was one of the major factors that caused the Palestine National Council, meeting in Algiers from November 12 to 15, 1988, to "declare the establishment of the State of Palestine on our Palestinian territory with its capital Jerusalem."[3] In the declaration, the Palestine National Council rejected the threat or use of force, violence or terrorism against the state's territorial integrity or political independence, as it also rejected their use against the territorial integrity of other states. An extraordinarily opaque paragraph indicated that the State of Palestine was established in pursuance of the resolutions adopted by the United Nations since 1947. This was widely interpreted (albeit not by the United States) as signifying PLO acceptance of Security Council Resolutions 242 and 338, which, while incorporating the principle of land for peace, refer to the Palestinians only in the context of the refugee problem and make no mention of a Palestinian state. In conversations with me in New York, the Permanent Observer of the PLO, Zuhdi Labib Terzi, made clear that the PLO very definitely had General Assembly Resolution 181 in mind. The new State of Palestine was the Arab state foreseen, along with the Jewish state, in that resolution; thus, with the establishment of the State of Palestine, the resolution now finally was being implemented.

Two days before the Algiers meeting of the Palestine National Council, Terzi raised two matters with me in anticipation of decisions the Council would take. The first was a proposal of Chairman Arafat to address either the regular session of the General Assembly (which was then in progress) or the Security Council on the decisions taken at Algiers. My good offices were requested in facilitating the issuance of the necessary entry visa by the United States. The second matter was the assignment of a Member State seat in the General Assembly to Palestine. He argued that one of the states foreseen in resolution 181 already had a seat. The Assembly should now assign a seat to the other state—Palestine.

Being very conscious of the negative perception of the PLO in the United States and some other countries, I found the proposal, which had been in the air for some time, unsettling. I was certain that a concerted effort to gain full UN membership for a PLO-created State of Palestine would increase hostility toward the United Nations in the host country and was, in any event, bound to fail. I said as much to Mr. Terzi and warned that if the PLO pushed too hard for a Palestinian seat, it might very well place in jeopardy its present Observer status.

To further complicate the situation, Yassir Arafat pursued his intention to come to New York. A visa application for him was submitted to the American embassy in Tunis on November 22, 1988. According to the application, the chairman intended to participate in the work of the 43rd session of the General Assembly. The Alternate PLO Observer in New York, Dr. Nasser Al-Kidwa, a relation of Arafat's, informed my office that Arafat would like to address the Security Council if it was prepared to adopt a resolution endorsing the principles of Resolutions 242 and 338, the concept of Palestinian self-determination, the right of Israel to exist and the nonuse of violence and terrorism. The U.S. Mission in New York said that it did not know what Washington's decision on the visa request would be. We heard from William Quandt of the Brookings Institute, who had served as a go-between for the U.S. Government with Arafat, that an arrangement was being made between Washington and the PLO. In a press conference Arafat would state that he accepted Resolutions 242 and 338 as the basis for an international conference and, in this connection, recognized the rights of all states in the area, including Israel, and a Palestinian state, to live in peace within secure and recognized boundaries free from threats or acts of force. The visa would then be issued. Knowing this and that Arafat had been given a visa in 1974, and being aware that the United States was interested under certain conditions in initiating a dialogue with the PLO, I could not imagine Arafat would be refused the visa. I was wrong. The United States, in a decision made personally by Secretary Shultz, denied the visa.

I did not think Arafat's appearance before the General Assembly immediately after the proclamation of an independent Palestine and in the heated atmosphere of the *intifada* would be helpful to the peace process. Yet, in my reading of the Headquarter's Agreement, he had every right to an American visa if his intention in coming to New York was to participate in the work of the General Assembly. Therefore, as a matter of principle, I had no choice but to take sharp issue with the position taken by the United States. In his memoirs, George Shultz writes that the decision derived partly from Arafat's terrorist associations, especially the murder of American tourist Leon Klinghoffer in the course of the hijacking of the cruise ship *Achille Lauro*. More fundamentally, he says, it was motivated by his strategy of maintaining a hard line with the PLO in order to bring the Organization to meet the conditions that the United States had laid down for beginning a U.S.-PLO dialogue.[4] I did not know his reasoning at the time. But even if I had, I would still have taken sharp issue with the U.S. action as a contravention of its legal obligation.

There was a major outcry in the General Assembly against the U.S. action, which, as in the attempted ban on the PLO Observer Mission, was supported only by the United States and Israel. In a near-unanimous vote, the General Assembly decided to move to Geneva for debate on the question of Palestine so that Arafat could speak. In Geneva, Yassir Arafat made a largely conciliatory speech to the general approval of Assembly Members. Nothing happened of great moment. The brief move to Geneva resulted only in a waste of a moderate amount of money. There were some calls from delegations to move UN Headquarters from New York, but they were hardly serious. Ironically, within a month the United States and the PLO had reached agreement on the initiation of a dialogue on the Middle East peace process. George Shultz suggests that denial of the Arafat visa was one of the steps that helped bring this about. True or not, the denial remains an act in contravention of a binding obligation of the United States.

PROTECTION FOR THE PALESTINIANS

As the maneuvering went on with regard to the PLO mission in New York, the establishment of a Palestinian state and the initiation of a US-PLO dialogue, the violent protest movement known as the *intifada,* centered among young Palestinians in the occupied territories, was gaining strength. Israel took forceful but unsuccessful measures to quell it. The situation was first brought to the attention of the Security Council by the Arab Group in December 1987. On December 22, 1984 the Council adopted Resolution 605 strongly deploring the "policies and practices of Israel" and calling on Israel to abide by the Fourth Geneva Convention relative to the Protection of Civilian Persons in Time of War. The Council requested me "to examine the present situation in the occupied territories by all means available . . . and to submit a report containing . . .

recommendations on ways and means for ensuring the safety and protection of the Palestinian civilians under Israeli occupation."

In order to obtain the necessary information, I sent Under-Secretary-General Marrack Goulding to examine conditions on the spot. To obtain the assessment of the Israeli Government, Goulding met with Foreign Minister Shimon Peres and Defense Minister Yitzhak Rabin. (Prime Minister Shamir declined to receive him.) The two ministers told Goulding that they were meeting with him as the representative of the Secretary-General "whom they regularly received" and not in connection with the Security Council resolution, which they rejected on the ground that the Council had no role to play in the security of the occupied territories. They admitted that the situation in the territories was serious. The Israel Defense Force had been surprised by the extent of the disturbances and had not been properly trained to deal with civilian unrest. The Israeli Government regretted the casualties that had occurred and was taking steps to minimize them in the future. They told Goulding that he was free to travel where he chose, except in areas under curfew or that were closed as military areas.

While travel in the West Bank and Gaza proved difficult, with many areas closed, Goulding was able to visit a number of refugee camps and witness at firsthand conditions in the territories. The picture he brought back was dismal and shocking. I reported his findings in unvarnished detail to the Council.[5] In my observations, however, I emphasized first and foremost that while more certainly should be done to ensure the safety and protection of the civilian population, such measures could only be palliatives. The only way to ensure the safety of both the Palestinians in the occupied territories and of the people of Israel was through a comprehensive, just and lasting settlement of the Arab-Israeli conflict.

A number of Palestinians, especially in the refugee camps, had suggested to Goulding that UN forces be deployed either to protect the inhabitants from the Israeli security forces or to replace the latter. I gave careful thought to both possibilities but concluded that I could recommend neither. Under the Fourth Geneva Convention the occupying power is responsible for the maintenance of law and order and for the protection of the civilian population. I felt that Israel should be held to this responsibility.[6] Moreover, without the consent of Israel, which was out of the question, the deployment of a UN force would be impractical.

In my response to the Security Council I suggested that the High Contracting Powers under the Fourth Geneva Convention, which included the United States and the Western European countries, ensure respect for the Convention by the Israelis. As an immediate means of affording some additional protection to the inhabitants of the occupied territories, I asked the Commissioner-General of UNRWA to appoint additional international staff to assist the Palestinian refugees. The draft resolution that was introduced by a number of nonaligned states in response to my report was vetoed by the United States. However, my request for additional international personnel for UNRWA was not subject to Security Council approval. New non-Palestinian personnel were hired and served as refugee affairs officers in the West Bank and Gaza for the next five years. Their presence provided considerable protection to the population and became a highly useful source of information when I was later requested to monitor conditions in the occupied territories.

I wrote to Secretary Shultz in March of 1988 concerning the suffering of the population in the Occupied Territories. I recognized that the situation caused by the *intifada* was a very difficult one for Israel and that under the Geneva Convention the occupying power was responsible for maintaining law and order. "But," I wrote, "the present reliance on force, and the lack of political response to the grievances of the Palestinians give cause for concern on both humanitarian and political grounds." I would therefore be grateful if the Secretary of State during his forthcoming trip to Israel could urge the Israeli authorities to reconsider their present practices and to act in accordance with the Fourth Geneva Convention. I wrote at the same time to Pope John Paul II appealing to him to use his great influence in a similar manner. These steps produced no evident results.

In May 1990 a series of events occurred that were in line with our worst expectation. On May 20 seven Gaza residents were murdered and ten others wounded by a deranged Israeli when they crossed the border for work in Israel. This sparked demonstrations throughout the occupied territories in which seven more Palestinians were killed and hundreds wounded by gunfire from the Israel Defense Force. This was followed immediately by an attack on Western tourists in Amman, Jordan, in which nine were wounded. There was a call for an urgent meeting of the Security Council, and the Permanent Observer of the PLO in New York wrote to me requesting that an entry visa be issued immediately for President Arafat so that he could address the Council on "the events of genocide" committed on Sunday, May 20.

Realizing that it was highly unlikely that the United States would issue a visa to Arafat, the majority in the Security Council, following the precedent set by the General Assembly, voted to hold a meeting in Geneva, so that he could be heard. This was only the third time in its history that the Council had held a meeting outside of New York. A draft resolution condemning the Israeli action and calling for the dispatch of a UN Mission to investigate the situation in the Occupied Territories was vetoed by the United States. The American Representative, Tom Pickering, said that the United States would support practical steps that would respond to the spiral of troubling events, including the dispatch of a special envoy of the Secretary-General "to look at the situation and to report back to the Secretary-General." The United States urged all parties to exhibit the necessary flexibility to permit such a mission.

Some months previously, hoping to find a way to alleviate the hardships faced by the Palestinians, I had appointed Francis Blanchard as special emissary to coordinate economic assistance in the occupied territories. Mr. Blanchard was the former Director-General of the International Labor Organization and was well and favorably known to many Israelis. However, the Israeli government refused to grant Blanchard permission to travel to the West Bank and Gaza to examine the humanitarian situation there. Given the greatly increased tensions that had followed the most recent incidents, tensions further exacerbated by the U.S. veto of the Security Council resolution, I felt it was imperative that I do something to calm the situation and permit the peace process to be restarted. I decided to do two things: to try again to send Mr. Blanchard, together with Jean-Claude Aimé, to the region to assess the situation; and once again to bring the five Permanent Members of the Security Council together to talk about the Middle East.

I discussed this with President Bush in Washington on June 4, 1990. Yassir Arafat had given me a confidential written communication while the Security Council was meeting in Geneva and asked that I give it personally to the President. I did this as soon as the subject of the Middle East arose. The communication contained several proposals for preserving the U.S./PLO dialogue and suggestions for the next steps to be taken on Palestine. Arab terrorists had just mounted a speedboat attack against a beach at Tel Aviv, an attack attributed to one faction of the PLO. I said that in my personal opinion Arafat was not associated with the attack. The President and Secretary Baker, in discussing this between themselves, concluded that the U.S./PLO understanding did not require that Arafat condemn terrorist acts against Israel but it did require him publicly to disassociate himself from such attacks. President Bush said that in considering Arafat's communication, they would take into account the fact that it was written before the speedboat attack.

I then told the President of my plan to send Mr. Blanchard and Mr. Aimé to examine the humanitarian situation in the West Bank and asked for his support with the Israeli Government. I planned to wait a decent interval to make clear that the mission was not a consequence of the Geneva Security Council meeting. The President said that the Israelis already knew that the United States supported such a mission. Parenthetically he remarked that he knew the current Israeli ambassador, "Bibi" Netanyahu, quite well and had considered him a friend. He and Secretary Baker had been greatly surprised and offended, however, by his attribution to the United States of lies and deception. Secretary Baker said that he and President Bush had tried to keep the focus on Israel's refusal to agree to a reasonable peace process. The PLO should realize that actions such as the terrorist attack on Israeli beaches served to obscure this refusal and made it much harder to bring pressure to bear against Israel.

General Brent Scowcroft, the National Security Advisor, confirmed to me later that the United States had sought to persuade the Israeli government to agree to the dispatch of the Blanchard mission. Perhaps as a result of the U.S. intervention along with my own repeated approaches, the Israeli authorities, while continuing to refuse a visa for Mr. Blanchard, agreed to a visit by my aide, Jean-Claude Aimé. Aimé was given full freedom to travel throughout the occupied territories, was permitted to visit the Ansar III prison in northern Israel where thousands of Palestinians were being held and was given access to the top members of the Government, including the Prime Minister, the Foreign Minister and, most important, Defense Minister Moshe Arens.

Based on his extensive conversations with Palestinian academics, intellectuals and community leaders as well as with refugee camp residents, Aimé judged the situation in the occupied territories to be worse than he had ever known it in his many years experience in the area. The Palestinians felt vulnerable and completely at the mercy of Israeli authorities. They had no security even in their homes. They felt stripped of their basic human and economic rights. Moreover, they were depressed by what they perceived as an impasse in the peace process and by the breakdown in the U.S./PLO dialogue. They were convinced that the international community knew about the conditions under Israeli occupation and was ignoring their plight. Aimé found that there was no interest in the West Bank and Gaza for yet another UN report or General Assembly resolution that would have no real effect. The Palestinians wanted action.

In two conversations with Aimé, Israeli Defense Minister Arens showed awareness of the growing hostility toward the Israel Defense Force in the occupied territories and said that he intended to reduce the army's presence in the major population centers (which he subsequently did). Arens acknowledged that the Palestinians had grievances and aspirations that should be addressed. He had already launched a review of defense force practices in the territories. The minister was quite negative, however, on the idea of a UN monitoring operation.

Aimé accompanied me to subsequent meetings with Chairman Arafat in Geneva and, after that, with General Scowcroft in Washington and reported on his findings in the West Bank, Gaza and Israel. Arafat was most interested in gaining some kind of protection for the Palestinians and strongly suggested that the United Nations should assume this responsibility. I said that sympathetic as I was, I had absolutely no mandate to undertake this responsibility. Aimé and I both suggested that the signatories of the Fourth Geneva Convention could take action. Arafat feared this would place action in the hands of the International Committee of the Red Cross, in which he had absolutely no confidence. General Scowcroft was particularly interested in whether Aimé had confirmed reports that armaments used by the *intifada* fighters were being upgraded. Aimé said he had not. (Interestingly, Arafat insisted that the youthful *intifada* protesters *[shebab]* were acting under orders from him not to use guns. He expressed amazement that his orders continued to be followed.) I told General Scowcroft that Arafat had instructed his colleagues not to press for a Security Council debate or resolution at this time. Quite frankly, I said, I was trying to give Arafat support because it was unlikely that anyone who would replace him would be as sensible. I felt that he needed something to show to his people in return for the concessions he had made. This was one reason I had initiated a meeting with the five Permanent Members on the situation in the occupied territories. I made clear, however, that such meetings would not be institutionalized and that I had no intention of establishing a new UN mechanism to deal with the Middle East.

General Scowcroft, for whom I had gained very high respect, seemed in general agreement with my meeting with the Permanent Members. He said that he understood what I was saying about Arafat, "but given the speedboat attack, our hands are tied regarding him today." Although he recognized that Arafat was in a difficult position, he considered that the main interest now was to get the new Shamir government to resume the peace process.

THE GULF WAR INTERVENES

Saddam Hussein's invasion of Kuwait in August 1990 moved the focus of attention of the Security Council and of the countries in the Middle East from the Palestinians to the Gulf. Saddam Hussein sought to portray his actions as aimed at bringing about a solution to the Middle East problem and defeating Israel in the process. The United States and its coalition partners were anxious to avoid any linkage between freeing Kuwait and resolving the Palestinian problem. In these much-changed and highly charged circumstances, the tragic Temple Mount incident occurred in Jerusalem on October 8, 1990. A group of Palestinians, apparently fearful that extreme Orthodox Jews were planning to take over the Al Haram mosque, began to throw rocks at Jews worshipping at the Wailing Wall. Israeli troops responded with unrestrained violence, killing 20 Palestinians and causing extensive damage in the holy Temple Mount area. I immediately decided to send a mission to Jerusalem to investigate the incident, having always in mind my sense of responsibility to do everything possible to afford protection to the Palestinians. However, before I could publicly announce my intention, the Security Council met and, on October 12, unanimously adopted Resolution 672, deploring the loss of life and calling on the Secretary-General to send a mission to the region. On the same day I summoned the Acting Israeli Permanent Representative, Johanan Bein, and asked what facilities the Government of Israel was prepared to extend to the mission. I told the Ambassador that it would be of short duration and would be composed of colleagues very close to me: Jean-Claude Aimé, Giandomenico Picco and Lisa Buttenheim.

Three days later Ambassador Bein brought me the text of a statement of the Israeli Cabinet totally rejecting Resolution 672 on the ground that it disregarded the attack on the Jewish worshippers at the Wailing Wall. Moreover, Jerusalem was not, in any part, occupied territory, and there was therefore "no room for any involvement of the United Nations in any matter relating to Jerusalem."[7] Given these considerations, the statement continued, Israel would not receive the delegation of the Secretary-General. I told Ambassador Bein that I would like to have certain clarifications from his government concerning this decision. The ambassador said, "We do not want the delegation in Israel. Full stop." He went on to say that Israel had appointed its own commission to look into the incident. It would not make sense to have two investigations conducted at the same time. I replied that, on the contrary, the two commissions could both investigate the facts. The UN mission would take account of the findings of the Israeli commission. I stressed that I wished to avoid informing the Council that Israel refused to receive the UN mission. I also would not like to present a one-sided report. I therefore appealed to Ambassador Bein to ask his government to receive my team, each member of which was known to its leaders.

The United States was understandably fearful that the Israeli defiance of the Security Council could jeopardize the unity that had been established in connection with the Iraqi invasion of Kuwait. Ambassador Pickering told me that the United States was proceeding from two assumptions: first, that the Israeli Cabinet decision could not be changed; and second, that the Security Council decision would have to remain as it was. The problem was to find a way between these two rocks. The United States hoped that it might be possible to delay sending the UN mission until after the report of the Israeli commission was completed. Under this arrangement, it might not be necessary for my mission to see any Israeli officials, since they would make available a copy of their report. According to Ambassador Pickering, Washington had informed Jerusalem that it would have to accept the UN team. President Bush was going to call Prime Minister Shamir, and it was understood that Prime Minister Thatcher would do the same. Ambassador Pickering asked if I would view an Israeli commitment to hand me the report of its commission as a sign of Israeli flexibility. I said no; I would consider the willingness of Israel to receive my mission as a sign of flexibility.

Israel did not relent. On the contrary, its Cabinet authorized the foreign minister to communicate an announcement to the United Nations that rejected the Security Council resolution, reiterated that Jerusalem "is not, in any part, 'occupied territory'" and stated that Israel would not receive the delegation of the Secretary-General.[8] I informed the Council orally of the Israeli government's decision. The Council nonetheless insisted that I submit the report requested in its earlier resolution. Since I was unable to send a mission to observe the situation firsthand, in the report I submitted[9] I reviewed the various resolutions adopted by the Security Council to protect the Palestinians in the Occupied Territories and I summarized the feelings that had been conveyed to me by Palestinians. I highlighted several themes that had recurred frequently in these contacts: a sense of vulnerability and fear even inside their own homes; resentment against the taking of land, especially for Israeli settlements; the denial of the right to education; and the overall exploitation of the territories. I stressed that for any measures of protection to be effective, the cooperation of Israeli authorities was essential. The numerous appeals to the Israeli government to comply with the provisions of the Fourth Geneva Convention had gone unheeded. Under these circumstances, I suggested that the Security Council might wish to call for a meeting of the high contracting parties to discuss possible measures that might be taken by them under the convention.

It took the Council almost three weeks to agree on a response to my report. On December 20, 1990, it finally adopted Resolution 681, which, inter alia, requested me, in cooperation with the International Committee of the Red Cross, to develop further my idea of convening a meeting of the high contracting parties to the Fourth Geneva Convention. I solicited the views of all the signatories to the convention, including Israel. The number of replies was disappointing. Those that were received were generally favorable but with the frequent comment "at an appropriate time." Israel categorically rejected the idea of convening such a meeting. Meanwhile, in November, I had an extensive conversation with President Chaim Herzog of Israel when we were in Tokyo for the funeral of Emperor Hirohito. President Herzog was an old friend, and the meeting was friendly and rewarding. He clearly had the task of finding a solution to the problem of the UN mission to investigate the Temple Mount tragedy. His proposal was that Israel would invite Jean-Claude Aimé to return to Israel in further pursuit of his earlier mission. Israel also would invite me for an official visit so that I could, in effect, follow up on Aimé's mission and obtain whatever additional information I wished. The only condition was that there should be no connection with the Security Council resolutions. I was already tentatively scheduled to visit Egypt in December and could easily add Israel to the trip. I decided that this proposal offered the best likelihood of being of any real assistance to the Palestinians. So I agreed, although I said I could not go if a war was in progress in the Gulf. While I was still in Tokyo, Jean-Claude Aimé received an invitation in New York to "visit Israel as the emissary of the Secretary-General to resume his June 1990 mission." The Gulf War intervened and Aimé was unable to make the visit until March 1991, at which time he once again traveled widely in the occupied territories and had extensive conversations with Israeli Government leaders as my representative. The demands of other crises prevented me from following with a visit of my own.

A major reason why it took almost three weeks for the Security Council to reach agreement on Resolution 681 was because a number of members were intent on including provision for the United Nations to monitor conditions in the occupied territories on a continuing basis. This was not a new idea, but it was one the United States had always resisted, given the strong Israeli objections. This time, however, an approach was developed under which reliance would be placed on personnel already stationed in the territories, rather than special missions, for information on the situation of Palestinians residing there. The requirement for Israeli entry visas would not arise. The unprecedented monitoring provision was set forth in Resolution 681 in the following language: "The Security Council also requests the Secretary-General to monitor and observe the situation regarding Palestinian civilians under Israeli occupation . . . and to utilize and designate or draw upon United Nations and other personnel and resources present there, in the area and elsewhere, needed to accomplish this task and to keep the Security Council regularly informed."

UNRWA was the only UN agency with a substantial presence in the occupied territories. I relied heavily on information provided by its international staff members in the preparation of Report S22472, which I submitted to the Council on April 9, 1991. The report gave a grim picture of the effect of the Gulf War on economic and political conditions in Gaza, the West Bank and East Jerusalem with extensive details on the impact of the curfew imposed by the Israeli authorities in the territories and of the continuing deportations, detentions and arrests. By July the draft of a second report was completed. However, the United States pressed me very strongly not submit it. By then the American-led peace process had gained momentum, with the promise of bringing the Palestinians directly into the negotiating process on a Middle East settlement. Washington felt that the submission of another report that would inevitably be critical of the conditions in the Occupied Territories would be prejudicial to the peace process. I did not feel that the report would, in itself, bring much benefit to the Palestinians at this point so I did not submit it, nor did I submit any further ones during my tenure. The principle had been established, however, that until such time as the Israeli occupation ends, conditions in the occupied territories are rightfully the concern of the United Nations and subject to its monitoring.

SIX

HOSTAGES!

I HAVE ALWAYS CONSIDERED THE TAKING OF HOSTAGES one of the cruellest forms of terrorism, showing utter disrespect for the most basic human rights of innocent persons. Far from serving any cause well, this practice has isolated and brought disrepute to any organizations or governments associated with it. I believe that now, finally, after so many appalling incidents in the Middle East, this fact is better understood by any who might be tempted to resort to this practice. In my endeavors to gain freedom for hostages, I was motivated first and foremost by humanitarian concern for the cruelty to which not only they but also their families were subjected. I sought to make this clear to all with whom I dealt. Shifts in power and political orientation had much to do with the ultimate release of most Western hostages in Lebanon. Without these shifts the efforts of the United Nations could hardly have succeeded. But something more was needed—the good offices of an independent third party, a trusted go-between and mediator, who could take advantage of an altered political constellation to bring finally a solution. I could be most effective by making clear that I was not acting in the interest of any one country or group, that my motivation was to bring freedom to all hostages and to remove this issue as an impediment to the development of more constructive relationships within the region. This, I felt, was my responsibility as Secretary-General and the necessary role of the United Nations.

ALEC COLLETT: THE UN HOSTAGE

My first direct involvement in the hostage problem began on March 25, 1985, when Alec Collett, a British journalist who was in Lebanon to write a number of articles for the United Nations Relief and Works Agency for Palestine

Refugees (UNRWA), was seized by unknown persons in Khalde, just south of Beirut. Khalde at the time was known as an "open" area in which all the armed factions in Lebanon came and went, using it as they wished. It was a particularly dangerous place in a country where danger could not be avoided. I had known and liked Collett as a good-humored and intelligent journalist who had long been a familiar figure in the corridors of United Nations Headquarters in New York. Collett was engaged in a legitimate job in Lebanon, completely uninvolved in the factional Lebanese strife, aside, ironically, from his evident sympathy for the Palestinian people. In the course of the long and ultimately futile efforts that were made to obtain Collett's return, I came to understand how, more than anything else, a hostage's fate is determined by the interplay of interests and incidents in which the hostage has no part.

The "Revolutionary Organization of Socialist Moslems," one of the many shadowy underground groups in Lebanon, identified itself as responsible for Collett's kidnapping, claiming that he was a British spy, working for the Americans on behalf of Israel—a lethal combination. We sought through the many channels that were open to the United Nations in Lebanon and Syria to penetrate the maze of armed groups and establish direct contact with this organization. At times success seemed near. We kept in close touch with British authorities who were making their own efforts to free Collett although they never informed the United Nations of what they were doing.

Ultimately, some 12 months after he was seized, the kidnappers announced that Collett was suffering from a serious kidney ailment and required dialysis treatment. They demanded that ten dialysis machines be provided, one of which would be used for him. It was also announced that a certain Mustapha Saad had been "authorized" to deal with the case. Saad was a prominent figure in the southern area who himself had earlier been the victim of a terrorist attack that had left him blind. He had visited the United Nations and was known to several staff members. I decided to ask one of them, Samir Sanbar, a native of Lebanon with many contacts in the region, to make the dangerous journey to southern Lebanon and meet with Saad.

When Sanbar arrived he found that the British ambassador in Lebanon had been there two days earlier. The kidnappers had made a number of demands on the British, including the release of four Palestinians who had been jailed in England. Saad told Sanbar that, "like the Secretary-General, he was dealing with the case only on humanitarian grounds." He said that following the ambassador's visit he had contacted the "organization." Saad had gained the impression that the positions of the two sides were hardening. He referred to the deteriorating atmosphere in the Middle East and said he thought there was real danger for Collett's life. Sanbar stressed my personal concern, emphasizing once again that Collett had been working for the United Nations, and suggested that the provision of the medical equipment that had been demanded by "the organization" might be pursued. While not optimistic on the outcome, Saad advised that if the medical equipment was provided, it should be seen as coming from the British. Shortly thereafter he contacted Sanbar and told him that there was no serious movement "in any area" and that time was running out. The danger to Collett persisted. On learning this, I asked Sanbar again to convey my personal request to Saad to do all he could to mitigate the threat to Collett's life. The situation was obviously extremely delicate.

In Damascus, Sanbar was in touch with the British embassy, passing on to the British representatives all that he had heard from Saad. He was told that the British were most grateful for the efforts of the Secretary-General but that since the demands being made by the kidnappers involved matters directly relevant to British interests, they would wish to handle the next stage without UN involvement. This same message was conveyed to me in New York. When Sandar saw Saad for the last time before returning to New York, Saad told him that he was ready to send someone to review the situation with British representatives at an agreed location. Immediately thereafter the United Nations assisted in arranging a meeting in Cyprus between the British and representatives of the kidnappers. The United Nations did not participate, and no further assistance in this matter was ever requested by the British.

On April 23, 1986, the Revolutionary Organization of Socialist Moslems delivered a statement to a Beirut newspaper announcing the execution of "British spy Alec Collett . . . in solidarity with the masses of our Moslem people in the Arab Libyan Socialist *Jamahiriyah,* and in response to the joint savage American-British raid [on Libya], and following the scandalous role of the British in participating in the murder of innocent sons of the Islamic Arab nation." The statement said further that "Our organization will deliver to the respected Beirut newspaper an-Nahar a footage of the ceremony of his hanging, emphasizing that the blood of our Islamic nation will not go to waste." The gruesome videotape was subsequently delivered showing a man in heavy clothing hanging by the neck. It was not possible to make a positive identification of the body from the videotape.

Until then, nothing had brought home to me so forcefully the brutality and utter senselessness of hostage-taking. I had little doubt that Collett was dead, but it seemed to me that as long as the slightest question remained, efforts should continue to determine his fate and, if he had been murdered, to recover his body. Again we sought information through all the channels open to the United Nations in the area. Sanbar once again made the dangerous journey to southern Lebanon to question Mustapha Saad. During a 90-minute conversation, Saad repeated several times that "there was no confirmation" of Collett's death. He mentioned that it had been determined that a body at the American University Hospital was not Collett's. His advice was "to keep possibilities open for the time being." He said that the meeting in Cyprus had been unproductive. The demands that had been made before were repeated and the British were unresponsive. He said the military events in the Mediterranean, referring presumably to the increased U.S. naval presence in the region, had further limited the possibilities of helping Mr. Collett.

Over subsequent years I used every opportunity to try to obtain information that would at least confirm Collett's death. Iranian authorities repeatedly denied any knowledge on the subject, as did the Syrians. As best we could determine, the Revolutionary Organization of Socialist Moslems was a radical Palestinian group. Like all the others, Yassir Arafat, whom I questioned on the matter, said, that he had nothing to do with Collett's kidnapping and knew nothing of his fate. There were some indications that Collett might have been handed over to an underground group with Libyan connections. When, in November 1991, my aide Giandomenico Picco traveled to Libya in connection with the release of other Western hostages, he asked the deputy of President Muómmar Gadhafi for Libya's assistance in determining Collett's fate. Picco was told that Libya had no connection with and no knowledge of the matter.

No kidney dialysis machines were provided for southern Lebanon. If the body shown in the videotape was that of Collett, apparently he had not been held in the south, for the body was clothed in wool, suitable only for the mountains in that season. A good and friendly man, on an innocent mission for the organization established to assist Palestinian refugees, was engulfed in the flood of terrorism from which he could not be rescued.

LIEUTENANT COLONEL WILLIAM R. HIGGINS:
AN AMERICAN IN UN SERVICE

The fate of the second UN hostage, U.S. Marine Lieutenant Colonel William R. Higgins, was similar in its senseless cruelty. Colonel Higgins was chief of the UN Military Observer Group in southern Lebanon. Military observers are unarmed. The group occupies six observer posts on the Lebanese side of the armistice line between Lebanon and Israel (the area established as a security zone by Israel). It also conducts patrols and carries out liaison duties with parties in and around the area in which UN peacekeeping forces are deployed. This has been a hazardous area for military observers.

Before going to Lebanon, Higgins was an assistant to the American secretary of defense, Caspar Weinberger, something he made no secret of in his new assignment. He had volunteered for service with the United Nations.[1] He was returning from a courtesy call on an official of the main-line Shi'ite organization Amal in Tyre (the same city from which Collett departed on his fatal journey to Beirut) when, on February 17, 1988, he was abducted by a previously unknown group that called itself the Organization of the Oppressed of the World. Higgins had been driving the last Jeep in an Observer Group convoy.

As with Collett, we immediately followed a three-pronged strategy of seeking information through all the channels open to the United Nations in Lebanon, Syria and Iran, of publicizing my appeals that emphasized the peaceful UN mission in which Higgins was engaged and of coordinating action with U.S. authorities, given Higgins's nationality. It was quickly learned that the Organization of the Oppressed was a Shi'ite group linked to Hizbollah, or the Party of God, the fundamentalist organization in Lebanon. As in Collett's case, at times a breakthrough seemed at hand. Amal, whose representative Higgins had been visiting, publicly condemned the kidnapping, which had taken place in Amal-controlled territory, and reportedly arrested those who had actually seized Higgins. Initially sources in Amal indicated that the Colonel would be released very shortly. However, no specific information was forthcoming. The captors let it be known that they were interrogating Higgins and would thereafter put him on trial. I wrote to Iranian Foreign Minister Velayati on March 15 and to President Assad of Syria on April 22, requesting their assistance; I felt that, given the Iranian government's very strong influence on Hizbollah and Syria's extensive presence in Lebanon, they might know what was happening or could find out. Neither replied.

In December 1988 the Organization of the Oppressed announced that Colonel Higgins had been tried and found guilty of spying on behalf of the United States and Israel. Then, in relatively quick succession, an Iranian airliner was shot down by the *USS Vincennes* over the open sea, and on July 30, 1989 Israeli agents abducted a prominent fundamentalist Shi'ite leader in Lebanon, Sheik Abdul Karim Obeid. The next day, July 31, the Organization of Oppressed of the World announced that it had killed Colonel Higgins in retaliation for the abduction of Sheik Obeid.

I was profoundly shocked to hear that an officer clearly identified as a UN observer fulfilling a mission of peace should have been brutally murdered. I found it difficult to sleep that night, and during my long periods of wakefulness I determined to send a competent envoy to find the truth of what had happened and, if Higgins's was dead, to try to recover his body. President Bush called me the following day to ask if I could assist in determining Higgins's fate. I said that of course I would pass on any and all information we obtained, as we had consistently done from the time the Colonel was abducted.

On the same day, August 1, Under-Secretary-General Marrack Goulding, the senior officer on my staff in charge of peacekeeping, a man with much experience in the Middle East, left on this difficult mission. He met with a wide variety of people in Lebanon, Syria and Israel, including senior government officials and Shi'ite leaders, although not with any of the clandestine armed groups. By this time, as in the Collett case, a videotape had been delivered to a newspaper in Beirut showing what was alleged to be Colonel Higgins's body hanging from a scaffold.

None of the persons with whom Goulding spoke admitted to any direct knowledge of Higgins's fate. All but three believed he was dead, but they differed as to when death most likely took place. Israeli Defense Minister Rabin was convinced that the execution actually took place in December or January, after the guilty verdict had been handed down by the Organization of the Oppressed "court." This was a convenient assumption for the Israelis since it relieved them from the opprobrium of having caused the execution by their kidnapping of Sheik Obeid. The American chargé in Tel Aviv confirmed, however, that Israel had passed an intelligence report that Higgins was dead to the United States about the time of the sentencing. Another theory was that a Shi'ite guard had become so enraged on hearing of the U.S. downing of the Iranian airliner that he killed Higgins in a fit of anger. When I subsequently pursued the question directly with Iranian Foreign Minister Velayati, he told me he had heard that this was what had happened.

The other contention—that the execution had been carried out in retaliation for the abduction of Sheik Obeid—was dismissed as impossible by some who felt that there had been no time for the necessary clearance to have been obtained from Tehran. The body shown on the videotape was fairly clearly that of Colonel Higgins, but it did not show the normal signs of recent death by hanging.

I do not know what, if any, independent action U.S. authorities took to obtain the Colonel's release. They were extremely firm in opposing any deal. Subsequently, I repeatedly asked the assistance of senior Iranian officials in obtaining the return of the body. Ultimately it was returned in conjunction with the 1991 release of the Western hostages for which Iran was primarily responsible.

Death was thus the final wage paid the two UN hostages.

THE OTHER HOSTAGES IN LEBANON

When, in 1985, we were pursuing the various channels available to the United Nations in Lebanon and Syria to seek Alec Collett's release, I told American authorities and stated publicly that such facilities as we had would be available for use in seeking information about the Americans and others then being held prisoner in the area. Subsequently I told George Bush, shortly after he became President, that I was ready to help in any way I could to resolve the hostage problem. There was no American response until August 1989, when President Bush contacted me to ask if I could communicate a number of thoughts to Iranian President Hashemi Rafsanjani. I immediately sent Giandomenico Picco to Washington to meet with General Scowcroft, the National Security Advisor.

Picco was a career international civil servant of Italian nationality whom I had first come to know well and to trust when he was serving as political officer in the UN operation in Cyprus. When I became Secretary-General, Picco joined my office where he dealt with such highly sensitive issues as Afghanistan, the Middle East and the Iran-Iraq war. In the course of this work he established wide contacts with government officials in the Middle East. While not imagining how large a role Picco would play in freeing the hostages, I knew that he had the initiative, courage and total discretion required for this work. Brent Scowcroft gave Picco a "nonpaper" containing suggestions on a message that I might convey to the Iranian President. I concluded that the message should not be put in writing and decided instead to send Picco as my personal envoy to convey the message orally to the Iranian President in complete secrecy. Knowing the subject matter in advance, Rafsanjani received Picco on August 26, with considerable reluctance. The jist of my message as conveyed by Picco was that I had known President Bush well for a good many years and was familiar with his thinking. I knew he would like to see improved U.S.-Iranian relations. In his inaugural address, he had stated that "There are today Americans who are held against their will in foreign lands and Americans who are unaccounted for. Assistance can be shown here and will be long remembered. Goodwill begets goodwill. Good faith can be a spiral that endlessly moves on." This was one of the very few statements in the address referring to individual foreign policy issues and underscored the importance he attributed to this issue and to improved U.S.-Iranian relations.

I was convinced, in my own mind, that if the Western hostages in Lebanon were released, President Bush would act swiftly to free Iranian assets blocked by the United States or respond with other appropriate gestures. I realized that President Rafsanjani had publicly called for the reverse sequence. The reality was, however, that, in view of the political sensitivities surrounding the Iran-contra affair, it would be impossible for President Bush to proceed in other than the sequence I was suggesting.

I assumed that President Rafsanjani was interested in improved U.S.-Iranian relations. I felt confident that an Iranian initiative on the U.S. hostages would elicit a positive response from the United States. In addition to these points stemming from General Scowcroft's suggestions, Picco conveyed to Rafsanjani the offer of my good offices for the benefit of all concerned and expressed my hope *for humanitarian reasons* of pursuing the dialogue directly with him.

Rafsanjani's response was not helpful. He said that for some time Iran had had no relations with those holding the hostages. They were not the traditional Hizbollah, they had no address and were not easy to find. In the last few days they had let Tehran know that they were not prepared to discuss the matter unless Sheik Obeid was freed. Rafsanjani insisted that the United States had frozen Iranian assets without a legal basis but nonetheless expected Iran to get involved in something in which it had no interest. He said, "We also have internal concerns. For us to help the United States we need signals that they will halt their unreasonable animosity toward us." The President added that Iran also had hostages in Lebanon. Bush, he stated, could pressure the Maronites, a Christian group against whom the Shi'ites were fighting. Their release of Iranian hostages could be seen as an incentive.

Rafsanjani ended the conversation by saying coolly that he had accepted the message conveyed by Picco only out of respect for the Secretary-General. Iran had expected the Secretary-General to take a firmer and more resolute attitude on implementation of Security Council Resolution 598, which sets forth the conditions for ending the Iran-Iraq War. (The text, which is discussed in chapter 7, provides, inter alia, for the withdrawal of "all forces to the internationally recognized boundaries without delay.") Had the Secretary-General been blunter Iranian territory would not still be occupied by Iraq.

Rafsanjani's response was promptly communicated to President Bush through General Scowcroft. Shortly thereafter I was asked to convey as a "signal" to the Iranian leadership that 19 Iranians who had been held in Lebanon had been released to the International Committee of the Red Cross. I so informed Iranian Foreign Minister Velayati on September 4, during a Non-Aligned Summit conference in Belgrade. Velayati showed no particular interest in this news. This did not greatly surprise me since I had already learned from the ICRC that all 19 Iranians had chosen to go to Canada and not to return to Iran. Velayati spoke rather of the Iranian chargé d'affaires and four other Iranian diplomats who had been kidnapped in Beirut. The foreign minister said that if the United States *really* wished to send a positive signal to Iran, the release of even 10 percent of the frozen Iranian assets would suffice. For its part Iran would continue to try to help with the release of all the hostages as I had requested.

While in Belgrade, I also spoke with Vice President Abdel al Halim Khaddam of Syria, asking Syria's assistance, as I had done before, in gaining the release of all the hostages. Khaddam's reply was oblique. He said first that no one in Lebanon was afraid of either American or Soviet troops. Both nationalities had already suffered from hostage-taking. Five Soviets had been kidnapped, and it had taken Syria three long months to secure the release of four of them. The fifth was killed. Khaddam said that Syria and Iran were together doing what they could to solve the hostage problem. However, it should be kept in mind that Iran did not have full control over the groups that were holding the hostages. I suggested to the vice president that "some good advice from Syria to Iran would be helpful."

From these conversations (which were communicated to the Americans through the U.S. ambassador in New York, Thomas Pickering), from the earlier remarks of Rafsanjani and from the experience we had gained in the case of

Lieutenant Colonel Higgins, I concluded that the Iranians, despite their disclaimers, could bring about the release of those hostages in the hands of Shi'ite groups in Lebanon; until Iran decided to be helpful, there was little hope of accomplishing anything through Hizbollah or its dependent groups; and the time was not yet ripe, partly because of internal rivalries in Iran, for Iran to do what was necessary to free the hostages. I felt it was worthwhile to continue pushing the Iranians—without ever accusing them of controlling the hostages—and I did so during the ensuing months on every suitable occasion.

On January 19, 1990, at 8:30 A.M. (which for a Latin American is quite an early business hour), I received at my residence an urgent telephone call from President Bush. After congratulating me on my birthday, which it happened to be, he expressed enormous concern over information he had received from what he considered an absolutely reliable source. The U.S. Government, he said, had learned that Hizbollah, with apparent help from Iran, was dispatching sophisticated weapons to Europe for the purpose of hitting American and other Western targets. According to this information, persons tasked to assassinate the novelist Salman Rushdie had already entered the United Kingdom. Spanish authorities had seized a cache of weapons in Spain. Bush said, as he had told me earlier, that he wanted to ameliorate relations with Iran, but actions such as those being reported would completely destroy any chances of doing so. He wanted President Rafsanjani to know that he had received this information and asked me to get through to him, if I could. I immediately got in touch with President Rafsanjani through Foreign Minister Velayati. In due course Rafsanjani replied that the information received by President Bush was false.

When I passed this word to Brent Scowcroft on January 29, I summed up from my perspective where the hostage matter stood. I believed that Iran could well have strong influence on the release of the hostages. Rafsanjani had suggested that since I was respected as Secretary-General by both sides, I might be able to find a formula that could be considered. In this context I thought some concrete steps would be needed on bilateral U.S.-Iranian issues. I mentioned specifically the release of some Iranian assets and compensation for the weapons purchased by the previous Iranian regime in the United States but never delivered. I also noted that American support in bringing about the withdrawal of all Iraqi forces from Iran could be helpful.

There was no direct American response to these suggestions. Aside from the message that I transmitted to President Rafsanjani and the release, as a "signal," of the 19 Iranian prisoners in Lebanon (prisoners in whom Tehran was not interested), the Bush Administration never to my knowledge made any offer of compensation to gain the hostages' freedom. The United States did make payment to Iran for the undelivered weapons at a fortuitous time in the hostage release process, something that the Iranians very much wanted. However, this did not figure in the negotiating process in which I was engaged, and, as far as I know, there were no other negotiations in train at that point.

THE INFLUENCE OF THE GULF WAR

The disintegration of the Soviet empire and the concomitant decrease in Soviet power had major repercussions in the Middle East, as in most other parts of the world. But it was the Gulf War and its outcome that bore directly on the hostage problem. Iran was certainly a major gainer from the war. Saddam Hussein, no doubt to protect his eastern flank, reached an agreement with Iran in which Iran's border claims were accepted, all Iraqi troops were withdrawn from Iranian territory and all prisoners of war were to be returned. Thus, while Iran claimed that several thousand Iranian prisoners were still held in Iraq, it won implementation of three provisions of Security Council Resolution 598 on which it had not been able to obtain satisfaction at the end of the Iran-Iraq war. In addition, in a case of profit blooming from perversity, the invading Iraqi troops freed 15 Shi'ite terrorists who had been imprisoned in Kuwait. Shi'ite groups in Lebanon, certainly with the support of Iran, had long demanded that these 15 be released as part of any arrangement for the release of the Western hostages.

The Gulf War left Iran the most powerful country in the region. Moreover, its reputation as a respected member of the international community was at least partially restored through the simple fact that it had been the first victim of Iraqi aggression and had resisted at enormous sacrifice. It could reasonably hope for doors to be opened in the West and, in particular, for Western investment and economic cooperation. Even President Bush had signaled a desire for improved relations. The main obstacle in Iran's way was the terrorist image that derived from the hostage issue. By the early spring of 1991, I detected in the frequent contacts I had with Foreign Minister Velayati and with the newly appointed Iranian ambassador in New York, Dr. Kamal Kharrazi, a distinct change of attitude. A primary objective had become the removal of Iran from the list of countries promoting terrorism that is compiled by the U.S. State Department and submitted each year to the U.S. Congress by the Department of Commerce. In the course of my conversations, the suggestion emerged from the Iranian side that I should become directly engaged in resolving the hostage problem. Picco participated in most of these conversations and became my main agent in the intricate negotiations that followed. All activities connected with the hostages were kept secret, no mean achievement in the United Nations. For the most part, only Picco and I knew about developments. Picco was ideally suited for the challenge of lengthy and devious negotiations in which pride and hatred, faith and distrust were intermingled. He gained and retained the confidence of all the parties in this secret game—a signal achievement, and one essential, I believe, to the ultimately fortunate outcome.

One of the first things I discovered after deciding to become directly involved in efforts to free the hostages was that I was not alone. There was a Swiss connection. The Swiss government, as the protecting power representing the United States in Iran, had been engaged for some time in a plan to gain freedom for the Western hostages in Lebanon and simultaneously of the Lebanese who were being held directly or indirectly by the Israelis. The plan also foresaw the return to Israel of three Israeli soldiers, dead or alive, who were missing in action in Lebanon. I made clear that I did not wish to interfere with the Swiss efforts, but the Iranians insisted that I continue. Iran preferred the UN channel since it would lessen the impression of U.S.-Iranian negotiations. The Swiss actually continued to be active well into the summer of 1991. At that time the involvement of two different channels threatened to confuse further an already extraordinarily complex set of circumstances and on my suggestion the Swiss withdrew, I think quite happily.

By this time the Iranians had developed a strong interest in the implementation of article six of Resolution 598, which requested the Secretary-General "to explore, in consultation with Iran and Iraq, the question of entrusting an impartial body with inquiring into responsibility for the [Iran-Iraq] conflict and to report to the Council as soon as possible." Iran wanted the Security Council to establish unambiguously that Iraq was to blame for the Iran-Iraq war. Action on my part would be necessary to bring this about.

CONTACT WITH THE TERRORISTS

In March 1991 the Iranians agreed to assist Picco in establishing contact with persons in Lebanon connected with the hostage situation. On April 13 Picco arrived in Beirut for this purpose. On the evening of his arrival, two cars of the Iranian Embassy picked him up at 8:30 P.M. to take him to the office of Sheik Muhammad Hussayn Fadlallah, spiritual leader of Hizbollah, in the heart of the Hizbollah quarter of Beirut. The first car was fully armored and manned by armed security guards. In the second there were four persons, also fully armed, along with Picco. This was the beginning of a series of meetings that was to bring Picco into direct, albeit masked, contact with the groups in control of most Western hostages and who had knowledge of some of the Israelis who were missing in action. In this first meeting, Fadlallah, with whom the United Nations had earlier contact in connection with the kidnapping of Lieutenant Colonel Higgins, said that he wished to see the hostage matter solved sooner rather than later but he was not the one who made decisions. The problem, he suggested, should be solved on "its merits," outside the spotlight of media attention, with no "financial attachments." Fadlallah insisted that no one in Beirut could really help in establishing direct contact with the responsible "groups" except the Iranian government. He considered the involvement of the UN Secretary-General essential. Neither the United States nor the United Kingdom could deal directly with "these people," whereas the Secretary-General, with the help of Iran, could. The Secretary-General should profit from his relations with Iran and proceed further. He cautioned, however, that the issue of Lebanese "prisoners of war" in Israeli control had to be addressed.

Several days later Picco met again with the political leaders of Hizbollah. The main points that emerged from the lengthy and polemical discussion were that Hizbollah was not responsible for the hostages; was saddened by the hostages lack of freedom and also by the imprisonment in Israel of some 300 Lebanese and Palestinians; was holding Israeli prisoners of war. It was not specified whether they were dead or alive.

As contacts proceeded with the Iranians in Tehran, New York and Geneva and with the groups in Lebanon, it became clear that the list of things that the Iranians wished to achieve in connection with the freeing of the hostages had changed. They had already gained part of their *desiderata* as a result of the Gulf War. They were no longer emphasizing the freeing of Iranian assets in the United States; now they were concentrating on the release of Shi'ite prisoners held by Israel, including Sheik Obeid; removal of Iran from the list of terrorist countries maintained by the United States; and UN confirmation that Iraq was to blame for the Iran-Iraq war. In addition, the Iranian government was eager to have me visit Tehran, as it viewed such a visit as a further step in Iran's reentry into the community of responsible nations. I felt that the keys to a settlement were now identified. One of these keys obviously belonged to Israel. If negotiations were to be successful, it would be necessary to reach an understanding with the Israelis.

Seven Israelis were missing in action in Lebanon: one navigator and two infantrymen who were believed to have been in the hands of Hizbollah; three soldiers who were captured in 1982 in Syrian-controlled territory in Lebanon by the Syrian army; and one captured in Lebanon by Palestinian units. The Israelis believed that at least one, the navigator, whose name was Ron Arad, was alive. The Israelis and their surrogate, the South Lebanese Army, in turn, were holding prisoner some 400 Lebanese and Palestinians. Most of the prisoners were in Al Khiam prison in southern Lebanon, while Sheik Obeid was known to be held by the Israelis in Israel.

In early June I put down on paper a simple and direct plan according to which all the Western hostages would be freed by their captors, the seven Israeli soldiers would be returned to Israel and then all Lebanese being held by Israel would be freed. I outlined this plan orally to Iranian Ambassador Kharrazi as a means of exploring Iranian thinking. It had not been cleared with Israel or shown to the United States or the United Kingdom. The Iranian reaction was given by Deputy Foreign Minister Mahmoud Vaezi in a meeting with Picco in Switzerland on June 22. He said he had tried a similar approach some months earlier. It had not worked because Israel had insisted on the release of Arad, which Iran could not guarantee. Vaezi insisted that Arad was not in Iran and that his whereabouts were not known. But he also said specifically that "the group with which Iran had relations" was in control of nine hostages: six Americans and three British. Two German hostages were in the hands of the Hamadi family; Iran had no information on a missing Italian, which was particularly regretted since both Rafsanjani and Velayati would like very much to do a favor to Italy. As a possible approach, Vaezi suggested that the Lebanese group would return the bodies of two Israeli soldiers and the Israelis would free Sheik Obeid and the other Lebanese prisoners. Then, he said, the nine Western hostages would surely be freed. The problem was to make something work without the Israeli navigator.

This was clearly a key problem, one that would remain until the very last stage of the hostage release. We developed several approaches to try to get around it. One, which became known as 9 plus 2 plus 500, was that the nine Western hostages and two Israeli bodies under Shi'ite control be exchanged for the Lebanese held under Israeli control. Picco briefed General Scowcroft on this plan on June 28 at the White House. Scowcroft thought that if the releases were to be implemented simultaneously, it smacked of a "deal," which was against American policy. If, on the other hand, the release of the 9 plus 2 was to take place first, as I was proposing, the United States was prepared to look at it closely. General Scowcroft said that the United States could not tell the Secretary-General that the release of the Western hostages would be reciprocated; but when Picco suggested that the Israelis, at U.S. prompting, could commit themselves to release the Lebanese prisoners, he did not reject the idea. The United States, he stressed, was in favor of the release of all hostages by all parties who held them. Including Israel. This desire could be communicated to the Iranians.

During the summer the Iranians continued to press me to visit Tehran. It was clear that President Rafsanjani was increasingly anxious for action on my part that would place blame on Iraq for starting the war with Iran. Realizing that this was one of the few levers I had that could be used in connection with the hostages, I suggested the possibility of a visit in late August but avoided agreeing on a specific date. I had already arranged for several highly reputable European scholars to prepare an independent report on the origins of the war with the idea that I would use their report as the basis for my own report to the Security Council. I had little doubt that the scholars would conclude that Iraq bore the major blame.

In late July I was informed through the Deputy Iranian Ambassador in New York, Dr. Javad Zarif, that a total release of the hostages was not feasible at that point. A partial release—two Americans and one British—was possible provided

Israel would be prepared to reciprocate. If I could determine this and present something concrete on paragraph 6 of Resolution 598, then my expected visit to Tehran would be "very successful." A few days later, on August 1, in meeting with the senior Iranian ambassador, Dr. Kharrazi (who was quite influential with President Rafsanjani), I said that from my point of view, the best solution would be that both sides would release all the hostages, all remains would be returned and agreement would be reached for a continued search for those unaccounted for. Kharrazi said that my plan had been well received and had been discussed with the Lebanese groups. The problem was Arad. If any additional information on him could be furnished, Iran was prepared to follow it up. The groups in Lebanon were convinced that without Arad, a full exchange would not be possible. That was why Iran had reverted to the partial release approach. At this point the idea developed of a mutually agreed upon search for Arad in which the United Nations would participate. This might satisfy the Israelis and permit the release of all Western hostages and the other Israeli military personnel held by the Shi'ite groups and all Lebanese prisoners held by Israel.

Realizing that there would most likely be a need for American intervention with the Israelis, I reviewed the state of play in detail with General Scowcroft on August 7, including the prospect of my visit to Tehran. I told him that Iran wished me to be the instrument for reaching a solution. It had accepted in principle my position that there should be a release in a short time of all hostages and prisoners held on both sides; Iran would help in securing the return of remains in the possession of Shi'ite groups in Lebanon; and it would assist in a search for any unaccounted for. However, I would need to obtain assurances that Israel would reciprocate—ultimately release all Lebanese prisoners being held under its control, including Sheik Obeid. The search for Arad would be linked to such assurances. Iran would expect that after the release of the first two American hostages, the United States would reciprocate by putting pressure on Israel to release some Arab prisoners.

I asked General Scowcroft for President Bush's support in my efforts, in particular with Israel. I hoped that the United States could influence Israel to make a commitment to release Sheik Obeid and the other Lebanese prisoners under its control if it obtained satisfactory information on its missing in action. I made clear that the United States did not need to pay anything for the release of its hostages apart from some possible gesture of appreciation at a later date. I would pay the bill with my visit to Tehran and through implementation of paragraph six of Resolution 598. Scowcroft said that President Bush's support was "a fact" but that he could make no promise concerning U.S. influence on the Israelis. Jim Baker, he noted, was opposed to U.S. involvement in any form.

In the first days of August Giandomenico Picco traveled via Tehran to Lebanon to meet again with the Lebanese groups. Several years previously the

United Nations had established a program for the reconstruction of Lebanon. Very little had ever been done because of the prevalence of violence in Lebanon and a lack of funds. In earlier meetings Sheik Fadlallah had asked whether funds could now be made available for reconstruction projects, a request the Iranians seconded. Unspoken was the implication that this could facilitate progress on the hostages. Since the aid program had been authorized by the General Assembly and the need for it in Lebanon had grown rather than diminished, I did not feel that the provision of reconstruction funds would constitute payment for the hostages. So I authorized Picco to inform his Lebanese interlocutors that I had contacted the major donors and had received indications of readiness to contribute to the reconstruction of Lebanon. The UN fund that had been established for this purpose would be used for the benefit of *all* communities. Picco also informed them that I had requested the former Italian Prime Minister, Bettino Craxi, to serve as my Special Representative for Lebanese Reconstruction.

On August 5, Ambassador Kharrazi confirmed to me in New York that two hostages might well be released unilaterally as part of what we had been discussing. This would mark the beginning of a process. Picco, in the meantime, was on his way to Beirut. Then, on August 6, the Islamic Jihad, one of the groups associated with Hizbollah, issued a communiqué that it intended to send an envoy to meet with me and ask that I work for a settlement of the hostage problem. The envoy turned out to be one of the hostages, John McCarthy, a young Irishman of intelligence and remarkable good humor in light of what he had been through, who was released on August 8. I flew to England and met alone with him at the Royal Air Force Base at Lyneham on August 11. On the same day, but before my meeting with McCarthy, American hostage Edward Austin Tracy and a Frenchman, Jerome Leyraud, who had been seized only three days before apparently by a group that was opposed to the hostage releases, were freed.

McCarthy handed me a lengthy letter from the Islamic Jihad that consisted mainly of polemics against the United Nations for failing to support the struggles of the oppressed people of the world, beginning with the Palestinians. The hostage seizures constituted the reply of Islamic combatants to the imprisonment of thousands of Lebanese and Palestinian fighters. The operative sentences came only at the end and read "Convinced that it is necessary to act in order to liberate our fighters who are rotting in the prisons of occupied Palestine and of Europe and to resolve the affair of the persons we hold, we ask that you [the Secretary-General] work personally, within the framework of a global solution, for the liberation of all of those detained in the world. In this case, we would be ready to bring to an end the process that we have begun today and to liberate within 24 hours the persons whom we hold."

More revealing than the letter was what McCarthy told me orally. He said that the Hizbollah was in serious difficulty since it no longer was receiving much support from Iran or other patrons. It was convinced that the time had come to end the hostage problem. McCarthy, Tracy and Leyraud had been released as a sign of goodwill. The remaining hostage problem could be resolved on the basis of an exchange of the hostages they held for those in the hands of Israel. The Islamic Jihad was seriously concerned about those Arabs imprisoned in Europe as terrorists, but it understood that they could not be released immediately. Some commitment, however, that they would be released in one, two or three years or transferred to a friendly country was needed.

According to McCarthy, the Jihad sought my involvement alone to avoid duplication of effort. The hostage problem would end if the Secretary-General could guarantee publicly that Israel would release all those it was detaining and that appropriate arrangements were being made that would permit the early release of those being held as terrorists in European countries.

Speaking only for himself, McCarthy said that Hizbollah was holding two Israeli soldiers but he did not know whether they were alive or dead. He understood that Arad, whom the groups in Lebanon realized was the crux of Israeli interest, was held by Amal. McCarthy had the impression that he was alive but had no direct evidence.

On the basis of this information and further conversations I had with Iranian Ambassador Kharrazi, I felt that developments were moving toward a full resolution of the hostage problem. I concluded that direct consultations with authoritative Israeli representatives were urgently needed at this point. Accordingly I met in Geneva on August 11 with the Coordinator of Lebanese Affairs in the Israeli Defense Ministry, Uri Lubrani, and the deputy director-general of the Israeli Foreign Ministry, Johanan Bein. Lubrani, who had served earlier as Israeli ambassador to Iran, was clearly the man in charge of the Israeli missing-in-action problem and, because of its direct relevance, the hostage issue. He was single-minded in his determination to obtain the return of the Israeli soldiers lost in Lebanon or their bodies if they were dead. This was a sacred duty of the State of Israel. He made clear to me from the beginning that Israel would use whatever bargaining chips it had to obtain the return of the missing Israelis. If the Western hostages could be liberated as part of the same bargain, fine and good, but there would be no bargain without the return of the Israelis. Lubrani had been working on the problem for many months and had been deeply involved in the Swiss channel. I had the impression that he was a man who did not extend his trust lightly and who was not, by nature, inclined to extend it to the Secretary-General of the United Nations.

In this first meeting with the Israeli representatives, I said that from what I had heard from McCarthy and Iranian Ambassador Kharrazi, I felt that Iran and the Shi'ite groups in Lebanon were interested in getting rid of the hostage problem and were prepared to help me accomplish this. But Iran was asking two things from me: a visit and full implementation of Resolution 598, especially paragraph 6, on blame for the Iran-Iraq war. From Israel, Iran and the groups in Lebanon wanted all Lebanese detainees to be freed. In other words, both the Secretary-General and Israel were being asked to pay a price. I told the Israeli representatives that in contacts with the Iranians I had urged that there should be an overall release of the hostages, emphasizing that I viewed this as a humanitarian, not a political, question and that I gave equal importance to all who were being held—Westerners, Israelis and Arabs. I had asked for Iran's assistance in helping to locate those who were missing and the bodies of those who had died, including Collett and Higgins. Iran had accepted these points and had now for the first time indicated a willingness to cooperate in a search for navigator Arad. But this would be linked to an Israeli statement on the release of Arab detainees. I had told the Iranians I was ready to send one of my close aides, such as Picco, to accompany them in the search for Arad.

I informed the Israelis further that if the International Committee of the Red Cross were permitted to visit Sheik Obeid, Iran would arrange for Israeli representatives to see the Israeli detainees or their bodies. Iran also wanted the United States to make a gesture in response to the positive role Iran was playing, but it was not asking the United States to pay a "price."

Lubrani remarked at this point "there is a lot of money involved in this affair. You cannot imagine how much." I never discussed the meaning of that remark. Lubrani then recounted that a year and a half earlier, the Swiss government informed the Israeli government that it had been approached by Iran to mediate the hostage issue. Israel had agreed to accept Switzerland as interlocutor. Eight months later the Swiss informed Israel that Iran had asked for a gesture, as a confidence-building measure, to establish Switzerland's credibility as interlocutor. Israel then persuaded General Antoine Lahad, the Commander of the South Lebanese Army, to release 40 detainees from Al Khiam prison even though all were implicated in terrorist activities against Israel. Israel conveyed to Iran well in advance a list of those to be released, including time and place. "We waited for a response. But there was none." Foreign Minister Velayati only remarked to the Swiss secretary of state for Foreign Affairs that the gesture was good but that more was needed.

Lubrani clearly attributed special importance to Arad. According to Israeli information, he had bailed out over Lebanon and was captured by Amal. Subsequently he was transferred to the control of the Iranian Revolutionary Guards in the Beka'a Valley under the control of a Mr. Ali Askari, Iran's representative in Lebanon. Since then Israel had heard nothing. Israel needed to know whether he was alive or dead. "We have been dealing with this issue for a long time," Lubrani said, "and occasionally they have approached us either to extort money or exert political pressure. But whenever we have asked them what they have to sell, they have been silent."

Since I was to see Ambassador Kharrazi the next day, I asked Lubrani to state exactly what the terms of an agreement would be. He defined an acceptable agreement in this way: in exchange for a "clear solution" on the six Israeli servicemen, Israel would be prepared to release the Lebanese and Palestinian prisoners captured in Lebanon, including Sheik Obeid. Although Samir Assad, the seventh Israeli soldier missing in action, was mentioned, no provision on him was necessary in an agreement, since separate arrangements were being made in his regard. There had to be a sign of life regarding Arad; the Prime Minister would insist on this. Once that happened, everything else would be "easy." I asked which side should go first. Lubrani replied that Israel should first receive some indication about the status of its missing soldiers.

On the following day, August 12, I conveyed the Israeli position to Ambassador Kharrazi. I underlined that from the Israeli perspective, the freeing of one British and one American hostage was an important, but insufficient development. Kharrazi clearly understood quite well that Israel was entitled to receive something concrete in exchange for what it was being asked to give.

When I next met with the Israeli representatives two days later, Lubrani first handed me a letter that he said Prime Minister Shamir had asked that he convey to me. The letter stated that Israel welcomed my role in furthering the release of the hostages and prisoners detained in Lebanon. The letter reiterated in precise terms the Israeli position that Lubrani had expressed to me with one point added. Israel was ready to enable immediate access of ICRC representatives to the Lebanese prisoners and detainees under the control of Israel and General Lahad, on condition that similar access be granted to Israeli prisoners of war (POWs) and those missing in action (MIAs) and South Lebanese Army captives in Lebanon. Lubrani insisted that in pursuit of my efforts to obtain a general release of hostages, Israel should not again be asked to make a unilateral gesture. It was essential that I obtain tangible proof of the status of the missing Israeli soldiers that could be passed to Israel.

Since the required evidence entailed technical details, it was agreed that Giandomenico Picco would travel to Israel for a full briefing. I asked what Israel would do once I obtained such evidence. Lubrani replied that once Israel had the evidence and was satisfied that neither I nor it was "being led down the garden path," Israel would free a considerable number of detainees. The proposal for a search for those Israeli soldiers not accounted for was also pursued. The Israelis said that three of their men had been captured in Syrian-controlled territory, and the search for the soldiers or their graves would have to include Syria. They could give Picco full details on what to look for. I agreed that I would seek Syrian agreement. Picco would travel to Israel very shortly—

as soon as he had something to convey from the Iranians. I would inform the Iranian side of the Israeli position precisely as it was contained in the Prime Minister's letter. The Israeli representatives said that there was no reason to keep the position of the Israeli government secret. I felt differently and told my Israeli friends that we were all diplomats. The only difference was that I was older and therefore inclined toward old-fashioned ways. I felt that if the letter were made public, it could be misused. I would therefore convey the contents verbally "but without changing a comma."

Before the meeting ended, the Israeli representatives stressed once again that Israel would not give in to pressure for another unilateral gesture. Lubrani revealed that after the release of McCarthy, British Prime Minister John Major had written to Prime Minister Shamir asking that Israel make a humanitarian gesture by releasing a number of detainees. Israel was aware that it would be under increasing pressure of this nature, but it would not buckle. To be sure that the Israelis understood my approach, I stated emphatically that I would never put the onus on them to make all concessions. I realized quite well that Israel was not the only party holding a key.

When Picco went to Israel a few days later, he was given a full briefing on the technical aspects of confirming the identity of the missing Israeli soldiers, whether dead or alive. The Israelis presumed that all except Arad were dead. They had made an investigation regarding the four Iranian diplomats about whom Foreign Minister Velayati had earlier expressed concern. According to their information, the diplomats had been killed immediately after capture in 1982. The Israeli intelligence service provided written and photographic material that could be given to Iran on where the Israelis believed the diplomats were buried. Detailed information was also given to Picco about South Lebanese Army soldiers that were in the hands of the Shi'ite groups. During the meeting, Picco said that, in order to get the identification information on the Israeli soldiers from the sources in Lebanon, he would need assurance that Israel would reciprocate with a partial release of Lebanese prisoners. Lubrani gave this assurance not in the larger meeting but subsequently when speaking alone with Picco.

On the following day I told Ambassador Kharrazi in Geneva that the provision of definitive identification on the two Israeli soldiers in Hizbollah's (or another group's) control would prompt a partial release of the Lebanese detainees under Israeli control. I also gave him the information on the four Iranian diplomats that had been provided by Israel and the name and location of the Iranian citizen who the Israelis had reason to believe knew where Ron Arad was. I further indicated that since three of the missing Israelis seemed to be outside the purview of Iran, I intended to write to the Syrian Government on the matter. I proposed to send Picco to Tehran to provide any further details that might be needed and to receive the definitive Iranian reaction.

The response of Iran and of Hizbollah was positive. The transaction could take place the following week. However, the Iranians insisted that Israel release 100 Lebanese prisoners. When Lubrani met with Picco to hear what the Iranians had said, his first reaction was negative. The next day, August 31, however, he called and said that perhaps it would be possible to free 100 Lebanese if definitive identification of the two bodies was provided. Then on September 1, Prime Minister Shamir's Inner Cabinet met to consider the matter. On September 2, Mr. Lubrani informed Picco that it had approved the exchange but instead of information on the Israelis, their bodies would have to be turned over and, in addition, information would have to be provided on Arad. This could be given to the Secretary-General during his visit to Tehran. The release of the Lebanese detainees also could take place during the visit. Under these circumstances, Israel would release 60 detainees from Al Khiam and 20 others from Israel, for a total of 80, and, in addition, it would return 15 Lebanese bodies.

Plans already had been made for Picco to proceed to Lebanon on September 4 to receive the identifying information on the two Israelis. I had to consider what course to follow in light of the new Israeli position. The Iranians had informed me that linkage of any other condition to the "minipackage" that I had proposed probably would stop the hostage release process for the foreseeable future. We decided that the search for Arad that had been agreed to earlier could provide a way out of the impasse. Following consultations, Ambassador Kharrazi agreed on September 5 that I could state the following to the Israelis: "The Secretary-General will start a search so that he can say in the end whether Ron Arad is alive or dead. The Secretary-General has been assured by Iran that it will provide all available tools to make him successful." Kharrazi told me the search could last 10 to 15 days, but this information was not included in the statement.

I reached Lubrani in Paris the next day and read him the statement. I said I thought that this met the requirements that Israel had set and that therefore I expected that the Israeli government would proceed with the "minipackage" as it had been discussed in Switzerland. Any other decision by Israel would suggest that it no longer wished to cooperate in my efforts. This prompted an immediate response from Israel containing a detailed counterproposal. The operative provisions, which were to prove highly significant in the subsequent negotiations, were as follows:

In order to facilitate the Secretary-General's initiative, Israel was willing to make an additional humanitarian gesture by releasing and returning 70 Lebanese detainees including a number of corpses, in exchange for: irrefutable evidence concerning the fate of its POWs and MIAs and that of South Lebanese Army POWs and MIAs; and an approach by the Secretary-General to President Assad of Syria on a thorough and intensive search operation for Israeli MIAs lost in Syrian-controlled territory.

It was proposed that Israel would release 35 Lebanese after information, to be verified by Israel, was received on the Israeli and South Lebanese Army MIAs and the approach had been made to President Assad. Israel would release 35 more prisoners when the results of the Secretary-General's search on the whereabouts of Ron Arad were known. Thus, the Israeli proposal foresaw the release of some Lebanese before the search for Arad was completed.

Meanwhile the date for my visit to Tehran had been set for September 10-11. In the interim matters developed rapidly. Picco made yet another secret trip to Lebanon to receive the material identifying the two Israeli bodies being held by a Hizbollah group. Then on the evening of September 8 Picco and I met in Paris with Lubrani and four other Israeli representatives. The Israelis were clearly concerned that in the forthcoming meeting with President Rafsanjani I would give the Iranians what they wanted before they had provided the desired information on Arad. I assured them that Iran had definitely agreed to the search for Arad. The Israelis were aware from their own sources that the Iranian leadership was expecting me to reveal the decisions I had taken with regard to Security Council Resolution 598. Their information indicated that Iran would try to split the issue of the Western hostages from that of the Israeli POWs. They reiterated that from their sources they were sure that Arad was being held by the Iranian representative Askari in the Sheik Abdullah Camp in Baalbeck and that the Iranian Government was aware of this. I said I intended to discuss the Arad case directly with President Rafsanjani and that, as always, I would insist that the hostages, POWs, and detainees were a package.

Lubrani then stated that Israel had already agreed on how many detainees would be released in the event the bodies of the two Israeli soldiers were returned and information was provided on Arad. Israel realized that the Secretary-General would need some further "device" in his talks in Iran. Therefore, if the identifying information Israel received proved satisfactory, by September 11—the day I would be meeting with Rafsanjani—60 Lebanese would be released and 30 more when the two bodies were turned over and information about Arad received. There was an exchange about these figures—60 plus 30, 70 plus 75 at one point, 80 plus 10 at another. I felt that none of the figures was entirely firm but that there would be a substantial release if the material provided on the Israeli soldiers proved satisfactory.

When the Israelis examined the material that Picco brought from Lebanon, they found everything that was needed to identify one soldier but insufficient material on the other. Accordingly, on September 11, 51 detainees were released from Al Khiam and 9 bodies were returned from Israel. The spokesman of the Israel Ministry of Defense, in announcing these steps, said that Israel believed this humanitarian gesture "will also facilitate the Secretary-General's efforts to resolve the problem of the Western hostages."

A DISCUSSION WITH PRESIDENT RAFSANJANI

I met with President Rafsanjani in Tehran later on September 11. I was struck again by his quickness and animation. Unlike most other personages of religious status in Iran, he had no beard, just a suggestion of whiskers on his chin. When I first met him in the course of the Iran-Iraq war, he was reserved, giving very much the impression of a fundamentalist *mullah*. In a subsequent meeting, but still during the war, he was more outgoing and responsive. On this occasion he was warmly welcoming. He listened intently and his dark eyes flashed with interest. He responded immediately and authoritatively to ideas and suggestions. In the quickness of his reactions and his readiness to listen he reminded me, surprisingly, of Mikhail Gorbachev.

The conversation began not on the hostage question but on implementation of Security Council Resolution 598. Rafsanjani, as expected, placed particular emphasis on the paragraph relating to blame for the Iran-Iraq war. I told him that a group of independent professors was preparing a report on this matter, which would be ready by October. I hoped then to be in a position to submit a report to the Security Council. The President, noting that my term of office would end on December 31, insisted that I must finish the report myself since I knew Iraq and Iran well and what had happened during the war. In response, I recalled that by invading Kuwait, Iraq had violated a basic principle of international law. In the Iran-Iraq context, the existence of the two countries' bilateral treaty of 1975 would have to be considered. I then turned the conversation to the hostages. After thanking the President for his assistance, I stated that the release that day by the Israelis of 60 Lebanese could be an important step in resolving the whole hostage problem. If information was forthcoming on Israeli navigator Arad, a real breakthrough was in sight. Solution of that one case could lead to the release of almost all of the Lebanese detainees— one man against 400! Rafsanjani replied that they had done a lot of work on this problem. He thought there were two possible approaches: They could go into Lebanon and question the people who might know, as they had done in the case of the Frenchman who had been kidnapped. In that case, they had to apply much pressure through the Lebanese. The other approach would be through Syria, for there was a small possibility that Arad was there. Rafsanjani promised that one of the two approaches mentioned would be followed.

In an effort to make clear the larger importance of resolving the whole hostage issue, I suggested that an improvement in Iran's relations with the United States was desirable so that Iran could become a full participant in the solution of the problems of the Gulf region and the Middle East. The stumbling block was the hostage issue. Rafsanjani was optimistic that the course I was following on the hostages could lead to a solution of the problems between the

United States and Iran. He related that earlier he had been in touch with Presidents Reagan and Bush. The Americans first did something very unwise. To gain money for the contras in Nicaragua, they sold arms to Iran at a very high price. He said "This stopped the whole thing." Since then President Bush had sent messages to Iran that the hostages should be released and the Iranian assets in the United States could be unfrozen later. Rafsanjani stated clearly that the link between the two issues had now been cut. Iran was putting no conditions on the release of the Western hostages other than a satisfactory response to the Lebanese request for the release of all Lebanese detainees.

I said that Israel wanted an exchange for its own people. The issues of the Western hostages and the missing Israeli soldiers were not, strictly speaking, the same. I then asked directly if Iran could obtain the release of the remaining Western hostages. Rafsanjani's reply was somewhat obscure, seeming to contradict what he had said earlier. "After the release of some further hostages," he said, "others had to be released." This would come after the Israelis had received full information on the bodies. "After all of this, if the U.S. wanted to improve relations with Iran, it should lift the freeze on Iranian assets. . . ." Rafsanjani's last request was that I not forget the Iranian hostages in making public statements on the issue. Apparently he had not been informed that I had already passed on to Iran the information provided by Israel on their deaths and burial and that I was meeting with their families while in Tehran to inform them and to express my sympathy.

THE HOSTAGE RELEASE PROCESS CONTINUES

During the ensuing two weeks Giandomenico Picco was engaged in intensive secret negotiations that kept him moving repeatedly between Israel and Lebanon. Two obstacles had to be overcome before further progress could be hoped for. The Israelis were insisting on further definitive identification material on the second Israeli body held by the Shi'ite groups. Hizbollah and the groups had been under the impression that Israel would turn over 80 detainees when the first identification material was provided. Since only 60 were returned, they considered that Israel had gone back on its commitment. It was necessary for Picco to maintain continuing contact with the underground groups in Lebanon to overcome this impasse.

The release of hostages and detainees resumed on September 24, 1991, with the freeing of the English longtime Beirut resident Jack Mann. Two days later, on September 26, the Israelis released 15 more Lebanese detainees, even though they still had not received what they considered definitive material on the identity of the second body being held by Hizbollah. On the same day the American hostage Jesse Turner was released. This was in line with President

Rafsanjani's earlier statement to me that other hostages would be released. I must say a word here about the Syrian role. The Syrians did not give much assistance in obtaining the release of the hostages. They were helpful, however, in providing logistic support when releases took place. For the most part, arrangements for the release of the Western hostages were made between the Shi'ite groups and Picco. The Syrians were determined, however, to be seen as receiving the hostages when they were freed and escorting them to safety in Damascus. When, the Shi'ite group insisted on turning over hostage Tracy to Picco themselves, the Syrians complained bitterly to the Iranians and, through them, threatened to end their cooperation with Picco.

Following the release of Jack Mann and Jesse Turner further progress on the American and British hostages seemed again to depend on news of Arad. While the Iranians had agreed to cooperate in a search for him, the timing of the search had not been established. The Israelis had agreed to release a substantial number of detainees in connection with the search, but they insisted that most would be released only on its completion. On October 8, Lubrani presented a new detailed plan according to which the timing of releases on both sides and progress in the search would be precisely correlated. The process would extend over 30 days from the beginning of the search for Arad. Included in the plan was a provision for the Syrians to search for the bodies of the three Israeli MIAs who had been captured in the part of Lebanon under Syrian control. At the end of the 30 days Ron Arad, Sheik Obeid and all remaining Lebanese prisoners in Al Khiam prison and in Israel would be released and the Secretary-General would make a statement that the search for the Israeli MIAs would continue.

The Iranian reaction to this plan was negative, on the ground that, as before, the number of Lebanese being released at the various stages was too limited. I sought to proceed on the basis of an earlier interim package we had developed that foresaw the release of an additional Western hostage followed by completion of information on the second Israeli body and finally the Israeli release of 10 more Lebanese prisoners. This approach was not successful. Picco again moved quietly in the area trying to bring the parties together. Word was received in Tehran that Libyan President Gadhafi was willing to be helpful in the hostage affair. Picco was invited to go to Libya and the Libyan Government chartered a plane for the trip. I personally was not sanguine on the likelihood of Libyan assistance, but Iranian authorities hoped that Gadhafi might be able to exercise a positive influence on the groups in Lebanon that were still holding Western hostages. This could be important since three underground Shi'ite groups were taking turns releasing them. The group whose turn it was to make the next release was ideologically mixed and not completely subject to Iranian influence. However, the trip to Libya was not productive. Picco did not see the

President. His deputy told Picco that while Libya would like to be helpful, it had nothing to do with the hostages and had no direct contact with the groups holding them.

During this period repeated reports emanated largely from Lebanese and Iranian sources that Israel's refusal to release more Lebanese detainees was jeopardizing continuation of the hostage release process. The Israelis, for their part, were becoming concerned that I would satisfy the Iranian expectations on Security Council Resolution 598 and the Western hostage problem would be resolved without any satisfaction for Israel. Their concern was increased by the fact that the promised search for Ron Arad had not started. The result was that on October 26, Lubrani gave Picco a revised Israeli proposal for a comprehensive settlement of the hostage problem, under which all further progress in the release process would depend on receipt of irrefutable information on the whereabouts of Ron Arad. When the proposal was passed to the Iranians, they rejected it as totally unacceptable. I met with Lubrani two days later in my residence in New York and suggested that the plan be modified so that 75 Lebanese would be released at the beginning of the search for Arad and another 75 at its completion. Lubrani was convinced that the Iranians now wanted the hostage situation resolved quickly. He thought it was best to wait several days, after which I might write another letter to the President of Iran. Israel was not prepared to revert to its earlier proposals. I believe that making all progress dependent on information on Arad was a tactical error on the part of the Israelis, since it encouraged the Iranians to move ahead to resolve the Western hostage problem separately from the issue of missing Israeli soldiers and Lebanese detainees.

The Iranians now suggested that I was not doing enough to get the Americans to apply pressure on the Israelis, but more important they emphasized anew the desirability of moving ahead with implementation of article 6 of Security Council Resolution 598. They also began to ask if funds could be found to go ahead with assistance programs for the communities in Lebanon—in other words, to find some justification for Iran to insist that the groups in Lebanon proceed with the release of the remaining Western hostages.

On November 4, we were informed that President Rafsanjani viewed the Israeli position as unacceptable and felt that other strategies would have to be found to achieve what he and I had agreed on: the liberation of the Western hostages. I looked into the possibility of obtaining funds from the European Community to be added to the trust fund already established (but poorly funded) by the General Assembly for assistance to Lebanon. I made clear, of course, to the Iranians that the funding of special projects in Lebanon could come only after all hostages were released and could not be depicted as payment. In any event, it proved impossible to obtain additional funding in time to be of use in connection with the hostages, although the European funds would come into play later in efforts to obtain the release of the two German hostages who were still captive after all the other Western hostages were freed.

Lubrani was certainly correct in part of his assessment of the situation in Tehran. The Iranians were anxious to get rid of the hostage problem quickly. Having decided that a new strategy was required that would not be dependent on the Israelis, they moved ahead expeditiously on an alternate approach. This approach amounted to obtaining as many of the Iranian political objectives as possible without making resolution of the hostage issue completely dependent on any one of them. At this point four objectives remained: (1) restoration of Iran's position as a responsible member of the international community, an objective only partly accomplished by the visit I had paid to Tehran in September; (2) the submission by me of a report to the Security Council that would establish that Iraq bore the blame for starting the Iran-Iraq war; (3) removal of Iran from the list maintained by the United States of countries subject to sanctions for harboring terrorists; and (4) some UN financial support for reconstruction in Lebanon. The Iranians returned to these points frequently as they began in early November to set a timetable for the release of the remaining Western hostages (with exception of the Germans).

On November 11, Ambassador Kharrazi informed me of the release schedule as foreseen in Tehran. In doing so, he stressed how useful it would be if the United Sates responded favorably to the releases. I indicated that I expected to be in contact with the United States and the likelihood that the process would be over by the beginning of December should be useful. I committed myself to state publicly that I would continue to work for the liberation of the detainees in Al Khiam prison and for the resolution of other related humanitarian problems. With regard to Resolution 598, I stated specifically that I had already approved conceptually my report on paragraph 6.

Giandomenico Picco left for Damascus and Lebanon immediately after this conversation in order to provide the Shi'ite groups with a number of reasons why they should complete the releases as Iran was urging. He also needed to be present for the next release, which was expected shortly after November 15. I must emphasize here that while the Iranians exercised strong influence on Hizbollah and the underground groups associated with it, their control was not complete. The groups required some direct persuasion—they needed, to use an American term, to be massaged. The details of the releases also had to be worked out. This is the task that Picco accomplished with remarkable skill and a great deal of courage. He will tell his own story, but I can say here that he put his life on the line venturing to meetings in Lebanon that even the Israelis, who are no strangers to that country, counseled against.

On the day after my meeting with Kharrazi, General Scowcroft came to New York at my suggestion. I told him that our negotiations had made substantial progress and that we now had a tentative schedule for the release of all the American hostages—that all should be home by early December. If all the American hostages were released, as now expected, it would be due to the major role played by Iran. The Iranians recalled President Bush's phrase that "goodwill begets goodwill" and expected a favorable American response. I indicated their particular interest in having Iran removed from the list of terrorist countries that President Bush would be submitting to Congress at more or less the time of the release. President Rafsanjani had asked me to transmit to President Bush a message containing his assessment of a recent conference on Palestine held in Tehran. (I gave that message to General Scowcroft.) I suggested that this was a further indication of his interest in closer relations with the United States. General Scowcroft was, of course, highly gratified to hear about the hostages and expressed the warmest appreciation for what the United Nations was doing. He could give no response, however, on Iran's exclusion from the list of terrorist countries.

On November 18, Terry Waite and Thomas Sutherland, one Englishman and one American, were released. At the same time agreement was reached between the United States and Iran at The Hague on payment to Iran of $278 million in compensation for military equipment purchased by Iran during the Shah's regime but never delivered. The United States also announced that neither Iran nor Syria was involved in the bombing of Pan Am flight 103 over Lockerbie, Scotland. The United States has said that these developments were not related to the release of hostages. I can state categorically that the United States never informed me that these moves were pending or suggested that they were in any way relevant to the hostage negotiations for which I was then the principal and, I believe, only channel. But even if the timing was entirely coincidental, it was nevertheless fortuitous, since two Iranian desiderata were met at least in part: Some Iranian assets were released and the terrorist stigma was reduced.

THE STILL-MISSING ISRAELIS

I was, by this time, confident that the other American hostages would be released, but I was also conscious that Israel had not obtained information on Ron Arad or its other missing soldiers and had gained the return of only one body. Several hundred Lebanese detainees remained in Israel's control. It had been, and remained, my hope and determination to resolve *all* aspects of the hostage problem before my term as Secretary-General expired. Giandomenico Picco had been in continuing contact with the Israelis, and I was aware of their dissatisfaction over the way in which the release process was developing. On November 23, I went to Rome to meet with Israeli hostage negotiator Lubrani. It was not an easy meeting. I emphasized my desire to close the hostage file by the end of the year and to accelerate the momentum so that we could obtain information on Ron Arad. I was mindful of the Israeli resolve to make no more gestures without a guarantee of reciprocation. Nonetheless, I suggested that if Israel would release a relatively small number of detainees at this point—as few as ten—the entire process could be accelerated and Israel reintroduced as an active party. Lubrani recalled his earlier understanding that a common strategy would be developed that would take full advantage of the political levers available to the Secretary-General as well as those held by Israel. He did not think this had been done. He took my point about expanding the momentum but stated that almost all of Israel's objectives were still unmet. He thought that before Israel took any further steps, the outcome should be assured. I reiterated my strong desire on humanitarian grounds to see the whole hostage issue resolved before the end of my term.

On November 30 Picco received from Hizbollah in Lebanon a timetable for the release of the three remaining American hostages. On the following day Israel released 23 detainees from Al Khiam prison, stating that this was done in response to my request. The release of the remaining American hostages then took place; Terry Anderson was the last on December 3. Each was received by Syrian representatives in Picco's presence and taken to Damascus in accordance with by-then well-established practice. All American, British and French hostages were now free. The goal I had set for a complete resolution of the whole issue of hostages, detainees and of soldiers missing in action or held prisoner before my term of office ended was not, however, to be achieved. Amid the satisfaction I felt on what had been accomplished—on the joy so evident on each hostage's face on liberation—I could not, and cannot, forget that the two United Nations hostages did not survive. They must be remembered both as victims and as martyrs: victims of a conflict that no amount of violence can resolve; martyrs to the cause of ending this conflict through reason, compromise and international cooperation.

The release of all the Lebanese detainees under Israel's control was within reach. The notorious Al Khiam prison could have been emptied. This depended on only one thing: the provision of information on the whereabouts of Ron Arad. The Israelis have compelling evidence that he, at one point, came into the hands of the Iranian representative in Lebanon. Why the Iranians were unable or unwilling to provide information on the fate of this one man, or to start the search for him on which agreement had been reached, remains a sad and destructive mystery. I did all in my power to persuade them to do so. I did not in any way suggest that the freeing of the Western hostages was a matter of greater concern than the return of Arad. In the end, Iran was ready to bring about the liberation of the Western hostages without reciprocity in the form of the release of all Lebanese being held under the Israeli control. This had the effect of also eliminating Arad and the return of the bodies of all the Israeli missing in action from the equation.

WHO WAS GUILTY?

The groups that seized the hostages were shadowy to the end. The nine Western hostages that were released between August and December 1991 were all being held by three underground Shi'ite groups functioning in association with Hizbollah, a public organization of fundamentalist Shia that had strong ties with Iran. At various times the groups identified themselves as the Islamic Jihad, the Revolutionary Justice Organization and the Organization of the Oppressed of the Earth. None of the groups ever asked the United Nations to provide assurance against pursuit or retaliation. It is doubtful whether they ever existed in a structured sense. I believe that they operated under the guidance, if not complete control, of Hizbollah. Hizbollah, in turn, was clearly dependent on support from Iran and accordingly was subject to strong Iranian influence. Neither Hizbollah nor Iran can be free from blame for these senseless kidnappings. Yet it is equally true that Iran, under the leadership of President Rafsanjani, was the major factor in bringing about the hostages' release. This signified an important change of direction for Iran, one motivated, to be sure, by its own pressing economic and political interests—interests that were not in conflict with those of the wider international community. Peace and stability in the region could only be strengthened if Iran reentered the community of responsible countries.

On the ninth of December 1991, six days after the release of the last American hostage, I submitted to the Security Council my report placing responsibility for initiating the Iran-Iraq war squarely on Iraq. This, I believe, was an accurate statement of fact, not influenced by the support given by Iran to my efforts to resolve the hostage problem. I have no doubt that I was justified in holding out the hope of such a finding—an honest finding—in order to encourage Iran's support on the hostages. (A further account of my report is in chapter 7.)

Understandably, the Bush Administration would not make concessions to Iran as part of a deal to obtain the hostages' release. U.S. policy was, as far as I knew, completely consistent on this throughout the process. I felt, however, that some positive response from the United States after the hostage release would be justified in light of President Bush's stated interest in improving relations with Iran and would be helpful in influencing Iran's policies in the region. In particular I thought that President Bush would be well advised to omit Iran from the list of countries against which trade sanctions would continue because of their policy of harboring terrorists. I suggested this when I last saw President Bush while still Secretary-General. Mr. Bush's response was vague but positive. Jim Baker, who was present, was negative because, he said, the

Iranians were still encouraging terrorism. How can they be taken off the list? he asked. I did not have knowledge of any Iranian actions in support of terrorism elsewhere in the world, although I was, of course, much disturbed by the continuing death sentence against Salman Rushdie. But I was still convinced that Iran's role in the release of the Western hostages was of decisive importance, that it did represent a positive change in direction for Iranian policy under more constructive leadership that it would be wise to encourage.

THE WOMEN VICTIMS

I cannot conclude this chapter without recording the great respect I gained for the family members of the hostages with whom I met. They came in the hope that I could do something to free their loved ones. In some cases the assistance I could promise seemed meager, I know. Yet all were appreciative of whatever could be done. Alec Collett's wife was gentle and a little shy in approaching me. She was totally desolated by the loss of her husband. Her first expression was always one of gratitude for whatever efforts had been made, no matter how futile they proved to be. Yet she was fiercely determined that her husband be freed and held to her belief that he remained alive even when no real ground for hope remained. Left with no means of support for herself and her small child, she is now employed by the United Nations, where she nurtures still a faith that her husband is alive.

Colonel Higgins's wife, herself a major in the Marine Corps, was totally different. Firm, appropriately military in her bearing, she was ready to take things into her own hands to bring about her husband's freedom. Understanding the constraints under which the U.S. government must operate in negotiating for the release of hostages, she had decided to pursue an independent effort. With the help of an American lawyer, contact had been established with a prominent Lebanese businessman who said he had evidence that Colonel Higgins was alive and that negotiations for his release (presumably involving ransom) could be fruitful. Major Higgins's lawyer was on the point of leaving for Lebanon when the Organization of the Oppressed announced her husband's execution. As much as she deplored the action of the Israelis in kidnapping Sheik Obeid, this, she said, was not the time for anger against anyone. Her interest was to free her husband. When the reports that reached me left no doubt that he was dead, I called Major Higgins to express my deep regret before informing President Bush of the outcome of our investigation. Even in her grief, she was appreciative of the efforts that the United Nations had made.

The wife of Major Arad came from Israel to see me with their young child, who was still an infant when Arad parachuted to an uncertain fate in Lebanon. Still young—hardly thirty, I would say—and very much a *sabra*, as the Israelis call the native-born, she too was brave and grateful that the United Nations had joined in the efforts to bring about her husband's return. He had managed to send letters to her from his captivity in Lebanon so she knew that he had been captured alive and, for a considerable time, had been well. But then, after eight years of waiting, he had totally disappeared.

As we all took joy in the release of the other hostages, I could not forget these three brave women who had waited and fought and found no reward. Their lives, like those of so many in Lebanon and Israel, have been forever marked by the inhumanity that hatred breeds.

SEVEN

AN UNENDING WAR

ON SEPTEMBER 21-22, 1980, Saddam Hussein sent his army across the border into Iran, beginning a war that for many years seemed likely to end only with the total collapse of one country or the other and quite possibly of both. Mutual exhaustion did, in the end, figure prominently in the acceptance of peace. The horrors of earlier wars—human wave tactics, including children, by Iran, and chemical warfare by Iraq—were revived at a cost in lives and property still not accurately calculated. The war unleashed forces of Moslem Shi'ite fundamentalism that threatened the stability of the whole Moslem world, the very forces that Saddam Hussein presumably sought to control. The oil supply on which the rest of the world was heavily dependent was jeopardized, if only for a while. The war brought destruction to international shipping and the threat of direct great-power involvement in the conflict, a threat all the more dangerous since this contest of strength and will between regimes in which fanaticism and rationality were peculiarly intermingled began during the Cold War.

When the Iraqi forces crossed the border into Iran, no country moved in the Security Council to stop it. Other Arab governments supported Iraq. No non-Arab government was interested in prejudicing relations with Baghdad or in giving another country an advantage in this regard. Only the Secretary-General of the United Nations, Kurt Waldheim, took action. On September 22, Secretary-General Waldheim offered his good offices to both Iran and Iraq to assist them in settling their conflict by peaceful means. The next day, following the rarely used procedure authorized in Article 99 of the UN Charter, he brought the situation to the attention of the Security Council as threatening "the maintenance of international security." After consultations with Council members, the president of the Council issued a statement supporting the Secretary-General's offer of good offices and appealing to both governments to settle their dispute by peaceful means. The Council met formally only after the Secretary-General, on September 25, requested that it consider the situation with utmost urgency. Meanwhile, the Iraqi army was advancing rapidly in Iran, overrunning numerous Iranian villages and towns in the process, including Khorramshahr, a center of both economic and symbolic importance for Tehran.

Finally, on September 28, the Security Council adopted Resolution 479, unanimously calling upon Iran and Iraq "to refrain immediately from any further use of force and to settle their dispute by peaceful means and in conformity with principles of justice and international law." In other words, it called for a cease-fire in place on Iranian territory without demanding the withdrawal of Iraqi forces. It did not condemn Iraqi action, calling on both countries on equal terms to accept "any appropriate offer of mediation or conciliation." Iran, with good reason, vehemently rejected the resolution as biased in favor of Iraq. Thereafter, it adamantly refused to deal with the Security Council until the end phase of the war, consistently maintaining that the Council was dominated by countries supporting Iraq and was incapable of impartial action. The Council's actions in the ensuing years did little to regain Iran's confidence.

In his efforts to end the Iran-Iraq conflict through mediation, Secretary-General Waldheim appointed the then former Swedish prime minister, Olof Palme, as UN Special Representative. Palme, who enjoyed great personal prestige in the area, made repeated trips to Baghdad and Tehran between 1980 and 1982 during which he sought to mediate an end to the conflict on the basis of a "comprehensive" approach that foresaw a cease-fire, followed by the withdrawal of troops and negotiation of the outstanding differences between the two countries. This approach reached an impasse because the Iraqi side insisted that troop withdrawal be part of a negotiated agreement whereas the Iranians demanded that troop withdrawals be completed before negotiations began. Underlying this impasse was the far more profound Iranian objective of eliminating the Saddam Hussein regime. Iran was, and long remained, completely unwilling to negotiate with Saddam Hussein. The only progress made during this period was agreement in principle by both countries to free 63 foreign ships that had been caught in the Shatt-al-Arab and the exchange of a limited number of wounded prisoners of war. The Non-Aligned Movement and the Conference of Islamic States, plus a number of individual countries, also sought, during this period and later, to mediate a settlement but with even less success than the UN.

This was the situation with which I was confronted when I became Secretary-General. While I had not been involved with Iran or Iraq during my previous service with the United Nations, I was conscious of the cruel

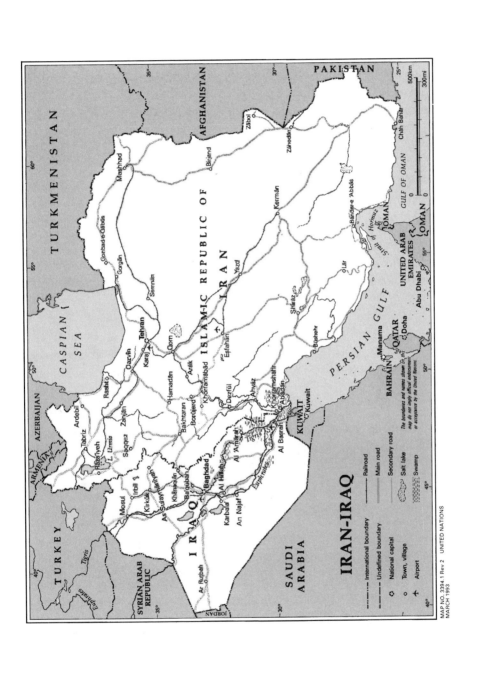

IRAN-IRAQ

International boundary
Undefined boundary
National capital
Town, village
Airport

Railroad
Main road
Secondary road
Salt lake
Swamp

The boundaries and names shown on this
map do not imply official endorsement
or acceptance by the United Nations.

MAP NO. 3394.1 Rev 2   UNITED NATIONS
MARCH 1993

destructiveness of this conflict, of the wider implications of the struggle between two autocratic and secretive regimes and, most of all, of the United Nations' responsibility to bring the war to an end. It soon became evident that my role would be central since only I was accepted as impartial by the two parties. It would be necessary for me to maintain a clear distinction between my position as Secretary-General and the actions of the Security Council. Yet I would need to work in close cooperation with the Council since the leverage required to bring an end to the war—if this should ever be possible—lay with it and its Permanent Members. This circumstance remained a controlling characteristic of my mediation efforts until, after long years of disappointment and frustration, agreement on a cease-fire was reached in 1988.

One of my first acts as Secretary-General was to state publicly my profound concern over the continuation of a war, which by then had lasted more than 15 months. I asked Olof Palme to continue as Special Representative for Iran and Iraq, and in February 1982 he made yet another trip—his fifth—to the warring capitals to see if rumors of increased flexibility had any foundation. He found that they did not. There was clearly no progress to be made in pursuing the "comprehensive" approach.

In a discussion with the U.S. Secretary of State, Alexander Haig, who visited me at UN Headquarters on March 15, I said that the only positive result of Mr. Palme's trip had been the maintenance of communication with both sides. I thought it was desirable to proceed cautiously so as not to impair the credibility of the United Nations. The secretary agreed. He stated that the Soviet Union was supplying arms to both sides—"the good stuff" to Iran, the "junk" to Iraq. He (like many others before and after) thought the best result would be a cessation of the war without a clear winner.

Shortly thereafter Iran mounted a strong offensive against the invading Iraqis. The Iranians succeeded in pushing the Iraqis out of most of the territory they had occupied and, on May 24, in retaking Khorramshahr. This was a major military and psychological achievement for Iran and a severe blow for Saddam Hussein. It seemed to me an opportune time for a UN initiative in which new elements could be introduced. I was quite wrong.

On May 25, 1982, one day after the Iranians reentered Khorramshahr, I sent identical letters to Presidents Saddam Hussein and Khameini in which I stated my strong belief that "a stage has now been reached where it is imperative to renew the search for an honorable settlement acceptable to both sides." My good offices were available to them in whatever form they desired. Saddam Hussein did not reply until July 6. Prior to that he took more direct action. On June 6 the Iraqi Revolutionary Command Council declared a unilateral cease-fire, which was promptly rejected by Iran. Saddam then announced on June 20 that the complete withdrawal of Iraqi troops from Iranian territory had begun and would be completed within ten days. The Ayatollah Khomeini, the supreme spiritual and temporal authority in Iran, immediately rejected this action as well, declaring that the war would continue even if Iraqi troops did leave all Iranian territory. It was evident that Iran was determined to eliminate Saddam's regime, something that, as Saddam claimed, it may have been endeavoring to achieve by nonmilitary means prior to the war. In his reply to my May 25 offer of good offices, President Khameini reaffirmed the previously stated Iranian position. In summary, it called for total Iraqi withdrawal; establishment of an Islamic Republic of Iraq (i.e., the ouster of Saddam Hussein); payment by Iraq of $150 billion in reparations; repatriation of all Iraqis who had been expelled into Iran (a substantial number of Shi'ites); and free passage of Iranian troops through Iraq en route to fight against Israel.

President Khameini asserted that any mediation efforts should be directed toward securing Iraq's acceptance of this position. Iran maintained then, as it did consistently even after its troops were occupying Iraqi territory, that it had no intention of seizing any part of Iraq.

In his July 6 reply, Saddam expressed his continued willingness to sit down at the negotiating table with Iran to seek a settlement of the dispute. There was no indication, in the letter or elsewhere, however, of any inclination to modify the previous Iraqi demand for sovereignty over the Shatt-al-Arab.

Through friends in the Non-Aligned Movement, at this point Iraq sought to encourage the Security Council to adopt a resolution setting out the main elements of a settlement that could provide a basis for negotiations. Eventually this was successful. The Permanent Representative of Guyana, when he assumed the presidency of the Council in July 1982, was able to bring the initially hesitant Council members to adopt Resolution 514, which called for a cease-fire, an immediate end to all military activities and the withdrawal of forces to internationally recognized boundaries. Further, the Council—optimistically— decided to dispatch a team of UN observers to supervise the cease-fire and withdrawal of forces. The resolution urged that mediation efforts be continued in a coordinated manner through the Secretary-General.

I had hoped that a further resolution would overcome Iranian distrust of the Security Council. My hope was in vain. The resolution called for a withdrawal of troops to internationally recognized boundaries, as Iran had earlier desired, but by now Iran was occupying Iraqi territory, which it intended to do until an overall settlement of the conflict was achieved. More important from Iran's point of view, the resolution still treated the two parties equally, without any suggestion that one was more guilty than the other of starting the war.

Iraq immediately accepted the resolution. Iran, equally as promptly, rejected it, in the process dissociating itself from any action taken by the Security Council. In October 1982, Iraq called on the Council to meet, claiming that Iranian forces had launched a major attack across the international border near the Iraqi town of

Mendali. The Council met and adopted Resolution 522 calling again for an immediate cease-fire and a withdrawal of forces to internationally recognized boundaries. This time, however, the Council welcomed "the fact that one of the parties has already expressed its readiness to co-operate in the implementation of resolution 514 (1982)" and called upon the other to do likewise, a provision guaranteed to infuriate Iran further precisely at a time when its military position had become more favorable. During the Security Council's informal consultations, I stated frankly that the text, as it was emerging, was not likely to bring the parties together or facilitate my task as mediator. Nonetheless, the resolution was adopted.

In its response (addressed to me since it refused to address the Security Council), Iran noted that the Sumar sector, which Iraq had identified as the location of an Iranian offensive, was well within Iranian territory and that Iran was proud to inform the international community that "with the help of God . . . this phase of our defensive operations against the invading army of aggression has been quite successful." The statement went on to ask if Iran was not justified "in doubting the impartiality and objectivity of this distinguished body [the Security Council] which had remained silent for more than 22 months of Iraqi occupation of our territories, and started deliberations only after the Islamic Republic of Iran was succeeding in forcing the aggressors to retreat." Under the circumstances, Iran considered Security Council resolutions relating to the situation between Iran and Iraq to be "non-binding on the Islamic Republic of Iran."[1] When I met a few days later with Iranian Foreign Minister Ali Akbar Velayati, I told him that I did not consider the new Security Council resolution particularly helpful and that undoubtedly he would understand that political influences present in the Council were beyond my control.

In October 1982 Olof Palme's party again came to power in Sweden, and he became Prime Minister again. I asked that he stay on as Special Representative notwithstanding the heavy national duties he was assuming. He accepted with grace and enthusiasm notwithstanding the seeming hopelessness of mediation prospects. I recognized the fact that failed missions undertaken by an official in high office could adversely affect his position at home. In informing the Security Council that Prime Minister Palme had agreed to continue as Special Representative, I stated that he would be asked to undertake further missions only when both parties indicated that they were prepared to enter into concrete, substantive discussions on a comprehensive settlement of the conflict. Unfortunately, these conditions were not met before Olof Palme was cut down by an assassin's bullet.

IMPASSE ON THE GROUND

By late 1982 the ground war had reached a stalemate. Thereafter repeated Iranian ground offensives were countered by increased utilization of Iraqi air power, where the Iraqis had superiority, and eventually by their resort to chemical weapons. My offer of good offices had gotten nowhere. The Iranians hinted that if they were to be responsive, something concrete would have to be proffered. I interpreted this to mean some form of Iraqi commitment to respect the Algiers Agreement on territory and to pay reparations.[2] No such commitment could be obtained. In May 1983 the Iranian government requested that I dispatch a mission to inspect civilian areas subject to Iraqi military attack. A month later Iraq requested a similar mission to investigate the situation of prisoners of war in both countries. I felt that for humanitarian reasons alone, I should respond favorably to these requests. Beyond that, by pursuing these avenues, it might be feasible to construct a basis for dialogue between the two countries and, possibly, to persuade Iran to restore contact with the Security Council. I therefore dispatched a mission to inspect civilian areas in both countries and initiated consultations with the ICRC, which has primary responsibility for the welfare of prisoners of war, on a mission to investigate the conditions of both Iranian and Iraqi prisoners of war.

The mission to inspect civilian areas reported that there had been heavy and intensive destruction of civilian areas in Iran by aerial, artillery and missile attacks and light damage in Iraqi civilian areas.[3] Iraq, while not happy with the report, did not seek to refute it nor did it show hard feelings toward me for having initiated the mission. Iran was understandably pleased with the report. The Iranian Permanent Representative informed me that his country hoped for constructive follow-up action by the Security Council that would justify Iran's reconsideration of its view of that body. The Council reacted in 1983 by adopting Resolution 540 condemning violations of international humanitarian law and calling for the immediate cessation of all military operations against civilian targets. It again requested me to continue mediation efforts and to consult with the parties on ways to sustain and verify the cessation of hostilities. This last point was hardly realistic since I had already made clear that there was no prospect of agreement on a cease-fire. The Iranian Permanent Representative let me know that the resolution, by failing to single out Iraq for criticism, had confirmed his country's opinion of the Council's prejudiced attitude.

Iraq, while suffering serious setbacks on the military front, carried out a skillful diplomatic policy at the United Nations, utilizing the friendship of other Arab countries, especially Jordan, and support within the Non-Aligned Movement, of which it was a member, to influence the texts of the resolutions adopted by the Security Council and by the General Assembly. While this diplomacy shielded Iraq from blame for having started the war, it did nothing to further the prospects of peace with Iran. As the war continued, with Iran demonstrating the will and the capability of launching repeated limited offensives and Iraq demonstrating an equal capacity to contain them, I felt that strong action by the Council would be necessary, including some judgment on the origins of the war and endorsement of the Algiers Agreement, to bring about negotiations between the two countries.

For the first—but not the last—time during this war, I considered following the procedure provided for in Article 99 of the UN Charter, as Secretary-General Waldheim had done earlier, and calling on the Council to meet to deal seriously with the war as a threat to international security. I did not do so, however, since I recognized that the Council, under the prevailing political circumstances, was no more likely to take effective action if called to meet at my initiative than it had been over the three preceding years. The United States and the Soviet Union, still locked in the rivalry and suspicion of the Cold War, showed no inclination to use their considerable influence to end the war, at least not if it would result in the victory of either country. Indeed, they were soon to reach agreement that the war could end in victory for neither side. The only realistic alternative appeared to be for the slaughter and destruction to continue until one or both sides was totally exhausted.

This prospect assumed an ever more ominous position, when, during the summer of 1983, France decided to, and eventually did, provide Iraq with five Super-Etendard aircraft capable of launching Exorcet missiles, which Iraq might conceivably use against Iran's Kharg Island oil terminals. In this eventuality, Iran threatened to block the Straits of Hormuz. It had become public knowledge that Israel was selling substantial quantities of arms to Iran.[4] Then, at the end of August, Iran accused Iraq of using chemical weapons against civilian areas and requested the United Nations to send an expert mission to inspect the evidence.

ESTABLISHING A BASIS FOR NEGOTIATIONS

At the end of September 1983, I met with the Iraqi foreign minister, Tariq Aziz, and with the Iranian foreign minister, Ali Akbar Velayati, both of whom had come to New York for the General Assembly. Olof Palme also had come to New York for the occasion and participated in the meetings. Both foreign ministers had their complaints about the UN. Tariq Aziz contended that it had suspended its efforts to bring the conflict to an end. I assured the foreign minister that there was no danger of the conflict becoming a forgotten war, the problem was that while all Member States agreed that the conflict was tragic, none was prepared to make a determined effort to end it. Mr. Palme was eager to help and prepared to go to the region at any time but, I said, it would not be helpful for me as Secretary-General, and even less for Mr. Palme in view of his high office, "to dive into an empty pool." It was essential to put water into the pool, which meant developing ideas that could lead to progress.

The Iranian foreign minister said that his country was grateful for my efforts and those of Olof Palme. However, Iran did not expect the Iraqi regime to "accept justice." He noted that while Iraq had announced 15 months earlier its complete withdrawal from Iranian territory, it continued to occupy 1,000 square kilometers. "It was not propitious," he said, "to keep a snake in one's sleeve that would eventually bite." I could only interpret this metaphor as another indication that Iran would be inclined to make peace only when the Saddam Hussein regime was deposed.

A BASIS FOR NEGOTIATIONS

Despite the less than propitious circumstances, I gave both foreign ministers a "nonpaper" that could serve as the basis for indirect negotiations between the two countries. If progress was made, direct negotiations might follow. The nonpaper was intended to facilitate discussions, not to provide a comprehensive recipe for ending the war.

The "points for discussion in relation to negotiated settlement" read as follows:

- Cease-fire and withdrawal of all forces to agreed lines.
- Monitoring and verification arrangements as necessary.
- Investigation into the responsibility for the initiation of hostilities.
- Reparation of war damage in accordance with the principle of state responsibility and established international practice.
- Return of prisoners of war and repatriation of all refugees and expelled persons.
- Conclusion of an agreement to reestablish peaceful and good neighborly relations between Iran and Iraq, including provisions to ensure noninterference and non-intervention in each other's affairs.
- Arrangements for the demarcation of the international boundaries between Iran and Iraq.

These same points later figured prominently in somewhat different form in Security Council Resolution 598, which brought the conflict to an end. That would only come after five more years—years that saw the war assume even more threatening dimensions.

At this point the nonpaper did not lead to a real dialogue. In view of the intransigence of the parties on substance, it was necessary to take another approach, one aimed at modifying the effect of the war as a necessary precedent to ending it.

Tariq Aziz and Akbar Velayati remained principal spokesmen and negotiators for their respective regimes during the full course of the war, and I was to have extensive contact with Tariq Aziz at the time of the Gulf War and with Velayati in connection with efforts to obtain the release of Western hostages in Lebanon. They were both able, rational and highly professional men. Velayati is a pediatrician, trained in the United States, and he continued his practice while serving as foreign minister. He was by inclination friendly, outgoing and full of energy. He sometimes began his day with a tennis match at 5:30 A.M. My sense was always that he tended to be flexibile and seek compromise, but his influence was limited. He showed none of the fanaticism of other Iranian leaders.

Tariq Aziz impressed me as a man of unusual capability. His English was excellent, and he was never less than totally prepared for any conversations in which he was involved. He knew exactly what he wanted to say and he said it. But he never showed any sign of disagreeing with his president. Both Tariq Aziz and Velayati could talk for hours in defense of their positions, and neither resisted repetition. Of the two, Tariq Aziz seemed the more willing to find ways to move beyond his instructions to overcome roadblocks, perhaps reflecting his more senior position in the national hierarchy.

The two men have survived until the present day as senior figures in their respective governments, no mean achievement. Both must have had, and retained, the full confidence of their less than predictable superiors. I judge them as more than survivors; each presumably felt a commitment to the cause he represented and each was prepared to overlook, or rationalize, weaknesses and inconsistencies in his government's policies that he was too intelligent not to perceive.

Reacting to continuing report of attacks on civilian population centers and to threats, mainly from Iran, to interfere with shipping in the Gulf, the Security Council at the end of October 1983 adopted Resolution 540 calling again for the immediate cessation of all military operations against civilian targets and, for the first time, calling upon the belligerents to cease immediately all hostilities in the region of the Gulf, "including all sea-lanes, navigable waterways, harbor works, terminals, offshore installations and ports. . . . " I considered the wording of the resolution unfortunate since in its references to hostilities in "the Gulf" it seemed directed more against Iran than to Iraq. Moreover, again it requested me to verify "the cessation of hostilities," something to which Iran had never agreed. Finally, omission of the adjective "Persian" before Gulf was bound to infuriate the Iranians, although in the circumstances it was the wording most acceptable to the other riparian states.

Olof Palme said publicly in Stockholm that the Council had acted too hastily in drafting the resolution. I could not disassociate myself from the resolution, but I could and did affirm my identity as separate from the Security Council.

The Iranian reaction was as negative as I had anticipated. The Iranian Government first formally requested my assistance in obtaining from the Security Council clarification as to "which gulf" was being addressed in the resolution. (No clarification was forthcoming.) In a written response, Iran said the Council's action was in the "same unbalanced tradition it has followed since the beginning of the Iraqi war of aggression. . . ."[5]

Iraq welcomed the resolution and said that it was ready to cooperate in "finding an effective system for ensuring a cease-fire and for ensuring that all the parties concerned benefit in a balanced manner from its results." However, it included a condition that was to constitute a continuing problem in bringing the conflict to an end. Its acceptance of the resolution was predicated on the premise that it was "an integrated and indivisible whole" with regard to substance, timing and procedures. All parties would have to benefit from its implementation immediately and in a balanced manner.[6]

CONFIDENCE BUILDING AGAINST ALL ODDS

Olof Palme was a strong supporter of the security and confidence process in Europe and placed a high value on confidence-building measures to reduce tension and build trust despite serious differences that might prevail between countries. He and I had extensive discussions (in part over the open transatlantic telephone wires, so they were hardly secret) on the desirability of encouraging such measures between Iran and Iraq. We concluded that if the two sides could be persuaded to cease attacks on civilian population centers, this could begin the process of confidence-building and possibly open the door to wider negotiations on ending the war. Beginning in the summer of 1983 and continuing through 1984, Iran repeatedly charged Iraq with instigating such attacks and called for the dispatch of a second UN team to confirm that the attacks were taking place. Iraq demurred on the ground that any mission also should have the mandate to discuss the political steps necessary to end the war, something that Iran rejected.

I felt that a solution might lie in sending a combined mission authorized both to inspect any damage caused by the bombardment of civilian areas and to discuss the political points related to ending the war that I had listed in the nonpaper given to both sides.[7] Both sides initially accepted this proposal, but then Iran, which had launched yet another offensive, withdrew its consent.[8]

Meanwhile the Iranian accusations that Iraq was using chemical weapons were growing ever more insistent. Increasing evidence emerged in the form of victims sent to Europe for treatment that the accusations were true. Many private and public organizations called for an impartial investigation, as did a number of governments, acting outside the United Nations. The Security Council took no action. However, the General Assembly, on December 13, 1982, had adopted Resolution 37/98D calling for measures to uphold the authority of the 1925 Geneva Protocol (which prohibits the use of chemical weapons).

The Iranian Permanent Representative met with me on March 6, 1984, and stated that under the Assembly resolution I had an obligation to investigate, with the assistance of qualified experts, any information that was brought to my attention by a Member State concerning activities that might constitute a violation of the Protocol. The resolution can be reasonably so interpreted but, since this was not the unanimous view, I decided to refrain from referring to it and to dispatch an expert mission on my own authority to investigate the situation.

The mission, which consisted of four experts from Sweden, Spain, Australia and Switzerland, traveled to Iran in March 1984. It found conclusive proof that bombs containing bis-(2-chloroethyl)-sulfide, or mustard gas, and a chemical nerve compound commonly known as Tabun had been dropped and that these had caused extensive casualties. Within the time limits imposed, the mission could not determine the extent to which the chemical agents had been used. The members noted that some of the bomb casings bore markings in Spanish. When I transmitted these findings to the Security Council, the Council forthwith strongly condemned the use of chemical weapons and all other violations of humanitarian law and called again for a cease-fire and a peaceful solution to the conflict. It did not, however, name Iraq as the perpetrator of the chemical attacks.

THE WAR ON SHIPPING

To the surprise of many, in the spring of 1984, Iran, whose air force was much weaker than that of Iraq, increased its air attacks in the Gulf on shipping headed for Arab states. The Security Council proceeded to adopt Resolution 552, which, while not mentioning Iran by name, condemned "recent attacks on commercial ships en route to and from Kuwait and Saudi Arabia and demanded that such attacks cease immediately." It decided further that in the event of noncompliance, the Council would meet again "to consider measures . . . commensurate with the gravity of the situation." I was requested to report on the progress of implementation of the resolution. The resolution served only to increase further Iran's disdain for the Council, if that was possible.

In the face of the continuing political deadlock, I was more and more troubled by the humanitarian dimensions of the war. On June 5, 1984, the Iraqis brutally attacked the Iranian town of Baneh; thereafter retaliatory and counter-retaliatory attacks on towns in both countries occurred. Following the ideas that Palme and I had developed earlier, I decided to act independently and call personally on the governments of Iran and Iraq to "declare to the Secretary-General of the United Nations that each undertakes a solemn commitment to end, and in the future refrain, from initiating deliberate military attacks by aerial bombardment, missiles, shelling or other means, on purely civilian populations centers." I appealed to both governments to respond by 1200 hours GMT on June 11, 1984.[9] Both governments replied affirmatively before the deadline and on June 11, 1984, the mutually accepted ban on attacks against purely civilian areas went into effect. This was a positive achievement that I hoped could be built upon, but I did not overestimate the prospects. In speaking to the press in Washington after a meeting with Secretary Shultz (who had been highly complimentary of this accomplishment), I said that we should be careful not to give too much importance to this first positive development. I added that, as "an old diplomat," I was very cautious.

The commitment of the two parties was eventually broken, with each side blaming the other. I could not judge the truth of the matter. But during the nine months in which attacks were suspended, thousands of lives were spared on both sides. This benefit derived from my capacity as Secretary-General to act independently when circumstances required and to maintain an identity separate from that of the other principal organs of the United Nations. This does not mean that the Secretary-General can act without the knowledge, or contrary to the wishes, of the Security Council. Doing so would jeopardize the Council's confidence in the Secretary-General, with devastating impact on his effectiveness. In this case, as in all others when I acted independently of the Council, I kept Council members fully informed. Without asking its permission, I always assured myself through quiet, informal consultations that there was no strong opposition to my actions, especially from any of the Permanent Members.

A SUMMER VISIT WITH OLOF PALME

In July 1984, I went to the summer residence of the Swedish prime minister in Harpsund to review the situation. I was brought to this rural location by helicopter. A large sheet had been placed on the ground to mark the landing field, as if in preparation for some giant's *déjeuner sur l'herbe*. This finest of Swedish midsummer days provided an invigorating atmosphere in which to discuss the humanitarian steps that had been taken and could yet be initiated. Mr. Palme went through a checklist: humanitarian steps *strictu senso,* as he said, such as cessation of attacks on civilian areas, prisoners of war, chemical weapons and shipping in the Gulf. This meeting has remained vivid in my mind as an indication of Olof Palme's immense humanism and commitment to peace. He had an inventive and restless intellect, imbued with an optimism that could not be defeated. He never lost faith in the possibility of dialogue between Iran and Iraq.

I suspect Mr. Palme sometimes felt he was being excluded from the action and that important information did not reach him. The latter may at times have been true, since the senior Secretariat official working with me on the Iran/Iraq conflict was Under-Secretary-General Diego Cordovez, who had a tendency to keep matters in his own hands. Even if Palme harbored this suspicion, he never allowed it to influence his generous goodwill toward the United Nations and his friendship with me. It was indicative of the man that when the United Nations faced a financial crisis in 1986, he quite spontaneously picked up the phone and called me to offer assistance—which he then proceeded to organize. Olof Palme was truly a force for a better world, and in his lifetime he accomplished a great deal toward this objective.

A NEW DEESCALATION EFFORT

On March 5, 1985, I received a letter from Iranian Foreign Minister Velayati notifying me that since "Iraq has left all international appeals to refrain from attacks on non-military and civilian areas unanswered, in spite of our numerous and sincere attempts to preserve the authority of the 12 June agreement, as of this moment we will assume a retaliatory stance vis-à-vis all such Iraqi attacks as the only means of stopping them."[10] After this notification, indiscriminate bombing resumed. Attacks on shipping in the Gulf also intensified. Under these daunting circumstances I put to the two sides a series of suggestions, in the form of eight numbered paragraphs, only seven of which were substantive, intended to lead to a deescalation of hostilities. This "eight-point proposal," which was to be the focus of mediation efforts over the next two and a half years, stated that both sides would:

- Cease all attacks on civilian population centers, thus reinstating the moratorium of 12 June 1984.
- Cease all interference with civil aviation in the airspace of the other side.
- Observe the provisions of the Geneva Protocol of 1925.
- Cease all attacks against unarmed merchant vessels of any flag or ownership.
- Refrain from attacking designated ports, terminals and related facilities.
- Cooperate with the ICRC in arranging an exchange of POWs.
- Maintain continuing contact with the Secretary-General on the observance of these arrangements and on further steps toward normalization of the situation.

These seven substantive steps brought together all the measures that might mitigate the lethal effects of the conflict, but they did not seek to resolve the basic issues in dispute between the two regimes. Iran initially agreed to the proposal but shortly thereafter stated that it could accept no strict linkage between the measures envisioned and a cease-fire within a specified time frame for which I had called. Iraq maintained its previous position, that such provisional measures could only be to the advantage of Iran and would not in any way hasten an end to the conflict.

Despite the rejection of my proposal, I informed both parties that I was prepared to travel to Baghdad and Tehran at any time for direct talks. I required only the assurance that they were prepared to enter into substantive discussions aimed at ending the war. Baghdad promptly agreed to such a visit; Tehran did not respond. Clearly I could not visit one capital without the other. Nonetheless, I decided to visit the area in the hope that by doing so—by holding conversations with Iran's neighbors in the Gulf—I might bring the Iranian government to invite me to visit Tehran for talks, which is what did happen, albeit at the last possible minute.

I left for the Gulf states at the end of March 1985, knowing full well that as a mediator, I was operating under severe handicaps. The most serious was the lack of support from the Permanent Members of the Security Council, particularly the United States and the Soviet Union, who despite their frequent appeals for an end in the fighting took no action to bring it about. Often I had been frequently tempted to renounce any further mediation efforts as pointless until the Council took some action that would meet Iran's demands that the aggressor be identified. In each of the Gulf states, I let it be known that direct talks with the Iranian and Iraqi leaders could be useful. While in Muscat, I indicated to the Iranian ambassador that I had been invited by the Iraqi government to go to Baghdad; while I was prepared to do so during my stay in the region, obviously I would not wish to visit one of the two warring capitals without the other. On arriving in Doha, Qatar, I was informed by the Iranian chargé d'affaires that his authorities had taken account of my remarks in Muscat and he was instructed to say that they would welcome a visit by the Secretary-General for the purpose of serious conversations. The chargé expressed his certainty that once I observed the bloodshed of which Iran was the victim, I would carry out my responsibilities "as guardian of peace" with a better understanding.

Arrangements were quickly made. The Emir of Qatar made his plane available for the trip to Tehran and Baghdad. Iraqi assurance of safe passage through the Iraqi-declared war zone was obtained. En route we were escorted first by Iraqi fighters and then Iranian ones, a nerve-wracking experience since it was difficult to be sure which was which. I was able to arrive in Tehran the next day, April 7, 1985. Within 24 hours I met with the principal Iranian leaders, with the exception of the Ayatollah Khomeini himself. My first talks were with Foreign Minister Velayati, with whom I was, by then, well acquainted. I suggested that there were signs that the Security Council was taking a more open-minded approach and that it would be a good time now to develop a timetable for implementing my eight-point proposal. Perhaps a three-month truce could be agreed upon to provide time to work out the details. The foreign minister was noncommittal, stating only that the implementation of the measures in the eight-point paper should not be related to "other issues."

The President of the Iranian Republic, Seyed Ali Khamenei, was not an easy man with whom to establish rapport. He has the use of only one arm, having been injured by a terrorist bomb, which increased a sense of distance in approaching him. I found him to be the most polemical and hard-line Iranian with whom I spoke, a man one could easily picture giving a fiery sermon in a mosque. He said, in effect, that there could be no solution as long as Saddam Hussein remained in power. Iran accepted unconditionally my eight points because of their humane intent. But, as Velayati had already said (repeatedly), they could not be linked to other matters.

Prime Minister Hossein Mousavi also proved to be a difficult conversation partner. While making generally the same points as the other Iranian leaders, he asked me specifically to convey to the Iraqis that the Iranian missile that had recently hit Baghdad was not, as had been reported, the last one in Iran's possession. Iran was well equipped to send more. If Saddam thought that he could save himself through violent attacks, including chemical weapons, he was wrong. Doing so would only force Iran to continue the war and would further unify the Iranian people.

The last senior Iranian official with whom I met during these hectic hours was the then speaker of the parliament (Majlis), Hojjat-ol-Eslam Hashemi Rafsanjani, who was to assume a highly influential role in the negotiations on ending the war and, later, in freeing the Western hostages in Lebanon. I would get to know him well. His appearance is at first surprising. His beard consists of only a few long strands of hair on his face, which makes him look somewhat like a Chinese of the old school. His demeanor was on this occasion stern; his whole attitude was that of a fundamentalist mullah, an attitude he may have wished to display to the large group of journalists who were present during our initial introductions. I had a sense that he did not wish to be outdone in this regard by Khamenei.

Rafsanjani's first comment after wishing me success in my task "of rendering service to humanity" was that revolution made the task of the United Nations more difficult since revolution created new conditions. "A revolutionary personality" at the head of the United Nations would help, he added. This was an unsettling suggestion since I patently was not one. I responded that if revolution was in behalf of justice and development, then I was for it. In emphasizing that the war was imposed on Iran, Rafsanjani said there was no way of comparing the situation of Iran with that of Israel (which it would never have occurred to me to do), since Israel was surrounded by neighbors at war with it. The war against Iran started because of the Iranian revolution. The revolution itself required that the punishment of the aggressor could not be forgone. The speaker stated bluntly that Iran possessed advanced facilities to produce chemical weapons but did not wish to use them and would not do so even if Iraq continued to attack with chemical weapons. Foreign Minister Velayati interposed to correct the interpreter by saying that Iran did not want to *produce* chemical weapons. The speaker insisted, however, that what he meant was what the interpreter had said: Iran did not wish to *use* chemical weapons.

Rafsanjani was harshly critical of the Security Council, which, he said, did not even dare to state "the elementary reality that Iraq was the aggressor." On the other hand, he considered the reports that I had made to the Council on the attacks on civilian targets and the conditions of prisoners of war to be impartial. In his opinion, I was the only one who had spoken the truth. I said that I had exerted my best efforts to end the attacks on civilian areas and the use of chemical weapons, but it was my duty not only to reduce the effects of the war but to find a peaceful solution to the war itself. The eight points I had suggested should be seen in that light. I had no magic formula but wanted only to bring the parties together in a peaceful settlement. The speaker's response was stern. He said he had a recommendation for me: I should not repeat the mistakes of others. The aggressor and the victim should not be treated as equals. Therein lay the only solution to the war. He would pray for my success in this regard. I said that success would depend on the determination of all the parties concerned.

The next day I was in Baghdad and met without delay with President Saddam Hussein. While I had shaken hands with him at one or more international meetings, this was my first substantive conversation with the man who was playing such a fateful role in the region. Neither then nor in later meetings did I find Saddam charismatic. On this occasion Tariq Aziz and Ismat Kittani, who was then Under Secretary in the Ministry of Foreign Affairs, were present along with an interpreter and note taker. As was almost always the case in the meetings I had with Saddam, among the Iraqis, only the President spoke. He spoke fluently, without notes or guidance, obviously knowing quite well what he wished to say. He is not a bombastic type, but neither did he seem a very good listener. In conversing with him, I had the sense of a man clearly in command who spoke his lines in a rather didactic fashion, showing only surface interest in what his interlocutor had to say. His mission seemed to be to preach his perception of truth to others. In this, and only in this, may there have been some similarity between Saddam Hussein and his ayatollah antagonist across the border.

Inevitably Saddam professed his strong support for peace. As Secretary-General, I never heard anyone who did not. He expected, since he was for peace, that I would not press Iraq to accept anything that would affect the country's dignity and sovereignty. He contended that Iran had always tried to expand at Iraq's expense. The present leadership had treated his government with contempt. When Iraq had sent congratulations on the establishment of the Islamic Republic, Tehran had replied using a salutation that in the Islamic world is reserved for infidels. While he had advised the Gulf States to respect the Iranian revolution, Iran, even under former President Abolhassan Bani Sadr, had let its intentions to "reach Baghdad" be known. Iran had attacked Iraqi border stations and interfered with navigation well before September 22, when Iraq reacted by moving troops into Iran. Since Iran had long made clear its intention to topple his government, he would have to ponder very carefully whatever word I brought from Tehran. The Iraqi Government, for its part, would cooperate with any action that would shorten the war and be part of a plan to bring hostilities to an end. His government demanded only the withdrawal of both armies to the international borders and the commitment of both sides not to interfere in the internal affairs of the other. He, Saddam Hussein, was ready to give Iran the chance to work in the direction of peace. He would not agree to any action, however, that might prolong the war.

Saddam spoke at length and with evident pride of the economic progress that his regime had brought to Iraq. When his government assumed power, he said, "Baghdad was no more than a village with a legendary past." Now the malnutrition, illiteracy and poverty that had once ravaged Iraq were things of the past. It was obvious that the people supported his government. Otherwise they would not continue to fight, after five years of war, as they were doing. The Iranian regime, he contended, wanted war because it had built nothing and had nothing to lose.

I suggested that the political aspects of the problem might be tackled on one track and the cessation of hostilities pursued on another. But I acknowledged that this was not likely to occur until the Security Council took some further action to demonstrate to Iran its impartiality. Saddam did not pursue this opening. Instead he expressed again his confidence that "the Secretary-General would not submit ideas that would infringe on the sovereignty of Iraq" or that would not be in accord with international law. He ended the conversation by declaring, rather patronizingly, that Iraq was prepared to save the Iranians from themselves—provided it did not jeopardize Iraq's own security.

The two subsequent extensive conversations I had in Baghdad with Tariq Aziz did not lessen my sense that the visits to Tehran and Baghdad had led nowhere.

THE WAR INTENSIFIES

Saddam Hussein sought to put pressure on Iran to accept his position by intensifying the war in the Gulf, especially by stepping up air attacks against the major Iranian oil terminal on Kharg Island. This strategy did not succeed. Out of 35 air attacks in 1985, only 2 caused significant damage, and Iran was able to make the necessary repairs expeditiously and resume full oil shipments. But the attacks on Gulf shipping seriously threatened to internationalize the conflict. On December 27, 1985, I reported to the Security Council on 61 incidents in the Gulf of attacks on, and interceptions of, merchant shipping. In 1986, 105 ships, including 80 tankers, would be attacked with 88 fatalities.

Iraq had originated the attacks on shipping in the Gulf early in the war, officially announcing "exclusion zones" where vessels would be attacked without warning. Iran began to retaliate in 1984, without, however, acknowledging that it was doing so. Iraq claimed that its policy was justified on the basis of rules of international law relating to armed conflicts at sea, which permit attacks on vessels engaged in acts of trade or unneutral service with a belligerent in a situation of armed conflict. My position, from which the United Nations did not deviate, was that Iraq's contention was not supported by international law.

Ground conflict also intensified as 1986 began. While Iran complained that Iraq had initiated new chemical weapons attacks, it launched yet another major offensive against Iraqi positions in Iraq, seriously threatening to capture Basra. I conveyed my grave concern over these developments to the Security Council, which forthwith adopted a further unproductive resolution (Resolution 582, February 24, 1986). I also dispatched another technical mission to investigate the charges of chemical attack. As expected the mission found ample evidence that Iraq was using chemical weapons. In July I called again for a halt on attacks on civilian areas, and both sides indicated their intention to comply. The attacks decreased for a while, but the effect was small given the intensity of the conflict.

I had in these months a sense that the Permanent Members of the Security Council, while supporting repeated resolutions that, among other things, called on states to abstain from actions that might contribute to a continuation of the conflict, were, at another level, taking actions that contributed to a prolongation of the war. The French attitude toward Iran warmed noticeably, and France began to sell advanced weapons systems to Iran (as it had already sold to Iraq). It became known that the United States also had supplied weapons to Iran. Knowing nothing of the origin or extent of the American dealings beyond what appeared in the press, I concluded, quite incorrectly, that Washington was, for *raisons d'état*, implementing a long-range policy aimed at establishing a favorable relationship with Iran (in competition with the Soviet Union) once the war was over. I found some of the press accounts of actions taken by Oliver North and Robert MacFarland so outlandish as to be beyond belief. In my fairly extensive dealings with Iranian representatives, I had gained the impression that some were more reasonable than others. I placed the foreign minister, Ali Akbar

Velayati, in this category and, somewhat later, Rafsanjani. As long as the Ayatollah Khomeini was alive, however, it seemed clear to me that they were not free to follow any reasonable inclinations they might have. Therefore, the distinction between moderate and extremist elements in positions of power in Iran had for me no meaning.

Iran's policy was adamant and inflexible. At the same time, Iraq was evidently receiving sufficient financial support from other Arab states and adequate weapons from Western suppliers to enable it to fight on indefinitely. I have to state that while I had always blamed Iraq for starting the war, by the summer of 1985, I had reached the point of blaming Iran for continuing it.

With the increasing presence of U.S., Soviet and other warships in the Gulf region, the possibility for the involvement of other powers became ever more threatening. On October 3, 1986, I addressed the Security Council with total candor. I noted that beyond the human devastation caused by the conflict, the international community had a legitimate concern over the dangers of its expansion. The declared intention of Iran to bring a military conclusion to the conflict gave renewed urgency to the situation. The step-by-step approach to ending the war that I had put forward in the eight-point plan had not brought progress. Six Council resolutions were part of the record, but none had been implemented satisfactorily. Iraq, I continued, had indicated that it was prepared to comply with all the resolutions. Iran, on the other hand, had made clear it was not prepared to accept them on the ground that the Council had not dealt with the country's fundamental grievances. It was more necessary than ever for the Council to establish a basis on which both sides would cooperate with the United Nations to promote the prospects for a settlement.

On October 8, 1986, the Security Council reacted with Resolution 588, which largely repeated earlier ones and ended by asking me to intensify my efforts and report back to the Council. This did not mark a high point in my appreciation of the Council's work. The responses of the two sides to the resolution indicated no change in their positions.[11]

A CHANGE OF WIND

It is the custom of the Secretary-General to give a press conference soon after the beginning of each new year to discuss the general state of the world and the problems lying ahead for the United Nations. The 1987 conference was scheduled for the thirteenth of January, a day whose unlucky number struck me as in consonance with the bleak prospects of peace between Iran and Iraq. The number of victims could not be accurately counted then and probably never will be. Not since the Children's Crusade had so many young people been led to die for a holy cause. Not since World War I had chemical weapons been used to such devastating effect. Not since World War II had so many merchant ships been sunk by hostile arms. It seemed clear to me that the danger of escalation beyond the region grew with each additional warship that arrived in the contiguous seas. Unless some new element was introduced in the situation, the military stalemate, costly both in lives and resources, seemed likely to last indefinitely.

On the day before the scheduled press conference, I met with a small group of close advisors to consider what I should say on the war. The chef de cabinet, Virendra Dayal, and the press spokesman François Guilliani were there along with Alvaro de Soto, James Sutterlin and Giandomenico Picco from my office. It was generally agreed that one more appeal from the Secretary-General to the parties to end the war would be inadequate in the circumstances and would only encourage an impression of helplessness on my part. Only strong action by the Security Council could break the impasse in peace efforts; but the Council had no credibility with the Iranians and appeared unable to come up with the measures to end the war. I was aware that in Moscow, Mikhail Gorbachev was in the process of fundamentally reorientating Soviet foreign policy and was placing new importance on utilizing the United Nations to settle international disputes. I knew too that the American and Soviet foreign ministers had consulted on the Iran-Iraq situation but had only agreed (as far as I was aware) that there could be no winner in the war.

As these circumstances were being discussed, the idea emerged that now was the time to pressure the Security Council to reassert itself as the organ responsible for the maintenance of peace and to urge the five Permanent Members to meet the particular responsibility that their privileged position imposed on them in this regard. At Sutterlin's suggestion, I decided to call for the Council to meet at the foreign minister level (which it had only done twice before in its history) to deal with the Iran-Iraq war and to point to the special role that the Permanent Members should play.

As expected, at the New Year's press conference on January 13, 1987, (the press spokesman took steps to ensure that it would happen) a reporter asked "What does the United Nations intend to do [on the Iran-Iraq war]? Is the United Nations' silence an indication of a failure to do anything?" I replied that, in my personal opinion, what we needed at this stage was a "meeting of minds at the highest political level and that a way to be effective in putting an end to this tragic situation in the area could perhaps be an urgent meeting of the foreign ministers of the member countries of the United Nations Security Council. That is something which I think is now very much needed—a meeting of the minds— since the situation is extremely serious not only because . . . there are thousands of casualties but also because there is always the threat of the conflict expanding, something that the Security Council has to deal with as urgently as possible."

Other reporters returned repeatedly to my suggestion. One posed the question: "How do you expect a meeting of the minds to be reached by the members of the Security Council, particularly in the minds of the United Sates and the Soviet Union, whose positions on the Iraq-Iran war are very well known . . . and do not coincide?" I replied that I could not entirely agree with that assumption. I thought that the leaders of both countries were "conscious of their obligations and must realize that . . . they have obligations under the Charter and obligations to the international community. They are the two most powerful countries; they have to show that they can deal with problems where the Security Council has a role. . . . The five Permanent Members have an obligation to try to reach agreement on the solution of problems related to peace and security. That is their duty. Of course, they could start by having differences, but that is why they have to work until they agree on a solution to international problems. That is why they have the veto power. It is not something given to them generously by the membership of the United Nations. The veto power implies that they have to work in order to reach agreement for the peaceful solution of international problems."

One perceptive member of the UN press corps referred to the reported supply of arms to one or both warring parties and asked whether, for this reason, a meeting of the foreign ministers might not prove to be embarrassing. What indication, he asked, did I have that the governments concerned would consent to such a high-level meeting? I replied that such a meeting would perhaps "provide us with the best way of putting an end to military assistance to both sides. . . . The Members might realize that their duty was to provide the parties not with arms but with ideas for solving their problems peacefully."[12]

The regular monthly lunch meeting of the Security Council was held two days later, on January 15. During my customary toast I took the opportunity to pursue the subject further by stating that "as we view the intensification of the war in these last days, we must ask ourselves honestly whether the time has not come for new decisions that would harmonize national policies and actions with the repeatedly stated intent of the Council. . . ." I invited the president of the Security Council and the ambassadors of the Five Permanent Members to meet with me the next day at my residence to discuss what new steps might be taken to end the war. This was the beginning of a constructive and harmonious process of consultation among the Five, working with my encouragement toward a common goal of regional peace. It signaled a new era for the United Nations. The collective security concept on which the Organization was based is predicated on cooperation among the Permanent Members in dealing with threats to international security. Only at this point in 1987, 45 years after the founding of the United Nations, did such cooperation become—tentatively, at first—a reality.

The personalities and stature of the ambassadors representing the Permanent Members were bound to be of crucial importance in advancing this novel process of multilateral agreement among formerly opposing countries. They were a mixed group, each with his own style; sharing, as far as I could tell, only a common desire to find a way to end the war and a predilection for caution. The ambassadors were feeling their way in a new process. I never had reason to doubt, however, that they were dedicated to developing satisfactory terms on which peace could be restored.

The American Permanent Representative was Vernon Walters, known to his friends as Dick. Walters is a career soldier, having the rank of major general, and belongs to that rather rarefied breed of soldier-diplomats. There seemed to me nothing military in his bearing or attitude. A man who had assembled an extraordinary amount of information and influential friends in his varied assignments ranging from interpreter (for Dwight Eisenhower) to deputy director of the Central Intelligence Agency, he shone best as a linguist and raconteur. As he seems more convivial than acute, it was difficult for me to comprehend that this was a man who had been repeatedly entrusted by several American administrations with missions of the greatest sensitivity. Perhaps it was this conviviality—his loquacity in several languages—that was his best "cover." It would be easier to think of Walters as a buffoon than as a secret agent of American imperialism, as he was sometimes portrayed. But that would have been wrong too. He was, in his way, a very effective representative of the United States at the United Nations; more than that, he was a strong and influential defender of the United Nations when it was under severe attack in the U.S. Congress, where his reputation was high, especially among conservatives who were prone to distrust the United Nations as a "nest of Communist spies." He worked well, and hard, with his "P5" colleagues, seeing quickly the advantages to be gained for the United States and the world from cooperating with the Soviet Union in the framework of the Security Council.

Sir John Thomson, the British Permanent Representative, was a very different type. If Walters could be considered a soldier-diplomat, then Thomson could best be thought of as a scholar-diplomat. He had something of the aroma of the classroom, where he was the professor. Whereas Walters was inclined to tell stories, Thomson was inclined to give lectures—but nonaggressively and somewhat modestly. He, too, quickly appreciated the value of the new opportunity for cooperation among the five Permanent Members—even more quickly than his colleagues—and became so enthusiastic about the process that began in connection with the Iran-Iraq war as to claim credit for initiating it. Without doubt, he did much to encourage the process of consensus-building among the members on the elements of the approach that ultimately found expression in Security Council Resolution 598.

The Chinese member of the "Big Five Team" was Ambassador Li Luye. A pleasant man of traditional Chinese courtesy, he was, as is the Chinese diplomatic custom, brief in stating a position and nonforthcoming in the expression of personal views. Over time, it became evident that while he had no leeway to depart from fixed Chinese positions, he was under instructions to maintain those positions in a way that would not prevent the cooperative process from going forward and agreement ultimately being reached.

Neither the Soviet Ambassador, Aleksander M. Belonogov, nor the French Ambassador, Pierre-Louis Blanc, were strong personalities. They got along well with their colleagues and did not insist on taking the lead, which facilitated the productive relationship among the group.

In the initial informal meeting, I said we needed to explore whether a coming together on steps to end the conflict was feasible. If so, we should see if an agreed approach could be formulated to deal with specific elements. I raised as possibilities the establishment of an ad hoc working group to investigate which country bore responsibility for initiating the war; steps to provide protection for freedom of navigation in the Gulf; and the possibility of shutting off the supply of arms to both belligerents. Whatever was agreed, I emphasized, needed to be decided for implementation and not simply as the basis of further resolutions or presidential statements.

The reaction of the five ambassadors was muted but positive. All favored the idea of a foreign ministers' meeting, but all were firmly of the opinion that any such meeting would have to be carefully prepared. Whether coincidentally or not, at this point President Reagan issued a statement expressing concern that the war could spill over and threaten the security of the region. The United States, he said, "would regard any such expansion of the war as a major threat to our own interests." The President condemned the Iranian seizure and occupation of Iraqi territory and called on Iran to join with Iraq in seeking a rapid negotiated solution to the conflict.

Also at this time I was scheduled to visit Kuwait for a summit meeting of the Organization of Islamic States. Prior to my departure, Sir John, on behalf of the group, invited me to an informal meeting at his residence to discuss the whole question further. I believe Sir John has since identified this meeting as the beginning of the cooperative consultations among the Permanent Five on a solution of the Iran-Iraq war. It was indeed the first meeting on the subject that I had held exclusively with the Permanent Five. At this meeting in Sir John's apartment on Beekman Place, the member's positions remained more or less as expressed in our first meeting. All favored, in principle, the initiative I had taken in calling for a meeting of the Council at the foreign minister level; all felt the first objective should be a cease-fire in place; all, except the British ambassador, were in favor of an arms embargo, albeit with a distinct lack of enthusiasm. The

Chinese Representative said he had no instructions on the subject, while the others thought that the imposition of sanctions would depend on the warring parties' reaction to the other proposals in the package. I warned that Iran was certain to reject a cease-fire in place separate from agreement on other aspects of a settlement and that this might force the Council to impose sanctions.

While traveling to Kuwait, I recalled a statement of one of the great thinkers of the Moslem world, Muhammad Pebal: "Islam," he said, "finds the principle of human unification not in the blood and bones but in the minds of men. Indeed, its social message to mankind is: De-racialize yourself or perish in internecine war." The real possibility that two Moslem nations might well perish in such a war was a message that I felt compelled to bring to the assembled leaders of the Moslem world, who had been singularly unsuccessful in bringing peace between two brother states. So, in addressing the Organization, I risked the danger of lecturing in the hope of bringing ultimate benefit. My main point was that "Nothing could . . . be more repugnant to your common vocation, nothing more contrary to the spirit of our age and nothing more injurious to your individual national aims than inter-State disputes which promote no useful end and violent conflicts that can bring no victory to either side." With direct reference to the war between Iran and Iraq, I referred bluntly to the frustrations and failures thus far and said that the challenge had to be faced of "at least achieving a cease-fire to enable a sustained mediation effort which would bridge the chasm between the two sides . . . Such a move forward could be made, if it was unequivocally linked with a commitment by both parties to accept the findings of an ad hoc body that might examine the question of the initiation of the wars.[13]

I intended to use my remarks to put the central points for resolution before the Islamic leadership. Although Iran had refused to attend the summit, I was subsequently informed that the government had been pleased with my statement. The Iraqi foreign minister, Tariq Aziz, told me that Iraq accepted the proposal for a foreign-minister level meeting of the Security Council and was generally in accord with the remarks I had made in my statement. He made clear, however, that any cease-fire had to be accompanied by troop withdrawals. The prisoner-of-war issue also would have to be dealt with. Only after these steps were taken could negotiations begin on a concrete and durable settlement.

Meanwhile the Permanent Five Ambassadors continued intensive consultations albeit without yet defining exactly their objective. They maintained strict secrecy, which naturally created suspicion and apprehension among the other Council members. When I met with the five Representatives again on March 11, Sir John Thomson said first off that while their consultations had been constructive, they were having great difficulty dealing with the substantive issues. The only thing that they were in complete agreement on was that the

Secretary-General was the most acceptable mediator to both sides. I responded that I was always at their disposal, but if the Council were to pass the ball back to me without taking action, it would be interpreted as a cop-out. On the same day the Iranian ambassador informed the Five (through the president of the Security Council) that the Iranian position could be expressed in three points: (1) Saddam Hussein must be removed; (2) Iran had no desire to infringe on Iraqi territory; and (3) Iran was prepared to accept any Security Council initiative based on the Secretary-General's February 26 statement in Kuwait.

In response to insistent Iranian complaints regarding continuing chemical attacks, I dispatched a further expert mission in April 1987. The resulting report was devastating. It was amply clear that the Iraqis were using chemical weapons to compensate for the Iranian superiority in ground forces and that they would continue to do so to counter any threat of being overrun by Iranian forces. Chemical weapons had become an essential element in Iraqi defense.

THE PERMANENT FIVE AT WORK

By May 1987 the Permanent Five Ambassadors had succeeded in putting together the operative portions of a resolution that included the following main points:

- As a first step toward negotiation, Iran and Iraq should immediately observe a cease-fire, discontinue all military action and withdraw their forces to internationally recognized borders.
- There should be a comprehensive exchange of prisoners of war within a short period after the cease-fire.
- Iran and Iraq should cooperate with the Secretary-General to achieve a comprehensive, just and honorable settlement.
- The Secretary-General should explore, in consultation with the two countries, the question of establishing an impartial body to inquire into responsibility for the conflict.
- The magnitude of the damage inflicted during the conflict should be recognized, as should the need for reconstruction efforts with appropriate international assistance.
- The Secretary-General should examine, in consultation with Iran and Iraq and other states in the region, measures to enhance the security and stability of the region.
- The Council would meet again, as necessary, to ensure compliance with this resolution.

The only important difference among the Permanent Five was on the inclusion of enforcement measures in the event that one party did not conform with the cease-fire provisions. Four members agreed, but China refused. So no such provision was included. At this point the draft text was given informally to the other ten members of the Security Council for consideration. On June 30, 1987, President Reagan, in an official statement, urged that the Security Council meet before the middle of July to pass a strong, comprehensive resolution. He listed the same points for inclusion as had been agreed by the five ambassadors in New York. The President said that UN Secretary-General Pérez de Cuéllar "supported this effort."

The presidential statement added that the United States would be consulting intensively at the United Nations on a second resolution that would impose sanctions against any party that refused to comply with the proposed cease-fire/withdrawal provisions. The Reagan Administration's overriding goals in the Persian Gulf, according to the statement, were to help moderate Arab friends defend themselves; to improve the chances for peace by helping demonstrate that Iran's policy of intimidation would not work; to bring about a just settlement of the Iran-Iraq war that would preserve the sovereignty and territorial integrity of both parties; to curtail the expansion of Soviet presence and influence in this strategic area; and to prevent an interruption in the flow of oil.[14] The statement contained no criticism of Iraq.

On the day of President Reagan's statement, I was in Moscow on an official visit and had the opportunity to discuss the Iran-Iraq war and the related Gulf problems with Mikhail Gorbachev and Foreign Minister Edouard Shevardnadze. President Gorbachev, whom I found well informed and thoughtful as always, wondered whether it would be possible to begin negotiations through the United Nations aimed at securing free navigation through the Gulf. I said that the most important requirement in this regard was an understanding between the two major powers. This was also true of the prospective Security Council resolution. The full support of the two major powers was essential to make it effective. I recalled the most recent adamant statements of the Iranian leadership as a clear indication that Tehran would not heed the voice of the international community unless there was clear evidence of cooperation between Washington and Moscow.

Gorbachev said that my appeal was "very appropriate." He had just received word that the leader of the Iranian Revolutionary Guards had stated expansion of the U.S. presence in the Gulf would be tantamount to a declaration of war. Unquestionably one had to deal with fanatics in Iran. Moreover, Gorbachev noted, the Prime Minister of Iran appeared to be convinced that both the United States and the Soviet Union were afraid of the Iranian revolution. To complicate the picture, Secretary of State Shultz had just stated that it was important for the United States to maintain its position in the area. The United States, Schultz reportedly said, would not accept a possibility that the Soviet

Union could cut the oil supply line to the West. "Nevertheless," Gorbachev said, "the Soviet Union would be acting with a sense of responsibility." For the moment he thought the best thing was to concentrate on the Security Council resolution.

In the separate conversation I had with Mr. Shevardnadze, he noted the importance I attributed to cooperation between the United States and the Soviet Union and said that he had discussed the problem many times with Secretary Shultz. There had even been the idea of a joint declaration on the war, but "with the Irangate affair, all such moves had come to nothing."

CONTINUING VIOLENCE ON THE SEA

During the early months of 1987, as the Permanent Five began their work on a resolution, the attacks on shipping in the Gulf and the movement of warships to the region seemed more ominous than the stalemated land war. During the first five months of 1987, there were 48 incidents involving merchant vessels in the Gulf. The U.S. naval cruiser *Stark* was hit by an Iraqi missile with considerable loss of life. On June 4, 1987, President Zia al Haq of Pakistan telephoned me to say that he had just spoken with a high-power Iranian delegation sent by President Khameini and had gained the impression that Iran was very keen to implement the suggestion I had put forward the previous year on assuring the security of shipping in the Gulf. President Zia said that he had asked the delegation whether Iran was prepared to see the United Nations involved in an operation aimed at this objective. The answer was yes. President Zia had detected some indication that if progress were made on this subject, Iran might be willing to negotiate on the larger issues, but that only the mediation of the Secretary-General would be acceptable.

At the end of June, President Reagan announced that the United States would register 11 Kuwaiti-owned tankers under the U.S. flag and would afford them the same protection by the U.S. Navy as had historically been accorded to U.S.-flagged vessels around the world. At the beginning of July, the Soviet Union proposed that all foreign warships be withdrawn from the Gulf. The United States responded coolly to this proposal. The White House chief of staff, James Baker, said that the United States, while perhaps willing to take a fresh look at the matter if the Soviet Union removed its warships, intended to go ahead with its plan to reflag.[15] The only specific action that the Security Council had taken on the problem was the 1984 adoption of Resolution 552 demanding the cessation of attacks on merchantmen en route to and from Kuwaiti and Saudi ports, which proved totally ineffective.

In light of this dangerous situation, a confidential study was undertaken in the Secretariat early in 1987 on what the United Nations might do to enhance the security of merchant ships. At the beginning of June, I was advised by this group that two approaches might be taken. One would be to deploy naval forces under the UN flag to afford protection to merchant shipping. The vessels would operate as a naval peacekeeping force. The Secretariat group noted that this would be a high-risk operation, entailing formidable political, legal, military, logistic and financial obstacles. It recommended against this option, as did the legal counsel when I sought his views.

The other option was to extend symbolic UN protection to all merchant shipping by granting ships permission to fly the UN flag. The Secretariat group concluded that this approach would not entail insurmountable obstacles. Its success would depend on the willingness of the two belligerents to respect the UN flag and the Security Council's readiness to impose sanctions on any state that did not do so. A fairly detailed plan was drawn up for implementing this concept. I had reservations, primarily because I felt it would be challenged by Iraq, would probably not be approved by the Security Council, and could jeopardize the serious efforts under way in the Security Council to end the war. I believed that the only real solution to the problem lay in ending the war. I will say now what I could not say then: I was also convinced that continuing high tension in the Gulf would be an important factor in persuading the two major powers to combine their influence on the two parties to bring the conflict to an end. Use of the UN flag for merchant shipping in the Gulf was never raised officially in the Security Council. The question would arise again, however, at the time of the Gulf War.

ADOPTION OF RESOLUTION 598

On July 20, 1987, the Security Council met at the ministerial level to deal with the war between Iran and Iraq, as I had suggested it should do six months earlier. The French foreign minister, Jean-Bernard Raimond, was in the chair and the foreign ministers of all the other Permanent Members except the Soviet Union were present. The text of the resolution as agreed by the Five had been previously circulated to the Non-Permanent Council Members. The vote in favor of the resolution, adopted as Resolution 598, was unanimous. (The text is provided as an annex.) George Shultz remarks in his memoirs that "nothing like this unanimous vote on an issue of real importance and difficulty had ever happened before in the history of the United Nations. . . . Constructive action through the United Nations was now possible."[16] This, I think, was the profound significance of the action taken by the Council. The five Permanent Members had met for the first time the special responsibility they bear under the Charter to combine their strength in behalf of peace. The adoption of this resolution marked the beginning of the disintegration of the stultifying shroud of the Cold War that had so long enveloped the Security Council. In his statement, the British foreign minister, Sir Geoffrey Howe, called the Council's action "not only a sign of hope for the resolution of this conflict but also for the future in a broader sense.[17] While fully conscious of the positive significance of the adoption of Resolution 598, I chose to caution those present that to end the war, the national policies and actions of all Member States would have to be harmonized with the will of the Council as reflected in the resolution text.

On July 13, 1987, just a week before Resolution 598 was adopted, President Reagan had sent me an extremely warm letter. Anticipating the resolution's unanimous adoption (on which he had received Ambassador Walter's assurance), he wrote: "By this action, the United Nations is living up to the highest purposes set for it by its founders so many years ago. I wish to convey personally to you my support, and that of all Americans, for this resolution." He then went on to say, quite correctly, that adoption of a mandatory resolution was only the first step. Without effective implementation, and "if necessary, enforcement," the historic decision of the Security Council would be rendered meaningless. Much of the responsibility for implementation, including persuading the two parties to accept the resolution, would fall on my shoulders. The task was formidable but he did not "know anyone to whom it could be better entrusted." He assured me that American support, "including my personal help where needed," would be even greater in the crucial weeks ahead.

I was not accustomed to such praise and support from the American President and I was truly grateful, especially since I knew that the task ahead was a most difficult one.

Three months later, on September 26, during the session of the General Assembly, I had a working lunch with the Permanent Five foreign ministers at which I again reviewed the status of efforts to end the Iran-Iraq war, which I characterized as still something of a vicious circle unless there was new input from the Council. Secretary Shultz, who was, as always, sparing in his words, summarized the situation as follows:

- All of us want to see the war end.
- All of us support resolution 598.
- All of us have great confidence in the Secretary-General and support him fully as he undertakes his mission.
- We believe he should continue efforts to bring the parties into agreement and accept the resolution.
- At the same time we need to move ahead in the Security Council to plan enforcement actions. (Foreign Minister Shevardnadze nodded at this point.)

I asked if all agreed to the summing up by the Secretary of State. There was no objection.

THE PROBLEM OF IMPLEMENTATION

None of the provisions of Resolution 598 would happen of themselves. Each would have to be agreed to by both countries and, before that could happen, both would have to accept the resolution. In principle, a resolution of the Security Council is mandatory, as I had told President Reagan, and the parties have no choice but to accept it. But previous demands by the Security Council for cease-fires had been routinely ignored. Even though the circumstances of the present resolution were unique, it would have been unrealistic to expect that a cease-fire would occur without further mediation and persuasion. Enforcement measures, as the Americans repeatedly suggested, might be required, although I detected little readiness on the part of China or the Soviet Union—beyond Shevardnadze's nod—to go that far.

I interpreted the Council resolution to mean that the cease-fire and withdrawal of forces should come first, with the other steps to follow. My first objective, therefore, was to establish contact with the two parties and get agreement on the dates and arrangements for these first actions. I immediately transmitted the text of the resolution to the two governments and asked for their early response. The Iraqi Government replied within two days, welcoming the resolution and expressing readiness to cooperate in its implementation. However, the wording included intricately phrased conditions, the most troublesome of which was Iraq's insistence that its acceptance "was based on regarding the resolution as a complete and indivisible whole, be it in its content, its timing or the procedures relating to the implementation of all its paragraphs." Iraq proposed ten days as the time allowable for the withdrawal of forces after the cease-fire and eight weeks for the repatriation of prisoners, but insisted that the cease-fire could not begin until Iran had agreed to procedures for implementing all the other provisions of the resolution.[18]

No official response from Iran was forthcoming. However, in a press conference in Geneva on July 29, Iranian Foreign Minister Velayati made three points regarding the resolution—all negative. In Iran's view, the resolution was a U.S. ploy that reflected only Iraq's positions; it was intended to prepare the Security Council to become a party to the conflict and would serve only to aggravate tension and extend the conflict; and, finally, it limited the Secretary-General in his independent, positive initiatives.[19]

Instead of decreasing after the adoption of Resolution 578, tension in the region increased, partly as the result of the death of a large number of rioting Iranian pilgrims in Mecca at the hands of Saudi security personnel. Iran complained that Iraq was repeatedly utilizing chemical weapons, and Iraq accused Iran of renewing attacks on civilian targets. The Iranian Foreign Minister canceled a meeting with me in Geneva. Soviet and German officials had talked with various Iranian representatives and been told that I would be welcome in Tehran but not to discuss Resolution 598. The British Permanent Representative informed me in New York that Mrs. Thatcher felt the Iranians were wasting time and were unlikely to give a sensible response to the resolution. She therefore believed that serious thought must be given to "enforcement action" and that the Security Council should try to reach agreement on a second resolution, imposing an arms embargo. I emphasized then, as I did repeatedly in the next weeks, that it was essential to maintain the unity of the Five.

Finally, on August 11, the Iranians responded with a letter that seemed to have been drafted by two different factions in the Iranian leadership, one that took a totally negative view of Resolution 598 and another that saw in it a possible basis for negotiations to end the war. After a long series of accusations against the United States and the Security Council, the letter expressed Iranian interest is pursuing four subjects covered in the resolution: (1) stability and security in the Persian Gulf, freedom of navigation and the free flow of oil; (2) determination of the aggressor in the war (Iraq); (3) practical measures to end the bombardment of civilian areas and the use of chemical weapons; and (4) repatriation of prisoners of war. The letter contained no endorsement, or acceptance, of Resolution 598, nor did it make any mention of the cease-fire ordered by the Security Council. Instead, the Iranian Government endorsed my eight-point plan of March 1985 and said that it was prepared to continue to cooperate with me in the framework of my "independent efforts and initiatives." The final paragraph sounded quite a different note. It referred to "constructive and commendable endeavors of certain impartial members of the Security Council" and declared that grounds had been laid "so that the Islamic Republic of Iran would continue its co-operation in a manner that would lead the Security Council to a just position."

Cutting through all the verbiage and seeming contradictions, it seemed clear to me that the Iranian government was now saying that prior to agreeing to a cease-fire, it was prepared to negotiate with me on those aspects of Resolution 598 that were in its interest without accepting or rejecting the resolution as such. In an informal consultative session, I reported on my interpretation of the Iranian position to the Security Council and asked for the Council's guidance. I then met separately with the five Permanent Members and said that we were confronted with a very clear question: was the resolution they had drafted an integrated whole, or could the package be opened up and individual elements selected for independent implementation? I recommended that I be authorized to let the Iranian authorities know that I was prepared to discuss the issues they were ready to tackle, but only after Iran accepted that a cease-fire would be the first step in the implementation process. I did not wish to be drawn into discussion that the world would see as an excuse for the continuation of the war. The instructions of the Security Council were that the resolution should be treated as an integrated whole. The tedious, at times extremely frustrating, negotiations that were to last almost a year while the war continued its cruel and dangerous course revolved around this issue—the time sequence in which the various provisions of Resolution 598 would be implemented.

NEGOTIATIONS BEGIN

The negotiating process began in earnest almost immediately, on August 24 and 25, 1987, in conversations with the Iranian deputy foreign minister, Mohammed Javad Larijani, who had come to New York for this purpose. For the first time in these conversations, the Iranian side indicated that it was not necessarily opposed to resolution 598. It was only, as Larijani said, very simplistic to expect a yes-or-no answer. In essence, the Iranian position was that a cease-fire prior to agreement on implementation of the other provisions of the resolution would be to Iraq's advantage and could well result in the other provisions never being implemented. I made it as clear as I possibly could that the Security Council's intent was that agreement on a cease-fire must come first with agreement on the other provisions to follow and that I was bound by the Council's position. After going over this question repeatedly, I finally said (somewhat uncharacteristically, I think) that Iran seemed to see the cease-fire "as some kind of castration." But, in reality, Iran could resume fighting if things did not work out. Larijani argued that in such an eventuality, Iran would be at a military disadvantage. I agreed that Iran's acceptance of a cease-fire "as the first step" did not necessarily mean that it would be implemented before the other provisions had been agreed to. Larijani insisted on knowing the meaning of "as the first step." Could there be several first steps? I said yes—that I would, for instance, start work immediately on setting up an independent body to determine responsibility for the war and on dealing with the issues of security and reconstruction. Larijani thought this was a very positive message he could take back to Tehran. In an effort to gain clarity, I asked Larijani whether, on the basis of our discussions, I could inform the Council that: Iran accepted the *concept* of an *integrated* approach that would include a cease-fire as a first step, and we had agreed that, before any formal commitment to an actual cease-fire, I would discuss with both sides the possible approaches to the implementation of *each* of the provisions of Resolution 598. Larijani undertook to submit these points to his authorities in Tehran.

The Director-General of the Iranian Ministry of Foreign Affairs, Mohammad Jafar Mahallati, delivered the reply from the Iranian Foreign Minister. It first invited me to visit Tehran "to discuss matters concerning major international and regional issues, the situation in the Persian Gulf and all aspects of the Iran-Iraq war, including Security Council Resolution 598." It then stated that Iran's response to the question I had posed to Mr. Larijani was positive. I told Mahallati I would reply to the foreign minister that, in accordance with my understanding of his letter and my conversation with the director-general, I would come to Tehran and Baghdad "to discuss possible approaches to the implementation of each of the provisions of Resolution 598, on the basis of the acceptance by both governments of the resolution." Mahallati objected to the phrase "on the basis of the acceptance by both governments of Resolution 598," since, he said, Iran had never said it accepted it. I informed the Security Council of this development. The Council agreed that it would still be adequately clear that my purpose in visiting Tehran would be to discuss the implementation of Resolution 598.

In both Tehran and Baghdad I was again received with great courtesy at the highest levels. I had by then become familiar with the leading members of the cast in both capitals—President Khameini, Speaker of Parliament Rafsanjani and Foreign Minister Velayati in Tehran and President Saddam Hussein and Deputy Prime Minister and Foreign Minister Tariq Aziz in Baghdad. The only change I noted was a further increase in Rafsanjani's authority.

In both capitals I presented an identical plan, consisting of the following main points:

- From a specific date, to be agreed upon (D-Day), a cease-fire would be observed.
- On a specific date after D-Day, to be agreed upon, the withdrawal of all forces to internationally recognized boundaries would start, to be completed within an agreed time frame.
- On D-Day, a team of UN observers would be dispatched to verify, confirm and supervise the cease-fire and the withdrawal of forces.
- On D-Day, or on an agreed date thereafter, prisoners of war would begin to be released and repatriated.
- On D-Day, I would start negotiations with Iran and Iraq with a view to achieving a comprehensive, just and honorable settlement of all outstanding issues acceptable to both sides.
- On D-Day, or another date to be agreed upon, an impartial body would begin work on determining responsibility for the conflict.
- At a date to be agreed, the impartial body would complete its work.
- On a day after D-Day, to be agreed upon, I would dispatch a team of experts to study the question of reconstruction.
- On D-day, or on a date to be agreed upon, I would start consultations with Iran and Iraq, and with other states concerned, on measures to enhance the security and stability of the region.

I proposed that upon their concurrence with this plan, the two governments agree on the date of D-Day. This would be followed by negotiations on the required preparations to implement each of the measures envisioned, the negotiations to be completed by D-Day. I suggested that in case no agreement was reached on some of the preparations required, the parties should respect the decisions of the Secretary-General.

The concept of simultaneity of action on D-Day was similar to the plan that had been developed in the case of the Falklands/Malvinas war. I felt it maintained the intention of the Security Council that Resolution 598 should be implemented as an integral whole (which was also Iraq's position), and at the same time it offered the Iranians the assurance they desired that the provisions in which they were interested would not be left unimplemented once a cease-fire was in place.

All of the Iranian officials emphasized forcefully, and sometimes at length, that peace must be established on the basis of justice. It followed that the inquiry into the responsibility for the conflict must be given the highest priority. In effect, Iran's position was that observance of a *formal* cease-fire must be preceded by the process of the identification of the party responsible for the conflict. If this approach were to be accepted by both sides, an *undeclared* cessation of hostilities could come into effect during the process of identifying responsibility for the conflict. While this last point was part of the Iranian position as stated by the foreign minister, Rafsanjani did not share it. He was particularly adamant that the impartial commission should do its work and the Security Council announce its verdict before a cease-fire could come into effect. I asked him what would happen at the front while the commission worked. He replied calmly that there was no need for the war to stop; it could continue as it had done for seven years.

In Baghdad, the Iraqi authorities considered the plan that I presented to be in accordance with Resolution 598, which they were ready to implement as an integrated whole. In their view, the Iranian position that implementation of paragraph 6 of the resolution on determining guilt for the conflict prior to the declaration of a cease-fire represented a clear rejection of the resolution. Under no circumstances would Iraq accept an undeclared cease-fire. The cease-fire would have to be official and should be followed by the prompt withdrawal of all forces.

After having these positions confirmed to me in New York a few weeks later by President Khameini and Foreign Minister Tariq Aziz, I informed the Security Council that we faced a fundamental problem of the interpretation of the resolution. It was profoundly distressing—and no compliment to either government—that the war could be allowed to continue for lack of agreement on a question of largely symbolic importance. I told the Council that in my view, neither country was happy with the resolution although each claimed now to be its champion and accused the other of noncompliance.

During the remaining months of 1987, instead of progress I only saw evidence of retrogression. On October 15, I gave the two sides a detailed paper on measures required to implement the outline plan that I had provided them earlier and asked for their comments within 30 days. Since both sides had been escalating the ground and sea conflict, I simultaneously called on members of the Security Council to urge the two governments to exercise restraint in order to foster a more favorable climate for such talks. The responses from Tehran and Baghdad revealed that the differences between them on implementation of the resolution were even greater than had been apparent in my visits to the capitals. New preconditions and interpretations were stated that amounted to a retreat from their previous acceptance of my outline plan. Under the circumstances, I urged the two governments to send representatives to New York for intensive consultations. This produced yet another "sequential" problem. Iran indicated that it was prepared to have talks with me but not with Iraq and that the simultaneous presence of their delegations was not necessary. Put more directly, Iran would not accept proximity talks in which the two sides would be in the same city but communication between them would be solely through an intermediary. I told the Iranian Permanent Representative that I was not pushing proximity talks. My objective was implementation of Resolution 598 with specific focus on the question of D-Day. The problem was resolved by Iraq's acceptance of sequential talks.

At the beginning of our talks, I advised the Iranian representative that observations conveyed to me by both Iraq and Iran on the measures I had proposed to implement Resolution 598 had created formidable impediments to an early settlement of the conflict. It was essential that both parties reaffirm unequivocally their acceptance of my outline plan so as to improve the possibility of progress. I said that four main elements had to be fitted into an agreed package: the determination of D-Day, the modalities of the cease-fire, the timing of the withdrawal of forces and the commencement of the work of the impartial body to inquire into the responsibility for the conflict. Our consultations should concentrate on them in very specific terms. I said the same thing to Foreign Minister Tariq Aziz when we met on December 9. In both cases excruciatingly detailed discussion of these points took place but the parties were not brought closer together. In fact, further differences were introduced.

Following the official meeting with the Iranian delegation, its leader, Deputy Foreign Minister Larajani, requested a tete-à-tete exchange with me. During this encounter, he told me that the position that he had conveyed had been approved by the Ayatollah Khomeini. This was the first time in my dealings with the Iranians that such information had been shared with me. Larijani explained that not every point of policy was put to the Imam. However, the Iranian leadership believed that a pronouncement from Khomeini was required at this juncture. Larijani then went on to elucidate a much-conjectured question about the leadership in Tehran. A hard-line element within the leadership, he said, was committed to pursuing the war as the only realistic option. Another faction, to which Larijani claimed he belonged and that included Speaker Rafsanjani and perhaps Foreign Minister Velayati, was eager to continue working on the basis of Resolution 598, seeing in that text sufficient positive elements for a reasonable solution. In this context, Khomeini's endorsement of the present position could be seen in a negative light. It could be a signal that little further advancement could be expected in a position endorsed at the top.

In summarizing the situation to the Security Council almost five months after the adoption of the resolution, I said that Iran had stressed elements such as its particular conception of the impartial body, the need to determine the "international border," the demand for reparations and its linkage to the withdrawal of forces. Iran stressed this linkage because of the paramount importance it attached to the determination of responsibility for the conflict. Iran had thus introduced considerations that went beyond the wording of the resolution. Iraq continued to insist on the sequential approach, in particular as it related to implementation of the first three paragraphs of the resolution (cease-fire, troop withdrawal and prisoner exchange). It could not accept any process that would leave its territory and the fate of the prisoners hostage to Iranian conditions, and the Iranian interpretation of the provisions of the resolution, especially paragraph 6 (responsibility for the war). Iraq had confirmed acceptance of the "land" boundaries set forth in all previous treaties and agreements and protocols. This did not appear to cover the boundary in the Shatt-al-Arab. Before meeting with the Security Council to pass on the substance of the Iranian reply, I had met jointly, at their request, with representatives of the American and Soviet Permanent Missions. I gave them a full account of my talk with Larijani, including the exchanges during our private meeting.

On January 8, 1988, Deputy U.S. Permanent Representative Herbert Okun informed me that the Five had met on the previous day and that the United States and France had tabled for the first time the elements for an embargo resolution. Neither China nor the Soviet Union had taken clear positions, but the Soviet Representative had suggested that the question of a naval force to enforce any embargo be discussed in the Military Staff Committee.

A CEASE-FIRE ON THE HORIZON

The United Nations has no intelligence service. The Secretary-General must rely primarily on information in the media and on accounts of events given him by the

Permanent Representatives of member states. Both sources have evident weaknesses as a basis for developing mediation strategies or deciding what other action might be desirable at a particular point in a crisis. The diplomatic missions have always felt that security in the Secretariat is lax and that any confidential information provided to the Secretariat would quickly be widely circulated. In general, this is true; however, in the Secretary-General's Office, any information given me in confidence was handled with great discretion. This was a major reason why, in dealing with sensitive problems, I relied on the support of a very small staff in whose loyalty I had complete confidence. Aware of this, the U.S. government periodically provided my office with intelligence assessments of situations in which the interests of the United Nations and of the United States were mutually involved. One such incidence occurred in early April 1988, when a representative of the Bureau of Intelligence and Research of the U.S. Department of State provided my chef de cabinet, Virendra Dayal, with a comprehensive assessment of the status of the conflict between Iran and Iraq. The information provided gave me reason to think that just possibly, after months of frustration, the time might be approaching when a cease-fire could be obtained.

The briefing consisted of five main points:

Despite impressive Iranian claims of a large new offensive, the level of ground fighting had declined markedly over the past year. Iran had succeeded in seizing a fairly large area in Iraq, but it was of little strategic importance. The Iraqi tactic was to maintain the main body of its forces well behind the front, thus avoiding losses, and to use chemical weapons to deflect any really serious Iranian advance. Iran had also used chemical weapons.

While the Ayatollah Khomeini continued to exercise strong influence on the general conduct of the war, Parliamentary Speaker Rafsanjani had gained greater influence. He was believed to oppose the human-wave tactics that were so costly in Iranian lives. Further Iranian advances on the southern front around Basra were therefore unlikely.

In the Gulf, the Iranian strategy had been to confine the conflict within the bilateral parameters of the war. This strategy had failed. The subsequent Iranian tactic of scattering mines had brought in more naval ships, instead of frightening Western ships from the area. Being at a disadvantage in the "war of the cities," Iran had sought to escalate retaliatory actions against Iraq in the Gulf, but there again it had miscalculated. Both sides, because of mutual advances in missile technology, had become more vulnerable to missile attacks. But the advantage here lay with Iraq. The Iraqi Scud attacks had hit the affluent areas of Tehran, causing the greatest losses among the *bazaaris*—the middle class merchants—who were already disaffected from the war effort.

The United States had had some success in restricting arms deliveries to Iran from Western Europe, although not from the communist countries. The

Soviet Union had told the United States that "at the end of the day," it would be prepared to vote in favor of an arms embargo, but the end of the day did not appear to be drawing much closer. In the U.S. estimate, Iran was fearful of the current unity among the five Permanent Members of the Security Council.

The American conclusion was that for the war to end: (1) the Iraqis had to do sufficiently well to preclude any prospect of an overall Iranian victory; (2) the war had to become even more painful for Iran; (3) the supply of arms to Iran had to be reduced through a second resolution of the Security Council; and (4) international pressure had to be maintained on a broad front.

This briefing was provided on the eve of a new round of talks in New York with the Iranian deputy foreign minister, Javid Larijani, and the Iraqi deputy foreign minister, Wasam Al-Zahawi. While I did not see any real prospect of Security Council action to embargo arms shipments, it seemed to me that the other conditions mentioned in the briefing were falling into place. Continuation of the war no longer had any logic, and while I was under no illusions that Khomeini was governed by reason, I felt that other members of the Iraqi and Iranian leadership were not immune to logic.

On April 18, 1988, the United States ordered military action against certain Iranian military targets in the Gulf. The statement transmitted to me by Secretary Shultz said that it remained the policy of the United States not to seek military confrontation with Iran, but it could not accept Iran's laying of mines in international waters, one of which had struck a U.S. vessel, the *Samuel B. Roberts*. Obviously the possibility of direct involvement of outside powers in the conflict was growing. I concluded that the time had come for a more aggressive approach on my part. Therefore, at the beginning of my talks with each party, I repeated essentially the same plan that I had proposed before for ending the war, but this time I suggested that I would set a specific date for "D-Day" and that from that date both parties would observe a complete cease-fire. On D-Day the impartial body to inquire into the responsibility for the conflict would begin its work. Both parties would commence withdrawing their forces on the day after D-Day. I also would set the date on which consultations would begin on the remaining elements of Resolution 598.

The reaction of the two sides was ambivalent but not as negative as in the past. Iran continued to avoid a formal statement of acceptance of Resolution 598, but it was ready to "co-operate with the Secretary-General for the implementation of all substantive provisions of the resolution as a continuous process and within as short a total time-frame as practicable." It continued to insist that justice required the determination of responsibility for the conflict. Iraq accepted the plan without reservations dependent only on Iran's formal acceptance in writing of Resolution 598. The key now lay squarely with Iran. Larijani had earlier informed me in Geneva that Iran had demonstrated in practice, if not in words, its acceptance of the resolution. Formal acceptance would open the way for me to set the date for a cease-fire that could end the war.

PEACE COMES AT LAST

At 12:30 A.M. on July 18, 1988, the Acting Permanent Representative of Iran, Amir Mahallati, delivered to me at my residence a letter from Iranian President Khamenei expressing Tehran's formal acceptance of Resolution 598. As one reason for accepting the resolution, President Khamenei cited the downing of an Iranian commercial airliner by the *USS Vincennes* in the Gulf and further use of chemical weapons by Iraq as showing that aggression against Iran had gained unprecedented dimensions, "even engulfing innocent civilians"[20] I believe, though, that these events were tangential to the Iranian decision, which stemmed from its recognition that its goals in the war were unachievable and that the cost of continuing the effort was unacceptable. This positive development represented a victory for peace and was the outcome of the efforts of many countries as well as of the United Nations. When I was asked at a press conference on the same day what had led to the Iranian Government's sudden decision, I recalled a saying that victory had many parents, while defeat was always an orphan.[21]

Baghdad reacted within two days. Tariq Aziz, in a letter addressed to me on July 20, proposed that representatives of the two countries enter into "formal and direct" discussions under my sponsorship to discuss the application of Resolution 598 "in accordance with the sequence of its operative paragraphs. . . ." He further requested that the United Nations undertake forthwith the task of clearing the Shatt-al-Arab and insisted that the full rights of free navigation in the waters of the Arabian Gulf and in the Strait of Hormuz be guaranteed forthwith.[22]

On the same day I informed the Security Council that I was dispatching a technical team to work out the modalities of implementing an immediate cease-fire. The team would be accompanied by a senior political advisor. I expected a report from the team within one week, after which I would be in a position to announce D-Day and the commencement of all the undertakings associated with it.

Given the long history of conflict and distrust, it could hardly be expected that no problems would arise. Iranian Foreign Minister Velayati, in agreeing to receive the technical team, recalled that the establishment of an impartial body to determine responsibility for the war was "among the first steps in the implementation of Resolution 598." This task, he added, should be undertaken without prejudice to "the observance of an immediate cease-fire. . . ." The Iraqis continued to insist on the official declaration of the cease-fire. Before accepting the technical team, they now demanded a clear reaction from the Iranians to their suggestion of direct talks under the auspices of the Secretary-General. To maintain as much momentum as possible and to sidestep the Iraqi demand for clarification, I invited the Iranian and Iraqi foreign ministers to come to New York for discussions at the earliest possible date. In the absence of any assurance of direct talks, I had to apply all my persuasive powers to get Tariq Aziz to come to New York. He finally agreed as did Velayati.

Since Iran continued to reject direct talks with Iraq, I met first on July 26 with the Foreign Minister of Iran and his party. I gave him a paper suggesting that the work should focus on two clusters of issues: the time frames and interrelationships during the implementation of the various paragraphs of the resolution; and the actions to be taken in order to give effect to the provisions of the resolution. I outlined the order and manner in which each of the operative paragraphs of the resolution could be implemented, making clear that I intended to state publicly on D-Day that I had begun preparations for the establishment of the impartial body to determine who had initiated hostilities.

On the following day I met with Tariq Aziz, giving him the same paper. When I stated that I would be glad to pass on to the Iraqi side the Iranian's reaction to the paper, Tariq Aziz said that he was authorized to discuss substantive matters only in direct talks with the Iranians. I next met again with the Iranians and provided a far more detailed operational plan for implementing all the provisions of the resolution, covering the interrelationship of dates, procedures for working with the International Committee of the Red Cross on the exchange of prisoners of war and so on. The Iranians agreed to study my proposals and provide their comments, which they did in very great detail. Velayati contended that the Iraqi insistence on direct talks was simply a pretext to obstruct my efforts to end the war. He said that President Khamenei had indicated that Iran, nonetheless, "was at the disposal of the Secretary-General. When one progressed past certain stages—for example, after the cease-fire and the withdrawal of troops—if the Secretary-General decides that Iran and Iraq have to meet directly, we shall be prepared to consider it favorably."

On this occasion, Velayati told me in confidence that his strong advocacy of ending the war was putting him in an increasingly exposed position domestically. Current reports that mujahideen forces from Afghanistan were mounting a major military campaign against Iran were nonsense. Nonetheless, hard battles continued on the front. Both President Khameini and Speaker Rafsanjani were in the field to inspire the nation's defenders.

When I next met with Tariq Aziz only a few minutes later, he again insisted that he was prepared to discuss substantive questions only in direct talks with the Iranian side. I said that Tehran now appeared prepared to accept this, but only after the cease-fire was in place and the withdrawal of forces had begun. Tariq Aziz dismissed this out of hand as an Iranian ruse, insisting that once Velayati got agreement on a cease-fire, he would go back home and "you would never see him again." He added that "if Velayati thinks that he can get his way by cheating and pressure and by playing certain cards, including the hostage card, he is wrong. If there is to be a cease-fire he cannot get it from Washington. He has to make peace with Baghdad and he has to sit down with the representative of Baghdad."

This was the first time the Iraqis had suggested that the Iranians were trying to use the problem of the Western hostages in Lebanon as a lever to gain American support for their position. During this period, I did appeal to the Iranians on humanitarian grounds for assistance in obtaining the release of the hostages (described in chapter 6). I did not connect the two questions, however, and I never saw evidence that Tehran was using the hostage issue in the context of ending the war with Iraq. The one aspect of Resolution 598 that became entangled in the release of the hostages was paragraph 6, relative to responsibility for the war.

In the next days, while engaging in intensive negotiations with the Iranian side on the details and legalities of the implementation plan, I sought in various ways to bring pressure on the Iraqis to agree to the cease-fire, with direct talks to follow immediately thereafter. I briefed the Security Council informally on the situation, making quite clear that in my view, the Iraqis, in demanding direct negotiations with the Iranians, were demanding something that was not in the resolution. I suggested that some form of assurance from the Council that the resolution would be implemented in its entirety was desirable. I met individually with the five Permanent Members, expressing the same views to each. The Soviet Chargé, Valentin V. Lozinskiy, informed me that the Soviet government had told Iraqi representatives both in Moscow and in Baghdad that Iraq was neither legally justified nor politically wise in insisting on direct negotiations with Iran prior to a cease-fire. Lozinskiy suggested that a guarantee from the Permanent Members that direct talks would take place could be helpful. In my subsequent talks with the other Permanent Members, I informed them of this Soviet suggestion and all were in agreement.

My colleagues and I passed this assurance to the Iraqis and simultaneously suggested there was a distinct possibility that the Security Council would set the date for a cease-fire and demand compliance. The Iraqis remained publicly adamant. When asked by the press what Iraq would do if the Secretary-General went ahead and declared a cease-fire date, the Iraqi Ambassador replied that Iraq would not accept a fait accompli, whatever quarter it might come from.

Then on August 6, with the impasse still seemingly insuperable, Saddam Hussein issued a lengthy statement that marked a clear change in the Iraqi position (as the Iraqi ambassador emphasized in delivering me a copy). The statement began, as usual, with a quotation from the Koran. In this case, the citation was "They schemed, and God schemed, and God is the best of schemers," which struck me as apt only if one could be sure on which side God stood. After pages of exposition on the Iraqi version of the war and on the villainy of the Iranians, the Iraqi President came to the point:

> We declare our readiness for a cease-fire, on the condition that Iran declares, clearly, unequivocally and officially, its agreement to enter into negotiations with us, in appreciation of this initiative, immediately after the cease-fire in order that we may discuss, reach agreement and implement all the provisions of Security Council resolution 598 other than those relating to the cease-fire, beginning with withdrawal to international boundaries, proceeding through to paragraph 8 and including all the operative paragraphs."[23]

In response to Saddam Hussein's statement, the Iranian government agreed that after the cease-fire came into effect, face-to-face talks with Iraq could be considered positively. To my surprise, Tehran did not repeat its earlier condition that withdrawal of troops would also have to begin before direct meetings with Iraq could take place. I moved quickly to establish August 20 as the date for the cease-fire and invited Iran and Iraq to send representatives to Geneva to begin talks on August 25 on implementing the other aspects of Resolution 598.

Announcing the date for a cease-fire in this seemingly endless war gave me a greater sense of fulfillment than any other action during my ten years as Secretary-General. A cease-fire would mean that the killing would stop, the horror of the use of chemical weapons against military and civilian targets would (I thought) end and the danger of escalation because of confrontations in the Gulf would be greatly reduced. Whatever difficulties lay still ahead—and I underestimated them at the time—my sense was that the war was over. This proved to be correct. As I arrived at the Secretariat building on the morning of August 8, a reporter asked how I felt. "I mean, this is a pretty big coup for you," he added. I replied, with all my heart, that to work for peace is really a beautiful effort and it is worthwhile—worth any effort, any sacrifice.

After the agreement between Iran and Iraq to begin talks was announced, I received, to my considerable surprise, a handwritten note from former President Richard Nixon, dated August 10, 1988. The letter, which, I must confess gave me a certain gratification, read as follows:

> Dear Mr. Secretary-General,
> As you know from my book *1999* I have in the past spoken highly of the quality of those serving at the UN but have not been impressed by its achievements in the field of diplomacy.
> For that reason I am delighted to congratulate you for your superb leadership in bringing about a cease-fire between Iran and Iraq.

In serving the cause of peace you have also rendered great service to the prestige of the UN.

With warm regards,

Richard Nixon

FINALLY, DIRECT NEGOTIATIONS

The direct talks between Iran and Iraq began under my auspices in Geneva on August 24, 1988. Iran was represented by Foreign Minister Velayati and Iraq by Deputy Prime Minister and Foreign Minister Tariq Aziz. The meeting, which opened with the widely publicized handshake between the representatives of two countries that had been at war for more than eight years, was an occasion of considerable drama and high expectations. I had by this time gotten to know both men extremely well, and while I had found the positions that they took on behalf of their governments frustrating, maddeningly stubborn and sometimes irrational, I esteemed both as highly professional and intelligent men with whom communication was easy. This gave me hope that these direct talks would lead to the comprehensive settlement foreseen in Resolution 598. From the beginning it was clear, however, that reconciliation would be neither easy nor quick.

In describing the atmosphere of the first two meetings to the Security Council, the best I could do was to characterize it as "fairly positive and nonacrimonious"; translated from diplomatese, this meant "unpromising and cool." The most encouraging development was that the cease-fire was in effect and the United Nations Iran-Iraq Military Observation Group (UNIIMOG) was in place to monitor it and to observe the withdrawal of the forces. In the direct talks, however, it was immediately clear that the perception of what constituted consolidation of the cease-fire differed sharply between the two sides. Again it was a question of sequence, but substance was inextricably involved. Iraq insisted that there could be no discussion on any other aspect of Resolution 598, including the withdrawal of troops, until agreement was reached on freedom of navigation and clearing of the Shatt-al-Arab. Iran took the position that since the cease-fire had been agreed and was in effect, it should not be among the subjects of the direct talks. Rather the two sides should seek common understanding on the other provisions of the resolution. Withdrawal to the internationally recognized boundaries should, in the Iranian view, already have started. While accepting the principle of freedom of navigation in accordance with international law, the Iranians denied that the right of search and boarding prevailed in conditions short of peace. It accepted the need to clear the Shatt-al-Arab, but insisted that this be done in accordance with the Algiers Agreement of 1975. Iraq refused to consider inclusion of any reference to the Algiers Agreement. At the conclusion of the talks, both sides made hostile press statements, which were not helpful.

I decided that at the next session of bilateral talks that were to begin in New York on October 1, I would present specific formulas as a basis for agreement on four issues: freedom of navigation, withdrawal of forces, procedures for the release and repatriation of prisoners of war and clearance of the Shatt-al-Arab. Before the talks began, I invited the foreign ministers of the Permanent Members of the Security Council to meet with me so that I could gain their support. They were all in favor of my strategy and afterward issued a joint statement calling on both sides "to display restraint, flexibility and readiness to search for mutually acceptable solutions."[24] The U.S. secretary of state and the Soviet foreign minister were especially supportive of my approach. Hearing Mr. Shultz and Mr. Shevardnadze speak with more or less the same voice concerning an area where they so recently had been hostile rivals made me realize how profound was the change taking place in the relationship between the American and Soviet governments.

My strategy for the October session did not bring progress. The only significant agreement was that the talks would resume on November 1. At that meeting I again reverted to a technique I had used in the Falklands/Malvinas mediation by listing the points on which I found the two sides were in agreement. Both sides, I noted, were prepared to continue the process toward implementation of the Security Council resolution in good faith. Both accepted in principle the concept of freedom of navigation on the high seas and in the Strait of Hormuz. They were both committed to the withdrawal of their forces to the internationally recognized boundaries within a short time frame. And, finally, they recognized the utility for both sides of restoring the Shatt-al-Arab for navigation. I confirmed with satisfaction that the cease-fire was holding. It needed, however, to be consolidated. I hoped that on the basis of the agreement that already existed we could move on to the rapid implementation of the resolution as an integral whole.

Following intensive contacts with both sides and with the International Committee of the Red Cross, a memorandum of understanding was signed covering the release and repatriation of approximately 1,500 sick and wounded prisoners. Both sides were favorably disposed toward the establishment of a mixed military working group comprising representatives of the two sides and chaired by the chief military observer of UNIIMOG; such a group, established shortly thereafter, was helpful in resolving the military incidents that continued to occur. However, the differences on the issues of sequence and substance were not narrowed.

In repeated subsequent sessions in Geneva, I and my Special Representative, Jan Eliasson, who demonstrated admirable skill and patience as a negotiator, sought to resolve the differences by reordering the sequence of implementation of the various points in the resolution, by demonstrating that the technical resources were readily available for clearing the Shatt-al-Arab, by direct approaches in visits to both capitals and by seeking to bring pressure to bear from the Security Council and from the five Permanent Members on both sides. Over the months, however, the attitude of the Iraqi and Iranian representatives became more abrasive and with the fighting stopped, the interest and concern of the international community declined. I was constantly fearful that the cease-fire would collapse. I was especially concerned when the Iraqis accused the Iranians of encouraging rebellion among Iraq's Kurdish population, an accusation not lacking in plausibility. Saddam Hussein chose, however, to attack the Kurds directly rather than renew the war with Iran.

THE GULF WAR INTERVENES

The situation changed dramatically with the forceful international response to Iraq's invasion of Kuwait. Clearly wishing to reduce the incentive that Iran might have to join in the UN-authorized military action to free Kuwait, Iraq, in direct contacts with Iran, conceded the principal points that had prevented progress in the United Nations' mediation efforts. On February 20, 1991, the UNIIMOG was able to confirm that the last of the disputed military positions along the internationally recognized boundaries had been withdrawn. Paragraphs 1 and 2 of Resolution 598 regarding the cease-fire and withdrawal of troops had finally been implemented. Thus the mandate of UNIIMOG, deriving from those two paragraphs, was completed.[25]

Under the circumstances, I recommended to the Security Council that UNIIMOG be replaced by small civilian offices in Tehran and Baghdad that could assist me in carrying out the remaining tasks entrusted to the Secretary-General by other operative paragraphs of the resolution. I had in mind in particular the need to develop measures to enhance security and stability in the region. I looked to the offices to keep me informed of measures that might be taken to begin a process of confidence-building. The Gulf War obviously imposed severe restrictions on what could be accomplished. Nonetheless, I thought it of value to have a continuing political presence in the region. My successor had a different perception of their value, however, and given the stringent budgetary conditions under which the United Nations must operate, decided to close the two offices.

One further paragraph of Resolution 598, paragraph 6, concerning determination of responsibility for the war, was implemented while I was still in office. Under my first plans for the implementation of Resolution 598, I proposed that on D-Day, when the cease-fire would come into effect, I would begin work on the formation of an independent group to examine where the blame lay for starting the war. Because of Iraq and Iran's differences of opinion on the sequence in which the resolution should be implemented, I was not able to carry out this intention as scheduled. The consultations I held with the two governments on the subject were not productive. The Iranian Government never reduced its pressure for the implementation of this paragraph, however, and eventually introduced it as an element in the complex negotiations to obtain the release of the Western hostages in Lebanon. As described in chapter 6, I gave assurances to the Iranians in this context that I would meet my responsibility in connection with paragraph 6.

I knew that any impartial investigation was bound to conclude that Iraq was the guilty party. However, with the troop withdrawals completed, I felt that implementation of paragraph 6 could no longer imperil the cease-fire that had been in effect for three years. Therefore, in August of 1991, I requested the governments of Iran and Iraq to provide me with their detailed views on the subject. At the same time I consulted a group of independent experts composed of eminent Belgian jurists. Their conclusion was that, in the course of the war, both parties were guilty of violating international law. However, Iraq, by penetrating Iranian territory, committed the initial aggression and should be held responsible for all the damages that Iran suffered as a result.

Taking the views of the impartial experts into account, along with the various communications I had received on the subject from the parties and other documents that were available to the United Nations, I submitted my report to the Security Council on December 9, 1991, regarding responsibility for the Iran-Iraq war.[26] I concluded that "the war was started in contravention of international law, and violations of international law give rise to responsibility for conflict. . . . Accordingly . . . the outstanding event is the attack of 22 September 1980 against Iran, which cannot be justified under the Charter of the United Nations, any recognized rules and principles of international law or any principles of international morality and entails responsibility for the conflict." My conclusion was thus a clear condemnation of Iraq. Having stated it, I suggested that further pursuit of paragraph 6 would serve no useful purpose. Rather, the objective should be construction of peaceful relations between the parties and of peace and security in the whole region.

The dynamics of this tragic war, which brought gain to neither side, changed markedly during the eight long years of conflict. Saddam Hussein, I believe, invaded Iran for two understandable, if perverse, reasons. First, he wished to gain full control of the Shatt-al-Arab as the essential sea lifeline for Iraq's economy. Judging that the Iranian military establishment was in disarray and that internationally Iran was isolated, he considered the time propitious to accomplish this objective. Second, as Iraq has a large Shi'ite minority, he wished to eliminate the avowedly evangelical regime of the Ayatollah Khomeini before his own authority was threatened by a contagious Iranian-style fundamentalism. Faced with far stronger resistance than he had anticipated, he quickly decided to cut his losses and seek peace through UN mediation. As the Iraqi military position improved over the course of the war, Saddam's terms for peace hardened but the objective of eliminating the fundamentalist regime in Tehran was dropped.

The Iranian objectives, beyond the obvious one of resisting foreign invasion, were to eliminate Saddam Hussein, to gain international acknowledgment that Iraq had started the war and to obtain compensation for the losses suffered as a result of the Iraqi attack. Only after years of debilitating military impasse and in the face of a clearly renascent Iraqi military capacity did Tehran abandon the first objective.

The external dynamics also changed with the coming to power in the Soviet Union of Mikhail Gorbachev and the resultant growing cooperation between it and the United States in resolving regional conflicts. I do not believe, however, that even in the early stages of the conflict, when the Cold War still prevailed, the actions taken by the Security Council were greatly influenced by East-West hostility. The United States was traumatized by its devastating experience with the Khomeini revolution. Until the peculiar misadventure of Irangate, it was unremittingly hostile to Iran, and therefore it was not inclined to support any Security Council action that might be favorable to Tehran. The Soviet Union, because of its long-standing close association with Iraq, was of a similar view. Finally, the other Arab states and Third World countries represented in the Council, for their own reasons, clearly favored Iraq. The result was first inaction by the Council at the time of the invasion and then a series of resolutions that were essentially unhelpful since they made no distinction between Iran and Iraq in terms of culpability for the war. The Council did not act with distinction in dealing with the Iran/Iraq conflict until the five Permanent Members recognized the wider danger that the conflict posed. Then, led by the Permanent Five, the Council acted with vigor and provided evidence of how effective it can be when the Permanent Members are ready to work together toward a common purpose.

In the end, it was the United Nations, rather than either of the parties to the conflict or any of the other countries involved, that was strengthened by the Iran/Iraq experience. I believe the mediation potential of the Secretary-General as an impartial UN organ gained credibility that would strengthen the position in the future. The Security Council showed a decision-making capacity and an authority that were to be instrumental in the resolution of other crises. Even though the United Nations could not fully resolve the causes of the Iran-Iraq war, it did end it. This seminal event marked the beginning of a new era in the United Nations' history.

ANNEX

RESOLUTION 598 (1987)
Adopted by the Security Council at its 2750th meeting on 20 July 1987
The Security Council,
Reaffirming its resolution 582 (1986)

Deeply concerned that, despite its calls for a cease-fire, the conflict between Iran and Iraq continues unabated, with further heavy loss of human life and material destruction,

Deploring the initiation and continuation of the conflict,

Deploring also the bombing of purely civilian population centers, attacks on neutral shipping or civilian aircraft, the violation of international humanitarian law and other laws of armed conflict, and, in particular, the use of chemical weapons contrary to obligations under the 1925 Geneva Protocol,

Deeply concerned that further escalation and widening of the conflict may take place,

Determined to bring to an end all military actions between Iran and Iraq,

Convinced that a comprehensive, just, honourable and durable settlement should be achieved between Iran and Iraq,

Recalling the provisions of the Charter of the United Nations and in particular the obligation of all member states to settle their international disputes by peaceful means in such a manner that international peace and security and justice are not endangered,

Determining that there exists a breach of the peace as regards the conflict between Iran and Iraq,

Acting under Articles 39 and 40 of the Charter of the United Nations,

1. Demands that, as a first step towards a negotiated settlement, Iran and Iraq observe an immediate cease-fire, discontinue all military actions on land, at sea and in the air, and withdraw all forces to the internationally recognized boundaries without delay;

2. Requests the Secretary-General to dispatch a team of United Nations Observers to verify, confirm and supervise the cease-fire and withdrawal and further requests the Secretary-General to make the necessary arrangements in consultation with the Parties and to submit a report thereon to the Security Council;

3. Urges that prisoners of war be released and repatriated without delay after the cessation of active hostilities in accordance with the Third Geneva Convention of 12 August 1949;

4. Calls upon Iran and Iraq to cooperated with the Secretary-General in implementing this resolution and in mediation efforts to achieve a comprehensive, just and honourable settlement, acceptable to both sides, of all outstanding issues in accordance with the principles contained in the Charter of the United Nations;

5. Calls upon all other States to exercise the utmost restraint and to refrain from any act which may lead to further escalation and widening of the conflict and thus to facilitate the implementation of the present resolution;

6. Requests the Secretary-General to explore, in consultation with Iran and Iraq, the question of entrusting an impartial body with inquiring into responsibility for the conflict and to report to the Security Council as soon as possible;

7. Recognizes the magnitude of the damage inflicted during the conflict and the need for reconstruction efforts, with appropriate international assistance, once the conflict is ended and, in this regard, requests the Secretary-General to assign a team of experts to study the question of reconstruction and to report to the Security Council;

8. Further requests the Secretary-General to examine in consultation with Iran and Iraq and with other states of the region measures to enhance the security and stability of the region;

9. Requests the Secretary-General to keep the Security Council informed on the implementation of this resolution;

10. Decides to meet again as necessary to consider further steps to insure compliance with this resolution.

EIGHT

AFGHANISTAN:
A VICTORY BETRAYED

WHEN I REFLECT UPON MY INVOLVEMENT IN THE AFGHAN PROBLEM, I recall the consternation and fear that the Soviet invasion caused and the optimism—and surprise—felt in April 1988, when the Geneva Accords were actually signed. For the first time since 1946, the Soviet army was withdrawing from an occupied territory! I was conscious that the internal situation remained unresolved. It had been left to the United Nations to bring the contending factions together, a task that I did not believe properly belonged to the Organization. Arms continued to be supplied to the Mujahideen and to the government.

Still, I hoped that with the help of the powers that had been so deeply involved in the war, the people of Afghanistan would find a way peacefully to determine the future of their country. Instead, Afghanistan faded from the international agenda and was abandoned to the fragmentation and power struggles that were the bitter heritage of the Cold War. I hope that this account will serve to recall that the withdrawal of the Soviet army was not the only objective of the difficult negotiations that spanned eight long and painful years. An objective of equal importance was to help the people of Afghanistan to achieve national reconciliation and the reconstruction of their country. The country suffers still from the failure to achieve those goals.

INITIAL UN INVOLVEMENT

The Soviet invasion of Afghanistan in November 1979 was immediately brought before the Security Council, where action, predictably, was blocked by a Soviet veto. Utilizing the provisions of the "Uniting for Peace" resolution adopted by the General Assembly at the time of the Korean war—377(v)—a majority of the Council, in a move not subject to the veto, called for an emergency special session of the General Assembly to consider the Soviet action. The Assembly adopted a Resolution, ES-6/2, deploring the armed intervention and calling for the immediate, unconditional and total withdrawal of all "foreign" forces. It appealed for humanitarian aid, to be coordinated by the UN High Commissioner for Refugees, to alleviate the plight of the many thousands who had fled from Afghanistan.

During its regular session in the fall of 1980, the Assembly adopted a further resolution, 35/37, repeating these same points and, in addition, expressing appreciation for the efforts of the Secretary-General in the search for a solution to the problem and the hope that he would continue to extend assistance "including the appointment of a special representative, with a view to promoting a political solution."

The Soviet Union denied the legitimacy of the resolutions, which, being Assembly resolutions, did not have mandatory effect. Nonetheless, this action of the General Assembly was very significant for the future course of events. Having been adopted by an overwhelming majority under the leadership of the Islamic countries, they demonstrated to Moscow the near-universal rejection of its action, as did similar resolutions that were passed each succeeding year. The resolutions also provided the basis for the High Commissioner for Refugees to extend assistance to more than 6 million refugees who fled to Pakistan and Iran. Finally, the resolution led to the appointment of a representative for Afghanistan, a post I was to fill before becoming Secretary-General. Secretary-General Kurt Waldheim appointed me as a "personal representative" rather than a "special representative," thus permitting Moscow to pretend that the appointment was unrelated to the Assembly resolutions. This was the basis on which the Soviet government dealt with UN representation on ending the war in Afghanistan. Secretary-General Waldheim considered that under the terms of the Assembly resolutions, he had a responsibility to do everything he could to find a peaceful resolution for the Afghan crisis. I felt the same responsibility when I succeeded him.

In January 1981, I accompanied Secretary-General Waldheim to a Non-Aligned Summit meeting in New Delhi. At this meeting the first signs emerged that the parties were interested in pursuing a political solution to the Afghan war. President Zia ul-Haq of Pakistan hosted a reception for the diplomatic corps during which he and the Soviet Ambassador had an exchange that revealed that both sides were open to discussions. When Secretary-General Waldheim and I learned of this, we decided to include in Waldheim's scheduled speech an offer of the Secretary-General's good offices. I felt it would be better for the Secretary-

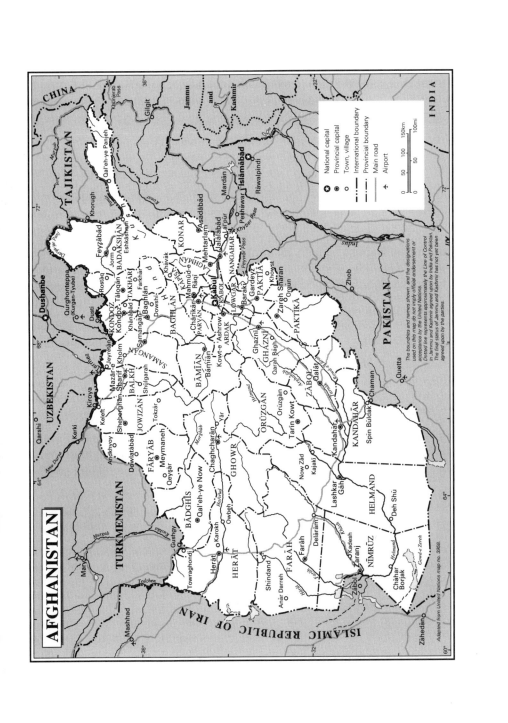

AFGHANISTAN

CHINA

TAJIKISTAN

UZBEKISTAN

TURKMENISTAN

ISLAMIC REPUBLIC OF IRAN

PAKISTAN

INDIA

Jammu and Kashmir

National capital
Provincial capital
Town, village
International boundary
Provincial boundary
Main road
Airport

0   50   100   150km
0   50   100mi

The boundaries and names shown and the designations
used on this map do not imply official endorsement or
acceptance by the United Nations.
Dotted line represents approximately the Line of Control
in Jammu and Kashmir agreed upon by India and Pakistan.
The final status of Jammu and Kashmir has not yet been
agreed upon by the parties.

Adapted from United Nations map no. 3958.

Dushanbe
Islāmābād
Rāwalpindi
Mardān
Peshāwar
Khyber Pass
Jalāl'pūr
Jalālābād
'Asadābād
Mehtarlām
Khāvāk
Feyzābād
Jorm
Eshkāshem
Farkhār
Khorugh
Qal'eh-ye Panjeh
Baghlān
Dowshī
Pol-e Khomrī
Khānābād
Kondoz
Tāloqān
Rāgh
Rostāq
Qurghonteppa (Kurgan-Tyube)
Dusti
Gilgit
Khavāk
Jorm
Mahmūd-e Rāqī
Chārīkār
Kābol
Bārak
Gardēz
Khowst
Orgūn
Zareh Sharān
Kowt-e 'Ashrow
Ghazni
Qarah Bāgh
Bāmīān
Shulgarah
Kholm
Mazār-e Sharīf
Sheberghān
Dowlatābād
Andkhvoy
Qeyşār
Meymaneh
Tokzār
Yār
Chaghcharān
Qal'eh-ye Now
Karokh
Owbeh
Gushgy
Towraghondī
Herāt
Shindand
Anār Darreh
Farāh
Delārām
Kadesh
Zaranj
Chāhār Borjak
Deh Shū
Lashkar Gāh
Kajakī
Now Zād
Tarīn Kowt
Oruzgān
Qalāt
Kandahār
Spīn Būldak
Chaman
Quetta
Zhob
Zābol
Zāhedān
Mashhad
Mary
Qarshī
Kerki
Keleft
Kirova
Jeyretān
Samangān
Nāyak
Dowshī
Khārān
Orgūn
Khowst

PROVINCES:
BADAKHSHĀN
TAKHĀR
KONDOZ
BALKH
JOWZJĀN
FĀRYĀB
BĀDGHĪS
HERĀT
FARĀH
NĪMRŪZ
HELMAND
KANDAHĀR
ZĀBOL
ORŪZGĀN
GHOWR
GHAZNĪ
PAKTĪKĀ
PAKTĪĀ
LOWGAR
KĀBOL
KĀPĪSĀ
PARVĀN
BĀMĪĀN
SAMANGĀN
BAGHLĀN
LAGHMĀN
NANGARHĀR
KONAR

HINDU KUSH

General to take the initiative than to respond to a request from the Non-Aligned countries, which we had heard was under consideration.

Immediately following his speech, the Secretary-General held consultations with the Foreign Ministers of Afghanistan and Pakistan. Both sides informed him that they accepted the offer of his good offices. The next morning over breakfast Secretary-General Waldheim told me he would like to appoint me as his Personal Representative for Afghanistan. I could scarcely decline, feeling as deeply as I did that the Soviet invasion, whatever its motivation, had raised tensions dangerously in an already volatile region and profoundly disrupted the lives of the Afghan people.

While my appointment was not officially announced until our return to New York, it became known while we were still in New Delhi and I was able to have useful discussions there with Pakistani representatives. I learned to my satisfaction that Pakistan would not object if, on my return to the region in April, I would visit Kabul on an *official* basis. This was significant because Pakistan, along with many other Member States, refused to recognize the regime headed by President Babrak Karmal as the legitimate government of Afghanistan. They viewed Karmal and the People's Democratic Party of Afghanistan (PDPA) as anti-Islamic Soviet puppets, placed in power under extremely dubious circumstances by the Red Army. The Pakistanis never dealt face to face with representatives of the Democratic Republic of Afghanistan until the signature ceremony of the Geneva Accords in 1988.

Despite widespread rejection of the Kabul government among Member States, the credentials of the Afghan delegation to the United Nations were never officially challenged. I was therefore in a position to negotiate with the Karmal regime. This permitted the United Nations to play the essential role of go-between in developing the eventual agreement. Only the United Nations was able to speak to all sides.

We began to consider how mediation could best be undertaken on the plane returning to New York from New Delhi. Four points emerged that were to remain the focus of negotiations in the ensuing years and that were to define the contents of the Geneva Agreements: withdrawal of foreign troops, noninterference in internal affairs, appropriate guarantees and voluntary return of refugees.

I brought this formula with me to Pakistan in April of 1981, where I met with President Zia ul-Haq, Foreign Minister Agha Shahi, and Deputy Foreign Minister Shah Nawaz, who would later become the Permanent Representative of Pakistan to the United Nations. I found President Zia ul-Haq then and in all subsequent meetings to be a gracious and personable man of profound religious convictions. He had a disarming quality that reflected the confidence of autocracy. I believe he genuinely wished to resolve the Afghan problem, although his commitment to the particular interests of the Pakistani military establishment and to the cause of the Islamic Mujahideen led him at times to take uncompromising positions. Foreign Minister Shahi, a former colleague at the United Nations, was far more rigid in his attitude and was not an easy man to deal with. Pakistan became a principal party, along with the government of Afghanistan, in negotiations for an Afghan settlement primarily because more than 3 million Afghan refugees had fled there. Pakistan represented their interests. Beyond that, however, Pakistan had its own interests in Afghanistan. It did not welcome a Soviet army on its borders and was fearful of possible further Soviet expansion in the region. This was an interest it shared with the United States, for whom it served as a surrogate in the negotiations, just as the Communist regime in Kabul did for the Soviet Union. Pakistan was rewarded for its policy on Afghanistan by substantial economic assistance from the United States and Saudi Arabia. President Zia was personally rewarded through enhanced international respect despite his seizure of power through a military coup.

During my meetings with President Zia and his advisors, the Pakistanis accepted three of the four points that I posited but insisted that noninterference in internal affairs should not be part of the agenda. They were obviously and understandably motivated in this by concern for the views of the Afghan refugees who were now settled in Peshawar and were able to exert strong influence on the Pakistani government. President Zia's refusal to deal directly with the Afghan government seemed to me to reflect more this "Peshawar" pressure than personal animosity toward the Soviet-installed regime of Babrak Karmal. Certainly he went out of his way to facilitate my contact with the regime by providing his personal plane for my trip to Kabul. This was a most welcome gesture, since there was no other way to get from "there to there."

In Kabul I met for the first time with President Karmal and the foreign minister, Shah Mohammad Dost. Karmal was a polite, unsmiling man who lived up fully to his reputation as a puppet of Moscow. His frequent reiteration of the standard Soviet position, his noncommittal stance on our proposals and his repeated defensive assertion that he was an Afghan nationalist gave me the impression that he was largely a figurehead. Foreign Minister Dost was more forthcoming and helpful, even though adjacent to his office was the office of the Soviet proconsul, who at that time was Vasiliy Safronchuk. The Soviet Union later sent Safronchuk to the Secretariat to serve on my staff as Under-Secretary-General for Political and Security Council Affairs. While in the Secretariat Safronchuk never spoke of his role in Kabul, although he acknowledged having served there as a diplomat. He did not impress me as a man who could have controlled the events that brought Babrak to power.

Not surprisingly, the position taken by the Afghans was diametrically opposed to that of the Pakistanis. They insisted that the issue of noninterference must be addressed whereas the question of withdrawal of foreign troops should not. My overall impression from this trip was that neither the Pakistanis nor the Afghans were in a rush to resolve the situation. Babrak must surely have calculated that his hold on power depended on the continued presence of Soviet troops. And the Pakistanis, quite apart from the economic assistance received from the United States and Saudi Arabia, were seeing a great deal of money flow into their country for refugee assistance and for the arming of the Mujahideen.

In August, I returned to the region to try again to bring the parties together on the agenda for negotiations. This time President Zia ul-Haq and Foreign Minister Shahi both agreed that the proposed four-point agenda corresponded with the intention of General Assembly Resolution 35/37, of which Pakistan had been a sponsor. I interpreted this as implicit acceptance of inclusion in negotiations of the issue of noninterference in internal affairs. At this time Foreign Minister Shahi also raised a fifth point, the issue of self-determination, a matter that would increase in importance over the course of the Geneva negotiations. For the time being, however, I was able to convince the Pakistanis to leave this question outside the context of the formal negotiations.

Having obtained at least implicit Pakistani acceptance of the agenda and an expression of their desire to continue the process, I went to Kabul and met again with President Karmal and Foreign Minister Dost. The foreign minister accepted my argument that my four points had been included in proposals that the Afghan government itself had put forward the previous May. Both Afghanistan and Pakistan were thus persuaded that the proposed agenda for negotiations was consistent with positions that they had taken previously. Foreign Minister Dost added a condition, however, that at first seemed relatively minor. Negotiations could begin, he said, when agreement on the format of the talks was reached. This proved to be a more difficult task than reaching agreement on the substantive agenda. The procedural problem would impede the negotiating process until the very end.

CHOOSING A NEW PERSONAL REPRESENTATIVE

After assuming the post of Secretary-General in January 1982, I immediately turned to the question of appointing a new Personal Representative for Afghanistan in order to maintain the diplomatic momentum that had gathered over the course of the year. The person should come from a country that was not involved in any way with the situation in Afghanistan. He had to be acceptable to all of the parties directly involved: Afghanistan, Pakistan and the Soviet Union. Because of my own personal involvement and interest in this matter, I wanted someone who would keep me well informed about the status of negotiations. After several candidates were reviewed with the parties, I chose

Diego Cordovez, a long-time Secretariat member of Ecuadorian nationality who had succeeded me as Under-Secretary-General for Political Affairs. I knew through what might be called the wives' channel that he wanted the job. The Soviet Union and Afghanistan initially opposed this choice. After I sent Giandomenico Picco to the two capitals to persuade them of Cordovez's merits, they both came on board. Cordovez thus met the requirements.

Cordovez, who subsequently became foreign minister of Ecuador, is a man of sharp intelligence and a keen sense for negotiating strategy. He is also a man who appreciates—and seeks—full credit for his accomplishments. There were times when both Moscow and Washington let it be known that they did not consider Cordovez entirely trustworthy, each suggesting that he was too much under the influence of the other. I calculated that this was evidence of his impartiality. Just as I did under Waldheim, Cordovez, as my Personal Representative, assumed primary responsibility for the UN mediation effort. He deserves credit for shepherding the talks through extended periods of frustration to the successful conclusion of the Geneva Accords. I never considered replacing him, although I was told repeatedly that he was given to deprecating my contribution to an Afghan settlement and, beyond that, to my performance as Secretary-General. In essence, I tolerated him despite his apparent disloyalty because I thought this was in the best interest of an Afghan settlement.

THE GENEVA TALKS BEGIN

Cordovez's first task was to obtain clarification of the agenda and agreement on the format for talks on a settlement from Pakistan and Afghanistan. This he successfully accomplished in repeated visits to the capitals, including Moscow and Washington. The first round of negotiations was held in Geneva from June 16 to 24, 1982. While the negotiating parties were Pakistan and Afghanistan, Soviet and U.S. representatives were always close by to monitor developments. The negotiating procedure was exceedingly awkward. Because of Pakistan's strict nonrecognition policy, the Pakistani delegation would not enter the building to meet with the Personal Representative until the Afghans had left the premises. While this first session was largely preliminary, both parties agreed to pursue a comprehensive settlement of the conflict; I considered this significant since a comprehensive settlement would have to include withdrawal of the Soviet troops.

In my own meetings and trips over the course of 1982 and 1983, I sought to gain a sense of the positions of the other interested parties, particularly Iran, the United States and the Soviet Union. By then Iran was host to over 2 million Afghan refugees. It had close ties with the fundamentalist Islamic resistance group. I had been quite pleased when the Iranian authorities agreed to meet with

Cordovez during his trip to the region in March of 1982. However, Teheran then chose to limit the discussion strictly to the delivery of humanitarian assistance by the United Nations High Commissioner for Refugees (UNHCR). In my contacts with Iranian representatives, I found that while they did not oppose UN mediation, they had great difficulty with the exclusion of the refugees from the negotiating process. This attitude did not change.

We were careful to maintain direct contact with Washington and Moscow during the course of negotiations, even though their representatives in Geneva were kept well informed. Initially I believe the American attitude was wary. No great importance was attributed to the Geneva negotiations. During a brief meeting I had in June 1982 with President Ronald Reagan at UN Headquarters, the subject was hardly mentioned. In the course of the next years Washington gave more positive support to our efforts and, to a limited extent, kept us informed of its bilateral contacts with the Soviets on the subject. These contacts became very active after Gorbachev came to power. The United States clearly attributed greater importance to them than to the UN negotiations.

The attitude of the Soviet Union was not dissimilar to that of the United States. When I visited Moscow in September 1982, I stated to General Secretary Brezhnev and Foreign Minister Gromyko in the frankest terms the need for Soviet withdrawal and a change in the Karmal regime. Brezhnev seemed not to comprehend what I had said. Foreign Minister Gromyko confined himself to agreeing to study the four-point proposal being considered in Geneva. When I returned to Moscow for Brezhnev's funeral—an event that did not surprise me— I had the opportunity to talk briefly with Yuri Andropov, Brezhnev's successor. Unlike Brezhnev, Andropov was well informed on the subject and gave me a clear hint of Soviet interest in achieving a political settlement, an interest that would flower when Gorbachev came into office.

THE AFGHAN REFUGEES

In the Geneva negotiations we chose to focus first on the issue of refugees on the assumption that it was the least controversial of the four points. This was a false assumption. It quickly became a point of contention because of the question of consultations with the various refugee groups. Almost a third of the Afghan population had fled and was now living outside of the country. They understandably wished to be part of the negotiating process that would determine the future of their country. In the context of the negotiations the term "refugees" had two meanings, even while referring to one and the same population. In one sense it connoted the community of Afghans in Pakistan and Iran. The term also served, however, as a euphemism for the leadership of the Afghan resistance. I considered that both categories had to be associated, in some way, with the Geneva negotiations, something on which the Pakistanis insisted and to which the Afghans were naturally opposed.

The first UN contact with the resistance took place at the thirteenth Islamic Conference of Foreign Ministers in Niamey, Niger, in August 1982. There the head of the United Nations delegation, Isoufou Djermakoye, an Under-Secretary-General in the Secretariat, held a confidential meeting with Sebghatullah Mujajadidi, Said Ahmad Pir Gailani, and Mohamad Nabi Mohamadi, all Afghan resistance leaders. This meeting was also attended by Giandomenico Picco, and thus marked the establishment of direct contact between the office of the Secretary-General and the resistance. I later told President Zia ul-Haq that I saw no objection to having the resistance meet Picco again, an offer that the resistance leaders accepted in August 1983. Regular meetings then took place on a strictly confidential basis.

Consultations with the refugee communities also proved a difficult issue to resolve. The Kabul government felt that communication by UN representatives with either the resistance or the refugee communities would serve to legitimize the opposition. For purposes of the UN mediation, however, it was clearly desirable that the refugees should be informed of the conditions for their return that were being discussed in Geneva. The Pakistani foreign minister, in a letter to me in April 1982, proposed that UNHCR assume responsibility for this task. In early 1983 the Afghans agreed that consultations with the refugees were necessary and that the possibility of a UNHCR role in these consultations should be explored. However, at this point, Pakistan raised the stakes by calling for the direct association of my Personal Representative in the consultations. This proposal was completely unacceptable to Kabul for the reasons just outlined.

It then developed that UNHCR was unwilling to serve as the contact for consultations with the refugees, since it would inject the High Commissioner into a political role and thereby jeopardize the humanitarian operation. Diego Cordovez and I both sought to persuade UNHCR of the importance of this mission, but to no avail. Subsequent efforts to convince the Afghan government of the importance of having the Personal Representative visit the refugees met unyielding opposition.

THE SPRING OF 1983: RAPID PROGRESS

During a trip to the region in January and February of 1983, Cordovez submitted to the parties the draft of a comprehensive settlement he and his staff had developed. Discussion of the draft in the Geneva talks in April 1983 led him to report that the text was "90 percent complete," although the parties were deadlocked on the question of consultations with the refugees. Increased Soviet interest in the Geneva negotiations was reflected in the assignment of a new "shadow" Soviet negotiator. I also received a letter in May of 1983 from U.S. Secretary of State Shultz expressing support for my efforts. At the conclusion of the further session of Geneva talks, from June 12 to 24, a Note for the Record was adopted, which called for another trip by Diego Cordovez to the region to "complete the draft text" and for him to approach the Soviet Union and the United States as possible guarantors of a settlement.

In order to capitalize on these favorable trends, we decided to seek agreement on a "Memorandum of Understanding" (MOU) outlining a course for future negotiations that would lead to a final agreement. A proposed agenda was included that reflected our confidence and optimism. This agenda involved commitments *not to reopen some issues* and to *complete* others; *finalizing* arrangements regarding consultations of the refugees; and *finalizing* the guarantees (emphasis added).

I met with the foreign ministers of Pakistan and Afghanistan during the general debate of the General Assembly that autumn to secure their agreement to the MOU. Foreign Minister Sahabzoda Yaqub-Khan of Pakistan found the MOU "too ambitious" and rejected it as a basis for future negotiations; the Afghan foreign minister objected, as a matter of principle, to the linkage of Cordovez's next visit to the region with acceptance of the MOU. Both sides, fearful of making the commitments implied in the MOU, were only willing to consider the draft MOU as a "program of work." The Afghan "spring" was quickly reverting to winter.

NEGOTIATIONS STALL

In January of 1984, I met with President Zia ul-Haq in Casablanca and suggested that the Afghan negotiations had come to a stalemate. President Zia, on the contrary, expressed satisfaction with the progress that had been made so far. He noted that a "signal" on the withdrawal of Soviet troops may have been sent in the form of a press report suggesting that Moscow had proposed an 18-month timetable. He then raised again the vexing question of consultations with the refugees. He believed that a methodology for conducting such consultations could be arranged. I expressed my readiness to see the contacts between the "refugees"—the leadership of the Afghan resistance—and my aide, Gianni Picco, continue. However, I also noted that formal consultations with a nongovernmental entity, such as the refugee communities, on a political settlement would set a dangerous precedent. The question therefore remained unresolved.

In the spring of 1984, Diego Cordovez was able to settle a number of procedural problems. Most important, a general understanding was reached on what became known as proximity talks. Rather than waiting for one delegation to leave the Palais des Nations, the UN headquarters in Geneva, before inviting the other delegation to enter, the two delegations would now be at the Palais simultaneously but in different rooms. The Personal Representative would henceforth "shuttle" back and forth between the two rooms. President Zia ul-Haq signaled that he would be willing to engage in direct talks with anyone on the Afghan side other than President Karmal. This progress on procedural issues, however, could not compensate for the lack of substantive progress on the main issues at hand, which by now consisted of the timing of the withdrawal of Soviet troops and noninterference in internal affairs.

Two trips to Washington in 1984 did not produce anything new. In May, I met with Secretary of State Shultz and emphasized my intention to press the new Soviet President, Konstantin Chernenko (my third), during my forthcoming trip to Moscow, on a timetable for Soviet withdrawal. I reminded the Secretary of State that only the United Nations was engaged in an ongoing attempt to secure Soviet withdrawal. All other efforts had failed. The Secretary did not comment on my presentation, and the question of Afghanistan was not discussed at a subsequent meeting with him in June.

My discussions with President Chernenko in Moscow proved equally disappointing. Chernenko, seemingly as remote from the subject as Brezhnev, expressed vague support for my efforts but insisted—reading from notes—that it was up to the West to provide the guarantees of noninterference that were necessary for Soviet withdrawal. Unilateral Soviet withdrawal, he read, would not solve anything. The Soviet position had evidently hardened with Andropov's death. Before going to Moscow I had been told by a Soviet member of my staff (who, according to the Americans, held high rank in the KGB) that Chernenko was only a transitional figure. In talking with Chernenko, I found it easy to believe that he would not head the Soviet Union for long. He was stolid to the point of immobility.

By the fall of 1984 the negotiations had become a vicious circle: Afghanistan complained about interference in its internal affairs while Pakistan complained about the presence of Soviet troops. I felt the continued deadlock placed the credibility of the Office of the Secretary-General at risk. Some movement would be required before further UN involvement could be justified. I therefore met with the Foreign Ministers of Pakistan and Afghanistan in November to ascertain the possibility of breaking the deadlock.

In my conversation with Foreign Minister Yaqub-Khan, I attempted to determine Pakistan's "price" for direct talks. He reiterated the position previously stated by President Zia, that a change in the Kabul regime was a necessary precondition. Noting that it would be difficult for the United Nations to make such a proposal to a government recognized by the General Assembly, I asked him whether Pakistan might agree to direct talks on the basis of an

Afghan commitment to discuss Soviet withdrawal. I urged him to float the idea of such a possibility. The Foreign Minister remained cautious and only agreed to report the conversation to President Zia ul-Haq.

Two hours later, I met with the foreign minister of Afghanistan and repeated my concerns about the lack of progress. I appealed for an Afghan demonstration of some flexibility in the next round of talks, particularly with regard to foreign troop withdrawal. Troop withdrawal was an essential element in any comprehensive settlement. The foreign minister rejected my argumentation.

Neither side seemed willing to test the other's desire for a settlement. It was therefore all for the best that the Pakistani Government requested the postponement of the next talks until after the completion of national elections in May 1985. The Americans and others in the West questioned this decision, and the Soviet government labeled it a demonstration of Pakistan's lack of sincerity. I felt, though, that it was pointless to continue the talks unless there was a significant change in the position of one or the other of the parties. I sensed that the Soviet government was coming under increasing pressure because of mounting losses in Afghanistan. We therefore decided to wait until the parties expressed the desire for the resumption of UN efforts before taking further action. Fortunately, there was a very significant change! Mikhail Gorbachev came to power in Moscow.

NEGOTIATING SOVIET WITHDRAWAL

My first meeting with Mr. Gorbachev was in March of 1985 at the funeral of President Chernenko. On previous such occasions, the new General Secretary had invited the heads of delegations in attendance to meet with him briefly, singly for the more important countries, in groups for the less important ones. I was always in the second category. However, Gorbachev invited me to meet with him singly, not as part of a group. This was the first time I (or any other Secretary-General) had ever received such an invitation. I was immediately, and no doubt naturally, impressed. We sat at a small table. Gromyko was present at the beginning but was called away, leaving Gorbachev and me with only an interpreter.

We did not specifically address the question of Afghanistan in our conversation. Mr. Gorbachev chose instead to discuss the role of the United Nations in the maintenance of peace and security and that of the Security Council in dealing with regional conflicts. He spoke with evident conviction and knowledge of the subject. He expressed the full support of the Soviet Union for the United Nations and for my own activities as Secretary-General. I sensed that these were not mere platitudes but represented something new in Soviet policy. Unlike some of his predecessors, he merely glanced at his briefing notes. He was expressive, smiling easily but not excessively. While I am not conversant in Russian, I could tell that he spoke fluently and with ease. It is not hindsight to say that I came away from the relatively brief encounter with a sense that Afghanistan—and other problems as well—might now open up.

I was briefed by the U.S. Permanent Representative on the Reagan-Gorbachev summit held in Geneva in November 1985, including their exchange on Afghanistan. I found it encouraging that Gorbachev had expressed support for "the solution emerging around the UN." He said the Soviet Union was prepared to cooperate on a package, including a cease-fire, international guarantees, return of refugees, and withdrawal of all foreign troops. He did not mention any necessity for direct talks between the Pakistanis and the Afghans. There was agreement that there would be follow-up bilateral talks between the United States and the Soviet Union on Afghanistan.

Despite this relatively encouraging report, we resisted pressure from both of the negotiating parties to resume the Geneva process until there should be some specific signal that progress would be made. In the late spring of 1986 Diego Cordovez, while visiting the region, was able to gain agreement on important procedural questions, which gave promise of breaking the impasse. The two sides agreed on the format of a settlement, which was now to be comprised of four documents rather than a single comprehensive one. The Afghan side finally accepted the direct linkage between the withdrawal of Soviet troops and guarantees of noninterference. The Soviets and the Americans both renewed their support for the UN process, and Andrei Kozyrev, who was in charge of UN affairs in the Soviet foreign ministry and was known to be among the "new thinkers" around Gorbachev, indicated that he would be in Geneva, presumably to help the negotiating process along.

On this basis, another round of proximity talks was held in Geneva in June 1986. My Personal Representative submitted drafts of the four instruments that together would constitute a comprehensive settlement of the Afghan problem. Agreement was reached on the instruments on noninterference and on the voluntary return of refugees. Both sides also accepted the text of the guarantees to be provided by the Soviet Union and the United States, on condition that the guarantors needed to be consulted (even though they were hovering nearby). Although Pakistan accepted the instrument on interrelationships, or linkages, between the other instruments, the Afghan side insisted that this instrument could only be agreed upon directly with Pakistan. This was the instrument in which the timetable for the Soviet withdrawal would be set. It became the key to the conclusion of a comprehensive settlement.

I attempted, unsuccessfully, to find a way to break the deadlock between the two parties. In talking to Foreign Minister Dost of Afghanistan, I suggested that persistence on a procedural point typically raised questions about a party's willingness to agree to a substantive point. (I realized, of course, that it was very much a substantive issue that was at stake.) The Foreign Minister insisted that direct talks would not imply recognition of the Kabul government. He was willing to accept a Pakistani disclaimer to that effect. When I conveyed this to Foreign Minister Yaqub-Khan of Pakistan, he remained unconvinced.

As the deadlock on the timetable for the withdrawal of Soviet troops persisted through two more negotiating sessions in Geneva, I came to realize that the critical negotiations were now between the United States and the Soviet Union. Until they reached agreement on the troop question, Geneva was only a sideshow. I therefore spoke directly to American and Soviet representatives in an effort to promote progress. I stressed to the American Deputy Secretary of State, John Whitehead, the need for both countries to make basic decisions regarding the situation in Afghanistan. Otherwise, no settlement could be reached. He indicated that nothing new had resulted from discussions between Secretary of State Shultz and Foreign Minister Shevardnadze. In my own discussion with Shevardnadze, I requested Soviet help in providing the impetus for some movement. The foreign minister noted his government's withdrawal of several divisions and called for a signal from Pakistan to demonstrate its willingness to cease interfering in Afghanistan. I communicated the Soviet request to Foreign Minister Yaqub-Khan.

Having received private assurances of flexibility from the Pakistani foreign minister, I proceeded to meet with the representatives of Afghanistan and the Soviet Union to prepare the way for yet another trip by my Personal Representative to the region. Afghan Foreign Minister Dost refused to indicate any Afghan flexibility, commenting instead on his government's efforts toward national reconciliation and the need to address the question of Iranian intervention in support of the fundamentalist resistance faction. I then met with Soviet Deputy Foreign Minister Vladimir Petrovsky, who said that his Government's position was to secure a settlement of the situation in Afghanistan as rapidly as possible. Shortly thereafter agreement was reached on a mechanism of implementation, which was significant because it reflected Soviet acceptance of a UN military Observer Force to monitor the withdrawal of Soviet troops.

THE ISSUE OF NATIONAL RECONCILIATION EMERGES

As the number of outstanding issues associated with the four points was gradually reduced over the years, the unspoken "fifth item" of national reconciliation, sometimes referred to as self-determination, began to loom larger. Although discussion of this issue dated back to the beginning of the negotiations, it did not assume much significance in the agenda until 1986, when the Babrak government was ousted and Najibullah became Afghan President.

In January 1987 the Najibullah government issued a "Declaration on National Reconciliation" announcing a cease-fire effective January 15 and a "Declaration on the General Amnesty." The Pakistanis (and the Afghan refugees) did not find these moves convincing. For them, the Najibullah government was as unacceptable as its predecessor had been.

National reconciliation was obviously an essential element in restoring peace to Afghanistan. I felt, however, that this was very much a domestic question, one in which the United Nations should not be involved. Despite my reservations, the subject was introduced into the Geneva process. It became known as "track two." Differences on the timetable for Soviet withdrawal were narrowed significantly, but now withdrawal became linked with the question of national reconciliation. Meanwhile, there was an unhelpful increase in tension between Afghanistan and Pakistan. Afghanistan accused Pakistan of hindering the voluntary return of refugees and called upon me to request an investigation by UNHCR and later to use my good offices to arrange, on a bilateral basis, a visit by an Afghani delegation to the refugees in Pakistan.[1] Pakistan denied those allegations and charged Afghanistan with bombing Pakistani territory, an accusation that Afghanistan rejected.

Another round of discussions in September 1987 further narrowed differences on the timetable for the Soviet pullout, but the linkage persisted between the timetable for withdrawal and national reconciliation. President Gorbachev had previously argued that the withdrawal of troops would not resolve the situation in Afghanistan, particularly given the attitude of the United States. However, in a meeting in Moscow on December 15, 1987, Soviet Foreign Minister Shevardnadze informed Diego Cordovez that the timetable for Soviet withdrawal could be reduced to 12 months. With this concession, Shevardnadze said, the Soviet side hoped that the next round of negotiations in Geneva would be the last. Although it would be a protracted session, this hope became a reality.

THE GENEVA ACCORDS

The final talks were scheduled to begin in March 1988. On February 8 the Kabul government announced that if the Geneva agreements were signed by March 15, the withdrawal of Soviet troops would commence on May 15 and be completed within 10 months.[2] Kabul and Moscow also indicated their acceptance of the front-loading of the withdrawal—more troops would be withdrawn in the first phase of the timetable than in the latter half. New complications emerged, however, and the March 15 deadline passed with no agreement. The United States was now insisting on the termination of Soviet military assistance to the Kabul government before the agreement could take effect. Pakistan, for its part, continued to insist on the establishment of an interim government in Afghanistan.[3]

Both of these issues were papered over temporarily; and with agreement finally reached on a nine-month timetable for the withdrawal of Soviet troops, the Geneva Accords were opened for signature in my presence on April 8, 1988. Eight years of effort by the United Nations and separately by the United States and the Soviet Union to achieve a political settlement of the situation of Afghanistan had seemingly reached a successful conclusion. Unfortunately, the success was to prove illusory for the Afghan people.

The Geneva Accords consisted of bilateral agreements between Afghanistan and Pakistan covering the four points that we had defined in 1981 as essential for a settlement: (1) nonintervention; (2) the voluntary return of refugees; (3) international guarantees (by the United States and the Soviet Union); and (4) the withdrawal of foreign troops. The United States would provide a memorandum of understanding on the arrangements for monitoring the withdrawal of the Soviet forces. The two crucial issues of national reconciliation and the supply of arms to the combatants remained unresolved. The foreign ministers of all the parties were present in Geneva for the signing ceremony: George Shultz for the United States, Edouard Shevardnadze for the Soviet Union, Zain Nourani, Minister of State for Foreign Affairs for Pakistan and Abdul Wakil for Afghanistan. The four foreign ministers warmly praised Diego Cordovez and me on the achievement of the accords. In a meeting between Secretary Shultz and his large delegation and the UN representatives, the secretary of state commented at length on the arms issue. He stressed quite strongly that, in the American understanding, it was the right of the United States to continue supplying arms "to those whom they considered to be the legitimate representatives of the Afghan people." The United States would have preferred to negotiate an agreement with the Soviet Union on symmetry of supply based on mutual restraint, but this had been rejected. If the Soviets exercised restraint, "the U.S. was prepared to act in a similar fashion."

In the last stage of negotiations an understanding had been reached at the insistence of Pakistan that the Personal Representative of the Secretary General would assist "in a personal capacity" in the national reconciliation process, which meant in the formation of an interim government in Kabul representative of the various resistance factions. In this regard I commented to Secretary Shultz that it was against the philosophy of the United Nations to become involved in the internal affairs of member countries. ordovez would be my representative for monitoring implementation of the Geneva Accords. I thought it might be difficult for him to perform this function and also serve as go-between or mediator for the internal parties. The secretary responded that he too wondered how it could work. Nonetheless, he said, all the pieces fitted together—a sense of an emerging legitimate government, the return of refugees and restraint in arms supplies. He thought it important that ways be found for Cordovez to continue what he had set out to do.

I considered the fact that an arms cutoff was not included in the Geneva Accords to be a major weakness. How could national reconciliation be brought about when the various factions were continuing to receive arms to carry on their search for victory? The provision of arms to the combatants, even on a basis of symmetry, was hardly compatible with peace. But this subject was never within the control or influence of the United Nations during the negotiations.

Iran was not represented at Geneva and, of all the interested countries, was the only one to assess the Geneva Accords negatively. Tehran complained that the Accords were the work of the two superpowers and were intended to realize their objectives against the interests of the Muslim people. The Acting Permanent Representative of Iran addressed a letter to me stating that "exclusion of Mujahideen, refugees and Muslim people of Afghanistan from a process of determination of the destiny of Afghanistan, has not been acceptable to the Islamic Republic of Iran."[4]

PURSUING A COMPREHENSIVE SETTLEMENT

After Geneva, pursuit of a comprehensive Afghan settlement still involved three interrelated activities:

- Monitoring by the United Nations of the observance of the Geneva Accords by the parties, particularly the withdrawal of Soviet troops and Pakistani compliance with the agreement on noninterference, which was understood to mean prevention of the movement of resistance fighters across its border. Noninterference, to which both the United States and the Soviet Union also were pledged, was an especially difficult problem, given the indications that the United States would continue to supply arms to the resistance and the Soviet Union to the Kabul regime. In my view this constituted intervention in the domestic situation.
- Promotion of an internal political settlement based on national reconciliation. The United Nations, in the person of the Personal Representative, was given a vaguely defined responsibility for this function.
- Repatriation of refugees and the provision of humanitarian assistance to the Afghan people. This responsibility was given to UNHCR, which had been remarkably successful in caring for a historically unprecedented number of refugees over the previous eight years.

Peacekeeping operations are normally authorized by the Security Council. However, in this case a resolution acceptable to all the parties was clearly not attainable. The Soviets would wish to emphasize the monitoring of compliance with the agreements on noninterference. The Americans and the Pakistanis would, on the contrary, want the operation to focus exclusively on monitoring the Soviet withdrawal. The United Nations Good Offices Mission in Afghanistan and Pakistan (UNGOMAP) was therefore established on the basis of an exchange of letters between the president of the Security Council and me.[5] My letter, which was cleared in advance by all the parties, is a notable example of diplomatic circumlocution. As was required by the circumstances, it states that the parties "have requested the Secretary-General to provide assistance for the purpose of investigating any possible violations of the instruments that comprise the settlement." For this purpose, I wrote, I intended to dispatch 50 military officers "and set them up, as envisaged in the agreements, as inspection teams in Afghanistan and Pakistan." The letter contains no direct reference to the withdrawal of Soviet troops. This procedure represented a clear expansion of the powers of the Secretary-General. Recognizing this, the Security Council requested that it not be considered a precedent for the future.

In the months following the deployment of UNGOMAP, the Soviet Union and Afghanistan complained bitterly of Pakistani violations of the Geneva Accords. Afghanistan alleged 400 instances of border violations between May 16 and June 30 and also charged Pakistan with hindering UNGOMAP operations. The Soviet Union resented the establishment of UNGOMAP posts along its border with Afghanistan to monitor the withdrawal of Soviet troops when no posts were established along the Afghan-Pakistan border to monitor Mujahideen infiltration. Reports from UNGOMAP made clear that, while exaggerated, Afghan and Soviet complaints had substance. However, UNGOMAP was responsible for investigating reports of violations, not preventing them. To monitor effectively the withdrawal of an entire Soviet army and the very porous border between Pakistan and Afghanistan would have required thousands of peacekeeping troops; UNGOMAP consisted of 50 military observers.

Fortunately, these developments did not lead the Soviet Union to suspend its withdrawal. By August 15, 1988, the Soviet Union had withdrawn half of its forces from Afghanistan. Fighting between the Mujahideen and the forces of the Soviet Union and the Kabul government intensified as Soviet troops thinned out. The Soviet Union charged that Pakistani violations continued, and Soviet Deputy Foreign Minister Petrovsky warned me about resultant negative consequences for peacekeeping operations in general and the overall credibility of the United Nations. By November 1988 the Soviet Union was suggesting that Pakistan's persistent violations of the Geneva Accords might force it to reconsider its plans for withdrawal. At this time we were able to improve UNGOMAP's coverage.

At the end of October, inspection posts were finally established along the Afghan-Pakistani border; they had been delayed by the Pakistani contention that they could not guarantee the safety of the monitors in tribal areas.

As the February 15, 1989, deadline for the completion of the Soviet withdrawal approached, the future of UNGOMAP became increasingly uncertain. I maintained that UNGOMAP had a responsibility to monitor compliance with *all* aspects of the Geneva Accords, not just the withdrawal of Soviet troops. The Soviet Union held a similar position, insisting that UNGOMAP's mandate be renewed and that there be no reduction in the number of personnel after the withdrawal was complete. The United States was more reserved in its support for the operation. Furthermore, as the fighting intensified and Kabul came under Mujahideen attack, the troop-contributing countries showed growing concern about the safety of their personnel.

Diego Cordovez urged that the strength of UNGOMAP be maintained (it had already declined from 50 to 39 as a result of a rotation of personnel); at a troop contributors' meeting on April 5, 1989, I personally appealed to troop-contributing countries to continue supporting UNGOMAP. However, given the obvious weakening in support for the operation, I stated that the situation would be reviewed within the next 60 days. UNGOMAP's mandate was reviewed by the Security Council for the last time in January 1990. When the mandate expired in the spring I was able to gain the agreement of the Geneva signatories to deploy five military observers each in Kabul and Islamabad to serve as military advisors to Benon Sevan, a senior member of the Secretariat whom I had appointed to succeed Diego Cordovez and designated as my Representative on the Implementation of the Geneva Agreements. Through the activities of Sevan, who is an energetic and politically perceptive officer of Armenian Cypriot origin, and of the small offices that he headed in Kabul, Islamabad and Peshawar, a UN presence was maintained in the area. The operation was renamed the Office of the Secretary General in Afghanistan and Pakistan (OSGAP), with Sevan serving also as my Personal Representative in Afghanistan and Pakistan.

The Soviet Union and the Kabul government were extremely unhappy with the disbandment of UNGOMAP. I agree that its mandate to monitor compliance with the Geneva Accords was not completed. As the situation developed in Afghanistan, however, its task became impossible. What had been a resistance fight against the Soviet invaders had now become a civil war between the Kabul regime and the various Mujahideen factions. To investigate reports of thousands of violations of the Geneva Accords under these circumstances could have had little, if any, significance. As long as it lasted, UNGOMAP served as a valuable symbol of the commitment of the parties to the implementation of the Accords. Given its size and mandate, its operational effectiveness was limited from the beginning.

TRACK TWO: RESOLVING CONFLICT WITHIN AFGHANISTAN

With the signing of the Geneva Accords, the search for a political settlement in Afghanistan, or "track two" as it had come to be known, came to the forefront, since the Kabul regime was widely expected to collapse once the Soviet troops departed. As has been noted, Pakistan strongly urged that Diego Cordovez be given the task of promoting national reconciliation, which was a euphemism for the formation of a broad-based government in Afghanistan that in the Pakistani view should be made up of representatives of the various Mujahideen factions. Given the divisions within the resistance groups and the existence of a weak but determined regime in Kabul, UN involvement represented a considerable risk to the reputation of the Organization. This was a price that had to be paid to gain Pakistan's agreement to the Geneva Accords. The statement that Diego Cordovez made on the occasion of the signature of the Geneva Accords was carefully drafted to provide a defensible basis for the UN role.[6] It read in part as follows:

> Throughout the negotiations, it has been consistently recognized that the objective of a comprehensive settlement implies the broadest support and immediate participation of all segments of the Afghan people and that this can best be ensured by a broad-based Afghan government. It was equally recognized that any questions relating to the government in Afghanistan are matters within the exclusive jurisdiction of Afghanistan and can only be decided by the Afghan people themselves. The hope was therefore expressed that all elements of the Afghan nation, living inside and outside Afghanistan, would respond to this historic opportunity. At this crucial stage, all concerned will, therefore, promote the endeavors of the Afghan people to work out arrangements for a broad-based government and will support and facilitate that process.

This text served as a mandate, granted by all of the Geneva signatories, for Cordovez to pursue national reconciliation in a *personal* capacity. As my Representative, his mandate would be restricted to the implementation of the Geneva Accords. Initially "track two" was not strictly speaking a UN undertaking. This fine legal distinction quickly lost whatever significance it might have had since in November 1988, the General Assembly adopted Resolution 43/20, which gave me a direct mandate to pursue a "track two" solution. The operative paragraph requested that the Secretary-General and his Personal Representative "encourage and facilitate the early realization of a comprehensive political settlement in Afghanistan." The resolution was supported by both the Soviet Union and Afghanistan. I now had a clear responsibility to assist the Afghan parties in their search for a solution to their conflict.

I undertook consultations with the parties immediately after the resolution was passed. On November 7, I met with the Prime Minister of Afghanistan, Dr. Mohammed Sharq, and on November 10, 1988, I talked with Professor Burhanuddin Rabbani, then chairman of the Islamic Unity of the Afghan Mujahideen. The difficulties of the task before me became immediately apparent during my meeting with Professor Rabbani. He first criticized the Geneva Accords for their failure to bring peace to his people and the United Nations for not consulting with the Mujahideen during the negotiating process. He suggested that Cordovez was biased against the Mujahideen and had misrepresented my position. I explained to Professor Rabbani that as an intergovernmental organization, the United Nations could not meet officially with the Mujahideen earlier and that it was the signature of the Accords themselves that allowed this meeting to occur. The professor's attitude was one of complete confidence in the ability of the Mujahideen to impose a military solution after the Soviet withdrawal was complete. The conversation offered little prospect for the achievement of a diplomatic solution in the near future.

Anticipating victory over the Kabul government, the Mujahideen had taken several steps toward the formation of a future Afghan government. They had proposed the convening of a *shura,* or consultative council, which would enable the Afghan people to participate in the formation of a new government. More important, they had agreed to enter into direct talks with the Soviet Union, represented by Ambassador Yuri Vorontsov. New proposals were also forthcoming from the Soviet Union and Afghanistan. On November 20, 1988, the Soviet Union and India issued a joint statement calling for the United Nations to convene an international conference on Afghanistan. I also received a letter from Afghan President Najibullah with the same request. Pakistan rejected the proposal as a propaganda ploy and an attempt by those in Kabul to present themselves as the legitimate government of Afghanistan.

When President Gorbachev came to United Nations Headquarters to deliver a speech to the General Assembly on December 7, 1988, he told me he was sure that once the Soviet troops left Afghanistan, bloodshed would ensue. According to his information neither the government nor the Mujahideen were strong enough to triumph. Moscow's objective, he said, was an independent and neutral Afghanistan. Gorbachev compared the United States' position on Nicaragua, where Washington was in favor of elections in which the Sandinista government would participate, to its position on Afghanistan, where Washington was insisting that the Najibullah government be dissolved before elections were held. Gorbachev characterized this as a double standard. Interestingly, Jim Baker, during a luncheon conversation at the White House six months later, on June 4, 1990, commented that the Soviets were always raising what they called the Nicaraguan model. The U.S. reply was that if all the parties involved in

Afghanistan, including the Mujahideen, could agree to elections, as the Contras, the Sandinistas and the civilian opposition had done, this would be quite acceptable. The Secretary elaborated by pointing out that Najibullah was installed in power by foreign intervention which was different "from the Sandinista take-over from Somoza." This was the only positive comment on the Sandinistas I ever heard from Jim Baker or other members of the Bush administration.

In his speech before the General Assembly, in addition to the convening of an international conference on Afghanistan, President Gorbachev proposed a cease-fire effective January 1, 1989, a halt to arms supplies to the belligerents effective that same date ("negative symmetry") and the deployment of UN peacekeeping forces in Kabul and other "strategic centers."[7] President Gorbachev's proposals, including the cease-fire, received a negative reaction from the other interested parties, with the exception, of course, of Afghanistan. The United States, supported by Pakistan and the Mujahideen, insisted that a cease-fire *follow* the formation of a broad-based government. Meanwhile it became increasingly clear from Cordovez's contacts with the Mujahideen groups that no single interlocutor could speak authoritatively for *all* of the Mujahideen.

Completion of the Soviet withdrawal on February 15, 1984 was greeted with general relief, but it did nothing to bring agreement on a government of national reconciliation or to halt the fighting between the Mujahideen and the Kabul regime. The much-anticipated *shura* was convened by the Mujahideen but the results were anticlimactic. A declaration was issued establishing the "Afghan Interim Government" (AIG) but the "government" was patently devoid of reality. It did nothing to unify the Mujahideen.

In March the Soviets launched another initiative, this time calling for the formation of a group of "experts" consisting of representatives from the United States, the Soviet Union, Pakistan, Iran, the Kabul government and the Mujahideen.[8] This group would meet to consider various approaches to a comprehensive settlement of the conflict. This proposal was also rejected because the Mujahideen were not prepared to negotiate directly with representatives of the Kabul government. From contacts we had with the Americans, including a meeting I had with Secretary of State James Baker, it was clear that the United States continued to believe that the Mujahideen would eventually win a military victory. They were not prepared to accommodate the Soviets by encouraging the formation of a new government that would include representatives of the Najibullah regime.

But the Najibullah regime did not fall, as it had been expected to do. The inability of the Mujahideen to take Jalalabad in the summer of 1989 raised questions as to the likelihood of their military victory. There was a change, too, in Pakistan where Benazir Bhutto became Prime Minister. When I met with her in Paris on June 9, she emphasized her government's desire for a political solution, a solution that she believed was possible if the Soviet Union dropped its insistence that the Kabul government remain in power. I explained to her that I was trying to identify the points on which the different Afghan parties were in agreement in the hope that such agreement might lead to an intra-Afghan dialogue. This dialogue, which would begin with the Mujahideen and then be broadened to include other Afghans, might then serve as the basis for the formation of a broad-based government. Prime Minister Bhutto did not appear to be very familiar with the problem. She seemed responsive to my suggestions, however, and I left the meeting with the impression that Pakistan would no longer hold out for a military victory by the Mujahideen. I shared the evaluation of my meeting with Prime Minister Bhutto with Edouard Shevardnadze during a conversation in Paris on July 29, 1989. The Soviet foreign minister said that he had received similar indications from other sources, but he wondered how firmly Bhutto controlled the Pakistan military. He mentioned that the Soviet Union had sought to cultivate contact with Iran on the Afghan conflict.

In August we received information that both the United States and Pakistan would be reevaluating the desirability of a military solution in Afghanistan. The Soviet Union, meanwhile, had decided not to resupply the Sandinista government in Nicaragua with arms, and it appeared possible that the United States and the Soviet Union were moving toward mutual restraint in the level of military assistance they were providing to the Afghan belligerents. Under these seemingly propitious circumstances, I called for a gathering of all Afghan opposition groups (an intra-Afghan dialogue) for the purpose of assembling a "structured Afghan delegation" that the guarantors and the neighboring countries would recognize as the authorized representative of the Afghan opposition. On September 19, I outlined the initiative at a press conference; I then followed this up with broad and intensive consultations, including meetings with the President and the foreign minister of Afghanistan, the Prime Minister of Pakistan, the deputy foreign minister of the Soviet Union and representatives of the Afghan opposition groups. Throughout the fall of 1989, Benon Sevan, who by now had succeeded Diego Cordovez, and Giandomenico Picco briefed various governments on my proposal. The proposal—unfortunately, I still believe—encountered objections from both sides. The Americans and the Pakistanis feared that recognition of the structured Afghan delegation as "the opposition" might imply acceptance of the Kabul authorities as the legitimate government of Afghanistan. They were also concerned that the creation of such a delegation might significantly diminish the legitimacy of the Afghan Interim Government that had been proclaimed by the *shura*. The Soviet Union and Afghanistan feared that a structured Afghan delegation would unify the opposition, giving them a political advantage over the Kabul representatives at the negotiating table and possibly also on the battlefield. The Soviets accordingly stuck to the idea of an international conference.

Given the apparent stalemate on a political solution and the continuing fighting in Afghanistan, I decided to appeal directly to Presidents Bush and Gorbachev. On November 27, 1989, prior to their summit in Malta, I wrote to both to call their attention to the tragic situation in Afghanistan and to my proposals for an intra-Afghan dialogue. In their replies, both men expressed the view that a political solution was needed. This was heartening insofar as it went. But neither supported my specific proposal, and President Gorbachev continued to advocate the idea of an international conference. At the beginning of 1990 I went to Moscow for further discussions with President Gorbachev and Foreign Minister Shevardnadze. In talking with the foreign minister, I emphasized the need for international consensus and specifically urged in this context that the Soviet Union reach agreement with the United States on halting arms deliveries to the belligerents. Shevardnadze referred to the "positive changes" in the positions of the United States and Pakistan that resulted from their realization that the Najibullah government was politically viable. But, beyond that, he only reiterated the Soviet proposal for a UN-sponsored international conference. President Gorbachev also called attention to the new attitude of the Americans and the Pakistanis and expressed the hope that a compromise could be achieved. He believed that the United Nations was certain to have a role in the settlement that eventually would be worked out. Most interesting, however, was his reference to President Najibullah's willingness to step down at the end of the process. Despite the lack of any positive response to my proposals, this suggested some flexibility on one of the most contentious issues in the negotiations.

I had the opportunity to discuss Afghanistan with Secretary of State Baker in Windhoek in March of 1990, on the occasion of the Namibian independence ceremonies. I referred to my impression that the Soviet Union no longer insisted that Najibullah retain power at the end of the political process. The secretary responded that this still left the question of how and when Najibullah would leave. In June, while on an official visit to Washington, I had a further opportunity to discuss Afghanistan with both President Bush and Secretary Baker. The President told me that his talks on the subject with Mikhail Gorbachev during their recent summit meeting had been, on the whole, quite positive. Each side recognized the interests of the other. Still, he and President Gorbachev shared a sense of frustration at not being able to reach complete agreement. Secretary of State Baker emphasized that the only remaining outstanding issue was whether President Najibullah would resign prior to or after an election. Both men then went on to a general discussion of how elections should be conducted, whether through a *shura* or through another mechanism, and the relationships among Pakistan, Saudi Arabia and Iran and the different Mujahideen groups.

Given the apparently expanding area of agreement between the United States and the Soviet Union, I circulated an informal paper on the necessary elements of an international consensus in a letter to all of the parties in July 1990. My staff had been working on a draft of this paper for several months. Benon Sevan and Giandomenico Picco had discussed it in Moscow, and the Soviets had voiced no major objections. I listed the following elements to bring an end to the fighting: a transition period and acceptable transitional arrangements leading to the establishment of a broad-based government; a cease-fire; a halt to arms supplies to the belligerents (negative symmetry); and the provision of assistance by the United Nations during the transition period and the electoral process.

I sent the paper to the foreign ministers of Afghanistan, Iran, Pakistan and the Soviet Union and to the U.S. secretary of state. The Soviet response was positive. The only reservations expressed were that it be clear that a transition not be interpreted as a transfer of power and that elections should be held in Afghanistan. Sevan and Picco traveled to Tehran in August. Their conversations with Foreign Minister Velayati and his staff suggested that the Iranians also had a favorable reaction to the paper, although they sought some clarification on the transition and elections. The United States found the paper generally acceptable and hoped that the United Nations would assist the Afghans in the formulation of arrangements regarding the transitional authority and elections.[9] By the end of the summer, the only party not to have expressed a formal position on my initiative was Pakistan.

When I met President Najibullah during the first week of September 1990, at a Non-Aligned Summit in Belgrade, he specifically accepted the need for a transition period and the holding of elections and proposed that the United Nations supervise these stages of the process. He described at some length the steps that had been taken to democratize political life in Afghanistan. He asserted that the privileged position of one party had been removed, political pluralism accepted and free market and free enterprise introduced. I called attention to the growing rapprochement between the United States and the Soviet Union and voiced the hope that the forthcoming summit between Presidents Bush and Gorbachev would produce an agreement that would accelerate the pace of developments. We shared the belief that positive changes in the positions of several of the parties gave promise of a settlement in the near future.

In the meetings I had with him, Najibullah did not conform with the image normally associated with the secret police chief in a Communist state. Tall, well built and soft-spoken, he had a rather warm and pleasant personality. Although there was no doubt that in the past he was associated with very cruel acts, for which he was widely hated by many of his countrymen, in my dealings with him he always sought to be obliging and gave evidence of a sharp understanding of the complex political forces at play in Afghanistan, forces he was adept in manipulating. During our meeting in Belgrade, I requested his assistance in gaining the release of a French national associated with the Handicap International Organization who had been taken prisoner in Afghanistan. Eventually, albeit only after lengthy negotiations with Benon Sevan, Najibullah saw to it that the man was freed.

In a meeting at the end of September 1990, more than two months after the dispatch of my letter, Foreign Minister Yaqub-Khan was still unable to provide me with Pakistan's position. To a certain extent, this could be attributed to the domestic political situation in Pakistan, which was in a state of flux, and to the Gulf crisis. Nevertheless, I warned the Foreign Minister that Pakistan risked being seen as the sole obstacle to an Afghan settlement.

For the remainder of 1990, the crisis in the Gulf monopolized world attention. In the spring of 1991, however, with Kuwait freed, I sought to revive efforts to bring peace to Afghanistan. With the end of my term as Secretary-General drawing near, I felt a deep sense of responsibility to the Afghan people and to my successor to try at least to put the Afghan tragedy on a course toward resolution. The fighting on the ground continued to intensify. In April the Mujahideen launched an offensive to capture the city of Khost, and efforts of the Kabul government to defend the city using Scud missiles produced tremendous civilian casualties. Many refugees fled the area immediately surrounding the city. At this point the Permanent Representative of Pakistan advised me that, although his government supported the initiative I had taken with my letter, Pakistan felt that the points on the supply of arms and the formation of an interim government should be avoided. Even though he assured me that, whatever the outcome in Khost, Pakistan no longer favored a military solution to the situation, this represented a significant hardening of previous Pakistani positions.

After the fall of Khost to the Mujahideen, neither Kabul nor the Mujahideen would consider a cessation in hostilities. I saw President Bush in Washington in early May of 1991 and informed him that I was attempting to build support among the parties for a statement on my part calling for a cutoff in all arms deliveries and a cease-fire. Benon Sevan undertook similar consultations with the Afghan Government, the Soviet Union, Iran, Saudi Arabia, with the U.S. Ambassador to Pakistan, Robert Oakley, the former Afghan king, Zahir Skak and the Mujahideen. On May 21, I issued the proposed statement that disclosed publicly for the first time the elements of the international consensus proposed to the parties in my letter of July 11, 1990. The positive reaction to the statement of all of the governments addressed as well as some of the Mujahideen factions strengthened my resolve to pursue a solution during the remaining months of my term.

Consultations with ambassadors from Iran, the United States, the Soviet Union, Saudi Arabia and Pakistan during June confirmed their support for my approach. The Pakistani position remained that President Najibullah had to be removed, but they indicated a renewed willingness to consider negative symmetry on arms deliveries. During a meeting in August, Sevan explained to President Najibullah that the opposition continued to reject any forum in which he would be present at the negotiating table. After an extended discussion, Najibullah indicated that he would not demand to participate personally in the intra-Afghan dialogue. He suggested that a number of options were available for his resignation after the gathering had met. This appeared to remove the primary obstacle to the convening of an intra-Afghan gathering.

I went to Tehran in September hopeful that such a dialogue might be close at hand. Iranian officials agreed that current international conditions were particularly favorable for a settlement. In Tehran, I also met with Mujahideen leaders, emphasizing the positive atmosphere and Najibullah's willingness to be excluded from the intra-Afghan dialogue. The Mujahideen leaders, in turn, indicated their willingness to participate in the gathering. That same evening I spoke with President Ghulam Ishaq Khan of Pakistan. He and I shared the view that the search for an Afghan settlement should be accelerated given the uncertainty in the Soviet Union, where an attempted coup against President Gorbachev had taken place, and President Najibullah's recent signals of flexibility. We discussed the various elements in a settlement and also dealt with formulating a list of participants in an intra-Afghan dialogue.

On September 13, 1991, the Soviet Union and the United States reached agreement on the cessation of arms shipments as of January 1, 1992. Buoyed by this latest development, I pursued my consultations with the parties, emphasizing to all the readiness of the Mujahideen to move forward with an intra-Afghan dialogue that would lead to the establishment of a transitional government to replace the administration of President Najibullah.

On September 23, President Bush, accompanied by Secretary Baker and General Scowcroft, came to the United Nations to address the General Assembly. There was an opportunity for a *tour d'horizon* of the international situation in which Afghanistan figured prominently. I said that I was generally encouraged about the situation in light of the conversations I had had the previous week. I had particularly urged the President of Pakistan to follow the good example of the United States and the Soviet Union in embargoing arms shipments to the combatants. I informed President Bush that I intended to invite all the Afghan factions to a meeting in Geneva in the hope that they could agree on a transitional administration. Jim Baker, clearly skeptical, asked when I expected the conference to be held. I replied, "Hopefully by the end of October." Secretary Baker stated that I had the strong support of both the U.S. and Soviet governments. I turned to President Bush and asked that he persuade Pakistan to give similar support. Again Jim Baker replied, saying that the Pakistanis "were not persuaded. . . . We have tried with them." He was confident that Saudi Arabia, on the other hand, would come along.

THE END OF THE ROAD

My decade-long effort to facilitate a solution to the situation in Afghanistan came to a conclusion in October 1991. I began my final month of work on this problem by meeting with the Pakistani Minister of State for Foreign Affairs, Mr. Mohammad Saddique Khan Kanju. Our conversation, although positive, confirmed an earlier impression that I had gained from my meeting in Tehran with the Pakistani President, that Pakistan was still not fully satisfied with my proposals. I emphasized the need to take advantage of the momentum that was building and indicated my readiness to convene, perhaps in Geneva, the gathering of Afghans that would lead to a transition period and then a transitional government. I needed the support of the interested countries and wished to hold a "tea party" for their Permanent Representatives—as I had suggested earlier in the summer—during which a consensus could finally be developed. Mr. Kanju merely noted the need for clarification of the transitional mechanism and the divisions among the Mujahideen.

The following day I received a delegation of Mujahideen and informed them of the current state of affairs. I appealed to them to exercise restraint and further clarified some aspects of the transitional mechanism, in particular the need to transfer all power to this mechanism. I emphasized my willingness to convene a gathering of Afghans and reiterated my assurance that President Najibullah would not attend. Benon Sevan then discussed with the delegation their views on details of the proposed gathering. Some of the Mujahideen groups, it seemed, were ready to participate in an intra-Afghan dialogue, but not all. On October 18, I finally welcomed the ambassadors of Pakistan, Saudi Arabia, the United States and the Soviet Union to the long-planned "tea party" on Afghanistan. Each expressed support for my efforts. Soviet Ambassador Vorontsov and U.S. Ambassador Alex Watson described how their U.S.-Soviet agreement on discontinuing arms deliveries would be implemented. I took this opportunity to appeal to all of the parties to comply with this agreement. I also expressed the hope that a gathering of Afghans could be held before the end of November. This would ensure that by the time my successor had assumed office in January 1992, the reconciliation process would be moving in the right direction.

Perhaps the emerging consensus on steps to be taken toward a political solution and the imminence of a weapons cutoff spurred the Mujahideen to intensify their military campaign to take Kabul and eliminate the Najibullah regime. That, in any event, is what happened. During the last months of 1991 and in early 1992 (after the end of my tenure), Najibullah continued to support a political settlement and the formation of a nonpartisan interim government. After extensive consultations with Benon Sevan, he issued a formal statement on March 18, 1992, expressing his full support for the proposed Afghan gathering in which he would not insist on participating. He declared further that once an understanding was reached "through the United Nations process" for the establishment of an interim government in Kabul, all powers and all executive authority would be transferred to it on the first day of the transition period. The president's statement was largely drafted by Benon Sevan.

This statement, combined with the Mujahideen's military advances, intensified pressure for the immediate formation of an interim government. The date was set for April 15. New alliances were formed within the opposition that included some members of the Kabul regime. The time had obviously passed for the proposed intra-Afghan gathering. Representatives of the opposition groups met on the deadline date in Islamabad in the residence of Pakistan's Prime Minister to agree on the makeup of the interim government. Benon Sevan was waiting at the Prime Minister's residence to fly the members of the new government to Kabul in a UN plane. But the opposition groups were not able to reach agreement. Seven flew back to Kabul only to be surrounded by the militia of Rashid Dostun, a former close ally of Najibullah's, who, with other former associates of the President, including the foreign minister, Abdul Wakil, had taken possession of the airport.

The Mujahideen groups were never able to form a united force or agree on a single policy. Looking back, I have concluded that, despite their reassuring words to the contrary, the only thing on which the Mujahideen factions were in agreement was the desirability of eliminating the Kabul regime by force. I do not believe Pakistan ever discouraged them from pursuing this objective. Had the Americans agreed to cut off the arms flow to the Mujahideen earlier, a political solution might have been possible, but this is by no means certain, since very large amounts of arms were already available. The major American mistake was to believe that the Mujahideen factions, once they were successful in overthrowing the Kabul regime, would be able to agree together, as joint victors, on a government in which they would be united. As it turned out, victory eliminated the single objective that united them.

As for Najibullah, he had sent his wife and family out of Afghanistan on Sevan's advice a few days prior to the collapse of his regime. After midnight on April 15, he tried to reach the airport but was blocked by hostile militia. He then took what eventually proved to be the fatal course of seeking refuge in the UN office in Kabul. Benon Sevan, who was at the airport surrounded by Dostum's militia, concluded that he had no choice but to grant him refuge as the President (still) of a UN Member State. Najibullah remained in the UN office until September 29, 1996, when the Taliban insurgent forces took over Kabul, dragged the former president from his UN sanctuary and hanged him a few blocks away. While far distant by then from events in Afghanistan, I felt shock and despair when I heard of this further tragic episode in the sad history of Afghanistan.

HUMANITARIAN ASSISTANCE

By 1982, 6.3 million people fled from Afghanistan to Pakistan and Iran—almost one-third of Afghanistan's population of 20 million. The High Commissioner for Refugees had the responsibility for providing assistance and protection to these millions of refugees. It was an enormous and successful operation that involved not only the provision of relief assistance but also extensive negotiations with the two governments to ensure that the status of the refugees was adequately protected. If the High Commissioner, Prince Sadrddin Aga Kahn, had been willing to serve as a channel for political consultations with the refugees during the course of the Geneva negotiations, our negotiating problems would have been eased. As I mentioned earlier, he staunchly refused to do this on the ground that political involvement would jeopardize accomplishment of his primary humanitarian task. This is the long-established position of UNHCR, and I believe it is fully justified. It was possible in other ways to be cognizant and take account of the refugees' views, albeit never to their full satisfaction.

When the Soviet withdrawal became imminent, accompanied as it was by the wide expectation of the collapse of the Kabul government, the possibility of large-scale repatriation arose. However, the devastation wrought by almost nine years of war meant that the country could not sustain such a massive influx of people. At the signing of the Geneva Accords, I promised the Afghan people that the international community was ready to assist them with the massive task of reconstruction that lay ahead. Michael Armacost, an under-secretary of state in the U.S. Department of State, repeatedly urged me to make the provision of humanitarian assistance a personal priority and to consider the appointment of a special coordinator for UN programs. Perhaps most important, he stated that financial support for the effort would be forthcoming from the international community. Secretary of State Shultz reiterated these assurances of U.S. cooperation and financial support during our conversation in Geneva at the signing ceremony of the Geneva Accords.

I shared the American assessment that an overall coordinator was needed. I asked Prince Sadruddin to take on the further task, which he did with his customary energy and dedication. He became responsible for the coordination of all assistance programs being conducted in Afghanistan by the UN system. Less than three weeks after his appointment, Prince Sadruddin led a high-level delegation of UN officials on a mission to the region in order to survey the needs of the population. They met with the parties involved and secured their understanding on the nonpolitical nature of the assistance to be provided. Based on the results of this mission, we launched an appeal for $1.16 billion for the first 18 months of operations.[10] Half was to be used to meet the immediate needs of the refugees and half was allocated to the rehabilitation of Afghan territory to foster conditions that would promote and sustain returnees. It was clear that the distribution of assistance would have to be handled extremely carefully. The provision of aid could not be seen either as strengthening the ability of the Kabul government to maintain its control within Afghanistan or of sustaining the Mujahideen. I assured the prospective donors as well as the Permanent Representative of Pakistan that the aid would be completely nonpolitical.

The initial response to my appeal was disappointing. On the day prior to the donors' meeting, the coordinator had gone to Washington only to learn that U.S. budgetary difficulties precluded the commitment of a specific contribution at that time. Two weeks after our meeting with donors, contributions totaled only $33 million. Prince Sadruddin spent the rest of June and most of July meeting with potential donors to generate additional contributions. By August total contributions had increased to $100 million.[11] Eventually, with the receipt of a Soviet donation of 400 million rubles (approximately $600 million at the official exchange rate), contributions totaled about $1 billion, although most of the donations were in kind rather than in cash.[12] By then, because of the continued fighting and the lack of any significant repatriation, humanitarian assistance was becoming a point of contention between the two sides.

Perhaps the most heroic moments of the humanitarian assistance effort came in the months immediately prior to the deadline for the completion of the Soviet withdrawal. As the deadline approached, the situation in Kabul became extremely dangerous. Relief agency administrators were deeply concerned about the personal safety of their staffs. However, the suffering of the Afghan people required a response. Prince Sadruddin organized an airlift of food and other supplies and recommended that I urge UNICEF and the United Nations Development Program (UNDP) not to evacuate their personnel.[13] Given the humanitarian, political and psychological importance of our efforts, I agreed and prevailed on the executive directors of these agencies to maintain their presence. As a result of personal bravery and commitment of UN personnel, many lives were saved.

The continued fighting between the regime and the Mujahideen prevented the massive flow of returnees that we had feared would overwhelm the country and result in a humanitarian disaster. At the same time, the continuation of the conflict prevented the implementation of large-scale reconstruction and rehabilitation programs. Nevertheless, the coordinator developed a plan for reconstruction and relief efforts in the spring of 1989, called Operation Salam, that was feasible even in conditions of continuing hostilities. Over the course of the next year, all of the parties expressed their support for the activities of Sadruddin Aga Khan and their satisfaction with the humanitarian assistance programs being coordinated by his office. By the end of 1990, Prince Sadruddin, feeling that he had gotten the relief program well under way, relinquished the coordinator post. Conditions had been created that permitted 3.9 million of the refugees eventually to return and resume productive lives. Given the circumstances, this was a remarkable achievement.

WHY WAS THE AFGHAN CONFLICT NOT RESOLVED?

The Geneva Accords succeeded in facilitating the Soviet withdrawal but did not, and could not, overcome the internal divisions within Afghan society. I knew that UN involvement in promoting an internal political settlement was highly risky, but I came to realize that only the United Nations could undertake the task. Given the importance of a settlement to the well-being of the Afghan people, the effort had to be made. We were unsuccessful in part because it was impossible to build a supportive international climate for political reconciliation. The influential parties—the United States, the Soviet Union, Pakistan, Iran and Saudi Arabia—all had their separate agendas. More important, however, was the absence of a sense of national purpose and national responsibility on the part of the Mujahideen factions. This, too, was a casualty of the war.

I was asked by a journalist from *Le Monde* in 1988 what my conclusions were on the "Afghan affair." I replied that I would be totally honest. "We have been used by the superpowers. Our role has been important. We prepared the ground. But it was thanks to the determination of Moscow and Washington to end the war that we succeeded [in mediating]. At the same time we proved that the UN can be an ideal instrument for the achievement of an agreement between the great powers. We saved face for both." This remains my view today. It was not the negotiating skill of the United Nations that persuaded the Soviet Union to withdraw its armed forces from Afghanistan. This was the result of the invincible resistance of the Mujahideen, the effective arms they received from the United States and the support for their struggle extended by Pakistan, Iran and Saudi Arabia. The timing of the withdrawal of the Soviet troops was settled between the Americans and the Soviets as was the belated agreement to cutoff arms deliveries to the combatants.

There is no doubt in my mind, however, that the UN role was essential. Diego Cordovez and his team devised the proximity negotiation procedure and developed the texts for a set of agreements between Pakistan and Afghanistan, a crucial element of which was the withdrawal of the Soviet army, something totally out of the control of either country. The United Nations provided the forum, the negotiating skill, the legitimacy and the patience required to permit the Soviet Union to withdraw from Afghanistan with its national dignity preserved. Of equal, or even greater, importance in human terms was the assistance provided under the leadership of the United Nations to the more than 6 million Afghan refugees. The task of repatriation has never been completed. That most of the refugees survived the rigors of exile is in no small measure thanks to the United Nations, as is the return under tolerable conditions of the more than 3 million who have gone home. The international community retains a responsibility to assist the Afghans to rebuild their country and to find the way to national reconciliation. The greatest responsibility rests, however, with the leaders of the competing factions who fought determinedly against the Soviets and then, tragically, with equal ferocity against each other.

1. Secretary-General Javier Pérez de Cuéllar meets with Prime Minister Margaret Thatcher of the United Kingdom.

UN Photo 176533 / M. Grant

2. Javier Pérez de Cuéllar, Permanent Representative of Peru with George Bush, Permanent Representative of the USA.

3. The President of Cyprus, Archbishop Markarios, UN Special Representative Javier Pérez de Cuéllar, and Turkish Cypriot leader Rauf Denktash. Bringing the two sides together.

UNFICYP photo 77/0904.

4. The Secretary-General welcoming Soviet President Mikhail Gorbachev.

UN photo 172524 / Y. Nagata.

5. Secretary-General Pérez de Cuéllar discussing matters of peace with Pope John Paul II.

L'Osservatore Romano Cittá del Vaticano. Servizio Fotografico. Arturo Mari.

6. Secretary-General Pérez de Cuéllar in a refugee camp at Korem, Ethiopia, 9 November 1984. Pledging UN support for the drought-stricken areas of Africa.

Be one heart full of love in the Heart of Jesus through Mary. God bless you
Mc Teresa

7. Marcela Pérez de Cuéllar and Javier Pérez de Cuéllar with Mother Teresa.

8. Secretary-General Pérez de Cuéllar in conversation with President François Mitterrand of France, 24 April 1985.

Presidénce de la République Française. Service photographique. Photographie no. 5589.

9. Secretary-General Pérez de Cuéllar meeting with Palestine Liberation Organization Chairman Yasser Arafat in Geneva, 8 July 1990.

UN Photo 176070.

10. Javier Pérez de Cuéllar discussing his peace mission to Baghdad with journalists gathered at the entrance of the UN Secretariat building in New York. 15 January 1991.

11. The Secretary-General discusses Iraq's invasion of Kuwait with Iraqi Deputy Prime Minister and Foreign Minister Tariq Aziz. Amman, Jordan. 2 September 1990.

UN Photo 176156.

12. Secretary-General Javier Pérez de Cuéllar with the representatives of the Five Permanent Members of the Security Council on the occasion of the adoption by the Council of Resolution 678 authorizing the use of all necessary means in driving Iraq from Kuwait. From left to right are foreign ministers Edouard Shevardnadze (USSR), Roland Dumas (France), Javier Pérez de Cuéllar, Qian Qichen (China), James A. Baker III (USA), and Prime Minister John Major (UK).

UN Photo 174704/E. Debebe.

13. President George Bush urges Javier Pérez de Cuéllar to accept a third term as Secretary-General during a stroll in the Rose Garden.

Official White House photograph.

14. The Secretary-General meeting with Nelson Mandela, Vice-President of the African
National Congress after the latter's release from South African detention.

UN Photo 157242 / J. Isaac.

15. Secretary-General Pérez de Cuéllar delivers the oath of office to Sam Nujoma as the first president of Namibia.

16. Midnight signature of the El Salvador Peace Accord, 31 December 1991. From left to right are General Mauricio Vargas (El Salvador), Oscar Santamaria (El Salvador), Dr. Eduardo Torres (El Salvador), Alvaro de Soto (Special Representative of the Secretary-General), Javier Pérez de Cuéllar, Pedro Nikken (Un Secretariat), Eduardo Sancho (El Salvador/FMLN), Francisco Jovel (El Salvador/FMLN).

CYPRUS: LABYRINTH
WITH NO EXIT

THE CYPRUS PROBLEM would seem at first glance to be easily susceptible to a reasonable solution. It should be a matter of finding the right formula that would afford the Turkish Cypriot minority—about 14 percent of the population—a satisfactory degree of cultural and political autonomy and a proportionate share of the island's territory while preserving the integrity of a federated Cypriot state government, in which both the Greek and Turkish Cypriots would participate. Finding the formula and gaining its acceptance by the two deeply mistrustful ethnic communities, however, has proven until now impossible. After my own sustained effort of more than 12 years, I would characterize the Cyprus problem as a maze in which each promising pathway leads back to the starting point.

In my years of UN service, I had more direct and continued involvement with the situation in Cyprus than with any other issue. Appointed Special Representative for Cyprus by Secretary-General Waldheim in 1975, I spent two years on the island seeking to facilitate agreement between the leaders of the Greek and Turkish communities to restore the unity of the island. I was neither the first nor the last to try. Despite the frustrations involved, I came to have a deep affection for the island and a very personal concern for its future.

When I first arrived on Cyprus, Archbishop Makarios was President and Rauf Denktash was the leader of the Turkish Cypriot community—as he remains today. All contact between the two had been broken. The archbishop was clearly the only Greek Cypriot with the personal authority to reach an agreement with the Turkish community. I therefore saw it as my first task to bring him and Denktash together so that talks on the future of the island could be resumed. This took much quiet persuasion with each man, but eventually I was able to arrange a meeting at a small restaurant in the buffer zone that divides the two parts of the island.

The archbishop was an impressive man whose devotion to Cyprus was so profound as to have a spiritual as well as political dimension. He enjoyed extraordinary admiration and loyalty among the Greek Cypriot community. While he was of humble origin, he was regal in his episcopal robes, so much so that his Turkish Cypriot counterpart, Rauf Denktash, who himself is not troubled by insecurity, patently feared that he would be at a negotiating disadvantage when faced with Makarios in full churchly array. However, when Makarios entered a negotiating session, he quickly removed his robes and set to work, with great energy, in his simple blue surplice. After observing his negotiations with Denktash in January 1977, I was convinced that he had realized, partly as a result of the earlier forceful overthrow of his government, that a settlement with the Turkish community was necessary for the future of the island. But, the archbishop's sudden death left a void that has never been filled.

Rauf Denktash, who remains today the unchallenged leader of the Turkish Cypriot community, is as impressive in his way as was Archbishop Makarios. His large girth is matched by a sharp and logical mind. His appetite for good food is boundless and, while I cannot confirm it, he is said to find respite from the summer heat of Cyprus by sitting in a tub of ice water sipping ouzo. Denktash was frequently excruciatingly prolix in expressing his positions, but his train of thought was always logical and clear even when his intent was to block or delay a reasonable settlement. At times he was sharply critical of my conduct of good offices. Yet I never ceased to admire the clarity of his expression even while becoming exceedingly impatient with its substance.

The third major political figure at the time was Glafcos Clerides, leader of the Greek Cypriot conservatives, who since 1993 has been President of Cyprus. Clerides was at times a direct participant in negotiations and even when not in government, an indirect one, since no settlement was likely to be approved without the concurrence of his party. Clerides is a man of *raison*. After Makarios's death, I felt he offered the best hope of an eventual agreement since he was forthright, not given to emotional outbursts and seemingly open to compromise. He enjoyed considerable respect beyond his own party, even among the Turkish Cypriots—he and Denktash have been friends since the time of British colonial administration. It is a mark of the intractability of the Cyprus problem that even though Clerides has now been president for four years, a Cyprus settlement appears as far away as ever.

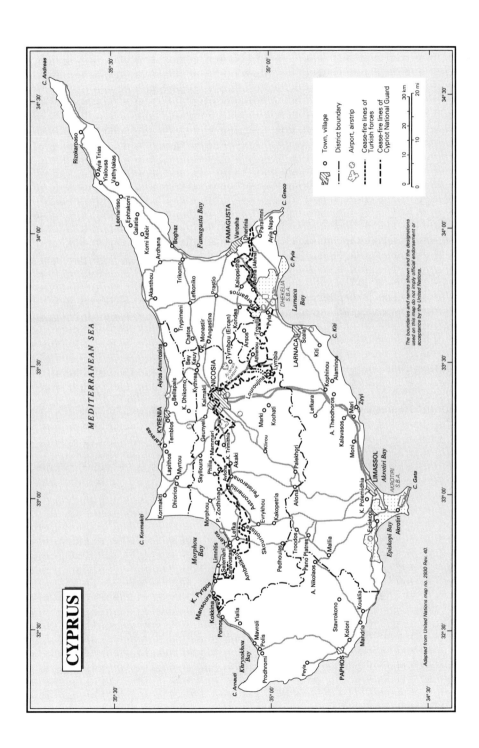

CYPRUS

MEDITERRANEAN SEA

Town, village
District boundary
Airport, airstrip
Cease-fire lines of
Turkish forces
Cease-fire lines of
Cypriot National Guard

0 10 20 30 km
0 10 20 mi

The boundaries and names shown and the designations
used on this map do not imply official endorsement or
acceptance by the United Nations.

Adapted from United Nations map no. 2930 Rev. 40.

THE GUIDELINES FOR A SETTLEMENT

After the quiet and generally friendly meeting in the restaurant on neutral ground, it was possible to bring the two sides into substantive negotiations to define the basic elements of a settlement. While retaining the posture of good offices, my staff and I presented a series of suggestions to help Makarios and Denktash to find their way to an agreement. Finally, in early 1977, after lengthy negotiations, the two met in my presence and reached agreement on four basic guidelines. The guidelines provided that:

- Cyprus should be an independent, nonaligned, bicommunal federal republic.
- The division of territory between the two communities should take into account economic viability, productivity and land ownership.
- Three freedoms—of movement, of settlement and for the right of property—were to be open for discussion.
- The powers and functions of the central federal government should safeguard the unity of the country, having regard for the bicommunal character of the state.

Subsequently, under the personal auspices of Secretary-General Waldheim, who had come to Cyprus for the purpose, six additional points were agreed as a basis for the resumption of the intercommunal talks that had been broken off. These included the following:

- There should be respect for human rights and fundamental freedoms of all citizens.
- The talks would deal with all territorial and constitutional aspects of a settlement.
- Priority would be given to reaching agreement on the resettlement of Varosha, a resort town that has remained unoccupied ever since it was overrun by the Turkish army.
- The two sides would abstain from any action that might jeopardize the outcome of the talks.
- Consideration would be given to the demilitarization of Cyprus.
- The independence, sovereignty, territorial integrity and nonalignment of the Republic of Cyprus would be guaranteed against union in whole or in part with any other country and against any form of partition or secession.

These guidelines and agreed points encompass practically all the issues that have been under negotiation off and on for 20 years. One additional issue raised subsequently and insistently by the Greek Cypriot side was the withdrawal of the Turkish troops and the Turkish nationals who had been settled in the part of the island controlled by the Turkish Cypriots (with the help of the Turkish military). The guidelines were incorporated in resolutions of the Security Council that called on me to use my good offices in facilitating a Cyprus settlement so that I, too, was bound by them—more, in fact, than were the two parties. Given the important part we had played in their development, I could hardly object. When I relinquished my post in Cyprus, I received warm expressions of appreciation from both communities.

WHEN AN OLD CYPRUS HAND BECOMES SECRETARY-GENERAL

Within days of my swearing-in as Secretary-General, Cypriot President Spyros Kyprianou (who had succeeded Archbishop Makarios), Foreign Minister Nicos Rolandis and Rauf Denktash all called to propose meeting with me at my earliest convenience. Each side seemed to see advantage in my appointment and each clearly felt they had a special call on my time and attention. The Turkish President, General Kenan Evren, also sent word of his "joy" on receiving word of my election. In Greece, George Papandreou had just become Prime Minister. He was viewed with misgivings by the Turkish Cypriots with some justification. I had a meeting with him in Moscow, a year later, in which he sounded as adamant as the Greek Cypriot leaders.

At the beginning of 1982 the talks between the two communities were again under way, and some progress on constitutional issues had been achieved. But not much. Hugo Gobbi, who had succeeded me as Special Representative for Cyprus, had put forward the first phase of an "evaluation" of where things stood. The paper was more than a summary since it included specific suggestions for dealing with the outstanding differences, including the suggestion that the island might be split between the two communities on the basis of 70 percent for the Greeks and 30 percent for the Turks. Any such suggestions had to be put forward officially only after the two sides had had an opportunity to see them informally in draft. Even then, they were always characterized as informal ideas that might provide a basis for discussion between the parties. I was only to extend my good offices, never to "mediate."

The distinction between mediation and good offices is a tenuous one, but one to which the Cypriots attached inordinate importance, as did the Turkish government. At an early stage of the conflict, the Special Representative for Cyprus had been designated as "mediator"; as such he put forward formulas for an agreement intended to bridge the gap between the Turkish and Greek sides. The Turkish Cypriots and the Turkish government felt that the formulas favored the Greek side and insisted that the Special Representative had exceeded his mandate in acting as a mediator. The Special Representative's effectiveness was destroyed, and subsequently he resigned. Thereafter, the term "mediator" was never used. Even so, at times one or the other of the parties accused me of exceeding my mandate and assuming the unacceptable role of mediator. The distinction was, at most, a matter of nuance, depending, I found, largely on whether one side or the other disliked a suggestion I put forward.

A tactic of which the Greek Cypriots were especially fond was to threaten to "internationalize" the Cyprus problem if the Turkish Cypriots were not more forthcoming. This meant that the Cypriot government would seek support from prominent international leaders in putting pressure on the Turkish side or that it would raise the problem again in the General Assembly. In our first meeting, in April 1982, President Kyprianou told me that he intended to ask the West German Chancellor, Willy Brandt, "to play the role of catalyst within the international community for a solution of the Cyprus problem." Kyprianou's government wished to create a sense of urgency on the Cyprus problem; otherwise the Turkish side would be able to cement the division of the island as a fait accompli. The Government of Cyprus was a member in good standing of the Non-Aligned Movement. Therefore it could count on strong support in the General Assembly for its positions as well as in the annual meetings of the Non-Aligned Movement. The Turkish Cypriots, on the other hand, had little access to international organizations, enjoying only occasional vicarious support from some Moslem countries. Moreover, Turkey, by sending and retaining a large number of troops to Cyprus to protect Turkish Cypriots, had gained the condemnation of the Security Council and wide opprobrium among UN members.

I sought repeatedly, with little success, to dissuade the Greek side from taking the problem to the General Assembly, since the result was greater resentment and intransigence on the Turkish side. This is precisely what happened in the spring of 1983. The regular session of the General Assembly was resumed to consider the Cyprus problem as a result of pressure from the Cyprus government, which also had circulated the idea that the Assembly should establish an advisory committee "to assist the Secretary-General in his search for a solution of the Cyprus problem." Concerned that the intercommunal talks were making very little progress and that the General Assembly debate was unlikely to help, I decided to intensify my personal involvement in the effort to find a Cyprus solution.

In talks in New York with both President Kyprianou and Rauf Denktash, I indicated my intention, making clear that whatever initiative I might take would end up on the negotiating table of the intercommunal talks, which remained the chosen forum for negotiating a solution to the problem. In a dinner toast to the Cypriot foreign minister, Nicos Rolandis, I stated that "my function, and that of my Special Representative, will be to stimulate the efforts of the parties to give shape to those elements which are needed to secure a just and workable solution." In a private conversation with President Kyprianou I gently suggested that a debate in the General Assembly was not the best way to encourage the constructive atmosphere that would be needed for my initiative. I doubted, moreover, that the establishment of an advisory committee to assist me would be very helpful.

President Kyprianou undertook to discourage the establishment of the proposed advisory committee in light of my intention to become personally involved in efforts to find a Cyprus solution. The debate in the General Assembly was already under way, however, and led inevitably to the adoption of another resolution (A/37/253, May 15, 1983) that supported the Greek Cypriot position. The Turkish Cypriot reaction was predictable. They again suspended participation in the intercommunal talks. Denktash insisted that by endorsing the Greek Cypriot position, the Assembly had "destroyed" the basis for intercommunal talks.

The Greek Cypriots declared that no solution would be possible until the Turkish troops were withdrawn from the island, a position also held by the Greek government. Greek Deputy Foreign Minister Carolos Papoulias told me in May 1983 that the withdrawal of the Turkish army was essential for the fruitful development of negotiations. He added that Greece would have to respond militarily if Turkey made any further military move.

This pattern was to be repeated again and again. One side or the other, and sometimes both, would adopt positions that were essentially nonnegotiable. Time and effort would then be required to find formulas to overcome these roadblocks. A useful technique in the resolution of conflict is to introduce new elements into the negotiations that permit the roadblocks to be bypassed. The Cyprus negotiations had been going on for almost 20 years, however, and every piece in the puzzle was well known. The only new elements that were introduced in the 1980s were the Unilateral Declaration of Independence (UDI) by the Turkish Cypriots and the relocation of Turkish nationals as settlers in the northern part of Cyprus controlled by the Turkish Cypriots. Both made a solution more rather than less difficult.

Thus the only possible recipe for a settlement was rearrangement of the well-known elements to give each side a modicum of satisfaction. This is what we tried to do—to develop trade-offs, for example, between the apportionment of land and the apportionment of control accorded to the central government, between the introduction of confidence-building measures and the initiation of the withdrawal of Turkish troops. There was ample room for reasonable compromise, assuming that each side desired a settlement that would reflect the central goal defined in 1977 of a federal, bicommunal, independent and nonaligned Cyprus. If this assumption proved invalid, reasonable compromise could not bring a settlement.

THE SEARCH FOR THE MISSING PERSONS

Thousands of Cypriots, both Greek and Turkish, were missing after the fighting that ensued after the Turkish military deployment to Cyprus in 1974. In 1981 a Committee on Missing Persons was established, made up of Turkish and Greek Cypriot representatives and, as a third party, a representative of the International Committee of the Red Cross. The purpose was to locate the missing persons or, at least, to determine their fate. It was hoped that resolution of this human tragedy could encourage reconciliation between the two communities. The result was just the opposite. The Cypriots became embroiled in procedural disputes that were beyond the capacity of the Red Cross representative, Claude Pilloud, to resolve. Pilloud lacked an appreciation of the essentially political nature of the problem and himself became a major bone of contention by advocating procedures that the Greek Cypriots considered pro-Turkish.

Resolution of the missing persons problem was the responsibility of the International Committee of the Red Cross, not of the United Nations. I felt, however, that in light of the broader responsibility of the United Nations for the peace of the island, this further cause of animosity between the communities should be brought under control. Accordingly I requested my Special Representative, Hugo Gobbi, to undertake intensive informal consultations with the Cypriot parties to find an amicable settlement of the procedural problems so that the committee could undertake the humanitarian mission for which it was created. At the same time I wrote to Alexandre Hay, the president of the International Committee of the Red Cross, to advise him of my action and to suggest that he consider replacing Pilloud. This he was unwilling to do. I could have insisted on Pilloud's removal; I concluded, however, that the level of distrust between the Cypriot parties was so high as to make progress in the committee unlikely with or without him. Moreover, most of those listed as missing were almost certainly dead, a reality that was bound to limit what the committee could accomplish.

The committee did not really begin its substantive work until 1984, and, as I expected, little was accomplished. During my entire tenure as Secretary-General, it was able to resolve less than 200 cases. Pilloud's successor as the Red Cross representative, Ambassador Paul Wurth, concluded as late as November 1990 that the committee was being used by both sides primarily as a propaganda tool, a poignant example of how distrust and hatred can defeat a humanitarian objective.

UNILATERAL DECLARATION OF INDEPENDENCE

Making good on the often-repeated threat of their leader, on November 15, 1983, the Turkish Cypriot authorities unilaterally declared their independence and the establishment of the Turkish Republic of Northern Cyprus. Three days later the Security Council adopted Resolution 541 deploring the declaration, which it termed legally invalid. The Council called for withdrawal of the declaration and asked all states to respect the territorial integrity and nonalignment of the Republic of Cyprus. Further, it called upon all states and the two communities in Cyprus to refrain from any action that might exacerbate the situation.

These developments seriously threatened the initiative I had undertaken to move negotiations between the communities forward. Over the next months I sought the help of other interested parties in countering their effect and in supporting my efforts. I met with Turkish President Kenan Evren for the first time in January 1984 and asked that he use his influence with the Turkish Cypriot community to discourage any follow-up to UDI while I was engaged in my "private diplomacy" on Cyprus. I also asked that he counsel Rauf Denktash to be more forthcoming on an arrangement for Varosha. The President responded by comparing Cyprus with Israel. The United States was not using its influence on Israel. Likewise, Greece was not using its influence on the Greek Cypriots; on the contrary, it was advising the Greek Cypriots to be intransigent. Turkey, he said, had always encouraged the Turkish Cypriots to make proposals and concessions. Unfortunately, those concessions had not been reciprocated. My conversations with Greek leaders tended to provide a mirror image of the foregoing.

I also sought to enlist the help of the five Permanent Members of the Security Council. Meeting individually with their ambassadors, I suggested that, in accordance with their special responsibilities, they jointly approach the parties to the Cyprus problem and emphasize to them both the need to preserve the territorial integrity of Cyprus and the necessity to cooperate with me in my efforts to bring a settlement to the problem. This was in May 1984, and the time had not yet come when the Five were willing to work together in the resolution of regional problems. The United Kingdom and France supported the idea of a joint meeting of the Five to coordinate an approach to the Cyprus parties. China agreed to proceed as I had recommended but to act individually. Foreign Minister Gromyko responded by restating the Soviet position on Cyprus and ignoring my proposal for joint action by the Five. The Soviet Ambassador told me that Soviet President Chernenko, when meeting with the leader of the Cypriot Communist Party, had strongly supported the position of the Cyprus government in its struggle to protect its territorial integrity. U.S. Secretary of State Shultz sent a letter expressing strong U.S. support for my initiative but rejected the idea of a five-power démarche.

I would have frequent occasion in the next years to talk to representatives of the Permanent Five, sometimes at the highest level, on the Cyprus problem. The British followed the subject closely partly because of their past association with Cyprus and partly because of the continued presence of two British bases on the island. On two occasions when I met with Queen Elizabeth II her principal substantive questions were directed to the situation in Cyprus. The Soviet Union's interests were concentrated on the Cypriot Communist party; Moscow did not become directly involved in the negotiations for a settlement.

The United States, on the other hand, was in continuing close contact with all the parties. Its interest was, in the first place, strategic. It saw the hostility between its two allies in the North Atlantic Treaty Organization (NATO), Greece and Turkey, which stemmed in good part from the Cyprus conflict, as threatening the security of NATO's southern flank. A second factor in the strong U.S. interest in Cyprus was the presence of an influential Greek lobby in Washington. In response to congressional pressure, ambassadorial rank was given to a State Department officer, Nelson Ledsky, whose sole responsibility was dealing with the Cyprus question as Special Cyprus Coordinator. While the frequent U.S. interventions with the parties sometimes caused confusion, they generally were supportive of the good offices role of the United Nations. Washington did not try to take over the negotiations but it monitored them critically, somewhat like a watchful mother. But not even the United States was able to persuade the Turkish Cypriots to rescind their unilateral declaration of independence.

TO THE PRECIPICE OF SUCCESS

After I indicated my intention to undertake a personal initiative to assist in the resolution of the Cyprus problem, we developed in the Secretariat a strategy to bring the two sides together, first through discussion of "elements" of a comprehensive settlement. The elements were put to the parties not as a UN-proposed text but rather as subjects on which I, in pursuit of my good offices mission (and not as a mediator), had concluded agreement would have to be found. The next step would be to move to high-level proximity talks for which I would provide a detailed "agenda," which in reality would constitute the outline of a comprehensive agreement with the more sensitive "elements," such as the division of territory, left open. The final step, following basic agreement in the high-level proximity talks, would be a high-level bilateral meeting between the two parties at which the comprehensive agreement, based on a further refinement of the "agenda" that I had provided, would be signed and the way cleared for the establishment of a provisional federal government. This strategy succeeded, albeit with agonizing resistance, up to the high-level bilateral meeting of the two parties.

The agenda that I proposed consisted of four broad "elements": confidence-building measures, governmental structure, territorial adjustments and additional matters, including such sensitive issues as the timetable for the withdrawal of non-Cypriot troops, the establishment of a provisional or transitional government and guarantees. The distrust between the two sides was intensified by their common habit of leaking confidential negotiating documents to the press and giving tendentious interviews, which they did again at this point. It was necessary to hold three sets of proximity talks, when only one had been contemplated, in order to obtain sufficient agreement to justify moving to the bilateral summit.

Nevertheless, in the course of the three sessions, sufficient convergence was reached on dealing with most issues to permit me to put together the elements of a comprehensive solution to the Cyprus problem. In announcing that the direct meeting between the two Cypriot leaders would begin on January 17, 1985, I was careful not to imply that a full agreement was ready for signature. I said only that I had reached the conclusion that enough progress had been made to justify the convening of a high-level meeting of the two sides. Nonetheless, the announcement was widely interpreted as an indication that the Cyprus problem was at long last on the point of resolution. The U.S. Department of State, in an official statement, said that a new opportunity had been created to end the division of Cyprus and to establish a reunited Cypriot government. President Reagan's earlier commitment to assist the Cypriots in rebuilding a united country when a settlement or major progress in that direction was achieved was reiterated. Unfortunately, that time had not yet come (nor am I confident that it ever will).

The Turkish side had been the more difficult (to the extent that this distinction was meaningful) in the proximity talks. Accordingly, I mobilized as much pressure as possible, including asking President Reagan to intervene with Turkey, to bring Denktash to accept the "agenda" prepared for the high-level meeting. This proved effective. When the summit meeting was convened in New York, Rauf Denktash accepted the documentation as a basis for agreement. However, even though the documentation was known to both sides in advance, President Kyprianou declared that it was unacceptable in its current form. He could agree to it only as a basis for further negotiation. To all intents and purposes, the President scuttled the meeting. Thus the first direct high-level meeting in five years collapsed. I believe that Kyprianou declined to proceed with serious negotiations at this critical point because of domestic considerations in Cyprus. Unlike Denktash, he was never a free agent. Kyprianou, who by nature was not inclined toward flexibility or adventure, was always constrained by pressures from within his government and from the opposition. Being politically vulnerable, he found it necessary to protect himself from accusations of conceding to the other side. His successor, George Vasiliou, who enjoyed a stronger political base, was more flexible. But by that time Denktash was moving to a position that was hardly subject to compromise.

REBUILDING A HOUSE OF CARDS

Following the failure of the high-level bilateral meeting, I thought it was essential to preserve the very considerable amount of agreement that had been achieved since 1984. Accordingly a draft agreement was prepared in the Secretariat with an accompanying statement consolidating all the points of convergence and setting forth a possible negotiating sequence. This time the Greek Cypriot side accepted the text and the Turkish Cypriots did not. Denktash refused even to consider it since he had not been consulted in its preparation. In September 1985 he came to New York to discuss the situation with me directly. After complaining bitterly that the Turkish Cypriot side had been portrayed as impeding progress ("even by President Reagan in his report to Congress"), he suggested that there should be three texts of a draft agreement for consideration: the original text prepared for the high-level meeting, the text subsequently worked out with the Greek Cypriot side and a third text to be worked out with his side. I commented that this approach would bring the negotiations well into the next century.

President Kyprianou identified three issues as of crucial importance: the withdrawal of the Turkish troops and settlers, the "three freedoms"—movement, settlement and property—and guarantees. He insisted that there could be no negotiations on other matters until these three issues were resolved. He proposed that the first two should be resolved in an international conference or all three in direct high-level negotiations between the two sides. Denktash rejected both alternatives with equal adamancy. Kyprianou did not help matters by threatening to bring the Cyprus question before the General Assembly once again with the objective of having the Assembly refer the problem to the International Court of Justice for resolution.

The Soviet Union also proposed that there should be an international conference on the Cyprus problem—a favorite tactic of Moscow. Since the Cypriot government continued to insist on such a conference, I had no choice but to consult the members of the Security Council. I did this despite my conviction that it was a bad idea, likely only to further infuriate Denktash, which it did. Four members of the Council favored an international conference while reiterating their support for my good offices mission; five members indicated that they could support the proposal only if all parties directly concerned agreed to attend; and four contended that a solution could be found only within the framework of the Secretary-General's good offices mission, and they therefore opposed the proposal. Accordingly I informed President Kyprianou that the conditions for holding a conference did not exist.

My consistent objective throughout these frustrating developments was to build the largest possible measure of agreement between the two sides and to devise procedures for resolving the outstanding differences. These procedures foresaw the holding of further high-level meetings, the agenda of which would include from the outset the questions of troop withdrawal, guarantees and the three freedoms, as Kyprianou was insisting. I also repeatedly suggested the concept of an integrated whole—that is, that neither side would be ultimately committed to an element of a solution until all issues had been resolved to its satisfaction. None of this brought the two sides closer to agreement. Distrust seemed to grow.

It had been my hope since serving in Cyprus that the UN peacekeeping force (UNFICYP) would be able to organize confidence-building measures between the two communities. UNFICYP had been deployed on the island since 1964 and, aside from the period of the Turkish invasion, had been very successful in preventing violence, in managing the buffer zone and in being of frequent assistance to the population on both sides. I proposed that a university be established in the buffer zone, which would afford an opportunity for young people from both sides to study together. Yet all efforts at confidence-building failed. Both sides frequently incited public hostility toward UNFICYP, which did not help. At one point Denktash denied UNFICYP entry to northern Cyprus in response to a statement I had issued criticizing the visit of the Turkish Prime Minister to the so-called Republic of Northern Cyprus. Greek and Greek Cypriot distrust of Turkish intentions increased in the mid-1980s when there was evidence—which UNFICYP confirmed—that the Turkish troops were being augmented and their equipment modernized. The inevitable result was a buildup of the Cypriot government's armed forces.

I suggested to the President of Turkey that a gradual reduction in the Turkish armed forces on Cyprus, monitored by UNFICYP, could do a great deal to improve the atmosphere for a settlement. While the Turkish government was generally forthcoming with promises to support my efforts and to use its influence to this end with Denktash, in the case of its troops there was no response.

In 1988 two incidents occurred in the buffer zone. In the first, a UN soldier was killed; in the second, a Turkish soldier was shot and the Greek Cypriot militia assumed control of a disputed part of the buffer zone despite the strong objections of the UNFICYP Force Commander. I informed the Security Council that there was cause for alarm since, while I did not believe that either side wished to initiate hostilities, the situation could easily get out of hand. Paradoxically, just at this point certain developments offered renewed hope that the long impasse in negotiations might be broken. A new president, George Vasiliou, took office in Nicosia. At more or less the same time, in February 1988, Oscar Camilión, a former foreign minister of Argentina, arrived in Cyprus to serve as my Special Representative. He was a skillful and seasoned diplomat, who I was confident could be of significant assistance in pursuit of my good offices mission.

George Vasiliou represented an unusual combination: a successful businessman who was the son of a former leader of the Cypriot Communist party. He had spent part of his youth in Czechoslovakia. An easy man to deal with, his style was informal and urbane. I found him to be a breath of fresh air after Kyprianou. We were quickly on a first-name basis although subsequently, when negotiations again faltered, he reverted to addressing me as Mr. Secretary-General.

In May of 1988, Oscar Camilión and my principal assistant in the Secretariat on Cyprus, Gustav Feissel, met separately with President Vasiliou and Rauf Denktash and reported back that both seemed disposed to respond favorably to a call from me to resume discussions on an overall solution of the Cyprus problem. Both were inclined to start afresh. Neither side would be held to concessions made in the documentation and draft agreement that I had earlier prepared. President Vasiliou was in New York in early June, and I proposed that he and the leader of the Turkish Cypriot Community come to a working lunch that I would host in Geneva in the following month. Vasiliou accepted. Denktash initially demurred on the ground that two brief papers on procedure that I had given to the parties were substantive and that I was thereby seeking to determine the outcome of the meeting in advance. When the Turkish President, Kenan Evran, visited me shortly thereafter, I explained the situation to him and asked that he use his influence to persuade Denktash to cooperate in the plan to resume high-level negotiations. Evran made the usual claims that the Turkish Cypriot side had made all the concessions in the past and asserted that it was now time for the Greek side to be more forthcoming. However, Evran said he would take what I had said into account in speaking with Denktash when the latter visited Ankara in the next days.

Thereafter Denktash quickly dropped his reservations and agreed to come to the working lunch on the terms I had suggested. In talking to the Special Representative, however, he referred to the "sovereign rights" of the two communities. This was enough to cause President Vasiliou to call me and express his concern that Denktash was intent on changing the essence of the High Level Agreement of 1977. This, he said, would be totally unacceptable to the Greek Cypriot side. The new beginning thus became quickly reminiscent of past set-backs.

The working lunch that took place on July 22, 1988, went well. (I gave personal attention to the menu, and selected the best wines hoping this would create a congenial atmosphere and encourage Denktash, whose gourmet tastes were well known, to be flexible.) An encouraging rapport seemed to be established between the two leaders both of whom formally reaffirmed their commitment to the 1977 and 1979 High Level Agreements. They jointly expressed their readiness to meet "without any pre-conditions and without delay to negotiate a settlement of all aspects of the Cyprus problem as an integrated whole through the efforts of the Secretary-General." I incorporated this agreement in a statement that I issued following the lunch.

After this moderately good beginning, the further talks between the leaders of the two communities, conducted in Cyprus in the presence and with the assistance of Oscar Camilión, quickly soured. Midway in their second round (the first round included 40 hours of talks), President Vasiliou wrote me on a personal and confidential basis expressing his suspicion that Denktash was being intentionally obstructive in order to cause him to walk out of the negotiations. Denktash, he predicted, would then go around the world asking for recognition since there was no possibility of agreement. Unfortunately, Denktash provided ample ground for this suspicion.

After 80 hours of unproductive talks, the two leaders, in June 1989, came to New York to meet with me for the second time. I took the occasion to summarize the ideas that had been discussed with them by the UN representatives and that could be included in a draft outline of an overall agreement that they had agreed to prepare. These were the ideas that I felt could and should form the basis of a comprehensive settlement. This was as far as I could go in my good offices mission in pushing the two sides to a reasonable settlement.

The ideas that I summarized, while not all-inclusive, were quite comprehensive. They provided for:

- A federal republic that was bicommunal in constitutional terms and bizonal in its territorial aspects.
- Equal roles for the two communities in the establishment of the federation, the need for their joint approval in adopting or amending the federal constitution, and equality and identical powers and functions of the two federated states.
- Administration of each federated state by one community that would be guaranteed a clear majority of the population and of the landownership in its area.
- Effective participation of both communities in all organs and decisions of the federal government.
- Prohibition of the federal government from encroaching upon the powers and functions of the federated states and from adopting measures against the interest of one community.
- Single sovereignty, single citizenship and a single international personality for the federation.
- Effective participation of the two communities in the legislative, executive and judiciary branches of the federal government.
- Jurisdiction of the two federal states over all functions not vested in the federal government.

- Provision in the federal constitution for the three freedoms for regulation by the federated states.
- Pending demilitarization of the federation, a prompt and drastic reduction in the presence of foreign troops but with the retention of a reasonable number of Greek and Turkish troops on the island.
- Satisfactory arrangements on territorial adjustments and displaced persons, including recognition of the rights of Greek and Turkish Cypriot displaced persons.
- Promotion of a balanced economy benefitting equally both communities.

I gave to the two sides a paper incorporating these points. President Vasiliou expressed his willingness to pursue negotiations on this basis; Rauf Denktash rejected the proposed procedure out of hand. In a letter addressed to me, he termed the negotiating process deeply flawed and accused the UN Secretariat of producing a document that should have been prepared by the two leaders themselves. After further excoriating "the Secretariat" and rejecting most of the concepts I had listed, Denktash, as his last point, emphasized "the Turkish Cypriot people's inalienable and imprescriptable right to self-determination."

Needless to say, the planned third session of the bilateral talks between the leaders of the two Cypriot communities did not take place. I was under some pressure from Washington immediately to invite Denktash to meet with me to get negotiations back on track. I felt that it was preferable to let him sit for a while and meanwhile bring as much external pressure as possible on the Turkish government to exert its considerable influence on the Turkish Cypriots. Oscar Camilión was dispatched to Bonn, London and Paris to request their assistance. Ambassador Ledsky promised to try to convince Denktash to resume negotiations on the basis of the ideas that I had put forward. I had no doubt that eventually there would be further negotiations. But at this point I viewed the prospect without enthusiasm. I told President Vasiliou quite candidly when he came to see me in October 1989 that for the past eight years I had listened to friendly governments assure me of their full support. Except for the United States, I never had the sense that they were really interested in the subject. I was against talks simply for the sake of talks. I was tired of my mission going nowhere.

By February 1990, enough pressure had been brought to bear on Turkey and on the Turkish Cypriots to cause Rauf Denktash to agree to a further round of high-level talks in New York with my participation. Jim Baker had written me in mid-January first to assure me that the United States regarded the UN good offices mission and my personal involvement as absolutely essential in reaching a peaceful, negotiated settlement. The secretary of state then added that the United States had been told by both Cypriot leaders that they were ready to respond favorably to an invitation from me to restart the negotiations. The United States favored a new negotiating session on the basis of the proposals I had outlined at the last high-level meeting and subsequently had described to the Security Council. Secretary Baker recognized that some serious preliminary spadework was needed. He indicated that the U.S. Special Cyprus Coordinator had already spoken to President Vasiliou and Denktash "on this theme," and Washington planned to pursue the question both with Turkish President Turgut Ozal and with the Greek government. By February 16 I was able to inform the secretary of state that the two Cypriot leaders had accepted my invitation for an extended session beginning on February 26 to prepare the outline of an overall agreement.

In my opening statement to the renewed high-level session, I sought to put to rest the fundamental issues that underlay the differences between the two communities with the following words:

> Cyprus is the common home of the Greek Cypriot Community and of the Turkish Cypriot Community. Their relationship is not one of majority and minority, but one of two communities in the state of Cyprus. The mandate given to me by the Security Council makes clear that my mission of good offices is with the two communities. My mandate is also explicit that the participation of the two communities in this process is on an equal footing. The solution that is being sought is thus one that must be decided upon by, and must be acceptable to, both communities.

I emphasized that the outline of the overall agreement that they were committed to prepare had to cover all the issues that make up the Cyprus problem. Then once again I listed the ideas that I had presented at the previous high-level session, all of which had been explored with the two leaders on a noncommittal basis, as possibly helpful in the direct talks that were now beginning.

From the very first session, Rauf Denktash's attitude was intolerable. When I finished my opening statement, he said that I had incorporated facts in the text that were not correct. After an intemperate exchange on this subject, Denktash read out his draft outline of a comprehensive settlement; its first words referred to "the reality of the existence of two peoples as partners in the sovereignty of the island" and to "the separate right to self-determination for these two peoples."

Introduction of the concepts of two peoples and self-determination ran counter to the basic Makarios/Denktash guidelines of 1977 and the Denktash/Kyprianou agreement of 1979, the bedrock on which any settlement would have to be built. Both concepts were totally unacceptable to the Greek Cypriot side, as Denktash well knew. Moreover, the Security Council, in according me my good offices mission, had specifically directed that this mission was with the "two communities." I could not, as Denktash insisted, substitute the word "peoples" for "communities" in my opening statement.

The meeting continued through three more days but President Vasiliou refused to discuss other topics until Mr. Denktash retracted his insistence on inclusion of the concepts of "two peoples" and "self-determination," which he adamantly refused to do. I met separately with each of the two leaders prior to the final session, but I was unable to find a way to bridge the differences that now were more profound than they had been when I began my good offices mission. There was no escaping the conclusion that Rauf Denktash had come to the meeting intent on preventing an agreement. In my closing statement I expressed the conclusion that, regrettably, we faced a substantive impasse that raised questions regarding the good offices mandate given me by the Security Council and, therefore, regarding the basis of the talks.

After I gave a full, but restrained, account of the meeting to the Security Council, it adopted Resolution 649, on March 12, 1990, calling on the leaders of the two communities to pursue their efforts to reach freely a mutually acceptable solution based on the 1977 and 1979 high-level agreements and providing for a bizonal, bicommunal federation. The Council requested that I pursue my mission of good offices in order to achieve the earliest possible progress and to assist the two communities by making suggestions to facilitate the discussions. This was precisely what I had been doing for eight years. The resolution was important, however, because it reiterated with the full authority of the Council the basic premises on which a settlement should be based. Both President Vasiliou and Rauf Denktash pronounced themselves satisfied with my report to the Council and with the Council's resolution.

So once again together with the Cyprus team in the Secretariat, I began an effort to bring the leaders of the two communities to agree on the outline of a comprehensive settlement. I approached the new effort with a strong conviction that there would be no point in holding another high-level meeting unless both leaders had agreed in advance to the principles of a settlement and the topics to be discussed and that this would not happen unless very strong pressure was placed on Turkey to use its full influence to bring Denktash in line.

The first significant step that I took was to telephone President Ozal toward the end of May to inquire how he thought progress might be achieved, given the outcome of the most recent high-level meeting. The President said he had concluded that a broader meeting under my chairmanship, which would include both Greece and Turkey as well as the two communities, could give new impetus to the negotiating process. This appeared to be a constructive idea, offering hope of a better outcome if Turkey was, as the President indicated, ready to support my position. It was hard to see how Denktash could remain the odd man out under such circumstances. Given this new prospect, I asked Oscar

Camilión, assisted by Gustav Feissel, to undertake discussions with all concerned, including the Greek and Turkish governments, to work out a set of ideas that would bring the two sides "within agreement range" on the main points of a settlement.

In June I discussed Cyprus very frankly with President Bush and Secretary Baker in Washington in order to get them to give strong support to my new effort with both the Greeks and the Turks. In presenting my assessment of the situation, I made two initial points: first, the Greek Cypriot leader, Vasiliou, was a reasonable man who wanted a solution to the Cyprus problem; and second, the Turkish Cypriot leader, Denktash, was too rigid and gave the impression of not wanting a solution. I made clear that I did not mean to imply that the Greek Cypriot side caused no problems. Its proponents were masters of publicity and made a point of attending every possible international meeting and stressing that they were there as the government of the entire island of Cyprus. This was a constant provocation to the Turkish Cypriot side. I asked the President and the secretary of state to push the Turkish government to restrain Denktash and to push the Greek government to get the Cypriot government to be less noisy.

Secretary Baker complained that Greek Prime Minister Constantinos Mitsotakis seemed to think that "we can snap our fingers and turn the Turks around," which was not the case. President Bush commented that U.S. relations with Turkey tended to go in cycles, in good part because of an Armenian genocide resolution that Congress regularly adopted. For the time being the Turks had gotten past this and relations were good. The President said he would do what he could and would support me in every possible way. A month later President Bush visited Turkey and Greece and spoke to the leaders of both countries along the lines that we had discussed. Shortly thereafter it was announced that Greece and Turkey had agreed to attend "a well-prepared meeting concerning Cyprus chaired by the Secretary-General" and that the Greek and Turkish leaders would work to help narrow the differences between the two Cypriot parties in advance of the meeting.

In these seemingly propitious circumstances Camilión and Feissel, in talks in Ankara and Athens, were able to develop an agreed draft covering the ideas to be included in an overall framework agreement on Cyprus. From Ankara, they reported to me that they were leaving for Cyprus much encouraged. Everything now depended on the leaders of the two Cypriot communities. I was very conscious that this was the last chance during my mandate for a settlement of the problem with which I had been longest associated and knew most intimately. We all wanted to believe that Rauf Denktash would not defy the Turkish government, the government on which his community depended so heavily for security.

This was wishful thinking. George Vasiliou, while cautioning that there were a number of differences that still needed to be resolved, concurred that the ideas in the text provided a basis for working out a final agreement. Rauf Denktash, on the other hand, sought extensive changes in the text but, more important, stated again very firmly that each side possessed sovereignty that it would retain after the establishment of a federation, including the right of secession. This position, as long as held, would eliminate any basis for agreement.

President Bush quickly sent a very strong message to President Ozal and Prime Minister Mesut Yilmaz stating that it would be unrealistic to think that a collapse of the negotiating process would not damage Turkey in Europe or elsewhere. Since the high-level quadripartite talks had been a Turkish idea, failure to see them through would raise doubt about Turkey's commitment to a settlement. The President asked the Turkish leaders to confirm that they would do their utmost to secure Mr. Denktash's acceptance of the draft text worked out in Ankara. By then Turkey was preparing for elections in which it was felt that Cyprus might be a factor. This was generally seen as a major reason why the Turkish leaders apparently ignored the U.S. plea and placed no further pressure on Denktash to modify his position on sovereignty.

I informed the Security Council on October 8, 1991, that the concept introduced by Denktash would fundamentally alter the nature of the solution that the Council had consistently foreseen. I indicated that I was asking my representatives to resume their discussions with the two sides in Cyprus and with the Greek and Turkish governments. If the discussions were productive, I was confident that it would be possible to convene the high-level meeting before the end of the year. However, while I did not say so to the Council, it was quite clear to me that Denktash had no interest in returning to these basic principles. I knew quite well that I would not have the satisfaction of seeing the Cyprus problem settled during my tenure.

WHAT OF THE FUTURE?

There is still today no Cyprus settlement nor has there been any reconciliation between the two communities. Provocative demonstrations still occur. UNFICYP has now been deployed for more than 30 years and has become the longest-lasting peacekeeping mission in history. There remains a near-unanimous feeling in the Security Council that withdrawing UNFICYP would seriously risk renewed conflict between the two communities. The Turkish troops and the Turkish settlers also remain, with the latter having become by now permanent residents.

In my opinion, there are two basic reasons why a settlement has not been reached. The Turkish Cypriot side, especially its leader, Rauf Denktash, has more to lose than to gain from integration into a reunited Cyprus. The Turkish Cypriots would have to surrender a substantial portion of the land they control, part of which is choice agricultural land. They would lose the satisfaction of living in a territory totally under Turkish Cypriot control. The leaders who function as president and cabinet ministers enjoy a status and freedom of action they could not hope to have in a united Cyprus. The major attraction of a settlement would be the possibility of sharing in the prosperity of the Greek Cypriot portion of the island, which now has one of the highest growth rates in the world. Besides that, some in the Turkish community might prefer to see the Turkish troops depart, even though their cost appears to be borne mainly by Turkey. But undoubtedly more see the Turkish troops as protectors from the more numerous Greek Cypriots, which is reason enough to tolerate their presence.

For the Greek Cypriots, the attraction of unification is not sufficient to cause them to accept a settlement that would acknowledge a right of the Turkish Cypriots to self-determination. In their perspective, this would deny the main purpose of a settlement. While they could expect to gain additional land, their economic growth is more than satisfactory without it. The greatest pressure for a settlement has come from the refugees and displaced persons from the north, who long hoped to regain their property. By the 1980s, however, few actually would have returned. The generation that was removed from their homes and businesses in the north is dying out. Any Cypriot government, no matter what its leadership, is likely to lose politically if it enters into a settlement entailing concessions on the central principles of unified sovereignty and unified identity for the island.

I found the intentions of the Turkish government most difficult to judge. In my experience, the Turkish leadership, while supportive of the Turkish Cypriots, always encouraged my good offices mission. President Ozal, in particular, spoke to me in favor of a settlement, and his government cooperated in preparing the de facto draft text of an overall settlement that complied with the high-level agreements reached in 1977 and 1979. The question was—and, for me remains—"Was this a dissimulation?" Turkey certainly had no interest in straining its relations with the United States, its NATO partners or the members of the European Community over the Cyprus question. This consideration dictated at least the appearance of reasonableness. The Turkish government seemed to contemplate with equanimity a substantial reduction of its troops in Cyprus. Yet the tactical military advantage that it gains from their presence must figure in the definition of Turkish policy.

In the last direct conversation I had with George Vasiliou, he—not surprisingly—contended that the Turks had never wanted, and had not expected, to see a Cyprus settlement. Under strong pressure from the United States they had to appear cooperative, knowing that they could depend on Denktash to prevent an agreement. This view is perhaps too cynical. My sense is that no

Turkish government is prepared to face the domestic political backlash that would result if it forced Denktash to accept an agreement that he would portray as endangering the Turkish Cypriot community. Thus Turkish governments, which are fragile in their composition, really are not in a position to control Denktash. Barring some outbreak of violence that UNFICYP is unable to control, the present status quo in Cyprus is likely to endure at least until there is a change in the Turkish Cypriot leadership and quite probably into the next century.

Should UNFICYP, under the circumstances, remain indefinitely on the island, serving, in a sense, as guardian of the status quo? UNFICYP has done a great deal during its long stay to prevent the violence that, given the animosity between the two communities and the arbitrary nature of the line dividing the two, otherwise would surely have occurred. While the Cypriot population has recognized UNFICYP's contribution to the peace of the island and to the well-being of its inhabitants, its presence has at times been the source of resentment. The media on both sides have printed inflammatory articles attacking UNFICYP for partiality and for improper intervention in internal matters. Fortunately, for most of its history UNFICYP has been under stable and responsible command. During my tenure I had frequent occasion to commend its performance under continuing pressure and occasional attack.

The very effectiveness of its performance has done a good bit to relieve the communities from the necessity of reaching a settlement. It can be reasonably argued that if UNFICYP were to be withdrawn the parties would face the bleak prospect of devastating conflict, unless a settlement were forthcoming. But after giving much thought to this, I have concluded that withdrawal of UNFICYP would carry too great a risk of war to be consonant with the purposes defined in the UN Charter. This is why I repeatedly recommended its extension and would still do so were I in office.

TEN

WAR IN THE GULF

THE MASSIVE IRAQI INVASION OF KUWAIT on August 2, 1990, flagrantly contravened international law and the Charter of the United Nations to which Iraq, as a member state, was committed. There was never a question in my mind that this aggression must be repelled. I believe that the United Nations emerged from the Gulf War a stronger force for peace in the world and that the basic principle on which the United Nations is founded, that of collective security, was shown to be achievable. These results outweigh any doubts that I harbored as the crisis moved rapidly toward war and that I still harbor concerning a number of aspects of the way the military campaign was conducted.

I would also like to state at the beginning, that I believe Saddam Hussein's aggression might well have been prevented. The major powers knew in advance that a very large Iraqi force was moving toward the Kuwaiti border. I did not have such knowledge, being dependent largely on press accounts of growing tension in the area. Either the United States or the Soviet Union could have warned the Security Council of a threat to peace; or, if they had given me the benefit of their satellite intelligence, I could have gone to the Security Council. In either event, the Council would likely have issued a warning statement and possibly sent a fact-finding mission to the area. I believe this would have had a restraining influence on Saddam Hussein. In the meeting that I had with him on January 12, 1991, only three days before the deadline set by the Security Council for the Iraqi withdrawal from Kuwait, he repeatedly referred to the fact that the Council had not acted for almost a month after Iraq had invaded Iran. He almost certainly moved against Kuwait on the assumption that the Security Council reaction would be equally slow and hesitant. A strong Council warning before August 2 would have disabused him of this notion.

I do not record this to place blame or to lessen in any way the guilt that Saddam Hussein must bear. Like so many others, I failed to anticipate his aggressive intent. My purpose here is rather to provide a lesson for the future. The United Nations and the Secretary-General, in particular, should have better sources of information on developments such as large troop movements that pose a threat to peace. And the United Nations, as much or more than national governments, should have the skill and insight to understand the import of such information and take appropriate preventative action.

IRAN MOVES AND THE SECURITY COUNCIL REACTS

The United Nations had not been a party to the various discussions that took place between Iraq, Kuwait, the United Arab Emirates and Saudi Arabia in the summer of 1990, during which Iraq had forcefully and repeatedly complained about Kuwait's oil marketing practices. I was aware, however, that there was a problem and that Iraq, in the context of its dispute with Kuwait, had deployed some troops along the Kuwaiti border. I understood the number was limited. On July 31, two days before the invasion, Dr. Clovis Maksoud, the expansive Permanent Observer at the United Nations of the League of Arab State, called on me to discuss the general situation in the Middle East. At the beginning of the conversation I expressed my concern about these Iraqi military moves. Maksoud did not condone Saddam Hussein's "ominous" actions but suggested that this was the nature of inter-Arab politics. He did not believe the Iraqi-Kuwait dispute would evolve into a serious crisis. The conversation then moved on to the Arab-Israeli problem, to which Maksoud attributed greater urgency. I also met that day with the Romanian Permanent Representative, a man who had very limited experience with the United Nations and who would on August 1 assume the presidency of the Security Council. The purpose was to review subjects that were likely to come before the Council during the month. I do not recall that the dispute between Iraq and Kuwait was among the subjects discussed. It is, then, no wonder that he was hardly prepared for the maelstrom that struck the Council on his second day in office.

The news of the invasion came in the late evening of what was still August 1 in New York. The Security Council convened at 2:00 A.M. on the morning of August 2. Once again, as so often in the past, August had brought war. The Council acted swiftly, adopting on the same day Resolution 660, condemning the Iraqi invasion and demanding the immediate and unconditional withdrawal of Iraqi forces from Kuwait. It also called upon Iraq and Kuwait to begin intensive negotiations on their differences.

The resolution did not call on the Secretary-General to take any action. The exercise of my good office in seeking a peaceful solution was never

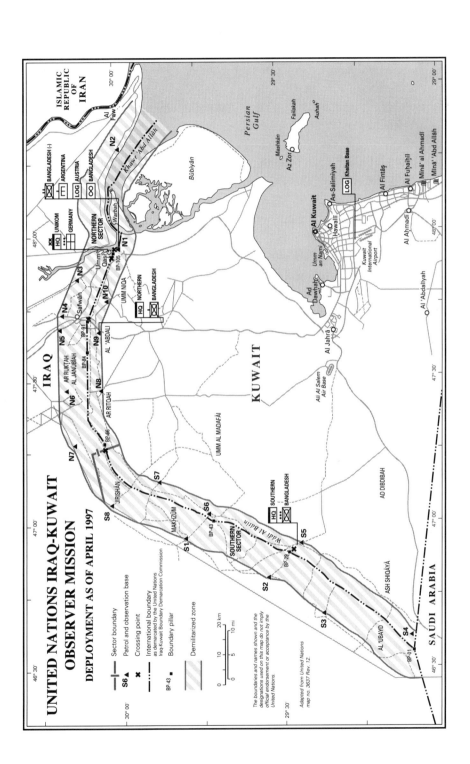

UNITED NATIONS IRAQ-KUWAIT OBSERVER MISSION

DEPLOYMENT AS OF APRIL 1997

Sector boundary

▲ S6 Patrol and observation base

✕ Crossing point

International boundary as demarcated by the United Nations Iraq-Kuwait Boundary Demarcation Commission

■ BP-43 Boundary pillar

Demilitarized zone

0   10   20 km
0   5   10 mi

The boundaries and names shown and the designations used on this map do not imply official endorsement or acceptance by the United Nations.

Adapted from United Nations map no. 3637 Rev. 12.

ISLAMIC REPUBLIC OF IRAN

IRAQ

KUWAIT

SAUDI ARABIA

Persian Gulf

Khawr 'Abd Allāh

Būbiyān

Warbah

Faylakah

Auhah

Mashtān

Az Zōr

Al Fāw

NORTHERN SECTOR

BANGLADESH (-)
ARGENTINA
AUSTRIA
BANGLADESH

UNIKOM
HQ
GERMANY

LOG

N1
N2
N3
N4
N5
N6
N7
N8
N9
N10

Umm Qaşr
BP-105
Şafwān
BP-91
BP-84
AR RUKTAH
AL JANŪBIAH
AR RITŌAH
BP-46
AL 'ABDALI
UMM NIQA

HQ NORTHERN
BANGLADESH

S1
S2
S3
S4
S5
S6
S7
S8

JIRISHAN
MAKHZŪM
BP-43
BP-29
Wadi Al Bāţin
SOUTHERN SECTOR

HQ SOUTHERN
BANGLADESH

BP-01

UMM AL MADAFĀI

AD DIBDIBAH

AL 'UBAYD

ASH SHIQĀYA

Al Jahrā
Ali Al Salem Air Base
Al 'Abdalīyah

Ad Dawhah
Umm an Naqj
Al Kuwait
As-Salimīyah
Hawalli
Kuwait International Airport

LOG Kheitan Base

Al Fintās
Al Fuḥaiḥīl
Mina' al Ahmadi
Mina' 'Abd Allāh
Al Ahmadī

specifically called for. Nonetheless, I felt it my duty to do whatever I could to alleviate a highly dangerous situation. One of the most critical problems in the period following the invasion was the refusal of Iraq to allow third-country nationals, including the many UN staff members who were stationed there, to leave either Iraq or Kuwait. On August 17, at a meeting of the Security Council, the members expressed their anxiety over this situation. Knowing that the Council would pass a resolution on the subject, I acted immediately to send the chief of my office, Virendra Dayal, and the head of the Secretariat personnel office, Kofi Annan, to Baghdad to try to arrange for the departure of all those being held hostage. By then some of the hostages had been moved to various locations throughout Iraq to serve as human shields against bombing by the American-led coalition forces. Dayal and Annan were both senior officers, and I thought they would be able to discuss broader aspects of the crisis with high-level Iraqi representatives. I intentionally announced their mission before the Security Council resolution was adopted, since I felt their chances of success would be better if their mission was not seen as the direct result of a Council action. The humanitarian objectives of the mission were to a substantial extent achieved. Permission for all UN staff members to depart, including those of coalition nationality who had been sent out as human shields, was given shortly after the UN representatives visited. Many non-UN Third World nationals and all women and children also received permission to leave. It is not clear whether the decision regarding women and children was the result of the UN mission.

Dayal, a highly intelligent and experienced officer of Indian nationality who was one of my closest associates, had extensive conversations with Iraqi Deputy Prime Minister and Foreign Minister Tariq Aziz in which he sought to make clear the serious and immutable nature of the Security Council resolutions. He emphasized that unless Iraq complied with them, a grievous outcome was to be expected. There were reports at this point that Iraq was moving stocks of chemical weapons to Kuwait as if in preparation for an attack, and in Baghdad there was an ominous sense of imminent danger. Dayal accordingly cabled a recommendation that I urgently invite Tariq Aziz to meet with me at a location outside of Iraq in order to allow the situation to cool down and enable rational dialogue. As soon as I received Dayal's message, I invited Tariq Aziz to meet with me in New York or Geneva. While I was confident that he would agree to neither location, the time needed to find an acceptable location could give the Iraqi government a further opportunity to assess the seriousness of the situation it faced. We agreed, with relatively little difficulty, to meet in Amman, Jordan, on August 31. By this time the Security Council had adopted four resolutions related to the Iraq invasion, 660 of August 2, 661 of August 6, 662 of August 9 and 664 of August 18. They imposed comprehensive economic sanctions; declared the annexation of Kuwait null and void; demanded that Iraq permit and facilitate the immediate departure from Kuwait and Iraq of all third-country nationals and that Iraq take no action that would jeopardize the safety, security and health of such nationals; and, finally, called on states having maritime forces in the area to use "such measures as may be necessary . . . to halt all inward and outward maritime shipping" to ensure strict implementation of the economic sanctions.

Prior to leaving for Amman, I met with the ambassadors of the five Permanent Members of the Security Council. I told them I had invited Tariq Aziz to meet with me to discuss how best to defuse the crisis and begin the withdrawal of Iraqi forces from Kuwait. I assured the five ambassadors that I would, of course, pursue the problem of the thousands of third-country nationals still trapped in Iraq and Kuwait and other humanitarian concerns. But my principal objective would be implementation of Resolution 660. I stressed that I was acting entirely on my own initiative and that I asked nothing from the Security Council. In fact, I preferred that no Council statement of endorsement or support be made, since I felt my chances of success with Tariq Aziz, whom I had come to know well in the course of the war between Iran and Iraq, would be better if I were seen to be acting independently. I anticipated the possibility that Tariq Aziz might ask me to travel on to Baghdad to meet directly with Saddam Hussein, which I was quite prepared to do. The only thing I would rule out would be a visit to Kuwait, since I would not wish to give any recognition whatsoever to Iraq's annexation of the country.

The five ambassadors welcomed my intention. The U.S. representative, Tom Pickering, commented that diplomacy should be given every chance—that it was a natural counterpart to the Council's action. I did not get in direct touch with President Bush. However, Brent Scowcroft, the president's National Security Advisor, when interviewed on the Cable News Network (CNN), said that the President had no problem with my initiative. I was armed, he said, with the five Security Council resolutions, which should serve as the basis of my negotiations. The United States would not back down from its position that it would not talk peace with Saddam Hussein until the Iraqis withdrew from Kuwait and all foreigners were released.

As I approached the meeting with Tariq Aziz, I was very much aware, even without General Scowcroft's admonition, that I was bound by the Council resolutions—that Iraqi unconditional withdrawal from Kuwait and restoration of the country's legitimate government were the sine qua non conditions for a nonmilitary resolution of the crisis. I met initially with the minister alone for two hours. Jordan's King Hussein, who placed much hope in the outcome of the talks, had made available a gracious residence within the royal compound known as Raghadan Palace, so our discussion took place in a congenial atmosphere. Tariq Aziz was quite as I had known him before—courteous, calm and highly articulate.

His English is almost flawless, better than my own in grammar if not in vocabulary, so communication was easy, I would almost say relaxed. I commented at the beginning that the five Security Council resolutions must be kept in mind but I had not come under any mandate from the Council. In proposing the meeting, I had acted entirely on my own initiative. I noted that "even the United States" had not given me any advice, except to wish me good luck.

I suggested that the best way to approach the problem would be to turn the clock back and start with Security Council Resolution 660, which had demanded the immediate withdrawal of Iraqi forces from Kuwait. If Tariq Aziz or President Saddam Hussein would make a statement—to me, or in some other forum—that the Iraqi presence in Kuwait "was not irreversible," it would certainly help defuse the tension in the area and would make it easier for an "Arab solution" to the problem to be found, as the Iraqi Government had repeatedly said was desirable.

Tariq Aziz was well rehearsed. He spoke for almost an hour, presenting, without notes, a remarkably well organized account of the background of the crisis as Saddam saw it. Saddam was to make essentially the same points to me on January 12 in Baghdad, three days before the military action began to drive him out of Kuwait. I will record them here because I think they provide an understanding of the immediate rationale for Saddam's action, although I am convinced that the reasons for his decision to invade Kuwait extended well beyond these events of the summer of 1990.

The unifying strain in Tariq Aziz's remarks was the Iraqi anger over Kuwait's oil pricing policy. At a summit meeting of the Arab Co-operation Council in Amman in February 1990, Saddam Hussein had strongly protested against the action of the Kuwaiti government in flooding the international market with oil, thereby bringing about a decrease in its price, causing serious damage to the Iraqi economy. Nevertheless, the Kuwaitis continued their policy; as a result the price of oil fell from $21 to $11 a barrel with catastrophic results for the Iraqi population, which was already living in difficult conditions. In May, at an extraordinary Arab summit meeting in Baghdad, Saddam Hussein had said that the Kuwaiti policy was "equivalent to war." When Kuwait and the United Arab Emirates continued to flood the market, Saddam sent a special emissary to Saudi Arabia to inform the Saudi government that Iraq could not sustain the damage being done to it, damage done to the people who had fought so hard to protect Kuwait and the other Gulf states during the Iran-Iraq war. The emissary also visited Kuwait and the United Arab Emirates and pressed for a summit meeting to deal with the problem.

It was only possible to gain agreement to a meeting of the oil ministers, which took place on July 10. At that time both Kuwait and the United Arab Emirates agreed to stop flooding the market, but the Kuwaiti minister said the agreement could only last until October, at which time Kuwait would raise its quota. Then on July 15, Tariq Aziz himself delivered a letter to the Secretary-General of the Arab League outlining all of Iraq's difficulties with Kuwait, including their long-standing dispute over the border. The next day Saddam Hussein announced publicly that countries in the region were conspiring to weaken Iraq and warned that there were other than diplomatic means to deal with the problem. Iraq had begun to mass troops along the border with Kuwait. At this stage President Hosni Mubarak of Egypt decided to mediate and proposed that there should be a bilateral ministerial-level meeting between Iraq and Kuwait in Jeddah, to be followed by a summit meeting in Baghdad. The meeting in Jeddah took place on July 30, but Kuwait would not budge on either the oil or the border issue. Iraq then concluded that "some countries" were trying to bring it to its knees. On August 2, the Iraqis invaded Kuwait.

Tariq Aziz's account of the action of Arab states in the ensuing days was as follows: King Hussein of Jordan rushed to Baghdad on August 3 and proposed an immediate summit meeting to include Iraq, Kuwait, Saudi Arabia, Egypt and Yemen. Saddam Hussein had agreed with the proposal, which already had Saudi concurrence. For reasons that were not clear to Iraq, a ministerial-level meeting was then proposed instead of the summit. The "mini-summit" never took place, but an Arab League Summit was held in Cairo on August 9. Saddam did not attend for security reasons, but three senior Iraqi officials were present. At the meeting a resolution hostile to Iraq was adopted by majority vote at Egypt's urging but eight states did not concur. The Arabs were thus divided, and the attempt to find an Arab solution failed although King Hussein still continued his efforts to resolve the crisis in a way that would take account of Iraq's interests.

Tariq Aziz concluded his presentation by stating that in Iraq's analysis, Israel and the United States had not been able to destroy the Iraqi economy themselves, so they had decided to use Kuwait for the purpose. Iraq was forced to act. "We are not adventurous," he said, "we are a serious government, open-minded, and we have been in power for 22 years. We are prepared to negotiate, but we insist on an Arab solution." The minister agreed with my view that the main objective now was to defuse the situation. But he insisted the region's problems could not be solved through gimmicks. The United States was foolish. Iraq recognized the American military superiority, but its planes could not win the war. Iraq was fighting on its own territory; it had 1 million men under arms and could double the number. Moreover, no political leader would be weakened by fighting against the United States. Egyptian President Gamal Nasser had lost a war but remained the most popular Arab leader until his death.

This, then, was the justification for the fateful action Iraq had taken. Nothing in Tariq Aziz's demeanor suggested that he had any doubts as to its validity. I recognized that it would be useless to argue with him on any specific point. Instead I said that, speaking as a lawyer, I felt that, quite apart from the resolutions adopted by the Security Council, international law had been broken by Iraq's action against Kuwait. Regardless of the validity of Iraq's claims, invasion and annexation were not in compliance with the principles of the United Nations Charter or with international law. The minister replied only with further justification of Iraq's action against Kuwait. He did say that Iraq was not closing any doors. He had a "boss," however, and was not in a position to make decisions independently. I expressed understanding that he might need to consult with his president and offered to meet again with the minister in Europe or Amman, if that would be helpful. I was ready to travel to Baghdad at any time to speak directly with President Saddam Hussein. Tariq Aziz did not respond to these openings. It was agreed only that we would meet again in Amman the following day.

During the conversation, the minister spoke passionately about Security Council Resolution 661, which had imposed a comprehensive embargo on shipments to and from Iraq, with exceptions made only for such food as was proven to be essential and for medicine. He insisted that if the sanctions were applied so as to interfere with the supply of food and medicine, it could lead to the strangulation of his country. He therefore asked that the resolution be implemented flexibly in so far as its humanitarian aspects were concerned. He recalled that in an earlier letter addressed to me he had drawn attention to Iraq's need to export a certain amount of oil to cover the purchase of normal humanitarian needs, principally foodstuffs and medicines. I told Aziz that I would convey his request to the Council. My feeling was that if Iraq gave a clear statement of its intent to withdraw from Kuwait, the Council would be inclined to be flexible in implementing the resolution. I welcomed Iraq's decision to allow the women and children of third countries and all the nationals of some countries to leave Iraq if they wished. I insisted, however, that Iraq should lift the restrictions on the movement of all third-country nationals.

The next day's meeting was scheduled for 6:00 P.M. in order to allow ample time for communications with Baghdad, although Tariq Aziz said that current conditions precluded any communications. We met alone for about an hour. I emphasized at the beginning that if I left Amman without any positive results, extremely dangerous developments might ensue. I again suggested the possibility of meeting later in the week in Geneva after he had an opportunity to consult directly with his president. Once more the minister failed to respond to this invitation. Instead he asked me to convey three points to the Security Council:

- Iraq pledged that it had no intention of initiating hostilities.
- There must be an Arab solution to the crisis.

- Iraq had taken a number of humanitarian measures, such as allowing third-country women and children to leave Iraq.

Tariq Aziz asked that I advise the Council to interpret Resolution 661 on sanctions in a generous way. He also requested that I obtain from the United States a guarantee that it would not attack Iraq. I responded that if the minister would express Iraq's intention to withdraw unconditionally from Kuwait, I would be in a better position to convey Iraq's request to the U.S. government. He said there were limits to what he could do.

I left Amman with a sense of doom. I could only assume that Tariq Aziz's lack of interest in a follow-up meeting in Baghdad or elsewhere meant that Saddam Hussein was unwilling to withdraw from Kuwait, even if this meant war. A more favorable opportunity for Saddam to take this action as part of a face-saving package was not likely to arise. While still in Amman, I stated publicly to the press, with Tariq Aziz at my side, that I was returning to New York "emptyhanded."

En route back to UN Headquarters, I met in Paris with King Hussein, whom I briefed fully on my conversations with Tariq Aziz. The King said that following the Arab Summit meeting in Cairo, which he characterized as one of the worst experiences he had ever been through, he had decided to visit President Bush. His talk with the President had been "very frank" but reassuring. He had found that the position of the United States was not to initiate military action, but rather to defend Saudi Arabia, something the King considered superfluous, since he never believed that Saudi Arabia was under threat. Subsequently, he had talked with most of the Arab states and believed that an Arab solution was possible. He considered Iraq's withdrawal from Kuwait a strong possibility, but now that Iraq was reaching agreement with Iran under terms that would leave control of the Shatt-al-Arab passage into the Gulf with Iran, Iraq would need better access to the Gulf. This would have to be arranged. The King said that the only government he had found "utterly impossible" during his travels was that of the United Kingdom. He had found Margaret Thatcher "on the warpath," which he thought quite shocking. The Prime Minister had told him that it was not purely a question of freeing Kuwait. Saddam Hussein must be deposed and his army and weapons destroyed. The Jordanian king considered this a dangerous attitude, and he feared its influence on the United States.

On returning to New York on September 5, I received a telephone call from President Bush, who congratulated me on my efforts in Amman. He felt that it was crucial that I should have gone. It enhanced not only my image but also that of the United Nations. I told the President that I had undertaken the trip with two aims: either to obtain flexibility on the part of Iraq that would lead to a peaceful resolution of the crisis, or to expose Iraq's intransigence.

Unfortunately, the latter objective was the one achieved. The President said that he was pleased that I had been so direct in my statements to the press, but he added "You know, I don't know where we will go from here." I suggested that if there were to be a solution, some form of Arab involvement would be required. I referred to my discussion in Paris with King Hussein and mentioned the difficult encounter that the King had with Prime Minister Thatcher. President Bush replied, "I know," in a tone that seemed to indicate regret.

In the detailed report that I gave to the Security Council, I said that I had not expected that the fundamental issues could be resolved in a matter of hours in Amman. I had hoped, however, to start a diplomatic process that would lead to a speedy resolution of the conflict. Regrettably, this had not happened.

By mid-September a large American force had arrived in Saudi Arabia and in the neighboring waters. Many rumors were in circulation of impending military action. On September 28, I was reliably informed that William Webster, the head of the Central Intelligence Agency (CIA), believed that Saddam Hussein had concluded that war was inevitable. The CIA, I was told, was convinced that Saddam, having arrived at that conclusion, would launch a preemptive strike against U.S. forces to inflict as much damage as possible. The CIA was said to believe that Iraq had a nuclear device that, while not deliverable by missile, could be dropped from an aircraft. Such reports were especially disturbing since no concerted diplomatic action was taking place to try to find a peaceful solution. Colombia, Cuba, Malaysia and Yemen introduced a draft resolution in the Security Council calling for renewed efforts for a peaceful political solution of the crisis, but the text received little support. Among major world leaders, only President François Mitterrand of France, in an address to the General Assembly, emphasized the need for diplomatic action. I felt that there was a vacuum and that an unintentional incident on the ground could lead to a tragic conflagration. I expressed this concern to President Bush when he came to the United Nations on October 1. The President responded that he was preoccupied with another matter, namely the need to hold together the international consensus in order to ensure that the Security Council sanctions against Iraq were effective. I mentioned the disturbing report I had received that Iraq might have a nuclear device that could be dropped from an airplane. The President said that he did not discount this possibility.

President Mitterrand, in his Assembly address, had specifically suggested that talks with Iraq should be possible, but only after Iraq had withdrawn from Kuwait and all hostages being held by Iraq released. President Bush noted that Mitterrand had not included restoration of the legitimate government of Kuwait, as called for in the Security Council's resolutions, among his conditions. He said with considerable emphasis that there were a good many "op-ed writers" in the United States who were calling for free and fair elections in Kuwait. But he felt strongly that "we should fulfill what the United Nations had set out to do." The United States could not and would not back away. I volunteered the thought that in order to ensure Iraq's complete isolation, the United States might begin a dialogue with Iran. As it was, Saddam Hussein undoubtedly was feeling the sting of King Hussein's decision to go along with the UN-imposed sanctions. If an American-Iranian dialogue were launched, it could further limit Saddam's room for maneuver and counter any temptation in Tehran to play the Iraqi game. President Bush said that if I were to meet again with Iranian Foreign Minister Ali Akbar Velayati I could mention that "In this new world order, he envisaged much better relations between Iran and the United States." He said this message had already been conveyed to Tehran by two friendly countries. Quite civilized responses had been received from both President Hashemi Rafsanjani and Foreign Minister Velayati, "despite the continuing anti-American demonstrations in downtown Tehran." But both had indicated that it was too early to enter into "more visible contacts" with the United States.

During late September and October a series of international statesmen went to Baghdad in the hope of gaining freedom for their nationals and of finding, with Saddam Hussein, a peaceful solution to the crisis. Of these, potentially the most important was Evgeni M. Primakov, who traveled twice to the region—and to Washington, as well—as the special representative of Soviet President Gorbachev. The Soviet Union had long been a principal supplier of arms for Iraq, and the two countries were bound in a treaty of friendship and cooperation. Thousands of Soviet military advisors and technicians were in Iraq and, like many other third-country nationals, were not being allowed to leave. I was not directly involved in Primakov's efforts, but the Soviet Permanent Representative in New York gave me an extensive account of Primakov's discussions in Baghdad. From this it was clear that Saddam Hussein was extremely resentful of the withdrawal of Soviet technicians for whom no Iraqi replacements were available and agreed to let the first 1,500 depart only after some very forceful language on Primakov's part. Primakov was under instructions to try to find some compromise solution that would preclude the use of force to drive Iraq from Kuwait. During his first visit, he concluded that this might be possible but he never departed from insisting that Iraq's withdrawal from Kuwait was the prerequisite for any compromise. Saddam was never willing to make such a commitment, claiming that even if he did withdraw, he would remain in an isolated position, unable to exert the influence throughout the region that was his ambition. So, like all the other special missions, Primakov's mission failed.

The Gulf crisis posed very special problems for Arab countries, to whom Saddam Hussein claimed to look for a solution. They were divided on what to do even though none condoned Saddam's action in invading a brother Arab state.

Egypt, which traditionally had competed with Iraq for leadership of the Arab community, was quick to join the American-led coalition to defend Saudi Arabia against an Iraqi attack. It clearly hoped to get rid of Saddam Hussein but wished to avoid making him into a hero for the Arab masses in the process. The deputy prime minister of Egypt, Boutros Boutros-Ghali, who was to be my successor as Secretary-General, expressed the problem very clearly in speaking to me in early October in behalf of President Mubarak. The objective, he said, must be to find a compromise formula that would not enhance the position of Saddam Hussein, whom many Arabs viewed as the only leader in the region concerned for the Palestinians. It was essential to make a distinction between the Iraq-Kuwait problem and the Arab-Israeli problem. In both cases a retreat was necessary, by the Iraqis and Israelis respectively. How, he asked, was one to establish the linkage while maintaining that no linkage existed?

Boutros-Ghali suggested that the answer was through the establishment of clearly separate schedules for the two operations. Egypt's position was firm; there must be an unconditional withdrawal of Iraqi forces from Kuwait. It rejected President Mitterand's suggestion that there should be a plebiscite to decide on the future government of Kuwait, since this would constitute intervention in the internal affairs of a sovereign country. As the matter turned out, the United States was able to impose, through military means, a schedule for Iraq's withdrawal from Kuwait and, through persuasion and pressure, a separate schedule for Arab/Israeli talks that were bound to touch on the question of Israeli withdrawal from the Occupied Territories.

ENFORCEMENT MEASURES BEGIN AGAINST IRAQ

The adoption of Resolution 665, which called on "those Member States cooperating with the Government of Kuwait which are deploying maritime forces to the area to use such measures commensurate to the specific circumstances as may be necessary . . . to halt all inward and outward maritime shipping in order . . . to ensure strict implementation of the provisions related to such shipments," marked a significant departure. It was only the second time in the United Nations' history that the Council had authorized the use of military means to enforce sanctions; the first time had been in 1950, in the Korean War. The application of sanctions by the United Nations (as by the League of Nations before it) had been considered of doubtful effect, since there were no means of enforcement. Now the Council authorized military enforcement measures by individual Member States acting "under the authority of the Security Council." This is the principle that was followed to much broader effect when on November 29 the Security Council adopted Resolution 678, authorizing "Member States cooperating with the Government of Kuwait, unless Iraq on or before 15 January 1991 fully implements the [previous] resolutions, *to use all necessary means* to uphold and implement Resolution 660 (1990) and all subsequent relevant resolutions and to restore international peace and security in the area" (italics added). There were only two negative votes on this fateful resolution, from Cuba and from Yemen, and one abstention, by China. I was not consulted while Resolution 665 was being drafted, even though it opened the way for an extraordinary departure in UN practice. The Secretary-General was given no role in designing or carrying out the strategy to defeat the Iraqi aggression and bring peace.

For the United Nations to go to war to maintain peace may seem inherently contradictory. Yet the concept of collective security on which the United Nations is based presupposes that the security of any country threatened by aggression will be protected by all other member nations, using force if necessary. The League of Nations failed primarily because it was unable to take effective action to stop aggression. At the ministerial-level meeting of the Security Council when Resolution 678, authorizing the use of "all necessary means," was adopted, the American secretary of state, James Baker, recalled the League's failure to respond to the plea for assistance from Emperor Haile Selassi of Ethiopia when his country was invaded by forces of Italy's Benito Mussolini. With the Cold War over, Baker said, history had given the United Nations and the Security Council "another chance" to act as "true instruments for peace and for justice across the globe."[1] It was historically apt that Ethiopia was a member of the Security Council and voted in favor of the resolution.

The Iraqi invasion of Kuwait constituted the first aggression that the United Nations needed to meet in the post–Cold War era. Quite remarkably, the five Permanent Members of the Security Council were able to agree, as they had never done before, on the use of force to implement its decisions. The Council was doing what I had warned nine years before in my first Annual Report must be done to avoid international anarchy.

The Council, however, had no military force available with which to bring about the unconditional withdrawal of Iraq from Kuwait. The United Nations Charter provides that Member States will make "armed forces, assistance, and facilities" available to the Council in accordance with special agreements to be negotiated with them. Because of profound disagreement between the United States and the Soviet Union on many aspects of the proposed force, no agreements were ever reached with Member States. Thus when the Gulf crisis arose, the Council had no alternative, if force was to be used, other than to turn to Member States to provide it. The United States, which already had a very large armed force in Saudi Arabia poised to take action against Kuwait, urged that the Council take this action; that is what the Council did.

It is highly likely that the United States plus the other countries that were joined in the coalition would have undertaken military action to free Kuwait even had authorization from the Security Council to act in its behalf not been forthcoming. The United States clearly chose to seek sponsorship for several reasons. To act under a Security Council mandate would ease President Bush's problem in gaining congressional approval to go to war with Iraq. It made it easier to maintain unity among the coalition countries, a number of whom found it far more convenient to fight on behalf of the United Nations than of the United States. I believe that President Bush also sincerely wished to take advantage of the United Nations' potential as an element of the new world order that he envisioned, however vaguely.

Just before Resolution 678 was adopted on November 29, Secretary Baker called on me in my office. Baker first ceremoniously handed me checks totalling more than $185 million, covering a portion of the U.S. indebtedness to the United Nations. The secretary then observed that it was exciting to be involved in making the dream of the UN founders come true. While the United States was to some extent responsible for this, "the lion's share of the credit," he said, "should go to the Soviet Union." I agreed that it was important to credit Mikhail Gorbachev personally because of the very great and courageous changes he had made. Mr. Baker continued that the end of the Cold War had made it possible for the U.S. administration to convince the American political establishment that the United States should work through the United Nations in matters of international security. He recalled that when the embargo of Iraq was under consideration, it had been widely argued in the United States that Article 51 of the Charter, covering the right of self-defense, provided sufficient legal grounds for the United States and other countries to take military action to enforce the sanctions. But President Bush had sought the wider support that could be gained through a resolution specifically authorizing the action. The secretary thought that President Bush had been influenced by his earlier experience as U.S. Permanent Representative to the United Nations. He had made the same "correct decision" with regard to the resolution that would be adopted by the Council that afternoon.

I expressed the hope that the resolution would send a clear, understandable message to Baghdad. At the same time I suggested that one must never lose sight of the possibility of a peaceful solution. Baker agreed, insisting that those who say that the United States sought this resolution "in order to spill the blood of U.S. boys and girls were wrong." Yet such a resolution could not be adopted, without demonstrating the military resolve to carry it out. A force the size of the one then in Saudi Arabia was not mobilized without realizing you might have to use it." Secretary Baker emphasized that the United States was serious about showing Iraq "that we mean business."

I told Baker I would do my best to convince the Iraqi authorities that what the Security Council was asking for was a *just peace,* without appeasement.

The secretary suggested that at some point following the adoption of the resolution he would want to talk to me about "whether, if and when" another effort on my part would be called for. President Bush had expressed the same thought to me when we met briefly in October in Paris at the summit meeting of the Conference on Security and Cooperation in Europe.

The Security Council met at the ministerial level to adopt Resolution 678. Of the 15 Council members, 13 were represented by their foreign ministers. Those present fully appreciated the significance of the step being taken. The American secretary of state served as Council president. In his introductory statement, he specifically stated that "if Iraq does not reverse its course peacefully, then other necessary measures, including the use of force, should be authorized. We must put the choice to Saddam Hussein in unmistakable terms." The British foreign minister, Douglas Hurd, stated, "The military option is reality, not bluff. If it has to be used, it will be used. . . ."

A number of members urged that the six weeks prior to January 15, the deadline that had been given for the withdrawal of Iraqi troops, be used for further efforts to find a diplomatic solution. The foreign minister of Malaysia Abu Hassan, expressed this sentiment with particular clarity. "Even with the present resolution, the most serious in the history of the Council," he said, "it is Malaysia's hope that force does not have to be inevitable." He insisted that any proposed use of force must be brought before the Council for its prior approval and considered that the absence of a clear requirement for this in the resolution might constitute a precedent that "may not bode well for the future." He warned against any action "purportedly taken under this resolution that would lead to the virtual destruction of Iraq." Still, Malaysia felt obliged to vote for the resolution because of its duty to support and uphold the Council's unity and resolve to reverse aggression and restore peace.

This statement coincided closely with my own views. After the resolution was adopted and all the national representatives had spoken, I asked for the floor. Given the responsibility inherent in my office, I stated, I felt duty bound to express the hope that the 45 days until January 15 would be used to the most constructive purpose. To my mind the situation demanded that diplomatic efforts be undertaken with renewed determination. In requiring compliance with the resolutions of the Security Council, the United Nations was not seeking surrender but the most honorable way of resolving a crisis in a manner conducive to the wider peace and the rule of law. I warned that a collective engagement requires a discipline all its own.

The United States, having decided to go the UN route, exercised strong leadership in setting the course that the United Nations was to follow. It worked with the other four Permanent Members of the Security Council to great effect. The result was a remarkable demonstration of how effective the Security Council can be when the Permanent Members are in agreement. The cause was clear: A small country, a member of the United Nations, had been invaded and annexed by a far larger neighbor, and one under dictatorial rule. No UN member could condone this. Nonetheless, it was an extraordinary feat of American diplomacy to keep the Permanent Members together (or, in the case of China, to keep it from blocking the desired action) and to gain sustained majority support in the Security Council for action against Iraq that was in important respects without precedent. Even so, American diplomacy (and pressure) would not have been successful without the notable changes introduced in Soviet foreign policy by Mikhail Gorbachev. In the pre-Gorbachev era, it can be assumed that the Soviet Union would have supported its ally Iraq at least to the extent of preventing adoption of a Security Council resolution authorizing the use of force. As the crisis progressed, it was evident that the Soviet Union still sought to pursue a policy that would take into account its previous close relationship with Iraq. It found itself restricted, however, by its commitment to the resolutions adopted with its affirmative vote by the Security Council and also by the intransigence of Saddam Hussein.

For its part, the Security Council, if it was to restore its credibility in maintaining international security, needed very badly to bring Iraq to comply with its various decisions. The Security Council had the responsibility to act against aggression, yet it had no means to undertake the military action that would most likely be needed to dislodge Iraq. This reality made members susceptible to the intense and skillful campaign mounted by the United States for the Council to authorize the use of military power by those countries able to do so. I am convinced that if the Security Council had voted against the use of force, and if military action was taken outside a UN framework, unfortunate consequences for the United Nations would have ensued. The blow to the concept of collective security could have been fatal.

This is not to say that the nature of the decision taken by the Council to authorize the use of force did not entail dangers and disadvantages. The Council's action in giving carte blanche for the conduct of military action without retaining control or influence on the command of operations, on overall strategy or on conditions for terminating military action raises serious questions. The Charter established a Military Staff Committee, composed of senior military representatives of the five Permanent Members, which was to be responsible "for the strategic direction of any armed forces placed at the disposal of the Security Council." But the United States and the United Kingdom made very clear that any direction, strategic or otherwise, by the Committee of the action against Iraq would be unacceptable. This was understandable, since the Military Staff Committee is a body that acts, if it acts at all, only on the basis of consensus. To rely on such a decision-making process for the strategic direction of a major military action would be of doubtful practicality.

Since the United States was providing the overwhelming majority of forces and equipment, the Council was hardly in a position to challenge it on the command of the military operation or on the military strategy to be followed. I do not believe the situation would be different in any comparable effort in the future. Nonetheless, the serious disadvantages inherent in this practice need to be recognized. A force over which the United Nations has little or no influence inevitably takes on the identity of its major component, as happened to a large extent in the Gulf. This lessens the image of collective responsibility and risks, in the course of time, losing the support of a sizable number of countries. During military actions, there is always the possibility that the force commander, under guidance from a national government or governments, will take action of which a substantial number of UN members disapprove. As a result, the United Nations, in effect, may disassociate itself from the operation. This could well have been the case in the Gulf War had the blanket bombing continued much longer or had the United States decided that the campaign should be carried to Baghdad in order to destroy Saddam Hussein.

Again, reality has to be faced. If one country is fielding a major armed force including land, air and sea contingents, it is not likely to accept UN control of that force. In such circumstances, the Security Council will not be able to impose very stringent conditions on how the force is commanded or the strategy that is followed. But the challenges that must be anticipated in the future are not likely to be of comparable size to that posed by Iraq with its large, well-equipped army. Nor will the interests of a major military power necessarily be involved, as was true in the Gulf. As I view the possibility of conflict between small, less-developed states, I am convinced that a multilateral UN force under UN command can be an effective instrument for peace. Certainly this option should be available. Otherwise the United Nations will remain dependent on one or two major countries in meeting future aggression, which means that it will be constrained to act in accordance with the interests of those countries.

FINAL EFFORTS FOR A PEACEFUL SOLUTION

Following the action of the Security Council to set January 15 as the deadline for the withdrawal of Iraqi forces from Kuwait, the United States took a unilateral initiative in seeking to arrange a meeting between Secretary of State Baker and Iraqi Deputy Prime Minister Tariq Aziz. It was announced in advance that Baker had no intention of negotiating any kind of compromise. His purpose would be to make clear beyond any doubt the determination of the United States to ensure the implementation of the Security Council resolutions. While welcoming the American initiative, I felt that Iraq was unlikely to make significant concessions directly to the United States. The loss of face would be too great for a man of Saddam Hussein's megalomanic pride to accept. In light of my experience with Tariq Aziz in Amman and the unsuccessful efforts of Gorbachev's special emissary, of Chinese Foreign Minister, Qian Qichen, of the former German Chancellor Willy Brandt and of the other dignitaries who had traveled to Baghdad and talked directly with Saddam, I did not have much hope that war could be avoided, especially given the massive buildup of American forces in Saudi Arabia that by then had taken place. Still, every possibility had to be explored, and I felt that if Saddam were to make the necessary concessions, it would be easier for him to do it to a UN representative than to the United States or another country friendly to it.

MEETING WITH TWO PRESIDENTS:
BUSH AND SADDAM HUSSEIN

Recalling the extensive and eventually successful discussions I had with Saddam in seeking an end to the Iran-Iraq war, I began in early December to think of seeking a meeting with him in a last effort for peace. I would do this only if Baker's talks with Tariq Aziz produced no positive results. With the help of my closest advisors, I developed ideas for a settlement that were built around a specific timetable for Iraq's withdrawal from Kuwait, the deployment of a UN peacekeeping force in Kuwait and the initiation of talks between Iraq and Kuwait to settle their differences. In the same time frame broader talks would begin to work out a structure for security and cooperation in the Gulf region, as was foreseen in Security Council Resolution 598 ending the Iran-Iraq war, which Iraq had accepted.

In mid-December, I quietly let the Iraqi government know through the Iraqi ambassador in New York that I was ready to come to meet with President Saddam at any time, if this might be helpful in resolving the crisis without further military action. On December 22 word was passed to me through the Chinese Permanent Representative in New York that Tariq Aziz, on behalf of Saddam Hussein, welcomed the prospect of a visit by the Secretary-General to Baghdad. I should propose a date and Baghdad would then consider whether it was appropriate. Tariq Aziz according to the Chinese, wished me to take two points into consideration: first, how to deal with the "unfair and punitive" resolutions of the Security Council, and second, implementation of the UN resolutions on Palestine and the exercise of the right to self-determination of the Palestinian people. A senior aide to Tariq Aziz had told the Chinese ambassador in Baghdad that while these points should be kept in mind, they were not preconditions to my visit.

I did not wish to interfere in any way with the exchanges that were then going on to establish a date for a meeting between the American secretary of state and Tariq Aziz. It would have been highly unfortunate if the Iraqi government was able to use my possible visit as justification for not meeting with Baker. Thus I did not suggest a date for a visit and I said nothing publicly about the Iraqi approach, although there was increasing speculation in the press that I might be making a trip to Baghdad. I simply passed word back through the Chinese that I was giving serious consideration to a possible visit. I informed General Scowcroft of these developments and suggested that it would be advisable for me to meet with President Bush before undertaking a trip to Baghdad.

When I returned to UN Headquarters on January 3, after a brief vacation, I was met at the entrance by a throng of press representatives who asked if I was in touch with Baghdad. I replied that in my quiet way I was in touch with all the parties and that I would go to Baghdad if the Iraqi authorities considered this useful. However, it was important not to duplicate efforts, not to create confusion by having too many cooks in the kitchen. I said that I felt that the initiative of the Americans and their allies for the meeting with Tariq Aziz was a heartening indication that everyone wanted to avoid a military conflagration. I added that I would be seeing the Iraqi ambassador, who was just returning from Baghdad the next day, and would explore with him all possibilities for a peaceful solution. On the same day President Bush called and invited me and my wife to go to Camp David for lunch on Saturday, January 5.

When I met with Iraqi Ambassador Abdul A. Al-Anbari on January 4, he informed me that Iraq had accepted January 9 as the date for a meeting between Deputy Prime Minister Tariq Aziz and Secretary of State Baker. He then conveyed to me an invitation to travel to Baghdad to meet with the President and minister Tariq Aziz at a time of my choosing. I expressed my thanks for the invitation but said that it would be wise to await the outcome of the meeting between Baker and Tariq Aziz before deciding on a possible visit to Baghdad. I hoped that the contacts between the Iraqi foreign minister and the American secretary of state would begin a process that would lead to peace. Ambassador Al-Anbari said he was authorized to make totally clear that Iraq would never respond to intimidation and threats. The world, he continued, could not afford to fail in its search for a peaceful solution. He had just read a scientific article in a British newspaper saying that it would take one to two years to extinguish the fires that would burn, to devastating environmental effect, in the Kuwaiti oil fields. This was the first authoritative indication I had received that Saddam intended to set the Kuwaiti oil fields on fire in the event of military action by the coalition forces. I told the ambassador that I had met President Bush, with whom I had a long personal relationship, in Paris in October, and my impression was that the President truly sought a peaceful way out of the crisis. It was significant, I suggested, that I had been invited to Camp David since in no sense was I a member of the coalition.

The luncheon meeting with George and Barbara Bush at Camp David was thoroughly pleasant. My wife and I were flown there by helicopter from the Pentagon and were met by the Bushes with all their customary cordiality. I had not been to Camp David before, and I found its sophisticated simplicity was conducive to a relaxed atmosphere free from the rigors of protocol. It was a cold day, with a frigid wind, which struck me as less than perfect for travel in the open golf carts that is customary at the presidential retreat. The President, however, had thoughtfully provided extra jackets for his Peruvian guests so that my shivering was kept to a minimum. During the substantive talks before lunch, the President was accompanied only by General Scowcroft. A gifted young American from the Secretariat, Lisa Buttenheim, was with me as note taker. The President, obviously concerned over the danger that lay ahead, had an anxious air. In the course of our discussions, I gained the impression that the basic decision to use the full coalition force deployed in the Gulf region to drive Iraq out of Kuwait had been made— that, barring a last-minute Iraqi decision to withdraw unconditionally, war was inevitable. Yet, at the same time, I detected in George Bush a genuine reluctance to go this route. He certainly was not fearful or lacking in confidence, but I believe that he hoped, against his own rational expectations, that a peaceful solution, involving no appeasement of Saddam Hussein, would be found.

The substantive discussion began on the subject of the Western hostages in Lebanon and the attitude of the Iranian Government. The United States stood ready to improve ties with Iran, but the President had recently heard from the Omanis that the Iranian Government still felt it was a bit early. I suggested that President Rafsanjani had to be extremely cautious in light of the buildup of American forces in Saudi Arabia. The President acknowledged that Iran might have reservations about the U.S. forces in the region. He encouraged me to continue my quiet dialogue with the Iranian foreign minister in which I could make clear that the United States did not wish the coalition forces to remain in the region for an extended period. "Not one American wants us to stay there," he said. It should be realized, however, that as long as U.S. and other Western hostages in Lebanon remained in captivity, "about whose fate Iran knew a great deal," relations between the United States and Iran could never be normal. When I suggested that Syria, which controlled a good part of Lebanon, could assist in freeing the hostages if it so wished, Mr. Bush said that President Hafez Al-Assad, when they had met in Geneva, had assured him that he was doing all that he could. I expressed some doubt as to the reliability of President Assad, a sentiment with which both President Bush and General Scowcroft vehemently concurred. The President thought that a whole cloud could be lifted on the Palestinian issue "if this hostage thing could be resolved."

After an inconclusive discussion of the Middle East problem, in which the President showed no great affection for Israel's Likud-led government, the conversation turned to the Gulf—"the main question," as President Bush said. At the beginning of this discussion, the President expressed his serious belief that the new world order could be more than a dream and that the United Nations could be a model for that new order. "The United Nations today has the opportunity to fulfill its peacekeeping role," he said. But the Security Council resolutions needed to be implemented "to the T." President Bush was convinced that if the objectives of the 12 Security Council resolutions relative to Iraq's invasion of Kuwait that had by then been adopted were compromised in any way, the United Nations would be rendered impotent. He felt that Saddam Hussein believed that force would not be used against him, or if it were used, it would result in a stalemate, and he would be able to do great damage to the coalition forces. General Scowcroft stated, in confirmation, that the "endless emissaries" who had visited Baghdad had all brought back word that Saddam Hussein did not believe the United States was prepared to use force. "Well, I am prepared to use force," President Bush said. He very much hoped that the meeting between Secretary Baker and Minister Tariq Aziz would produce something, but he was not optimistic.

President Bush dwelt with evident concern on the moral issues involved in the use of force. He said that he was a "WASP" Episcopalian. The presiding bishop of the Episcopalian Church had recently visited him and told him to pray about the morality of a decision to use force, which he had done. But he also had drawn the bishop's attention to the Amnesty International report on Iraqi atrocities and asked him to answer that "moral question." If the United States had stood up during the Hitler threats of 1938-39 instead of retreating into an isolationist stance, perhaps millions of lives could have been saved. Speaking as a friend, the President wanted me to know that he had thought a great deal about the moral question. He had 12 grandchildren, and he received mail every day pleading not to cause a husband or a son to die. Still, he felt very strongly that "if we do not achieve what Resolution 678 is all about, we will live to regret it." A huge force had been moved to the Gulf precisely "to ensure that the risk to every U.S. kid was minimized." There would be a surgical strike, no stalemate, no Vietnam. With this force, the President said, "the man" would not be there very long, or "the man" might still be there but his army would not.

I commented that it was important for the President to be seen as exhausting all possibilities for peace and, precisely for this reason, it was excellent that Jim Baker would be seeing Tariq Aziz in Geneva. I wondered why, for this same purpose, the President didn't consider sending Baker on to Baghdad. President Bush was very firm in stating his reasons. First, Saddam Hussein would thereby buy time; second, with any stalling, the UN resolutions would become meaningless; and third, there would be divisions in the coalition. The real loser, the President continued, would be the "peacekeeping function of the UN."

I noted that two scenarios seemed possible after the Baker–Tariq Aziz meeting. The first was that Iraq would react sensibly and begin to pull out of Kuwait. In such an eventuality, contingency plans (which we were making) for the deployment of UN peacekeeping forces to monitor and supervise the Iraqi withdrawal presumably would have to be implemented. This idea seemed to take both the President and General Scowcroft by surprise. The President asked if I really thought that was going to happen. He said that what the coalition was most worried about was a partial withdrawal. I pursued the concept further, explaining that the UN force could be made up of contingents from neutral Moslem countries and could include military observers from the Security Council's permanent members. This concept clearly intrigued General Scowcroft, who commented that whatever happened, the U.S. forces eventually should be replaced by UN troops. The President said that even with an Iraqi pullout, the sanctions would have to continue until the issues of Iraq's nuclear capability and its proven chemical weapons capacity were dealt with.

I then said that the second scenario was that the Secretary of State would return emptyhanded. What would then be the next step? I had told the Iraqi ambassador the day before that I would be meeting with the President and that I would be glad to convey any message the Iraqi President might have. None had been forthcoming. The ambassador had told me, however, that I would be most welcome in Baghdad at any time to meet with President Saddam Hussein. I felt now that if the Baker–Tariq Aziz meeting did not produce a favorable outcome, it was my responsibility as Secretary-General of the United Nations to do something before the January 15 deadline. Were I to travel to Baghdad, I could convey personally the position of the United Nations as contained in the Security Council resolutions. The President concurred, as long as Saddam could not use such a move as a ploy, "because we could not be deterred at that point from what we have decided." I replied that if I received a second negative response, as I had in Amman, then the President would be in a "clean" position to use force, "although I would not be happy to have my visit serve as a trigger for the war to begin." "So you would be going the extra mile," the President commented. I said yes, but that I was not sure it would lead anywhere. If I came back empty-handed I would say so publicly, just as I had after the meeting with Tariq Aziz in Amman.

General Scowcroft expressed the fear that Saddam would try to use me by asking to continue the talks and to appear before the Security Council. President Bush commented that if I told Saddam, as I had told Tariq Aziz, that my mandate was the 12 Security Council resolutions, "that might be okay. You are free, of course, to do what you think best." The President then said that if Saddam sought a delay of the UN deadline until February 15 or decided on a partial pullout, that would not be acceptable. "Nothing," he emphasized, "will deter us. We, the UK, and the Arab coalition partners won't change our thinking." He commented somewhat ruefully that he had to take some responsibility for being wrong about Saddam Hussein. He had tried to move in a better direction with Iraq but it hadn't worked.

At this point Brent Scowcroft asked specifically whether I proposed to go to Baghdad if Jim Baker's meeting with Tariq Aziz produced no results. I said that by going I could make a final effort. A direct approach to Saddam Hussein might offer the only chance—no matter how slight—to avoid war. As Secretary-General, I had to exhaust all possibilities for peace. Once this was done, a "just war" would be permissible. The President promised that I would be given full details on the content and atmosphere of the meeting between Secretary Baker and Minister Tariq Aziz.

I left Camp David with the distinct feeling that the die had been cast; barring capitulation by Saddam Hussein, military action by the coalition forces under the strong leadership of the United States was inevitable, and it would begin as soon as the January 15 deadline expired. I concluded that President Bush would welcome a peaceful solution if it included Saddam Hussein's acceptance of all the Security Council's demands without delay but that he did not expect this to happen. What he feared was that the clarity of the demands might be compromised, that some appeasement might be offered to Saddam in exchange for peace. That was why he did not particularly encourage me to journey to Baghdad and gave me nothing to offer Saddam Hussein should an opening for serious negotiations arise. The sense I had gained of the terrible imminence of full-scale war increased my conviction that the United Nations, under whose authority the war would be waged, should be seen as making a final effort for peace. For this, a direct meeting with Saddam was essential.

Shortly after I returned from Camp David, the ambassador of Kuwait, Mohammad A. Abulhasan, called at my office. The main purpose of his visit was to urge that if I went to Baghdad, I should do so before January 15 and that, in any talks with Saddam Hussein, I should stay strictly within the limits of the Security Council resolutions. He recalled that American Vice President Dan Quayle had told the Kuwaiti Emir that the world would witness up until January 15 "a marathon of Nobel Prize seekers." I refrained from replying to this sally, but I did promise to let the Emir know in advance if I decided to go to Baghdad, and I also promised that any trip would be before January 15 and any conversation with Saddam Hussein would be within the framework of the Council resolutions.

From the statements made by Secretary Baker to the press following his lengthy meeting with Tariq Aziz in Geneva on January 9, it was evident that no progress had been made. Given Saddam's apparently adamant stand as reflected in the position taken by Tariq Aziz, no further initiative for a peaceful solution on the part of the United States or the coalition members could be expected.

My intention to travel to Baghdad was announced the evening of January 9, just after the negative results of the Baker–Tariq Aziz meeting were made known. Only six days remained before the likely initiation of a mammoth military action, which I feared would be larger and deadlier than any military engagement since World War II. I was asked by the press if I felt I had much room for maneuver. I replied that the only sources of strength I had were the moral force inherent in the post of Secretary-General and the political support of the international community as a whole. Although I did not say so, I knew that these were not forces that would necessarily bring Saddam Hussein to see reason.

The next day I received a letter from Secretary Baker giving an extensive account of his talks with Tariq Aziz. He started by saying that, like President Bush, he welcomed my forthcoming mission to Baghdad. He then described the meeting in notably measured terms. The decisive sentence, however, was—as he had stated publicly immediately after the meeting—that he "saw no sign whatsoever of flexibility or readiness to comply with the 12 Security Council resolutions on the crisis." He had conveyed the clear message from President Bush that Saddam Hussein would either withdraw peacefully and unconditionally from Kuwait in accordance with the expressed will of the international community or be expelled by force. In the meeting with Tariq Aziz, Baker had offered the following assurances:

- The United States would not attack Iraq or its forces if it withdrew completely and restored Kuwait's sovereignty and legitimate government.
- The United States had no intention of maintaining ground forces permanently in the region or of maintaining an offensive capability against Iraq if Iraq complied with the Security Council resolutions.
- The United States supported the provision in Security Council Resolution 660 calling on Iraq and Kuwait to negotiate their differences peacefully.
- Once Iraq demonstrated its intention to comply with these resolutions, the United States intended to consult with Security Council members and coalition partners on the relaxation of sanctions against Iraq, although the continuing concern about Iraq's disproportionate military capabilities, especially in weapons of mass destruction, would have to be factored in.
- While compliance with the Security Council resolutions must be unconditional, the United States had a genuine and continuing commitment to peace between Israel and its Arab and Palestinian neighbors and was ready to make a further effort for an Arab-Israeli dialogue after an Iraqi withdrawal.

After describing Tariq Aziz's unwillingness to depart from the previously held Iraqi positions and his failure even to mention withdrawal from Kuwait, the secretary closed his letter by stating that "as the embodiment of a great world institution, poised on the brink of the most promising period in its history, I hope that you can reinforce to the Iraqi leadership the severity of the situation. . . . President Saddam Hussein . . . must know that the January 15 deadline is very real." When I was asked during an informal press conference that day whether, in going to Baghdad, I felt my hands were tied, I replied that everybody's hands were tied because we had security Council resolutions, but still, I thought, there was room to make some progress.

I left immediately for Baghdad on the Concorde. During a brief stop in Paris, President Mitterrand asked to see me. He had earlier made an informal remark that was interpreted as a French proposal to link Iraqi withdrawal from Kuwait to a settlement of the Arab-Israeli conflict, a position that the United States firmly rejected. Before I reached Paris he had already denied that this was his position in a press conference; during our brief meeting at the Elysée the President made no such suggestion. In effect, he wished me well without stipulating any limitations on my freedom of maneuver in talking with Saddam Hussein. He was very firm, however, that unconditional Iraqi withdrawal from Kuwait was the sine qua non for any peaceful solution.

I arrived in Baghdad in the afternoon of January 12, just three days before the time limit set in Resolution 678 would expire. To the limited extent I could observe, the city seemed normal with no sign of particular preparation for an imminent attack. At seven in the evening a meeting began with Deputy Prime Minister and Foreign Minister Tariq Aziz that lasted for three hours. The minister devoted most of the time to repeating Iraq's position. At the outset I stated that I had traveled to Baghdad on my own initiative, with no specific proposals. (In point of fact, I preferred to save the proposals I had in mind for the meeting with Saddam Hussein.) My sole intention was to search, in cooperation with the Iraqi government, for a peaceful solution to the present crisis. I suggested that our discussion be devoted to preparing for my forthcoming meeting with the President. Tariq Aziz was his usual composed self, speaking at length, in a well-organized, rational manner. But he had nothing to offer with regard to the meeting with Saddam Hussein. I have found that like the Bible, the Koran can be cited as the authority for many different actions. In this case Tariq Aziz, who is Christian, cited a passage that seemed ominously fatalistic. As stated in the Koran, he said "Fighting may be forced on you even if you hate to engage in it. And even if you hate it, it could be good for you." So, he concluded, if God has decided we must have a war, we will submit to the will of the Almighty.

I had proposed to meet twice with Saddam, thinking that this would afford him an opportunity to consider what I had to say before making his reply.

However, Tariq Aziz confirmed only that there would be a meeting with the President on the following day, January 12. He did not specify the time. Since it was known to the Iraqi side that I would have to depart on the twelfth in order to report to the Security Council before January 15, I assumed that the meeting would be early in the day. However, as the morning passed, I received no word on the time of the meeting with Saddam, who was said to be engaged in consultations with his advisors. Instead, first the former Nicaraguan President, Daniel Ortega, and then PLO leader Yassir Arafat—neither of whom was likely to be a particularly useful conversation partner under the circumstances—called on me. Ortega was pessimistic and full of gloom. He saw no escape from war.

Arafat, on the other hand, assured me that Saddam Hussein wanted peace. The important thing was that a binding linkage be established between resolution of the Kuwait problem and the holding of an international conference on the Middle East. Asserting that he knew the local mentality (he had talked with Tariq Aziz before and after my conversation with the foreign minister), he contended that the action by the U.S. Congress in authorizing the use of force gave a highly negative sign at the very time of my peace mission. Saddam was prepared to face the challenge and say, "Okay, let's go to war!" Linkage, he repeated, was the magic word. What was necessary was to find a linkage between Iraq's withdrawal from Kuwait and a solution to the Palestinian problem that would save face both for Saddam and George Bush. That was the way to avoid war. After all, he continued, the holding of an international conference would not be a concession to Saddam Hussein. But clearly more time was required. I would need to come back to Baghdad again. Arafat suggested that I could tell the Security Council that I had heard a number of ideas from European, Palestinian and Iraqi sources and ask for more time to explore them.

I replied that a fisherman must have some bait to attract the fish. Referring to my meeting with President Bush the previous week, I said that I had never met an American president who was so understanding with respect to the Middle East, including the Palestinian question. My chef de cabinet, Virendra Dayal, asked Arafat whether in conjunction with discussion of a Middle East negotiating mechanism, Saddam would be prepared to spell out his position on withdrawal from Kuwait. Arafat said that at a recent meeting of Islamic leaders in Baghdad, Saddam had said he was prepared to offer concessions. "But he, like me, was worried about giving concessions and receiving nothing," the chairman added.

I found Arafat's performance on this occasion distressing. It was all too transparent that he was seeking to utilize Iraq's invasion of Kuwait as a means of gaining advantage for the PLO. He seemed to overlook entirely the inadmissibility of Saddam Hussein's brutal invasion and annexation of a small neighboring state. The thousands of Palestinians resident in Kuwait would pay a heavy price for Yassir Arafat's support of Saddam Hussein. My sense, perhaps unjustified, was that Arafat had been delegated to suggest to me that a bargain was possible if more time were provided and some means could be offered to save Saddam Hussein's face.

Only in the late afternoon did I receive word that the President would receive me at 7:00 P.M. It was later suggested in the press that I considered it a personal insult to have been kept waiting all day to see the Iraqi President. It is true that I was extremely unhappy, but not from *amour-propre*. It seemed to me irresponsible for Saddam Hussein to give no indication even of when the meeting would take place, having full knowledge of the fatal time limit under which we were operating and of the necessity of my departure in the evening.

I have never overestimated my own ability as an individual to alter the course of history. As I approached the meeting with Saddam Hussein that evening, however, I did have the sense that this was the last chance to avoid a war that would bring enormous destruction and the likelihood of even greater instability in a highly volatile region. This chance was clearly small, yet in my previous dealings with Saddam Hussein I had found a rational man. If reason was to triumph over pride, then working through the United Nations Secretary-General could make retreat easier for him. This was my only hope. Knowing that I could offer no compromise on the explicit provisions of the operative Security Council resolutions, I put together a package that was simply a reworking of the points that Secretary Baker had made to Tariq Aziz. Saddam was bound to see the close resemblance between what I was offering and what Baker had offered in Geneva. The question was whether it would be more acceptable as a UN proposal, presented in my language. I wrote down the following points on a small piece of paper, which was all I took with me to the meeting:

- The United States will not attack Iraq if it withdraws from Kuwait and the legitimate government of Kuwait is restored.
- The United States does not intend to maintain ground forces or an offensive capability in the region.
- The United States will support negotiations between Iraq and Kuwait on their differences.
- Sanctions against Iraq will be relaxed once it complies with the Security Council resolutions, although there is concern about excessive military capabilities and arms of mass destruction.
- The United States is committed to work for peace between the Arabs and Israel.
- President Bush has made a clear statement to this effect in his speech to the General Assembly.
- The United States has encouraged my visit to Baghdad.

When the word finally came that Saddam Hussein would receive me, we set out in a convoy to the President's office. We traveled through darkened streets in heavy rain. We emerged from the dispiriting gloom to be confronted at the entrance to the presidential compound with a huge, brightly lit, rather primitive wall painting showing Saddam in military uniform astride a distinctly phallic missile in full flight. It spoke well neither of Saddam's taste nor intentions.

I was received by Saddam in the relatively modest reception room in which I had met with him on previous occasions. Present with the President were Tariq Aziz, Latif Jassem, the Minister of Information, and several aides. As I entered, Saddam extended his arms to his entourage and said "Here, Mr. Secretary-General, are your hawks. Do you consider the Iraqi head of state to be a hawk, too?" I took this as meant in jest and replied only that I was very pleased to have this third opportunity to meet with the President of Iraq. In opening the substantive conversation, I emphasized to Saddam, as I had previously done with Tariq Aziz, that I was in Baghdad on my own initiative, without any specific mandate from the Security Council or the General Assembly and carrying no messages from anyone. My visit had, however, received strong support from world leaders, including President Bush, with whom I had spoken four times since meeting with him at Camp David. While under no instructions from the Security Council, I had an obligation to report to the Council on our conversation and therefore would have to leave Baghdad that night. I was confident that the President "as a military man" would understand that obligations must be respected.

Saddam quickly interjected that he was *not* a military man and had never "for a single day" followed military studies. He was, he said firmly, a lawyer. Making what I hoped was a quick recovery, I responded that I was happy to know that we shared the same legal background. As a lawyer he would understand the importance of UN resolutions and the distinction between those of the General Assembly, which constituted recommendations, and those of the Security Council, which were compulsory on member states. I added that I had no intention of repeating the Security Council resolutions that were relevant to the present crisis because I was certain that the President was entirely familiar with them. What I hoped to discuss was how a military conflagration in the area, which I was confident the President did not wish to see, could be avoided. I said that before coming to Iraq, I had sought to determine whether President Bush truly desired a peaceful solution. I could not serve as a "guarantor" of the President's sincerity, but it was my clear impression that he wished to see a peaceful solution. I had spoken to him just prior to leaving New York and specifically asked him whether he would authorize me to say to President Saddam that he sought a peaceful solution. President Bush had replied, "I, who am responsible in my country for peace and war, would prefer a peaceful solution."

I acknowledged that Saddam had taken some helpful steps. His unilateral decision to release all foreigners was a constructive move. It was to his credit that the international community attached new urgency to dealing with the Palestinian problem. I mentioned, in this context, that I had decided to appoint a new Special Representative to deal with the Middle East. There was now an opportunity to do more for the Palestinians that should not be missed. But to move ahead on Palestine, the present crisis had to be brought to an end. To do so, Resolutions 660 and 678 of the Security Council had to be implemented. I suggested that it would be helpful to think of the postcrisis situation. In this connection, I felt that guarantees could be obtained from the Permanent Members of the Security Council that Iraq would not be attacked if it withdrew its forces from Kuwait.

Saddam had been taking notes throughout my remarks and, when I paused, invited me to continue. After quoting President Mitterrand to the effect that if the Security Council resolutions were implemented, "everything was possible," I proceeded to read the points I had written down. Saddam then rather brusquely told the translator to take the paper from me and read it to him, which the translator did. I told Saddam that President Bush had conveyed these points to me before I left for Baghdad, which was not quite true, but I felt justified in saying this on the basis of my telephone discussions with Bush and knowing they were substantively the same as those Baker had offered. I said that for my part, I could ensure that certain steps, such as the deployment of UN peacekeeping forces, could be taken to guarantee Iraq's safety following the crisis. Work also could begin on a security regime for the region as foreseen in Security Council Resolution 598. In summing up, I said I was not so naive as to think that the problem we were discussing could be resolved in a single meeting, but it was my strong hope to be able to return to New York with something on which a solution could be built.

Saddam replied at length. His manner was calm and his thoughts well organized. He alone spoke, using always the monarchial "we" rather than "I" or referring to himself in the third person, as "Saddam Hussein" who did this or that or was treated thus and so. He began by saying that he would make no secret of the fact that he was reluctant for me to come to Baghdad. He wanted me to come because I knew Iraq and was familiar with Iraqi traits. On the other hand, if I failed to take anything with me that would deter those who were threatening to use their weapons against Iraq, it would give them a pretext for waging war. The President recalled that it had been Iraq that had consistently sought to end the war with Iran. He returned several times to the point that in that case and others, withdrawal of forces had been connected with negotiations rather than set as a precondition for them. He contended that Kuwait was not occupied but was reunified with Iraq, a process that was expedited when the United States moved massive threatening forces to Saudi Arabia. While Iraq had not recognized the legitimacy of Resolution 660, it had responded to its content by declaring unequivocally that it would withdraw from Kuwait; it actually had withdrawn a mechanized brigade. "When the United States escalated its threats against us, we had to halt our withdrawal." Had it not been for the precipitous intervention of the American government, he stated, "the reunification would have taken a longer time and all legal aspects would have been accommodated."

Saddam restated at length but without noticeable passion the by then familiar Iraqi complaints against the United States and Israel. Referring to the points I had read, Saddam maintained that President Bush spoke only of procedural things and never went into the fundamental issues that were important to Iraq as a nation that had suffered injustice. "He refers to the withdrawal of U.S. ground forces but not naval and air forces. He speaks of relaxing sanctions. . . ." I interjected that the sanctions were a United Nations' decision, but Saddam Hussein insisted that they were a U.S. decision "because we are living in an American era. What the U.S. wants, it gets." I said that was certainly not true as far as I was concerned. In rejecting "American domination," I was on the same side as the president of Iraq. Saddam insisted that to understand the complexities of the issues involved in the crisis, dialogue was essential and Iraq was ready for dialogue. However, they had been told to do this and do that, which was not dialogue but imposition. That was the tone of President Bush's letter. "How could Mr. Bush believe that Saddam Hussein would be intimidated even one-millionth of a possibility by threats?" he asked. When Saddam expounded again on Iraq's legal claim to Kuwait, I suggested that this was an appropriate matter for consideration by the International Court of Justice.

I said that careful note had been taken of all that the President had said, and it would be communicated to the Security Council. I then asked whether he still had doubts about my visit. He said that he had not had doubts, "he was hovering." I suggested that he was rightly worried that the outcome of our meeting might go against peace, and this was a valid concern. If I returned from this meeting with nothing, those who sought war could use this as a means of achieving their objective. I was therefore asking, on behalf of the international community, that the President agree to a step that would defuse this crisis, which otherwise could lead to a catastrophe for the region and for the world. Saddam Hussein insisted that in every point he had made there was something for me to carry back. I replied unequivocally that there had been nothing sufficiently tangible in what he had said to decrease the very imminent threat to peace. He recalled then that I had stated at the beginning that I had come without any mandate or message other than that war be avoided. It appeared, though, that I was seeking one thing: that Iraq should declare its withdrawal from Kuwait and then everything would be possible. I said that it was President Mitterand who had made a statement along those lines. "And yet you quoted him and not George Bush," he exclaimed. With more emotion than he had displayed at any other time during the meeting, he declared that all Iraqis know that Kuwait is the nineteenth province. "No Iraqi,' he said, "would whisper the word withdrawal." To do this would mean a psychological preparation for the adversary to achieve victory. What is possible, he continued, is discussion of a package deal, just as was done during the war with Iran. There had to be a comprehensive approach— no loser and no winner.

As there must be no misunderstanding on either side, I stated that if I understood the President correctly, his position regarding Kuwait was firm and irreversible, in which case I saw no possibility for a package deal. Under this condition, any package deal was a nonstarter. Saddam Hussein replied abruptly that what he had said was not what I had said. "I said what I said." If, he continued, the United States is looking for a way to come out neither as a loser nor as a winner and still achieve all of its objectives, then "we can lay down principles and accommodate them." Perhaps, he said, I, as Secretary-General and as an experienced diplomat, could come up with proposals. To make the point crystal clear, Tariq Aziz made his only comment of the meeting, stating that "the President would like you to produce a package." I asked whether the President authorized me to inform the Security Council that he wished to continue discussion through the Secretary-General. He said yes, commenting that was why he gave me such a long exposé.

Saddam walked with me to the entrance of the building as we left and told me almost jocularly that the package I had brought was not good enough. "Come back with something better next time." I responded that any package would have to start with Iraq's withdrawal from Kuwait. He did not react.

There was no doubt in my mind that Saddam Hussein knew perfectly well, as I did, that his adamant refusal to withdraw from Kuwait made war inevitable. He could not have believed that there was still time for negotiation without a firm withdrawal commitment on his part. Yet he showed no sign of nervousness or doubt. The contrast between him and George Bush was extraordinary. Bush, at Camp David, was fully persuaded of the rightness of his position and confident of the power of the coalition forces. He had already made firm decisions on the action to be taken. Yet, conscious of the consequences that the action could have in terms of human lives, especially American lives, he was not a man at ease. I do not believe that George Bush wanted war. He was determined that Iraq would be forced from Kuwait and would pay a price for its aggression. If this required war, then the war should be fought under the most favorable circumstances, which meant under UN authorization and without delay. Saddam Hussein, on the other hand, in his meeting with me gave an impression of serenity, incongruous as that might seem in the circumstances.

He asked few questions and displayed no doubts. His manner, which was always courteous, had not changed from the earlier times we had met.

I have given much thought to the question of what impelled Saddam to adopt his course of action and to hold to it with such confidence in the face of his country's almost certain destruction. The roots, I have concluded, lie in the history of the region, both recent and ancient; in rational but misguided national ambition; in economic necessity; and in personal hubris. Saddam's experience in Iraq's war with Iran surely led him to a number of conclusions that contributed to his fateful decision to invade Kuwait. In all likelihood, they included the following points:

- The UN Security Council took no action against Iraq in 1980 when it invaded Iran; therefore it was not likely to do so now.
- The United States actually had supported Iraq during the Iran-Iraq war and would wish to maintain a tolerable relationship with Iraq as a barrier against Iranian influence in the Gulf.
- The Iraqi army had stood up well and was battle trained. It could be expected to conquer Kuwait before action could be organized to prevent it.
- Despite the relative success of the Iraqi army in the war with Iran, Iraq did not achieve its important objective of unimpeded access to the open sea through control of the Shatt-al-Arab.
- Finally, if Iraq was to recover from the bankruptcy caused by the war with Iran and carry forward ambitious military and economic development programs, a new and large source of funds needed to be found quickly.

Incorporation of Kuwait would, in effect, take the place of the full and quick victory over Iran that Saddam had failed to achieve. It must have seemed a safe operation—until the remarkably swift and unified international reaction occurred.

Kuwait's defiance of Iraq in refusing to maintain limits on the sale of oil and in allegedly pumping oil from Iraqi oil fields may have been a further important influence in Saddam's decision. I doubt, however, that it was the decisive factor. Even if Kuwait had been willing to compromise on these issues, Saddam Hussein still would not have obtained free access to the sea and Iraq's nationalist claim to Kuwait would not have been satisfied. No doubt these points figured in the hubris that triumphed over reason and, as in a Greek drama, brought Saddam to disaster. From my admittedly limited observation I would conclude that in Saddam Hussein's case, an identity with the ancient glory of Babylon was added to a near-maniacal personal ego to produce a man of boundless ambition who could not draw the logical consequences when faced with the certainty of disastrous defeat.

I departed Baghdad for New York immediately after our meeting and, on the next day, January 14, I gave a full report on the meeting to the Security Council, including the Iraqi President's suggestion that I engage the views of the parties in order to make proposals that could lead to a solution. But, in closing, I stated that "it must sadly be concluded that a most ominous situation exists at present. Despite the near-universal yearning for peace . . . the relevant resolutions of the Security Council remain unimplemented. . . . With January 15 upon us, members of the Council must once again consider whether there are any diplomatic measures that can still be taken . . . to secure full implementation of the Council's resolutions by peaceful means." France had prepared a draft declaration for issuance by the Security Council following my report on my unsuccessful mission calling on Iraq to announce immediately its intention to withdraw from Kuwait in accordance with a fixed schedule and giving assurance, in the Council's name, on essentially the same points that Secretary Baker had made to Minister Tariq Aziz and that I had made to Saddam Hussein. The draft, however, did not call for the implementation of all the relevant Council resolutions or for the restoration of the legitimate government of Kuwait, it could be construed as linking the holding of an international conference on the Arab-Israeli problem to the withdrawal of the Iraqi forces from Kuwait. The Council did not act on the draft but simply took note of my report and expressed appreciation for my efforts.

In the absence of further action by the Council, I issued an appeal on January 15, the deadline date, to Saddam to turn the course of events away from catastrophe, to signify Iraq's readiness to comply with the relevant resolutions of the Security Council and to commence without delay the total withdrawal of Iraqi forces from Kuwait. I assured him "on the basis of understandings that I had received from governments at the highest level" that, once withdrawal was under way, UN forces would be deployed to afford protection to all parties. I would urge the Security Council to review its decisions on sanctions, and I would encourage the phasing out of foreign forces from the area. Moreover, I had every assurance that with the resolution of the present crisis, every effort would be made to address the Arab-Israeli conflict in a comprehensive manner, including the Palestinian question. I pledged my "every effort" to this end. There was no response from Saddam Hussein.

Just after 6:00 P.M. on January 16, President Bush called me. After expressing appreciation for my efforts to find a peaceful solution to the Gulf crisis—for having gone the extra mile—the President informed me that American fighters would strike at Iraqi targets in Iraq and Kuwait within one hour. The maximum would be done to avoid civilian casualties. Referring to Saddam

Hussein, he said that it had been impossible to "make the man comply." He then added, "You are a good man. Say a couple of prayers for us. I am not asking for anything else." I expressed my deep sorrow that military action was necessary but said I understood the President's position. He had my warm affection.

Three hours later President Bush announced publicly that the attack by allied air forces had begun. "Our objectives are clear," he said. "Saddam's forces will leave Kuwait. The legitimate government of Kuwait will be restored to its rightful place and Kuwait will once again be free. Iraq will eventually comply with all relevant United Nations resolutions." When asked by the press the following morning whether I saw a prospect of peace any time soon, I replied that it depended on Iraq—"whether Iraq capitulates."

While the battle was waged against Iraq under authorization of the Security Council and in pursuit of implementation of its resolutions, those in command of the military effort did not consult with the United Nations on strategic objectives or inform the Security Council directly of the course of military action. General Norman Schwarzkopf was appointed commander of the coalition forces by the United States, not by the United Nations. Unlike General Douglas MacArthur and his successors during the Korean War, he was never designated as a UN commander, nor did he ever report to the United Nations. The coalition forces bore no UN emblems, and the UN flag was not carried. The countries participating directly in the coalition military force had their direct sources of information from the field. At the United Nations we were almost entirely dependent on the media. From this, however, there quickly emerged a vivid portrayal of the massive bombardment of Iraq and its armed forces from land, sea and the air and of the Scud missile attacks mounted by Iraq against Israel and coalition bases in the Gulf region.

As I watched the television coverage and read the reports of the comprehensive destruction of Iraqi targets, including the logistic backbone of the country, I was deeply torn. The objectives were clearly those defined very broadly by the United Nations Security Council, although whether the United States would interpret these objectives as going beyond the eviction of Iraq from Kuwait, the unconditional restoration of the Kuwaiti government and compensation for the losses inflicted by Iraq was not clear. The paragraph in Resolution 678 authorizing member States to use all necessary means "to restore international peace and security in the area" could cover the occupation of Baghdad and the capture of Saddam Hussein. I feared that if the military campaign took this course, there would be serious divisions within the Security Council that could weaken the effectiveness of the United Nations not just in this case but in others as well, where membership solidarity would constitute its greatest strength. It also seemed to me that the size and intensity of the coalition attack were out of proportion to the enemy's strength, although I understood perfectly well President Bush's determination to avoid another Vietnam.

There was considerable pressure on me from around the world to call for a cease-fire to give an opportunity for further diplomatic efforts. This I felt I could not do. In the first place, it would have been futile. Having undertaken this mammoth military effort, the United States and its coalition allies could not be expected to stop in midstream. But, I think more important, I could not call for a cease-fire during a military operation that was being conducted in the framework of Security Council resolutions. What I did do was to issue on January 22 a further appeal to Iraqi authorities to comply with the relevant resolutions of the Security Council "to prevent the toll in death and destruction from escalating any further and the suffering of the peoples in the region from growing even worse." I said that I was in touch with the main humanitarian agencies of the UN system and the International Committee of the Red Cross, with a view to ensuring that humanitarian help would be provided to those afflicted by the conflict.

There was no direct response from Iraq although, on January 24, Tariq Aziz sent a letter to me condemning the United Nations "for its shameful action in providing cover for the aggression against Iraq of the United States, NATO and the Zionists." I personally, he said, "bore responsibility to history for the heinous crimes being committed against the noble people of Iraq who are fighting for their freedom." Obviously any hope that I might serve as an impartial mediator to bring the conflict to an end had ended. The only thing I could do was to begin planning for the peacekeeping and humanitarian responsibilities that were certain to fall to the United Nations once the fighting was over. The UN organization would have more of a role in building a new peace than in fighting the war.

THE AFTERMATH OF WAR

After Iraq informed the Security Council on February 27, 1991, that all of its armed forces had withdrawn from Kuwait and that it had decided to comply fully with Resolution 660 and all other relevant resolutions, offensive combat activities of the coalition forces were halted and a provisional cessation-of-hostilities arrangement was agreed upon between the commander of the coalition forces, General Schwarzkopf, and Iraqi military representatives. A formal cease-fire was made dependent on Iraqi government acceptance of wide-ranging conditions. At this point the Security Council, having played no part in the military campaign, resumed the leading role in dealing with the Gulf crisis. The United States and the United Kingdom led the way, working closely with the other Permanent Five Council Members in defining the requirements that

Iraq must meet. The result was Security Council Resolution 687, adopted April 3, 1991, by a vote of 12 in favor, 1 opposed (Cuba), and 2 abstentions (Ecuador and Yemen). It is one of the longest resolutions ever adopted by the Council—so long that it quickly became known (in a backhanded compliment to Saddam Hussein's rhetoric) as the "mother of all resolutions." The adoption of the resolution amounted to the imposition on a defeated country of the conditions of peace, something the Security Council had never done before. These conditions, which I consider were well justified, were wide-ranging and severe. Iraq, in negotiations with the Council, sought to resist some of them, as it tried later to resist their implementation, but the choice was clear: Either accept the conditions or face the likelihood of a renewed coalition offensive that could destroy the substantial Iraqi army that remained in the field and Saddam Hussein himself. In effect, Iraq accepted an imposed peace, the provisions of which, as implemented by the United Nations, would prevent the country from again becoming a threat to peace and assure compensation to its victims. Specifically, Iraq was required to:

1. Respect the inviolability of the international boundary with Kuwait as previously agreed between them and accept the assistance of the Secretary-General in demarcating the border.
2. Accept the establishment of a 15-mile-wide demilitarized zone along the demarcated boundary, extending 10 miles into Iraq, in which a UN observer unit would be deployed.
3. Accept unconditionally the destruction, removal or rendering harmless under international supervision of all chemical and biological weapons stockpiles and missiles with a range greater than 150 kilometers and submit to the Secretary-General a declaration of the locations, amounts and types of all the specified items.
4. Renounce any future development or use of these specified weapons.
5. Agree unconditionally not to acquire or develop nuclear weapons and nuclear weapons–usable materials as well as related subsystems, components, research, development and support or manufacturing facilities; submit to the Secretary-General a declaration of the locations, amounts and types of all of these items; and accept their destruction, removal or rendering harmless.
6. Return all Kuwaiti property seized by Iraq.
7. Adhere scrupulously to all its foreign debt obligations.
8. Compensate for any direct losses suffered by governments, nationals or corporations, including environmental damage and depletion of natural resources, as a result of Iraq's invasion of Kuwait for which purpose a compensation fund would be established under the supervi-

sion of the United Nations to be financed from Iraq's petroleum export revenues.

9. Accept continuation of a full international arms embargo against Iraq and of the economic embargo imposed by the Security Council with the exception of medicines and health supplies, foodstuffs and supplies essential for civilian needs.

As Secretary-General I was given primary responsibility for planning the application of many of the requirements placed on Iraq and for overseeing their implementation. Totally new fields for the United Nations were involved. New inspection bodies had to be created, many technical experts recruited and a new peacekeeping mission organized. The Council directed that within 45 days I should present a plan for a special commission to oversee the destruction of Iraq's biological, chemical and missile capabilities and assist the International Atomic Energy Agency in the elimination of Iraq's military nuclear potential. The commission was promptly established as a subordinate body of the Council, as I recommended. These various tasks were accomplished expeditiously, for which the UN Secretariat deserves much credit.

AN URGENT CONCERN: HUMANITARIAN ASSISTANCE

With the end of hostilities, my first concern was to determine the conditions that prevailed in Kuwait and Iraq and to find the dimensions of humanitarian needs. I called on Marti Ahtisaari, who had led the UN Transition Assistance Group in Namibia (see chapter 11), to assess the situation and to report to me on action that the United Nations might take to lessen the suffering of the Kuwaitis and of the mass of Iraqis who, as in any dictatorship, had no voice in their regime's disastrous decisions. Ahtisaari's reports were alarming. The destruction in Kuwait was shocking but the Kuwaiti government had the resources to assist the population to reclaim a normal life. In Iraq, the Ahtisaari mission found that most means of modern life support had been destroyed or rendered tenuous. The national communications system was largely inoperable. Food supplies were inadequate, and new shipments were not coming in. The next harvest was threatened because the irrigation systems were not functioning and pesticides were unavailable. Sanitation disposal systems had been destroyed, which caused a serious threat of the spread of disease. Medical supplies were inadequate. The mission concluded that Iraq had, for some time to come, been relegated to a preindustrial age, but with all the disabilities of postindustrial dependency on an intensive use of energy and technology. While this conclusion, which was widely quoted in the press, proved overstated, the Iraqis urgent need for food and the means of producing it and for medical assistance were very real.

As a result of the Ahtisaari report, the Sanctions Committee of the Security Council determined that the import of foodstuffs into Iraq should be permitted automatically upon notification of the committee. Moreover, the import of fuel, energy items, spare parts and other equipment indispensable for food distribution, harvesting, sanitation and water supply also would be permitted.

The Iraqi situation was made worse by the regime's move to put down by force rebellions of the Kurdish population in the north and of the disaffected Shi'ite minority in the south. The international community suddenly was faced with the dual problem of providing humanitarian assistance to Iraqis in need and of providing protection for minorities under attack by the national government. The control exercised by a national government over the country's citizens is patently a domestic concern and, as such, excluded from UN intervention unless enforcement measures are imposed by the Security Council under Chapter VII of the Charter to preserve peace. Yet remaining passive in the face of a genocidal threat to a group or groups within a population poses a moral problem of profound dimensions. The Iraqi regime's campaign against the Kurds posed precisely this problem for the international community in especially vivid terms. In the face of brutal repression from the Iraqi military, a substantial portion of the Kurdish population fled into the mountains in the border area between Turkey and Iraq. Conditions there were devastating. In the south a large Shi'ite group, under similar attack, took refuge in marshes close to the Iranian border.

Under these circumstances, the Security Council on April 5, 1991 adopted yet another seminal resolution, 688, declaring that the Iraqi regime's repression of its civilian population constituted a threat to international peace and security in the region. The Council demanded that this repression end; that Iraq allow immediate access by international humanitarian organizations to all those in need of assistance in all parts of the country; and requested that the Secretary-General pursue his humanitarian efforts in Iraq and send a further mission to the region if necessary to report on the plight of the Iraqi civilian population, in particular the Kurdish minority. I was to use all the resources at my disposal to address the critical needs of the refugees and displaced Iraqi population. While articulating these various demands that entailed direct intervention in Iraqi domestic affairs, the resolution, in its preamble, reaffirmed the commitment of all Member States "to the sovereignty, territorial integrity and political independence of Iraq. . . ."

Given the need to mobilize various UN agencies and nongovernmental organizations to meet the vast human tragedy, I decided to appoint a high-level official to oversee the UN response. I turned to Prince Sadruddin Aga Khan, a man of long experience in humanitarian undertakings, who agreed to serve as Executive Delegate of the Secretary-General in a United Nations Inter-Agency

Humanitarian Program for Iraq, Kuwait and the Iraq-Turkey and Iraq-Iran border areas. Prince Sadruddin, a former UN High Commissioner for Refugees, had already served as my personal representative to assist third-country nationals when Iraq invaded Kuwait. The prince is a man of energy and compassion. Under his imaginative leadership, the humanitarian assistance program functioned well, saving hundreds of thousands from hunger and illness, facilitating the return of many to their homes, literally sparing thousands from death through privation. The UN membership gave strong political support, although the financial contributions were scarcely half of what was needed.

We developed a plan that foresaw the establishment of humanitarian centers throughout Iraq, where assistance from participating UN agencies and private organizations would be available. Relay stations would be established on the main transportation routes to aid thousands of displaced Iraqis as they returned to their homes. Since Iraq continued to be recognized as sovereign and independent, the government had to agree to any humanitarian projects undertaken in its territory. A memorandum of understanding was therefore sought covering implementation of the plan. The Iraqi government had an evident interest in obtaining assistance and was quite cooperative, even undertaking to provide logistic and local currency support for the program. It insisted only on avoiding any language or action that could infringe on its sovereignty or imply acceptance of Security Council Resolution 688, which it had rejected as invalid.

The memorandum of understanding was scheduled to be signed in Baghdad by the Iraqi foreign minister and Prince Sadruddin at 6:00 P.M. on April 17, 1991. However, signature was suddenly postponed because President Bush had just announced that France, the United Kingdom and the United States would move forces into northern Iraq to establish camps for Kurds returning to Iraq from refuge in the mountains of Turkey. After reexamining the text "at the highest level," the Iraqis agreed to go ahead after only a short delay; the memorandum, which was the basis of all subsequent humanitarian activities in Iraq, was signed on April 18. It contained no reference to Resolution 688 or to the Security Council. It was agreed to entirely under my authority as Secretary-General.

PROTECTING THE KURDS

President Bush had called me on April 16 to tell me of the planned military move into northern Iraq and to discuss possible courses of action on behalf of the Kurds. He explained that for the American Government and other Western governments, it was urgent to get the Kurdish refugees to return to Iraq, where humanitarian assistance could be provided. The Kurds would only return if they received assurance that they would not be attacked by the Iraqi regime. For this reason, a security zone was being established in northern Iraq by the coalition commander from which Iraqi military forces, including aircraft, would be excluded. Transit camps would be established where the refugees could be housed temporarily in safety pending return to their homes. The President expressed the hope that I would make clear publicly that the military action being undertaken by the three countries was fully consonant with the provisions of Security Council Resolution 688.

In a letter to me immediately after this move was announced publicly, President Bush emphasized that this "extraordinary and temporary measure" was being undertaken as a bridge until the United Nations could take over the humanitarian service of providing assistance and protection to the refugees and displaced persons. He again repeated his request that I publicly affirm that the action being taken was entirely in accord with Security Council Resolution 688. This I could not do. The action taken by the three powers was highly motivated and well executed. It successfully saved many Kurdish lives. However, I could not stretch the meaning of Resolution 688 so far as to attest that it constituted authorization for a Western military incursion that, however justified, amounted to an infringement of Iraqi sovereignty. The Security Council could, in principle, have authorized the action as an enforcement measure, but whether agreement could have been achieved in the Council remains an open question.

To facilitate the rapid withdrawal of U.S., British and French forces, the United States wanted the United Nations, acting under this same resolution, to establish a UN security zone or "safe haven" in northern Iraq and deploy a "police force" for the protection of Kurdish refugees. When I met privately with President Bush, Secretary Baker and General Brent Scowcroft at the White House on May 9, the President asked if I wished to raise anything in confidence before proceeding to a larger meeting in the Cabinet Room. Knowing the American interest, I referred to the idea of deploying a UN police force to protect the Kurdish minority. I said that I was entirely sympathetic with the need but after giving the matter most careful study with the assistance of my legal counsel, I had concluded that Resolution 688 did not provide an adequate legal basis to deploy a peacekeeping or police force on Iraqi territory without the consent of the Iraqi Government.

I cited two related difficulties: First, the financing of such a mission would have to be approved by the General Assembly, which would wish to know the legal basis for the proposed action and would likely pose objections. Second, Member States would be reluctant to provide troops or police if Iraq was not prepared to cooperate with the force. The idea of a UN civilian police force had already been discussed with Iraqi authorities, and they had totally rejected it. I suggested that if the United States, the United Kingdom and France wanted a UN protective presence in northern Iraq to serve essentially humanitarian purposes, they should seek the understanding of the other members of the Security Council on a new resolution establishing an appropriate mandate.

After paying high tribute to the "superb and historic role" played by the United Nations throughout the Gulf crisis, President Bush emphasized that American troops had been sent to northern Iraq "to save lives. . . . Our goal now is to get out. I am not going to get bogged down in a lasting quagmire. It's the job of the international community to save these people." The President said that the United States would seek another resolution if this were necessary to provide the United Nations with an appropriate mandate. Secretary Baker interjected that the United States would have to approach this matter with care and prudence. "We need to split the difference," he said, "between security for the Kurds and humanitarian relief . . . in order to avoid a veto over what might appear as UN interference in Iraq's internal affairs."

The President asked about the possibility of sending a "refugee relief force" to northern Iraq. I replied that Sadruddin Aga Khan had signed a memorandum of understanding with the Iraqi authorities enabling the United Nations to send humanitarian assistance and relief workers to Iraq. There were already 100 UN personnel in Iraq working within this framework, and Prince Sadruddin was holding further talks with the Iraqis with a view to expanding the agreement to allow a large number of UN personnel to be sent to the north. While the authorities were entirely negative regarding any form of UN peacekeeping or police operation within Iraq, they had been more open-minded on UN assistance to the Kurds if it was part of the general UN humanitarian assistance program in the country.

President Bush reacted enthusiastically to the news of Prince Sadruddin's negotiations with the Iraqis and urged that the prince continue his efforts. Secretary Baker asked whether the five Permanent Members would back a Security Council resolution establishing a refugee/relief operation. I said that in principle the Security Council could take any action it wished. But a new resolution would be necessary. Without that I would have no way of raising the money for the operation; nor would it be easy to persuade governments to provide the necessary personnel. The President thought the Iraqis would find it very difficult to stand up to an international police force. In the meantime, he asked, "Who would save the lives of the Kurds?" I commented that I did not wish to sound cynical, but it seemed to me that the United States and its allies were providing far more security than the United Nations could. To this, the President exclaimed with considerable emotion, "But we don't want to stay there."

Secretary Baker thought that the continued U.S. presence gave Saddam Hussein a rallying point with his army and other members of the population who "ought to be overthrowing him." The President acknowledged that the relief workers would need some form of protection. "I just wish," he said, "that 688 could be sufficient. . . . We've done a hell of a good job but we cannot stay much longer." President Bush clearly understood the reasons for my reservations and pursued the idea no further. I found that on matters such as this, the President's earlier UN experience led him to appreciate the factors at play in the Organization that officials directly charged with responsibility for United Nations affairs in the State Department often did not have.

THE UNITED NATIONS TAKES OVER

Following signature of the memorandum of understanding on the provision of humanitarian assistance, the United Nations was able to move ahead quickly with the establishment of humanitarian centers and relay stations in widely spread locations in Iraq. The three powers were insistent that the United Nations should also assume full responsibility for the transit camps they had established in northern Iraq and for the well-being of the Kurds. The problem was to find a way not only to provide safety for the Kurds in the camps but also to encourage them to leave the camps and return to their homes. On my behalf, Prince Sadruddin again broached with the Iraqi authorities the possibility of deploying a peacekeeping force. Their answer remained a resounding no.

Prince Sadruddin had had the idea of using a modest number of UN guards for security purposes. These guards are the uniformed personnel who stand at the entrances of the principal UN buildings in New York, Geneva, Vienna and Nairobi, checking the identity of visitors. They are generally responsible for security in the extraterritorial UN premises and are trained to deal with any disturbances, since the local police have no authority there. Many were policemen before joining the United Nations. They are regular Secretariat staff members and function entirely under the administrative authority of the Secretary-General. Sadruddin believed the guards could be posted in the humanitarian centers (and the transit camps once the United Nations took over) to provide protection for the many workers from the United Nations and private agencies that would be participating in the work of the centers and security for the supplies that would be brought in. This would be their official purpose. But, in addition, they could circulate throughout the Kurdish region, observe what was going on and, by their presence, provide reassurance to the Kurds that they were safe from harm.

Prince Sadruddin discussed with the Iraqis such utilization of the guards—solely for the protection of the staff and supplies of the humanitarian centers. The Iraqi government accepted, motivated, certainly, by its desire to get the tripartite troops out of northern Iraq, a desire it shared in this instance with the three powers themselves. The conditions governing the functioning of the guards were spelled out in a letter from the foreign minister of Iraq to Prince

Sadruddin that became an annex to the memorandum of understanding. Under this agreement, the guards could be assigned to UN humanitarian centers, transit camps, relay stations and suboffices as needed, up to a total number of 500, with no more than 150 in any one region. The guards could move freely in UN-marked vehicles and a UN-marked helicopter, for which the government of Iraq would make the necessary landing arrangements. They would carry sidearms supplied by the Iraqi government.

Utilization of UN guards to provide security in the field had not been undertaken since the first Secretary-General, Trygve Lie, had tried it in the Middle East. I was not sure that this modest number of personnel without experience in conflict situations could provide the degree of security that was expected and needed in northern Iraq. However, the large UN civilian presence in the humanitarian centers would provide some assurance that the Kurds would not again be subjected to attack by the Iraqi regime. Moreover, the Iraqi military would remain barred from the area, and the three Western powers would continue their protective overflights. The guards would serve primarily as a symbol of an effective UN presence. They could also observe what was going on and report back to senior UN representatives any untoward developments.

Shortly after the Iraqis gave informal agreement to the proposal and, before the written annex to the memorandum of understanding was completed, ten UN guards from UN Headquarters in Geneva who had volunteered for this duty were sent to Dohuk on Iraq's northern plain where a UN humanitarian center had just been opened. The transit camps, which were established by the three powers and would shortly be turned over to the United Nations, were nearby, and the Iraqis understood that the guards would also provide security for the UN staff and supplies there. The procedure worked well. The transit camps were turned over to the United Nations without difficulty and the allied troops departed. The humanitarian center at Dohuk and its suboffices became the principal source of food and medical assistance for the Kurdish population. The UN presence—with the UN guards much in evidence—proved sufficiently reassuring to cause those Kurds who were still in the mountains to return and for those in the transit camps to move back to their villages and towns. The camp tents could soon be folded. The Iraqi regime, fortunately, chose not to make difficulties. It certainly knew that the UN guards were serving a larger purpose than just protecting UN staff and supplies, but since the guards' first action had been to rescue an Iraqi official who had fallen into the hands of fierce Kurdish fighters, perhaps they were disinclined to complain.

The utilization of UN guards in Iraq as part of a United Nations humanitarian effort marked an innovation that may prove useful elsewhere. The United Nations has become increasingly involved in providing humanitarian assistance in internal conflict conditions. The Security Council has been reluctant to authorize the deployment of troops for peace keeping or peace enforcement without the consent of the government concerned. Under these circumstances, UN guards offer an alternative. Since they are regular employees of the UN Secretariat, they can be assigned to do guard duty at the pleasure of the Secretary-General. As has been shown in Iraq, their presence can make a difference. They cannot, however, be seen as an alternative to peacekeeping forces. In the first place, the number of guards available for field service is severely limited. To send 500 to Iraq, as was done, new personnel had to be recruited beyond the regular guard complement for which funds are available in the regular UN budget. The financing of the guards in Iraq was a problem notwithstanding the emergency conditions that prevailed and the enthusiastic (but nonfinancial) support for their use among major contributing countries. In the end, their cost had to be covered from the voluntary contributions for humanitarian assistance in Iraq. Moreover, the guards are civilians, not trained soldiers. They have no real command structure. They constitute only a limited tool but one that can nonetheless be useful in some of the varied humanitarian projects in which the United Nations is, or will be, engaged.

THE SHI'ITES

International attention was focused on the plight of the Kurds. As a result, a great deal was done to help them. Much less attention was given to the Shi'ite minority in southern Iraq, which had also risen up against Baghdad and been the victim of vicious attacks by the Iraqi government. They had fled into marshlands near Basra—some were resident there—and no one knew quite where they were or how large their number was. Their Moslem fundamentalism and association with Iran made the Western public less sympathetic to them than to the Kurds, who already enjoyed wide sympathy because of Saddam Hussein's earlier use of chemical weapons against them.

Still, a number of governments urged that the United Nations act to assist the Shi'ites. The British government, among others, expressed great concern, as did the Federal Republic of Germany. Both hoped the humanitarian centers that were being opened in the south of Iraq could help the Shi'ite victims of government persecution. I myself felt very strongly that the United Nations must help these people. I had some doubt, in fact, whether the assistance program for the Kurds in the north should be fully begun before something was also undertaken for these other victims in the south. Until then, the humanitarian center that had been opened in Basra had not been able to assist the thousands who had sought refuge in the marshes.

Prince Sadruddin shared my views. Accordingly, he had in late May requested one of his senior staff members, Stefan de Mistura, who had had a major part in establishing the UN humanitarian offices in the Kurdish area, to ascertain firsthand the situation in the south. De Mistura plus a small number of UN guards and colleagues from several UN agencies made a remarkable journey. All in all they traveled more than 3,000 kilometers, crisscrossing southern Iraq in an effort to avoid the attention of the Iraqi regime's Special Services.

The first problem was to find the marshes. In the 1980s the Iraqi government had built dams and military roads, which had served to drain the area. Available maps were out of date. What was shown as marshes was now dry land. At first the mission could not locate any stranded Shi'ites. Then, from conversations with local inhabitants, it emerged that some displaced people were concentrated in the area around the marsh town Hawr Al Hammar. Having heard this, de Mistura formed his group's vehicles into a convoy and proceeded ostentatiously, at midday on a religious holiday, toward Hawr Al Hammar. After passing through 44 roadblocks, they arrived at the town, which they found to be surrounded by machine gun posts placed at every 50 meters. The group discovered that an unknown number of people were hiding somewhere deeper in the marsh, partly on islands in a marsh lake, and that each day the Iraqi army launched a flotilla of 450 canoes in search of them. Besides Shi'ite dissidents, the refugees included many deserters who retained their weapons and also members of the Baath party who had fled from Basra at the time of the revolt in that city. Then, too, there were people who lived permanently in the marshes. One informant in Hawr Al Hammar put the number of people who had fled into the marshes at about 100,000. De Mistura concluded that the figure could be anywhere between 30,000 and 150,000. The number was certainly large enough to be of serious humanitarian concern.

When Prince Sadruddin heard de Mistura's report, he immediately called the Iraqi ambassador in Geneva. Expressing great concern regarding the situation, he reminded the ambassador that the humanitarian mission of the United Nations extended to all Iraqis. He requested the urgent concurrence of the Iraqi government in the establishment of a UN humanitarian center in Hawr Al Hammar and in the thinning out of the Iraqi military presence there. Information on the situation was given to the press in both Geneva and New York. Fearing that thousands of people in the marsh might be massacred unless urgent preventive measures were taken, Sadruddin decided to go himself to Hawr Al Hammar. He was able to gain the agreement of Iraqi authorities, and he proceeded to the marsh town on July 11, where he was met by a UN convoy carrying relief supplies from the World Food Program, the UN High Commissioner for Refugees and the UN Children's Fund, accompanied by a contingent of UN guards. The machine gun emplacements had been removed. Sadruddin learned that the Iraqi military had begun to withdraw from the area three days earlier. Some displaced persons had already started to return from their hiding places, reassured by the arrival of the UN representatives.

A small post, including several UN guards, was established in Hammar to monitor relief distribution and demonstrate a UN presence. UN staff members traveled by boat through the marshes to explain how assistance could be received and to show the UN flag. The results were as desired. As they had in the north, the coalition forces established a no-fly zone in the south to prevent Iraqi harassment from the air. And, as in the north, the displaced persons gradually returned to their homes. Here again was evidence of the enormous humanitarian benefits that the UN system brings to the world, a service that in my view alone more than justifies its existence.

AFRICA: A CONTINENT
OF TRIUMPH AND TRAVAIL

T H R E E

The decade of the 1980s was for Africa a time of continuing turmoil. From North to South economies were in decline, some in collapse. A succession of natural disasters brought misery and death to millions. Political leadership also failed in many of the countries. Nationalism remained strong, although the generation of charismatic leaders who had brought their countries to independence was disappearing from the scene, and in some countries the institutions of governance were disintegrating. Yet in southern Africa, Namibia achieved independence peacefully and in South Africa apartheid and minority rule were abandoned, a seminal event that brought brighter prospects to all of the region.

During my ten years as Secretary-General I visited some 30 countries in Africa, in the process traversing more than 300,000 miles. I experienced the enormous contrast between sumptuous palaces and the abject misery of refugee camps where millions suffered the special hardship of want and disease and death in exile. Again and again I found confirmation that in no other continent was the need for the United Nations as great, and nowhere else were the expectations and faith placed in the Organization larger.

I made my first official visit to the continent in November 1982, to attend the nineteenth summit meeting of the Organization of African Unity (OAU) in Tripoli. Despite several days of consultations by the heads of state and government who had already assembled, the summit did not take place since there was no agreement on the representation of Chad. This notwithstanding, the trip gave me an opportunity to meet individually within a two-day period with 12 African heads of state or government, as well as with Sam Nujoma, the leader of the SWAPO, the South West African resistance movement. I obtained a vivid sense of what the Africans saw as their principal problems and could assess the quality of leaders that the continent enjoyed or, in some cases, suffered.

I came away from Tripoli confirmed in my mind that the three political issues that demanded priority attention from the United Nations and on which the United Nations could be most useful were Namibia, the complex of southern African problems deriving from South African apartheid policies and the Western Sahara, which, I thought, lent itself to external mediation. Overshadowing all political problems, however, were the economic and humanitarian needs of a continent in crisis.

AFRICA'S BURDEN: UNDERDEVELOPMENT
AND NATURAL DISASTERS

The drought that was devastating Africa at the time of my first visit to the continent as Secretary-General had been endemic, with variations in intensity, for some 17 years. Many experts predicted that inadequate moisture was a phenomenon that African countries would have to learn to accept. I could witness for myself the incalculable consequences that the continuing drought would have on the conditions of life for millions of people. It was evident that communication between African governments and donor countries needed to be improved and that cooperation among the various UN agencies that were engaged in Africa— seldom in coordination with one another—needed to be enhanced. It took a further deterioration in the situation, however, to bring this about.

In 1984, as a result of the enduring drought and an invasion of locusts, famine threatened large areas of sub-Saharan Africa. Images of starving people, especially children, conveyed by British television, brought the world a shocked awareness of the desperate situation in the region. I had already established in Nairobi a special office to monitor nascent economic and humanitarian crises. The General Assembly adopted a Declaration on the Critical Economic Situation in Africa (A/RES/39/29). However, monitoring and declarations were inadequate responses to a desperate situation. I therefore established an Office for Economic Emergencies in Africa. I designated Bradford Morse, the Administrator of the UN Development Program, to head it and asked Maurice Strong, the former Executive Director of the UN Environment Program, to work with him in ensuring cooperation among all UN agencies. Morse and Strong were both dynamic and forceful leaders with experience in mobilizing government and public support for humanitarian needs. They were an extraordinarily effective team. I also appointed Special Representatives for Emergency Operations in both Ethiopia and the Sudan and, somewhat later, in Mozambique. Generous financial support was obtained from governments.

The specialized agencies and functional offices of the UN system and nongovernmental humanitarian organizations cooperated in a massive and successful program to alleviate the famine. Hundreds of thousands of lives were saved. It was a remarkable achievement. When the Office for Economic Emergency Assistance in Africa was terminated in 1986, as the crisis had by then eased, there were loud objections not only from the aid-recipient countries but also from the nongovernmental organizations that had been involved in the common humanitarian effort. It is one of the few instances that I can recall when the elimination of a UN office was greeted with dismay.

The assistance that was mobilized and organized by the United Nations to alleviate the famine in sub-Saharan Africa in 1984-1985 was an achievement of which I am especially proud. Yet the fact that the emergency arose and that it had to be handled on a crisis basis was indicative of an inadequacy in the UN system. Numerous signs of impending disaster were evident to the field representatives of the various UN agencies active in Africa. Ominous drought conditions could be traced back, as I have said, for 17 years. But the United Nations had no early-warning center to which information from the field offices could be fed and assessed. Until the Emergency Office was established, there was no authoritative entity capable of alerting the UN system as a whole to the impending danger and developing adequate preventive measures. It took disaster, brought into homes throughout the developed world by television, to prompt governments to make the generous contributions that they did and, I must add in all honesty, to cause the UN system to come together in a coordinated program to mobilize and deliver the desperately needed assistance. Prevention of human tragedies such as the one that occurred in sub-Saharan Africa requires the early application of resources in an amount that, until now, has not been available for such purposes.

Let me give but one example. Food to feed starving people is generally available on short notice. There was no great problem in finding the food to ship to Africa. In the years 1984-1985, 6.4 million tons were donated. The most serious problem was to get it to those in need who were beyond the reach of the few roads that existed in the area. To ensure that food is accessible to people in time of need, roads have to be built, a task undertaken in the wake of the sub-Saharan crisis by the UN Development Program together with other agencies in the Sahara region. But it should have been done much earlier, *before the crisis,* as part of the development process. The United Nations needs an early-warning capacity that encompasses all its agencies and programs, and it needs the sustained support of governments to permit the various agencies to undertake the measures required to limit the likelihood of such catastrophes as famine from occurring.

ECONOMIC AND SOCIAL DEVELOPMENT IN AFRICA

These tragic crises of drought and hunger, and the spreading desertification in Africa, plus the continent's vulnerability to the world-wide recession of the early 1980s, placed in stark relief the need not only for early warning but, more fundamentally, for long-term solutions to the underlying economic and social problems. This was widely recognized by the international community and by the main development institutions of the UN system—the World Bank, the

International Monetary Fund and the United Nations Development Program. The General Assembly convoked a ministerial-level conference in 1986 to examine the critical economic situation in Africa. Despite many predictions of failure, this conference, under the strong and expert leadership of Edgard Pisani, a former French minister of agriculture, succeeded in adopting the UN Program of Action for the Economic Recovery and Development of Africa.

This program committed the African governments to undertake long-term structural reforms that would free the most productive sectors of their economies from obstacles to growth, especially in regard to agriculture. For its part, the international community promised to provide increased assistance to Africa, beyond emergency humanitarian aid, and to support a process of economic reform that would inevitably entail heavy sacrifices for the populations of the affected countries. In concrete terms, the global cost of the Program of Action was estimated at slightly more than $128 billion for the period 1986 to 1990. The African countries offered to cover $82.5 billion of this; the remainder—about $9 billion annually—would come from external assistance. The United Nations undertook a commitment to mobilize these external resources.

It has often happened in the United Nations that important declarations and programs are adopted with no follow-up mechanism. I was determined that, in this instance, this should not be the case. Africa's needs were too great and too urgent. I quickly established a Lead Committee (comité directeur) under the Director General for International Economic Cooperation, Jean Ripert, to ensure the coordinated participation of all elements of the UN system in the program. Further, I requested the dynamic and articulate Canadian ambassador, Stephen Lewis, to assist me in a personal capacity in gaining the necessary support of member states. Lewis, who undertook an energetic tour of European and African capitals, quickly became known as the principal advocate at the United Nations for African development. He took much satisfaction in saying that Africa now had an important place on the global agenda.

I realized that successful implementation of such a large program would require wide public support and therefore arranged for an extensive information program with bimonthly bulletins to publicize the progress achieved in African recovery. This became a bitter irony since instead of progress most African economies continued to deteriorate. Commodity prices continued to drop and the flow of capital to the continent declined. Per-capita income fell despite improved climatic conditions. External assistance did not reach the target levels. Most devastating of all, foreign debt continued to grow, the interest on which in some cases exceeded a country's entire foreign earnings. The internal situation in a number of African countries was a further deterrent, with civil wars raging in some and corruption rampant in others.

In the face of this situation, I assembled an advisory group of experts to examine the financing of economic recovery in Africa. They concluded that the sub-Saharan region alone would require $5 billion annually to counter the effect of the declines in commodity prices and capital in-flows and the crushing cost of debt servicing. The group proposed that creditor countries reschedule the debts or, better still, reduce interest rates to zero for the next three years. But by 1987 Africa's external debt had reached $34 billion. The countries that were most in debt were obliged to take out new loans in order to service the old ones. Even though some members of the Club of Rome agreed to reschedule debts and Canada and France both canceled outstanding government loans, service charges continued to grow. Seventeen of the most indebted countries foresaw that by 1988 to 1990, the annual interest due on their debts would triple, rising from $2.3 billion annually to $6.9 billion. The debt problem had resulted in a vicious circle. The Group of Seven Industrial States, meeting in Toronto in 1988, decided unanimously to reschedule the debts of the poorest developing countries. Neither this, however, nor the draconian restructuring requirements imposed by the World Bank in the extension of loans was able to improve the situation greatly. Rather, the economies of many African countries continued to deteriorate, further strained in 1990 by a return of drought conditions, by the failure of tariff reduction negotiations in the General Agreement on Trade and Tariffs (GATT) and by the effects of the Gulf War.

Despite all the measures taken, external debt continued to grow, reaching $272 billion in 1990. In this same time frame, external assistance declined precipitously. Bettino Craxi, the former Prime Minister of Italy whom I had appointed as my Special Representative on the debt problem, reported to the General Assembly that the problem would remain insoluble in sub-Saharan Africa unless extreme measures were taken to reduce debt and the World Bank and the International Monetary Fund introduced exceptional concessional measures.

There was no escaping the conclusion that the ambitious and hopeful UN Program for the Economic Recovery and Development of Africa had failed. While I do not believe that the United Nations bears the primary blame, this failure was, nevertheless, one of my main regrets as I left office. It seems to me that no government or agency has found the right formula to resolve the endemic economic problems of the African continent.

There were, unfortunately, also other occasions in Africa when I felt a sense of failure—not personal failure but, far more important, a failure of the human community. This sense was never more oppressive than during a visit to a refugee camp in Ethiopia when the land was ravaged by drought. The haggard, resigned faces of the dying children, who should have been a vital asset to Africa's future, challenged the symbol of a universal morality that, as UN Secretary-General, I represented. I took great satisfaction in the humanitarian assistance that the United Nations mobilized to alleviate the natural disasters that repeatedly afflicted sub-Saharan Africa. Yet I have remained deeply conscious that the UN system, as the principal instrument for global cooperation, had failed to halt the grave deterioration in the conditions of life that set a good portion of the continent apart as a region where, despite the indomitable will of the population, hope is limited and solutions still unknown.

SOUTH AFRICA REBORN

No national policy was so unanimously and vehemently condemned in the United Nations as the South African policy of apartheid. Over the years there were differences as to how the common goal of its elimination could be achieved—whether through isolation and sanctions or through sustained contact, public pressure and persuasion. Ultimately all approaches were pursued. The General Assembly, in addition to its many condemnatory resolutions, excluded South Africa from participating in its sessions, held a special session devoted entirely to excoriating the racist policies of the South African government and established a Special Committee Against Apartheid to publicize its unacceptable racist actions. The Security Council embargoed the shipment of military goods to South Africa on the ground that its policies, which were aimed at destabilizing its neighboring states, constituted a threat to international peace and security. Regional organizations and, eventually, individual countries with effective economic leverage imposed additional sanctions in keeping with the many calls of the General Assembly for such measures.

I used every appropriate occasion to call publicly on South Africa to abandon its racist policies and to respect the human rights of its citizens. I maintained contact with prominent South Africans such as Bishop Desmond Tutu and Oliver Tambo, the president of the African National Congress, who were struggling to change the apartheid regime. But at the same time I avoided as far as possible polemical exchanges with the South African Government or its representatives. I wished to preserve my credibility with the South African leaders as an impartial interlocutor. This, in time, proved its value.

The long-sustained, multifaceted UN campaign did much to end apartheid—not alone, but as one of the many forces that came together to bring about change in South Africa comparable in its significance to the abolition of slavery in the United States. One of my most fulfilling experiences as Secretary-General was to stand between Nelson Mandela and Frederik de Klerk and sense the mutual respect in which these two South Africans, one black and one white, were newly joined. My proudest act was on the same day to administer the oath of office to Sam Nujoma as the first president of an independent Namibia, something that could not have occurred without those positive changes in southern Africa to which the United Nations had contributed a fulsome share.

It was and remains my hope that the extraordinarily favorable political change in South Africa will lead to comparable economic progress at least in the southern part of the continent and perhaps beyond. I am quite certain that economic progress will be achieved only where there is political stability.

ELEVEN

NAMIBIA:
INDEPENDENCE AT LAST

WHEN, IN 1966, the General Assembly terminated South Africa's mandate over South West Africa—a mandate that dated from the end of World War I—the territory became, in legal terms, the direct responsibility of the United Nations. The General Assembly officially christened it Namibia and established a council, assisted by a commissioner, in which, in theory, ultimate authority over the territory resided pending its independence. The reality was different. South Africa continued to control the territory essentially as a colony and extended to it the intolerable racial policy of apartheid.

By the time I assumed office, substantial progress had been made toward correcting this deplorable situation. In 1976 the Security Council defined the basic requirements for the independence of Namibia. The next year the five Western members then serving on the Security Council—Canada, France, the Federal Republic of Germany, the United Kingdom and the United States— initiated consultations with the South African Government, with SWAPO, the resistance group that had been officially recognized by the General Assembly as the legitimate representative of the Namibian people, and with the internal political parties and church and business leaders in Windhoek, the capital of Namibia. The result was agreement on a settlement plan. The principal provisions of the plan, which was endorsed by the Security Council in 1978 in the form of Resolution 435, were the following:

- Cessation of all hostile acts by all parties and the restriction of South African and SWAPO armed forces to base. Thereafter there would be a phased withdrawal of all but 1,500 South African troops from Namibia within 12 weeks.

- Free elections for a Namibian Constituent Assembly, under the supervision and control of the United Nations.
- The appointment of a United Nations Special Representative to work together with the official appointed by South Africa (the Administrator-General) to ensure the orderly transition to independence.
- The repeal, prior to the beginning of the electoral campaign, of all discriminatory and restrictive laws and the release of all political prisoners.
- Deployment of a United Nations Transition Assistance Group (UNTAG), consisting of both military and civilian contingents.
- Retention of primary responsibility for maintaining law and order in Namibia during the transition period by the existing police forces. However, the UN Special Representative would make arrangements for UN personnel to accompany the police in the discharge of their duties.

Martti Ahtisaari, a Finnish national who later became President of Finland, was appointed UN Special Representative for Namibia.

Thus, by the time I became Secretary-General the plan for Namibia's independence had long been in place. The Security Council had approved the proposed size, composition and functions of UNTAG. Plans for its deployment had for the most part been agreed with South Africa and the other parties concerned, including SWAPO. All that remained to be done was to set the date of the cease-fire that would inaugurate implementation of the plan. Progress had come to an impasse, however, because South Africa insisted that implementation of the plan be linked to the withdrawal of the Cuban forces that had been deployed in neighboring Angola at the request of the Angolan Government.

I could never establish whether the United States or South Africa first inspired the linkage between implementation of the UN plan for Namibia and the Cuban troops in Angola. Over the years the South African representatives had raised a multitude of issues, including their doubts as to the impartiality of the United Nations. They even walked out of an implementation conference held in Geneva. Prior to the inauguration of the Reagan Administration, however, they had never raised the question of the Cuban forces in Angola. The linkage policy was first announced by the South African Government following a visit to South Africa in June 1981 by U.S. Under-Secretary of State William Clark (subsequently President Reagan's National Security Advisor), Assistant Secretary of State for African Affairs Chester Crocker and Elliot Abrams, who at that time was assistant secretary of state for International Organizations and later for

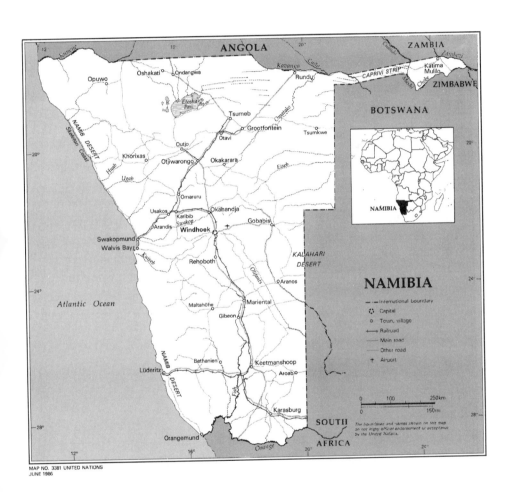

ANGOLA

ZAMBIA

Kunene

Kavango

Cuito

Chobe

Zambezi

Katima
Mulilo

CAPRIVI STRIP

ZIMBABWE

Opuwo

Oshakati

Ondangwa

Rundu

BOTSWANA

NAMIB DESERT

Skeleton Coast

Etosha
Pan

Tsumeb

Omatako

Tsumkwe

Grootfontein

Otavi

Outjo

Khorixas

Otjiwarongo

Okakarara

Eiseb

Huab

Ugab

Omaruru

Usakos

Karibib

Okahandja

Gobabis

Swakop

Arandis

Swakopmund

Windhoek

Walvis Bay

Kuiseb

KALAHARI
DESERT

Rehoboth

Omatako

Aranos

Atlantic Ocean

Maltahöhe

Mariental

NAMIBIA

Gibeon

— · — International boundary
⊛ Capital
○ Town, village
↔ Railroad
—— Main road
—— Other road
✈ Airport

NAMIB
DESERT

Bethanien

Keetmanshoop

Lüderitz

Fish

Aroab

0   100   250km
0   150mi

Karasburg

Orangemund

Orange

SOUTH
AFRICA

The boundaries and names shown on this map
do not imply official endorsement or acceptance
by the United Nations.

NAMIBIA

Latin America. Immediately after the South African announcement, the United States declared that it saw the negotiating process as dependent on parallel progress on the departure of Cuban troops from Angola. The United States stated further that it had initiated bilateral talks with the Government of Angola to discuss the question.

It did not really matter which of the two parties had first suggested the linkage. The South Africans had an evident interest in delaying an agreement on Namibia in order to assess what the effect would be in South Africa itself and possibly to see a more friendly government installed in Angola. For the Americans, the withdrawal of the Cubans would mean a victory in the Cold War and the restoration of Western influence there and possibly in Mozambique as well. Chester Crocker's untiring efforts over the ensuing years demonstrated that the United States was deeply committed to two objectives that at times seemed to work at cross purposes—the independence of Namibia and the withdrawal of the Cuban troops with the concomitant reduction of Communist influence in southern Africa.

I repeatedly insisted publicly and in private conversations that Namibia should be treated as a separate, independent problem and not tied to other issues. I came to realize, however, that desirable as this might be, it was not realistic. I never acknowledged the legitimacy of demanding prior agreement on the withdrawal of Cuban troops as a condition for implementation of Resolution 435, but in the interest of Namibian independence, which was clearly the paramount objective, I did my best to bring about conditions that would facilitate their departure.

INVOLVEMENT OF THE SECRETARY-GENERAL

Seven days after I took office, I addressed the opening session of a meeting of the Council for Namibia. My speech was consonant with UN policy on Namibia as defined in General Assembly resolutions. It reviewed the progress that had been made, noted that South African reservations had prevented agreement on a date for the initiation of a cease-fire and called for the release of political prisoners by South Africa. It contained a *de rigueur* reference to SWAPO, as the legitimate representative of the Namibian people, but this was not highlighted. The main thrust was the importance of the early implementation of Resolution 435 to which all the parties had agreed.

The next day the South African Ambassador communicated to me a message from South African Foreign Minister Pik Botha asking that his government be informed how I could reconcile my statement with the principle of impartiality that was an essential element in the agreed plan for Namibian independence. This was followed four days later by a letter from Prime Minister P. W. Botha accusing me of publicly demonstrating my "personal attachment to the political cause of ideological adversaries of the South African Government . . . thereby demonstrating [my] inability to act in a just and unbiased manner towards member states who are excluded from power blocs and who are made scapegoats for the inequities which are characteristic of the governments of the majority of the members of the United Nations."[1]

South Africa had long been distrustful of the United Nations, and understandably so. It had been excluded from participating in the General Assembly, had been subjected to sanctions by the Security Council and was the object of repeated resolutions in the General Assembly and other UN bodies condemning its policy of apartheid. Its racist policies invited nothing less. I found apartheid intolerable and the South African occupation of Namibia brutal and illegal. I could in no way, either officially or personally, refrain from criticizing South African policies. Yet, with regard to implementation of the plan for Namibia, the United Nations had pledged impartiality. I intended to honor this commitment and, within the limits that I have described, work to gain the confidence of the South African leadership in my objectivity. I made this policy clear in various meetings with the Front Line States, explaining to these neighbors of South Africa the importance of maintaining my credibility and usefulness with all sides. This position was well understood by African leaders.

I first came to know Pik Botha when we were serving as Permanent Representatives to the United Nations. He was an amiable colleague with a sharp mind. While a faithful servant of his government's policy, he was always good company. Over the next ten years I was to have many meetings and innumerable written exchanges with him as South Africa's foreign minister. While his language was sometimes demanding and accusatory, in all our direct encounters his attitude was as friendly as it had been in former days. I found him a likable man as long as I could disassociate him from the disruptive policies pursued by his government in southern Africa, policies that he skillfully represented but which almost certainly did not originate in his ministry.

In July 1982, the representatives of the Western Contact Group, who had continued their dialogue with South Africa despite the setbacks of 1981, transmitted to me the text of "Principles concerning the Constituent Assembly and the Constitution for an Independent Namibia," which, they said, all parties had accepted. The principles provided that Namibia would be a unitary, democratic state with executive, judicial and legislative branches, the latter to be elected by universal and equal suffrage. Human rights would be assured consistent with the Universal Declaration of Human Rights. The election of representatives to the Constituent Assembly would be either by nationally based proportional representation or on the basis of single-member constituencies. The decision on this question would be delayed until later. For my part I undertook productive consultations with all the parties concerning the conditions for the deployment of UNTAG. However, at the end of 1982, progress on implementing the plan for Namibian independence remained deadlocked. Vice President George Bush called me in December and emphasized that the United States was determined to see Resolution 435 implemented and was not pessimistic. However, the Cubans must leave. "The South Africans," he said, "are intransigent on this point." I understood this to mean the United States was too.

In August 1983, primarily at the instigation of the Front Line States, the Security Council called on me to undertake consultations with the parties with a view to securing speedy implementation of Resolution 435, which already was five years old. To carry out this mandate, I felt that direct discussions with the South African and Angolan governments and with SWAPO were necessary. Yet were I to go to South Africa and gain no positive results, it would be seen as a further reverse in the prospects for a settlement. In discussing the question with Chester Crocker, I said the visit could have only two purposes: to register progress or to report that all possibilities had been exhausted. I felt the need for U.S. support to persuade the South Africans to be more flexible. Crocker replied that progress now depended on the Angolans and the United States could give no assurance that the Angolan position had altered sufficiently to promise positive results from my visit. However, the United States saw several advantages to be gained. The South African government had boxed itself in with its rhetoric against the United Nations. A visit by the Secretary-General could help the government get out of this box by giving evidence to the population of UN impartiality. Moreover, South African assurances—if forthcoming—that real progress on Namibia was possible would enable me to report to the Security Council that the current negotiations were viable.

By this time, I had received several messages from both the Prime Minister and the Foreign Minister of South Africa expressing their confidence in me personally and indicating that they took no exception to the various statements that I was making with regard to Namibia. The terms of reference of my trip to South Africa needed, nevertheless, to be mutually understood in advance. I made clear to Ambassador Brand Fourie, the South African ambassador to Washington (who was clearly the senior South African representative in the United States) that the question of Cuban troop withdrawal could not be accepted as a precondition for a Namibian settlement. If South Africa was not prepared to discuss the other outstanding issues, there would be no point in making the trip. The reply came from Foreign Minister Botha who promptly cabled that, once firm agreement had been reached on Cuban withdrawal and a commitment obtained from the Angolan government regarding implementation of such an agreement, the other outstanding issues could be addressed and resolved reasonably quickly. In this regard, South Africa insisted that impartiality remained an essential requirement for the implementation of any settlement.

On this basis I traveled to South Africa in August 1983 and met in Cape Town with Prime Minister P. W. Botha, Defense Minister General M. Malan and Foreign Minister Pik Botha. The Prime Minister was cordial but impassive. All of the South African officials repeated the position that had been expressed to me in New York with regard to the Cuban troops, and I stated again and again that the United Nations could not accept the linkage. Pik Botha and I spoke jointly to the press at the end of the talks. He said that South Africa had found the discussions useful and positive, restated South Africa's commitment to Resolution 435 and confirmed that the major issue still to be resolved was the withdrawal of the Cubans from Angola. I said that we had made substantial progress on outstanding issues but that I was still not in a position to indicate a date for implementation of Resolution 435 since an issue outside the scope of my Security Council mandate remained unresolved.

During my subsequent brief visit to Luanda, Sam Nujoma reaffirmed that SWAPO was ready to sign a cease-fire with South Africa and cooperate with me and with UNTAG in facilitating the speedy implementation of Resolution 435 without modification, amendment or extraneous and irrelevant issues of linkage and reciprocity. SWAPO would accept either a proportional representation or single-member constituency electoral system. In this and other meetings I had with Nujoma prior to initiation of the independence process in Namibia, he was always cooperative and, like the leaders of the Front Line States, showed preference for the United Nations as mediator. He was inclined, however, to speak in leftist jargon and appeared to be under marked Communist influence, either Soviet or Cuban. In one of our meetings I advised him that in his struggle to achieve Namibian independence, it was of great importance to maintain his own independence. I suggested that Namibian independence depended primarily on two countries: South Africa and the United States. This had always to be kept in mind. I do not know how much effect my advice had on Nujoma. He is an intelligent man and no doubt could see for himself the realities of the situation. What I found remarkable, however, was his ability to change and to grow in stature. Nujoma did not initially impress me as a forceful or shrewd leader. I had serious reason to doubt his reliability when SWAPO armed fighters crossed into Namibia after the cease-fire finally went into effect in April 1989. Yet once the election campaign was under way, he conducted himself and led his party in a highly responsible manner. The extreme leftist orientation was gone. When he assumed the presidency of Namibia, he had become an impressive leader genuinely committed to democratic government.

On my return to New York, I informed the Security Council that virtually all the outstanding issues with regard to UNTAG had now been resolved. However, the position of South Africa on the withdrawal of Cuban troops from Angola made it impossible to launch the UN plan. I stated that "this difficulty can only be dealt with in its own context by those directly concerned, acting within their sovereign rights, and, above all, by a determined effort by all concerned to reduce the tensions and contentious issues and to put an end to conflict in the area as a whole."[2]

UNITED STATES MEDIATION

The United States took the lead in mediating an arrangement between Angola and South Africa that would bring about the elimination of the Cuban military presence in Angola. In this complex process, the assistant secretary of state for African Affairs, Chester Crocker, was the principal American actor. He showed determination, indefatigable optimism and courage in his efforts, all of which were necessary. At a time when relations between Washington and the United Nations were strained and Crocker's superiors in the State Department were expressing distrust of the UN role in Central America, Crocker made a genuine effort to consult with those of us in the United Nations who were dealing with Africa. While the United Nations was largely excluded from the negotiating process (until the need for UN monitoring of the Cuban withdrawal arose), Crocker was assiduous in keeping me informed. He was quite open in giving me personally his assessment of developments and of the personages involved, something he would not do, however, in meetings where other UN staff was present.

In the summer and fall of 1983, the Angolan insurgent movement, the National Union for the Total Independence of Namibia (UNITA), was in the midst of an apparently successful campaign to expand its already extensive area of control. One purpose of the South African military presence in Angola, besides combatting SWAPO, was to support UNITA. The Angolan government valued the presence of Cuban troops as an important defense against UNITA victory. In view of the apparent increase of South African troops in Angola in the second half of 1983 and the intensified level of fighting, pressure grew from the Front Line States for the Security Council to meet and take action. On December 5, 1983, Chester Crocker met with the South African foreign minister in Rome and strongly suggested that a withdrawal of South African troops from Angola was needed to get negotiations on Namibia going again, something that I had suggested to the South African government two months earlier. Apparently prompted by these various moves, Foreign Minister Botha wrote to me on December 15 informing me that "with a view to facilitating the process of achieving a peaceful settlement of the Southwest Africa/Namibia issue, the Government of South Africa is prepared to begin a disengagement of forces . . . in Angola on 31 January 1984 on the understanding that this gesture would be reciprocated by the Angolan Government which would assure that its own forces, SWAPO and the Cubans would not exploit the situation. . . . The proposed action by South Africa would last initially for thirty days, and could be extended on condition that the provisions of this proposal are adhered to."[3]

The withdrawal of the South African forces as proposed by Botha was completed in April 1985. The truce between SWAPO and South Africa was agreed in bilateral contacts through Zambian channels. With the South African troops gone and Cuban troops committed to move out of southern Angola, prospects for resolving the Cuban problem appeared to brighten. I had to continue to reject the Cuban linkage in principle; yet knowing that this was the sole issue preventing Namibia's transition to independence, I felt I should do all that I could to encourage its resolution. I told the Permanent Representative of Angola, Elisio de Figueiredo, in March 1984, that once the South African withdrawal from Angola was complete, I intended to ask Fidel Castro to make a symbolic gesture by withdrawing 2,000 or 3,000 troops from Angola.

DISCUSSIONS WITH FIDEL CASTRO

I paid an official visit to Cuba from May 28 to 30, 1985, during which I spent some 12 to 13 hours with President Castro. There was an extensive official meeting in his office, a "private" day's fishing and a visit to the *Isla de la Juventud,* an island where schools have been established for needy young people from Third World countries, one of Castro's favorite projects. Throughout, Castro was voluble and expansive. As I am a good listener, it was possible to establish a comfortable rapport with the Cuban leader whom I found to be both charismatic and surprisingly likable. His grasp of international affairs, while opinionated and colored by his strong feelings of hostility toward the United States, was wide-ranging. When we were returning from the *Isla de la Juventud* he turned to a huge briefing book that contained a daily summary of developments around the world. The entries consisted of reports from Cuban embassies and from major newspapers and news services. He boasted to me that he was the best-informed head of government in the world, a claim I had no reason to doubt. His interest in southern Africa was surprisingly intense. In his enthusiasm and energy there was much that I considered misguided, but as far as I could see, it contained no element of guile. After three days of close association, I could understand why even the many in Central and South America who strongly oppose Castro's policies refer to him with a certain affection simply as Fidel.

When the subject of southern Africa was broached, Castro was at pains to assure me that the agreement between South Africa and Angola on the withdrawal of South African troops had taken place in close collaboration with Cuba. He then commented ironically on the syrupy language *(lenguaje de almibar)* used by the United States with Angola and its efforts to appear as an impartial mediator when in fact it was supporting South Africa and UNITA. Cuba, he said, could only gain through a negotiated settlement since it had no interests in Angola; but it was prepared to remain there as long as was necessary. Cuba was in Angola purely on behalf of internationalism *(por puro internacionalismo)*. The stationing of Cuban troops in Angola posed no serious burden for Cuba since Angola covered the costs of food and lodging.

In noting that Angola had agreed to the withdrawal of 20,000 Cuban soldiers from the southern part of the country within three years, Castro said that UNITA might well rout the Government forces. Cuba, he said, was not favorably disposed toward any solutions negotiated by the United States and South Africa "because they were both bandits." Cuba, he boasted, could extend the same collaboration as it had to Angola to "four other Angolas." If he sent 100,000 men abroad, Cuba wouldn't notice the difference. On the eve of my arrival in Cuba, South Africa, which had just completed the withdrawal of its forces from southern Angola, made a military incursion into Cabinda, the oil-rich enclave in the north of Angola, where a U.S.-owned petroleum enterprise was operating. In view of Castro's vehement reaction to the new South African incursion and the Angolan commitment on the removal of 20,000 Cuban troops from the south of the country, I did not pursue my idea of the withdrawal of several thousand Cuban troops from Angola. It would obviously have been rejected.

RETROGRESSION

A series of negative developments took place in mid-1985. The South African government established a "Transitional Government of National Unity" in Namibia based on the six internal parties that were under strong South African influence. A movement among conservative members of the U.S. Congress to give greater support to UNITA led the Angolan government to cut off its bilateral negotiations with Washington. Throughout the region the level of violence increased. The United States claimed that large quantities of Soviet arms were reaching the area, while the Angolans claimed that UNITA and South Africa were receiving strong support from the United States and from African countries under its influence.

Faced with increasing internal violence, the South African government began a series of gradual steps to liberalize the apartheid regime. This preoccupied a great deal of its attention. I concluded that South Africa was reluctant to revise its position on the withdrawal of Cuban troops because it did not wish to face a Namibian regime armed with Soviet guns on its northern border while dealing with a volatile situation at home. The Angolan situation was not dissimilar. The government, threatened by continuing UNITA attacks, was unwilling to relinquish the protection of the Cuban troops before a friendly, independent Namibia was established on its southern border.

The outcry against the South African action in establishing the transitional government in Namibia was almost universal. The Security Council declared the action null and void. The only exception, surprisingly, was Sam Nujoma. In talking with the Under-Secretary-General for African Affairs, Abdulrahmanel Farah, he said he saw the decision by P. W. Botha (who now had the title State President) as a political ploy aimed at outmaneuvering white extremists in South Africa. Even though President Botha knew the interim government would not survive, he had taken the action to give the impression that he was doing everything possible to assist the internal parties against SWAPO. Nujoma contended, with considerable prescience, that Botha's action would strengthen his position in moving ahead on a settlement based on the UN plan.

There was one favorable development during this unhappy period. After the Security Council asked me in Resolution 566 of June 19, 1985, to obtain from the South African government its choice of the electoral system to be used in the Namibian elections, the government issued a statement declaring that, "in the interests of economy," the transitional government in Windhoek had requested the South African government to select a system of proportional representation. With this South African decision on the electoral process all the prerequisites for the implementation of Resolution 435 had been completed. In theory, all that needed to be done was to establish the date of the cease-fire that would initiate the plan. I wrote to Foreign Minister Botha on November 26, 1985, from a sense of duty rather than expectation, asking that the South African government name a preferred date for a commencement of the cease-fire. I received no reply.

In early 1986 the UNITA leader Marcus Savimbi visited the United States and was well received in Washington, to the great dissatisfaction of the Angolan government. President José Edurdo dos Santos informed President Reagan that the United States could no longer continue as a mediator in view of its interference in Angolan internal affairs. Simultaneously, dos Santos requested me to assume full responsibility for implementation of Resolution 435. While Chester Crocker had been helpful in keeping me generally informed of the course of U.S. negotiations with Angola and South Africa, I suspected that there was a good bit that I did not know. I asked whether the Angolan statement meant that they were breaking all contact with the United States. The answer was no but that all contact would be through me. The break in direct U.S.-Angolan contact lasted almost a year.

In March 1987, Crocker informed me that there was a growing likelihood that the United States would be meeting again quite soon with Angolan representatives. He suggested it would be useful if I informed President dos Santos that I had been told of this likelihood and welcomed it. I conveyed this message, and the President confirmed to me that Angola had decided to resume bilateral talks with the United States in order to break the impasse in the negotiations. Dos Santos made clear that Angola remained vehemently opposed to negotiating total Cuban withdrawal. He wanted the talks with the Americans to focus on Angola's security needs.

THE THAW IN THE COLD WAR REACHES SOUTHERN AFRICA

By the beginning of 1988, the improvement in U.S./Soviet relations began to be felt in southern Africa. During a visit to Moscow in March 1988, Secretary Shultz had tested the Soviets on the possibility of reconciliation between UNITA and the government in Angola. The Soviets expressed keen interest in the approach. Moreover, a victory for the governing party in South Africa gave State President Botha greater flexibility in dealing both with the internal South African situation and with the Namibian problem. South African troops, many of them young recruits sent to Angola to afford protection to UNITA forces, suffered extensive casualties, causing unease among the South African population. Coming together, these developments would make 1988 a year of decision.

In January 1988, for the first time, Cuban representatives joined in the U.S./Angolan talks and Angola confirmed its acceptance in principle of the total withdrawal of Cuban troops. The timing would be determined by Angola's domestic concerns and by South Africa's cessation of interference in Angola. When I visited the area in February, President dos Santos told me that now that the Angolans had accepted total Cuban withdrawal, it was for the Americans to solve the problem created by U.S. assistance to UNITA. He insisted that "the Americans had to find an urgent solution to the present political situation in Angola." I suggested the possibility of national reconciliation as the Americans had proposed in Moscow. The President resisted the idea, saying that the Angolan situation should not be confused with the one in Afghanistan. UNITA had no more than 30,000 troops and was not entitled to participate in the government. I confided to the President that in Zaire, President Mobutu Sese Seko had told me of his personal efforts to persuade Savimbi to withdraw from the political scene as a contribution to national reconciliation. Dos Santos thought this was an important development "if it was truly the case."

Rapid advances occurred in the summer of 1988 in which the United Nations was largely an interested bystander. After a series of meetings among Angola, Cuba and the United States, with the Soviet Union present as an observer, the three governments reached agreement in Geneva on August 5, 1988, to recommend to the UN Secretary-General the date of November 1, 1988, for the beginning of the implementation of Resolution 435. In talking with me a few days later, Chester Crocker elaborated that the Geneva agreement covered the complete verified withdrawal of South African forces from southern Angola. Crocker said that a *de facto* cease-fire was in effect in southern Angola and that Cuba would not undertake offensive operations in the defined area provided they were not the subject of harassment. Only the time frame for the complete withdrawal of the Cuban troops remained to be agreed. Angola and Cuba had offered complete withdrawal within four years while South Africa was insisting on seven months. I offered to use my good offices with the Cubans. Crocker accepted this offer but said that the real problem was with the Angolans, who were indecisive. Cuba, on the other hand, had shown the capacity to take firm decisions. When Crocker was asked to clarify the U.S. position on the issue of national reconciliation, he replied that as long as there was no national reconciliation, the United States would continue to aid UNITA.

WORKING OUT THE FINAL
DETAILS ON UNTAG WITH SOUTH AFRICA

By this time, I received an invitation to visit South Africa for three or four days at a minimum. The proposed agenda was limited to largely technical issues such as the budget for UNTAG and guaranteed bank loans for Namibia, plus the question of UN impartiality. A special envoy, Derek Auret, was sent from Pretoria to emphasize that the invitation came from President Botha, "who held the Secretary-General in high regard."

I was reluctant to travel to South Africa if the agenda was limited to these technical questions and to UN impartiality, which I considered already settled. Auret insisted that the main purpose of the visit would be to move forward the process for a settlement, the prospect of which was now at hand. After discussing this with my colleagues and with Chester Crocker, in whom I had come to place much confidence, I concluded that the South African government desired my presence as a means of encouraging the white South African population and the internal political parties in Namibia to accept the agreement that was emerging with Angola and, most important, the looming reality of Namibian independence. I obviously wished to facilitate these objectives in any way I could and therefore accepted the invitation, arriving once again in South Africa on September 21, 1988.

The timing was propitious. At the end of August, I had been informed by the South African Permanent Representative that the withdrawal of South African troops from Angolan territory had been completed. South Africa and Angola had agreed that the withdrawal of Cuban troops would be sustained and continuous over a period extending beyond the Namibian elections. The precise time frame was still not decided, but the two governments had agreed to consider a plan under which the withdrawal would begin on November 1, 1988, at a rate of not less than 3,000 troops per month. Under this plan all Cuban troops would depart Angola by October 31, 1990.

My visit, which lasted only two days, met the principal objectives of both the United Nations and the South African government. For me, given the apparent imminence of the initiation of the UN plan, it was very important to gain a firm South African commitment to cooperate with UNTAG and concurrence in the dispatch of a UN survey mission to Namibia to see if UNTAG's logistic and administrative requirements remained more or less the same as had been assessed eight years earlier. I also wanted to give strong public support for the early implementation of Namibian independence and urge that the spirit of reconciliation that had made agreement between Angola and South Africa possible be extended to South Africa's relations with the other Front Line States. All of these objectives were attained. For the South Africans, I believe the most important thing was to obtain for public consumption a strong reiteration of the UN pledge of impartiality once the implementation of Resolution 435 began. In a meeting with the foreign minister, I stated categorically that "all the parties in Namibia will be treated equally." I would include in my final report to the Security Council a paragraph on impartiality in order to ensure that my position would be reflected in the enabling resolution to be adopted by the Council.

The conditions on impartiality that had been agreed to by the Western Contact Group and the Front Line States were extensive: The General Assembly would suspend consideration of the question of Namibia during the transition period; the United Nations would not provide funds to SWAPO or any other party; the UN Council for Namibia would refrain from engaging in public activities once the Security Council met to authorize implementation of Resolution 435; and the activities of the Office of the Commissioner for Namibia would be strictly limited. SWAPO, for its part, would forgo the exercise of the special privileges granted to it by the General Assembly. Compliance with these conditions would evoke considerable controversy. The UN organizations that had grown up over the years to represent the interests of Namibia found it difficult to relinquish their accustomed activities. The South Africans kept close watch well before implementation started and were quick to complain of perceived infractions. I, too, had to keep these offices under close control.

THE SECURITY COUNCIL COUNTS PENNIES

The five Permanent Members of the Security Council undertook to draft the resolution authorizing implementation of Resolution 435. When I met with them as they began their work, they read a prepared statement declaring that in order to obtain the necessary support, the five Permanent Members "believe it is necessary to reexamine the plan for UNTAG. . . . They are convinced that UNTAG can carry out its primary function—to ensure free and fair elections . . . in a substantially more economical manner. The Five therefore hope that the Secretary-General will now begin a thorough review of existing UNTAG plans, particularly with respect to the size of the military component. . . ." The insistence on cost-cutting would have serious consequences. I reminded the Five that Resolution 435 endorsed specific resource requirements for the tasks assigned to UNTAG. If any major reductions were sought, the Council would have to change the originally defined tasks. I stressed that the African and other nonaligned countries had expressed their strong opposition to any cuts in the size of UNTAG. Just at this time I was informed of a seemingly most favorable development. South Africa had reportedly disbanded the hated secret police unit, the Koevoet, in Namibia.

SIGNATURE OF THE ENABLING AGREEMENTS

At the request of the United States as mediator, the ECOSOC chamber at UN Headquarters was made available on December 22, 1988, for signature of the agreements among South Africa, Angola and Cuba foreseen in the Geneva Protocol. Secretary Shultz chaired the signing ceremony to which all the members of the Security Council were invited. In my brief remarks I noted that April 1, 1989, had been recommended to me as the date for the implementation of Security Council Resolution 435 of 1978. "For my part," I said, "I welcome this recommendation wholeheartedly." The date was thereby established. In light of subsequent developments, I came to see this momentous date as premature.

On January 16, 1989, the Security Council, in Resolution 629, requested that I arrange a formal cease-fire between SWAPO and South Africa and reexamine the requirements for UNTAG in order to identify wherever possible cost-saving measures "without prejudice to its ability fully to carry out its mandate . . . to ensure the early independence of Namibia through free and fair elections under the supervision and control of the United Nations." This wording was intended to bridge the gap between the Permanent Members of the Security Council who wished to see the cost of UNTAG reduced and the African and other nonaligned states that feared a reduction in the size and resources of UNTAG would prejudice its ability to accomplish its mission. The Security Council did not alter the UNTAG mandate on which the original estimates were made and approved by the Council.

As was often the case, the effect of the Council's wording was to transfer the problem to the Secretary-General. I had intensive consultations with both sides in the debate, realizing that time was short before the operation was to begin. I was unable to bring them together. I therefore presented to the Council a compromise proposal that had been developed with much ingenuity by the peacekeeping staff and my military advisor, Brigadier General Timothy Dibuana, I stated candidly in my report to the Council that it was unlikely to please either side. Under my proposal, the authorized upper limit of the military component of UNTAG would remain 7,500, as agreed originally in 1978. However, taking into account, among other things, the views expressed by some Council members that recent progress in the southwestern Africa peace process had reduced the need for border surveillance and the prevention of infiltration, budgetary provisions would be presented to the General Assembly on the basis of a military component of 4,650. If it became apparent during the transitional period that a military component of this size was insufficient, I would so inform the Council and, subject to its concurrence, deploy as many additional troops within the 7,500 limit as was necessary.[4]

Before the budgetary request could be presented to the General Assembly, an enabling resolution was required from the Security Council expressing approval of my revised plan. The African and other nonaligned Members of the Council continued to have reservations about the reduced number of UN troops to be deployed. Without their votes, adoption of the resolution was impossible. The president of the Security Council undertook frantic consultations with Council members, as did I. I repeatedly expressed my concern that unless the enabling resolution was promptly forthcoming, the United Nations could not be prepared to begin implementation of Resolution 435 as scheduled on April 1. In order to overcome the African and nonaligned reservations, I made a further explanatory statement to the Council, reaffirming that the mandate of the military component of UNTAG remained unchanged and that I would inform the Council immediately if additional forces were required for the accomplishment of this mandate. My estimate for the cost of UNTAG was $416 million, excluding the cost of repatriating Namibians who were in exile. To overcome fears that the necessary funds for the repatriation program could not be raised through voluntary contributions, I stated that should that prove to be the case, I would not hesitate to recommend alternative arrangements. Finally, on February 16, 1989, the Security Council adopted the enabling resolution. The General Assembly then took until March 1 to approve the UNTAG budget. Thus the six to eight weeks lead time that I often had stated as the absolute minimum necessary to permit UNTAG to be fully effective on April 1 was reduced to four weeks.

Because of the serious financial crisis with which the United Nations was afflicted, owing primarily to the withholding of a substantial portion of the U.S. budgetary contribution, no money in the reserve fund could be used to initiate a peacekeeping operation pending the receipt of the contributions assessed from member states for the Namibia operation. These contributions were due only within 30 days of the General Assembly's expenditure authorization for the operation, and often they were delayed well beyond the due date. In this case, given the large startup funds that were needed and the urgency of the operation, I wrote to Member States on February 23—a week before the General Assembly approved the UNTAG budget—requesting that, once the assessments were established, payment be made immediately and that those states able to do so make voluntary contributions over and above their assessed contributions, to be repaid when all the assessed contributions were received. Despite these efforts, insufficient funds were on hand to purchase the necessary equipment and transport it and the bulk of the UNTAG force to Namibia by air before April 1. By then, my Special Representative and his senior staff together with the force commander, General Prem Chand, and his senior staff were in Namibia. Also in place were 280 of the 300 military monitors. That was all that had arrived, and their effectiveness was limited by the lack of communication facilities and transport, which also could not be flown to Namibia.

The Under-Secretary-General for Peacekeeping Operations, Marrack Goulding, made a trip to southern Africa in March 1989 and on the twenty-third met in Harare with SWAPO president Sam Nujoma. Nujoma referred immediately to a working paper that had been drafted earlier in the month for talks among the parties on implementation of Resolution 435 on the monitoring by Angola of the confinement to their bases in Angola of the SWAPO fighters. He insisted very forcefully that this was wrong. Quoting a report made by Secretary-General Waldheim in August 1978, Nujoma contended that the plan approved in Resolution 435 provided for the monitoring of South African and SWAPO bases in Namibia but *not* of SWAPO bases in Angola. Goulding pointed out that an agreement of July 1982 clearly provided that SWAPO bases in Angola and Zambia would be monitored. Nujoma said that SWAPO did not accept the agreement. Goulding reiterated that it had been agreed that Angola and Zambia would monitor the SWAPO bases in the two countries, although it was now accepted that there were no SWAPO bases in Zambia. UNTAG was to have a liaison function. If SWAPO did not allow its bases to be monitored, Goulding said, there would be no implementation of Resolution 435. The South Africans had made brutally clear that if there was no monitoring of SWAPO bases, they would suspend implementation of the independence process. The SWAPO president then asked what about SWAPO bases in Namibia. If SWAPO personnel were being humiliated, he would give orders that they resist the South Africans or anyone else. Goulding asked where the SWAPO bases in Namibia were. Nujoma replied, "We will tell you where they are."

Goulding then said that he was compelled to make absolutely clear that the plan approved by the Security Council did not allow for either SWAPO bases or gathering centers for SWAPO guerrillas inside Namibia. Nujoma again insisted that the 1982 plan was unacceptable to SWAPO. He contended that South Africa was training UNITA troops to attack UNTAG, which would then be blamed on SWAPO. He claimed that in the Caprivi Strip, South Africans dressed as game wardens were helping to supply UNITA; he warned that UNTAG personnel needed to be on high alert for such activities.

Goulding's account of this conversation did not reach me until March 28. In retrospect, it is clear that Nujoma's determined objection to the monitoring of SWAPO bases in Angola and his reference to SWAPO bases in Namibia should have warned us of a possible intent to infiltrate fighters into Namibia. Goulding did not see the conversation as sufficiently significant to alert Headquarters, however; even if we at Headquarters had interpreted it in this light, we did not have the means to move additional UNTAG personnel to the northern border area. It was too late to postpone the April 1 implementation date.

SWAPO INFILTRATION

At 9:45 A.M. on April 1, Martti Ahtisaari, the UN Special Representative for Namibia, called Headquarters to say that the South African Administrator-General had been continuously in touch with him for the last several hours regarding the infiltration from the north of four groups of armed insurgents totalling at least 143 persons. Clashes had occurred in the course of which 15 insurgents had been killed and 1 captured. Eight South West African police had been wounded, and reportedly the number of casualties was rising. Ahtisaari had agreed that South African helicopters could be sent to evacuate the wounded. He considered the incidents to be very serious and deliberately provocative. I immediately contacted the president of the Security Council, Soviet Ambassador Alexander Belonogov, and the representatives of Angola and SWAPO.

Two hours later Foreign Minister Botha called me and said that "a very critical and grave situation" had arisen, with many killed and wounded as a result of the infiltration of SWAPO insurgents. The State President of South Africa felt that unless "the Secretary-General made his position clear," he would have no choice but to ask for the withdrawal of UNTAG. I agreed that the incidents appeared serious but I did not see the logic of asking for UNTAG's recall. Botha then said that given the inadequacy of UNTAG, the South African Defense Forces should be allowed to leave their bases in order to protect the people. He was, in fact, authorizing the South African Defense Forces, as an emergency measure, "to take guard on the border." I said that there should be no unilateral measures. I intended to be in touch again with Mr. Ahtisaari and the UN force commander to determine the best course of action. I relayed to Ambassador Belonogov and to the representatives of Angola and SWAPO the import of this conversation and asked that each do whatever he could to affect the situation positively.

Shortly thereafter, still on April 1, Ahtisaari called to say that the South African Commanding Officer in Namibia, a General Meyer, had informed him that the South Africa Defense Forces were "going to the border." General Meyer implied that this was being done in light of my conversation with Foreign Minister Botha from which the Foreign Minister had "gained the impression" that I "understood" the necessity of this action. I made clear to Ahtisaari that this was far from an accurate reading of the conversation. Quite to the contrary, I had told Foreign Minister Botha that there should be no unilateral action by South Africa. I told Ahtisaari that he should be "tough" with the South Africans and stay firm against the movement of South African troops to the border.

This conversation was hardly completed before Ahtisaari called back to say that according to the South African administrator-general, one of the captured SWAPO insurgents had revealed that some 4,000 to 6,000 SWAPO fighters would try to infiltrate that night. Both Ahtisaari and General Prem Chand considered this to be an extremely grave threat. They felt that they had no alternative but to seek my agreement to the following: Certain specified units of the South African Defense Forces, to be agreed on, would be released from restriction to base to provide such support as may be needed by the existing police forces in case they cannot handle the situation by themselves. The situation would be kept under continuous review and the movement out of existing bases would be monitored throughout by UNTAG military observers.

The 280 UNTAG military observers who had arrived in Namibia could not cope with a threat of this dimension. The infantry battalions had yet to reach Namibia. I was convinced the situation, as described by the Special Representative and the Force Commander, posed a severe threat to the entire independence process. I saw no choice but to give my agreement to this proposal, and I did, albeit with misgivings. The President of the Security Council and the representatives of Angola and SWAPO were immediately informed. The Angolan ambassador said that President dos Santos had no information concerning the incident. The Front Line States, SWAPO and the African National Congress (ANC) were meeting in Luanda. All, he said, were surprised by what had happened. Nujoma had suggested that the SWAPO people involved in the fighting were not from "outside" but were from inside Namibia.

A senior team of UNTAG officials, including military personnel, civilians and police, hurried to the border area. The officer commanding the South West Africa Police told the team that the police were no longer able to handle the situation. The UN team also interviewed two prisoners captured by the security forces. They confirmed that they belonged to SWAPO armed units and that they had been told by their regional commanders to enter Namibia. Each said that he had been instructed not to engage the security forces because a cease-fire was to be in effect and there was to be no more fighting. However, the unit to which each belonged was to bring all of its arms, even rockets and antiaircraft guns, with them. One man had entered alone; the other in a group of between 40 and 50 personnel. One said that he had been told by his detachment commander that he would be instructed in Namibia where he should go so that the United Nations would supervise him and his colleagues. The other said that he had been sent to find out whether the security forces were still hunting SWAPO fighters or were observing the cease-fire. The further purpose of the infiltration, he said, was to establish bases inside Namibia. When asked whether the bases were for fighting or for peace, the prisoner replied that it was necessary to have a base inside Namibia where UN personnel would take care of them. This account differed markedly from the hostile and aggressive objectives attributed to the infiltrators by the security forces.

Following receipt of the team's report, Ahtisaari and General Prem Chand met with the Administrator-General and representatives of the local military and police to urge maximum restraint while the situation was being resolved. SWAPO, for its part, issued a press release on April 2, denying that it had violated the cease-fire. It claimed that its personnel, who were celebrating the implementation of Resolution 435, were attacked inside Namibia by South African soldiers. In the midst of this deplorable situation, the Government of Canada, always a strong and committed supporter of UN peacekeeping, offered to help in any accelerated deployment of UNTAG to Namibia or in the redeployment to the north of any UNTAG personnel already there.

Obviously it was essential to stop the fighting and get the SWAPO infiltrators out of Namibia or the prospect of Namibian independence would evaporate—a development that would not be entirely unwelcome to the more hard-nosed elements in Pretoria. On April 5 I made proposals to the South African Government and to SWAPO for the restoration of the cease-fire on a specified date; the cessation of all cross-border movement; the return, under UNTAG supervision, of all armed SWAPO soldiers to Angola beginning 24 hours after the restoration of the cease-fire; and the return to their homes in Namibia as unarmed civilians of those personnel who wished to do so and were prepared to hand over their weapons to UNTAG.

On the following day Ahtisaari called my chef de cabinet, Virendra Dayal, and informed him that the South Africans intended to move additional troops out of the bases where they were restricted, because they were convinced infiltration was increasing. Dayal stated categorically that the United Nations could not be associated in any way, shape or form with a South African decision of this sort. Speaking on my behalf, he advised Ahtisaari to ensure that UNTAG conduct itself in such a way as to preclude any likelihood of its colluding with the South Africans in a search-and-destroy mission. Ahtisaari suggested that the proposal to increase the number of unrestricted South African forces be at least brought to the attention of the Security Council. This was vigorously rejected. The Special Representative and the Field Commander were told to tell the South Africans that if they pursued this policy, it could destroy the whole Resolution 435 operation.

SWAPO quickly accepted my proposals but with an important modification. Nujoma insisted that rather than being returned to Angola, the SWAPO fighters be assembled in camps where they would remain under UN supervision until after the election. This was completely unacceptable to the South Africans, who continued to circulate alarming reports about SWAPO preparations in Angola for a full-scale armed invasion. In reality, they had the situation well under control in Namibia (as they had inflicted heavy casualties on the SWAPO fighters), but undoubtedly they were taken by surprise by the initial infiltrations and were understandably unimpressed by the United Nations' capacity to stop it.

I am certain that Sam Nujoma did not wish to risk the prospect of becoming the leader of an independent Namibia. That is why I have never been able to understand why the SWAPO fighters were sent across the border into Namibia in clear contravention of the cease-fire agreement and the Geneva Protocol. He must have felt that SWAPO encampments in Namibia were needed to counter any pressure that the presence of South African encampments might exert on the electorate. It was, by any measure, a foolhardy move. To his credit, Nujoma, seeing the danger of the situation, swallowed his pride and made the concession necessary to get the independence process back on track. On April 8, just one week after the crisis began, Nujoma announced to the press that in the interest of the implementation of independence process, SWAPO had decided to order its troops in Namibia to stop fighting, regroup and report to the People's Republic of Angola within 72 hours under the escort of UNTAG. The next day a joint commission consisting of Angolan, Cuban and South African representatives met at Mount Etjo in Namibia, with the United States and the Soviet Union present as observers, and agreed on a withdrawal procedure that aimed at restoring the situation that existed on March 31, 1989. The withdrawal would be jointly verified by the Administrator-General and the UN Special Representative. With this agreement in place, the process of transition to independence could go forward.

By May 4, 540 UN troops were in Namibia. Agreement had been reached with the Angolan government that UN military observers would have a permanent presence in each of the locations in Angola where SWAPO armed personnel were to be restricted. Thirty-two were already on duty. The Angolan government retained the responsibility, however, for ensuring that the SWAPO soldiers did not leave their bases. The Angolan control proved to be lax, whether intentionally or not, which was a legitimate cause for frequent South African complaints.

The joint commission also agreed that the South African Defense Forces in Namibia would remain released from restriction two more weeks in order to verify that SWAPO armed personnel had returned to Angola and to locate and destroy its arms caches. I strongly opposed this decision, which contravened the responsibility already given to UNTAG to monitor the withdrawal of the SWAPO forces and was certain to lead to further tension and possibly to conflict with the local inhabitants. I informed the Security Council that renewed clashes between the South African forces and SWAPO had already occurred and that the South West African Police was also a serious cause of concern. As the UNTAG operation was planned, it was assumed that this police force was a normal police organization. It proved, however, to be a paramilitary organization equipped with arms and vehicles associated with military action. Moreover, it included members of the dreaded Koevoet. I informed the Council that UNTAG police monitors were investigating a number of killings allegedly perpetrated by the South West African Police.

Inevitably an account of my remarks to the Council reached the South African government, and Foreign Minister Botha sent me the rudest letter I ever received as Secretary-General. As a further discourtesy, the letter was released to the press before it was delivered to me. At least that gave me the advantage of being prepared when the South African ambassador delivered the text. The minister accused me of having lost sight of the "elementary fact that SWAPO and SWAPO alone was responsible for the current disruption of the settlement process." My attitude, he wrote, "was not acceptable to the South African Government." He implied that until I made it clear to SWAPO that it should comply immediately with its commitments, the settlement process could not continue. I categorically rejected the foreign minister's accusations (some of which he repeated to me by phone) and in my eventual written reply said that I could not accept any implication that the South African government or any other party to this delicate process could unilaterally resort to any measures or means that were not provided for in the UN plan.

Pik Botha's letter was the strongest but by no means the only expression of distrust resulting from the SWAPO incursion. The Secretary-General of the Organization of African Unity sent word to me that I should have anticipated and alerted Member States that there was not enough time to deploy UNTAG. Zimbabwe President Robert Mugabe, who has never been known for restraint in his rhetoric, wrote to me in his capacity as chairman of the Non-Aligned Movement that he had observed with sadness and surprise that the UNTAG leadership was "totally unsuspecting and unprepared to respond appropriately" to the initiative of the racist South African occupation forces. Mugabe contended that certain decisions and actions taken by the Special Representative constituted monumental errors of judgment. His agreement to the release of South African military from their camps cast serious doubt on his suitability for his position in Namibia. The Front Line States also blamed Ahtisaari for agreeing to the utilization of South African troops and distrusted him as favoring South Africa. This view was shared, I must admit, by a few of my colleagues at Headquarters. This was not my opinion. I did feel, however, that greater oversight should be exercised from New York and that Ahtisaari needed a deputy to relieve him of some of the administrative burden. I decided to appoint an African to this post. Ahtisaari resisted the proposed appointment. It also prompted yet another disturbed telephone call from Foreign Minister Botha and caused the force commander, Prem Chand, who considered himself to be filling the role of deputy, to submit his resignation. I nonetheless appointed Mr. Joseph Legwaila, the Permanent Representative from Botswana, to the position. He provided much-needed assistance to Ahtisaari and, as I had hoped, strengthened African confidence in the impartiality of UNTAG.

I traveled to Namibia, South Africa and Angola in mid-July 1989. By this time UNTAG was fully deployed and its police strength reinforced; the South African Defense Forces had been reduced to 1,500 persons and the South West African Territorial Force had been demobilized. An amnesty had been declared for Namibians in exile, half of whom had been repatriated, and much discriminatory legislation had been repealed. Voter registration had begun on July 3 and much of the SWAPO leadership had returned peacefully and was campaigning without incident. I spoke with representatives of all the Namibian political parties and civic organizations—the first time such a joint meeting of the parties had ever been held—and reviewed with them the progress that had been made since the unfortunate developments at the beginning of April. I was greatly impressed by the mature conduct of all candidates. They were avoiding accusations that might incite hatred and distrust among the disparate elements of the population. I also spoke candidly of remaining problems related to the activities of the South West Africa Police and the electronic media, which were influenced by the governing authority. I pursued these problems during a lunch with the Administrator-General, Louis Pienaar, especially the many complaints that UNTAG had received about barbarous police actions in the north and the presence of former Koevoet personnel in the police. Pienaar denied that there was a problem, insisting that there was no such thing as "Koevoet," since it had been disbanded. When I traveled to the north the next day I was told repeatedly that Koevoet personnel were everywhere in the shadows. It was like an evil ghost threatening the Namibian population. This was in sharp contrast to the generally positive atmosphere throughout the rest of the country.

I met with Foreign Minister Botha a day later in Pretoria and found him in an unusually upbeat mood. He observed that southern Africa was moving away from using violence to solve its problems. The main concern he raised was with regard to detainees being held in Zambia by SWAPO; reportedly they were being tortured and women raped and killed. Ahtisaari intervened to say that he had been informed that SWAPO had released 153 detainees. Botha contended that there was a bit of a trick in the numbers since not all of the 153 had been detainees. Some were actually members of the People's Liberation Army of Namibia (PLAN). All together, he said, there were 1,577 PLAN members among those who had returned to Namibia, and they were becoming an intimidating force in the reception centers. When later in the conversation I raised the issue of the continuing presence of Koevoet personnel in the South West Africa Police, the foreign minister did not deny their presence but said that if I could do something about the "numbers" that concerned him, it might be possible to alleviate my concern on the Koevoet matter.

When I reached Lusaka, I spoke to both President Kenneth Kaunda and Sam Nujoma about the SWAPO detainees. President Kaunda assured me in the strongest terms that there were no remaining detainees on Zambian soil. We also made exhaustive checks concerning PLAN personnel in Angola who, the South Africans repeatedly claimed, were planning armed attacks into Namibia. The Special Representative concluded that there were no PLAN personnel in southern Angola. The great majority had returned to Namibia peacefully on refugee flights. It was clear that PLAN no longer posed any military threat.

On returning to New York, I passed this information to the South African Ambassador while at the same time expressing the strongest possible objections to the continued Koevoet presence in northern Namibia. Four days later, on August 15, Administrator-General Pienaar announced in Windhoek that, in light of the assurances I had given to the South African Government concerning PLAN, he was removing from duty 1,200 members of the South West Africa Police. That number, he said, "represents the remnants of the counter-insurgency component re-integrated in SWAPOL following the incursions of SWAPO on April 1." The Koevoet problem was thus finally resolved.

INDEPENDENCE AT LAST

The independence ceremony was the culmination of an effort stretching back over two decades in which the indigenous forces of national liberation were complemented by the support of the international community on behalf of a free and independent Namibia. The presence of the new state president of South Africa, F. W. de Klerk, as honored guest rather than master, of Nelson Mandela and representatives of the Front Line States and of the Organization of African Unity seemed to me a harbinger of hope for all of southern Africa. In the joy of the occasion the bitter struggle of the past appeared forgotten. Pride and hope had replaced hatred and violence.

UNTAG truly served as midwife for the birth of this new country. It had arrived poorly equipped for the job at hand with near-disastrous results. Its recovery was, under the circumstances, remarkably swift. The United Nations was never "in charge" in Namibia. Administrative authority during the transition period rested with the South African–appointed Administrator-General; security was the respon-sibility of the South West African Police. UNTAG's job was to monitor, to be the impartial chaperone and to ensure that the police respected the human rights of the population, that the election laws and procedures were fair and that the cease-fire was properly observed. UNTAG worked closely with South Africa, the political parties and local authorities on the various laws and legal instruments required for holding free elections and establishing the new state. The key instruments needed clearance from the United Nations. The views of UN legal and constitutional experts had a strong influence on their content. This was especially important in the case of the constitution, which in its final wording provides full protection for the freedom and human rights of the population.

Special Representative Martti Ahtisaari and his staff had to maintain a satisfactory working relationship with the South African authorities while at the same time encouraging and protecting the political parties, including, of course, SWAPO, in the role they were assuming in a new, democratic country. Ahtisaari had the calm but authoritative personality that permitted him to meet these requirements extremely well. UNTAG included over 8,000 military and civilian personnel from more than 100 countries. They were widely spread throughout the country. Managing this operation was not easy, and, especially in the early months, it was less than perfect. But while Ahtisaari and Force Commander General Prem Chand sometimes lost patience with what they saw as unnecessary interference from New York Headquarters, they never lost their composure or their clear understanding of UNTAG's mission.

DE KLERK AND NELSON MANDELA

I had my first substantive meeting with State President de Klerk in Windhoek during the independence celebrations. I was deeply impressed by his evident strength of character. He struck me as a revolutionary with both feet firmly on the ground, a rare combination. De Klerk was intent on bringing a basic change in his country's social and political structure. He saw the future of South Africa as linked to the health of the other countries of southern Africa—the Front Line states that had been South Africa's foes. It was South Africa's responsibility to assist these countries to prosper, even while recognizing that they could never match South Africa's level of development. Surprisingly, de Klerk made me think of Gorbachev, even though he resembles the Soviet leader neither in appearance nor in personality. Yet both were ready to take very large risks in pursuing their vision of the future of their countries. I sensed, too, that, like Gorbachev, de Klerk was bringing about a fundamental change in human society.

In our conversation, the State President's first comment was that after many decades the United Nations and the Republic of South Africa had become partners in bringing Namibia to independence. That undertaking had brought honor to all concerned. He was now mainly concerned about the economic prospects of the new state. He asked that I not permit the wealthier countries to lose sight of Namibia's needs. I said that I fully agreed and intended to convene a pledging conference to raise funds. I noted that the United States had appropriated the very unsatisfactory amount of $500,000 for aid to Namibia. The day before I had pursued this with Secretary of State Baker, and he had promised to secure increased funding from Congress.

President de Klerk was forthright in his comments on Walvis Bay, the only port on Namibia's coast. His government, he said, desired to have a situation "where Namibia would have a feeling of full security that Walvis Bay will be there for safe use in conducive circumstances and, as a corollary, that Walvis Bay will never be used as an instrument of destabilization nor for putting Namibia in a corner nor for exerting pressure on Namibia." With regard to South Africa itself, de Klerk stated that his government was "in a hurry . . . to get away from negative ground." The new constitutional dispensation would "assure full participation of South Africans in all levels of government in a manner that is both just and equitable." At the same time he cautioned that the situation in South Africa was in no way comparable to Namibia. Good government had to continue within the framework of the present constitution until the new dispensation had been negotiated and promulgated. We cannot, he said, "suspend government and thereby create a vacuum." He urged that I use all of my good offices to prevent discussion from moving in that direction.

The General Assembly, during a special session on apartheid the previous December, had requested that I provide a report by the end of June 1990 on the situation in South Africa. I assured the President that my approach to this task would be completely impartial. In order that the report would reflect only the truth about what was going on, I hoped de Klerk would accept a quiet UN mission led by Under-Secretary-General Farah, who was well known to South African authorities. Again President de Klerk's response was direct and forthright: "You or anybody acting in your behalf will be very welcome in South Africa but it must not be on the basis that South Africa accepts the right of the United Nations to interfere in our internal affairs. . . . We shall cooperate in a practical way." He added—and it impressed me deeply—that he had a mandate from his people to ensure that South Africa returned to its rightful place in the international community. He recognized that it was necessary to fill an information void. "I keep asking our opponents to stop knocking at the door," he said. "It is already open."

While in Windhoek I also met with Nelson Mandela. What a fortunate eventuality that these two great men, de Klerk and Mandela, should come at the same time into positions of power and influence. With Mandela, one has the sense of being in the presence of a very wise man, a vigorous leader who has the courage both for bold action and for restraint. He has the charisma of extraordinary humanity. He gave me his assessment of developments in South Africa and, like de Klerk, spoke of the urgency of moving ahead in negotiations for a new constitution. He listed various areas of difference between the African National Congress and the government. His major concern, however, was who would take part in the negotiations. He opposed the government's position of relying on existing political structures. If all the homeland leaders, who had no mandate of any kind from the South African people, were to be seated at the negotiating table, the African National Congress automatically would be outnumbered. He wanted to unite all the antiapartheid forces in the negotiations to dismantle apartheid. As we discussed the report that I needed to submit to the General Assembly, Mandela said that he could confirm to me "that de Klerk is an honest man. He wants progress. The question is, can he carry the National Party with him?" He thought that at present the "pillars of apartheid" remained in place.

I met again with Nelson Mandela four months later in New York. By this time Farah and his team had completed their information-gathering mission in South Africa and were preparing to draft my report to the General Assembly. I felt that this report would have more than usual importance since many Member States were trying to get their bearings in light of the rapidly changing situation in South Africa. The general conclusion reached by the Farah mission was that the forward-looking statements made at the higher political levels had not yet resulted in an abandonment of apartheid or in the public attitudes that sustained it. I was anxious to hear Mandela's views.

Mandela's response was clear and statesmanlike. There had been very significant political developments in South Africa. Negotiations between the African National Congress and the government were in progress. There remained serious difficulties, but Mandela was convinced that the government was serious and wished, like the African National Congress, to reach agreement on a new constitution that would quickly eliminate racist policies. He felt that if the existing sanctions were lifted at this stage, it would not help de Klerk but would encourage the far right opposition. The government had made clear to him that the international sanctions had devastated the economy.[5] Mr. de Klerk, in a conversation just before Mandela's departure, had asked him to "cool it" on sanctions during his trip. He had rejected this advice. "In our view," he said, "the sanctions had been instrumental in bringing the government to the table . . . sanctions should be maintained."

On another issue that I raised Mandela showed a sensitive understanding for the government's position. The United Nations High Commissioner for Refugees was assisting in repatriating African National Congress members and their families. The South African Government objected to UNHCR support of the refugees once they had returned to South Africa. When asked for his views, Mandela said that de Klerk had discussed this matter with him and explained that, in the government's view, UNHCR had no jurisdiction within South Africa. The returnees should be looked after by a South African organization. Mandela said he would like to know what the precedents in other countries were. But he suggested that we "must understand the sensitivity of the government on this question." The government had said it was ready to let the African National Congress mobilize organizations to look after the returnees. "I would therefore proceed with some caution," he said.

This was a small matter, but Nelson Mandela's attitude raised my confidence that there would be an orderly transition when the African National Congress assumed leadership of South Africa.

Namibian independence became possible only through the combined efforts of the United Nations and of national governments—in particular the United States and the Western Contact Group—working separately but within the framework of objectives defined by the UN Security Council. Despite its interest in the proceedings, the United Nations was on the sidelines of the negotiations undertaken by the United States with South Africa, Angola and Cuba on the withdrawal of the Cuban and South African troops from Angola. It was impossible for me not to feel somewhat excluded. Yet the Western powers had the leverage to bring South Africa to accept a settlement and to gain Angolan agreement to the complete withdrawal of Cuban troops. Western powers had the capacity—which they eventually exercised—to put pressure on the financial and economic institutions of South Africa and to exclude it from association with the Western cultural community of which the white minority considered itself a part. The United States, together with South Africa and also the Soviet Union, could influence the Angolan government by manipulating internal Angolan forces.

The United Nations had long championed the cause of self-determination for the people of Namibia. Over a long period it mobilized global pressure against the racial policies of South Africa that certainly was a potent factor in bringing that country to see the necessity of a Namibian settlement even before the apartheid system collapsed. The settlement plan for Namibia could not have been implemented without the United Nations. The successful negotiations undertaken by the Western Contact Group, within the framework of principles defined by the Security Council, stands as a model for the utilization of the disparate capacities of the Organization and of its Members toward a commonly agreed goal.

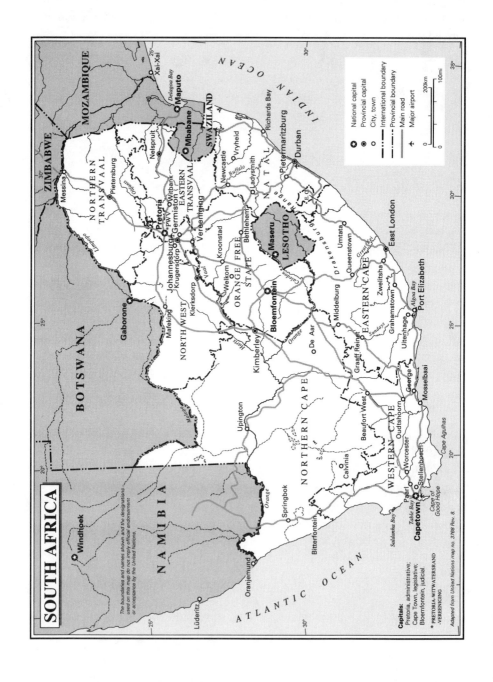

SOUTH AFRICA

National capital
Provincial capital
City, town
International boundary
Provincial boundary
Main road
Major airport

0   200km
0   100mi

Capitals:
Pretoria, administrative;
Cape Town, legislative;
Bloemfontein, judicial.

* PRETORIA-WITWATERSRAND
-VEREENIGING

The boundaries and names shown and the designations used on this map do not imply official endorsement or acceptance by the United Nations.

Adapted from United Nations map no: 3768 Rev. 8.

ZIMBABWE

MOZAMBIQUE

Xai-Xai
Delagoa Bay
Maputo

SWAZILAND
Mbabane

INDIAN OCEAN

Richards Bay
Pietermaritzburg
Durban

Messina

NORTHERN
TRANSVAAL
Pietersburg

Nelspruit

Vryheid
Newcastle
Ladysmith

Limpopo
Olifants

Pretoria
PWV
Witbank
Germiston
Johannesburg
Krugersdorp
EASTERN
TRANSVAAL
Vereeniging

NATAL
Buffalo

Maseru
LESOTHO

Bethlehem

Kroonstad

NORTH WEST
Klerksdorp

Welkom
ORANGE
FREE
STATE

Bloemfontein

Drakensberg

East London

Umtata
Queenstown
Zwelitsha

EASTERN CAPE

BOTSWANA

Gaborone

Mafeking

Vaal

Kimberley
De Aar
Orange

Grahamstown
Great Kei
Sundays

Uitenhage
Algoa Bay
Port Elizabeth

Upington

Molopo

NORTHERN CAPE

Beaufort West

Middelburg
Graaff Reinet

George
Oudtshoorn
Mosselbaai

WESTERN CAPE

Worcester
Calvinia

Springbok

Orange

Bitterfontein

Paarl
Stellenbosch
Capetown
Table Bay
Cape of
Good Hope
Cape Agulhas

Saldanha Bay

NAMIBIA

Windhoek

Lüderitz

Oranjemund

ATLANTIC OCEAN

TWELVE

ANGOLA AND MOZAMBIQUE: COUNTRIES IN CRISIS

THE INTERNAL CONFLICTS THAT DEVASTATED ANGOLA AND MOZAMBIQUE during the 1980s were strongly affected by external forces. In Angola, the government enjoyed the support of the Soviet Union and, more directly, of Cuba, which had sent troops to help the government defend itself from the insurgent forces of the National Union for the Total Independence of Namibia (UNITA) and to repel South African incursions. UNITA, in turn, received support from South Africa and the United States with the cooperation of Zaire. RENAMO, the ill-defined insurgent movement in Mozambique, was supported by Southern Rhodesia and subsequently by South Africa, which long pursued a policy aimed at destabilizing the country's political cohesion. The eventual resolution of these conflicts was also heavily influenced by external events: in the case of Angola by the waning of the Cold War and by South Africa's decision to agree to the independence of Namibia; in the case of Mozambique by the domestic changes in South Africa, which resulted in a more constructive policy toward its neighbors.

The United Nations was not involved in mediating these conflicts. It was an essential element, however, in their resolution. As in the case of Namibia, national governments (and in Mozambique a nongovernmental organization) were better able to bring the parties in conflict to terms than the United Nations because of the special relationship they enjoyed or the leverage they could apply. The United Nations need not be jealous in sharing responsibility for conflict resolution. There are enough problems to go around. It is important, however, that third parties that assume the mediating responsibility recognize that the United Nations is likely to figure in the settlement terms and that for this reason the Secretary-General should be kept informed of the course of negotiations. When this is not done—as was the case in Angola—problems in implementing the settlement are likely to occur.

ANGOLA

A crucial element in implementation of the UN plan for Namibia was an agreement between Angola and Cuba providing for the staged withdrawal from Angola of the estimated 33,000 Cuban troops in the country. Cuba and Angola requested that the United Nations verify the withdrawal. The Under-Secretary-General for Peacekeeping Operations, Marrack Goulding, developed an operational plan that foresaw the stationing of UN observers at the ports and airports to be used for evacuation and around the country to verify that the movement of Cuban troops was proceeding according to schedule. The plan was approved by the Security Council in 1988, in Resolution 626, as the UN Angola Verification Mission (UNAVEM).

The Chief Military Observer in Angola, Brigadier General Ferreira Gomes from Brazil, was initially unhappy with the operational procedures for the withdrawal of the Cuban forces, feeling that he had to rely totally on information provided by Angola and Cuba and had no independent powers of verification. Unfortunately, he let his concern be known to the press, which resulted in unwarranted doubts about the effectiveness of the UN operation. The operation actually went exceedingly well under General Gomes's very competent command. The Cubans moved northward and out of Angola on schedule in a disciplined manner. I was able to confirm to the Security Council on May 25, 1991, that all Cuban troops had left Angola.

The United Nations was also to observe the monitoring by Angolan soldiers of the camps in which SWAPO soldiers were gathered. In other words, the United Nations was to monitor the monitors, a practice that is seldom fully satisfactory. UNTAG was to establish "liaison posts" at the sites of SWAPO encampments. The UNTAG observers were not in place by April 1, 1989 when the incursion of SWAPO fighters into Namibia made it apparent that Angola was not doing an effective monitoring job. After the United Nations registered strong concern with President dos Santos and the liaison posts were established, the situation improved, but only slightly. The UNTAG observers did not have the authority or the strength to maintain the security of the camps. They reported that many SWAPO soldiers were continuing to move freely about the country. This caused frequent and understandable South African complaints, although

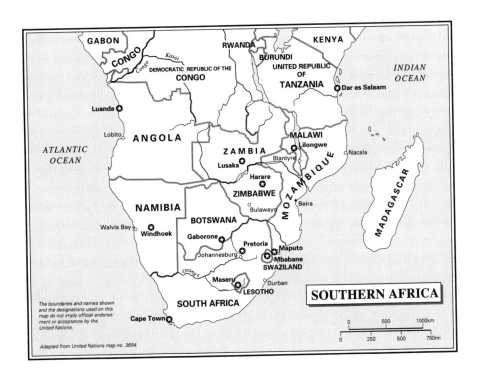

GABON

CONGO

Kasai

DEMOCRATIC REPUBLIC OF THE
CONGO

Congo

RWANDA

BURUNDI

UNITED REPUBLIC
OF
TANZANIA

KENYA

INDIAN
OCEAN

Dar es Salaam ⊕

Luanda ⊕

Lobito ○

ATLANTIC
OCEAN

ANGOLA

ZAMBIA

Lusaka ⊕

MALAWI

Lilongwe ⊕

Blantyre ○

Nacala ○

Harare ⊕

NAMIBIA

BOTSWANA

Bulawayo ○

ZIMBABWE

M O Z A M B I Q U E

Beira ○

MADAGASCAR

Walvis Bay ○

Windhoek ⊕

Gaborone ⊕

Pretoria ⊕

Johannesburg ○

Maputo ⊕

Mbabane ⊕
SWAZILAND

Orange

Maseru ⊕

Durban ○

LESOTHO

SOUTH AFRICA

Cape Town ⊕

The boundaries and names shown
and the designations used on this
map do not imply official endorsement or acceptance by the
United Nations.

Adapted from United Nations map no. 3654.

SOUTHERN AFRICA

0   500   1000km

0   250   500   750mi

South Africa itself had reached the agreement with Angola providing that Angolans would do the monitoring.

THE SEARCH FOR INTERNAL RECONCILIATION

As the Cold War ebbed and South African policy changed in the late 1980s, both UNITA and the Angolan government lost much of their external support. The United States and the Soviet Union were clearly interested in a resolution of the Angolan civil war. Chester Crocker, on behalf of the United States, had for some years been pressing the Angolan government (and presumably UNITA) to seek a "political solution," which meant bringing the two together in some form of government of national unity. I, too, suggested this to President dos Santos as early as 1987, but at that time he rejected the idea outright. By 1990, however, it had become evident that without external assistance neither side could attain a military victory and that the economic and social disintegration of the country—in large part the result of the civil war—had reached a disastrous stage.

At this point the government and UNITA accepted Portugal's offer to mediate a settlement. The United States and the Soviet Union had the role of observers, which, I think, could more accurately have been described as godfathers. The United Nations was not involved in the negotiations, but when its participation in monitoring the proposed cease-fire was broached, the United States began to fill us in on developments. According to the Americans, the Angolan government had at first strongly opposed UN involvement but had been prevailed upon, mainly by the Soviets, to accept it. The proposed verification structure was complex. The cease-fire would be monitored on the ground by joint government/UNITA military groups, which would be supervised by a Joint Verification and Monitoring Commission composed of the Angolan government and UNITA plus the United States and the Soviet Union as observers. This commission would be under a Joint Political and Military Commission of the same composition. The UN Angola Verification Mission (UNAVEM) would observe the functioning of this machinery and verify the overall implementation of the cease-fire. My staff pointed out to the Americans that these arrangements were very different from those that normally prevailed in peacekeeping operations. It was suggested then and in subsequent conversations that greater clarity would be needed on the mandate of the UN observers, on the required resources and the expected duration of the operation. However, the provisions on monitoring the cease-fire that were included in the peace agreement signed in Lisbon on May 31, 1991, remained essentially unchanged. Provision was only added that a UN representative could be invited to participate in the two commissions.

The joint government/UNITA monitoring groups did not perform effectively. UNAVEM was increasingly expected to carry out their monitoring function.

At the request of the Americans and the Portuguese, the UN observers assumed responsibility for counting the troops that were assembled. Initially the UNAVEM observers often met resistance from the local commanders on both sides who had not received appropriate instructions from their headquarters. By October, Marrack Goulding, in visiting the area, found that both the Angolan sides as well as the three observer countries welcomed an ever larger UNAVEM verification role.[1]

The conditions in the camps where the troops of the two sides assembled were abominable. In many, the UNAVEM representatives had to sleep in grass huts that the Angolan soldiers made for them. UNITA clearly lacked an adequate logistical system to provide for its troops. The shortage of food threatened the whole peace process. Therefore, in October 1991, the United Nations undertook an urgent program to provide food for the soldiers and their dependents in the assembly areas pending their demobilization. (This program was in addition to a special relief program that had been introduced in 1990 when some 2 million Angolan civilians were threatened with starvation.) UNAVEM estimated that approximately 250,000 people were in the assembly areas, including 130,000 government troops and 50,000 UNITA soldiers. The reports from the UNAVEM observers indicated that despite these harsh conditions, the peace process was going forward. There was concern that neither side had turned over many of their arms to UNAVEM (an ominous sign for the future), but, nevertheless, the cease-fire was holding. UNAVEM detected no inclination to resume fighting. Still, on his return from Angola, Goulding reported to me that there were disturbing signs for the future. Marcus Savimbi, the UNITA leader, was accompanied by a large and assertive group of bodyguards. His supporters seized buildings and still showed pretensions of being the "government" of the *Terras Livres de Angola.*

When he called on me in New York at the end of September 1991, the Angolan foreign minister, Pedro De Castro Van Dunem "Loy", raised the possibility of UN assistance with the elections to be held in one year. My immediate (unstated) reaction was relief that this would not be my problem. Given the devastated condition of Angola and the almost total lack of infrastructure, observing elections would be a formidable prospect. I explained to the minister that, on my own authority, I could extend technical assistance for preparation of the elections but that more extensive participation in the electoral process would involve the General Assembly or the Security Council and possibly both. I reiterated my conviction that if the United Nations was to assist in the electoral process, it should be involved at an early stage and not be brought in at the last minute. The foreign minister said that he would bear this in mind. Three months later President dos Santos sent letters officially requesting that the United Nations provide technical assistance and observers to help prepare and verify the electoral process.

In the few weeks remaining in my term I was able to begin preparations for the dispatch of a technical mission and to inform the Security Council of Angola's request for election monitors. I had real hope that Angola had emerged from 31 years of war and that reconciliation of the opposing political forces would open the way for the reconstruction of the country. This hope turned out to be premature. But as I write, there is again a prospect of peace; this time the United Nations is more experienced in the requirements for the restoration of stability in the wake of civil war and is better equipped for the job than it was in 1992, although the achievement of national reconciliation remains daunting.

MOZAMBIQUE

In the 1980s, Mozambique was surely one of the most tragic countries in the world. Miserably poor, it was beset by drought and insurrection and was the object of destabilization programs of the Southern Rhodesian regime and South Africa. The centralized economic structure introduced by the Marxist government only intensified the problem.

I first met the President, Samora Machel, at the Organization for African Unity summit in Libya in November 1982. I expected a hardened Marxist revolutionary but found instead something of a visionary. He was a man of impressive presence, clearly a leader. He hardly spoke of the problems of his own country, showing greater concern for Namibia and for East Timor, which, like Mozambique, had suffered Portuguese colonization and in Machel's view was in worse condition than Mozambique. When I visited Maputo, the Mozambique capital, a year later he had every reason to be under great stress. There had been direct attacks by South Africa inside Mozambique's borders. The insurgent organization Resistência Nacional Mocambicana (RENAMO) was laying large areas of the country to waste. The government distrusted its neighbors, especially Kenya and Malawi. Yet Machel showed no signs of a siege mentality. He was ready to put ideology and past history aside in the interest of Mozambique's well-being. Three days after Mozambique accused South Africa of plotting to assassinate the President, his foreign minister opened talks with the South African foreign minister aimed at normalizing their relations. Subsequently, President Machel, to the shock of his Front Line neighbors, signed an Agreement on Non-Aggression and Good Neighborliness with South Africa. The South African government later made public that the agreement was based on a package deal under which Machel would remain the leader of Mozambique, a cease-fire would be signed between the government and RENAMO and joint commissions would be established to deal with further problems. Whatever its intent, the agreement had little affect on conditions in Mozambique, which continued to deteriorate, or on South Africa's policy of destabilization.

The United Nations was in no way involved in these developments. As conditions in Mozambique continued to deteriorate, however, I expressed my growing concern and sent a mission to Maputo to assess the needs of the country. Its findings were dire. There was an imminent threat of mass starvation. Thereafter, in February 1987, I launched an appeal to governments for assistance to cover food aid, transport and logistical assistance, survival items, health needs and agricultural inputs. At the same time I appointed a Special Coordinator for Relief Operations in Mozambique. The response was gratifying; $330 million was pledged.

At this time, General Olesegun Obasanjo, the Nigerian leader, approached me to suggest that, while the pledging conference was valuable, he thought the United Nations should do more at the political level. Mozambique had become the test case, he said, for the international community's readiness to help the Front Line States resist destabilization by South Africa. My staff had already been working on plans to help with the restoration of the Beira corridor, which was the main transportation route between Zimbabwe and the sea and which RENAMO had seriously disrupted. These plans envisioned three stages: first, the Secretariat would advise the Front Line States on how to establish a multilateral African force to protect the corridor; second, these states would ask the Security Council to approve the establishment of the force and to set up a voluntary fund for contributions to support it; and third, the Council could establish an observer group to report on the progress of the African force. When this plan was outlined to General Obasanjo, he said that President Joachim Alberto Chissano, who had succeeded Machel, would be very interested in stages 1 and 2 but that he would oppose any UN military presence in Mozambique.

Word of these plans leaked out and news stories appeared in Canada that the Canadian government might be asked to participate in a peace force to protect Mozambique from South African–backed guerrillas. It was just at this time, in 1987, that Zimbabwe substantially increased the number of its troops in Mozambique to protect the communication routes to the sea. UN involvement therefore remained confined to assistance activities until peace was established between the government and RENAMO.

The UN aid program focused on four objectives: to prevent starvation; to link emergency assistance with economic recovery programs; to ensure the government's central role in the execution of the emergency program; and to provide continuing coordination among the government, the bilateral donors, the nongovernmental organizations and the United Nations. Problems derived mainly from the failure of some donors to meet their pledges and from the tying by others of their pledges to particular relief areas that were not always of top priority. The response at a second pledging conference that I called in 1988 was even more generous than the first. After that, donor generosity declined, partly because of reports of government officials' misuse of relief goods and by government inefficiency in the relief operation. The program remained, however, highly valuable. It was nothing less than the life blood for a people in agony during a period of domestic turmoil and conflict and of repeated natural disasters. The annual per capita income at this time was $150—very nearly the lowest in the world—and infant mortality was the world's second highest.

In 1990 there was a sea change in the situation in Mozambique. Peace talks between the government and RENAMO brought about through the efforts of a Roman Catholic lay organization, the Community of Sant' Egidio, began in Rome, and the government endorsed the adoption of a multiparty system and a mixed economy. Multiparty parliamentary elections were scheduled for 1991. In October of that year, the Foreign Minister of Mozambique, Pascoal Mocumbi, raised with me the possibility that his government would request the assistance of the United Nations in monitoring the elections. At the same time, he described the difficulties being encountered in the talks with RENAMO and the continuing acts of terror in which RENAMO was engaged. He complained of a persistent flow of assistance to RENAMO from right-wing elements in South Africa and the United States. I told the minister, as I had told his Angolan counterpart, that the Secretary-General could offer only technical assistance for the preparation of the elections. It was clear that the time for this would not come until my successor was in office.

As I dealt with these problems of southern Africa, I was constantly struck by the heritage of colonialism, by the invidious effect of racism and by the misguided intrusion of Cold War objectives. It was a lethal combination. It was my good fortune to be Secretary-General when two of these—the Cold War and apartheid—markedly decreased. The results were quick and extraordinarily positive. Great change requires strong leaders, and Nelson Mandela and F. W. de Klerk came on the scene to fill this need and to change the history of southern Africa. Sam Nujoma has been able to give strong, democratic leadership to newly-independent Namibia. Samora Machel, crippled by a failing Communist ideology, was nonetheless an inspiring leader and a realist when realism was required. His successor as President of Mozambique, Joachim Alberto Chissano, has gone further along this route leading his country to peace and democracy.

Among these leaders in southern Africa, my personal rapport was closest with President dos Santos of Angola. He much appreciated my ability to converse with him in Portuguese, and we became good friends. He is a cautious man and, given the circumstances of his government, understandably always on guard. While courteous, his watchful eyes convey distrust. The course that he steered was sometimes serpentine as he adjusted to the contradictory pressures on him from South Africa, from his not always welcome SWAPO guests, from the United States, from the other Front Line States and, not least, from his internal opposition. That he has survived, given the challenges he has faced, says a great deal.

The task of all these men is enormous given the economic need and the social tensions that will long remain. Yet de Klerk and Mandela's vision of a southern African community with the strong South African industrial economy at its core is extremely hopeful; unfortunately, such a vision is still lacking for the rest of sub-Saharan Africa.

THIRTEEN

THE WESTERN SAHARA

THE WESTERN SAHARA, a large expanse of desert stretching along the northwest coast of Africa, has a population of less than 150,000. Largely nomads, in their history they have had little appreciation for the concept of national borders. Yet this land, whose only major resources are large phosphate deposits and plentiful fish along its shores, has become a nationalist cause, giving rise to an armed conflict that has remained unresolved for a quarter of a century. The problem was first one of decolonization from Spanish control; thereafter it evolved to be one of nationalism and the struggle between Morocco and the liberation group that seeks independence for the territory.

Morocco has argued that the Sahrawi people have long made known through their traditional tribal chiefs their wish for reintegration into the Moroccan kingdom. The nationalist movement POLISARIO *(Frente Popular para la Liberación de Saguia-el Hamra y Rio de Oro)* maintains that the territory constitutes an independent entity totally separate from Morocco and fully entitled to statehood. In the United Nations, where the Western Sahara has figured on the agenda since 1963, the position established by the General Assembly is that the Sahrawi people should decide their own future and exercise their right of self-determination. This is the intent of repeated resolutions adopted by the General Assembly and was the point of reference in all of the actions I took in seeking to facilitate a settlement of the Western Sahara problem.

The Organization of African Unity initially took the lead in calling, in 1981, for a cease-fire among POLISARIO, Morocco and Mauritania, which at that time still claimed a part of the territory, and for the holding of a referendum on the future of the territory. The General Assembly later in the same year reaffirmed, in Resolution A/36/46, the inalienable right of the people of Western Sahara to self-determination and independence and endorsed the efforts of the OAU. It requested that the Secretary-General take the necessary steps to ensure that the United Nations participate in the organization and conduct of the referendum and cooperate closely with the OAU Secretary-General in the achievement of the other OAU objectives with regard to the Western Sahara.

Realizing that it did not have the resources to finance these objectives, especially the peacekeeping operation that would be required, the OAU at a summit meeting in 1983 decided that the referendum should be held under the joint UN/OAU auspices. It also requested that the United Nations, "in conjunction with the OAU," station a peacekeeping force in the territory to ensure peace and security while the referendum was organized and conducted. From this point on the United Nations became the primary force in seeking to resolve the Western Sahara conflict. As mediator, the OAU was handicapped by its admission of the Sahrawi Arab Democratic Republic (SADR) to membership, which caused Morocco to withdraw from participation in the organization. I was always careful, however, to operate in tandem with the successive African heads of government who served as OAU chairs. The General Assembly has never recognized the Sahrawi Arab Democratic Republic (SADR) as a state although it recognized POLISARIO as the legitimate representative of the Sahrawi people. I dealt with the POLISARIO leaders only in their party capacity and not as government representatives.

MOROCCO'S POLICY

King Hassan II personally defined and directed Moroccan policy on the Western Sahara. He is an extremely shrewd and determined man, highly cultivated, with a quick intelligence, full of nervous energy, who seldom sits still during a conversation. With him one has to be alert and find the right opening to make a point, because the King, verbally at least, is always on the offensive. The King is also a very human man, of elegant expression and great courtesy. During one of my rare tête-à-tête meetings with him, his beautiful young granddaughter came in. He immediately interrupted our conversation to play with her and seemed to forget for the moment what we were talking about.

Politically, Morocco faced the disadvantage of having the OAU and the Non-Aligned Movement be supportive of POLISARIO and of the independence of the Western Sahara. Its military position, on the other hand, was increasingly strong as it successfully walled off the better part of the West Saharan territory from POLISARIO attack. The King could engage in diplomatic tactics relatively immune from military pressure. In addressing the General Assembly in September 1983, he reiterated Morocco's commitment to the holding of a

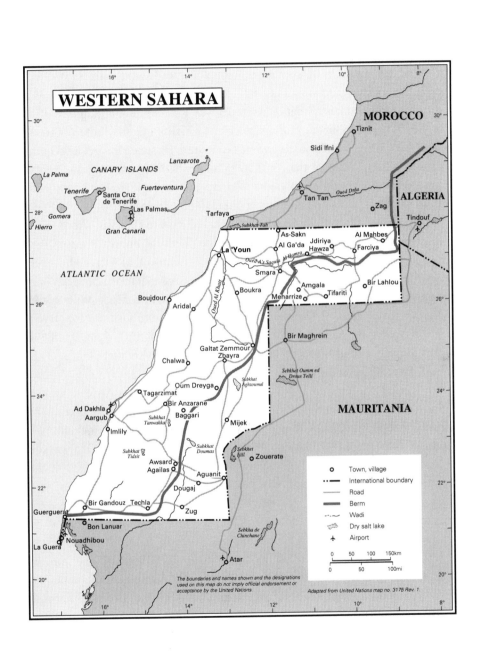

referendum, "tomorrow, if you wish it, in the presence of observers from the OAU and the UN." He solemnly undertook to consider Morocco bound by the results of the referendum. At almost the same time, however, at a meeting of the OAU Implementation Committee on the Western Sahara, the Moroccan representative refused to sit at the same table with the POLISARIO representative and the meeting broke up in disarray. Hassan II declared in October 1984 that if the Sahrawi Arab Democratic Republic attended the scheduled OAU summit, Morocco would walk out of the OAU, which it subsequently did. My sense was, and remains, that Hassan II was sincere in his support of a referendum, but only under circumstances in which a majority vote for some form of association with Morocco would be assured. He stated this position quite clearly at the beginning of the conflict. I doubt whether, in the ensuing years, he has ever seriously contemplated a Western Sahara separate from Morocco. This, in his mind, would be contrary to the will of his people.

Morocco's Permanent Representative to the United Nations, Ali Benjelloun, called on me in February 1985 and stated with the utmost firmness that Morocco would never agree to direct negotiations with POLISARIO. However, the Mahgreb needed peace, and it had to be recognized that peace currently was threatened by the tensions caused by the Western Sahara conflict. With this in mind, the government of Morocco wished to invite me to visit the country in order "to open the way for cooperation in the Mahgreb." I accepted the suggestion and visited Morocco in July in conjunction with attending an OAU summit meeting in Addis Ababa.

During the summit I had conversations with various African leaders concerning the Western Sahara, the most important of which were with the Algerian president, Chadli Bendjedid, and with Mohammed Abdelaziz, the Secretary-General of POLISARIO. I found President Chadli then and always to be a reasonable and helpful statesman. He was genuinely committed to the concept of a peaceful community of Mahgreb states. While he was consistent in his support of Western Sahara independence and was critical of Morocco for resisting bilateral talks with POLISARIO, he clearly was not motivated by personal hostility toward King Hassan II. I gained the impression at this meeting and later that Chadli preferred to see Hassan II remain on the throne. POLISARIO was heavily dependent on Algeria for financial, diplomatic and military support as well as for refuge. While the Algerian government would never confirm that POLISARIO had most of its military bases in Algeria, it was generally known that the POLISARIO headquarters was at Tindouf, well inside the Algerian border. Under these circumstances, Algeria was in a position to exert strong influence on the POLISARIO leadership. I repeatedly found that the best way to obtain greater flexibility from POLISARIO was through President Chadli or members of his government.

The POLISARIO leader, Mohammed Abdelaziz, was a very different sort. He had the habit of beginning conversations and correspondence with professions of admiration and trust for me as Secretary-General, followed by a lengthy list of demands. Surprisingly, this man who pretends to be the leader of what was formerly the Spanish Sahara speaks no Spanish. He and I conversed always in French. If I said something in Spanish, he was entirely lost.

FINDING A NEGOTIATION FORMAT

In our meeting in Addis Ababa, Abdelaziz's main point was that the only solution to the conflict in the Western Sahara lay in direct negotiations between POLISARIO and Morocco, endorsed by the OAU and the United Nations. I asked whether he expected me to pursue this question, to which he replied in the affirmative. I pointed out that Morocco's withdrawal from the OAU raised a number of unresolved problems. For one, it would be more difficult to find a formula for a cease-fire if one party would not deal with the OAU. I suggested that Abdelaziz give thought to this question as well as to how the referendum should be organized and who should be allowed to participate. Abdelaziz's immediate reaction was to object to my forthcoming visit to Rabat. I pointed out that the only means of mediation at my disposal was contact with the two parties. I hoped that he, as leader of POLISARIO, would have confidence in my impartiality; otherwise it would be impossible for me to exercise my good offices.

When I saw King Hassan II the next day, he was adamant that Morocco "could not and would not" have direct negotiations with a "phantom" entity such as POLISARIO. No one could expect a government to negotiate and sign an agreement with its own people *(resortissants)*. He insisted that while Morocco continued to support the principle of self-determination and favored a referendum, it could no longer accept the OAU as a proper framework in which to consider the problem of the Western Sahara. I asked the Moroccan sovereign how he foresaw the withdrawal of the Moroccan administration and the Moroccan troops from the territory during the referendum. The King replied that he could imagine the establishment of a demilitarized zone in the territory within which the referendum could take place. He did not go beyond that. I suggested to the King, as I had to Abdelaziz, that he give further thought to these questions, since I was sure they were bound to arise in the future.

The King did not attend the Fortieth Anniversary session of the General Assembly in 1985, but his prime minister read a statement on his behalf in which the King announced an immediate and unilateral cease-fire that Morocco would cancel only if attacked. POLISARIO's reaction was entirely negative, calling the King's initiative a stillborn maneuver. POLISARIO demanded the total withdrawal of the Moroccan army and administration and, for the first time, called for the "withdrawal of 100,000 Moroccan settlers from the towns and coast of Western Sahara." After the Fourth Committee of the General Assembly approved a draft resolution again calling for direct negotiations between Morocco and POLISARIO, Morocco announced that it would no longer participate in discussions of the Western Sahara in the United Nations. Nevertheless, as Foreign Minister Abdellatif Filali wrote to me, Morocco remained entirely open to any initiative I might find useful in order to achieve peace in the region. At the same time, in a press interview prior to visiting France, King Hassan II declared with magisterial certainty that "The Sahara is Moroccan and this will be freely expressed by its inhabitants."[1]

The General Assembly continued to pass fruitless annual resolutions calling for the two parties to negotiate a settlement of the Western Saharan conflict. Since Morocco refused to meet directly with POLISARIO, I decided, in consultation with the current OAU chairman, President Abdou Diouf of Senegal, to invite the parties to New York to see what could be achieved through proximity talks. Both sent representatives in April 1986, but nothing was achieved. In July, I again visited King Hassan II in Rabat, this time without being accompanied by anyone from the OAU. The King specifically agreed that the United Nations should organize a referendum in the Western Sahara "without administrative or military restraints." Morocco was prepared to discuss with me—but not with the current chairman of the OAU—the modalities of the referendum, including the presence of Moroccan troops and the Moroccan administration in the territory. Beyond that he said only that Morocco would take such measures with regard to its troops and administration as necessary to permit the United Nations to organize the referendum.

A member of the POLISARIO Executive Committee, Bachir Mustapha Sayeb, was sent to New York to tell me that POLISARIO saw only two ways to overcome the present impasse: either direct negotiations between the parties to agree on a cease-fire and a schedule for the referendum; or transfer of responsibility for administering the territory to the United Nations, which, together with the OAU, would organize the referendum.

PLANNING FOR THE REFERENDUM

Since the United Nations was to have principal responsibility for organizing an eventual referendum, there was a clear need to have firsthand information concerning conditions in the Western Sahara. It was therefore decided that a joint UN/OAU technical mission should be sent to the territory to look into such matters as the availability of communication facilities, housing and all the logistical requirements for a free referendum. Initially POLISARIO strongly objected to the idea, claiming in a lengthy letter to me that conditions were too dangerous because of the Moroccan "occupation" and, more to the point, that the mission was likely to come under Moroccan suasion and its findings prejudiced. In my reply, I stated bluntly—also at considerable length—that the POLISARIO Secretary-General was under a misapprehension concerning the purpose of the visit and concerning the susceptibility of the mission to pressure from any of the parties. I noted that the mission could hardly complete its task while military action was under way. Its dispatch therefore would not be finally decided until satisfactory assurances were received from the parties relating to its security. Abdelaziz promptly replied that the dispatch of the mission would be appropriate *after* POLISARIO and Morocco had reached a written agreement affirming in principle the withdrawal of the Moroccan troops and administration from the Western Sahara and after UN assumption of responsibility for administering the territory and organizing and monitoring the referendum.

Two senior members of my staff traveled to Tindouf to explain personally to Abdelaziz the limited purpose of the mission and its importance for organizing the referendum that both parties agreed should be held. Since they made no headway, I asked the POLISARIO Secretary-General to meet with me in Geneva. There I told him that the United Nations was not requesting permission of the parties to send the mission. Were one or the other to be in a position to dictate to the mediators their course of action, this would negate our role. We had wished only to inform the parties of our intention and request their cooperation, particularly with regard to security. Despite this line of argument, I was unable to obtain assurance from Abdelaziz that he would order a cessation of hostilities while the mission was in the territory. King Hassan II, when told of our intention to send the technical mission, said that Morocco would cooperate in every way possible. This was welcome even though it patently served Morocco's interest to show who was in a position to be of assistance in the Western Sahara.

The decision to send the mission to the Western Sahara was publicly announced in September 1987. Because of difficulties in deciding its composition and the continuing concern over its security, the mission did not arrive there until November 25. One day earlier POLISARIO announced that it would observe a cessation of hostilities for the 20 days that the technical mission was expected to be in the Western Sahara. The mission went forward without incident and produced a comprehensive report detailing the almost total lack of facilities in the territory, the wide dispersal of the population and the severe problems that were likely to be encountered in monitoring a cease-fire. With the completion of the technical mission's survey, I felt that we had successfully reached an important stage in the peace process. Both parties had been brought to agree that there would be a transition period during which the United Nations, in cooperation with the

OAU, would organize and monitor a free and impartial referendum on the self-determination of the Sahrawi people. Both were committed to comply with the results of the referendum and both had promised to cooperate with the UN Secretary-General and the current OAU chairman in the elaboration and implementation of the appropriate measures for the referendum. Morocco had agreed that these measures would cover the presence of its troops and its administration in the Western Sahara. POLISARIO, in turn, had pledged that there would be no military interference or intimidation during the voting.

The next step was to fill in the details of a peace plan, which we then undertook to do. The old saying that the devil lies in the details again proved its accuracy. In collaboration with the current chairman of the OAU, we prepared Proposals for a Settlement of the Question of Western Sahara. They provided that the Security Council, assuming for the first time an active role in regard to the Western Sahara, would call on the Secretary-General to appoint a Special Representative who, during the transition period between the cease-fire and the referendum, would have full and exclusive authority for all questions relative to the voting. He could take whatever measures were necessary to guarantee the security and freedom of movement of the population and the impartiality of the referendum. Under the plan I would set the date of the cease-fire. Prior to the cease-fire Morocco would "appropriately and substantially" reduce its troops in the territory. All POLISARIO troops and the remaining Moroccan troops would be confined to their bases, which would be monitored by UN peacekeepers.

The referendum, as foreseen in the plan, would pose two choices: independence or integration in Morocco. All Sahrawis over 18 who were listed in the census taken by the Spanish colonial administration in 1974 would have the right to vote. A new census of refugees outside the territory would be taken with the assistance of the UN High Commissioner for Refugees. Prior to the initiation of the electoral campaign, the Special Representative would ensure the release of all political prisoners and detainees. All refugees who had been identified as legitimate Sahrawis would be free to return to the territory. The referendum campaign would begin only when the Special Representative was convinced of the fairness and appropriateness of the procedures that would govern the voting. Maintenance of public order during the transition period would be the responsibility of the Special Representative with the assistance of a UN police unit.

Under the plan the Special Representative would certify the authenticity of the referendum results and transmit them to the UN Secretary-General who, in consultation with the Security Council and the current chairman of the OAU, would take the necessary steps to ensure that the wishes of the Sahrawi people, as reflected in the referendum results, were realized. These were and, with minor modifications, remain today the main points of the peace plan. On this basis I undertook along with two close collaborators, Under-Secretary General Farah and my Special Counselor Issa Diallo, a long and laborious process of negotiations with the parties. During a four year-period, I visited Morocco six times, Algeria three times, Tindouf twice and Mauritania once. I had 128 bilateral conversations with Algerian authorities, 132 with those of Morocco, 33 with representatives of POLISARIO and 50 with representatives of the OAU, all devoted to the Western Sahara.

In May 1988, I traveled to Rabat again in order to present an advance draft of the peace plan to King Hassan II. During a very brief initial interview the King's only comment was that he hoped I would not ask him for the impossible. On the following day I met alone with him and sought to explain my good offices role. I was acting as an honest broker, not as a judge. The plan that I had presented represented a compromise that I realized would not entirely please either party. When I broached the provision in our proposals for the confinement to bases of Moroccan and POLISARIO troops, the King reacted sharply, insisting that POLISARIO had no bases in the Western Sahara. If any existed, Moroccan forces would have destroyed them. POLISARIO, he said, knew this very well. The King, while expressing agreement with the "spirit" of the proposals, highlighted in particular the problems entailed in determining who would have the right to vote in the referendum. He thought that it would be premature to deal with operational problems relating to the referendum before such a fundamental question was resolved. There was always the risk, he said, that the United Nations might run into serious financial difficulties if the operation were begun and its troops and civilians had to remain until such problems as the criteria for determining who could vote were settled. Morocco would not want the United Nations to stay in the Western Sahara "eternally" under the cover of organizing the referendum. The King thus identified, perhaps on the basis of his own intentions, the problem that was to prove the greatest hinderance to the referendum: the problem of identification.

In our earlier conversation I had briefly suggested to that one solution to the Western Sahara problem might be to accord the territory an autonomous status within the Moroccan kingdom. The King quickly rejected this on the ground that other groups would claim the same privilege, leading to the disintegration of Morocco. Surprisingly, at the end of this conversation—after, as I mentioned earlier, we had been interrupted by his granddaughter—the King told me "on a very confidential basis" that he had an idea that could facilitate a settlement. The idea was to offer to the Sahrawis, within the framework of the referendum, "a third path," that of "a territory integrated federally with Morocco."

When I met President Chadli Bendjedid a few days later, I sounded him out on the possibility of including a third option in the referendum, something between full independence and full integration. The President thought this was not a bad idea. He told me in strict confidence that he expected Morocco to win the referendum mainly because of the large amount of money that the Moroccan government had spent to improve conditions and encourage development in the territory. I, in turn, was candid in saying that POLISARIO was unrealistic in the demands it was placing concerning conditions for the referendum. I had told Abdelaziz it was impractical to imagine that the United Nations would assume responsibility for the administration of the entire territory. As I saw it, the existing Moroccan administration in the territory would retain responsibility for law and order except on the actual polling day. I suggested that it would be helpful if the Algerian President would impress on the POLISARIO leadership the impracticality of insisting on a total withdrawal of Moroccan forces from the territory. It should be sufficient for the Moroccan forces to withdraw from the populated areas during the actual period of the referendum and to be confined to their bases. President Chadli promised to impress these points on POLISARIO. I realized his task would not be easy.

When the plan was officially presented to the two sides in August 1988, they both accepted it but at the same time expressed extensive "comments." Moustapha Béchir, the intelligent and sensible POLISARIO official responsible for foreign relations, informed me that the organization considered the propositions acceptable "in their spirit." He then proceeded to list 12 demands and observations. The demands included bilateral negotiation of a cease-fire between POLISARIO and Morocco, enhancement of the role foreseen for the OAU and the abrogation during the transition period of all Moroccan laws in the territory. There was one surprise among the comments. POLISARIO had long objected to giving voters a choice in the referendum between independence and integration, insisting that they be asked to indicate only whether they were for independence. Abdelaziz had expressed anger on learning earlier that I intended to include the two choices in my plan. Now POLISARIO accepted the two-option voting plan. I told Béchir that I would do what I could on bilateral negotiations but I needed a definitive answer on whether POLISARIO accepted the peace plan as presented to it. He replied that POLISARIO accepted the propositions "with his remarks and comments."

The main reservations of the Moroccan side pertained to the powers of the Special Representative during the transitional period. It rejected, in particular, the proposition that the Special Representative would have responsibility for the maintenance of public order. I sent a note to the King clarifying why the Special Representative would have to have this authority, but I refused to change the propositions, being convinced that if the plan, which represented a compromise between the positions of the two sides, were altered in its details, the agreement in principle that both sides had expressed would collapse.

I informed the Security Council on September 20, 1988, that the Kingdom of Morocco and the POLISARIO Front, "while making remarks and comments, have . . . given their agreement to the proposals for a peaceful settlement submitted by the current Chairman of the OAU and myself within the framework of my mission of good offices." The Security Council took note of the agreement in principle and authorized me, in Resolution 621, to appoint a Special Representative for Western Sahara. To proceed in this way, knowing the reservations of both parties, was risky. There seemed no other hope, however, of moving forward toward the referendum that both POLISARIO and Morocco said they favored.

As a result of the coordinated persuasion of President Chadli and myself, King Hassan II invited POLISARIO to meet with him in Marrakesh for direct talks in January 1989. No tangible agreements resulted but the atmosphere was surprisingly positive. Both sides announced that there would be further meetings within the framework of the Secretary-General's good offices. Unfortunately, POLISARIO then publicly portrayed the meeting as recognition of its status as representative of the Sahrawi people, which alienated the King and, I think, caused him to decide never to meet bilaterally with the POLISARIO leadership again. Despite repeated efforts, I was unable to change his mind.

I traveled to the area in late March 1990 to give a fresh impulse to negotiations, taking such advantage as I could from the new spirit of international cooperation that had led to the successful transition to independence in Namibia and to free elections in Nicaragua. I had already decided to submit a report to the Security Council before mid-summer setting forth an action program for implementation of the peace plan. The draft of the program was almost complete, but there were a number of open questions to which I hoped to find answers in talking to King Hassan and to POLISARIO Secretary-General Abdelaziz.

My first stop was in Rabat. In an earlier visit to the territory, my military advisor had confirmed that there were approximately 159,000 Moroccan troops in the Western Sahara, most of whom were in fixed positions along the sand wall. I sought Hassan's agreement to reduce the number of his troops in the Western Sahara by a specific amount, preferably 80 percent. After recalling that the peace agreement only called for an appropriate and substantial reduction in the number of troops, Hassan finally indicated that Moroccan troops in the territory would be reduced by 50 percent. This would leave about 80,000 troops, which was a high number for the United Nations to monitor and was certain to be unsatisfactory to POLISARIO, but I could not persuade the King to cut his troops more. I was able, however, to gain his agreement to a cessation of military activities in order to improve the atmosphere for a renewed dialogue between the two sides. I informed the king of my intention to convoke informally a session of the Identification Commission that was charged with determining eligibility to vote in the referendum. About 40 tribal chiefs were scheduled to participate in the meeting to provide advice on this very delicate matter. The

King repeated his desire that the referendum be held without further delay but warned once again of the problems entailed in identifying those Sahrawis with the right to vote. He insisted that many who were not included in the 1974 Spanish census must be allowed to participate.

It had been arranged that I would meet with the POLISARIO leader, Abdelaziz, in Tindouf's Town Hall. However, I was met in the desert about 10 kilometers from the town and we held our conversation there in a tent. The POLISARIO head exhibited his perennial distrust of the Moroccans, whom he described as fighters, intent on making war. When I told him that King Hassan II had agreed to renewed contact with POLISARIO, his immediate reaction was that a meeting with bureaucrats from a government ministry would imply that the Western Sahara was an internal Moroccan matter. He was somewhat assuaged when I told him I would do my best to persuade the King to designate a representative from his personal entourage. Abdelaziz was reluctant to make a firm commitment to cease hostilities, claiming that POLISARIO had ceased all military action a month earlier. However, on returning to New York, I received written confirmation that POLISARIO agreed to cease military engagement.

In giving Abdelaziz a general summary of my meeting with King Hassan II, I did not mention the King's proposal to withdraw 50 percent of the Moroccan troops from the Western Sahara. I indicated only that I had found his ideas on withdrawal unsatisfactory. I described to Abdelaziz and his sizable entourage the role the United Nations had played in Namibia and Nicaragua as proof that the organization's impartiality could be trusted. This seemed to make an impression. I left this desert rendezvous with a sense that Abdelaziz, though distrustful as always, had become more realistic and more cooperative. On June 18, 1990, I submitted, as planned, a comprehensive report to the Security Council on the implementation of the peace plan (Document S/2130). As I did so, I recognized that two omissions were bound to raise questions:

- No figures were included on the number of Moroccan troops to be withdrawn. To have included the 50 percent figure advanced by King Hassan would have invited rejection of the report by the Council.
- The place where POLISARIO troops would be confined was not defined, nor was the role of the Algerian and Mauritanian governments in monitoring encampments within their borders. This was because POLISARIO claims notwithstanding, there were no POLISARIO camps within the Western Sahara. POLISARIO refused to agree that its troops would be confined in camps in Algeria and Mauritania.

Five years had passed since my good offices had begun and two years since Morocco and POLISARIO had accepted in principle the UN/OAU peace proposals. Both parties had agreed to suspend military hostilities. But there was a risk that POLISARIO might resume its attacks at any moment. Morocco had postponed its national elections for two years to allow the United Nations time to organize the referendum. If there were no progress in the peace process within this period, Morocco's reaction could not be predicted. In November 1989 King Hassan II had declared that if, after two years, the United Nations did not organize the referendum, Morocco would draw its own conclusions. In these circumstances, it was important that the Security Council convey in clear terms the determination of the international community to find a solution to this problem. I held a special meeting with the five Permanent Members and emphasized the need for a new impetus to the implementation of the peace plan. The Permanent Members concentrated on the need to restrict the cost of the operation. I emphasized the political need for the Council's endorsement of the present report even though a number of clarifications were still needed. As to the cost, I pointed out that much would depend on my success in persuading King Hassan II to withdraw more of his forces from the territory so that fewer UN troops would be needed to monitor those who remained. This was a matter on which the assistance of the Permanent Members would be most welcome.

THE IMPLEMENTATION PLAN

The Security Council approved the report unanimously on June 27, 1990, in Resolution 658. Implementation of the plan as described in the report was to be in two distinct phases. The first would be the cease-fire, monitored by UN peacekeepers, the date of which I would set. During this phase the Identification Commission would complete its work in the refugee camps and in designated locations in the territory. The second phase would begin with the termination of the commission's work. At that point those who had been qualified to vote would be authorized to return peacefully to the territory, without arms, at special entry points designated by the Special Representative. This stage would end with a limited electoral campaign period and the holding of the referendum. The civilian contingent of the UN Mission for the Referendum in Western Sahara (MINURSO) would be present only for the second phase. The referendum would be held 24 weeks after the cease-fire went into effect. The Special Representative could determine whether circumstances required that this schedule be altered. He would have responsibility for the maintenance of law and order during the transitional period between the cease-fire and the completion of the referendum. The United Nations would monitor the total withdrawal of Moroccan troops or the demobilization of the POLISARIO Front, depending on the outcome of the referendum.

The Moroccan reaction to the implementation report was sharply negative while that of POLISARIO was highly cautionary. The main Moroccan objections were:

- The interim period leading to the referendum could be prolonged indefinitely.
- The United Nations might intervene in the Moroccan administration of the territory, including the maintenance of internal security, whereas its sole functions should be to monitor the cease-fire and establish the electoral lists.
- The cease-fire seemed to be confused with an armistice. A cease-fire could not entail neutralization of forces or disarmament.
- There was no provision for UNHCR to interview refugees located outside of the Western Sahara so that their status could be determined for purposes of the referendum.

POLISARIO's concerns were more or less the mirror image of the Moroccan objections. POLISARIO objected to any continuation at all of Moroccan administration, insisted that only those listed on the 1974 Spanish census would be eligible to vote and contended that not only should the Moroccan forces be neutralized, the United Nations should assume responsibility for controlling the northern frontier of Morocco as well as the sea coast.

IDENTIFYING ELIGIBLE VOTERS

The United Nations first established the Identification Commission on an unofficial basis, made up of a population expert knowledgeable on Sahrawi society assisted by other experts familiar with countries with nomadic populations and by Secretariat staff. Its purpose was to review the 1974 Spanish census, calculate the growth of the Sahrawi population and assess the movements of the population in preparation for the authentication of the electoral lists. It quickly became evident that the best means of identifying the Sahrawi population in the absence of official documentation was through the tribal chiefs. In May 1990 the commission met with 40 of these "notables" in Geneva. The meeting served more to demonstrate the complexity of the problem than to resolve it. Many of the tribal chiefs had been living in exile in Morocco, Algeria or Mauritania and had not seen each other for 15 years. Those coming from Morocco assumed an air of superiority, refusing to accept any reimbursement from the United Nations for their expenses. Each chief was clear on who belonged to his tribe, but many reasons were offered as to why tribe members' names did not appear on the Spanish census. The most serious problem at the meeting was the lack of clearly agreed criteria for determining eligibility to vote. My Special Representative at the time, Ambassador Johannes J. Manz of Switzerland, later informed me in a confidential assessment of the meeting, with typical Swiss caution, that while a comprehensive solution to the Western Saharan problem was not to be excluded, success was by no means guaranteed.

DEPLOYMENT OF MINURSO

Before approving the deployment of MINURSO, the Security Council wished to have a precise estimate of the number of personnel that would be needed and the cost of the operation. Another survey mission was therefore sent to the territory under the leadership of Issa Diallo. The mission met with senior representatives of POLISARIO, Morocco, Mauritania and Algeria. Its purposes were well accomplished. During this period I became aware of contentions within POLISARIO that Diallo was overly influenced by the Moroccans. Given the profound distrust that existed between the two parties, any advisor who was as closely involved in the effort to overcome the various differences as Diallo was would be thought partial to one side or the other. Nonetheless, it further complicated an already difficult situation.

Following the July completion of the technical survey, preliminary estimates were made of the size and cost of MINURSO. They could not be definitive, however, until King Hassan's final position was known on how many Moroccan troops would be withdrawn from the territory. His current proposal to leave 85,000 troops there would mean one soldier for every two inhabitants. I strongly and repeatedly suggested to the king that 40,000 would be an appropriate figure. Finally, in November, he agreed that instead of 85,000, 65,000 Moroccan troops would remain in the Western Sahara during the transitional period. I accepted this as satisfactory.

Meanwhile, the five Permanent Members of the Security Council had become alarmed over the possible cost of the operation; by then it was estimated at $250 million. They urged, in particular, that the refugee repatriation program to be undertaken by the UN High Commissioner for Refugees be covered by voluntary contributions rather than included in the assessed cost of the operation. I rejected this since the return of the refugees, which was essential to the referendum, could not be dependent on uncertain contributions by Member States. Unfortunately, the most logical economy measure entailed political problems with the parties. Substantial funds could be saved if the voter identification process began in the territory (as it had outside) before the cease-fire came into effect and MINURSO was deployed. POLISARIO strongly objected to this approach, claiming that the Identification Commission, in the absence of MINURSO, could come under strong Moroccan pressure.

All of this caused further delay, which was compounded by the fact that in this case the Secretariat task force for the Western Sahara, many of whose members were preoccupied by other current regional conflicts, including the Gulf War, did not function as efficiently or harmoniously as I would have wished. The most serious problem, however, was continuing Moroccan and POLISARIO resistance to the implementation procedures that I had outlined in my May report to the Security Council.

THE CEASE-FIRE IS SET

I had set November 1990 as the deadline for submission of my follow-on report to the Council requesting authorization for the establishment and deployment of MINURSO. Largely because of the crisis in the Gulf that erupted just at this time, I was not able to submit the report, document S/22464, until April 19, 1991. The report provided a detailed timetable for the various actions leading to the referendum. A period of 36 weeks was foreseen between the General Assembly's approval of the MINURSO budget and the holding of the referendum. The overall cost of MINURSO was estimated at $200 million, including the repatriation program, which, as I pointed out to the Council, represented a considerable reduction from earlier estimates. The Security Council, in approving the deployment of MINURSO, required in Resolution 690 that the cease-fire should begin "no later than 16 weeks after the General Assembly approves the budget for the Mission." The General Assembly approved the budget on May 17, almost a month after the Security Council's action, a further example of the delay that can—and frequently does—occur in obtaining the budgetary authorization needed to begin a peacekeeping operation. If the full 16 weeks were taken, the cease-fire would begin on September 6, 1991. Under this schedule, the referendum could not be held until after I had left office. Having invested so much time, effort and hope in a settlement of the Western Sahara conflict, I would have liked to see the process largely completed while I was still Secretary-General. I asked the Special Representative, Ambassador Manz, whether it might be possible to set the cease-fire somewhat earlier, perhaps on the first of September. Feeling that the identification process was so complex and controversial that the full 16 weeks would be required, he strongly advised against it. I accepted this judgment and set September 6 as the date for the cease-fire. The Moroccan government and POLISARIO each informed me that it "accepted the conditions of the cease-fire and would take all necessary measures to bring all military measures to an end." I was quite conscious that they remained in sharp disagreement on two major points: the location of POLISARIO encampments and the criteria for establishing eligibility to vote in the referendum. I hoped that the establishment of a deadline in the form of the cease-fire would pressure the two to compromise. I felt it was urgent to move ahead since the de facto cease-fire that had been in effect for two years was threatened by a new outbreak of hostilities.

POLISARIO, misguidedly I think, began the construction of a number of buildings in the part of the territory that lay beyond the sand wall, presumably to establish evidence of its sustained presence there. The Moroccan military quickly reacted by sending troops to destroy the construction work. Thereafter the Moroccan air force initiated surveillance flights over the area, generating strong and repeated protests from the POLISARIO side. Given the deteriorating situation, it was clearly advisable to get UN observers in place to monitor a cease-fire and stabilize the situation. This purpose was achieved. The cease-fire went into effect on September 4. The prospect of a settlement, however, was promptly clouded by another development.

On September 15, 1991, King Hassan II sent me a private letter with the startling news that Morocco intended to facilitate the return of 170,000 Sahrawis to several locations in the Western Sahara where camps were being prepared to receive them. Morocco immediately published the contents of the "private" letter, causing consternation on the part of POLISARIO. I discussed the matter with President Bush and Secretary Baker shortly thereafter when they came to New York for the meeting of the General Assembly. The Secretary of State's reaction was that sending 170,000 people into a territory that was inhabited by only 75,000 to 80,000 was a very thin disguise for rigging the results of the election. The king had told him the previous July that he was determined to cooperate fully with the Secretary-General. Baker's comment was "I think we need to hit him again." President Bush said that he would be seeing Hassan II later in the week and would speak privately with him on the subject.

The United Nations had no means of preventing the movement of Sahrawis to camps in the territory. MINURSO, which had only 200 observers in place, was not authorized to police the borders (although POLISARIO insisted it should be). Its mandated task was to monitor the cease-fire. At the beginning of October 1991, King Hassan II arrived in New York for the General Assembly. The announced move was of course raised with the king and his senior advisors. My legal counsel, Carl-August Fleischhauer, pursued the matter initially with Ambassador Driss Slaoui, who had accompanied the King. Ambassador Slaoui sought to justify the action by claiming that Sahrawis who had left the territory for whatever reason had the right to return. This, he said, did not mean that they necessarily had the right to vote. Fleischhauer stated emphatically that the Implementation Plan stipulated that all refugees and other nonresidents wishing to return to the territory could do so only after the United Nations had established their right to vote. Ambassador Slaoui contended that this provision of the plan applied only to the POLISARIO side and not to Morocco. Fleischhauer responded that there was no such distinction in the plan.

Two days later Moroccan Foreign Minister Filali, in discussing the subject with me, took a distinctly different if equally uncompromising line. His government, he said, had taken the initiative to regroup the Sahrawis in order "to facilitate the work of the Identification Commission." His government did not see how the commission could travel all over—*un peu partout dans la région*—looking for Sahrawis. Morocco agreed, of course, that it was for the commission to judge according to its criteria who was eligible to vote. Further, the Foreign Minister argued, when the Spanish had left the Western Sahara, they transferred Tarfaya Province to Morocco. The Sahrawis who lived in that province had a clear right to return to the territory.

I did not feel it was worthwhile to dispute this point. Instead, I insisted that under no circumstances could I accept a tribal association alone as a sufficient basis to establish voting eligibility. Minister Filali conceded that some geographic link with the territory was essential. Rather than pursuing this further, I suggested that the ideal solution would be for Morocco and the POLISARIO bilaterally to reach a settlement that could then be confirmed by the referendum. The minister said only that he would pass this interesting suggestion on to King Hassan II.

When the King discussed the subject with me two days later, he confirmed that Morocco was entirely ready to agree that a link should be established between "blood and territory." He used the words *jus sanguini* and *jus soli*. He then confided that he had made a commitment, in speaking to Algerian President Chadli, to grant to the Western Sahara an autonomous status "once the Sahrawis had opted for integration with Morocco." It was understood that President Chadli would quietly let POLISARIO know the King's position. I said that I was all the happier to hear his idea, since I had found that the King's Mahgreb colleagues supported a political compromise as constituting the ideal solution for the Western Sahara.

My impression, from reports received from MINURSO, was that the number of persons resettled did not exceed 40,000. Even so, this was more than half again the number of Sahrawis documented as living in the territory in 1974. The Moroccan motivation in resettling these people may have been to establish the necessary geographic tie with the territory to assure their eligibility to vote in the referendum. Certainly their movement made more sensitive than ever the criteria that still had not been agreed upon for establishing voting eligibility. Morocco insisted that until there was agreement on this, the Transition Period foreseen in the Implementation Agreement could not begin (even though the cease-fire had come into effect). This meant that the time schedule for the referendum could not be met.

The disagreement between POLISARIO and Morocco on the criteria for establishing voting eligibility was basic and intractable. The differences could not be overcome in the extensive consultations that we held with both sides. Given the failure of mediation, I issued instructions to the Identification Commission that defined the following criteria to be applied in determining eligibility to vote:

- All persons whose names were included in the revised 1974 census together with immediate family members are eligible to participate in the referendum.
- Persons living in the territory in 1974 but who for various reasons were not included in the census are eligible, together with their immediate family members. In each such case, testimonies or documents must be submitted in support of each application.
- Persons who claim to be Sahrawis and who were living outside the territory in 1974 must prove a solid and demonstrable link with the territory to gain voting eligibility. Such persons may fall under any of three categories: (1) Persons and their children who had fled colonial rule; (2) members of a Sahrawi tribe who had resided for six consecutive years prior to December 1, 1974, in the territory; and (3) (to take account of the nomadic nature of the Sahrawi society) tribal members who had intermittent residence in the territory for 12 years prior to December 1, 1974.

It was my hope that the parties would accept these criteria as an *obiter dictu,* and the impasse could thereby be broken. This quickly proved a vain hope. POLISARIO considered the criteria too liberal and Morocco considered them too rigid. They both refused to proceed on this basis.

In a December 19 report—document S/23299—to the Security Council, which would be my last on the subject, I noted that of the planned 500 military observers, 200 had been deployed and were effectively monitoring the cease-fire, although the Force Commander had strongly recommended that the number be increased. Each side had complained of infringements of the cease-fire, but far more important was the fact that no violence had occurred since it began. While a revised list of the 1974 census had been completed on the basis of information provided by the two parties, it had not been possible to gain the parties' agreement to publication of the list in the territory. The place of confinement of the POLISARIO troops had not been established. I concluded that serious efforts would still be needed at the political and technical levels to keep the process going. In other words, my successor would have to carry on with an unfinished and frustrating task.

I was never convinced that independence promised the best future for the inhabitants of the Western Sahara. Their number, however counted, is less than 150,000, and aside from its phosphate deposits the land is poor, offering meager prospects of economic viability as a separate country. Such political leadership as exists is not impressive and in some cases not Sahrawi in origin. A reasonable political solution under which the Western Sahara would be integrated as an autonomous region in the Moroccan state would have spared many lives and a great deal of money. The Mahgreb countries were in the best position to pressure POLISARIO to accept such a solution since POLISARIO was largely dependent on them, especially Algeria, for support. They chose not to do so even though in conversations with me President Chadli seemed prepared to support such an outcome. I do not know whether he discussed a political solution with Abdelassiz.

Neither the Cold War nor its demise was an important factor in efforts to resolve the conflict. The United States and the Soviet Union were both supportive of the UN Implementation Plan. Their main interest was to restrict the cost of MINURSO as much as possible, an objective that a political solution would have served.

As the years passed, Morocco was able to strengthen its position in competing with POLISARIO, first militarily but subsequently in its political position within the Western Sahara, which it cultivated with substantial economic assistance. I believe that King Hassan II can have considerable confidence that if the referendum is ever held, there will be majority support for integration with Morocco. I am doubtful that he would acquiesce in any other decision. This does not mean that the extensive time and resources that the United Nations, in partnership with the OAU, has devoted to Western Sahara has been without positive results. First of all, the parties were persuaded to cease hostilities and then to comply with a cease-fire, which has brought peace to Western Sahara for eight years. The presence of a UN peacekeeping mission in the territory has unquestionably served to stabilize the situation and lessen the likelihood of renewed fighting. The assumption by the United Nations, together with the OAU, of responsibility for achieving a settlement to the Western Sahara problem did a great deal to remove it as a source of friction among the Mahgreb states and thereby facilitated the notable growth of friendship and cooperation among them.

So I do not look back on the time and energy that I devoted to the Western Sahara as wasted. Certainly to have come so close to the long-sought referendum and find the parties unwilling to accept my guidance on the last serious issue dividing them was frustrating. But there was satisfaction in the achievement of agreement between these distrustful parties on practically all other aspects of a settlement. The guns were silent and economically the Western Sahara was better off than ever before in its history. This surely was of importance to the Sahrawi people who had never known independence and perhaps never will.

WAR AND PEACE
IN LATIN AMERICA

At the time of my appointment as Secretary-General, Central America was racked by long-enduring political instability and violence. Throughout Latin America, economies were in decline. As a Latin American, I was especially sensitive to the region's problems. I felt the United Nations should do more than observe "with concern," which was the current phrase, as a group of its members sank ever deeper into conflict, social disarray and debt that brought immeasurable suffering to their people and intensified hostility and distrust among countries outside the region.

During my first days in office, I wrote down on a sheet of notebook paper—which I still have—my impression of the situation in the region. It included four points:

- In El Salvador, elections will take place in March in an atmosphere of internal and external tension. Acceptance of the outcome of the elections is uncertain.

- In Nicaragua, the Sandinista regime is resisting, with the support of Cuba and, indirectly, of the Soviet Union, insurgent forces that are armed and financed by the United States.

- Guatemala is in the hands of a military dictatorship that shows little, if any, respect for the human rights of its inhabitants.

- Incidents are frequent on the border between Honduras and Nicaragua with each side accusing the other of military incursions.

Missing from my list was the dispute between Argentina and the United Kingdom over the Falkland/Malvinas Islands, which would shortly bring full-scale war to the region, a crisis I did not foresee.

I also noted on my *bout de papier* the various plans then in circulation to resolve the Central American conflicts. Mexico called for global détente and the achievement of peace, stability, development and democracy through mutual concessions and mutual recognition of vital interests. Nicaragua proposed nonalignment, nonaggression pacts with its neighbors, mutual patrolling of its borders with Costa Rica and Honduras, friendly relations with the United States and pursuit of the Sandinista revolution within the framework of a mixed economy, ideological plurality, nonalignment and democratic elections in 1985.

The United States saw economic and social development and democratic government as the way to peace in the region and sought to build cooperation with Canada, Mexico and Venezuela to this end. It struck me that almost everyone had a plan except the United Nations and the responsible regional organization, the Organization of American States (OAS). This thought no doubt underlay the last notation on my sheet of paper:

UN involvement?!

1st, Information Mission. 2nd, Inform the Security Council?

I never doubted that the prevailing conflict and instability in Central America were rooted in the economic and social conditions that had long prevailed in El Salvador, Nicaragua, Guatemala and Honduras. In the long run, no lasting solution would be possible until these conditions were improved substantially. From the beginning to the end of my tenure, I emphasized this in almost every public statement I made regarding the region. Yet there was little chance of getting at these basic problems while armed insurrection was in progress, external intervention persisted and a major Latin American country was embroiled in a debilitating war.

FOURTEEN

THE FALKLANDS/ MALVINAS: A NINETEENTH-CENTURY WAR IN THE TWENTIETH CENTURY

THE FALKLAND ISLANDS were an unlikely object of war in the late twentieth century. Known in Spanish as the *Islas Malvinas,* they are situated in the South Atlantic on the continental shelf of South America, just over 300 miles from the coast of Argentina. South Georgia and the South Sandwich Islands, located more than 600 miles to the south and well off the continental shelf, are among the "dependencies" that the British have administered from the Falklands. All are claimed by Argentina. The Falklands are neither rich nor particularly hospitable. Their initial value as a sealing and whaling station has long since disappeared. By the beginning of the 1980s, the islands were populated by approximately 1,800 people, almost all of whom were engaged in sheep farming, the islands' only industry. The inhabitants were British and determined to remain so.

Repossession of the Malvinas has never ceased to be a nationalist cause in Argentina and a source of friction between Buenos Aires and London. In 1947 Great Britain proposed to submit the dispute to the International Court of Justice, but Argentina declined to accept the Court's jurisdiction. Instead, Argentina brought the matter to the United Nations, and in 1965 the General Assembly invited the two countries to enter into discussions that would lead to a peaceful solution of their differences. Such discussions were initiated and continued off and on until February 1982. Various possible solutions were considered and agreements were reached on such matters as communications, postal services and the provision of petroleum supplies by the Argentine state petroleum company. A basic agreement on the status of the islands could not be found, however, because of Argentina's insistence that its sovereignty over the islands be recognized and Britain's commitment to respect the freely expressed "wishes" of the islanders, and their wish was to remain British. This dispute, long-standing though it was, hardly seemed a likely cause of war between two friendly countries, a war that would cause thousands of deaths and cost billions of dollars. This was the main reason, I think, why the international community took no preventive measures, even though warning signals were not lacking.

At the end of a further fruitless session of talks between British and Argentine representatives in New York in February 1982, a communiqué was issued stating that the meeting took place in a cordial and positive spirit. The two sides reaffirmed their resolve to find a solution to the sovereignty dispute. On March 1, however, the Argentine Foreign Ministry, in an official release, stated that unless there was an early solution, Argentina would choose freely "the procedure that best accorded with its interest."

At this point an Argentine scrap metal merchant arrived in Leith Harbor on South Georgia to salvage scrap metal from an abandoned whaling station. Earlier he had notified the British embassy of his planned operation and, after checking with the governor of the Falklands Islands, the embassy expressed no objections. However, the merchant arrived in Leith Harbor on an Argentine naval vessel and promptly raised the Argentine flag. Observers at the British Antarctic Survey Base on the island noticed the Argentine flag and reported this to the Falklands governor. The British government filed a formal protest, claiming that the scrap metal workers were illegally occupying British territory. It dispatched the survey ship, *HMS Endurance,* the sole British naval vessel in the area, with 24 marines aboard, to South Georgia to remove the scrap metal workers peacefully. Before the *Endurance* arrived at Leith Harbor, the Argentine naval vessel that had brought the workers departed, leaving only ten of the workers on the island. The incident quickly escalated, however, when Argentina sent another naval vessel with a small detachment of marines to protect the remaining workers. Amid reports that Argentina was assembling a naval task force to invade the Falklands, Prime Minister Margaret Thatcher authorized the dispatch of three nuclear submarines to the Falklands. (Eventually two were sent.)

On March 31, 1982, the British government received word that Argentina was in the process of invading the Falklands. The first new international crisis in my tenure as Secretary-General was clearly at hand. It was especially unwelcome to me since, as a Peruvian, I had always felt a particular friendship with Argentina and sympathized with its claim to the Falklands, given their close proximity to

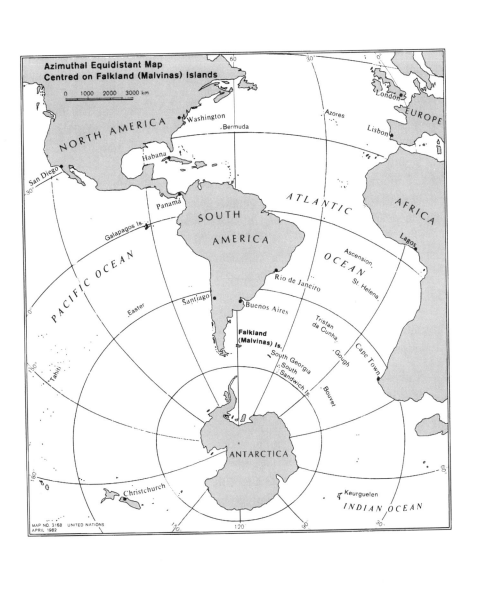

Azimuthal Equidistant Map
Centred on Falkland (Malvinas) Islands

0   1000   2000   3000 km

NORTH AMERICA

Washington
Bermuda

San Diego

Habana

Panama

Galapagos Is.

SOUTH
AMERICA

PACIFIC OCEAN

Easter

Santiago

Buenos Aires

Falkland
(Malvinas) Is.

South Georgia

South
Sandwich Is.

Tahiti

ATLANTIC

OCEAN

Rio de Janeiro

Tristan
da Cunha

Gough

Bouvet

Ascension

St. Helena

Azores

Lisbon

London

EUROPE

AFRICA

Lagos

Cape Town

Christchurch

ANTARCTICA

Keurguelen

INDIAN OCEAN

MAP NO. 3168   UNITED NATIONS
APRIL 1982

the South American continent. I resolved immediately to put aside these personal feelings and to maintain the strictest impartiality in any involvement I would have in the crisis. In this, I believe I succeeded. The British were doubtless somewhat wary initially of the direct involvement of an untested South American Secretary-General in mediation efforts. However, I was quickly able to develop a relationship of confidence and trust with Mrs. Thatcher—I later learned this had something to do with my earlier experience in Southern Rhodesia. I had been appointed by Secretary-General Waldheim to lead the UN mission to observe the elections in 1980, at the time of Rhodesian independence. I stopped in London and talked with Lord Carrington, whose forthrightness and integrity I greatly admired and, subsequently in South Africa spoke with the British senior representative, Lord Soames. Soames told me with evident sincerity that the British had no interest in influencing the outcome of the elections. The decision was strictly for the Rhodesian people. Two other observer missions, one led by India, criticized the elections as unfair. I was personally in three locations and found the conduct of the elections completely in order. This was also the verdict of all the members of the UN team, most of whom were African. Accordingly I submitted a positive report on the elections, which presumably had come to Mrs. Thatcher's attention. She is not a woman to forget.

In an interview before his death in 1992, the Argentine foreign minister at the time of the Falklands War, Nicanor Costa Mendez, said that Argentina would have preferred not to have a Secretary-General from South America since the junta felt I had gone so far in my impartiality as to be disadvantageous for Argentina. I took this as a compliment.

ARGENTINA ATTACKS AND THE SECURITY COUNCIL REACTS

On April 1, I received a call in Italy from the U.S. secretary of state, Alexander Haig, informing me of the Argentine action and of the readiness of the U.S. to mediate a peaceful solution to the crisis. He said that President Reagan had telephoned President Leopoldo Galtieri, the leader of the Argentine junta, to urge that the invasion be halted, only to be told that the invasion was already under way and could not be stopped. I immediately issued a statement urging maximum restraint on both sides. Through my office in New York, I was in touch with the President of the Security Council, who issued a statement calling on both countries to refrain from the use or threat of force and to continue the search for a diplomatic solution.

Early on April 3, the Security Council adopted Resolution 502 in which it determined that there had been a breach of peace, demanded an immediate cessation of hostilities and the withdrawal of all Argentine forces from the Falkland Islands and called on the two governments to seek a diplomatic solution to their differences. The resolution had been drafted by the British. By determining that a breach of peace had occurred, the Argentine action was placed within the scope of Chapter VII of the UN Charter, meaning that the United Kingdom, even though a party to the conflict, could veto any further resolutions if it chose to do so. The resolution called for no action by the Secretary-General. I was given no mandate. The British and the Argentines both accepted the U.S. offer to assist in finding a peaceful solution in accordance with Resolution 502, and Secretary Haig began his energetic shuttle mediation that was to last almost a month. Ironically, the American Permanent Representative in New York, Jeane Kirkpatrick, had sought to discourage the British from calling for a meeting of the Council to condemn the Argentine action; according to the account of the British Permanent Representative, she told him that she thought he had taken leave of his senses. Ambassador Kirkpatrick did not attend the Security Council meeting at which the resolution was adopted, sending instead a relatively junior officer to sit in the American seat with instructions neither to help nor to hinder the British in their initiative. (The United States did, however, vote affirmatively on the resolution.)

Secretary Haig, while he was acting as mediator, did not keep Ambassador Kirkpatrick informed of developments, which meant that I had no authoritative source in New York on the negotiations. This was no doubt in part the result of the dyspeptic relationship between Mrs. Kirkpatrick and General Haig that I witnessed throughout the Malvinas crisis. I suspect this relationship was a factor in Haig's eventual removal from office. At a late stage in the war Haig came to see me in New York, accompanied by a number of his staff and by Ambassador Kirkpatrick. I assumed that she would be accompanying him into the meeting. Clearly this was also her assumption. But as they moved to enter my office, General Haig came in first and closed the door in her face. Our conversation turned out to be rather inconsequential.

Jeane Kirkpatrick would be the first to say that she is a political scientist, not a diplomat, and I must confess that I had never before in my diplomatic career encountered anyone quite like her. We had a good working relationship, based, I think, on mutual respect. I admired her energy and determination, and I appreciated her influence as a member of the Reagan Cabinet. Still, I could not help but feel that she lacked the political sensitivity that one would expect from the representative of a major power in the complex world of the United Nations. On one occasion, in the midst of my mediation efforts on the Falklands, she invited me to have coffee at her residence. Upon arriving, I found that another guest was a close associate of the air force member of the junta in Buenos Aires, which for me was embarrassing and potentially prejudicial. On another occasion, also related to the Malvinas, Ambassador Kirkpatrick called me from President Reagan's office and asked that I confirm for the President's benefit something I had told her that differed from a version that General Haig had given to the President. She never sought to hide her skepticism about many of the activities of the United Nations, which, unfortunately encouraged the criticism of the Organization in the U.S. administration and Congress.

THE AMERICAN MEDIATION

It was logical and positive that the United States should assume the mediatory role in a conflict between two countries with which it had friendly relations and much influence. It seemed to me unlikely, however, that the Argentine junta would have confidence in Secretary Haig's impartiality, given the close alliance between the United States and the United Kingdom and Haig's own association with the North Atlantic Treaty Organization. Subsequently I found that this assumption was wrong; the Argentine leadership trusted Haig and were appreciative of his efforts until he announced that the United Sates would support the United Kingdom. His mediation failed primarily because of the disparate positions of the two parties on the future status of the Falkland Islands and their dependencies. I was right, nonetheless, in my assumption that the Haig effort would probably fail and that the time would come when I would need to extend my good offices in seeking a peaceful solution. With this in mind, I adopted a three-pronged policy: to interfere in no way with Secretary Haig's mediation but to be of such assistance as I could; to maintain close contact with the parties through their representatives at the United Nations; and to make preparations for the contingency that it would fall to the United Nations to try to negotiate a solution of the conflict.

For this last purpose I established a task force in the Secretariat, made up of members of the various departments having relevant expertise under the chairmanship of Under-Secretary-General Rafeeuddin Ahmed, a Pakistani national. The first job of the task force was to collect information on the military moves of Argentina and the United Kingdom and on the details of Secretary Haig's mediation. From the information that was available as Secretary Haig shuttled between London and Buenos Aires, it was clear that the positions of the two countries were very far apart. Argentine representatives informed me that their country could not accept a return to the status quo, nor was Secretary Haig's proposal for self-determination by the people of the islands acceptable. Argentina could accept the principle of withdrawal provided the British navy withdrew and the withdrawal process was linked with a global agreement. Argentina would never renounce sovereignty over the Malvinas, but it would be flexible on their administration, including the exploitation of the minerals in the area. Argentina could accept an international presence provided it included Argentineans. Any inter-American force should include the United States.

Simultaneously, the British Permanent Representative in New York, Sir Anthony Parsons, told me that he had spent three hours with Prime Minister Thatcher in London and had also met with the new foreign minister, Francis Pym. There was complete unanimity in the government that the United Kingdom could not yield to Argentina. The Argentine action had prompted the greatest show of national unity since 1940. The United Kingdom could not accept anything short of the withdrawal of Argentine troops from the islands and the restoration of the British flag. Once Security Council Resolution 502 had been implemented, the United Kingdom was prepared to hold discussions on the Falklands/Malvinas, but it could not accept third-party mediation on the substantive dispute between the two countries on the future status of the islands.

It appeared that no account was being taken in the Haig mediation of the possible contribution of the United Nations to a solution of the crisis. With this in mind, I provided the Argentine, British and U.S. Permanent Representatives with an informal note on April 19 suggesting that the United Nations could be used for any of the following purposes, singly or in combination:

- To observe, verify and certify the withdrawal of armed forces and/or civilian/administrative personnel from the area;
- To observe and verify any administrative arrangements for the islands as might be agreed;
- To provide a United Nations "umbrella" for such administrative arrangements;
- To provide a temporary United Nations administration.

When I gave this informal note to Ambassador Parsons, he said that it could be a useful contribution to the U.S. efforts. He hoped that it could be kept entirely confidential. The Argentine and American representatives received the paper without comment. None of the three countries reacted officially to the note or gave any indication that its suggestions were being taken into account. After the war was over, Nicanor Costa-Mendez stated that Buenos Aires considered the note quite important as signaling the availability of a UN mediation option.[1] But the Argentine government was aware that the United States had some misgivings about UN intervention, and Argentina did not wish to interfere with the U.S. effort. Moreover, the Argentine Foreign Ministry suspected that the United Kingdom would not agree to UN mediation. For its part, Argentina could not forget that the United Kingdom had veto power in the Security Council. Ambassador Parsons recalled the British reaction to my note as being neutral. London realized that it had been put on notice that the Secretary-General was ready and willing to act if Haig failed, but the suggestions were regarded as fairly routine, "the kind of thing we were expecting, knowing what the Secretary-General's task force had been up to during the previous few weeks."

On April 25, I was informed by the Argentine ambassador that an Argentine submarine had been attacked by British naval forces and that the British had reoccupied South Georgia by force. The ambassador suggested that this action would bring an end to the Haig mission. In view of this further armed exchange, I issued a statement on April 26 emphasizing that the escalation of the situation must be halted. However, on the April 28 the United Kingdom announced the closure of Stanley airport and the imposition of a total exclusion zone around the island. By this time it had enough ships and planes in the region to make the exclusion a reality. Troops and equipment necessary for landing in the Falklands had begun the long journey across the South Atlantic.

With military tension steadily increasing, Secretary Haig announced on April 30 that the United States could not and would not condone the use of unlawful force to resolve disputes. Further, in light of Argentina's refusal to accept a compromise that had been offered, the United States was imposing economic sanctions on Argentina and would respond favorably to requests from Britain for material support. The secretary described the American proposal for a solution of the crisis as having involved the following points:

- A cessation of hostilities
- Withdrawal of both Argentine and British forces
- Termination of sanctions
- Establishment of a U.K./U.S./Argentine interim authority to maintain the agreement
- Continuation of the traditional local administration with Argentine participation
- Procedures for encouraging cooperation in the development of the island and a framework for negotiation on a final settlement, taking into account the interests of both sides and those of the inhabitants

The secretary of state said that he had had reason to hope that the United Kingdom would consider a settlement along the lines of this proposal, but Argentina had stated it could not accept it. Argentina's position was that it must receive an assurance of eventual sovereignty or an immediate de facto role in governing the islands that would lead to Argentine sovereignty.

Just as Secretary Haig made his press announcement, I was meeting in New York with Argentine Foreign Minister Costa Mendez. I had known him slightly for a number of years. He was a highly successful lawyer who had served as foreign minister in a previous Argentine military regime. He was obviously a close collaborator with the current junta, although I was never sure to what extent he was involved in its decision-making process. Aristocratic in back-ground, widely read and highly articulate in both Spanish and English, he had some of the attributes of the English "gentleman." With a ruddy complexion and graying reddish hair, he even looked English. He seemed a strange choice to be leading the diplomatic aspects of the struggle against England. I could never warm to him, as I could not decide whether his nationalist fervor stemmed from conviction or opportunism. He seemed too shrewd a man to have advocated such a risky undertaking as the invasion of the Falklands Islands. Yet even after Argentina's defeat and the imprisonment of the junta leaders, he never disassociated himself from the policy or from his loyalty to General Galtieri. I believe he probably calculated that the Americans would put irresistible pressure on the British to accept Argentine sovereignty out of fear that the Soviets would profit from the situation and gain a foothold in the South Atlantic, this notwithstanding the fact that Costa Mendez clearly had an abiding distrust of the Soviets and of communism.

At the beginning of our conversation, the foreign minister emphasized that acknowledgment of Argentina's sovereignty in the Malvinas Islands was of capital importance to Argentina and was supported by the overwhelming majority of Latin American countries, as had been expressed in their vote in the Organization of American States. Argentina was prepared to abide by Resolution 502 and felt that implementation should begin with the withdrawal of forces. But the basic condition, he insisted, was recognition of Argentina's sovereignty. Argentina accepted that it would be necessary to go through a period of transition before its sovereignty could be fully exercised. It was quite prepared to enter into negotiations on this. It was ready to take into consideration the *interests* of the island residents, but it rejected the idea that their *wishes* should dictate the future status of the islands. Costa Mendez said that, as I must be aware, most of the islanders were agricultural workers on land owned by a large corporation in England. Argentina was prepared to purchase the company and to consider accepting a form of municipal government that would allow for the representation of the local inhabitants so that they could maintain their "British flavor." "Except for the issue of sovereignty," he said, "Argentina's generosity would know no limits." The foreign minister said that the Argentine government believed that the United Nations, and the Secretary-General in particular, could make an important contribution to a peaceful solution of the problem. It was ready to listen to any suggestions that I might have.

As this discussion was under way, a note was brought in summarizing the statement that Haig had just made to the press. Costa Mendez reacted immediately, saying that with this statement, Haig's capacity to serve as mediator had clearly ended. Under the circumstances he saw no inconvenience in the United Nations' assuming responsibility. I told the minister that there would be some initiative either from me or from the Security Council to fill the void that had now arisen.

Later on April 30, I met with the British Permanent Representative. I first gave him a summary of my earlier discussion with the Argentine foreign minister. Parsons said that the British foreign secretary had just set out his government's views in a public statement. A solution to the crisis would have to include the withdrawal of Argentine troops, the establishment of an interim administration and the setting up of a framework for negotiations on the future of the islands that would, of course, have to respect the *wishes* of the islanders.

From Secretary Haig's statement and the indications given to me by both Foreign Minister Costa Mendez and Ambassador Parsons, it was evident that Argentine insistence on sovereignty in the Malvinas was the nub of the crisis. If this could be managed, war might still be avoided. The logic of this conclusion was unassailable. Logic, unfortunately, did not determine the outcome. In the ensuing negotiations, this issue was removed but agreement did not follow.

Secretary Haig sent me a letter that repeated almost verbatim his statement to the press, but a final paragraph was added expressing the hope that I would continue to "support our efforts to achieve a peaceful solution of this crisis in the South Atlantic." There was no suggestion that the United Nations or anyone else should assume the mediatory role nor was there a clear statement that Haig was ending his mission. It was evident to me, however, that he could no longer serve as mediator and that unless someone else stepped in, a dangerous vacuum would occur. I had gained the impression that neither side would welcome the Security Council assuming the mediatory role; in any event, that would be impractical, because of the inevitable divisions within that body. Under the circumstances, I considered it morally incumbent on me to undertake whatever action I could to bring about implementation of Resolution 502 and to restore peace, even though the Security Council had given me no mandate. With the help of good work by my task force, I already had in mind an approach that I intended to put to the two countries. I met separately with the outgoing and incoming presidents of the Security Council to tell them of my intention. The response of each was encouraging. Therefore, later on the same day, my press spokesman announced that I was willing to be of assistance to both governments in the solution of their conflict.

THE PERUVIAN INITIATIVE

On the evening of May 1, I had a working dinner with British Foreign Secretary Pym at Ambassador Parsons's residence. Mr. Pym insisted that Argentine compliance with Resolution 502 was the primary requirement for peace. There could be no negotiations on that. However, he asked a good many questions about the possible makeup of a UN interim administration of the islands and about other ideas I had put forward in my note of April 19. I felt the secretary was open-minded.

Throughout the evening aides kept bringing in news bulletins about an initiative of President Fernando Belaunde Terry of Peru. The Peruvian government had not forewarned me or provided any information concerning its intention to launch new proposals. Pym was also completely in the dark, although, in Washington on the previous day, he had heard something about the possibility of a Peruvian move. When I left Ambassador Parsons's residence that evening I was bombarded with questions by the many press representatives who had been waiting all evening at the entrance. I could only say truthfully that I knew nothing about the Peruvian move.

Five days later I received a letter from the foreign minister of Peru. It detailed a draft proposal developed by the Peruvian Government consisting of the following four points: (1) a period of truce; (2) mutual withdrawal of forces; (3) immediate opening of negotiations between the parties with reference to the relevant resolutions of the General Assembly and the OAS on the Malvinas; and (4) temporary administration of the islands by the United Nations with the support of an international peace force. These points had been presented to the U.S. government several days earlier.

As a result of this initiative, a joint Peruvian/U.S.proposal was prepared, consisting of the following seven points:

1. Immediate cessation of hostilities
2. Mutual withdrawal of forces
3. The presence of representatives other than the parties involved in the dispute to govern the islands temporarily
4. Recognition by the two governments of the existence of divergent and conflicting claims concerning the status of the Malvinas Islands
5. Recognition by the two governments that the points of view and interests of the local inhabitants had to be taken into account
6. Establishment of a contact group to participate in the negotiations for implementing the agreement, consisting of Brazil, Peru, the Federal Republic of Germany and the United States of America
7. Achievement of a definitive agreement under the responsibility of the contact group before April 30, 1983.

The Peruvian foreign minister stated that these seven points were presented to the President of the Argentine Republic, who "noted" the presence of the United States among the members of the contact group and who requested that in point 5 the reference to the "points of view" of the local inhabitants be deleted, leaving reference only to their "interests." Accordingly points 5 and 6 were reformulated as follows:

5. The two governments recognize that the aspirations and interests of the local inhabitants have to be taken into account in the definitive solution of the problem

6. The contact group which would participate immediately in the negotiations for implementing this agreement would consist of several countries to be designated by mutual consent.

Subsequently, according to the foreign minister, Peru proposed the following revised wording to Argentina for point 4:

4. The two governments recognize the existence of divergent and conflicting claims concerning the status of the Islands and will take into account the resolutions on the Malvinas adopted by various international organizations.

In a later interview, Argentine Foreign Minister Costa Mendez gave a somewhat different account of the "Peruvian" initiative. He stated that he felt, on first seeing the Peruvian plan, which was sent from President Belaunde to General Galtieri by telex, that a peaceful settlement of the crisis might be in sight since the words "aspirations and interests" of the islanders were used rather than "wishes." This implied that something other than continuation of the British colonial status of the islands was a possibility. Costa Mendez called it a *"muy buen papelito."* However, according to Costa Mendez, very shortly after the original text was received, President Belaunde telephoned Galtieri. Galtieri asked Costa Mendez to speak to Belaunde since Costa Mendez was familiar with the technicalities. Belaunde said that the paper had been drafted by General Haig, who had asked him to push it with Galtieri. Costa Mendez told him that the text was being studied and Galtieri would have to consult the other members of the Junta; but he, Costa Mendez, thought it was a positive move. Then, in Costa Mendez's account, 14 minutes later, Belaunde called again. Again Galtieri asked Costa Mendez to speak with him. Belaunde said that there had been a very slight change—perhaps two changes—but only one of importance. Haig had asked that the word "aspirations" be changed to "wishes." Costa Mendez, according to his account, said, "Mr. President, that puts an end to everything." He was convinced that the British had seen the document. Belaunde argued that it was only one word, but Costa Mendez replied that although the dictionary definition of "wishes" might not be very different from "aspirations," "wishes" nonetheless connoted a lot of unacceptable things.

THE UN PROPOSAL

On May 2, I presented to the two sides an aide-mémoire proposing that they agree to take the following steps simultaneously at an agreed time, which I designated as Time T:

1. Argentina would begin to withdraw its troops from the Falklands/ Malvinas and the United Kingdom to redeploy its naval forces and begin their withdrawal from the area of the Islands, with withdrawals to be completed by an agreed date.
2. Both governments would commence negotiations to seek a diplomatic solution to their differences by an agreed target date.
3. Both governments would rescind their respective blockades, exclusion zones and economic sanctions, and cease all hostile acts against each other.
4. Transitional arrangements would begin to come into effect to supervise implementation of the above steps and to meet interim administrative requirements.

I assured the governments that practical arrangements for any UN role such as I had earlier suggested—for example, in the interim administration of the islands—could be completed expeditiously. In light of the urgency of the situation I expressed the hope that the two governments would speedily accept this approach and said that I would appreciate written confirmation in time to make a public announcement on May 5. I proposed that Time T be set for 11:00 A.M. New York time on May 6, 1982.

On May 2, 1982, the same day that I presented the aide mémoire to the two governments, the Argentine cruiser *General Belgrano* was torpedoed outside the 200-mile exclusion zone by a British nuclear submarine. Out of a crew of 1,042, 321 men were lost. Two days later the British destroyer *Sheffield* was sunk by an Exorcet missile fired from a Super-Etendard plane—French arms were being used against France's ally. British planes had begun to bomb the airport at Port Stanley.

Despite the sinking of the *Belgrano* and the *Sheffield* and other evidence of a widening conflict, both Argentina and the United Kingdom replied positively to my aide mémoire. Neither accepted the specific proposals as such but both took the position that the aide mémoire provided a framework for negotiations. Argentina, in its response, referred to "the fundamental need for a cease-fire and truce" so that negotiations could be started without the pressure of military attacks by either side. The British, understandably, were not of a mind to agree to a cease-fire while Argentine troops were occupying the islands.

Meanwhile there had been informal consultations by the Security Council during which I had emphasized that my proposals were essentially procedural in nature. I had not made suggestions on the substance of the problem, which I recognized could be resolved only in negotiations between the two countries. There was full agreement on this point. Jeane Kirkpatrick, speaking for the United States, commented that the Security Council was really *the* United Nations and she welcomed its present concern with the Falklands/Malvinas crisis. She insisted that the substantive issue of sovereignty went back hundreds of years and said that it was not a matter on which the Council should express an opinion. It was generally agreed that a formal meeting of the Council would not be helpful since it would inevitably be the forum for inflammatory statements. I was able to discourage several initiatives to convene a meeting, and none was held until May 21, when I had concluded that my mediation efforts had failed.

I undertook to mediate under the relentless pressure of the steady progress of the British landing force across the South Atlantic and mounting air attacks against Argentine troops and installations. Obviously there was insufficient time to continue the shuttle diplomacy that Secretary Haig had followed which I felt, even with the transportation at the Secretary's disposal, had been overly time (and endurance) consuming, given the great distances involved. Instead I resorted to the technique of proximity negotiations, meeting separately in New York with the two delegations. I sought in these talks to build through my suggestions a text on which the two sides could agree.

The senior representatives for Argentina and the United Kingdom in the negotiations were respectively Enrique Ros, the deputy foreign minister of Argentina, and Sir Anthony Parsons, the Permanent Representative of the United Kingdom to the United Nations. Both were experienced and skillful diplomats with whom I was personally well acquainted. But they represented very different governments and were of decidedly different personalities. Sir Anthony Parsons, whom everyone called Tony, was an outgoing man of easy charm and evident honesty. He had been the British ambassador in Tehran at the time of the Iranian revolution and had earned a reputation for strong nerves and vast expertise. Parsons was one of the most senior members of the British Foreign Service, and the United Nations was to be his last post before retirement. His manner was direct and he put no store on protocol. Without being egotistical, he had the self-confidence that derived from knowing that his views were respected in London and that his ability was recognized by his diplomatic colleagues and by his own staff. During the negotiations on the Falklands he was always fully and quickly informed on developments in the British government. Most important, it was evident that he had the full confidence of Mrs. Thatcher, whom he subsequently served as foreign policy advisor.

Enrique Ros was also a diplomat of skill and wide experience. As deputy foreign minister, he held the senior career position in the Argentine diplomatic service. He had served in this post under two previous foreign ministers as well as under Costa Mendez. He had also been Argentine Permanent Representative to the United Nations. Ros was clearly nonpolitical but evidently not unwilling to serve in a senior position under the Junta regime. If he had differences with his government and the instructions he received—and I believe he did—he kept them to himself. His greatest difficulty may well have been getting clear and timely guidance from Buenos Aires, since there was continuing evidence of confusion and incompetent leadership in the Argentine government. Ros and Parsons had served together previously and personally were good friends. Both have suggested that it would have been helpful if they could have sat together and sought to come to a better understanding. I personally doubt this, since the Argentine regime patently allowed Ros no flexibility.

Throughout my mediation effort, I was conscious that the United States remained an important player in the drama, capable of exercising significant influence on the parties, especially the United Kingdom. I kept Washington fully informed on a confidential basis of all developments. Secretary Haig obviously wished to continue to be directly involved. It was perhaps natural that he did not believe the United Nations could succeed where he had failed and that he continued to work on his own sometimes without informing me of his initiatives. I sensed that he did not understand the United Nations very well. Yet he showed respect for the Secretary-General as an institution and did not exhibit the antipathy toward the United Nations that was evident elsewhere in the Reagan Administration.

On May 5, three days after I had presented my aide-mémoire to the two sides, the secretary telephoned concerning the state of play. After I told him that Argentina had accepted my démarche, he said that he did not think that the proposals made so far would gain the agreement of either side, particularly the British. Reverting to the "Peruvian initiative" (on which I had not yet received details from the Peruvian government), he said that he felt agreement had almost been reached on that basis. President Belaunde believed that had it not been for the torpedoing of the *Belgrano,* his proposals would have been accepted. Haig informed me that President Reagan had contacted Prime Minister Thatcher over the previous weekend and strenuously urged her to consider a cease-fire. She had promised to consider "the timetable for a cease-fire." Haig was convinced that, under the circumstances, the Peruvian proposals (which, he said, the Peruvians could portray as their own) provided the basis for an agreement that could be signed at the United Nations under my auspices. The secretary of state asked that I not move "too fast." He was not opposed to anything I was doing and he wished to strengthen the United Nations, but his main goal was to stop the shooting; he felt that within the next 24 hours a cease-fire would be achieved.

With the British task force moving inexorably toward the Falklands, time was obviously of the essence if war was to be avoided. I therefore sought to speed up the talks. I would meet first with one delegation and then the other, communicating to the one the position of the other on the points in dispute. Neither Parsons nor Ros could proceed without instructions from their respective capitals. This is a cumbersome negotiating technique, which inhibits the development of a dynamic momentum. Nonetheless, progress was made.

The approach that I took differed in three essential ways from that followed by Secretary Haig. First, any agreement reached was to be of the nature of a *provisional measure,* that is, without prejudice to the substantive position of either party on matters of principle such as sovereignty; second, all actions to be taken under the proposed agreement would begin simultaneously; and third, the United Nations would assume responsibility for the interim administration of the islands, to be symbolized by the flying of the UN flag with the Argentine and British flags flying on either side, symbolizing that the question of sovereignty was open.

It was my hope that Argentina could be persuaded to reach an interim agreement, understanding that it could maintain its claim to sovereignty but that recognition of this claim would not be the guaranteed outcome of future substantive negotiations with London. From the beginning of the talks, Ambassador Parsons stated clearly and repeatedly that this point was absolutely crucial for London. Agreement on all other points under discussion would be dependent on the inclusion of a "no-prejudgment" clause. "Five previous negotiations," he said, "had collapsed on this point." Britain needed to know whether it was entering into a genuine period of negotiation or whether it was again merely engaged in an exercise aimed at the automatic transfer of sovereignty to Argentina.

A BREAK-THROUGH ON SOVEREIGNTY

In the first talk with Enrique Ros, I made as clear as I possibly could that if Argentina held to its insistence on recognition of its sovereignty, there could be no interim agreement and war would be inevitable, a war that I did not believe Argentina could win. I acknowledged that Argentina would be taking a calculated risk concerning the outcome of future bilateral negotiations on the status of the islands. There was at least the possibility, however, that future circumstances would be more propitious for Argentina's claim. When we met with the Argentine delegation three days later, on May 11, Ros asked first to speak with me alone. In this private conversation he told me that Argentina had decided to accept the "no-prejudgment" clause. This had been an extremely difficult decision, which had not been easily reached. He emphasized that it had the approval of *all* elements of the government—meaning, I assumed, all members of the Junta. Subsequently, in the meeting in which my staff and the full Argentine delegation took part, Ros repeated Argentina's agreement that any interim agreement reached would be without prejudice to the substantive positions of either side. This, he said, was a great sacrifice that could be detrimental to Argentina's interests. In return, Argentina insisted that Britain must agree to references in the text of the proposed agreement to the UN Charter and to "relevant General Assembly resolutions." Ros suggested the following text for inclusion, a text that had first been developed with slightly different wording in the Secretariat task force:

> The parties undertake to enter into negotiations in good faith under the auspices of the Secretary-General of the United Nations for the peaceful settlement of their dispute and to seek, with a sense of urgency, the completion of these negotiations by 31 December 1982, taking into account the Charter of the United Nations and the relevant resolutions of the General Assembly. These negotiations shall be initiated without prejudice to the rights, claims or position of the parties and without prejudgment of the outcome.

The reference to the UN Charter had special significance for Argentina since Chapter XI, Article 73, entitled "The Declaration Regarding Non-Self-Governing Territories" (into which classification the Falkland Islands fell), states that "Members of the United Nations which have or assume responsibilities for the administration of territories whose peoples have not yet attained a full measure of self-government recognize the principle that the *interests* of the inhabitants of these territories are paramount, and accept . . . the obligation to promote to the utmost . . . the *well-being* of the inhabitants of these territories" (italics added). There is no obligation to respect the *wishes* of the inhabitants. Reference to the General Assembly resolutions was considered important since they tended to favor the Argentine position by calling for an end to colonial control of the islands. I realized that reference to the Charter in this context could be difficult for the British, but such a reference entailed no British commitment *not* to respect the wishes of the islanders. I felt that a crucial breakthrough had been achieved. The sovereignty question, on which the Haig effort had foundered, had been put aside. In a meeting on the following day, Ambassador Parsons referred to the Argentine move as an extremely encouraging development.

The concept of simultaneous initiation of troop withdrawals, the termination of economic sanctions and the initiation of bilateral negotiations on a diplomatic solution of the differences between the two countries was accepted by both sides in principle. However, there were serious differences on the modalities of withdrawal and on the form that the administration of the islands should take. Prior to the Argentine invasion, there were three levels of governance in the Falklands/Malvinas: (1) the governor general, who represented the queen as head of state; (2) the Executive Council, which functioned as the governor general's cabinet; and (3) the Legislative Council, consisting of eight representatives, four of whom were appointed by the governor general and the remainder elected by the inhabitants. The United Kingdom placed major importance on the continued functioning of the Legislative Council, as the elected representative body of the islanders. The Argentine side insisted that the members of the council should serve only as advisors to the UN Administrator, and this only if there were an equal number of Argentine advisors. It also called for the relaxation of restrictions imposed by the British on communications, residence and the acquisition of property. Inevitably the British saw this as a way of changing the demographic makeup of the islands with evident implications for the future "wishes" of the islanders. The British, at a session on May 12, did agree, however, that the UN Administrator would assume the functions of the British governor. He "would administer the government" and have the "authority to ensure the continuing administration of the territory." But there should be no "significant alteration in the character of life" of the islanders during the interim period.

From the beginning of my mediation, the Argentine side insisted that an interim agreement on the Falklands must also extend to South Georgia and the South Sandwich Islands. The Argentine delegation pointed out that, as dependencies, they had been administered together with the Falklands. The British insisted that the dependencies had a different status and were not included in the negotiations. There was also a serious difference over the rather elusive question of a cutoff date for the substantive negotiations to be undertaken by Britain and Argentina on the future status of the Falklands/Malvinas. What would happen if, by an agreed target date, no agreement had been reached? The British held that a legal vacuum had to be avoided and that the interim administration of the islands continued until an agreement was reached between the two parties. Argentina held a contrary view that the bilateral negotiations could not be extended beyond an agreed termination date.

During these crucial days, the United States continued to play a role in the search for an agreement that would end the crisis. Secretary Haig informed me on May 12 that he had been in direct touch with British Foreign Secretary Pym with suggestions regarding a schedule for the interim administration. He thought Ambassador Parsons would be receiving new instructions soon. Haig continued to offer to be of any possible service to me in my mediation. Then, on the following day, Jeane Kirkpatrick suggested that I telephone President Reagan and advise him to call Prime Minister Thatcher and President Galtieri in order to urge them to make the necessary compromises to reach agreement along the lines I had proposed. Feeling that the application of U.S. influence at the highest level could be useful at this point, I followed Ambassador Kirkpatrick's suggestion and telephoned the President. Apparently he had been briefed by Mrs. Kirkpatrick, for he was familiar with the three main stumbling blocks to an agreement—the termination arrangements for the bilateral negotiations, the geographic area covered in an interim agreement and the extent of Argentine participation in the interim administration—and immediately agreed to be in touch with the two parties. That same evening Ambassador Kirkpatrick informed me that the President had called Mrs. Thatcher and that they had had a long talk on the crisis. Mrs. Thatcher had explained that she was in a difficult position with the House of Commons, which was totally opposed to the government's backing down. She, nonetheless, was still hopeful for peace through the Secretary-General's efforts. Ambassador Kirkpatrick added that a senior, Spanish-speaking aide to the President was expected to call President Galtieri. Without telling me the source of her information, she also said that Argentina would show flexibility on the number of Argentine advisors in the interim administration.

Meanwhile, Secretary Haig had telephoned me from Turkey. He had learned about my phone call to President Reagan and was distinctly unhappy about it. I explained that I had made the call at the suggestion of Mrs. Kirkpatrick, who told me that she had been keeping the President informed on the status of negotiations. Since the negotiations were at something of a standstill and time was very limited, I had felt that the President's intervention could be helpful. I feared that there was some possibility that the British might make some kind of attack on the Argentine mainland, which could be disastrous. It was my hope that the President could discourage such a move. Secretary Haig said the President should make such a call only if it would produce results. He did not feel that the President should have called until at least two of the stumbling blocks were removed. I cannot say whether the President's call to Mrs. Thatcher made any difference; probably it did not. My sense, though, was that the real source of Secretary Haig's unhappiness was what he considered Ambassador Kirkpatrick's interference in his business.

On May 12 and 13 the British Representative presented his government's further views on the three major differences. These views were not forthcoming. I had to tell Ambassador Parsons that the British position was not encouraging. I feared that unless there were greater flexibility on the British side, Argentina might withdraw its acceptance of the no pre-judgement clause. Obviously there would have to be greater flexibility on the Argentine side as well, a point that I emphasized with equal force in the next meetings with the Argentine delegation. I told both sides that I was asking them to make concessions not to each other but to peace. My main concern was that escalation of the armed conflict was bound to result in terrible bloodshed. I told the British specifically that I was not asking for compromise on principles. It was evident that Argentina had resorted to force and, for me, that was simply as a matter of international law unacceptable. I was totally committed to implementation of the position set forth by the Security Council in resolution 502. Within this context I appealed to the British, as one of the cofounders of the United Nations, to give me their maximum concessions by the next day.

On that same day I described to the Argentine delegation the request I had made to the British and put the same request to them. I stated my intention once these positions were received to make an evaluation, which I would submit within 48 hours to both sides to consider. I made clear that my role was not simply to deliver mail from one side to the other, stating bluntly that I did not wish to be used by anybody as an instrument for endless manipulation.

As a bloody armed conflict became ever more likely, I received without any prior warning a remarkable call from Mrs. Thatcher. The Prime Minister appealed to me to keep "her boys" from being killed. I sensed that this was the woman and the mother who was speaking to me—a very different person from the firm, seemingly belligerent leader of the British government. From this call I was certain that Margaret Thatcher was not, as so much of the press was reporting, hell-bent on war.

I had now been involved in the mediation effort for 15 days. Obviously a critical stage had been reached in the negotiations. I have always felt that a Secretary-General does not have the right to be either optimistic or pessimistic in dealing with a crisis situation. But in this case, despite the warnings I gave to both sides, I allowed myself a degree of optimism. By May 13 all of the members of the Secretariat task force who were working so closely with me felt that the situation was hopeful, that major obstacles had been overcome and that true negotiations between the parties were in progress. Momentum, that elusive factor in negotiations, was perceptible. It seemed to all of us that given the extent of agreement that had been achieved, the remaining differences, while by no means simple, should be surmountable. There was, of course, the question of whether the British government, having mounted a large and costly military effort that was proving politically extremely popular, was determined under all circumstances to carry through with the military defeat of Argentina and of the aggression that its invasion of the Falklands represented. I was conscious that the intensification of air attacks on the Argentine forces was obviously in preparation for a British landing, and with the increasing proximity of the British task force, time was running out. I knew that Mrs. Thatcher was totally determined to bring about the unconditional withdrawal of Argentine forces from the Falklands. Yet, from her private call to me, which I had not revealed even to my closest associates, I had reason to think that she was prepared to accept a peaceful solution even while telling Parliament, as she did on May 14, that the British battle fleet was ready to launch a major assault. Ambassador Parsons also made some remarks that strengthened this conclusion.

I told the Security Council, which met for informal consultations on May 14, that substantial progress had been made toward an agreement to end the crisis in a manner consistent with Resolution 502. The agreement would provide for an immediate cease-fire accompanied by a mutual withdrawal of forces, termination of all hostile acts, an interim administration of the territory by the United Nations and negotiations on a diplomatic settlement under the auspices of the Secretary-General. I added that differences remained that had so far proved difficult to bridge and I warned that time was not, in this case, "on the side of peace."

A BRITISH PROPOSAL: COMPROMISE OR ULTIMATUM?

Anthony Parsons was not at the Security Council consultations because he had suddenly been called back to London for consultations. My colleagues and I were surprised and disconcerted by this development, since it inevitably meant a hiatus in the New York talks at a very sensitive and hopeful point and there was no time to spare. Nonetheless, I told the press, on leaving the Headquarters building, that I viewed Ambassador Parsons's trip to London as a hopeful sign.

Sir Anthony flew back to New York on the Concorde on the morning of May 17 with what he has said was the only complete copy of a British draft of an interim agreement. It had been worked out in a six-hour meeting that Prime Minister Thatcher had held with her War Cabinet in which Sir Anthony was a major participant. He came to my office with the text immediately upon his return. He said that the basic views of the British government were the following: The United Kingdom was the victim of clear aggression. There was only one adequate response—restoration of the *status quo ante*. Argentina had had plenty of time to withdraw since the adoption of Security Council Resolution 502. However, for the sake of peace, the British government had participated in repeated rounds of negotiations. Now, in a final effort, the United Kingdom was making a proposal for an agreement that the entire War Cabinet viewed as containing significant concessions. The British government could not do more.

Ambassador Parsons listed the following as British concessions:

- A brief interim administration with a target date for a settlement of the basic dispute.

- Nonreintroduction of British administration during the interim administration, with administrative responsibility resting with the United Nations.
- Relinquishment of certainty of sovereignty, leaving the outcome of bilateral negotiations open.
- Parallel withdrawal of forces rather than the prior withdrawal of the invading forces.
- Downplaying the islanders' participation in the interim administration.
- The introduction of two Argentine representatives, one each in the Legislative and Advisory councils, representing a total Argentine population of only 30 people.
- Reliance on the United Nations for verification of the nonreintroduction of armed forces.
- Acceptance of Argentine observers during the period of interim administration.

Parsons emphasized that the British government regarded these as major concessions. It took account of the fact that Argentina also agreed to the inclusion of a "no-prejudgment clause" although it did not consider this a major concession on Argentina's part.

The British text was more forthcoming than anything I had expected. It covered all of the proposals that I had made in my aide-mémoire of May 2 and included much of the language that had been developed during the proximity talks in New York. Its major provisions, which encompassed the concessions that Sir Anthony had listed, were the following:

- Nothing in the agreement would prejudice in any way the rights, claims and positions of either party in the ultimate settlement of their dispute over the islands.
- Within 24 hours of an agreed date (Time T) mutual withdrawal of armed forces to at least 150 nautical miles from any point on the islands would commence and would be completed within 14 days.
- With immediate effect as of Time T, exclusion zones and economic measures would be lifted.
- Immediately after the adoption of an appropriate resolution by the Security Council, a United Nations Administrator, acceptable both to Argentina and the United Kingdom, would be appointed by the Secretary-General to administer the government of the islands. He would discharge his duties in consultation with the representative institutions of the islands.
- The parties would enter into negotiations under the auspices of the

Secretary-General for the peaceful settlement of their dispute and seek, with a sense of urgency, the completion of these negotiations by December 31, 1982.

The preamble to the proposed agreement made specific reference to the "obligations with regard to non-self-governing territories set out in Article 73 of the Charter," the entire text of which was annexed to the draft. In a letter officially transmitting the proposed agreement to me, Ambassador Parsons stated that the Falkland Islands (Islas Malvinas) as referred to therein excluded the dependencies.

Ambassador Parsons stated firmly that this draft agreement was the "bottom line" as far as the British were concerned. He requested formally that I pass it on to the Argentine delegation as the final British position. The United Kingdom required an Argentine response within 48 hours. Any request for additional time would be interpreted as purely delaying tactics. I asked whether the draft text and the deadline should be considered confidential. He answered affirmatively. I also asked whether even minor changes were excluded. Was it strictly a take it or leave it situation? The ambassador replied that any insistence on substantive changes would mean the end of negotiations. I told Parsons that while I was favorably impressed by the text, I very much feared that if it were presented as an ultimatum, Argentina would automatically reject it. It was a matter of national pride. I suggested it might be better if I presented the paper as my own assessment of the best that could be gotten from the British side. Parsons replied that the paper would have to be made public by the British government shortly, possibly within two days, given the pressure in the House of Commons. He suggested instead that I might present the U.K. deadline as a UN deadline.

Some points in the British proposal that obviously were going to be difficult for Argentina to accept, in particular the geographic limitation, the continuation in effect of the restrictions on the movement of Argentine nationals to the Falklands and on their purchase of property there and the lack of a definite commitment that negotiations on the future status of islands would be completed by a specific date. But the text offered very basic advantages in terms of Argentine aspirations. Most important, there was no commitment by the United Kingdom to be bound in future negotiations on the status of the islands by the *wishes* of the islanders (although Mrs. Thatcher was to use that word in explaining the U.K. position a few days later in the House of Commons). The very prominent reference in the preamble to Article 73 of the UN Charter clearly signaled that the United Kingdom was prepared to be guided only by the islander's *interests*. This was the very issue over which the Peruvian initiative apparently collapsed. Moreover, acceptance of a UN Administrator to administer the government of the islands with observers from both Argentina and the United Kingdom would clearly symbolize that the question of sovereignty was open. Yet I felt certain that Argentina would reject the text if presented as an ultimatum. When I met a few hours later with the Secretariat task force, I expressed my conclusion that the game was lost. Looking back now, I feel that when Parsons gave me the text, I might have expressed even more forcefully my conviction that the Argentine leadership would reject anything that appeared to be an ultimatum. Tony Parsons has since said that in deciding on their tactic, the British had not considered Argentine pride. Pride was now joined with shortness of time as an enemy of peace.

I immediately transmitted the British proposal to the Argentine delegation, describing all the concessions that the British government considered it had made. I made clear that the British considered this their final effort at agreement. The British side might accept some cosmetic suggestions, but nothing more than that. I asked to have the Argentine response by the next evening. It should be the final Argentine position since if success was not achieved within the next two to three days, I intended to withdraw from my mediation effort. To ensure that there could be no misunderstanding in Buenos Aires, I privately gave Ambassador Ros my briefing notes, which contained in Spanish a summary of the British proposal and the list of British concessions.

At 9:30 P.M. the next day, within the time limit I had set, the Argentine delegation delivered to me the Argentine response. Like the British draft, it took the form of a proposed agreement. While it incorporated most of the points on which agreement had been reached in the proximity talks and which were also included in the British text, it offered no concessions on the points that had remained in dispute. In fact, it presented a harder statement of the Argentine position than that put forward orally in the proximity talks. The geographic scope was specifically defined as including both South Georgia and the South Sandwich Islands; there were to be no discriminatory restrictions of any kind for the parties, "including freedom of movement and equality of access with respect to residence, work and property"; British forces would have to be withdrawn to home ports; and, most discouraging of all, bilateral negotiations on the future status of the islands could be extended only once, until June 30, 1983. If by that time no agreement was reached, the General Assembly would determine the terms to which the final agreement should conform. The Argentine response was obviously unacceptable. I told Ambassador Ros that the two positions remained so far apart that a minimum of two weeks would be required to negotiate the differences. And two weeks were not available. The United Kingdom would feel relieved of all restraint as of the next day and would be free to attack with full force. Under the circumstances, the next day, May 19, would obviously be critical.

When I showed the Argentine paper to Ambassador Parsons, his immediate conclusion was that the negotiations had finished. In reporting this to Ambassador Ros, I said that regardless of the British view, my own efforts had not yet ended. I intended to put forward suggestions to overcome the remaining differences in a last attempt to avert war. I planned first to telephone President Galtieri. If that conversation offered any encouragement, I would telephone Prime Minister Thatcher. Ambassador Ros commented that in putting forward their proposed agreement on a take it or leave it basis, the British had left no possibility for anything other than the counter paper that Argentina had presented.

As soon as the Argentine paper was received, the task force that had been supporting me with great diligence and ingenuity throughout the negotiations began to develop suggestions on ways to bridge the stark differences between the British and Argentine proposals. Their first suggestions leaned more toward the Argentine position than the British. Here I feel compelled to say that the British delegation had developed an evident distrust for the head of the task force, Rafeeuddin Ahmed. Ahmed led the task force with great efficiency, and his counsel was almost always impartial. But being a Pakistani, he could not help but be hostile to colonialism in any form, and the Falklands were unquestionably a colonial possession. I felt strongly that the Argentine position was completely unrealistic and, under the circumstances, self-destructive. The British draft offered Argentina a fair chance of gaining sovereignty in the Falklands and the reality of a non-British administration of the islands for an indeterminate period. The British military position was obviously very strong, and I was convinced that they were entirely serious in saying that they would accept no substantive changes in their proposal. Therefore it seemed to me that the best course—in the interest of peace and of both parties—was to devise suggestions that would offer some cosmetic satisfaction to soothe Argentine pride without changing the substance of the British proposal. The members of the task force and I set around a conference table and hurriedly drafted such suggestions. They were to be treated as highly confidential; surprisingly they did not leak to the press or to the other delegations.

My suggestions were the following. Regarding the geographic scope, the status of the dependencies, South Georgia and the South Sandwich Islands, would be included within the framework of the bilateral negotiations that were foreseen on the status of the Falklands. However, provisions of the interim agreement relative to the withdrawal of forces and the interim administration would not be applicable to the dependencies.

Concerning force withdrawals, the parties should rely on the United Nations to establish the modalities of the mutual withdrawal of forces in the understanding that the withdrawals would be simultaneous and would be accomplished in phases. This responsibility would be assumed with the goal of completing the withdrawals within two weeks.

Regarding termination of bilateral negotiations, if the Secretary-General determined that the negotiations could not be completed by the established deadline, he could set a new deadline that would be compatible with the urgency of reaching a diplomatic settlement.

Finally, regarding interim administration, the UN representative would assume full authority for administration of the territory. In carrying out his functions, he would consult the representative institutions of the islands. One representative from the Argentine population normally resident in the islands would be appointed by the UN Administrator to each of the two institutions. The Administrator would exercise his powers in accordance with the terms of the agreement and in conformity with the laws and practices traditionally obtaining in the islands.

The wording on the interim administration was essentially the same as that contained in the British draft. However, the following points were added:

- The United Nations flag would be flown in the territory. The United Kingdom and Argentina would each establish small liaison offices on which their respective flags would be flown. (This had been tentatively agreed to in the proximity talks but was not included in the British draft).
- During the period of interim administration, all communications and other provisions for cooperation in the economic, social, cultural and scientific-technological fields that were in force on March 31, 1982 would continue and be further encouraged, as appropriate. (The British text contained a comparable provision, but it was tied to an exchange of notes between Argentina and the United Kingdom dating back to 1971.)
- Reductions in the restrictions on residency and the acquisition of property would be considered, taking account of the need to respect and safeguard the customs, traditions and way of life of islanders.

I telephoned the Argentine President, General Galtieri, in the late afternoon on May 19. After describing the seriousness of the situation, I emphasized that in the talks that had been conducted with Ambassador Ros and the British representative in New York, an advance had been made that had not been achieved in previous negotiations: It had been agreed that there would be no return to the earlier situation on the *Islas Malvinas*. Everything else was of minor significance compared to this achievement. There remained, however, several unresolved points. The matter was urgent since the United Kingdom considered the negotiations as having terminated. I did not feel this was necessarily the case. I had suggestions to make that I hoped might serve to overcome the remaining problems. I was inclined to call Prime Minister Thatcher but did not wish to do so without first receiving the President's encouragement.

Galtieri seemed somewhat confused, as if he had been drinking. I had the impression that he was being prompted by others on what to say. His first response was that it was not Argentina that was setting deadlines, it was Britain. Argentina was ready to continue negotiations. Argentina had gone to extreme limits in making its position ever more flexible. The same goodwill did not exist on the other side. I expressed appreciation for Galtieri's willingness to continue negotiations and said that I was thinking of sending an envoy to Buenos Aires to discuss the formulas that I had in mind. The President agreed but only if an envoy were also sent to London, since otherwise Argentina would be placed in an unfavorable light. I said that I saw no difficulty in this but it seemed best to start with Argentina. Galtieri asked if I had thought of inviting the two foreign ministers to New York. I suggested that would be premature until there was greater certainty that an agreement would be reached. Galtieri then repeated that it was not Argentina that was setting deadlines for the Secretary-General's efforts but if there were a massive British offensive it would be more difficult to continue negotiations.

I immediately called Prime Minister Thatcher (it was already 11:30 P.M. in London) and told her that I had just spoken to President Galtieri and appealed for his help in overcoming the impasse in negotiations. He had said that he was interested in seeing a solution of the problem and was prepared to consider the three suggestions I was making in the hope of avoiding a military confrontation. I asked the Prime Minister to allow a further 36 hours to see if agreement could still be found. Mrs. Thatcher replied that while she was very grateful for my efforts, the views of her government had been clearly stated in the proposed agreement that it had put forward. There had been seven sets of discussions with the Argentine regime and each had ended with the same point: "confuse and delay." The Prime Minister was convinced that the Argentine government was using the negotiating process as a ploy for delay. The most recent Argentine response was a total rejection of the British position. If they were serious about negotiating, they could do two things: first, comply with the resolution of the Security Council and withdraw their forces; second, accept the British proposals. Mrs. Thatcher said that she would have to make a statement to the House of Commons the next morning and at that point would have to make public the British proposal.

I told the Prime Minister that this most recent Argentine response was not their final word. It was still subject to reconsideration. She was not impressed. She said that it was clear to her that even if there were 107 more rounds of negotiations, the conclusion would still be the same. I replied that even so, I did not consider my own efforts as terminated and if she did not mind,

I would like to convey to Ambassador Parsons some new ideas that might bring a peaceful solution. Her response was that I should do as I saw fit. She was willing to look at fresh proposals. But she would have to present the British draft agreement to the House of Commons very soon.

Later on the same day I called in the British and Argentine representatives and gave them separately, on a confidential basis, an aide-mémoire that first listed those points on which I felt that agreement existed and then put forward the four suggestions that I had developed with the task force to overcome remaining differences. I stated that the extent of agreement was clearly substantial and important. Unless the remaining differences were resolved in the immediate future, all that had been achieved would be lost. I stressed that the time for achieving an agreement must now be measured in hours. This could be the last opportunity to avoid war. I then issued a statement to the press, declaring that at this decisive moment "a last urgent effort is needed to reach the accommodation necessary for a reasonable settlement. . . . We must continue to work for peace without jeopardy to principle." I thought it important to place the last sentence on record to avoid any impression that I favored compromise on the principles of Resolution 502. I was *not* working for peace at any price.

On May 20, I waited for an Argentine reaction to my four suggestions. None came. When Nicanor Costa Mendez was asked some years later why Argentina had not responded, he said that he was then in Washington and had intended to respond in person but the British invasion intervened. When Enrique Ros was asked the same question, he said that in the midst of the intensive British air attacks that were then taking place and in the face of an imminent British landing, the government simply could not put a response together. Ambassador Parsons informed me on May 20 that he had received a response from London but was under instructions to deliver it only after Argentina had replied. In the absence of an Argentine response the British instructions were never communicated to me. However, in addressing the sixth debate on the Falklands crisis in the House of Commons on May 20, Mrs. Thatcher said that my suggestions (which she did not reveal) differed in certain important respects from the British position contained in the British draft of May 17, which her government had made clear was "the furthest we could go." Some of my suggestions, she added, were the very ones that Argentina had already rejected. Even if they were acceptable to both parties as a basis for negotiation, that negotiation would take many days, if not weeks, to reach either success or failure. It was inconceivable, she continued, "that Argentina would now accept those ideas which closely resemble our own. . . . Even if we were prepared to negotiate on the basis of the aide-mémoire, we should first wish to see substantive Argentine comments on it, going beyond mere acceptance of it as a basis for negotiation. These are the points that we are making in our reply to the Secretary-General. At the same time we are reminding him . . . that negotiations did not close any military options." This no doubt was the essence of the undelivered British response to my aide-mémoire.

When, in the course of May 20, I heard nothing from Argentina, I concluded that my mediation effort was at an end. It was evident that British forces were on the point of landing at some location in the Falklands within the next two days. I felt that it was desirable that I report to the Security Council, which had not met formally on the results of my good offices, before the land war began. So, in the late evening of May 20, I addressed a letter to the President of the Security Council to inform him that the efforts in which I had been engaged "did not offer the present prospect of bringing about an end to the crisis or, indeed, of preventing intensification of the conflict." I held a brief press conference in conjunction with the release of the letter to the press. One correspondent said that earlier in the day Sir Anthony Parsons had said that the patient had been dead since yesterday. What did I think? I replied that Sir Anthony was a British doctor while I was an international doctor. Our assessments on the patient's condition were different. For me, the patient had been alive up until now.

On the following day, May 21, I provided a full report to the Security Council in which I expressed my continuing belief that an agreement along the lines developed in the exchanges over the past two weeks, incorporating the suggestions I had made on May 19, could restore peace in the South Atlantic. I had to report, however, that the necessary accommodations had not been made. The prospect that faced us now was one of destruction, continuing conflict and the loss of many, many young lives.

WAR AND CALLS FOR A CEASE-FIRE

By the time I made my report to the Security Council, the British had begun landing troops for their major assault against the Argentine forces in the Falklands. While the landing was successful in eventually establishing a bridgehead, there was a substantial loss of ships and aircraft on both sides. The Security Council met daily to consider what could be done to bring the fighting to an end. There were widespread calls for a cease-fire both within the Council and in the broader international community. Pope John Paul II, the foreign ministers of Brazil and Uruguay and others issued appeals for an end to the fighting. The foreign ministers of Argentina, Nicaragua, Panama and Venezuela issued a declaration confirming Latin America's rejection of the British military offensive. The Soviet Union, which had been notably restrained with regard to the Malvinas crisis, issued a statement expressing its anxiety over the dangerous development of events for which, it said, the United Kingdom bore full responsibility, as it had refused to decolonize the islands. It too demanded an immediate end to the bloodshed.

The challenge for the Council was to produce a resolution calling for a cease-fire that would not be vetoed by the United Kingdom. The word from London was that despite the initial losses, Mrs. Thatcher remained determined to gain victory. There would be absolutely no cease-fire without Argentine withdrawal from the Falklands. Finally, on May 26, the Council adopted, as Resolution 505, a modified version of an earlier Irish draft, which called on me to enter into immediate contact with the parties to negotiate mutually acceptable terms for a cease-fire. I felt that the resolution was completely unrealistic, as it shifted to me a responsibility that could not be fulfilled. I warned that "when war is in full sway, as is now the case, the early achievement of a cease-fire and a return to negotiations is certain to be of extreme difficulty." I would nevertheless do all in my power to bring about peace.

Immediately following the Council meeting, I met with the British and the Argentine Representatives and requested that each obtain within 24 hours his government's definition of "mutually acceptable terms" for a cease-fire. In meeting with the British delegation, I spoke first privately with Sir Anthony Parsons and said candidly that the conditions he had stated at the Council meeting for a cease-fire did not leave much room for negotiation. If the United Kingdom maintained that position, I would have no choice but to go back immediately to the Council. Sir Anthony explained that he had spoken on the basis of written instructions from his government. He would report back to London immediately and try to "improve" those instructions to facilitate my task. During the subsequent meeting with the full delegation, Ambassador Parsons said that London would certainly be very interested in the Argentine reaction. If there was some movement, the British government would consider it very seriously. When I met with Ambassador Ros and the Argentine delegation, he said that he would transmit my request for his government's views to Buenos Aires immediately, but he implied that it was up to Britain to state its definition first.

It was evident that a cease-fire could be obtained only if the British position was modified. I concluded that London might be influenced in this direction if its closest allies urged it to show flexibility. Therefore, I asked the Permanent Representatives of France and the Federal Republic of Germany to convey my hope to their governments that they would make appropriate démarches to the British government. I then spoke by telephone with Secretary Haig in Washington and I asked if he, or perhaps President Reagan, might try to persuade London to be more flexible. The secretary said he shared my view that if there was no mutuality of force withdrawal a cease-fire would be difficult to obtain. He thought deployment of a peacekeeping force might permit simultaneity of withdrawals. He promised "to get busy" and do what he could. On the following day Haig called back to say that he had contacted London and the response had not been encouraging. There had, however, been some modification in the British position, and the response that Ambassador Parsons would be giving would perhaps not be quite as negative as expected.

The initial Argentine definition of acceptable terms for a cease-fire was: immediate unconditional cease-fire; discussions on mutually acceptable terms for a continuing cease-fire together with the modalities of an interim administration; and rejection of a unilateral Argentine withdrawal. These terms did not change greatly in the ensuing days. The British position was communicated to me in a confidential letter from Foreign Secretary Pym on May 27. The foreign secretary stated that a cease-fire would be acceptable to the United Kingdom if it was inseparably linked to the commencement of the withdrawal of Argentine forces and the completion of this withdrawal within a fixed period. Simultaneous withdrawal of British forces was not acceptable. The United Kingdom was willing to consider the possibility of eventual British withdrawal, but prior to that wished to achieve (1) repossession of the islands; (2) restoration of British administration; (3) reconstruction; and (4) consultation with the islanders. Once these four stages were completed, withdrawal of British forces might take place in the context of international security arrangements for the islands in which the United States must be included.

In presenting the letter, Ambassador Parsons drew particular attention to the reference to eventual security arrangements, which, he said, contained a "nuance" that offered a certain glimmer of hope. He said that I was still the "only horse in the race." On the way out of the building, he told the press that "we were still in business." I later sought further clarification of the implications of "international security arrangements." Ambassador Parsons's deputy, Marrack Goulding, who was later to become Under-Secretary-General in charge of peacekeeping in the United Nations, said only that Mr. Pym's message should be read in light of Prime Minister Thatcher's statement of May 27 in the House of Commons, when she had said that the objective of sending British forces to the Falklands was "first, repossession; second, the restoration of British administration; third, reconstruction, followed by consultation with the Islanders—a true consultation about their *wishes and interests for the future*" (italics added). A House Member asked the Prime Minister whether that was all she was going to say about the approaches made by the Secretary-General. She replied that "the talks with the Secretary-General will be about unequivocal withdrawal of Argentine forces in accordance with Resolution 502 as a condition for a cease-fire."

When the British terms for a cease-fire were received, it was clear that if the mounting intensity of the war was to be stopped and a devastating defeat for Argentina to be avoided, Argentina was going to have to agree quickly to comply with the terms of Resolution 502. I made tentative plans to fly secretly to Washington, where Foreign Minister Costa Mendez was attending a special session of the Organization of American States. Through him, I would make the situation entirely clear to the Argentine Junta and suggest as strongly as I could that unconditional Argentine withdrawal was the only sensible course. However, after I received a full statement of the Argentine position, I concluded that a meeting with Costa Mendez would be pointless. Foreign Secretary Pym, in a further personal letter to me on May 31, confirmed my expectation that the United Kingdom would find the Argentine position unacceptable.

The only remaining alternative was to present a UN proposal to the two parties, something on which the Secretariat task force had been working. So, late on the evening of May 31, one of my senior aides, Alvaro de Soto, who had been directly involved since the beginning of my mediation effort, went to the two missions and handed over a paper that foresaw an immediate cease-fire with the terms arranged on the spot by a UN representative, the interpositioning of UN observers between the opposing forces, the withdrawal of all Argentine forces with only a token British withdrawal and resumption of negotiations on an interim agreement under the Secretary-General's auspices. Argentina responded that it was prepared to begin discussions on this basis and that it was willing to withdraw its forces following agreement on a cease-fire. It accepted that Argentine forces would have to be withdrawn first in implementation of Resolution 502. I informed the British side of this immediately.

The British reaction to the terms I had put forward was negative. The British Permanent Representative said that London felt that at this stage of military operations, a cease-fire could be worked out satisfactorily only by the military commanders on the spot. It considered that the injection of UN Observers would complicate the situation. Argentina might use an "interposition force" to freeze the withdrawal process. It was unclear to the British what was meant by a "token" withdrawal of its forces. It could not accept the concept of parallel withdrawal. As for the resumption of negotiations, the British government considered the positions reached through my mediation no longer relevant. Substantive negotiations could begin only after life had returned to normal on the islands. I asked whether in the British view the idea of a UN administration was still workable. The ambassador replied that he could not say 100 percent no. The restoration of British administration did not necessarily mean restoration of the *status quo ante*. But any substantive negotiation would be inappropriate until the islanders had a chance after the fighting was over to think about their future. After further discussion of various modalities, Sir Anthony agreed to put the following ideas to his government: a UN political presence to help stage-manage a cease-fire that would be arranged between the field commanders; the gradual "trickling in" of UN forces at a late stage in the

Argentine withdrawal; and restoration of British administration on an interim basis, perhaps with a military governor rather than the "plumed hat" governor who would symbolize a complete return to the former status.

The Argentine response to these refinements of the earlier UN suggestions was equivocal. Buenos Aires still insisted on some form of British withdrawal and on the handing over of territory to the United Nations as Argentine forces withdrew. The British considered this unacceptable, since it constituted Argentine conditions for implementing Resolution 502. London also found the refinements that had emerged from the meeting with Ambassador Parsons unacceptable. A UN presence at cease-fire talks was simply not practicable. The idea of a British military administrator for the islands was not attractive. The presence of UN military observers was rejected.

After receiving this information on June 2, I reported to the Council that in my considered judgment, the positions of the two parties did not offer the possibility of a cease-fire that would be mutually acceptable. In the ensuing days several further efforts were made in the Council to bring about a cease-fire. On June 5 a draft resolution submitted by Panama and Spain calling for an immediate cease-fire and implementation of Resolutions 502 and 505 in their entirety came to a vote and was vetoed by the United Kingdom and the United States. Confronted by the impasse in the Council and the continuing escalation of the war, I decided to make a final attempt to bring an end to the fighting. On the same day I sent identical urgent messages to Prime Minister Thatcher and President Galtieri suggesting a specific plan for resolving the conflict between their two countries. Since further exchanges with the parties were not likely to be productive, I said that the plan should be considered as an integral whole. The plan foresaw the following:

- A truce on June 7 to be followed on June 9 by a meeting between the two military commanders, in the presence of a representative of the Secretary-General, for the purpose of agreeing on the modalities of a cease-fire that would come into effect on June 11.
- The commencement, simultaneously with the cease-fire, of the withdrawal of Argentine forces from the islands, to be completed within 15 days. Within this time frame, the United Kingdom would inform the Secretary-General of plans for the reduction of its forces in the region. In the light of these plans, the Secretary-General would undertake consultations on security arrangements under United Nations auspices.
- An undertaking by the parties to enter into negotiations, without prejudice to their rights, claims or positions, for the peaceful settlement of their dispute for completion by December 31, 1982. If the Secretary-

General determined that completion by that date was not possible, he could establish a new target date.

In presenting this plan, I emphasized that the conflict threatened to enter into an extremely dangerous phase that was likely to result in a heavy loss of life and would gravely prejudice any prospect for a settlement of the underlying dispute. To be effective, the plan would have to receive the unqualified acceptance of both governments by 8:00 P.M. on the following day, June 6. At 7:00 P.M. on the sixth, Sir Anthony Parsons conveyed to me the British government's rejection of the plan. It had decided that at this stage "it must confine itself to a single objective: Argentine withdrawal." The Argentine reply came late, but it was also negative. Henceforth the field would be left to the military, and the British forces triumphed fairly quickly.

I made one further attempt to bring the Argentine leadership to realize that the disastrous Falklands adventure should be stopped without further pointless loss of life. It was a far-out chance, but even a far-out chance had to be taken. Pope John Paul II, because of a commitment to visit England, had also found it necessary to schedule a visit to the Catholic faithful in Argentina. Through an extremely awkward chance of scheduling, he would arrive in Buenos Aires on June 9. It had been publicly emphasized that the Pope's sole intent was religious. He would not engage himself in any way in the conflict between Argentina and the United Kingdom. However, the Vatican secretary of state, Cardinal Agosto Caseroli, came to New York en route to Argentina, and we discussed the tragedy of the war then in progress in the Malvinas at length. It was clear to me that the only remote possibility of stopping the senseless loss of life was by making clear directly to President Galtieri that continuation of the war could only lead to further tragedy for Argentina. The only rational and humane choice was to accept the British terms for a cease-fire. This was the most patriotic thing he could do for his country. I knew that the Pope would be seeing the President.

I am not sure now whether it was Cardinal Caseroli or I who first suggested that the Pope might make this final effort with Galtieri. I believe it was in both of our minds, and once the idea was voiced, it was quickly agreed upon. The cardinal said that he would make arrangements for an envoy whom I would send to put the case directly to the Pope. I immediately called Alvaro de Soto to my office, and as the cardinal left I introduced him to "my envoy."

De Soto arrived in Buenos Aires on June 11, 1982. He immediately found that other members of the Pope's entourage did not share Cardinal Caseroli's view on the Pope's political intervention. De Soto was brusquely turned aside. Eventually he was received by the Pope and, in a show of devoutness, kissed the pontif's ring, as is customary. But it was too late, the Pope had already seen Galtieri.

I met with Mrs. Thatcher in London on June 14, the day that she announced the surrender of the Argentine forces. She told me that since word had been received from Argentina that they regarded hostilities as having de facto ceased, Britain was returning remaining prisoners of war and the bodies of Argentine troops killed in the fighting. All of the islanders who had been forced to leave at the time of the invasion had since been returned. There remained, however, a great deal of reconstruction to be done, and extensive supplies were on their way across the South Atlantic. I recalled that I retained a mandate under Resolution 505 and would at some point need to report again to the Security Council. Mrs. Thatcher replied that hatred of the Argentines in the Falklands was understandably intense. By its resort to force, Argentina had forfeited any prospect of greater friendship with them. She did not think there would be any possibility of negotiations for some time. She noted emphatically that the UN Charter emphasized self-determination, and this would be the key for the United Kingdom's future actions. Foreign Secretary Pym, who was also present, said that in due course it would be necessary to work toward normal commercial arrangements on such matters as transport with Argentina. Mrs. Thatcher expressed doubts in this respect. She was not entirely confident that the Argentine air force was committed to the cessation of hostilities. This was why she had decided not to lift the exclusion zone yet. I stated that I felt Argentina had made a tragic error in not accepting the agreement that the British had proposed on May 19. The Prime Minister concurred and stated that she had thought the proposal would be accepted.

During my ten years as Secretary-General, I would have many further occasions to meet with Margaret Thatcher. Along with Mikhail Gorbachev, I found her among the most impressive of all the world leaders with whom I had occasion to deal. Even when I did not agree with her—as for example, in her views on nuclear disarmament—I had to respect her intelligence and the logic of her argumentation. She was always fully in command of all subjects under discussion—she never used briefing cards—and certainly, in my experience, she was a careful listener. She seemed to respect dissent when it was well founded. I was especially pleased to find that she recognized and, I believe, respected my own impartiality, beginning with the Falklands War, when my South American origins might have caused her to doubt. The argumentation in her speeches at the United Nations was always cogent and coherent and reflected so clearly her convictions as to suggest that she had written them herself, or at least devoted a great deal of attention to them. Certainly she was firm in her views. Even in informal, off-the-record conversations, there was never doubt as to where she stood on any issue or, for that matter, on fellow leaders. I am convinced that Mrs. Thatcher would have preferred a peaceful solution in the Falklands/

Malvinas but only on the basis of unconditional implementation of Resolution 502, which her ambassador, Sir Anthony Parsons, had largely drafted.

The Argentine invasion of the Falkland Islands was the tragic and misguided act of an inept military regime, too ineffective and irresponsible to minimize the cost of its blunder even while that was still possible. The Argentine claim to the *Islas Malvinas* was not, however, an artificial issue invented by the ruling junta for its own political purposes. The belief among the Argentines that these treeless islands belong to Argentina is deeply held and practically unanimous. In rejecting and condemning the military leadership that embarked on this reckless adventure, the Argentine people did not reject the goal that the leadership was pursuing: the recognition of Argentine sovereignty over the islands. The most tragic aspect of the Falklands War was that it was fought at great human and economic cost without bringing any closer a resolution of the basic dispute between Argentina and the United Kingdom over possession of the territory. It could have been otherwise.

"If" is a fatal word in reliving history; yet in this one case I will use it. If there had been more time to pursue the course of mediation before the British task force drew so close to the islands that the military operation could not reasonably be reversed, I believe diplomacy could have triumphed over war. I have no criticism of the tactics followed by Secretary Haig, as far as I am familiar with them, in seeking to settle the dispute between two countries with which the United States had close friendship and extensive mutual interests. After his own failure, the secretary, without rancor, gave me support (albeit very little information) in my mediation effort, as did President Reagan. My only reservations about the secretary's endeavor are the time that it took and his failure to keep me informed of developments during his mediation.

Two critical points in my good offices endeavor opened the way to a peaceful settlement. The first was the decision of Argentina not to make agreement dependent on recognition of Argentine sovereignty over the Falklands; the second was British acceptance of an interim administration of the Falklands under a UN Administrator. UN administration would mean the flying of the blue UN flag as the symbol of the Falklands government. Had this been accepted, Argentina would have accomplished at least half of what it sought: British administration of the islands would have been removed at least temporarily and, with it, a substantial advantage for the British in the projected negotiations on the ultimate status of the islands. The shortness of time compelled the British to present their proposed agreement, which incorporated to a gratifying extent wording that I had put forward and that had been discussed and agreed in the proximity talks, as an ultimatum with a short deadline. Had it not been presented in this form—had there been more time in which I myself might have gone to Argentina to increase the leaders' understanding of the value of the proffered agreement—I believe the British draft that emerged from the New York proximity talks could, with minor cosmetic changes, have brought peace. Time, had it been available, would have been a precious asset in the quest for a peaceful settlement. The shortness of time was a fatal enemy. Time, healer and tyrannical master, has now been sufficient to heal the wounds of war but not yet to bring two friendly countries to a reasonable accommodation on a dispute that has already endured for centuries.

FIFTEEN

THE PATH TO PEACE IN CENTRAL AMERICA

THE FIRST LATIN AMERICAN HEAD OF STATE whom I received as Secretary-General was Daniel Ortega Saavedra, who then, in March 1982, had the title of "Co-ordinator of the Governing Junta of National Reconstruction of Nicaragua." Nicaragua had decided to take its complaints about U.S. intervention to the Security Council. The *commandante* said that Nicaragua's sole purpose in doing so was to enlist international support against greater intervention in Central America. He contended that he had knowledge of U.S. plans for military action that would include the participation of forces from Argentina, Colombia and Honduras. I told him that the U.S. Secretary of State, General Haig, had informed me the United States was disposed to negotiate directly with Nicaragua. I hoped that Commandante Ortega's speech to the Security Council would contribute to the prospects of a negotiated solution.

This was the first of many meetings with Daniel Ortega, the last of which, as I have recorded in chapter 10, was while I was waiting to see Saddam Hussein on the eve of the Desert Storm action. He always struck me as a man remarkably lacking in charisma. He showed none of the intellectual vigor and forceful personality of Fidel Castro. He may have had strong qualities as a military leader (although I believe his brother was more impressive in this regard), but I could not imagine him as a popular politician. While UN staff members in Managua expected a Sandinista victory when free elections were held in Nicaragua, it did not surprise me that he lost. Like so many observers, he, too, surely expected victory. Even so, he deserves great credit for having agreed to the elections and for having given up power peacefully. The intent of the economic and social reforms that he introduced, especially land reform, was constructive. Failure was the result of misguided implementation and of the disregard for human rights that so often accompanies revolution.

At the time of Commandante Ortega's visit, a resolution was drafted in the Security Council in response to Nicaragua's complaint of U.S. intervention. The wording was restrained, making no mention of the United States, but appealing to "all Member States" to refrain from "the direct, indirect, overt or covert use of force against any country of Central America and the Caribbean." The United States nonetheless vetoed the resolution. Its representative, Charles Lichtenstein—who was later to express his satisfaction at the prospect of the United Nations' disappearing across the East River "into the sunset"—said that the resolution was unacceptable because the text was not supportive of either the Security Council or the Organization of American States (OAS). This statement was ironic since the United States during the entire Reagan Administration was opposed to active UN involvement in Central America. The Sandinistas, for their part, were opposed to OAS involvement because they considered it dominated by the United States. As a result, for a long time both the OAS and the United Nations were excluded from an active role in resolving the Central American problems.

THE CONTADORA PROCESS BEGINS

In January 1983 the foreign ministers of Mexico, Venezuela, Panama and Colombia met on the Panamanian island of Contadora and, in an agreed note, expressed deep concern over foreign interference in the conflicts of Central America. They emphasized the need to remove such external factors and called on the countries of Central America to reduce tensions and establish a basis for friendly relations and mutual respect through dialogue and negotiation. Subsequently the ministers undertook a series of consultations with the five Central American governments—Costa Rica, El Salvador, Guatemala, Honduras and Nicaragua—with the purpose of encouraging negotiations to achieve peace in the region. This marked the beginning of the Central American peace process. The Security Council was content to express support, in Resolution 530, for the Contadora agreement and to request that I keep the Council informed of developments in the region, something that I was already doing. The General Assembly also expressed support for the Contadora group and urged it to persevere in its peace efforts.

By September 1983 the Contadora foreign ministers had agreed on a "Document of Objectives" consisting of a list of lofty principles, including pluralism, social justice and respect for human rights. This was followed in mid-1984 by the Contadora Act on Peace and Cooperation in Central America, which the group presented to the five Central American states for signature and

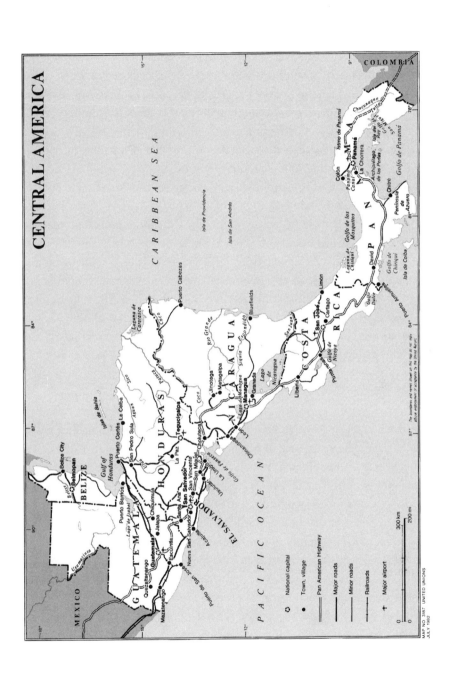

CENTRAL AMERICA

MEXICO

BELIZE
Belize City
Belmopan

GUATEMALA
Guatemala
Quezaltenango
Mazatenango
Escuintla
Jalapa
Chiquimula
Santa Ana
Nueva San Salvador
San Salvador
San Vicente
San Miguel
La Unión

EL SALVADOR

HONDURAS
Puerto Barrios
Puerto Cortés
San Pedro Sula
La Ceba
Tegucigalpa
La Paz
Choluteca

NICARAGUA
Puerto Cabezas
Jinotega
Matagalpa
León
Chinandega
Managua
Granada

COSTA RICA
Liberia
San José
Cartago
Limón

PANAMA
Colón
Panamá
La Chorrera
David
Puerto Armuelles
Chitré

COLOMBIA

CARIBBEAN SEA

PACIFIC OCEAN

Gulf of Honduras
Gulf of Mexico

Lago de Izabal
Laguna de Caratasca
Islas de Bahía
Isla de Providencia
Isla de San Andrés
Río Grande
Coco
Río Coco
Lago de Managua
Lago de Nicaragua
Golfo de Nicoya
Golfo de los Mosquitos
Laguna de Chiriquí
Golfo de Chiriquí
Isla de Coiba
Golfo de Panamá
Península de Azuero
Archipiélago de las Perlas
Istmo de Panamá
Panama Canal
Golfo Dulce

○ National capital
● Town, village
Pan American Highway
Major roads
Minor roads
Railroads
✈ Major airport

0   300 km
0   200 mi

MAP NO. 3187 UNITED NATIONS
JULY 1982

The boundaries and names shown on this map do not imply
official endorsement or acceptance by the United Nations.

ratification. The Contadora ministers spent the next year and a half seeking, without success, the agreement of the five Central American states to this document. In the process the early momentum evaporated. By mid-1986 the Contadora process had reached a dead end.

The Contadora initiative was a noble and much-needed effort to bring peace to Central America, but it suffered three serious weaknesses. First, it was an external effort, which the Central Americans resented as interference. Some Central Americans suspected—I think incorrectly—one or another of the Contadora countries of not being impartial. More important, while the need in Central America was to resolve internal conflicts, the Contadora proposals provided no means for incorporating guerrilla groups into the negotiations. The effort was flawed by its very ambition. By seeking to deal in the same context with the conflicts in Nicaragua, El Salvador and Guatemala as well as the socioeconomic problems of the entire region, the Contadora group overreached the limits of the possible. Finally, the United States, while expressing lukewarm support for the Contadora negotiations, clearly viewed them with suspicion, fearing that they would lead to agreements that were overly favorable to the Nicaraguan Sandinista regime. This attitude did not change when the United Nations became directly involved in seeking a solution. For the Reagan Administration, the Sandinista government was an instrument of Havana and Moscow and had to be eliminated.

A UN/OAS INITIATIVE

In June 1983 I met in New York with representatives of the Contadora group and emphasized the importance of persisting in their efforts. I suggested that if the military situation continued to worsen, I might feel compelled to raise the problem in the Security Council under the provisions of Article 99 of the Charter. I knew, though, that such a step could have little effect, given the negative attitude of the United States at that time toward UN involvement. When the Contadora foreign ministers subsequently called on me in New York to review the situation, as they did from time to time, they were reluctant to speak of the more sensitive aspects of their activities. They, too, patently did not want the United Nations to become very deeply involved in what they considered their affair. So as the Contadora effort foundered, the United Nations remained largely passive.

The meetings that I had during these years with the heads of the Central American governments were more productive. I was particularly impressed by the President of El Salvador, José Napoléon Duarte. He seemed to me to be an honest and committed man who, in trying to establish a pluralistic government in his country, found it necessary to resist both the attacks of his enemies and the embrace of his friends. In talking with me in the summer of 1984, Duarte said that he had had to establish clearly with the U.S. Administration that he would not accept the existence of three governments in his country, his own, that of the U.S. Agency for International Development (USAID) and that of the military.

The seemingly endless violence that had engulfed Central America was much on my mind as I was hospitalized in the late spring of 1986 for heart surgery. While I was still in the hospital, Alvaro de Soto, my highly skillful and trusted aide of Peruvian nationality, came to see me with a proposal. He was aware of my sense that something should be done to overcome the impasse in the peace process. Moreover, we shared the perception that the advent of Mikhail Gorbachev to leadership in the Soviet Union could have a significant impact on regional disputes. We felt there might now be an opportunity for the United Nations to play a more useful role in Central America. With this in mind, de Soto suggested that I seek the agreement of the Secretary-General of the OAS, Jao Baena Soares, on a joint UN/OAS initiative to reinvigorate the peace process.

As simple and direct as this suggestion sounded, I recognized its hazards. As I recuperated, I reviewed them repeatedly: the Contadora powers were jealous of their initiative and would not welcome extra partners in the search for peace; the United States would likely be unenthusiastic about UN involvement; the Central American countries themselves, other than Nicaragua, had not asked for UN involvement; the OAS traditionally had been reserved, to say the least, about UN activities in "its territory"; and, finally, I had no mandate from the Security Council to act and probably would not receive one if I asked.

On the other side were three considerations of overriding importance. The first was the simple fact that the United Nations and the Secretary-General as its representative have a moral responsibility to act in the interest of peace if there appears to be any chance of success. Second, a new impetus was obviously needed in the Central American peace process. Finally, joint action with the OAS could lessen suspicion that I was making an overly ambitious bid and reassure those who were suspicious or jealous of the United Nations as an actor in the Central American drama.

Alvaro de Soto went to Washington in May 1986 and began a series of conversations with Baena Soares, with whom he had long been on friendly terms. It took almost six months to bring him along. He had only recently become OAS Secretary-General and brought to the post an optimism that experience had withered in his predecessor. He is a highly intelligent man whose friendship I greatly value. In one respect, however, he followed in the tradition of earlier OAS leaders. He was almost pathologically concerned that the OAS not be seen as playing a secondary role to the United Nations. The OAS loyalists never forgot that the OAS (in an earlier form) predated the United Nations. Even with Latin American colleagues at the head of both organizations, some of the traditional tensions remained.

Once Baena Soares was persuaded of the desirability of a joint initiative, he came to New York, where we met first with the Central American representatives, since it was their countries that were directly involved. In this case, contrary to my usual custom, I took no prior soundings—not with the Permanent Members of the Security Council or with the Contadora group or with the Central American parties themselves. I knew that to do so would be to invite objections. Our general approach harked back to the technique I had used in the Falklands/Malvinas crisis as described in chapter 14. We simply outlined to the Permanent Representatives the services that the United Nations and the OAS could offer "to complement and consolidate what has developed until now within the Contadora framework." The two organizations could establish an appropriate civilian or military presence to observe the borders, the withdrawal of forces, the dismantlement of military bases and the demobilization of armed forces. They could verify agreements on the reduction of arms, provide protection and assistance for refugees, observe elections and referenda and investigate allegations of infringement of human rights.

All five Central American countries replied positively to the offer of assistance. We next saw the representatives of the Contadora countries. Their reaction was decidedly cooler. They asked if I had a mandate to make this offer, a question to which they knew the answer. Very shortly thereafter, as a way of reinvigorating the peace process, the Contadora group expanded to include the so-called Support Group, consisting of Argentina, Brazil, Peru and Uruguay. The Contadora members also may have seen this as a way of protecting their turf from UN invasion. However, almost immediately after the establishment of the Support Group, the foreign minister of Peru called me and said that the eight foreign ministers of the Contadora and Support groups were organizing a joint excursion to the five Central American countries to "give them a good jolt." He invited Baena Soares and myself to join them. I had considerable doubts as to the wisdom of appending myself to this kind of excursion, which I suspected would be more of a sideshow than a productive enterprise. Still, as it provided a legitimate opening for the United Nations and the OAS to become directly involved in the peace process and to further the initiative that we had taken in New York, Baena Soares and I agreed to join the group.

The U.S. reaction was immediate and extremely negative, imputing far more importance to the enterprise than I felt it deserved. The U.S. Representative, Jeane Kirkpatrick, called on me and rehearsed Washington's view that the Sandinistas were seeking to consolidate a repressive, Marxist-Leninist regime aligned with Cuba and the Soviet bloc. In response, the United States was following a two-track policy: negotiations and pressure, including military pressure. While the United States had supported the Contadora process, it was concerned that under the influence of Mexico and a few others, Contadora was tilting in favor of Nicaragua. It was in this context, Ambassador Kirkpatrick said, that the United States was particularly concerned over my participation, along with the OAS Secretary-General, in the visit to Central America. She also took the occasion to express Washington's reservations about the joint initiative on Central America that Secretary-General Baena Soares and I had taken in New York. It was feared, she explained, that our action could be exploited by the Sandinistas "by seeming to support inadequate piecemeal solutions." The United States felt that it should have been consulted before the initiative was taken and before we had agreed to go on the trip to Central America. Reading from her position paper, the ambassador said that the American concern had already been expressed in the OAS Permanent Council. The United States believed that Baena Soares had understood the point. Lest I should miss it, the ambassador left with me the text of her talking paper.

The mission to Central America consisted of three different levels—the foreign ministers of the Contadora countries, the foreign ministers of the Support Group and the two Secretaries-General. I suggested to the group that the three levels should be thought of as the three letters *PAZ*, standing for peace. I made clear that I was going on the mission primarily because of Security Council Resolution 350, which supported Contadora and requested me to keep the Council informed on developments in the region. I saw the main value of the trip as affording a firsthand opportunity to take the political temperature among the Central American leaders. For this purpose I would need to differentiate myself from the eight foreign ministers. Therefore I arranged for a separate plane and, with Alvaro de Soto accompanying me, I managed to arrive in most of the capitals a few minutes before the foreign ministers' plane. In each capital I insisted on a separate appointment with the President. Of these meetings, the only one of real interest was with President Oscar Arias Sánchez of Costa Rica. While he did not reveal to me his peace plan for Central America, he hinted rather clearly that he had a proposal in mind. He emphasized repeatedly the close relationship between democracy or pluralism and peace in the region. The Contadora proposals included democratic government among their objectives. Arias's thinking clearly went beyond this rather abstract concept to the necessity of measures to ensure the development of pluralistic governance *within* the states of the region. This was to be a central element in the Arias peace plan that was announced less than a month later.

My talks during the trip with the other presidents revealed no departure from their long-established positions that had prevented agreement on the Contadora peace plan. They were decidedly less than overwhelmed by the uninvited visit of the eight Latin American foreign ministers. I thought it could spur some change if I stated my pessimistic assessment of the situation openly and candidly. Therefore, on the last day of the trip in Mexico City, I gave a separate press conference in which I expressed my assessment that the necessary political will was lacking in the governments concerned to complete the peace process at this time.

THE ARIAS PEACE PLAN

In an extraordinary way the Arias peace plan, which the Costa Rican President announced at a meeting of the Central American presidents in San Jose on February 15, 1987, restored a dynamism to the peace process that led ultimately to success. As he dramatically put it, "Peace has reclaimed its hour . . . and will bring an end to the remaining dictatorships in the region."[1] This was all the more remarkable since, with all his good qualities, his deep belief in democracy and respect for human rights, his personal honesty and his true commitment to peace, Arias was not well liked by his Central American colleagues. He tended to preach to them in a patronizing way and was seen as having an ego that exceeded his intellect. Most irritating to the others was his tendency to seek the limelight. Nonetheless, they recognized, as did the broader international community, that Oscar Arias, through the formulation and timing of his plan, brought peace closer in Central America. For this reason the Nobel Peace Prize that he received was well deserved.

The Arias peace plan incorporated the principles of the Contadora plan. It went further, however, in defining the procedures for bringing an end to civil conflicts within the countries of the region and in setting time limits for their implementation. It provided in specific terms for amnesties, dialogue by governments with internal opposition groups, cease-fires and, most significantly, a verification commission to be established by the UN Secretary-General composed of the foreign ministers of the Contadora and Support groups. The plan foresaw that pacification had to go hand in hand with democratization, thus recognizing that fundamental social problems had to be addressed in restoring a durable peace in the region. It was taken over with very few changes in the Guatemala Procedure, better known as Esquipulas II, that was signed by the Central American Presidents on August 7, 1987. This agreement was a turning point since now Central Americans took over their own peace process, a process in which the United Nations would become a major participant.

ESQUIPULAS II

The verification body foreseen in the Arias plan and established in the Esquipulas II agreement was called the International Verification and Follow-up Commission (CIVS). Its intended purpose was to monitor the implementation of the Esquipulas agreement. Unfortunately, it was not a success. As a first step in this enterprise,

Secretary-General Baena Soares and I sent a technical mission to the region to assess what would be needed to monitor the implementation of the various stages in the agreement. Then, in early January 1988, a CIVS mission was sent to assess the political and social situation in each of the Central American countries. Alvaro de Soto was my representative and served as de facto chair of the team. In each capital the group held informal hearings in their hotel accommodations with representatives of all segments of society—from the armed forces to human rights organizations. The witnesses spoke quite freely. The resulting CIVS report, even though watered down from the first draft, gave a bleak portrayal of social and political conditions in the Central American countries, with the exception of Costa Rica. The governments were intensely displeased with the report. As de Soto reported to me, they were furious about being opened up for dissection without even the benefit of anesthesia. The result was the prompt disbandment of the International Verification and Follow-up Commission.

The United Nations' major role in the Central American peace process began in 1989. In February of that year the five Central American Presidents in the Costa del Sol Declaration took three important steps. They requested their foreign ministers to arrange technical meetings to establish, with the participation of the United Nations, a mechanism for verification of the Esquipulas II security commitments. The government of Nicaragua announced its decision to call general and free elections, to amend its electoral law and to invite international observers, in particular the Secretaries-General of the United Nations and the OAS, to verify that the electoral process was genuine at every stage. Finally, the five Presidents agreed to draw up a joint plan for the voluntary demobilization, repatriation or relocation of members of the Nicaraguan resistance and their families. They requested technical advice from specialized bodies of the United Nations. In response, the Security Council, in Resolution 637 of July 27, 1989, officially welcomed Esquipulas II and other agreements made by the five Presidents and lent its full support to the Secretary-General "in his mission of good offices in the region." After seven years, and well into my second term, I finally had a mandate from the Security Council with regard to Central America.

The affirmative vote of the United States on this resolution marked a major shift in U.S. policy. It was reported to me that until this time, the US Permanent Mission had standing instructions to keep the United Nations out of Central America. This was certainly the impression I gained in the various conversations I had with Secretary Shultz and President Reagan. They always expressed general support for the Contadora process and for a negotiated settlement, but they clearly put little credence in the possibility of serious negotiations with the Sandinistas. The attitude of President Bush and Secretary Baker was quite different. In talking with them, I gained quickly the impression that they wanted to see the Central American problem settled. The U.S. Congress had long been resistant to continued U.S. assistance to the Contras, which no doubt had been a troublesome problem for Jim Baker when he was President Reagan's chief of staff. By the time of George Bush's inauguration, it was clear, too, that the Cold War was coming to an end—that there was no need to fear the extension of Soviet influence in the Western Hemisphere through Nicaragua.

These considerations surely influenced the readiness of the Bush Administration to accept an active UN role in the most sensitive aspects of the peace process. Some of my staff referred to the positive U.S. vote on Security Council Resolution 637 as the end of the Monroe Doctrine. This was surely a hyperbole. The United States continued to exercise a strong unilateral influence on the peace process. Moreover, U.S. representatives not only monitored UN actions closely, they also frequently cautioned me and my staff on the necessity of maintaining complete impartiality in our mediation efforts, clearly fearing that we would not. Still, there can be no question that the change in U.S. policy that this vote represented was of major importance in the ultimate success of the peace process.

NICARAGUA

The five Central American Presidents rightly saw that the conflicts in the region were inter-related. Peace required that the political and social problems in each country be tackled as part of the overall effort that had begun with Contadora. Primary concern was directed, however, to Nicaragua and El Salvador, since that was where internal wars were raging and where external powers were most directly involved. Resolution of the conflict in Nicaragua was identified as the key to progress in El Salvador and elsewhere. Moreover, the other central American countries saw the leftist, authoritarian Sandinista regime, with its close ties to Cuba and the Soviet Union, as a threat to the region. Therefore, the requests for UN assistance emanating from the region related first of all to Nicaragua. They covered three broad objectives: the holding of free elections in Nicaragua; verification of compliance with the provisions of Esquipulas II; and demobilization, disarmament, repatriation and reintegration of the Nicaraguan Contra resistance.

The three were pursued simultaneously. In the process the United Nations entered new and unknown terrain, which gave me personally no little concern. What was accomplished in restoring peace to the region and how it was done constitute a seminal chapter in the United Nations' history. More flexible limits were established for the involvement of the United Nations in domestic developments within a Member State. New approaches were developed for bringing governments into negotiations with insurgent groups. Perhaps most important, the United Nations accepted and carried out a responsibility to strengthen democratic institutions and to monitor compliance with accepted human rights norms within a country. Article 2, paragraph 7, of the UN Charter, which prohibits intervention "in matters which are essentially within the domestic jurisdiction of any state," gained a new and broad interpretation.

Enlargement of the UN's Peace-Making Role

Just five months after I informed the Government of Nicaragua that the United Nations would provide a mission to observe the electoral process in that country, the Central American Presidents, in accordance with the Costa del Sol Declaration, invited the Secretaries-General of the UN and of the OAS to establish an international commission to support and verify their joint plan. Also, the Presidents requested that the United Nations establish an Observer Group to verify the cessation of aid to irregular forces and insurrectionist movements and the nonuse of the territory of one state for attacks against another. These actions would take place while preparations for the Nicaraguan elections were under way.

I welcomed these decisions as marking a new and hopeful phase in finally resolving the conflict in Nicaragua and in contributing to peace in the region as a whole even as I recognized the complexity of the responsibilities that were being placed on the United Nations. I immediately initiated consultations with Secretary-General Baena Soares on operational plans for the verification commission, which had the title International Support and Verification Commission (CIAV). The consultations were not easy—first, because of the complexity of the mandate, and second, because of Baena Soares's ever-present concern to ensure that the OAS and the United Nations had equal status.

CIAV was asked to carry out the following functions in support of the Presidents' joint plan[2]:

- Consult with the Nicaraguan government and the other Central American governments, with the Nicaraguan resistance and with humanitarian organizations.
- Visit the camps of the Nicaraguan resistance and of refugees in order to make known to them the benefits of the joint plan and organize the distribution of humanitarian aid.
- Take as much responsibility as possible for the distribution of food and medical supplies in the resistance camps.
- Carry out negotiations for the reception by third countries of those who did not wish to be repatriated to Nicaragua.
- Receive arms and military supplies from the Nicaraguan resistance and keep them in custody until the five Presidents decided on their disposition.

- Take the repatriated persons to the places of final settlement.
- Establish reception centers capable of providing basic services, including family counseling for the repatriates.
- Open follow-up offices to guarantee the security of repatriated persons.

CIAV was to submit a report on the implementation of the five presidents' joint plan within 90 days.

These tasks were for the most part unprecedented. One, the collection of weapons and matériel from the Contras, was unrealistic for an unarmed, largely civilian operation. I pointed this out in my report to the Security Council, noting that this task should be entrusted to military units equipped with defensive weapons. I also indicated that some of the tasks entrusted to CIAV would be best undertaken by special programs and agencies within the UN system.

OAS Secretary-General Baena Soares and I agreed that CIAV should be officially established on September 6, 1989. Arduous negotiations were required to work out a division of labor. Alvaro de Soto, who was the main negotiator, first proposed that there be a functional division of work, based on comparative advantage. This was not acceptable so we ended with a geographic distribution. The OAS would be responsible for the work to be done within Nicaragua, and the United Nations would take on those tasks that were to be accomplished outside of the country. As it turned out, this left the lion's share of the work to the OAS, which was probably for the best since the U.S. Government, which was deeply involved in the fate of the Contras, had greater trust in the OAS than in the United Nations. The UN High Commissioner for Refugees agreed to oversee the repatriation of the Nicaraguan resistance; this was accomplished with commendable efficiency.

It was just at this time, in October 1989, that the Soviet Foreign Minister, Edouard Shevardnadze, visited Nicaragua and reiterated the Soviet decision to interrupt arms deliveries to that country. He expressed the hope that this Soviet restraint would encourage a similar U.S. restraint with regard to other countries in the region. This move was especially welcome at this point since the ground conflicts in both Nicaragua and El Salvador had intensified. An estimated 2,000 Contras had moved across the border into Nicaragua, and the government canceled the cease-fire that had been in effect since March of 1988. Fighting was renewed. Almost simultaneously in El Salvador, the *Frente Farabundo Martí para la Liberación Nacional* (FMLN) initiated a major offensive against government forces. It was evident that arms were continuing to flow from Cuba to Nicaragua and from there to the FMLN in El Salvador. Despite the progress that was being made toward elections in Nicaragua, the whole Central American peace process appeared to be in jeopardy. It was clear to me that if the situation was to be saved, it would be necessary to engage the three parties who had great influence on the course of events but who were not part of the peace negotiations: the United States, the Soviet Union and Cuba. President Arias, during a long conversation I had with him in November 1989, agreed with my assessment of the danger of the situation and of the desirability of bringing Cuba—which would be assuming a seat on the Security Council at the beginning of 1990— into a constructive role in the negotiations.

Acting in my behalf, de Soto conveyed my thinking to representatives of Cuba, the United States and the Soviet Union and asked for their reaction. I also expressed this idea to Vice President Dan Quayle during a meeting in New York in December 1989, suggesting that by involving Cuba in the negotiating process, it might be possible to bring an end to the transfer of arms from Cuba to Nicaragua and the FMLN. A positive symmetry (as was being sought under similar circumstances in Afghanistan) should be sought under which no country would send arms to any of the parties. I referred to Foreign Minister Shevardnadze's statement that Soviet arms shipments would be halted.

The Vice President acknowledged that Shevardnadze had also recently told President Bush and Secretary Baker that the Soviet Union would stop arms shipments to the region. The fact was, however, that arms continued to flow in. Mr. Quayle did not respond to my idea of bringing the three powers into the negotiations. His interest with regard to Cuba was to obtain a commitment from me that I would issue a report critical of the human rights situation there. I said that if requested to do so, I would make a report. I noted, however, that at the time I was engaged in delicate negotiations with the Cubans to obtain the release of several political detainees. Just a month after my meeting with Vice President Quayle, the U.S. Permanent Representative, Tom Pickering, delivered a letter from Secretary Baker sharply criticizing my failure to take action with regard to the human rights situation in Cuba. I had, in fact, a few days earlier sent a letter to the President of the Human Rights Commission suggesting that the commission's report should be followed up with a full investigation of human rights violations in Cuba. Ambassador Pickering confided to me that the text of the Secretary's letter had been "put together" prior to my action and the "tone" did not reflect the U.S. Government's appreciation of my efforts to "open up the process." However, the United States continued to feel that I should issue a public report on my dialogue with the Cubans. "But," he said, "we agree to disagree." This illustrates a problem with which I was frequently confronted. The Secretary-General can quite often intervene confidentially with a regime and gain the freedom, or at least an improvement in conditions, of individual political prisoners. Yet a critical public report can jeopardize his ability to perform this useful service. A balance has to be drawn as to which course can produce the greater benefit for those suffering from a deprivation of their human rights.

On the eve of their meeting in San Isidro de Coronado on December 12, 1989, I wrote to each of the five Central American Presidents to express my alarm at the intensified conflict in the region. I stressed the obvious necessity of reviving the cease-fire in Nicaragua and restoring conditions for a productive dialogue between the government and the FMLN in El Salvador. Beyond that, I offered to be of any assistance I could in establishing a mechanism "appropriate to the Central American context" involving those external powers that could assist in the realization of peace and democracy in the region. The Presidents, in their San Isidro communiqué, accepted this offer and requested that I make the "necessary connections" directly into the peace process."[3] Shortly thereafter I gave separately to the US, Soviet and Cuban ambassadors in New York an informal paper requesting their reaction to the establishment of the mechanism I had suggested. As relevant models, I listed the advisory committee established to assist the Secretary-General in connection with the UN Emergency Force (UNEF I) at the time of the Suez War and the participation of the United States, the Soviet Union and Cuba in peace talks on Angola.

Only the Soviet Union was forthcoming in its response. The United States contended that since Cuba had not agreed to the commitments entailed in the Esquipulas II Agreement to refrain from giving aid to irregular forces or insurrectionist movements, it should not be given a role in the peace negotiations. Moreover, the United States had contacts with Cuba and very active relations with the Soviet Union and saw no advantage to be gained from my proposal. Cuba considered the agreement reached by the Central American Presidents at San Isidro (like Esquipulas II) to be hostile to the FMLN. It would cooperate with the Secretary-General but not within the framework of those agreements.

Notwithstanding these reservations, all three governments stated their support for my efforts. Thereafter, I felt free to maintain contacts with the three countries in the specific context of their roles in the peace process. This did not prove particularly productive in dealing with the conflict in Nicaragua, but it produced useful results in bringing an end to the fighting in El Salvador.

ONUCA

The United Nations Observer Group in Central America (ONUCA) was established by Resolution 644 of the Security Council on November 8, 1989. Its purpose was to verify the cessation of aid to irregular forces and insurrectionist movements and the nonuse of the territory of one state for attacks on other states. The Nicaraguan government, always wary of the influence of the United States in the Security Council, had wished that the General Assembly should be responsible for authorizing the establishment of ONUCA. I insisted, however, that action by the Security Council was essential if we expected to get the necessary troops from Member States. The Nicaraguans then suggested that we use only civilians. Brian Urquhart, who at that time was still in charge of UN peacekeeping operations, maintained that would be impossible for the intended purposes, and we told the Nicaraguans as much. We also took a firm line that because of the sensitivity and complexities of ONUCA's tasks, full control must be in the United Nations' hands. We could not, in this case, share responsibility with the OAS. I wrote to Secretary-General Baena Soares and invited him to assign a representative from the OAS Secretariat to ONUCA Headquarters so that we could maintain close liaison. No OAS representative ever appeared. ONUCA was an entirely UN operation.

ONUCA's verification mission can accurately be described as mission impossible. It consisted initially of only 260 unarmed military observers, 1 fixed-wing aircraft and 12 helicopters with their crews, a naval unit of some 8 small vessels plus medical personnel and a UN civilian staff of just over 100 people. The border terrain between the Central American states is heavily forested and largely impenetrable. The territory to be observed was far too extensive to be covered by 260 observers. The most serious weakness, however, was ONUCA's lack of an intelligence capacity, since intelligence gathering was considered to be strictly within the domestic jurisdiction of the Central American states.

ONUCA did not detect a single instance of cross-border arms shipments or personnel movements in violation of the Esquipulas II undertakings. (The FMLN leaders in El Salvador subsequently told Alvaro de Soto that they had continued to bring in large quantities of weapons during the ONUCA operation.) Still, I am convinced that even in this first phase, ONUCA served a useful purpose. For one thing, without its deployment, the other parts of the peace process could not have gone forward. Moreover, the "blue helmets" moved widely, if ineffectively, around the area, sometimes on horseback. There were even a few peacekeeping boats patrolling the rivers. The people in the region thus became accustomed to the presence of UN military personnel and saw evidence of the impartiality of the UN mission. For their part, UN personnel were afforded an opportunity to learn a good bit about local politics and culture. This would prove valuable later in connection with the peace settlement in El Salvador.[4] But the most important purpose ONUCA served was to establish an important precedent for the control by the United Nations of developments *within* a country's sovereign jurisdiction—in this case, control over the utilization of its territory. I believe this was justified—and could only be justified—by the threat that misuse of national territory for attacks against another state could pose to peace in the region. I stated to the Security Council when ONUCA was authorized that it would be an innovative operation that would require vigilant monitoring. Council members, and I believe the larger membership as well, were aware of the significance of the ONUCA undertaking as a further reinterpretation of the charter prohibition against interference in matters within the domestic jurisdiction of states.

In December 1989 the Central American Presidents in a declaration signed at San Isidro de Coronado, Costa Rica, asked that the mandate of ONUCA be expanded to include verification of any cessation of hostilities or demobilization of Nicaraguan resistance forces. Such agreement was reached only following the Nicaraguan elections when representatives of the newly elected President and the Contras met in Toncontin, Honduras, on March 23, 1990. It was understood that the United Nations would not only observe the demobilization but also provide security for the demobilization centers and collect the arms and military equipment surrendered voluntarily by the Contras. In response to my recommendation, the Security Council agreed, in Resolution 650 of March 27, 1990, that for this enlarged task, ONUCA should be expanded and its military component authorized to carry light arms.

While, in its first phase, ONUCA served a largely symbolic purpose, in this second phase its function was both real and effective. The demobilization process was divided into two parts. First, the Contras would be called on voluntarily to gather at designated demobilization areas in Nicaragua, Honduras and the border region of Costa Rica. There they would surrender their arms, matériel and uniforms and be demobilized from their units. Once this was accomplished, their repatriation or, if they were already in Nicaragua, their resettlement would be the responsibility of CIAV. This worked surprisingly well. By chance, Venezuela had an infantry battalion ready for deployment to the Western Sahara. As it was not needed there, it was free and ready to assume a large share of the oversight of the Contra demobilization.

Five "security zones" were established within Nicaragua where the resistance forces were to assemble and surrender their arms and equipment. (Two additional zones were established for the demobilization of the Misquitian Indian resistance.) The voluntary demobilization was supposed to begin on April 25 and be completed by June 10, 1990. There were immediate complaints, however, from resistance leaders of violations by the Nicaraguan army of the agreements reached between the Contras and the government. On my express instructions, the Chief Military Observer was able to clarify satisfactorily most of these complaints, but demobilization went very slowly until May 30. On that day President Violeta Barrios de Chamorro, "Commander Franklyn" of the Nicaraguan Resistance and Cardinal Miguel Obando y Bravo reached a new agreement that responded to the publicly stated concerns of the resistance. After that the demobilization proceeded smoothly and was completed not on June 10, as originally scheduled, but on June 29. Despite the slight delay, under the conditions prevailing in Nicaragua, it was a remarkable achievement.

In the course of the successful operation, there was one unfortunate incident. The Joint Plan of the Central American Presidents provided that the demobilization and repatriation of the Contras must be entirely voluntary. This provision, with which I was in complete agreement, was understandably of major concern to the United States as the Contras' principal sponsor. CIAV, under the terms of the five Presidents' request, was to visit the Contra camps for the purpose, inter alia, of "making known the achievements and benefits of the Plan"—in other words, the desirability of demobilization and repatriation. In October 1989 a CIAV mission visited a Contra camp at Yamales, Honduras, for this purpose. The senior UN member was Francesc Vendrell, a highly intelligent and articulate staff member from Spain whom I knew to be left-leaning in his political orientation and who had long been viewed with some suspicion by the U.S. Government.

Vendrell and his OAS colleague, a Peruvian diplomat named Hugo de Sela, were greeted by a Colonel Bermudez, who was later murdered behind the Intercontinental Hotel in Managua. The colonel suggested that Vendrell and de Sela talk to some of the resistance men to assess their attitudes. The CIAV representatives were then escorted to a nearby field where, to their surprise, they were confronted with some 3,000 armed Contras in formation along with a substantial press contingent. Bermudez gave an impassioned speech to the soldiers in which he considerably misrepresented the purpose of CIAV. He then invited the OAS and UN representatives to speak. De Sela, who spoke first, was quite circumspect, but Vendrell, as he reported to me later, decided to use this unique opportunity to try to persuade the Contras to accept the provisions of the Joint Plan. He devoted most of his remarks to an explanation of CIAV and its purposes, but at the end he added some thoughts that proved explosive in Washington and contributed to the suspicion there that the United Nations was less than impartial with regard to Nicaragua. He was quoted very prominently the next day in the Washington Post—more or less accurately, he later confirmed to me—as having told the Contras that they were patriotic and brave Nicaraguans who had fought because they believed the things they were told. However, they could stay in Honduras only as long as the Honduran Government permitted. They should not remain the instruments of an anachronistic policy that had been abandoned by the government that had helped them. His clear implication was that the Contras had lost their raison d'être, were about to be sold out by the U.S. Government and had little choice but to return to Nicaragua. While this may have been sound advice, it was extremely unpolitic under the circumstances.

The U.S. Secretary of State, Jim Baker, called me immediately after the press reports appeared and in unrestrained terms told me that what the UN representative had said was extremely harmful to the U.S. efforts to arrange a settlement in Nicaragua. He hoped I would promptly disassociate the United Nations from Vendrell's remarks. I found Vendrell's performance in this case insensitive, to say the least, and I asked him to return to Headquarters immediately to clarify the situation. However, I did not think it appropriate publicly to disavow a dedicated staff member who thought he was following the mandate given CIAV by the Central American Presidents. I therefore had my press spokesman say that the comments attributed to Mr. Vendrell in the press were selected from an impromptu statement. The comments had given rise to misunderstandings concerning the rigorously impartial position of the United Nations, something that I regretted.

Two days later the U.S. Assistant Secretary of State for International Organization Affairs, John Bolton, came to see me and delivered a letter from Jim Baker in which Baker shared with me his "deep concern about reports that some officials of the United Nations are attempting to interject an approach which is contrary to goals we all share—the achievement of democracy in Nicaragua." He concluded the letter by expressing the hope that "the mischaracterizations of the problems and potential solutions to those problems can be corrected promptly. The United Nations must be, and be seen to be, impartial in its conduct if there is to be success."

Something like the Vendrell affair was probably inevitable because of the contradictions between the Joint Plan, which expected demobilization of the Contras to take place in 90 days, and the American position that democratization in Nicaragua was a prerequisite to demobilization. Neither the United Nations, nor the United States, nor the Nicaraguan resistance was consulted when the five Central American Presidents set up the plan. In carrying out its assigned task, the United Nations was bound to look as if it were favoring to some extent the position of the Sandinista government. The suspicion that the Americans felt toward Alvaro de Soto, whom I had by then appointed as my Personal Representative for the Central American Peace Process, was to carry over to the negotiations for peace in El Salvador in which he was the principal mediator.

Monitoring the Electoral Process

Having announced in March 1989 its intention to hold free elections, the Nicaraguan Government followed up quickly by requesting the United Nations and the Organization of American States to monitor the electoral process. Given my training in international law and my commitment to the principle of nonintervention in the domestic affairs of states, initially I was hesitant to recommend compliance with this request. Previous requests to monitor elections in Member States had always been refused, the United Nations' having only assisted in the conduct of elections as part of the decolonization process. To oversee the electoral process in a sovereign state would take the United Nations into uncharted and, I thought, potentially treacherous waters. However, in the course of extensive discussions with Secretariat colleagues, I came to the conclusion that in this case, at least, the action was justified and desirable. Still, I preferred to articulate both the pros and the cons to the General Assembly before putting forward a specific proposal.

I accordingly sent a letter to the President of the General Assembly, who at that time was the foreign minister of Argentina, Dante Caputo, stating first the traditional UN position against monitoring elections in sovereign states. I then pointed out that the present case was somewhat different, since the request had been made within the context of an international agreement and could be seen as part of the Central American Peace Process. Successful elections in Nicaragua, properly verified, could contribute to the goals defined in Esquipulas II that the General Assembly had endorsed. I thought the members of the Assembly should have time to consider this question before taking a decision. I waited two months. Then, as no Member expressed any objection, I submitted to the General Assembly a proposal for the establishment of a United Nations Observer Mission for the Verification of the Electoral Process in Nicaragua (ONUVEN). A number of stipulations included in my proposal have since become part of UN doctrine on election monitoring. First of all, the United Nations would need to observe the whole electoral process, not just the balloting on election day. Second, there must be broad public support for UN involvement. Third, the United Nations should have the opportunity to make recommendations as to the legislative procedure to be followed. Finally, there should be ample reason to believe that a fair environment—a level playing field—would be assured for the elections.

After receiving the approval of the General Assembly, I informed the government of Nicaragua in early July 1989 that I was prepared to send a mission to monitor the electoral process in accordance with its request. This was the first time that the United Nations had monitored an election in a sovereign state. The precedent was thus established for a practice that has now become commonplace, no longer requiring such special circumstances as existed at that time in Central America. I now see this as a favorable development in an era when, fortunately, democracy is very widely accepted in principle as the desirable form of government. However, the conditions that were defined for the action in Nicaragua should always be maintained.

ONUVEN carried out its mission in three phases from August 1989 through the holding of the elections on February 25, 1990. The first phase covered the organization and mobilization of the political parties; the second encompassed the electoral campaign proper; and the third the elections themselves. I thought it of the utmost importance to have as my Special Representative for the verification of the elections in Nicaragua a person of high prestige and credibility and a reputation for fairness. Should the Sandinistas win in a fair election, which many of my colleagues thought likely, it would be essential that the assessment of the Special Representative be credible in Washington. With these considerations in mind, I asked Elliot Richardson, the eminent American lawyer and former attorney general and secretary of defense, if he would take on this task. He accepted and, as I fully expected, carried out his responsibilities admirably. He gained the trust both of the Sandinista government and of the Union Nacional Opositora (UNO), the opposition coalition, while strictly monitoring the conduct of both.

By the second stage of the ONUVEN operation, there were 39 UN observers in Nicaragua monitoring the electoral campaign. There was evidence that at times the government was misusing its power to influence the outcome of the elections. Elliot Richardson was in frequent contact with government officials, including President Ortega, to bring this to a halt. He urged Ortega, in particular, to instruct those in charge of radio stations across the country to stop slanting the news. There were complaints from UNO that the government was preventing funds from the Center for Democracy in the United States from reaching it and that government trucks were being used for Sandinista rallies. Richardson pursued all of these problems with the Sandinista authorities as they arose. He found, however, that UNO was more interested in making their charges public—and in communicating them through their own channels to Washington—than in producing evidence that could be used to eliminate improper government actions. Vice President Dan Quayle, when he called on me in December 1989, told me that through his channels he knew that the Sandinistas *had* disrupted the electoral process. Opposition rallies had been harassed. He was certain that the other Central American Presidents were worried. "Be aware!" he counseled me. I reminded him that Elliot Richardson was present in Nicaragua as my Special Representative and was keeping a close watch on the conduct of all the parties. Prior to the elections in Namibia, there had been speculation and complaints that the process would be unfair. As it turned out, the elections had been completely fair. I assured the Vice President that we would be following the same procedures in Nicaragua.

The Proposed Visit of a U.S. Presidential Commission

A particular problem arose with the U.S. government in connection with the proposed travel of a presidential commission including members of Congress from both parties to observe the elections. The Nicaraguan government refused to agree to the commission's entry. Elliot Richardson had learned in Nicaragua that there had been discussions with the assistant secretary of state for Latin America, Bernard Aronson, on a possible agreement that could serve as a basis for normalization of relations between the United States and Nicaragua even before the Nicaraguan elections. This would be dependent on clear evidence that the electoral process was heading in the direction of a pluralistic, democratic system with a guaranteed role for the opposition and assurance that the Nicaraguan government would cut off all assistance to the FMLN, the insurgent group in El Salvador.

When he returned to Washington, Richardson checked with Secretary of State James Baker to see if this idea reflected his thinking. Baker indicated that he was open to any understanding with the Nicaraguan government provided two conditions were met: that the government accept the bipartisan commission that President Bush had appointed to observe the Nicaraguan elections and that several American diplomats who had been declared *persona non grata* be allowed to return to Managua. When Richardson returned to Nicaragua, he discussed this with President Ortega who, in Richardson's words, was paranoid on the subject of the presidential commission. He was convinced that the commission was a key element in a Bush/Baker plan to eliminate the Sandinista government just as Manuel Noriega had been eliminated in Panama. It was not possible to dissuade Ortega from this fear even when it was pointed out that with the elections already scheduled to be the most observed in history, one more commission could hardly make any difference.

Elliot Richardson raised this problem with me to see if some compromise solution could be found. He was fearful that the elections would be discredited in Washington if the presidential commission was excluded. Following suggestions from several congressmen, I had already invited interested countries to place their parliamentary delegations to the elections under the ONUVEN umbrella. It was agreed that we should see if it would be possible for the presidential commission to travel to Nicaragua under the aegis of the United Nations. President Ortega replied that Nicaragua would not invite any delegation from the U.S. Congress. However, it had no objection if the United Nations, the OAS and the Carter Center, which had already announced that it would send a team headed by former President Jimmy Carter, wished to invite congressmen from the United States and parliamentarians from other countries to observe the elections. This arrangement was not acceptable to the U.S. government so the bipartisan presidential commission did not go to Nicaragua, although a number of American congressmen were present in other delegations. Had the Sandinistas won the election, the absence of the presidential commission might well have caused a good many in Washington to challenge the outcome. Given the UNO victory, the problem did not arise.

To monitor the voting, 207 ONUVEN observers traveled throughout Nicaragua. They visited 2,155 polling stations in 141 of the 143 municipalities. The OAS carried out a similar program, and many other observers were present as well. As soon as the polling stations closed on February 25, 1990, the UN observer team in Managua, using only one desktop and two laptop computers, made a rapid "quick count" of the outcome. By ten o'clock that evening Elliot Richardson knew that UNO had won. He immediately informed former President Carter and OAS Secretary-General Baena Soares and suggested that the three go together to inform President Ortega of the outcome, which would not be known from Nicaraguan sources until the following morning. Although the UN and OAS teams had pooled incoming information on the balloting, Baena Soares had insisted, in his desire always to maintain parity with the United Nations, that the OAS team make its own separate count. As this was not completed until much later, it took a good bit of persuasion to get the OAS Secretary-General to accept the reliability of the UN count. When this was done, the three senior statesmen called on Ortega, gave him the news and spent almost two hours with him. In what amounted to a cathartic session, they told him that he had lost and that for the good of the country he should swallow hard and accept it.

Finally Ortega said he would accept his defeat but that he would have to persuade his people to go along with good grace. He said that he needed one thing: Violetta Chamorro, the victor, must be persuaded not to go out and crow. He, Ortega, needed a few hours—until the following morning—to get his people in line. The three eminent observers spent the rest of the night shuttling between Mrs. Chamorro and President Ortega. Mrs. Chamorro did as she was asked and Ortega persuaded not only his Sandinistas but also the *Sandalistas*—the sandal-wearing supporters from many Western countries—to accept defeat peacefully. Thanks to this effort, the transition teams from the two sides met the next morning in a constructive mood to begin preparations for the transfer of power. There is no doubt in my mind that the UN quick count and the actions of Elliot Richardson, along with President Carter and Secretary-General Baena Soares, were, along with the monitoring of the electoral process, of crucial importance in the orderly return to democracy in Nicaragua. ONUVEN reported to me, and I reported to the General Assembly, that the electoral process had been "impartial and fair throughout" and that the elections had been conducted in a highly commendable manner.

EL SALVADOR: A VICTORY WITH NO LOSERS

The Esquipulas II Agreement foresaw a comprehensive solution for all the conflicts then raging in Central America. The fiercest and most deadly of these was in El Salvador, where for more than a decade insurgent forces had been waging war against the government. By 1987 the various insurgent groups had joined in a loose alliance called the *Frente Farabundo Marti para la Liberación Nacional* (FMLN). The freely elected government in San Salvador was headed first by a Christian Democrat, José Napoleon Duarte, and subsequently, during the difficult negotiations that led eventually to peace, by Alfredo Félix Cristiani-Burkard of the right-wing Arena party. In September 1989 the Salvadoran government and the FMLN, meeting in Mexico City, reached an agreement to initiate a dialogue aimed at ending the conflict in El Salvador through political means. Shortly thereafter I met with President Cristiani for the first time; he had come to New York for the annual meeting of the General Assembly. Knowing that the President came from a political party that had been under the dominant influence of extreme right-wing elements, including senior officers in the Salvadoran army, I was doubtful of the role he could play in bringing peace to his country. However, I was immediately impressed by Cristiani's evident commitment to achieving an end to the war that had brought so much devastation to his country. In my many subsequent conversations with the President, some of which were quite difficult, I never had reason to doubt his personal determination to reach an honorable settlement with the FMLN. Facing continuing opposition from the more extreme elements, he unquestionably had serious problems in holding his party together as the negotiating process went forward. That he succeeded was perhaps the most important factor in arriving at a settlement because only the Arena party could have brought the powerful right-wing elements, including the Salvadoran military, to accept an agreement that contained provisions that were distinctly not to their liking. Cristiani is a man of the right but not an ideologue. In substantive meetings that Cristiani had with me and with my Special Representative, Alvaro de Soto, his wife Margarita was usually present. A very clear-sighted woman, she had substantial and, I think, constructive influence on the course of events.

Having said this, I must add that Cristiani was initially somewhat distrustful of direct UN involvement in the negotiation process, feeling that the United Nations, especially de Soto, was overly sympathetic to the FMLN position. As I have said, this was a suspicion shared by the Americans. The suspicion was not difficult to understand. The FMLN leaders were young, intelligent and with a good sense of humor. Their principal negotiator, Joaquín Villalobos, was especially impressive. I always enjoyed my meetings with them, and I think de Soto developed a genuine affection for them. This was far less true of the government delegation. Cristiani followed the tactic of sending hard-line representatives with little flexibility in their instructions, so that at the crucial moment he, Cristiani, could step in as the reasonable person who could find a solution. This is a common technique but not one to inspire mutual affection between the delegation and the mediator.

A meeting in Costa Rica followed the Mexico meeting between the government and the FMLN. The United Nations was invited to be present as a witness (along with representatives of the OAS and the Catholic church) but not as a participant. It was decided in Costa Rica to pursue a two-track course under which the various political problems would be dealt with separately from negotiations on a cease-fire. The cease-fire would follow resolution of the political problems. This was in line with suggestions made earlier in Mexico by the FMLN and was to complicate negotiations enormously.

Despite the agreements reached between the government and the FMLN, the ground war intensified. The FMLN launched a major new offensive in November, penetrating, for the first time, the capital. All nonessential UN personnel had to be evacuated. Also in November, a number of Jesuit priests were murdered. Widely believed to be an act of the Salvadoran army, this prompted calls for remedial action from all over the world along with simultaneous appeals for an end to the FMLN offensive. In discussing the critical situation caused by that offensive with Alvaro de Soto, I concluded that it could be useful to consult directly with the FMLN leaders, partly to assess their intentions and partly to give them a sense of participation in the peace process and in responsibility for its outcome. I decided that de Soto should hold a quiet discussion with the FMLN commanders. Knowing the reluctance of the U.S. Government to issue visas to FMLN leaders (whom Washington categorized as terrorists), we decided it would be best to hold the meeting in Canada. The Canadian government was cooperative and on a snowy December 6, 1989, de Soto met in Montreal with the FMLN leadership. The talks took place in the building of the International Civil Aviation Organization, which provided a UN umbrella.

The FMLN offensive was still raging, but the leaders, in their comments, showed that they were clearly thinking of the period after the offensive was over. They thought that by then President Cristiani would probably be ready for serious negotiations. In their view, the Contadora group (which they had always seen as hostile toward the FMLN) had run out of steam. The same applied to the OAS. Secretary-General Baena Soares, who had come to the region after the offensive began, was, in their words, "a spent shell." They insisted that they were serious about negotiating a settlement and that the United Nations could help. They wanted, however, to know more about how the United Nations functioned, particularly about the dynamics of the Security Council. Rather ingenuously, they asked what the Secretary-General could do in extending his good offices and how verification could be implemented once a settlement was reached. De Soto returned with the impression that these were bright young men who were interested in achieving peace but who knew very little about the ways of diplomacy.

The five Central American Presidents, in their San Isidro declaration, requested the UN Secretary-General "to do everything within his power . . . to ensure the resumption of the dialogue between the Government of El Salvador and the FMLN, thereby facilitating the dialogue's successful conclusion."[5] A few days later President Cristiani called to express personally his support for my direct involvement in the Salvadoran problem. Commandant Shafik Handal, who served as spokesman for the FMLN, wrote to me on December 18 expressing the same sentiment but with many more details. Handal stated that it had been established in the meeting with Alvaro de Soto in Montreal that diplomatic mediation, in the strict meaning of the words, was needed to resolve the El Salvador problem. This would mean preliminary work by the Secretary-General with the parties concerned to delineate the area of possible political agreement before proceeding to the stage of direct negotiations. The FMLN favored the involvement of other governments with interests in the area, but warned that this would not guarantee satisfactory results. While respecting the position of Cristiani as President, the FMLN believed that the inclusion of other political parties in the negotiations would be necessary to produce a stable agreement.

With these decisions by the five Presidents, the government of El Salvador and the FMLN, the United Nations moved from the position of helpful bystander to central actor in the search for peace in El Salvador. Much of the mediation in different meeting places in the region was done by my Special Representative, Alvaro de Soto, assisted mainly by Secretariat staff members Francesc Vendrell and Blanca Antonini. De Soto did a superb job, combining imagination and courage with intuitive diplomatic skill. His considerable self-confidence never faltered under the criticism and suspicion to which he was subjected at times by sources in Washington and San Salvador. His loyalty and respect for me were impeccable. He never failed to seek my guidance or to keep me fully informed on the course of negotiations.

Despite the many other developments that demanded my attention during these years of expanded UN responsibilities, I gave very high priority to El Salvador, where it seemed to me a newfound potential of the United Nations was being severely tested. I was in daily touch with de Soto when he was in the field. When, in the course of the next months, difficulties arose, the United States and the Soviet Union repeatedly urged me to take personal charge of the negotiations. I explained that I was continuously involved through my Special Representative but felt it wisest to reserve my personal participation for times when the most senior representatives of the two sides were directly involved. Time was to prove the wisdom of this approach.

UN-Led Negotiations Begin

In September 1989 the FMLN had issued a "Proposal for democratization, a cessation of hostilities and a just and lasting peace in El Salvador." A cease-fire of short duration would occur after agreement on a number of immediate economic, social and political reforms, including the "self purification and professionalization" of the armed forces. With the achievement of a cease-fire, which would not entail disarmament of the FMLN forces, the FMLN would enter the legal political life of the country as a political party. After the cease-fire, negotiations would take place on a definitive end to hostilities, the principal requirements for which would be fundamental constitutional and electoral reforms, the establishment of a single national army and elimination of the special security forces, and the redirection of US military aid into a fund for economic reconstruction. For the next year, negotiations centered (and frequently faltered) on this agenda.

In January 1990, I had a most constructive meeting in New York with President Cristiani. The President accepted that in the extension of my good offices, I or my representative would be directly involved in the negotiations. I told the President that if the negotiations were to succeed, the respective military establishments would have to be represented in the two delegations. I assured him that the FMLN would have to do its part in preparing for the resumption of negotiations and in fostering an atmosphere of restraint and moderation. President Bush and Secretary Baker discussed the resumption of negotiations with President Cristiani the next day; subsequently Baker called to express the strong support of the U.S. government for my efforts to promote a negotiated solution of the war.

Arranging the first meeting under my auspices took three months. In mid-March the FMLN announced that it would cease attacks against a certain number of civilian targets. In return, the government dropped all preconditions to the negotiations. De Soto had repeated meetings with FMLN representatives in Mexico to resolve their problems. Finally, on April 4, 1991, I presided over a meeting between a government delegation headed by Oscar Santamaria and an FMLN delegation headed by Shafik Handal. It was largely pro forma. The two sides signed a paper on which we had listed various procedural points that would guide the conduct of the subsequent negotiations. They would be carried out either through direct dialogue between the two negotiation commissions with UN participation or through the Secretary-General or his Representative. Both sides agreed that the political parties and other representative social organizations in El Salvador had an important role to play in achieving peace and that each would maintain adequate contact with them. It was provided further that the Secretary-General could maintain contacts with Member States that might contribute to the success of the process through their advice and support. Strict confidentiality was to be observed.

The following month it was agreed in meetings in Caracas that sufficient progress on substantive issues would be achieved by mid-September to warrant proclamation of a cease-fire. The government would have to bring about reforms concerning respect for human rights, the judiciary and—most difficult—the military. Members of the FMLN set this high price since they saw a cease-fire as a major concession on their part that would require them to disengage from the cities, in which they had been free to move since their offensive the previous year. President Cristiani, for his part, had to deal with elements in his party that were less than enthusiastic about a negotiated solution to the conflict. By this time senior military officers had been included in the government negotiating commission, which introduced an element of realism that, I thought, could only benefit the process. But it was quite clear that the military would have to be "purified" and those bearing responsibility for the egregious crimes committed against the civilian population punished. The United States held the key to bringing the military under control through the large military assistance that it was providing.

At this point, in June 1990, the U.S. Mission in New York informed us that troubling reports had been received that the FMLN was planning another large offensive. I was asked to warn the FMLN that such a move would only strengthen the hard-liners on both sides of the table who did not want peace. De Soto had picked up similar reports in Mexico City, where he was meeting with the FMLN. He thought the rumors might be an FMLN tactic aimed at gaining concessions from the government. Even if it were only a tactic, however, it was dangerous; and a new offensive would be even more so. He advised that I warn both Soviet and Cuban representatives that if the FMLN undertook a new offensive or took other actions in violation of its previous commitments, I would find it very difficult to continue in the good offices role that had been endorsed by the Security Council. I promptly took this action and authorized de Soto to give the same warning to the FMLN directly.

U.S. Assistant Secretary of State Aronson, with whom Alvaro de Soto was in continuing contact, complained forcefully that the "troglodytes" in the FMLN were placing overly heavy demands on the government, particularly with regard to the military. He contended that if there were to be a comparable purge in the FMLN, no one would be left for the next round of negotiations. Secretary Baker wrote in mid-July to express his concern about actions of individuals who opposed a negotiated settlement, including the murdering of civilians (which he attributed largely to the FMLN). I replied that I had made clear both to the FMLN and to the government that I could continue my good offices role only if the two sides acted in good faith. Without naming either Cuba or the Soviet Union, I told the Secretary of State that others with whom I had discussed the problem had made their views known to the appropriate party.

In the midst of this threatening situation, the parties reached a notable and unprecedented understanding on human rights. In an agreement signed on July 26, 1990 in San Jose, the concept of which had been suggested by my Special Representative, the Cristiani government and the FMLN undertook immediately to avoid all acts and practices that threaten the life, integrity, security or liberty of individuals. The agreement also covered the legal procedures to be followed for the release of political prisoners. This remarkable six-page document amounted to a comprehensive pledge of unrestricted respect for human rights. It provided, moreover, for the establishment of a UN mechanism to monitor compliance with the accord once a cease-fire came into effect. The two sides were not able to agree on measures to reform and reduce the Salvadoran military, the second major requirement before a cease-fire could be realized. Nevertheless, I felt that the United Nations should make preparations to carry out the monitoring responsibility once circumstances permitted. I sought and obtained the concurrence of the Security Council to establish a small preparatory office in El Salvador to assess the local situation and make plans for carrying out the monitoring task in a systematic way. This was the first step toward the groundbreaking monitoring of human rights compliance within a Member State that the United Nations would undertake in due course.

Following the San José agreement, Secretary Baker wrote to me stating that the government of El Salvador was ready to accelerate the pace of negotiations. He suggested that the interval between the negotiating rounds might be reduced. Earlier I had asked that the United States facilitate the issuance of visas for FMLN representatives, since it would simplify the negotiations if they could be held at UN Headquarters in New York and would make my direct participation easier. On this the secretary remained cautious. The United States, he wrote, would be as accommodating as possible in handling FMLN visa requests, but it remained unable to grant blanket approvals in advance.

Unfortunately, the agreement on human rights did not lead to a wider breakthrough. The next round of talks was a failure and for some months a state of quasi impasse prevailed. The central issue was reform of the military, which included the sensitive issue of the dismissal of a number of senior officers. Other problems also made progress difficult. Parliamentary and local elections were scheduled for March 1991. It was widely believed that Cristiani's Arena party would benefit if a cease-fire was achieved by the target date of September 15. Some of the opposition parties, none of whom were included in the negotiating commission, had an interest in depriving Arena of this advantage and may have worked separately with the FMLN to delay matters. The FMLN did not consider the Arena party as truly representative of the Salvadoran population and, like the opposition parties, was not eager to see Arena get full credit for a cease-fire.

A further complicating factor was the continuing distrust of the UN good offices team by President Cristiani and the more rightist elements in his party and by influential officials in the U.S. Government. At the beginning of October, Bernard Aronson and Tom Pickering had a three-hour meeting with de Soto during which Aronson laid out in detail U.S. complaints about the way the United Nations was handling the negotiations. Mr. Aronson said that as the

Secretary-General had suggested, the U.S. government had given signals to the Cubans that it was willing to cooperate with them for the purpose of peace. It had now given visas to the FMLN. But it was frustrated that the Secretary-General was not playing the role of mediator for which he had been empowered by the Geneva agreement. The Secretary-General or de Soto should put forward proposals and force the parties to accept or reject them. De Soto responded that in the exercise of good offices, proposals could be put forward usefully only if both sides were receptive to receiving them. He had, however, long been making quiet suggestions to the two sides in behalf of the Secretary-General.

Mr. Aronson summarized the U.S. position in five points: (1) the Secretary-General should play a more visible role, stressing the urgency of the situation; (2) a strict calendar for nonstop negotiations should be put into effect, possibly, as de Soto had suggested, with the participation on the FMLN side of Joaquín Villalobos; (3) a multiparty negotiation commission, again as de Soto had suggested, should be established, "if the endgame scenario was in place"; (4) enhancement of de Soto's role as a mediator capable of threatening the parties that they would pay a price for not accepting his efforts; and (5) support from the Security Council as necessary.

I met with President Bush and Secretary Baker in my office in New York on the same day as Aronson's conversation with de Soto. When the discussion turned to El Salvador, I pointed to the conference room next door and said that the FMLN had assured me in that very room that they would not leave the negotiating table and would honor the unilateral commitments undertaken prior to the Geneva conference. Something more was needed, however, to get the negotiations back on track. I noted that I had discussed the problem recently with President Cristiani, who, I felt, was a good and honest man. He was making every possible effort despite his difficulties with the army and the right wing. I had suggested to him the idea of including some of the opposition parties in the government delegation in order to lend credibility to the government's position.

President Bush asked Secretary Baker to review the American position. Jim Baker's first concern was the U.S. Congress. It was essential to know what Congress was going to do about withholding military assistance from El Salvador. He agreed that Cristiani was a good man who had problems with the army and with the right wing of his party. Cristiani knew that he "must show something on the Jesuits." Baker felt that the FMLN was stalling. His hope was that if Congress attached strings to military assistance to El Salvador, the assistance could be releasable in the event the FMLN left the negotiating table. The United States had had good talks with Mexico, Venezuela and Spanish Prime Minister Felipe Gonzales. It had asked the Soviets several times to persuade the Cubans to stop funneling arms to the FMLN and encourage them to continue negotiating. Baker knew that some had suggested the atmosphere might improve if the United States were to engage in a dialogue with the FMLN. (De Soto had indeed been proposing this, with my concurrence.) But, Baker said, the United States would not talk to them until they declared a cease-fire and even then, "it would be up to President Cristiani to decide if he wished us to do so."

At the end of October, Alvaro de Soto, on my behalf, transmitted to the government of El Salvador and to the FMLN a working paper on the armed forces as a means of bringing negotiations forward on this most difficult subject. The paper covered the principal points at issue—"purification," immunity, special security forces, the notorious Atlacatl ready reaction battalion, death squads and verification by the United Nations. The government reaction was cautiously positive. While there were parts that it could not accept, it appeared ready to use the paper as a basis for negotiation as long as it remained strictly confidential. The FMLN said that it was definitely prepared to accept the working paper as a basis for negotiations. It insisted on making many formulations more precise, however, and when these changes were communicated to the government, the government contended that the FMLN had transformed the character of the working paper in a way that it could not accept. The government suggested that the Special Representative nevertheless continue discussions separately with the two sides looking toward the possibility of a round of direct confidential talks in December.

As was becoming a fateful habit, just at this relatively hopeful juncture the FMLN on November 21, 1990, initiated a new military offensive. Early the next morning the FMLN representative at the United Nations, Dr. Rafael Moreno, informed de Soto that the offensive would not be centered in the capital, as had been the case the previous November. The objective was to mount attacks in various parts of the country, including San Salvador, but in such a way as to minimize the effect on the civilian population. The action, limited in time and intensity, had the political aim of warning that military activity would increase if there was no progress in the negotiations and of demonstrating that the FMLN had not become weak, as some thought. The military aim was to respond to the increasing government attacks on areas under FMLN control.

However limited the intent of the FMLN action might have been, obviously it could have given ammunition to those on the government side who were opposed to a political solution; at the least, it was likely to delay the negotiating process. I quickly issued a statement expressing my concern and recalled earlier unilateral promises by the FMLN to refrain from certain categories of actions in order to strengthen confidence in its political will and in the Secretary-General's good offices. I addressed a fervent appeal for restraint, noting that a real possibility still existed of ending the conflict, of addressing its underlying causes and of attaining a positive transformation of

Salvadoran society. At the same time I instructed Alvaro de Soto to return to Mexico City in order to intensify negotiations, particularly on questions related to the armed forces. Just as he arrived there I received a letter from the FMLN Command stating that the working paper on the armed forces distributed earlier by de Soto could provide the basis for rapid progress in the negotiations. They could be completed by the end of December and agreement reached on all the other questions on which a cease-fire was conditional by January 31.

I believed that in these volatile circumstances, it could be helpful to build upon the most hopeful development that had until then occurred, namely the agreement between the two sides on respect for the human rights of the population. As I stated earlier, the United Nations was to monitor the implementation of this agreement. While making preparations, I had been reluctant to initiate field action in the absence of a cease-fire, given the dangerous conditions that persisted throughout the country. Various governments had urged that an Observer Mission be sent, however, and the General Assembly, in document A 45/15, had requested me to "continue to afford the fullest possible support to the Central American Governments in their efforts to consolidate peace, especially by taking the measures necessary for the maintenance, establishment and effective functioning of the appropriate verification machinery." I now decided that despite the dangers involved and the unprecedented nature of such monitoring action, an observer mission should be dispatched. Such a mission could discourage attacks on civilians and, I hoped, give a much-needed boost to the negotiating process. Late in December 1990 I informed the Security Council that I intended to send to El Salvador as soon as possible a technical mission to advise me on the conditions for establishing a United Nations Observer Mission in El Salvador (ONUSAL). I stated that as a first step, the human rights component of ONUSAL should be established as soon as the necessary preparations had been made on the ground, even in the absence of a cease-fire.

The technical mission went to El Salvador on March 31, 1991. It reported to me that there was a strong and widespread desire in the country that the United Nations should commence its verification of the Agreement on Human Rights without awaiting a cease-fire. Explicit assurances of support were received from the government, the military and security authorities and from the FMLN. On this basis I recommended to the Security Council that the human rights component of ONUSAL be dispatched without delay.

ONUSAL achieved remarkable results in monitoring human rights. Although it was deployed in conditions that amounted to continuing civil war, ONUSAL representatives were able to travel freely in territory controlled by both sides. Human rights violations dropped markedly to the point that few complaints were received. The results were unquestionably favorable for the

Salvadoran people and served, very directly, to bring the conflict to an end, even though a cease-fire was not reached until after further months of difficult negotiations. It was and remains an intrusive operation, going far beyond the monitoring of elections. Since it was undertaken with the consent of the lawful government and of the other major elements in the political life of El Salvador, I do not believe it constituted an infringement on the country's sovereignty. It accords with those provisions of the UN Charter that clearly define respect for human rights as a matter of international concern. Assistance such as that provided by ONUSAL can be very important in the restoration of stability and security in countries where civic order has failed.

Election Monitoring

The government of El Salvador requested the OAS and the United Nations to monitor the parliamentary and local elections that were held in March 1991. The OAS agreed. Despite considerable pressure from member states, including both the United States and the Soviet Union, I declined the request. Since the United Nations had just undertaken this task successfully in Nicaragua and Haiti, my response requires an explanation. As I have said elsewhere, I long felt that UN monitoring of elections in member states was inconsistent with the Charter provision prohibiting UN interference in the domestic affairs of states. But when improper conduct of elections could have adverse international consequences, the assistance of the United Nations in ensuring their fairness and honesty was warranted. As will be recalled, in Nicaragua I had suggested criteria that should govern the provision of electoral assistance by the United Nations. I did not consider that the situation in El Salvador met all these conditions, especially in the absence of a cease-fire, when parts of the country were not under government control. I explained this in detail to President Cristiani and also in letters to Secretary Baker and Foreign Minister Shevardnadze, who had written jointly to urge that the United Nations provide electoral assistance. If I were faced with the need to make such judgments now, I still would find valid guidance in the criteria I defined when the United Nations was faced with multiple requests in the last years of my mandate.

U.S. Criticism of UN Mediation Intensifies

In the early months of 1991, U.S. criticism of the UN role in ending the El Salvador conflict threatened to overshadow the mediation efforts in which we were deeply involved. On February 1, 1991, the *New York Times* carried an article that was highly critical of Alvaro de Soto's conduct as my Special Representative. Most damaging was the assertion that de Soto favored the

FMLN and pushed its positions while showing hostility toward the legitimately elected government. The criticism was attributed to unnamed "administration officials." Clearly it came in good part from the Bureau of Inter-American Affairs in the State Department. Bernard Aronson and his deputy, Joseph Sullivan, had been candid in expressing their dissatisfaction with UN efforts when talking directly to de Soto.

Ambassador Pickering telephoned me on the morning the *Times* article appeared to tell me that Secretary Baker was much disturbed by the story and wanted me to know that the U.S. Government supported my efforts and those of my Special Representative. We learned, however, that the Secretary had told the Spanish foreign minister that he was disturbed by de Soto's "tilt toward the FMLN." It also came to my attention that Deputy Assistant Secretary Sullivan had told the Soviet embassy in Washington that I and my Special Representative were supporting the FMLN in the negotiations. In the same time frame Secretary Baker wrote letters to the foreign ministers of the countries serving as my "friends" in supporting the negotiations in which he said that the position of the government of El Salvador was highly flexible and that the FMLN had hardened its position. He requested his colleagues, the foreign ministers of Spain, Mexico, Colombia and Venezuela, to approach the Secretary-General and his Representative to urge them to redouble their efforts to achieve an immediate cease-fire.

Washington's attitude was undoubtedly heavily influenced by information that it was receiving from its many contacts in the Salvadoran army and government, some of whom had no interest in making the concessions that would be required if the negotiations were to succeed. What worried me was that Washington's support of such allegations and insinuations could easily undermine the utility of de Soto and of myself as mediators in the very difficult and distrustful relationship between the government and the FMLN precisely at a time when there were serious indications of progress. I wrote to Jim Baker after the *Times* article and asked that the State Department spokesman publicly disassociate Baker from the criticism attributed to administration officials. This was not done. I then called Under-Secretary of State Robert Kimmitt, expressing my concern that the highest levels of the U.S. Government seemed to be misreading the status of the negotiations and what needed to be done to lead them to success. I asked that Kimmitt meet with Alvaro de Soto for a private discussion so that we might find a way of working around this stumbling block.

The meeting took place on March 4. Kimmitt contended that the FMLN had been dragging its feet, perhaps for understandable electoral reasons, but once the elections were over, fast progress was required. Time was of the essence. He stressed that the period between the elections on March 10 and the end of the current legislature on April 30 would be crucial. De Soto agreed on the importance of accelerating the negotiations but pointed out that the aim was not only to silence the guns but also to achieve democratization, respect for human rights and the reunification of Salvadoran society. Negotiations on such political issues were difficult to conclude under a tight schedule. De Soto informed Kimmitt in confidence that the FMLN would be willing to decrease the level of fighting and simplify its demands at the negotiating table in return for rapid movement to a stage in which it could carry out its struggle in the political arena. This would require the government to guarantee that it would not take advantage of the situation to gain by military means what it had hitherto failed to achieve. The Under-Secretary did not disagree with de Soto but emphasized that I should involve myself personally in the process during the ten months that were left in my term. He suggested that my cultural links with El Salvador gave me a greater chance to succeed there than on other issues with which I was dealing.

This meeting, unfortunately, did not stop the U.S. criticism of de Soto's handling of the negotiations, criticism that I realized was also intended for me. In late April, Deputy U.S. Permanent Representative Watson conveyed to us that Assistant Secretary Aronson felt de Soto had treated the representatives of the political parties in the government delegation at the meeting that was then taking place in Mexico as "interlopers," even though de Soto himself had suggested their inclusion. Further, de Soto reportedly had rejected an agreement that the party delegates had worked out with the FMLN and insisted that only his working paper should be the basis of negotiations. None of this was accurate. The following day the Acting Secretary of State, Larry Eagleberger, called me directly "on instructions from the President who had some concerns about the round of negotiations taking place in Mexico City on El Salvador." Eagleberger had the impression things had slowed down in the talks, and he wondered whether de Soto was pushing hard enough. The President had asked that I urge de Soto to accelerate the negotiations so that a cease-fire could take place by May 30. I expressed surprise, noting that I had talked with Alvaro de Soto just a few hours earlier and did not gain the impression that he was dragging his feet. Rather the contrary. Eagleberger said he did not wish to raise the question of de Soto's competence but, if things did not progress, I should enter into the talks at the next round.

When in May I went to Washington for talks with President Bush, I felt that I had to take the opportunity to eliminate these persistent differences on the El Salvador negotiations and, in particular, to reaffirm my full confidence in de Soto as my Special Representative. Obviously this was a matter of considerable delicacy, since the underlying intent of my remarks had to be that

BLAIR HOUSE
THE PRESIDENT'S GUEST HOUSE
1651 PENNSYLVANIA AVENUE, N. W.
WASHINGTON, D. C. 20006

EL SALVADOR

1 UNDERSTAND WE HAVE SOME DISCREPANCIES OF A TACTICAL NATURE REGARDING THE EL SALVADOR NEGOTIATION.

SOME MEMBERS OF YOUR ADMINISTRATION HAVE COMPLAINED TO GOVERNMENTS ABOUT THE CONDUCT OF THE PROCESS BY MY REPRESENTATIVE.

1 WANT YOU TO KNOW THAT MY REPRESENTATIVE HAS MY FULL SUPPORT, AND HE ACTS STRICTLY ON MY BEHALF.

1 HAVE A SLIGHT ADVANTAGE OVER YOU REGARDING EL SALVADOR: 1 AM IN CONTACT WITH BOTH SIDES.

SUCCESS TO DATE IN THE NEGOTIATION SEEMS TO INDICATE THAT WE ARE ON THE RIGHT TRACK.

1 HOPE THAT IN THE FUTURE, WHEN YOUR COOPERATION WILL BE ESSENTIAL, WE CAN DEAL WITH ANY DISCREPANCIES DIRECTLY. CRITICISMS TO OTHER GOVERNMENTS UNDERMINE MY EFFORT.

the President and secretary of state were receiving misleading information from their advisors. On the evening before the meeting I carefully wrote out what I would say. (See original note above.) Participation in the first part of the meeting, which took place on May 9, 1991, was limited to the President, Secretary Baker, General Scowcroft and Lisa Buttenheim, who accompanied me to take notes. When, after an extensive discussion of the situation in Iraq, the conversation turned to El Salvador, I referred to the criticism of the United Nations' handling of the negotiations and said I would like to clarify any misunderstandings. President Bush was very direct in his response. "We feel," he said, "that Mr. de Soto is leaning on Cristiani and not on the FMLN. Most leaders in South America believe that Cristiani is dealing in good faith. Our view is that Mr. de Soto, with all due respect to his good intentions, is leaning on him and not on the FMLN."

I answered that the United States, which had no direct contact with the FMLN, should understand the difficult position in which the United Nations was placed. My Representative had the unpleasant task of serving, in a sense, as the FMLN spokesman when conveying—not espousing—its position to the other parties. I stressed that arranging a cease-fire was an extremely complicated task. The FMLN wished to ascertain where the cease-fire lines would be drawn and what territory it would continue to control. "But I don't understand," the President exclaimed, "why these people should have equal standing. The elections in El Salvador were free and fair and Cristiani is doing his best. Why should the FMLN have the same standing at the table?"

President Bush's fully understandable outburst got to the core of the U.S. (and Cristiani's) distrust of the United Nations' mediation tactics. The Cristiani government was a legitimate, elected government. From this perspective, giving equal status and importance to positions of an insurgent group that resorted to violence to achieve its aims amounted to showing favoritism to that group. For the mediator, the perspective was quite different. For him (and for me) impartiality between the two parties was absolutely essential. The insurgent FMLN had to be treated with the same respect as the legitimate government of El Salvador.

Another consideration explained to some extent the criticism of U.S. authorities, which, being at a somewhat greater distance, I could more easily understand than de Soto. Because of the requirements of democratization, especially the reform of the military and security forces, greater demands were made of the government than of the FMLN. The FMLN was in the position of *demandeur.* Yet what the Front was demanding was clearly in the interest of sustained stability and freedom. As de Soto presented the FMLN demands, government commission members may have felt that they were being placed on the defensive. I am certain that de Soto and I were completely impartial in the ultimately successful efforts to bring a peaceful solution to the conflict in El Salvador. This would not preclude a personal sympathy on de Soto's part—*au coeur*—for the reformist positions of the FMLN. The American criticism, I must add, diminished after my conversation with President Bush—not so much, I think, because of the exchange, as because of the favorable direction taken by the negotiations. In the end the President and the Secretary of State were highly complimentary of both de Soto's and my own performance, and I believe genuinely so.

1991—A Time Limit for Success

Notwithstanding the impression given by U.S. criticism of the negotiating process, some progress, even if slow, had been made in the early months of 1991. Near agreement was reached on reform of the armed forces on the basis of the working paper that de Soto had prepared. Under-Secretary-General Marrick Goulding held useful discussions with both sides on the technical aspects of a cease-fire, once it was agreed. In March the FMLN proposed an intensified, concerted effort to reach agreement by the end of April on the armed forces, constitutional reforms and a cease-fire. Details on other issues, such as judicial and electoral reforms and economic and social questions, would be left until after the cease-fire was in place. Through de Soto's effort, agreement had been reached to hold unannounced direct talks between the two sides in Mexico starting on April 4 for an indefinite period in the hope of wrapping up a package agreement on the armed forces, constitutional reform and a cease-fire by April 23.

I asked the Friends of the Secretary-General—the Presidents of Colombia, Mexico, Spain and Venezuela—to undertake démarches with the FMLN, the government of El Salvador and the United States, urging that the necessary compromises be made on both sides to permit agreement. I myself wrote to President Bush to this effect and urged again that the United States establish direct contact with the FMLN in order to dissipate misunderstandings and clarify the respective positions. In all of these approaches the urgency of reaching agreement before April 30 was emphasized. This deadline resulted from a peculiarity of the Salvadoran constitution. Constitutional amendments required the approval of two consecutive sessions of the legislature. The current session would end on April 30. Should any constitutional reforms required by the agreement not be approved by the current session, their enactment would be delayed for at least two years.

The talks in Mexico City were tempestuous. Because of personal animosity between the two sides, most of the negotiation had to be done in proximity mode, with de Soto shuttling between delegations. President Cristiani, in response to a letter I had written to him asking for his personal support of the negotiations, sent a bitter reply accusing de Soto of introducing a proposed constitutional amendment to which his government could never agree. Nevertheless, almost miraculously, agreement was reached on April 27 on a package covering a series of constitutional reforms on the armed forces and their subordination to civilian control, on judicial power and on the electoral system. Agreement also was reached on establishing a Commission on the Truth to investigate serious acts of violence that had occurred since 1980 "and whose impact on society urgently demands that the public should know the truth."[6] The National Assembly approved the constitutional amendments at the eleventh hour on April 30, thanks to the courage and skill with which President Cristiani handled the matter in the face of harsh opposition from the extreme right.

As important as it was, the Mexico Agreement was not sufficient to bring about the long-sought cease-fire. The terms for a cease-fire were extremely delicate both for the government and the FMLN. It was impossible for the government to accept terms that would imply that some areas of the country were outside its sovereign control. The FMLN was reluctant to give up its arms during a cease-fire. By doing so it would lose its main means of pressure for the negotiations on the broad conditions of peace that would follow the cease-fire. Moreover, the cease-fire remained dependent on agreement on a process for cleansing (purification) of the armed forces. In the ensuing weeks some further progress—for example, on the establishment of a civilian police force— was made in continuing talks in Mexico City. It soon became clear, however, that the basic disagreements between the government and the FMLN leadership on the political aspects of a cease-fire were too deep to be overcome in isolation from the other political issues that were to be dealt with after the cease-fire came into effect.

Toward the end of June, prior to an Iberoamerican Summit Meeting in Guadalajara, Mexico, the FMLN suggested to de Soto the possibility of combining all the remaining issues in one negotiating phase prior to a cease-fire. At the Guadalajara Summit I discussed this approach with President Cristiani, with three of the five members of the FMLN Command, including Joaquín Villalobos, whom I considered the most impressive of the group, and with the Presidents of Colombia, Mexico, Spain and Venezuela. On the basis of these consultations I concluded that, even though President Cristiani had expressed reservations, the single-phase concept in which the concerns of both sides would be addressed together offered the best prospect of breaking the logjam. I explained the altered strategy in detail in letters to Secretary Baker and to Soviet Foreign Minister Alexander Bessmertnykh, who had sent a further joint U.S./Soviet letter to urge my personal involvement in efforts to achieve an early cease-fire. I explained that a single-phase agenda would cover all outstanding questions other than the FMLN proposal that its fighters be integrated into the Salvadoran army, a proposal President Cristiani had totally, and I was sure irreversibly, rejected. Under this plan all negotiations would occur in advance of a cease-fire, to be followed solely by implementation of the agreements. The uncertainties that were currently preventing agreement on a cease-fire would thus be removed.

After a further meeting with Alvaro de Soto, President Cristiani withdrew his reservations to the one-phase approach (although not to the substantive positions that the FMLN had put forward) and the U.S. government also informed me that it saw merit in the plan provided it did not delay a cease-fire by introducing new issues. Thus the way was clear for compressed negotiations. Another problem, however, had bedeviled the negotiations. Neither the government of El Salvador nor the FMLN was represented at an authoritative level in the negotiations; neither delegation could take decisions without referral to higher authorities; and the government delegation was particularly disinclined to be flexible. If this situation continued in the compressed negotiating phase, it offered small hope for quick progress. In late August de Soto went to Geneva, where I was at the time, to discuss this problem and other aspects of the next stage in the negotiations. We decided that it would be necessary to bring the top level on both sides directly into the talks. President Cristiani had repeatedly told me that he would be at my disposal whenever needed. The time now had come.

I was conscious that if I sounded out the Salvadoran government and the FMLN in advance about participation at the highest level, they might well say no. The U.S. government also might be disinclined to issue visas for all the FMLN leaders to come to New York, and I felt that for the kind of high-pressure negotiations I foresaw involving my own participation, it was important that the talks be held at UN Headquarters. So, conscious of the diminishing time left in my term of office, I wrote a brief letter to Cristiani on August 27, 1991, inviting him to New York on September 16 and 17 for consultations "on means to unblock and give new impulse to the stalled negotiations." (It was clear that the President would not agree to participate in direct negotiations with the FMLN.) At the same time de Soto wrote similar letters to the five commanders of the FMLN. We then informed the U.S. Ambassador what had been done and requested that he ensure that visas be issued to all five commanders, some of whom had been accused of various misdeeds. President Cristiani accepted, the United States issued the visas, and all five commanders came, each accompanied by several associates.

While there were many discrete issues that needed to be settled, the fundamental question was the reintegration of the FMLN, within the framework of full legality, into the civilian, institutional and political life of the country. The conditions and the guarantees for such reintegration had to be established. I stated this very strongly to President Cristiani in our first meeting after his arrival, suggesting that the FMLN was likely to abandon its insistence on the integration of its fighters into the army only if they were offered "a package of conditions and guarantees" that would satisfy their aspirations for full reintegration into civil society.

The New York negotiations lasted from September 16 to 25. President Cristiani and the commanders stayed in New York for the entire time. They never met face to face. I met repeatedly with each side separately, and de Soto and his team spent long hours, often sustained only by brought-in pizza, the aroma of which indicated to the perceptive observer in which conference room the talks were taking place. On the evening of September 25 the two delegations signed two documents—the New York Agreement and the Compressed Negotiations—which, as I announced the next morning to the press, "untied the Gordian knot."

The two agreements provided for the immediate establishment of a National Commission for the Consolidation of Peace (COPAZ) to supervise all the agreements reached by the parties. It would consist of two representatives of the government, two of the FMLN, and one member each of the political parties represented in the National Assembly. The archbishop of El Salvador and a member of ONUSAL would participate as observers. The agreements also contained provisions on the purification, reduction and reorganization of the armed forces, criteria for the recruitment and training of a civilian police force and a number of economic and social goals. What remained to be accomplished in the compressed negotiations were agreements on how these extensive understandings would be realized. These would open the way for the long-awaited cease-fire, which would be "brief and dynamic" and followed by the full restoration of peace. The two delegations would resume urgent direct negotiations in the understanding that if problems arose that required decisions at the highest level, the Secretary-General would call a further meeting at UN Headquarters. Thus while the Gordian knot had been untied, there were still loose ends to be taken care of.

Despite the agreements reached in New York, armed engagements were still taking place in El Salvador. Both sides were zealously guarding their military positions. I was fearful that elements hostile to aspects of the understandings might bring about an intensification of the fighting and thereby jeopardize completion of the outstanding agreements. Therefore, in informing the Security Council of the New York agreements, I suggested that the parties adopt a "modus vivendi" for the gradual cessation of combat that could be verified by the United Nations. This idea was not accepted as such, but in mid-November the FMLN announced that it would cease all offensive operations; and the government followed suit. The modus vivendi was thus in effect realized without agreement between the two parties.

The New York Agreement was not enthusiastically welcomed in San Salvador. President Cristiani was sharply criticized for having approved it. Rightist elements mounted public demonstrations and members of the newly established COPAZ were physically threatened as were foreign press representatives. Presumably this motivated the government to introduce a new position paper after the renewed bilateral talks had gotten off to a favorable start in San Miguel Allende, Mexico, that seemed in important respects to be in conflict with the provisions of the New York Agreement. Alvaro de Soto called me urgently and expressed the fear that a new government position regarding the civilian police force, which would exclude former FMLN members from enlisting, together with increased rigidity on other issues, could torpedo the still-delicate negotiating process. I called President Cristiani and expressed my profound concern over this development. I told him frankly that his government would be seen as acting in bad faith. The FMLN would almost certainly categorically reject the new government positions. We discussed possible reformulations to which the President promised to give sympathetic consideration. The talks in Mexico did not move forward, however, and the end of my tenure was fast approaching. I decided that the only possible course was again to ask President Cristiani and the FMLN commanders to come to New York and to use the imminence of my retirement as a lever to gain an agreement.

Initially President Cristiani did not come to New York with the government negotiating team. In the days before Christmas, negotiations appeared hopelessly bogged down, with neither side showing the flexibility required to overcome the impasse. I called President Cristiani and urged that he come and assume the leadership of his delegation since only he had the authority to make the decisions needed to bring the negotiations to a successful conclusion. Despite opposition from right-wing members of his party, he arrived in New York on December 28, three days before the end of my tenure.

By this time the newly elected Secretary-General, Boutros Boutros-Ghali, was already in the city. President Cristiani called on him patently to explore whether it would be advantageous to delay matters until the new Secretary-General was in office. Boutros-Ghali handled the situation with finesse. He gave Cristiani to understand that there were many other items on his agenda, and it would take him at least six months to get around to El Salvador. If the President wanted a peace agreement anytime soon, he should come to terms while Pérez de Cuéllar was still in office.

On the thirty-first of December, my last day in office, I participated directly in intense negotiations. With Cristiani able and willing to make compromises, the FMLN team also moderated its demands. At four minutes before midnight the deal was finally struck and the New York Act (I) was signed just before the clock struck in the New Year. In it the parties declared that they had reached agreement on all the substantive issues of the Caracas Agenda and the New York Agreement and that the implementation of these two documents would put a final end to the Salvadoran armed conflict. They agreed that the cease-fire would take effect formally on February 1, 1992, and would end on October 31, 1992. Thereafter all of the provisions of the peace treaty, which would be signed in Mexico City on January 16, 1992, would be in effect.

I was warmly invited by all the parties and by Secretary-General Boutros-Ghali to attend the signing ceremony in Mexico City. It seemed to me, however, that it would not be in the best taste to accept. There was now a new Secretary-General. I did not attend.

A POSTSCRIPT TO PEACE: GUATEMALA

The Central American peace process got a late start in Guatemala, beginning in earnest only in early 1990. The auspices were unusual, previewing in a way the more dramatic role that Norway would later play in bringing Israel and the PLO together. The Lutheran church of Norway, whose Secretary-General was a member of the committee charged with selecting the recipients of the Nobel Peace Prize, had become interested in the situation in Guatemala, which had been the scene of the grossest violations of human rights in the region. Through means that are still unknown to me, Norwegian church representatives were able to persuade the National Reconciliation Commission (CAP), which had been formed as a result of Esquipulas II, to meet in Oslo with representatives of the Guatemalan insurgency, *La Unidad Revolucionaria Nacional Guatemalteca* (URNG). The unstated objective was to prepare the way for an eventual meeting between the government of Guatemala and the URNG.

The National Reconciliation Commission was made up of representatives of the various sectors of Guatemalan society. Jorge Serrano Elias headed the representatives of the opposition political parties at the Oslo meeting; less than a year later he was elected President of Guatemala. Serrano is a man of very strong personality, highly intelligent and charismatic. He is a Protestant of fundamentalist persuasion, which no doubt eased his rapport with the Norwegian Lutherans, but had a contrary effect on his relations with the man appointed as "Conciliator" in the talks with the URNG, Monsignor Rudolfo Quezada Toruño. I met with President Serrano in New York and later in Guadalajara. Both times he impressed me as a man thoroughly committed to a political settlement of the insurgency in Guatemala. His meeting in Oslo with members of the URNG had encouraged him to believe that a settlement was possible and desirable.

The United Nations had no part in arranging the Oslo meeting nor was a UN representative present there. Given my good offices responsibilities for the peace process throughout the region, however, I felt that UN assistance should be available, if the parties wished, as the negotiating process went forward. Francesc Vendrell, who was already much involved in peace efforts in Nicaragua and El Salvador, had been following the situation in Guatemala. He was able to communicate to the parties who had met in Oslo my readiness to be of such assistance as might be desired. As a result, the participants agreed to invite an observer representing the Secretary-General at ensuing meetings. I designated Vendrell as my Representative for this purpose.

Vendrell served as far more than an observer, acting frequently as a channel of communication between the parties, providing impartial advice both to the President of Guatamala and to the URNG and even furnishing drafts to facilitate the negotiating process. Vendrell did an excellent job. Earlier I suggested that on one occasion in dealing with the Nicaraguan Contras, he showed questionable judgment. No such problem arose in connection with Guatemala. On the contrary, he showed consistent discretion, which earned him the confidence of all sides.

Following the positive outcome of the Oslo conference, a series of separate meetings was held between the URNG and representatives of the various sectors of Guatemalan society; at each meeting the UN Observer and the Conciliator were present. Following Serrano's assumption of the presidency, there were several moves to initiate talks between the government and the URNG, something encouraged by Monsignor Quezada. The Lutherans proposed that a purely ceremonial meeting be held in Oslo to mark the first anniversary of the earlier Oslo meeting. While President Serrano had met secretly with URNG representatives (with the assistance of Vendrell), he resisted the idea of a ceremonial meeting. He was fearful that it would result in an extended negotiating process such as was taking place in El Salvador, in which he felt the demands of the FMLN were continually expanding. He preferred a rapid negotiation of what he called "total peace." He agreed, nevertheless, to the initiation of talks between the government and the URNG; these talks were held in Mexico City in late April 1991. In these talks agreement was reached on a Procedure for the Pursuit of Peace through Political Means. The procedure, the draft of which was suggested by Vendrell, provided that talks would be held under the auspices of the Conciliator, Monsignor Quezada, as president of the National Conciliation Commission. The UN observer, as representative of the Secretary-General, would play an active role in both the direct and the indirect talks between the parties. Both the government and the URNG committed themselves not to abandon the talks and to negotiate in good faith on the agreed agenda items, which included (as in El Salvador) democratization, human rights, demilitarization, problems of the indigenous population, agrarian reform, revision of the constitution and of electoral procedures, and resettlement of refugees and displaced persons.

The procedure provided for the United Nations to verify the agreements to be reached between the parties. The government delegation originally proposed that this responsibility should be shared by the United Nations and the Organization of American States. By this time, the United Nations had experienced in Nicaragua the difficulties of carrying out the verification process in tandem with the OAS. Accordingly we suggested that the United Nations be given sole responsibility for this function in the Guatemalan peace process. Secretary-General Baena Soares never took issue with me on the exclusion of the OAS, nor, as far as I know, did he discuss the issue with the Guatemalan authorities.

In late September 1991, President Serrano was in New York and I was able to review with him the state of negotiations in detail. He gave me no reason to doubt his continuing personal commitment to the achievement of peace with the URNG through political rather than military means. It was clear, though, that his room for maneuvering was limited. His government was based on a fragile coalition in which his party was one of the smaller members. The army continued to have a major influence on government policy and on the actions of the President. (On one occasion President Serrano found it necessary to communicate with my representative, Vendrell, through a used car dealer because he knew that all of his telephone lines were tapped.) The President's major strength lay in the force of his personality.

By this time the most difficult issues in the negotiations were those related to human rights. The URNG was insisting on the establishment of a truth commission to look into, among other things, past human rights violations by the army. It also demanded disbandment of the civilian self-defense patrols (PACs) and verification by the United Nations of all agreements regarding human rights. President Serrano was not personally opposed to the establishment of a Commission on Human Rights; but he clearly was not free to agree to the establishment of a Truth Commission to investigate past actions of the army. I had the impression that he was genuinely opposed to it as incompatible with eventual civic reconciliation within Guatemala. I should note that the President, like his predecessor, depended on the military in part because, despite the notoriety of the Guatemalan army for human rights abuses, it contained some of the most efficient and best- educated people in the country. The President often turned to the army for advice or action quite simply because it could provide him with the most efficient response.

In speaking to me, President Serrano acknowledged the importance of verification by the United Nations. He interpreted this as the United Nations' providing technical assistance to Guatemalans who would do the on-the-spot monitoring. He rejected entirely the precedent established in El Salvador of the deployment of UN human rights observers before a peace agreement was achieved. This was another reason why the President viewed what was happening in El Salvador with suspicion. It could not be a model, in his view, for Guatemala.

Negotiations were not alleviated by the distinctly nonprofessional approach of the Conciliator, Monsignor Quezada, and his team of distinguished citizen-advisors. Quezada had an unfortunate tendency to tell each side what he thought it would like to hear. This produced continuing confusion. Since the negotiations frequently were conducted through indirect talks in which Quezada was the link, each side often gained a misleading impression of the other's position. The UN observer sought to lessen this problem by serving as a channel of communication between the delegations. This contributed to the negotiating process but not to relations between the Conciliator and the observer.

Monsignor Quezada came to see me in New York in the middle of November 1991. I found him to be cultivated, sincere and not lacking in a sense of his own importance. I could easily see that their differing religious orientations were not the only cause for the tension that marked the relationship between President Serrano and the Monsignor. At this time negotiations were still stalled on the human rights question. At the request of the parties, Monsignor Quezada had developed a "nonpaper" providing for the United Nations to establish a body to verify everything pertaining to human rights. This body would be an integral part of the mechanism responsible for verifying *all* the agreements reached between the parties. In the face of the continuing impasse on the human rights issue, the Monsignor had changed his position and urged that the United Nations should establish a human rights verification mechanism without waiting for the achievement of a cease-fire. Knowing the President's adamant opposition to this concept, I avoided endorsing it and instead emphasized the importance of patience in bringing full agreement between the two sides.

In the case of El Salvador, the imminent end of my term as Secretary-General could be used as a lever to bring a final peace agreement between the government of President Cristiani and the FMLN. The negotiations were not sufficiently advanced for this to be possible in Guatemala. I was convinced, though, that there could be no turning back from the search for a political solution. Neither the Government nor the URNG could expect much external assistance in continuing pursuit of a military solution. The democracy that had been restored in Guatemala needed peace to survive.

Now, I can record that, with the final agreements signed between the government of Guatemala and the URNG on December 29, 1996, following the package of peace accords signed earlier in Madrid, Mexico City, Oslo and Stockholm, peace has been fully achieved. As elsewhere in Central America the steps toward peace have been nurtured and verified by the United Nations. The peace process in all of Central America can be considered essentially accomplished. Still lacking, unfortunately, are the economic resources—the necessary cement—to ensure that the structure of peace throughout the region is secure for the longer term.

HAITI: A TRAGEDY IN MANY ACTS

The roots of violence in Haiti differ from those in other countries of the region. The efforts to bring peace to this country cannot rightly be considered part of the Central American Peace Process. Contadora did not encompass Haiti. Yet, no matter how different its history, Haiti is part of the Central American region. Its troubles mark the region just as do those of Nicaragua or Guatemala. I felt, both as Secretary-General and as a man of the hemisphere, a special sympathy for Haiti's people and a determination to help them toward a better life.

This was my immediate intention when, after 30 years, the disastrous Duvalier era came to an end in 1986. The military regime that replaced it did not come to power through a democratic process, but the man who became president, Lieutenant General Henri Namphy, quickly announced his government's paramount objective to be the establishment of democracy, the rule of law and fundamental freedoms for all. I felt that Haiti should be provided with every possible assistance in this period of transition to discourage Duvalier followers from regaining power.

The economy of Haiti was in disastrous condition. Mobilizing substantial assistance and helping the regime to organize its effective application were the immediate needs. To accomplish these, I asked the UNDP, as the most appropriate agency for the purpose, to set up an emergency assistance program for Haiti. A senior UNDP official, Orlando Olcese, who had been a successful minister of agriculture in Peru, was appointed as my Special Representative in Haiti. My schedule was revised to permit me to travel to Haiti in June with the primary purpose of encouraging early elections. In my comprehensive discussions with President Namphy he impressed me as an honest, rather simple man, well intentioned but without great strength of character. This remained my impression throughout the subsequent events in which he was involved.

At the time of my visit to Haiti, I was still opposed to UN action, which might be construed as intervention in the domestic affairs of Member States. Yet, because of the clearly desperate condition of Haiti and the inexperience of its new leaders, I found myself giving almost avuncular advice on clearly domestic matters to President Namphy and members of his National Council of Government. I promised UN technical assistance in preparing for elections, indicated that I would urge the Director-General of UNESCO to send an expert to Haiti to develop a literacy program and suggested that the government should give attention to the population problem, which, I explained, should involve more that just birth control measures. In all my conversations and public statements, however, the main emphasis was on the importance of democracy for Haiti's future and on the wide support that Haiti enjoyed in the international community. I said that Haiti, which so often had been isolated in its own region, should realize that in its struggle for democracy it was not alone.

The advent of the new regime did not bring calm to Haiti. During Namphy's first months in office, serious riots and demonstrations against the National Council Government—for allegedly trying to keep the country in the hands of Duvalier partisans—occurred. To counter this unrest, my Special Representative advised the president to call a constituent assembly to draft a new constitution by a specified date, to enact revised electoral laws and to fix a date for elections. Namphy took all of these actions. Elections were scheduled for November 29, 1986. However, before they could be held, he dismissed the Provisional Electoral Council that had been created to organize them—because of alleged mishandling of preparations. As a result rioting occurred, which forced the last-minute cancellation of the elections.

In a communication addressed to me on December 3, 1987, Namphy listed the reasons that had caused him to dismiss the electoral commission and stated that he had appointed a new council to prepare for elections. He wrote that the National Council Government undertook to transfer power to a freely elected president on February 7, 1988. I replied that I did not think, as some had proposed, that the Namphy government should immediately resign, nor did I think that the refusal of some candidates to participate in elections was a contribution to the return to democracy. The wise course, I suggested, would be to reconsider the decision to dissolve the earlier electoral council. This was not done. When the president subsequently requested that the United Nations send a mission to observe elections to be held on January 11, 1988, I declined. The election turned out to be a sham.

A NEW OPPORTUNITY FOR DEMOCRACY

Following a series of coups and short-lived military regimes, wide public unrest led to the formation on March 13, 1990, of a new government and the appointment of Ertha Pascal-Trouillot as provisional president. As one of her first acts, on March 15 President Pascal-Trouillot requested that I arrange for a UN mission to be sent to observe and verify elections, which she was personally committed to organize in a way that would be recognized by the Haitian people as honest and credible. On the basis of this request I immediately arranged for UNDP to send a technical mission to Port-au-Prince to advise on the preparation of elections. President Pascal-Trouillot subsequently requested the assistance of "advisors with experience in security matters" who would help the Haitian Armed Forces in developing and implementing electoral security plans and in observing their implementation. I fully supported the president's request. There was no doubt in my mind that, with the circumstances prevailing in Haiti, a UN security mission, including military as well as civilian personnel, was needed to assist in the provision of security—not only for the Haitian electorate but also for the members of the UN observation mission. The request led, however, to a time-consuming constitutional debate within the United Nations.

The question was whether the General Assembly or the Security Council should authorize the dispatch of the mission. Observation and verification of elections is clearly within the purview of the General Assembly. Security questions, on the other hand, especially when military personnel are involved, are viewed by Security Council members as being within their mandate. The problem was further complicated by the opposition of three members of the Security Council to the dispatch of a mission that would include a security component. They considered this would infringe on Haiti's sovereignty, even though President Pascal-Trouillet repeatedly emphasized that the function of the UN security personnel would only be to advise and observe; the Haitian Army would remain responsible for the maintenance of security, which it did.

I was careful to keep both the Council and the Assembly informed of all exchanges with the Haitian authorities.

Eventually a draft resolution was circulated in the General Assembly authorizing the dual mission. On this basis, I informed the Security Council, without requesting its agreement, that if the Assembly resolution was adopted I intended to send an electoral mission to Haiti that would include, as requested by President Pascal-Trouillot, a security component with military personnel. The Council, while still claiming responsibility for matters involving military and security personnel, expressed approval of the plan in a letter addressed to me by the Council President. The Assembly on October 10, 1990, adopted resolution 45/2, authorizing the establishment of the United Nations Observer Group for the Verification of Elections in Haiti (ONUVEH), entailing observation, verification and security functions.

Under the outstanding leadership of João de Medicis, who had become my Special Representative in Haiti, ONUVEH performed remarkably well.[7] Despite the initial coolness of the Haitian Army, a constructive relationship was developed and violence was avoided. The vote was conducted freely and the election of Jean Bertrand Aristide as president was unchallenged.

ONUVEH did not operate alone. The Organization of American States (OAS) also fielded an observer mission (but with no security function) and many NGO's were present. I believe, though, that ONUVEH was the most important and effective of the organizations involved in the electoral process. U.S. Secretary of State, James Baker, wrote to me afterwards that "much of the credit for Haiti's first free and fair elections goes to the United Nations."[8]

I had scant contact with President Aristide. I met him directly only once and that was when he put on something of a show, in addressing the General Assembly in several languages. He struck me as vain and something of a demagogue. Nonetheless I recognized that he had been freely elected by a large majority of the Haitian people. His subsequent overthrow could only be deplored as yet another sad act in Haiti's history. The OAS quickly sought to reverse the effect of the coup by sending a political mission to negotiate a restoration of democracy and a human rights mission to bring an end to human rights abuses inflicted by the new military regime. I proposed that there should be a joint UN/OAS human rights mission but this was rejected by the OAS Secretary-General, who felt that the crisis could best be dealt with on a regional basis, a view that was later to change.

While the ONUVEH operation was undoubtedly a major UN accomplishment, it had a serious failing. The mission departed as soon as the elections were over, leaving no residual force to assist the government in establishing and strengthening the institutions required to maintain a new and fragile democracy. It is satisfying to note that this lesson has been learned. The next mission that went to Haiti to restore democratic government remained there to protect it. I hope it will stay long enough to ensure a happy final act for the Haitian drama.

It should never be forgotten, however, that the root causes of the conflicts that so long afflicted this region were poverty, social discrimination and economic injustice. As great as the achievements have been, peace over the longer term in the region will remain dependent on a sustained process of economic and social development.

RESTORING PEACE ON TWO CONTINENTS

CAMBODIA: REBIRTH
OF A NATION

THE REBIRTH OF CAMBODIA was one of the remarkable triumphs of reason, and reasonable negotiation, that marked the end of the Cold War. The restoration of peace and democratic government there, as fragile as they may be, was a signal achievement of international cooperation, lengthy negotiations and complex planning, in all of which the United Nations played an important role—even if its role was not always visible.

In 1979 the General Assembly adopted the first of a series of resolutions on Cambodia, calling for the withdrawal of all foreign forces from the country and for self-determination for the Cambodian people. It also requested the Secretary-General to use his good offices to contribute to the problem's peaceful solution and welcomed his coordination of relief assistance. By the beginning of 1982 the International Conference on Cambodia, which had been established by the General Assembly as a forum for reaching a settlement of the Cambodian conflict, had reached a dead end. Vietnam, which had invaded Cambodia, driven the Khmer Rouge government out of office and installed a Vietnamese-dominated regime, had refused to participate in the conference as had its friend and ally, the Soviet Union. The Association of South East Asian Nations (ASEAN) had viewed the International Conference mainly as a means of bringing pressure on Vietnam to get out of Cambodia. Vietnam, on the other hand, contended that Cambodia was a regional problem that should be handled in a regional framework.

I was generally familiar with the situation and knew some of the principal players well, especially Prince Sihanouk and the Vietnamese foreign minister,

Co Thach, since Southeast Asia had been part of my portfolio as Under-Secretary-General and I had visited the area twice with Secretary-General Waldheim. I felt that the best course, on becoming Secretary-General, was to start afresh, to find out what the objectives and interests of each of the concerned parties were and see if in some way they could be brought into harmony to a sufficient degree to permit a settlement. My first action was to appoint Refeeuddin Ahmed as Special Representative for Humanitarian Assistance in Southeast Asia. This was a somewhat misleading title, determined in part by the fact that the UN role in relation to Cambodia had, for political reasons, to be seen as primarily humanitarian since the United Nations did not recognize the Vietnamese-installed government in Phnom Penh. However, the Special Representative had a highly political role, becoming the principal instrument for the exercise of the good offices of the Secretary-General in seeking a Cambodian settlement. I selected Rafee Ahmed without fully appreciating the importance of the work that lay ahead. However, it quickly became apparent that Ahmed was the right man in the right place. He is by nature soft-spoken and remarkably shrewd. If he is in temperament somewhat guarded, this equipped him well for the complexities of the positions and characters of the various parties in the Cambodian picture. Moreover, Rafee Ahmed had a talent for gathering highly competent people on whom he was prepared to rely heavily for advice and the formulation of positions. The most important members of his Cambodian team were a brilliant Tunisian, Hedi Annabi, in whom I developed the highest confidence, my military advisor Brigadier General Timothy Dibuama from Ghana, and a young American lawyer, Linda Hazou, who died some years later at a tragically early age. With his team, Rafee Ahmed was intimately involved as my Special Representative in every stage of the ultimately successful achievement of the Cambodian Peace Plan.

In the many meetings I had in New York with leaders from the region and with the Permanent Members of the Security Council, I sought to gain a clear understanding of their positions. Early in 1982 I asked Ahmed to make the first of what would be repeated visits to the area in order to explore the views of the leaders of Democratic Cambodia,[1] Thailand, Indonesia, the Philippines, Vietnam, Laos, China and the Soviet Union. We agreed that it could be useful to suggest to the leaders he met that a smaller forum limited to the countries of the region and other powers having a special interest in the Cambodian problem might be more conducive to progress than the International Conference had been. The ASEAN countries were generally receptive toward this idea. Vietnam was also well disposed. Only China showed reluctance, but even the Chinese were not entirely negative. We thought that we might be on the brink of a significant procedural step forward. Unfortunately, the Indochinese foreign ministers held a conference at this time and in their final communiqué proposed

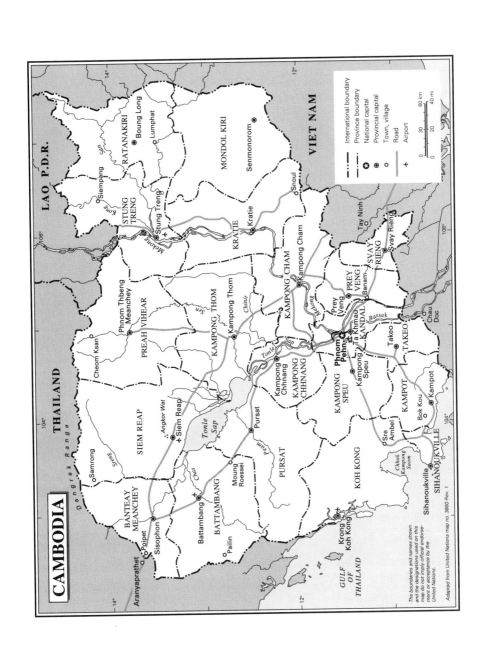

CAMBODIA

LAO P.D.R.

THAILAND

VIET NAM

Aranyaprathet

Dangrek Range

BANTEAY MEANCHEY
Poipet
Sisophon
Samrong
Sreng

SIEM REAP
Angkor Wat
Siem Reap

BATTAMBANG
Battambang
Pailin
Moung Roessei
Chas

PURSAT
Pursat
Pean

KOH KONG
Krong Koh Kong
Sihanoukville
SIHANOUKVILLE

GULF OF THAILAND

Cheom Ksan

PREAH VIHEAR
Phnom Thbeng Meanchey
Sen

KAMPONG THOM
Kampong Thom
Chinit

Tonle Sap

Tonle Sap

KAMPONG CHHNANG
Kampong Chhnang

KAMPONG SPEU
Kampong Speu
Sre Ambel
Chhak Kampong Saom
Bok Kou

RATANAKIRI
Siempang
Boung Long
Lumphat

STUNG TRENG
Stung Treng
Kong
Mekong

KRATIE
Kratie
Snoul

MONDOL KIRI
Senmonorom

KAMPONG CHAM
Kampong Cham
Mekong

PREY VENG
Prey Veng
Banam

SVAY RIENG
Svay Rieng

Tay Ninh

KANDAL
Ta Khmau
Phnom Penh
Bassak
Chau Doc

TAKEO
Takeo

KAMPOT
Kampot

Legend
- International boundary
- Province boundary
- ⊛ National capital
- ◉ ○ Provincial capital
- ○ Town, village
- Road
- ✦ Airport

0 30 60 km
0 20 40 mi

14° 106° 12° 104° 106°

the holding of a limited international conference on Cambodia exactly along the lines of the UN suggestion. Hostility among the ASEAN countries was so intense that Vietnamese sponsorship of the idea amounted to the kiss of death. It would be eight years before the concept was realized when the Conference on Cambodia (PICC) opened in Paris.

THE VIETNAMESE POSITION IS DEFINED

In March of 1984, Vietnamese Foreign Minister Co Thach, during a visit to Australia, agreed that a "partial solution" to the problem of peace and stability in Southeast Asia could be based on five points:

- Withdrawal of Vietnamese troops from Cambodia
- Elimination of Pol Pot and his associates as a political and military force and the creation of a safety zone on both sides of the Thai/Cambodian border
- Guarantee of the security of the Sino/Vietnamese, Sino/Laotian and Thai/Laotian borders
- Self-determination by free elections in Cambodia but with the exclusion of the Pol Pot faction
- International supervision and guarantees of all aspects of the foregoing.

Australian Foreign Minister Bill Hayden announced that Vietnam's acceptance of the five-point formula indicated its willingness to discuss Cambodia as a priority issue. It seemed to us in the United Nations, however, that several of the points were unrealistic. When Rafee Ahmed visited Hanoi a few months later, he pointed out to Co Thach that ASEAN could not reasonably be expected to discuss the security of the Sino/Vietnamese and the Sino/Laotian borders with Vietnam. He urged that these items be excluded from Vietnam's eventual dialogue with ASEAN. Co Thach agreed. So the five points agreed in Canberra were converted into the following four-point "agenda":

1. Elimination of Pol Pot and his accomplices and adoption of security measures along the Thai-Cambodian border.
2. Withdrawal of Vietnamese troops from Cambodia.
3. Self-determination by free elections, excluding Pol Pot and his accomplices.
4. International supervision and guarantees for all aspects of the foregoing.

In various public statements Co Thach subsequently reverted to the earlier Vietnamese position of linking the withdrawal of Vietnamese troops from

Cambodia to the cessation of the Chinese "threat." When challenged on this by Ahmed, the foreign minister said that he could not avoid perfunctory references to the Chinese "threat" and the Indonesian communiqué, but that his position as defined with Ahmed had not changed. During a meeting with me on October 11, 1984, Co Thach formally confirmed that Vietnam would be ready to enter into talks with ASEAN on the basis of the four-point agenda worked out with Mr. Ahmed. This, he said, should constitute the "first phase" of a global settlement of the problems of the region. This marked the first time that the Vietnamese foreign minister, whom I found to be shrewd and highly intelligent, had acknowledged that the Cambodian question had its international aspects.

Vietnam's modified position did not lead immediately to an improvement in its relations with ASEAN. On the contrary, ASEAN, at a ministerial meeting in July 1984, denounced Vietnam's attempts to impose a military solution in Cambodia and dismissed the partial withdrawal Vietnam had announced as simply another rotation of troops. Ahmed attended this meeting as my Special Representative and advised the foreign ministers to seek confirmation of the four-point agenda directly from Co Thach. The ASEAN members were disillusioned with Vietnam, however, in part because of the renewed Vietnamese offensive launched during the dry season along the Thai-Cambodian border. This offensive continued into the fall, leading to intensified fighting within Cambodia and repeated incidents between Thai and Vietnamese military forces. When Co Thach stated during the General Assembly meeting in September 1984 that conditions were ripe for a dialogue with the ASEAN countries, the ASEAN representatives replied that the problem of Cambodia was not between Vietnam and ASEAN but between Vietnam and the Cambodian people.

Meanwhile, efforts to encourage a dialogue between the government in Phnom Penh and the opposition factions that were loosely united in the Coalition Government of Democratic Cambodia (CGDK) under Prince Sihanouk had failed. The Prince informed me in October 1984 that France had tried to arrange secret contacts between him and representatives of Hanoi and Phnom Penh. He had told the French authorities that he was "a man of dialogue" and willing to talk to anybody. However, when China and the Khmer Rouge expressed strong opposition to the meetings, Sihanouk canceled them.

In this unpromising situation, I embarked in January 1985 on a visit to all of the capitals of the region except Phnom Penh, following a schedule I had adopted four months earlier. My principal purpose was to encourage a process of genuine negotiations on Cambodia. In Bangkok, Prime Minister Prem Tinsulanonda and Foreign Minister Siddhi Savetsila asked me to convey their desire for peace to the Vietnamese leadership. They stressed that Thailand did not view Vietnam as an enemy. At the same time, they were convinced that Vietnam's presence in Cambodia posed a constant threat to Thailand's security.

They were pessimistic about the prospects of an early negotiated settlement because they felt Vietnam was intent on imposing a military solution. In Hanoi, Prime Minister Pham Van Dong and Foreign Minister Co Thach reciprocated Thailand's message of goodwill and stressed that it would be "sheer madness" for Vietnam to undertake hostile action against Thailand, whose territorial integrity it respected. Co Thach promised that the Vietnamese army would not carry out hot-pursuit operations against Khmer resistance units in Thailand.

The Vietnamese leaders said they were eager to work toward a negotiated settlement in Cambodia and would withdraw their troops as soon as possible. However, such withdrawal had to go hand in hand with the elimination of Pol Pot. The Pol Pot "clique" was guilty of genocide (Co Thach put particular emphasis on the word) and could not be allowed to participate in Cambodian elections. The foreign minister reiterated his proposal—first made by Rafee Ahmed in his earlier conversations with South East Asian leaders—for an international conference on Cambodia restricted to the countries of the region, the Permanent Members of the Security Council and other countries that were prepared to contribute to peace in the area.

When I met subsequently with Prince Sihanouk and with Son Sann, the Prime Minister of the Coalition Government of Democratic Cambodia, they evidenced a quite different attitude regarding the Khmer Rouge. The Prince maintained that Hanoi wished to eliminate the Khmer Rouge because it was the main obstacle to Vietnamese colonization of Cambodia. China, he said, would never accept the elimination of the Khmer Rouge, and its views had to be taken into account. The Chinese had made this very clear to him. I marveled again at the equanimity with which Sihanouk accepted the necessity of cooperation with the Khmer Rouge, which was responsible for the death of two of his sons, the loss of vast amounts of his property and the near destruction of his country. In all our many meetings and in his sometimes mercurial actions, his total devotion to his country and its people was constant. I could believe that, on their behalf, he would deal, sometimes in the guise of a minstrel, with the devil incarnate.

A U.S. REQUEST

The U.S. government had asked me on a strictly confidential basis to raise several matters of urgent concern at the time with the Vietnamese authorities. These pertained to the fate of the American soldiers missing in action, exit permits for Amerasians, detainees in reeducation camps and an American citizen who had been arrested in Vietnam. I took each of these up directly with President Pham Van Dong and Foreign Minister Co Thach. On the day following my approach, the foreign minister gave me factual and generally positive responses on each issue. I do not need to dwell on the details, since these matters have now been dealt with in direct U.S.-Vietnamese contacts; however, I saw the Vietnamese action as evidence of a genuine interest in establishing satisfactory relations with the United States. Pham Van Dong personally stressed to me Vietnam's readiness for improved "mutual understanding" with the United States. Vietnam was willing to forget the past, make peace and establish good relations. He hoped "the White House" would reciprocate this readiness. I transmitted a full account of these exchanges to American authorities.

FORMULATING A UN STRATEGY

On returning from Southeast Asia, I sat down with Rafee Ahmed and Hedi Annabi to identify the points of convergence that emerged from my conversations with regional leaders. On this basis we were able to define for the first time the main elements of a comprehensive political settlement for Cambodia. I foresaw the following steps as leading to the establishment of an independent, neutral and nonaligned Cambodia:

- A cease-fire and the withdrawal of all foreign forces from Cambodia.
- National reconciliation on a basis of preventing a return of the universally condemned policies and practices of the recent past.
- Self-determination for the Cambodian people through free and fair elections.
- Establishment of an independent, democratic, neutral and nonaligned Cambodia.
- Guaranteed respect for the legitimate security concerns of all states of the region.
- Establishment of a zone of peace, freedom and neutrality in Southeast Asia.

My single difference of opinion with Rafee Ahmed in connection with Cambodia arose in the preparation of these points. Vietnamese officials were insistent in all conversations in calling the actions of the Pol Pot government "genocide." They frequently cited this as a reason why the Khmer Rouge could never participate in free elections in Cambodia. Many other governments had condemned Khmer Rouge actions in equally harsh terms. Ahmed, recognizing the legal significance of the noun "genocide," proposed that the past policies followed in Cambodia be referred to as "genocidal." He felt this would satisfy the Vietnamese without raising the question of the applicability of the Convention Against Genocide. While I had no sympathy whatever for the Pol Pot regime, I was convinced that we were going to have to gain the cooperation of the Khmer Rouge (and their Chinese friends) in order to reach a settlement.

Use of the word "genocide" in any form would, I was certain, make this far more difficult. I therefore rejected it and we worked out instead the phrase "universally-condemned policies and practices of the recent past," which was to become the standard locution utilized in reference to the Khmer Rouge's past record. Eventually it was incorporated into the Paris Peace Agreements.

Later I was to have an extensive conversation with Deng Xiao Ping on Cambodia that further confirmed my views in this regard. I met with this extraordinary man on May 11, 1987, in the Great Hall of the People in Beijing. When the conversation turned to Cambodia, Deng asked if I was going to Vietnam. I told him that I was not but that I had been urging Hanoi to cooperate in a reasonable solution of the Cambodian problem that would take into account the will of the Cambodian people. Deng agreed with my position but then went on to say that Vietnam simply had to withdraw its troops from Cambodia. Vietnam, he said, insists that China should not support the Cambodian resistance, which means that Vietnam should have the opportunity for its puppet regime to consolidate its position and then withdraw its troops. Vietnam wished to hold talks with China on the question. Such talks could take place but only if Vietnam withdrew its troops.

This small, wizened man, who was the supreme leader of China, then asked me to convey the following "positive" message to "our Vietnamese neighbors":

- The internal mistakes of individuals and foreign invasion cannot be equated. Which crime is more serious? Foreign invasion, by a long way. It is true that Pol Pot made many mistakes, by no means small ones, but, in comparison the Vietnamese foreign aggression was a greater mistake. This principle obtains not only in the case of Cambodia but has worldwide application. So, in order to resolve the Cambodian question, Vietnam should withdraw its forces and end its aggression.
- Vietnam should allow the Cambodian people to solve the Cambodian problem themselves.
- This should involve all four factions—Sihanouk, Son Sann whose faction was joined with Sihanouk in the Coalition Government of Democratic Cambodia, Khieu Samphan, who represented the Khmer Rouge, and Hun Sen, who represented the government in Phnon Penh. The Pol Pot forces should be only one part of a future government, headed by Sihanouk. China would not support a government headed by Pol Pot, only one led by Sihanouk.

I said that I would willingly transmit this message. I added that Mr. Ahmed had been in Hanoi earlier in the spring and gained the impression that the Vietnamese leadership was prepared to enter a dialogue on a peaceful solution. Deng expressed satisfaction and then proceeded to recount briefly China's sad experience with Vietnam, which he described as a "perfidious country." Laughing in good humor, he said this last was not a message for Hanoi but a briefing for me. If the Pol Pot forces are dissolved, the resistance in Cambodia would practically cease to exist. "The Pol Pot forces cannot be dissolved," he said. "If they were, Vietnam could rule Cambodia directly, declare victory and let off firecrackers. That would be the end of that." At this point Deng said "So, let's call it a day." I realized I had heard an authoritative articulation of the Chinese position on Cambodia that was not likely to change.

The United Nations was not alone in seeking a solution to the Cambodian problem. At times so many different countries and groups were involved that it was difficult to keep abreast of where things stood. American and Soviet representatives met and announced that the agreement they had just reached on Afghanistan could serve as a model for Cambodia, an idea that Vietnam quickly, firmly and, I think, wisely rejected. The Non-Aligned Movement, spurred on somewhat mysteriously by the PLO, met in Harare to discuss the Cambodian question. Indian Prime Minister Radjiv Ghandi and Romanian President Nicolai Ceausescu both paid quick visits to Vietnam in the hope of encouraging a Cambodian settlement. The Ad Hoc Committee of the International Conference on Cambodia continued to maintain contact with the parties. Indonesia, which had been designated by ASEAN as its interlocutor on Cambodia, began to pursue the idea of a "cocktail party" that would bring the four Cambodian factions together for dialogue. In brief, there was a great deal of motion between 1985 and 1988, but very little progress.

REFUGEES ON THE BORDER AND HUNGER INSIDE CAMBODIA

The United Nations had the task of bringing humanitarian assistance to the more than 300,000 refugees in camps just inside the Thai border with Cambodia and to the Cambodian people inside Cambodia even though the United Nations did not recognize the Vietnamese-installed government in Phnom Penh. My predecessor had appointed Sir Robert Jackson to coordinate all UN assistance to Cambodia, both inside the country and among the refugees abroad. This was a new position established at the strong suggestion of Rosalyn Carter, the wife of the American President, who had traveled to the border area and been deeply impressed by the plight of the thousands of people living in miserable conditions there. Sir Robert, who had had a long association with UN development and humanitarian programs, was a man of enormous energy and tempestuous temperament. He was absolutely unrelenting in his determination to get food to the needy in Cambodia, and he was largely successful. He alone among senior

UN officials was authorized to meet with the Hun Sen government until, in late 1986, Prince Sihanouk himself held direct talks with Hun Sen. Sir Robert developed a cooperative relationship with the Phnom Penh authorities that greatly facilitated food delivery to all parts of the country that were under the government's control. During the period of greatest need, the Western industrialized countries and Japan were generous in their assistance. I believe that more than a million lives were saved through the UN relief program in Cambodia.

By 1982 food production had recovered but pockets of severe need remained. Despite Sir Robert's energetic lobbying, the Western donor countries became less generous, insisting that it was time that the Communist countries assume a greater part of the burden. I sought to reinvigorate the donors' enthusiasm, but by 1984 the humanitarian program inside Cambodia was essentially over. Sir Robert's position was eliminated—not an easy undertaking—and he retired still fulminating against countries, especially the United States, that had allowed politics to interfere with the provision of food to the starving. I know that he was aware, however, of how great the humanitarian accomplishments had been in Cambodia.

While the humanitarian problem inside Cambodia decreased, the problems connected with feeding the refugees on the border became ever more complex. The refugee camps were largely controlled by the different Cambodian factions. Security in the camps was provided by special units of the Thai army that earned a reputation for vicious behavior. Corruption was widespread. The UN agencies that were providing assistance were well aware that a good part of the food intended for the refugees was being channeled back to the military forces of the factions in Cambodia. It was also clear that the Thai army was engaged doing business with the Khmer Rouge forces and was involved in delivering food intended for the refugees to the Khmer army. Seemingly this was being done with the full knowledge of the government in Bangkok. I deduced that the Thai government had concluded that the Khmer Rouge were the only fighting force in Cambodia capable of preventing Vietnam from gaining complete control there, something that Thailand greatly feared. Thus the Thais like the Chinese saw the Khmer Rouge, despite their reprehensible record, as a useful barrier against Vietnamese expansion.

The UN relief agencies faced a choice: cut off food deliveries to the refugees because part of it was being illegally passed on or sold to Cambodian military groups; or continue with the distribution programs, knowing that it was desperately needed and that it did alleviate the misery in the camps. Each time new evidence of dubious conduct was brought to my attention I discussed with my immediate staff what we could do to correct the situation. On one of these occasions Rafee Ahmed, who was very familiar with conditions in the camps, asked: If you lift a rock and reveal the slime underneath, are you going to be able to do anything to clean it out? The implication was that the United Nations could do very little to eliminate the corruption or the political control exercised by the Khmer Rouge and, to a lesser extent, by the other factions in the camps. Under the circumstances, it was better to leave the stone unturned.

ERRATIC PROGRESS—BUT PROGRESS STILL

At the end of 1987 and the beginning of 1988, a series of developments suggested the possibility of real movement on a Cambodian settlement. Vietnam announced in January that it would be ready to withdraw all of its troops from Cambodia by the end of September 1989. In a series of bilateral talks, China, Vietnam and Thailand achieved a convergence of views on a timetable for the withdrawal of the Vietnamese troops, the gradual cessation of foreign assistance to the Cambodian factions, the future sovereignty, neutrality and nonalignment of Cambodia and the convening of an international conference. The three countries agreed to encourage national reconciliation among the Cambodian parties in order to prevent civil war. Soviet Foreign Minister Shevardnadze visited Beijing in February and agreed with his Chinese counterpart on the need to establish an "effective international control mechanism" for Cambodia and that the United Nations might play "its appropriate role" in a Cambodian political settlement.

In this same time frame, the Coalition Government of Democratic Cambodia officially endorsed a five-point plan earlier advanced by Prince Sihanouk calling for a precise timetable for Vietnamese withdrawal; simultaneous dismantling of the People's Republic of Cambodia (PRK) and the CGDK; general elections under international supervision; formation of a provisional quadripartite government and national army; and deployment of a UN peacekeeping force. The CGDK paper also called for the establishment of a UN international control mechanism that would ensure that the Khmer Rouge could not come to power alone.

At the end of 1987, Prince Sihanouk initiated contact, in his personal capacity, with the Prime Minister of the Phnom Penh regime, Hun Sen. After only two meetings Sihanouk adjourned the talks *sine die* on the ground that Hun Sen could not act independently. He would be willing to resume the talks only if Phnom Penh agreed to two fundamental preconditions: dismantlement of the PRK and the CGDK and the formation of a provisional government; and the deployment of an international peacekeeping force. Following the second of his meetings with Hun Sen, the Prince, in a conversation with Rafee Ahmed, suggested that I should pursue my efforts to construct a scenario for achieving a comprehensive Cambodian settlement. This was something I had begun the previous year by placing the six elements of a comprehensive settlement that we had defined in 1985 within a time schedule, similar in some respects to the plan that we had developed for Namibia.

The most critical and difficult issues to be dealt with were the formation and functioning of a provisional government of national reconciliation, the modalities for the total withdrawal of foreign forces and the nature of international supervision and guarantees. Clearly some kind of a trigger mechanism would be required to set in motion a plan that covered these issues. In the "draft framework" that I developed, the initial trigger would be a firm commitment by Vietnam to withdraw all of its forces within a specified time frame. At that point, talks among the Cambodian parties would begin, with the purpose of achieving agreement on the establishment of a provisional government of national reconciliation under the leadership of Prince Sihanouk. Once established, this government would be recognized as the sole legal representative of Cambodia.

According to this draft framework, a comprehensive cease-fire would enter into effect simultaneously with the establishment of the provisional government, and all foreign forces and Cambodian armed elements should be regrouped and confined to bases. Consideration could be given to disarming and disbanding the Cambodian armed elements, so that they could peacefully participate in the political process that would ensue. Upon establishment of the provisional government, the international peacekeeping forces would be introduced to control the cease-fire and withdrawal arrangements and to assist the provisional government with the maintenance of law and order. Subsequently other international assistance would be provided, including a comprehensive program for the return of refugees and displaced persons and for the reconstruction and development of the country. During the final stages of the transitional period, free and fair general elections would take place under international supervision.

Two types of guarantees were foreseen. The first would be those guarantees that the Cambodians themselves would undertake regarding nonreturn to the policies and practices of the recent past and the international status of Cambodia. The second type would be those guarantees concerning the future of Cambodia to be undertaken by neighboring states and the international community.

By June 1988 this draft framework had been incorporated in a confidential paper to be used as a basis of discussion with all the parties involved. (See Annex, where a copy is provided since it was never published as an official document.) It presaged and, I believe, significantly influenced the Paris Agreements, which would take three more years to complete. Rafee Ahmed discussed the plan with the regional leaders during two trips to Asia in the summer and fall of 1988 and subsequently in Geneva with the representatives of the five Permanent Members of the Security Council. This was the first contact with the Permanent Five as a group on Cambodia. As we had agreed, Ahmed did not press for specific reactions, making clear that the paper was intended only to help the parties focus on the main issues to be addressed and to suggest ideas for resolving them.

I reviewed the ideas with Lieutenant General Colin Powell, the U.S. National Security Advisor, when I visited Washington in July 1988. It was the first time that I had met the general and I—like most others, I now realize—was favorably impressed. The general paid the courtesy of calling on me in my hotel when I arrived in the capital, something that had never happened in my previous visits to Washington. It was during this call that the subject of Cambodia first came up. The general wondered if I could explain the significance of Prince Sihanouk's resignation as president of the CGDC, which had recently been announced. I said the Prince was always hard to fathom but I thought it might have been his way of putting pressure on the Chinese. The Chinese had been making two main points to me recently: first, they did not want the Khmer Rouge to play a prominent role in a Cambodian settlement; and second, the Pol Pot "clique" must be gotten rid of completely. I suggested that Sihanouk, who, I was sure, harbored strong feelings against Pol Pot, might have had some influence on the Chinese in this regard.

While I did not mention it to General Powell, it was my feeling that the Chinese were disassociating themselves from the Khmer Rouge largely as a factor in their relations with the West, especially the United States. The Cold War was over. China's economy was just beginning to take off. It needed good relations with the United States. So it was convenient for their leaders to let it be known that they disapproved of Pol Pot. But there was never any doubt that the Chinese would never permit an agreement that did not include the Khmer Rouge.

General Powell turned the discussion rather quickly to the recent shooting down by the Americans of an Iranian airliner; understandably, this was of more concern to him than the motivations of Prince Sihanouk. He did comment favorably on Prince Sihanouk's son, Prince Norodam Ranariddh, who, he thought, was reliable and sensible and more likely than his father to make a constructive contribution to peace. My experience was that the son followed his father's directions closely. Sihanouk, his unpredictability notwithstanding, was essential to the peace process—not his son.

In accordance with its role as ASEAN's interlocutor on the Cambodian question, Indonesia organized an informal meeting of the four internal factions in Jakarta at the end of July 1988. There the faction leaders reached a loose consensus on the main features of a comprehensive settlement that reflected to a degree the main points in the UN paper. Differences remained among the various countries in the region, however, on such matters as the scope and timing of the cessation of assistance to the Cambodian factions. Hanoi and Phnom Penh continued to insist on the "military elimination" of the Khmer Rouge. Prince Sihanouk, while continuing to demand officially that both the PRK and the CGDK be dismantled, had concluded that any extensive dismantling of the PRK would lead to anarchy. He therefore began to suggest in talks with me and with others that initially a provisional government should rely on the existing administrative structure.

For his part, Hun Sen, in talking with Rafee Ahmed in the late summer of 1988, pushed for the establishment of a "national reconciliation council" comprising of the four Cambodian factions under the chairmanship of Prince Sihanouk. The council would not, he said, operate within the framework of the PRK but would discuss the adoption of a new constitution and the future political, economic and social systems of the country. By this time all parties were in agreement on the holding of a limited international conference. But one side strongly distrusted Vietnam, while the other was determined to eliminate the Khmer Rouge; and Hun Sen, supported by Hanoi, clearly retained a strong and understandable interest in preserving his own government, the PRK.

In April 1989, Vietnam announced, in a joint statement with the Lao People's Democratic Government and the People's Republic of Cambodia, that it would withdraw all of its forces from Cambodia by the end of September. The joint statement foresaw that the withdrawal of the Vietnamese troops and the cessation of foreign interference and provision of military assistance should be supervised by the International Control and Supervision Commission established by the Geneva Agreements of 1954, supplemented by the chairman of the Jakarta Joint Informal Meeting and a personal representative of the Secretary-General. Other countries were moving toward a larger UN role. When they visited UN Headquarters, senior State Department officials told us that the United States considered it logical that the United Nations should have principal responsibility in monitoring the terms of a Cambodian settlement. Prince Sihanouk and his coalition partners, the ASEAN countries, China and the Soviet Union all had a similar view. However, given the Vietnamese position, there was some talk among the delegations in New York of a "hybrid" operation, combining the International Control Commission and the United Nations. I immediately discouraged this, pointing out that the effectiveness of UN peacekeeping operations always depended on a single command and a clear line of authority running from the Security Council, through the Secretary-General, to the Force Commander or the Chief Military Observer. I repeatedly emphasized in private conversations and in official reports that if the United Nations was to undertake a peacekeeping mission in Cambodia, it was imperative that there be a clear, realistic and accepted mandate.

THE PARIS PEACE PROCESS BEGINS

In May 1989 Prince Sihanouk held talks in Jakarta with Hun Sen. The French gained the impression—which turned out to be mistaken—that the two had reached some kind of an understanding. Assessing the situation, partly on this basis, as favorable for completion of a Cambodian settlement, they took the initiative in convoking a peace conference in Paris. The Quai d'Orsay immediately came to me to ask for the United Nations' assistance. Between May and the end of July when the conference convened, Rafee Ahmed and his staff provided the French with advice and assistance. The Paris Conference on Cambodia took the form of a limited international conference, as we had suggested eight years earlier (with several additional non-Asian countries participating). All together, 18 countries plus the United Nations took part. France and Indonesia served as co-presidents. I attended in my capacity of Secretary-General rather than in the framework of the good offices responsibility given to me in the numerous General Assembly resolutions on Cambodia since the resolutions were generally hostile to Vietnam. The United Nations was a full participant in the conference from the beginning, even though I signed the Final Act only as a witness. The UN delegation was entitled to speak and to vote just as the national delegations were. Since all decisions were by consensus, the United Nations, like the other participants, had the right of veto. I know of no other instance where this was the case.

By the time the conference opened, there was general agreement that there should be some kind of International Control Mechanism (ICM) to supervise the implementation of the internal aspects of a Cambodian settlement. The UN staff wrote the basic paper on the subject that defined the responsibilities foreseen for the ICM. It did not identify the United Nations with the mechanism, but the wording was such that the United Nations could be inserted as the implementing agency. The functioning of the mechanism would clearly depend on conditions in Cambodia, which were largely unknown. Hedi Annabi had the idea that a UN mission should be sent to the country to assess the functioning of the bureaucracy, the state of infrastructure and the security situation. I put this idea forward in my statement to the opening session of the conference. I pointed out that the creation of a credible international control mechanism, under whatever auspices, was directly contingent upon the identification of a clear and realistic mandate, the adoption of an effective decision-making process and the provision of the necessary human, logistical and financial resources. A precise evaluation of such resources could be made only after a visit to the area by a fact-finding mission. This suggestion was quickly accepted by the conference, in the understanding that the mission would gather information of a purely technical nature without prejudice to the positions of any of the parties or states participating in the conference.

The UN fact-finding mission was in Cambodia (and briefly in Vietnam and Thailand) for just over two weeks. The mission traveled to all parts of the country. When the mission visited the forward location of the Sihanouk army (ANS), the commander-in-chief, Prince Norodam Ranariddh (Sihanouk's son), stated that only an ICM under the United Nations would be acceptable to him. His army would respect a cease-fire only if the United Nations could monitor and verify the Vietnamese withdrawal.

The technical mission returned with daunting information concerning conditions in Cambodia. In brief, it found that the existing infrastructure, sources of supply and services were not sufficient to support the deployment and operation of an ICM. Until this UN mission went to Cambodia, there was no clear conception among the Paris Conference participants of the composition of an International Control Commission. After the completion of the mission, it was generally accepted that whatever the mandate of the ICM might be, it should be a UN operation.

This first session of the Paris Conference on Cambodia lasted exactly a month. When it broke up it was widely, although unfairly, viewed as a total failure. The refusal of the Phnom Penh government to relinquish power and join in a coalition government that would include the Khmer Rouge had prevented progress on national reconciliation. Two other major points that were left unsettled were the modalities of a cease-fire and the nature of the International Control Mechanism. In my statement to the final session, I acknowledged that "the ship has not yet reached the shores of peace, even though it has caught occasional glimpses of them." Yet I felt that there had been significant accomplishments to which the United Nations had made major contributions. Working papers provided by the UN team served as the main basis of productive discussion in the three conference committees. They covered, in addition to the International Control Mechanism, the establishment of a cease-fire, electoral procedures and voter registration. The conference reached unanimous agreement on a plan of action for the recovery and reconstruction of Cambodia, which was based on a paper submitted by the UN delegation. There was also partial agreement on the repatriation of refugees and displaced persons, including the need to give the UN High Commissioner for Refugees a central role. The work done at this first session, based heavily on papers prepared by the United Nations and on the report of the technical mission, would figure prominently in the final agreement.

THE FIVE PERMANENT MEMBERS STEP IN

Nonetheless, there was a wide sense of frustration following the adjournment of the Paris Conference, marked by mutual recrimination among the Cambodian factions and some increase in military operations in the field. Son Sann, the

Prime Minister of the Coalition Government of Democratic Cambodia, visited me in New York and complained bitterly that Hun Sen remained too close to Vietnam. The Prime Minister had sent three messages to Hun Sen warning him that the policy followed by his government would ensure the Khmer Rouge's return to power. He advised that someone should get the Soviet Union, which had provided extensive armaments to Phnom Penh, to persuade the latter to accept the proposal for a coalition government of the four factions. I suggested to the Prime Minister that it would be useful for the Khmer Rouge, as a member of his government, to make a public statement that it did not seek to regain power. This would calm widespread apprehensions concerning the role that it might play in Phnom Penh. Son Sann said he would heed this advice. He recalled that Pol Pot had earlier declared he would leave Cambodia when the Vietnamese withdrew all their forces. The Prime Minister thought that Pol Pot and the notorious people around him should leave Cambodia as soon as Phnom Penh accepted the CGDK proposal for a coalition government.

In October 1989 the Australian foreign minister, Gareth Evans, circulated a proposal for a Cambodian settlement that called for the United Nations to take over the civil administration of the country until an elected government was established. The United Nations would, in effect, replace the Phnom Penh regime, which would cease to exist, thus solving the power-sharing problem among the four factions that until then had proven intractable. Evans did not consult with the United Nations before circulating his proposals. The concept of the United Nations' assuming administrative responsibility in Cambodia was not entirely new. Prince Sihanouk had suggested more or less the same thing as early as 1981, and U.S. Congressman Stephen Solarz later made a similar proposal to me.[2] But the Australian proposal received wide attention, as it was personally sponsored and pushed by Foreign Minister Evans. While it was unrealistic in its assumptions of what the United Nations could reasonably be expected to do, it served a major purpose: it broke the period of inaction that followed the adjournment of the Paris Conference on Cambodia and was instrumental in spurring the five Permanent Members of the Security Council to begin joint consultations on Cambodia. The idea of an "enhanced" role for the United Nations that the Australian paper had inspired provided a new basis for discussion.

At this time the United States, whether influenced by the Australian paper or not, began to support an ambitious role for the United Nations. A U.S. position paper that was given to us in confidence by the State Department foresaw a peacekeeping force of between 8,000 and 10,000 troops. It suggested further that the United Nations should oversee the establishment of a new national army and national police force and that, in the meantime, UN personnel should replace the senior Cambodian police officials. All government ministries would be under the authority of, and report to, a special representative of the Secretary-

General. The transitional period was to extend over two to three years. The Soviet Foreign Minister, Edouard Shevardnadze, in a meeting with me in July 1989, also spoke forcefully of the desirability of a "peacemaking role" for the United Nations in Cambodia, specifically through participation in the International Control Mechanism.

THE FIVE PERMANENT MEMBERS TAKE ACTION

The United States took the initiative to bring the five Permanent Members together for a series of highly visible talks on Cambodia. Meeting first in Paris, the Five agreed that they would be guided by 16 principles in working for a resolution of the Cambodian problem. These principles, following in many respects the Australian proposals, foresaw a major enhancement of the UN role. UN responsibilities would include verification of the withdrawal of foreign forces, assurance of internal security and the administration of free and fair elections. For the first time, it was proposed that a Special Representative of the Secretary-General be appointed to supervise all UN activities.

I welcomed the readiness of Australia and, then, of the Permanent Members to accord such large responsibility to the United Nations. Realizing that the United Nations was now clearly going to have a major role in Cambodia, I established a task force in the Secretariat to make preparations. At the same time, I was concerned that some of the tasks envisioned were beyond the United Nations' capacity or could infringe on Cambodian sovereignty, which, according to the principles designed by the Permanent Members, would rest with a Supreme National Council (SNC). I expressed these sentiments to the ambassadors of the Permanent Members when they called to brief me on their Paris meeting. The U.S. Ambassador, Tom Pickering, speaking for the Five, said that in the meeting the group had focused especially on the electoral process that would unfold in Cambodia. They had taken full account of the useful paper the Secretariat had provided on the subject during the Paris Conference. Now they would like to have my comments.

I first made clear how very much I welcomed the initiative of the Five. It was evident that important work had already been accomplished in the talks they had held in Paris. I was pleased that such confidence was being placed in the United Nations. The Secretariat would do its best to carry out whatever mandate was given it by the Security Council. I wanted to emphasize, however (as I had already done and would do repeatedly over the next months), that the mandate would have to be clear and that we would need constant political support from all the concerned parties plus adequate financial and human resources. I hoped, moreover, that the possible ramifications of the tasks foreseen for the United Nations would be given careful consideration. An example was internal security. The United Nations had never had responsibility for the maintenance of law and order within a sovereign state. Even in Namibia, primary responsibility for this function had rested with the South African - appointed Administrator-General.

My very able legal counsel, Carl-August Fleischhauer, carried this point further by noting that the United Nations had never been directly responsible for the conduct of elections in an independent country. The organization of elections would inevitably involve the United Nations in aspects of internal administration. How far would such internal involvement extend and how would it relate to the sovereignty of the Supreme National Council as described in the principles defined by the Five? Fleischhauer suggested that in their further meetings, the Five would need to give much consideration to such questions, a view that I endorsed while also emphasizing that we did not wish to be in any way negative toward what the Five were undertaking. It struck me, as we were talking, how far we had come in the short time since the end of the Cold War. For more than four decades, the Permanent Members had been reluctant to give the United Nations any independent authority at all. Now they seemed prepared to have it administer a whole country, a task that was, in my view, inappropriate and beyond its capacity.

The United Nations did not participate in the first meeting of the Permanent Members. Beforehand they had sought the advice of the Secretariat on various technical points, however, and after the first meeting a UN representative participated in at least every other meeting. As a result, the talks were frequently called the Five plus One. This was an accurate description.[3] I was fully briefed by the Five after every meeting and had the opportunity to offer comments and counsel.

The Permanent Members were making very slow progress toward agreement on the framework of a comprehensive settlement, when in early March 1990 a further informal meeting of the Cambodian factions and Vietnam was held in Jakarta. The factions were unable to come to any formal agreements. Neither the Vietnamese nor the Khmer Rouge seemed particularly impressed by the work of the Five. Rafee Ahmed observed one bitter exchange between the Vietnamese and Indonesian foreign ministers in which the former stated that the Five should mind their own business. Nevertheless, an understanding was reached on the need for the United Nations to have an enhanced role in dealing with the various aspects of the Cambodian settlement process and on the establishment of a Supreme National Council.

Until then the Phnom Penh regime had resisted a dominant UN role as had its Vietnamese sponsor largely because of the anti-Vietnamese tenor of the General Assembly resolutions. Now all the parties involved agreed on the concept. This lent new momentum to the Five who in their Paris meeting on March 12-13 adopted a "summary of discussions" that reaffirmed the need for UN involvement in a comprehensive political settlement, "including both military and administrative aspects." The summary called for effective measures to guarantee the human rights and fundamental freedoms of the Cambodian people and covered three other main issues: the organization of elections, the establishment of a Supreme National Council and the creation of a United Nations Transitional Authority in Cambodia (UNTAC). Ahmed, who participated in this session, reported that agreement among the Five had not been easy because the Chinese had insisted on language that made clear that the SNC could be established only with the agreement of the four Cambodian parties—that is, including the Khmer Rouge. China also insisted on giving the SNC a status that would at least imply the dismantling of the Phnom Penh regime. It obtained the deletion of language that would have allowed the United Nations to make use of "existing structures."

The assistance provided by Rafee Ahmed in connection with the meeting of the Five in Paris on July 16-17, 1990, is illustrative of the role the United Nations played in furthering these talks. This was one of the meetings to which the United Nations was not invited. However, Ahmed, feeling it would be useful to have direct contact with the Five before their talks, went to Paris and was able to meet each member separately. He found the three Western members rather despondent because they felt both China and the Soviet Union had hardened their positions. Ahmed told them that he had found both the Chinese and the Soviets seriously interested in furthering a settlement and that they would find it worthwhile actively to pursue their efforts to secure agreement, the course they then followed. Ahmed also briefed the Permanent Five representatives on his recent contacts with the Cambodian factions and informed them that he had explained to Hun Sen the procedures the United Nations would follow in bringing about the regrouping, cantonment and eventual disarming of the armed forces belonging to the four Cambodian parties. Ahmed told the Five that Hun Sen had appeared satisfied with his explanation. At a working lunch on the following day, Ahmed was told that during the morning, with the help of the information he had transmitted, the Five had agreed on a paper on military matters.

On August 28, 1990, the Permanent Five reached agreement in New York on the framework of a comprehensive Cambodian settlement.[4] Less than two weeks later, at a meeting convened in Jakarta by the co-chairmen of the Paris International Conference, the Cambodian parties accepted the framework document in its entirety as the basis for settling the Cambodian conflict. They also agreed on the nature and functions of the Supreme National Council as "the unique legitimate body and source of authority in which, throughout the transitional period, the independence, sovereignty and unity of Cambodia is embodied." The SNC was to consist of 12 members, including the leaders of the four Cambodian parties; if it chose, it would elect a chairman who would be the thirteenth member. On September 20 the Security Council endorsed the framework for a comprehensive political settlement and welcomed its acceptance by the Cambodian parties. On October 16, 1990, the General Assembly adopted essentially the same resolution, 45 to 3. There was still a good bit to be done before peace was in hand, but that it would come was no longer in doubt.

A NORTHERN DIVERSION

The Soviet member of the Permanent Five working group on Cambodia was Deputy Foreign Minister Igor Rogochov. Rafee Ahmed had found him to be flexible and responsive to suggestions. During the months when the Permanent Members were meeting, the long-standing quarrel between Japan and the Soviet Union over Japan's Northern Islands, which the Soviet Union had occupied since World War II, flared up, jeopardizing the prospect of better Soviet/Japanese relations. I had long felt that the United Nations should help in any way possible to resolve this last dispute deriving from World War II. Ahmed's frequent informal contacts with Rogochov in connection with Cambodia provided an opportunity to suggest some ideas on the Northern Islands in a discreet and unofficial way.

Thinking back to the ideas we had developed in the case of the Falklands/Malvinas conflict, we decided that Rafee Ahmed should put to Rogochov the idea of placing the islands under an interim UN administration with provision for both a Japanese and Soviet representation on the Islands. The UN administration would last until Moscow and Tokyo reached an agreement on the islands' ultimate disposition. Rogochov found the idea interesting and referred it to Foreign Minister Shevardnadze while he himself continued discussions on the subject with Ahmed. Given the apparent Soviet interest, Ahmed suggested that I inform the Japanese of the exchange and sound them out on the idea. I felt this could give the Japanese government the impression that I was making a formal proposal, which was not the case. I thought it better for Rafee Ahmed to inform the Japanese very quietly and informally of the exchanges with the Soviets, which he did. Their reaction was cautious. While not rejecting the idea outright, they gave no indication of wishing to pursue it. The dialogue with Rogochov was not continued after the Permanent Members completed their draft text for a Cambodian settlement. I understand, however, that Russian representatives have since occasionally referred to the idea in conversations with Ahmed as something that might still come to fruition.

THE FRAMEWORK FOR A SETTLEMENT

The framework for a comprehensive settlement was composed of five sections: (1) transition arrangements regarding the administration of Cambodia; (2)

military arrangements; (3) elections under UN auspices; (4) human rights protection; and (5) international guarantees. The resolutions endorsing the framework called for a resumed Paris Conference to transform it into a draft agreement and to draw up a detailed plan of implementation. Since the United Nations would be responsible for implementing most provisions of the settlement, I believed that we should be directly involved in the formulation of the plan and whatever final document emerged from Paris. By this time we had sent four fact-finding missions to Cambodia and a fifth was about to depart to assess the prospects for cooperation between the United Nations and nongovernmental organizations in the restoration of stability and respect for human rights. Since the United Nations had far more information about conditions in Cambodia than anyone else, I instructed the Cambodian Task Force to prepare detailed papers on each of the headings included in the framework text.

I met with the French Foreign Minister, Roland Dumas, shortly after the resolutions of the Security Council and the General Assembly were adopted with the intention of proposing that the conference ask me to provide a draft implementation plan. This proved unnecessary. The minister spontaneously asked that the Secretariat assist in the preparation of the operative parts of the final agreement. As it worked out, the French and Indonesian co-presidents did the major part of the drafting of Section 1 of the final act while the annexes covering the UNTAC mandate, force withdrawal, cease-fire and related measures, elections, repatriation of Cambodian refugees and displaced persons and principles for a new constitution were taken almost verbatim from papers provided by the UN Secretariat. Sections 3 and 4 of the final act on the sovereignty, independence and neutrality of Cambodia and on rehabilitation and reconstruction were also based on papers provided by the United Nations.

APPOINTMENT OF THE SECRETARY-GENERAL'S SPECIAL REPRESENTATIVE

In a meeting with the Permanent Five on the day after the Security Council and the General Assembly endorsed the framework agreement, I asked how soon they felt I should appoint my Special Representative. The French representative, Claude Martin, replied "as soon as possible." The American representative, Assistant Secretary of State John Bolton, suggested that the timing of the appointment could be used to prod the Cambodian parties to agree on the functioning of the SNC by indicating I would proceed with the appointment only when the Cambodians had resolved their differences. I said that I would try to find the right man which would not be easy. (In the Secretariat we had developed a profile of the person needed for the post.)

The next month when I was in Tokyo, Foreign Minister Taro Nakayama also mentioned the appointment of my Special Representative for Cambodia. The minister said that Japan would be interested in providing a suitable candidate. However, the next day the head of the UN Division in the Foreign Ministry suggested to a member of my staff that the minister did not necessarily have a Japanese candidate in mind for the Special Representative post. Japan, he said, would be providing substantial material backing for the UN operation and in this context had identified a good number of candidates who would be qualified to participate in UNTAC. There was never any further suggestion from Tokyo that a Japanese should be named as the Special Representative.

As the months passed I came under increasing pressure from the Permanent Five to appoint Rafee Ahmed to the position. Indeed, it was widely accepted among all the parties that, given the crucial role he had played in the achievement of an agreement, he was far and away the best choice for the post. My problem was that Ahmed did not want to be named Special Representative. He felt that the UNTAC operation would be a very complex one that would need extensive support and guidance from Headquarters. He could be of greater service as head of the responsible department or supervisory unit in New York, a post that he assumed my successor would give him. I could not disagree with him and yet I was reluctant to appoint anyone else, knowing his unique qualifications for the post and the strong support he had among the parties concerned. Finally, in October, I sounded out the Permanent Five and Prince Sihanouk on Ambassador Mohammed Sahnoun of Algeria and Ambassador Mahmoud Mestiri of Tunisia. The Prince's reaction to Sahnoun was favorable, but he left the choice entirely to me. The Five continued to express strong support for Rafee Ahmed and did not react to the other two names. By then there were barely two months left before the new Secretary-General took over, and I decided that the choice of his representative could best be left to him. Unfortunately, Ahmed was not named head of department in the Secretariat but instead was sent to head the UN regional economic commission in Bangkok. Secretary-General Boutros-Ghali's decision to name a Japanese, Yasushi Akashi, as Special Representative, did not stem from any Japanese pressure for the post while I was in office.

AGREEMENT IS REACHED

The Permanent Five, together with the co-presidents of the Paris Conference on Cambodia and the UN delegation, reached consensus at a meeting in Paris on November 23 to 26 on the text of a comprehensive political settlement. The text was an amplification of the framework that all the parties had already approved.

By this point the papers prepared by the United Nations were all incorporated into the text with one exception. The Soviet Union objected to the language we had proposed on the demobilization of the armed forces belonging to the four factions. They did not feel this could be sold to Phnom Penh or Hanoi, who contended that the national army of Cambodia could not be equated with the opposition factions' guerilla forces. After two separate meetings with Ahmed, the Soviet delegation accepted a formulation according to which all parties agreed "to undertake a fixed process of return to civilian life of all categories of their military forces, and to do so within a reasonable time frame, in accordance with a detailed plan to be drawn up by UNTAC in consultation with the parties." It was understood that I would have to spell this out more clearly when I submitted an operations plan to the Security Council.

The question of how any differences between the Supreme National Council and the Special Representative of the Secretary-General were to be settled was also resolved at this meeting of the Permanent Five, the co-presidents, and the UN delegation. After extensive discussion, the UN delegation proposed the following wording, which came to be of major importance to the Special Representative in exercising his responsibilities: "If there is no consensus on any given matter among the members of the SNC, the Secretary-General's Special Representative should make every endeavor to reach a consensus on such a matter. In case it is unattainable, the Secretary-General's Special Representative is entitled to make a final decision, taking fully into account views expressed in the SNC." This wording, in effect, gave the Special Representative supreme power if he chose to use it.

On April 22, 1991, the co-presidents and I issued a joint appeal for a temporary cessation of hostilities to create a favorable environment for a forthcoming meeting of the SNC and the co-presidents in Jakarta. In response, the Cambodian parties informed me that they intended to respect the appeal, voluntarily observing their first cease-fire in 12 years of fighting. At a meeting of the SNC in Pattaya, Thailand, later in June, there was a unanimous decision to call for an open-ended and unconditional cease-fire and for a halt to the receipt of outside military assistance. Prince Sihanouk, who, after a period of withdrawal from participation in the negotiations had once again returned to the fold, was elected president the following month. In mid-September, while meeting in New York, the SNC reached agreement on the remaining outstanding issues. Seventy percent rather than 100 percent of all forces would be demobilized prior to the elections. Further, to resolve a long-standing disagreement on the organization of elections, the SNC members accepted a UN-suggested compromise according to which the elections would be held on a provincial basis following a system of proportional representation. To meet a concern about Prince Sihanouk's inability or unwillingness to make decisions in the SNC in the absence of a consensus, the prince sent me a letter stating that he would always make decisions or, exercising the sovereignty vested in him, would delegate the authority to do so to my Special Representative in Cambodia.

At the end of the SNC meeting in New York, I met with Prince Sihanouk, now the President of Cambodia, and with the leaders of the four factions: Hun Sen, Son Sann, Khieu Samphan, and Prince Norodom Ranariddh. Sihanouk was in high spirits and did most of the talking. I asked him how he saw the future of his country. He said that he looked for the emergence of a liberal democracy, embracing political pluralism and respecting all residents of Cambodia. He cautioned, however, on the risks of "accidents." He felt strongly that UNTAC should remain in Cambodia after the elections so that the situation could be fully normalized. I said that I recognized that it would take time for the situation to be fully consolidated. In this respect, we were "in his hands."

With the final agreement now in sight, the Secretariat staff intensified planning for the deployment of UNTAC, which would likely be the largest field operation undertaken by the United Nations. For some time we had been considering the need for an interim UN peacekeeping operation to be on the ground as quickly as possible since it was clear that full deployment of UNTAC would take up to a year after the Paris Agreements were signed. I had sent a survey mission to evaluate personnel requirements and the modalities of control and to submit recommendations on a mine-awareness program. The experience of the survey mission, which did not receive adequate cooperation from the military elements in Cambodia, had made clear that an early UN peacekeeping presence would be essential. I informed the co-presidents of the Paris Conference and the Permanent Five that, initially, the United Nations could assist the Cambodian parties to maintain the present cease-fire by deploying a small good offices mission upon signature of the agreements. This was uniformly welcomed. The United States was concerned about the budgetary aspects, however, and both they and the French asked that the Permanent Members be shown in advance the draft of my report to the Security Council on the subject. The United States did not, in this case, pursue the financial question, and the United Nations Good Offices Mission in Cambodia (UNGOMIC) was authorized by Security Council Resolution 717 without controversy.

Aside from this initial U.S. concern about the cost of UNGOMIC, no serious questions were raised about the cost of UNTAG, which was estimated at $1 billion annually. This was all the more remarkable since at the very same time reservations were being expressed about the far lower costs of the peacekeeping operations in the Western Sahara, Angola and elsewhere. In my experience, Cambodia was the only peacekeeping operation where money was not a problem. This may have resulted in part from the fact that Japan voluntarily undertook to pay a larger share of the cost than it would have been assessed under the regular assessment formula.

REFUGEES UNDER PRESSURE

As prospects for a Cambodian settlement brightened in 1989, we began to make preparations for an orderly repatriation of the approximately 300,000 refugees living in camps just inside Thailand. As these preparations were getting under way, I received reports that refugees were being pressured and even forced by political bosses to return to Cambodia prior to a peace settlement and without the provision of suitable conditions for return. In late January the entire population of an encampment associated with the Khmer Rouge was relocated to unknown destinations across the border. More than half eventually made their way back on their own to UN-assisted border camps, many ill from malaria, malnutrition or injured in mine explosions. A reduction in the census of various camps showed that the same pattern was being repeated elsewhere.

For a good many years a special unit of the Thai army was in charge of security in the refugee camps. In the face of continuing complaints of brutality and corruption, many emanating from humanitarian organizations working to assist the refugees, the Thai government withdrew the army and deployed a specially trained civilian force to maintain order. While this brought a marked improvement in conditions in the camps, the presence of this refugee population entailed serious problems (as well as considerable profit) for Thai authorities. In February 1990 the Secretary-General of the Thai National Security Council, Suwit Suthanukul, published an article in which he stated that Thailand could send displaced persons back to Cambodia without waiting for a comprehensive settlement, which may take a long time, if there is a cease-fire and if it is safe to do so. The Thai Prime Minister denied that there was any intention to force the displaced persons to return to Cambodia. Still, it was evident that the Thais either could not or would not do anything to prevent Cambodian factions from pressuring refugees to return to their country without making any preparations for their reception. As peace grew nearer, the forced repatriations became more rampant. After the senior UN official in Bangkok stated publicly that the Khmer Rouge was guilty of forcing an entire encampment to return to an area in Cambodia under Khmer Rouge control, seven U.S. Senators wrote to me urging that the United Nations take action to prevent this from happening again.

One of my last actions regarding Cambodia was to try to correct this situation. Just prior to the signing of the Paris Agreements, I appealed directly to Prince Sihanouk, as president of the Supreme National Council, to secure the commitment of the parties not to organize any repatriation outside the framework of the draft agreements. Sihanouk quickly assented. While I was not in a position to observe the border situation closely in the following months, I was told that the situation improved. After the signing of the agreements, the extraordinary repatriation program supervised by the High Commissioner for Refugees got under way and removed any ground for forced repatriation.

The generous contributions given by governments over an entire decade to alleviate the plight of the Cambodian refugees remains as evidence of the spirit of humanity that sometimes motivates government policies. The care that was administered to these benighted people by the various UN agencies is likewise a tribute to what the UN system can accomplish in meeting urgent human needs. While I was no longer at the United Nations to witness the repatriation of these thousands of people and their safe resettlement, I am told that the accomplishment of UNHCR was hardly short of miraculous. This was a central element in the happy ending of the Cambodian tragedy.

THE PEACE AGREEMENTS ARE SIGNED

The Final Act of the Paris Conference on Cambodia, along with its associated agreements, was signed in Versailles in the presence of President Mitterrand, on October 23, 1991, the sixty-fifth birthday of Prince Sihanouk.[5] The agreements accorded to the United Nations responsibilities that were in many respects unprecedented. The UN mandate entailed the rehabilitation of a fractured and displaced society—the restoration of stability and freedom in a country in which governance was ill-defined and in transition.

The United Nations was charged specifically to:
- Supervise the cease-fire and the cessation of hostilities and verify the withdrawal of foreign forces.
- Bring about the regroupment and cantonment of all the armed forces in Cambodia and ensure that 70 percent were disarmed and demobilized.
- Assist in the detection and clearing of minefields.
- Supervise and control existing administrative structures, including the police.
- Organize and conduct elections for a constituent assembly.
- Ensure respect for human rights.
- Ensure the repatriation of refugees and displaced persons so that they might take part in elections.
- Launch, as a parallel measure, an international program for the rehabilitation and reconstruction of Cambodia.

In the course of the long negotiations, we had been able to modify the proposal that the UN assume full responsibility for the administration of Cambodia. The administrative structure of the Hun Sen government would remain in place, but not the government itself. Still, the functions to be undertaken by the UN would inevitably involve UNTAC in central aspects of domestic administration. It would have unprecedented responsibility to organize elections in a sovereign country. This could be—and was—seen as indicative of a new era in which the United Nations would assume responsibility for the restoration of states where the institutions of governance had failed. The risks were obviously great. That is why I repeatedly emphasized that the ability of the United Nations fully to discharge its responsibilities would depend on the extent to which the international community made available the required human and financial resources.

As I witnessed the signature of these Paris Accords, I was proud of the major contribution that the United Nations had made to their development. I was equally proud and a little wary of the confidence that the countries concerned, especially the Permanent Members of the Security Council, had come to place in the United Nations. Cambodia was bound to stretch to the limits the capacity of the Organization to bring peace and order and freedom to a country that had been severely fractured by conflict. The ultimate success of the UN operation derived in good measure from the following factors:

- Unity of the Permanent Members of the Security Council.
- The readiness of the international community to provide the resources required for successful fulfillment of the mandate defined by the Security Council for the operation.
- Familiarity with the political, social and economic conditions within which the United Nations would have to carry out its assigned responsibilities.
- Comprehensive plans prepared in advance for the operation.
- Participation of the Secretary-General or his representatives in the formulation of the mandate covering the operation for which he would be responsible.
- Superior field leadership.

These factors, when taken together, stand as a recipe for success that emerges from the Cambodian experience.

ANNEX

1. In my report to the fortieth session of the General Assembly on the Situation in Kampuchea, I had identified the main elements which should serve as a framework for a settlement of the Kampuchean problem. However, at that time, the procedural aspects of setting the process of dialogue into motion remained to be resolved. Since then, there has been some progress on this point. In particular, Prince Sihanouk has undertaken talks with Mr. Hun Sen of the Phnom Penh régime, and an informal meeting is envisaged between the Kampuchean parties and other States concerned, to take place in Jakarta, possibly next month. It would appear therefore that the procedural hurdle could be overcome in the not too distant future.

2. There remains a need to put forward more concrete ideas upon the basis of which a comprehensive settlement could be elaborated. Following his second round of talks with Mr. Hun Sen last January, Prince Sihanouk met my Special Representative and suggested that I should pursue the efforts I had undertaken last year to build a scenario for a solution. In this regard, I consider that the most critical issues to be addressed are the formation and functioning of a provisional government of national reconciliation, the modalities for total withdrawal of foreign forces, and the nature of international supervision and guarantees. In addition, a "trigger" mechanism may be needed to set into motion the implementation of a plan.

3. On the basis of a firm commitment by Viet Nam to withdraw all of its forces within a specified timeframe, talks between the Kampuchean parties could be envisioned. The purpose of these talks would be to achieve agreement on the establishment of a provisional government of national reconciliation under the leadership of Prince Sihanouk. Once established, this government would be recognized as the sole legal representative of Kampuchea.

4. Simultaneously with the establishment of a provisional government, a comprehensive cease-fire should enter into effect, and all foreign forces and Kampuchean armed elements should be regrouped and confined to bases. The total withdrawal of foreign forces would then take place, in phases to be completed within an agreed timeframe. Consideration could be given to disarming and disbanding the Kampuchean armed elements, so that they may peacefully participate in the political process which would ensue.

5. Upon the establishment of the provisional government, an international peace-keeping force would also be introduced to control the cease-fire and withdrawal arrangements and to assist the provisional government with the maintenance of law and order. Subsequently, other international assistance would be provided, including comprehensive programmes for the return of refugees and displaced persons and for the reconstruction and development of the country. During the final stages of the transitional period, free and fair general elections would take place under international supervision. Indeed, the United Nations has a rich history of involvement in such matters, which can be drawn from as appropriate.

6. It would appear necessary to envision two types of guarantees. The first type would be those which the Kampucheans themselves will undertake regarding the non-return to policies and practices of a recent past, as well as regarding the status of Kampuchea and its attitude towards its neighbours. The second type would be those which the neighbouring States and the international community would undertake vis-à-vis Kampuchea.

7. These ideas are, of course, flexible, and would require further consideration, particularly regarding their interrelationships and the modalities and sequence of their implementation. I believe, however, that the ideas are consistent with the recent developments and initiatives regarding the Kampuchean problem. It is my fervent hope that continued dialogue will lead to the initiation of a genuine negotiating process, with the aim of realizing the generally agreed objectives for a solution. Of course, I remain ready to be of assistance in any way which might be requested.

1 June 1988

SEVENTEEN

YUGOSLAVIA:
A EUROPEAN TRAGEDY

PRESIDENT MILAN KUCAN OF SLOVENIA called for an urgent meeting of the Security Council on June 28, 1991, in view of the air attacks launched against his country by units of the Yugoslav army. The Council did not respond. It first reacted officially to the conflict and humanitarian distress that accompanied the disintegration of Yugoslavia on September 25, 1991, when it adopted Resolution 713. This resolution, which was based on a draft prepared by the European Community (EC) members in the Council, placed first emphasis on the Council's support for the efforts of the Community to restore peace and dialogue in Yugoslavia. It specifically supported the deployment by the EC of cease-fire observers and its sponsorship of the Conference on Yugoslavia in The Hague to develop a basis for peace.

The resolution called for only two UN initiatives. First, it invited the Secretary-General "to offer his assistance without delay, in consultation with the Government of Yugoslavia" to all those promoting the efforts for peace and to report as soon as possible to the Council. Second, after characterizing the situation as a threat to international peace and security, the Council imposed a general and complete embargo on the delivery of weapons and military equipment to Yugoslavia. The Council also called on all states to refrain from "any action which might contribute to increasing tension and to impeding or delaying a peace and negotiated outcome to the conflict. . . ." This was generally understood to be an admonition against premature recognition of Croatia and Slovenia.[1]

The balance between the European Community and the United Nations was a delicate one. The EC had assumed responsibility for dealing with the

Yugoslav crisis, and its members had no intention of ceding this responsibility to the United Nations. Yet the Europeans themselves had concluded that UN endorsement of their efforts was needed, partly because the parties in Yugoslavia did not trust the EC as being completely nonpartisan. Furthermore, the EC had not been able, on its own, to impose effective sanctions. This could only be done with global effectiveness by the United Nations. The Parliamentary Assembly of the Council of Europe had requested its members to ask the United Nations Security Council "to consider sending an effective military force to Yugoslavia in order to secure a cease-fire and a sensible solution to the future of Yugoslavia and its republics." At this point such a request was unrealistic, but it indicated the Europeans' desire to see the United Nations more deeply involved in the crisis but not in competition with the EU.

It was appropriate that the EC, along with the other European organizations, should have the principal responsibility for dealing with Yugoslavia; clearly it was a European regional conflict. I was convinced that it was extremely important for the future of the EC that the European initiative succeed. I, of course, had been following the alarming developments in Yugoslavia with growing concern, but I did not wish to see the United Nations compete with the EC over Yugoslavia nor did I wish personally to interfere in any way with the work being done by Lord Carrington, the EC-appointed chair of the Conference on Yugoslavia. This is the spirit in which I undertook the vaguely defined responsibility given me in Resolution 713 to assist in the promotion of the various measures initiated by the EC and other organizations to end the conflict.

I decided that the most useful thing I could do in the short run was to talk with representatives of the organizations that were directly involved in the Yugoslav crisis so that I could provide a comprehensive and objective assessment of the situation to the Council. For this purpose I established contact with Lord Carrington and met with Hans Dietrich Genscher, the vice chancellor and foreign minister of Germany who was in the chair of the Conference on Security and Cooperation in Europe (CSCE) and the Western European Union (WEU); with the Netherlands Foreign Minister Hans van den Broek, the current president of the EC Council of Ministers; with Italian Foreign Minister Gianni de Michelis, who had an important role in the EC efforts; and with Budimir Loncar, the Yugoslav Federal Secretary for Foreign Affairs. All welcomed the addition of the United Nations to the organizations dealing with Yugoslavia but all were of the opinion, as Loncar put it, that the focus should be on supporting the EC effort and adding to its credibility. None felt that the deployment of a UN peacekeeping force was desirable while fighting continued. The Italian foreign minister was particularly emphatic on this point, stating that the Italian government viewed the idea of sending peacekeepers to Yugoslavia as "nonsense." There was general agreement that the Conference on Yugoslavia in

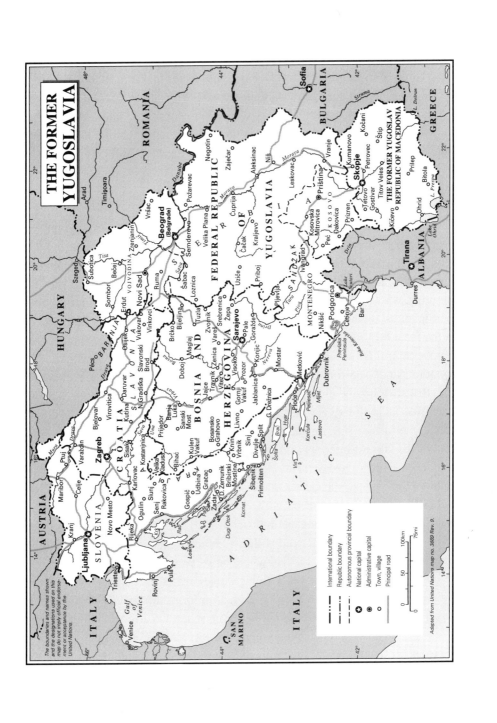

THE FORMER YUGOSLAVIA

The boundaries and names shown and the designations used on this map do not imply official endorsement or acceptance by the United Nations.

Legend:
- International boundary
- Republic boundary
- Autonomous provincial boundary
- ⊛ National capital
- ⊙ Administrative capital
- ○ Town, village
- Principal road

0 50 100km
0 75mi

Adapted from United Nations map no. 3689 Rev. 9.

Countries and regions:
AUSTRIA, HUNGARY, ROMANIA, BULGARIA, ITALY, SAN MARINO, GREECE, ALBANIA

SLOVENIA, CROATIA, BOSNIA AND HERZEGOVINA, FEDERAL REPUBLIC OF YUGOSLAVIA, VOJVODINA, KOSOVO, SANDŽAK, MONTENEGRO, THE FORMER YUGOSLAV REPUBLIC OF MACEDONIA, SLAVONIA, BARANJA

ADRIATIC SEA, Gulf of Venice

Cities and towns:
Ljubljana, Zagreb, Beograd (Belgrade), Sarajevo, Skopje, Podgorica, Cetinje, Tirana, Sofia

Kranj, Maribor, Celje, Ptuj, Varaždin, Novo Mesto, Trieste, Venice, Rovinj, Pula, Rijeka, Ogulin, Senj, Slunj, Karlovac, Sisak, Kostajnica, Virovitica, Bjelovar, Kutina, Daruvar, N.Gradiška, Slavonski Brod, Osijek, Erdut, Vukovar, Vinkovci, Pécs, Drava, Mura, Sava

Novi Sad, Sombor, Subotica, Szeged, Bečej, Zrenjanin, Ruma, Šabac, Loznica, Bijeljina, Brčko, Tuzla, Zvornik, Srebrenica, Žepa, Vareš, Zenica, Travnik, Jajce, Doboj, Maglaj, Dobój, Banja Luka, Prijedor, Sanski Most, Bosanski Grahovo, Kulen Vakuf, Bihać, Una, Vrbas

Zemunik, D. Zemunik, Bribirski Mostine, Knin, Vrlika, Sinj, Split, Brač, Hvar, Korčula, Lastovo, Mljet, Pelješac, Ploče, Metković, Mostar, Dubrovnik, Neretva, Konjic, Goražde, Pale, Visoko, Gornji Vakuf, Prozor, Jablanica, Livno, Vrbnik, Divulje, Šibenik, Primošten, Zadar, Gračac, Udbina, Gospić, Rakovica, Kornat, Dugi Otok, Cres, Lošinj, Krk, Vis

Podgorica, Nikšić, Bar, Durrës, Lake Scutari, Previaka Peninsula, Boka Kotorska, Tara, Piva, Drina, Pljevlja, Priboj, Užice, Velika Plana, Smederevo, Požarevac, Vršac, Timișoara, Arad, Danube, Tisa, Tisza, Morava

Negotin, Zaječar, Aleksinac, Niš, Leskovac, Vranje, Kumanovo, Petrovec, Štip, Kočani, Titov Veles, Gostivar, Tetovo, Prilep, Bitola, Ohrid, Kičevo, Lake Ohrid, L. Prespa, L. Doiran, Strama

Čuprija, Ćuprija, Čačak, Kraljevo, Kosovska Mitrovica, Novi Pazar, Peć, Đakovica, Prizren, Priština

SLAVONIA, FEDERAL REPUBLIC OF YUGOSLAVIA

The Hague could make little progress as long as fighting on the ground continued. Loncar suggested that it would have a useful political and psychological effect if I would make a high-profile trip to Yugoslavia. I responded that I did not wish to seem in any way to be duplicating the work of Lord Carrington.

I had been informed that Vice-Chancellor Genscher favored the early recognition of Croatia and Slovenia. He did not allude to this in our conversation but said that he had been in touch that morning (September 26) with President Franjo Tudjman of Croatia and advised him "very strongly" that no matter what happened the Croatians should stick to their obligations under the latest cease-fire. He had told Tudjman "it would be better for their future."

THE APPOINTMENT OF CYRUS VANCE

The adoption of Resolution 713 succeeded neither in slowing the fighting in Croatia nor in strengthening the effectiveness of the EC efforts to control it. A cease-fire brokered by the EC representative in Yugoslavia in early September was quickly disregarded like the many others before had been, and the EC monitors, who were unarmed and limited in number, were increasingly shown to be helpless, unable even to travel to the areas where fighting was taking place. In the face of this deteriorating situation, the EC issued a public statement on October 6 urging that I consider sending a personal envoy to Yugoslavia. The appointment of a personal envoy had been suggested to me earlier by the French and British Permanent Representatives, so I was not surprised by the EC statement. I had already decided that the best person for this job would be Cyrus Vance, the former U.S. Secretary of State and a Democrat whom I knew as a man of the highest integrity and keen judgment. I knew, too, that he had been associated with Yugoslav developments in the past and was acquainted with many of the country's leaders. On the day following the EC statement, I called and asked him if he would be willing to serve as my Personal Envoy in the context of the mandate given me in Resolution 713. Despite his numerous prior commitments, Mr. Vance agreed within 12 hours to take on what proved to be an extremely onerous mission. He would be very pleased, he told me, to do all he could to help in what was a tragic situation. As a courtesy I called the American Secretary of State, Jim Baker, to inform him of this appointment. Baker said that "from our point of view" Cyrus Vance was an outstanding choice.

Arrangements were quickly made for Mr. Vance to travel to Yugoslavia for what, we agreed, under the terms of Resolution 713, would be essentially a fact-finding mission to continue the talks I had initiated in New York. Before his departure we met with Lord Carrington in New York. In welcoming Carrington, I said that Cyrus Vance had agreed to help him out on the problem of Yugoslavia. However, there would be no duplication of effort. I noted that my mandate was a low-key one and that the EC had asked me to appoint a special envoy. Lord Carrington welcomed these remarks and Vance's appointment. He had already invited Mr. Vance to attend the next meeting of the Conference on Yugoslavia. The only thing we needed to be careful of, he said, was to make sure that neither the press nor anyone else should get the impression we were working at cross purposes.

Cyrus Vance and Lord Carrington were old friends and had long been on a first- name basis. This was fortunate. The relationship between the two could have become extremely awkward since, in the course of events, Vance became an active participant, on behalf of the United Nations, in the negotiations for a Yugoslav settlement and for a cease-fire. Within months it was Vance, with Lord Carrington sitting in almost as an observer, who negotiated a cease-fire in Croatia that ultimately held. But because of the high character and wide experience of both men their relationship was at all times cooperative and mutually supportive. Both men's prior foreign policy achievements had been such that neither needed to fear a loss of credit in the Yugoslav case. Both were generally in agreement in their assessments of the situation, although Carrington was the less patient and the more cynical in his judgment of some of the Yugoslav leaders. While Vance was patient, he also could be stern and did not hesitate to give a strong lecture to the Serbian and Croatian leaders when needed.

During our meeting on October 10, 1991, Lord Carrington gave Cyrus Vance and me a vivid, personal perspective on the Yugoslav state of play. At this point, he was moderately optimistic. While there had been seven failed cease-fires, he thought that the latest one that had been negotiated *sur place* in Zagreb had a chance of holding. More important, there had been a real breakthrough in a meeting in The Hague on October 4 with Presidents Slobodan Milosevic of Serbia and Tudjman of Croatia and General Veliko Kadijevic, the Federal Yugoslav Secretary of Defense.

Milosevic, whom Carrington characterized as an unreconstructed Communist, had affirmed that he was prepared to see an independent Croatia on condition that foolproof, satisfactory arrangements were made for the security of the Serbian minority; by this he said he meant that the Serbs should be independent in their own right. Lord Carrington had made clear to him that there could be no involuntary change in the borders. He had gained the impression that this was Milosevic's "extreme position" and that a way could be found, short of independence, to afford the Serbs in Croatia sufficient protection to satisfy the Serbian President. All three Yugoslav participants had agreed that a general settlement would have three components: a loose association or alliance of sovereign or independent republics; adequate protection of minorities with possibly a special status for certain areas; and no unilateral changes in borders. The three also agreed at the meeting in The Hague that to create a more favorable environment for the negotiations, the Croatian authorities would immediately lift the blockade of Yugoslav army garrisons and other facilities and the Yugoslav People's Army (JNA) would relocate and regroup its units in Croatia with the assistance of EC monitors.

In Lord Carrington's judgment, the Slovenes wanted nothing to do with anyone else in Yugoslavia. They posed no real problem. The Macedonians had declared independence, which Carrington characterized as silly since unless Macedonia was closely associated with Serbia, either the Greeks or the Bulgarians might march in. Bosnia was also worrisome but, on the positive side, its president, Alia Izetbegovic, was not a Communist. The Albanian minority in Kosovo could bring a further serious explosion. Furthermore, the "hijacking" of the Federal presidency on October 3 by Milosevic and other radicals had complicated the mediation process since there was no longer a legitimate or effective Yugoslav government with which to deal.

Lord Carrington thought Vance would be wasting his time in seeing Federal Yugoslav officials as though Yugoslavia still existed. Now made up only of Serbia and Montenegro, Yugoslavia was only a shell. When Vance asked him about the current views of the German foreign minister, Carrington said that Genscher was pushing very hard for recognition of Croatia and Slovenia. From Genscher's point of view, the Croats were "whiter than white." Carrington reported that the coordinator of the Conference on Yugoslavia, Dutch Ambassador Henry Wijnaendts, considered the Croatians as much to blame for the breakdown of the successive cease-fires as the Serbs, a view Carrington obviously shared.

THE FIRST VANCE MISSION

During his first mission to Yugoslavia as my Personal Envoy, from October 11 to October 18, 1991, Cyrus Vance met with all members of the Federal Presidency, the Federal Prime Minister, the Federal Secretary of Defense, the presidents of the republics, the EC monitor mission and representatives of the International Committee of the Red Cross and the UN High Commissioner for Refugees. In his conversations with the various Yugoslav officials, Vance explored their attitudes toward the three political principles that had been agreed on at the meeting in The Hague on October 4. He found that the presidents of all the republics except Milosevic professed general support for the principles. Milosevic viewed the October 4 principles as only one of several options, none of which had been agreed on. He could perhaps live with the three principles option but only if the special status of the Serbs in Croatia was fully assured. He envisaged that the relationship between the Serbs resident in Croatia and the Croatian government would be identical to the relationship between the Republic of Croatia and Yugoslavia.

President Alija Izetbegovic considered the settlement package viable but said that it must be fleshed out quickly since time was short. He asked Vance to urge the Yugoslav People's Army to refrain from active involvement in Bosnia, which Vance did in a subsequent conversation with General Kadijevic. Both Izetbegovic and President Vladimir Gligorov of Macedonia insisted that international recognition of newly independent republics must be extended as a package. Izetbegovic did not want to be left behind in a rump Yugoslavia with Serbia and Montenegro.

Of all the presidents, Tudjman came closest to equivocating on the principle of no unilateral changes in borders. In a tête-à-tête conversation with Vance, Tudjman stated clearly that he had reached a verbal accommodation with Milosevic under which Croatia would receive satisfaction in regard to the areas of Croatia most heavily populated by Serbs (the Krajina and eastern Slavonia), meaning that Serbia would not seek territorial adjustments there. In return, Tudjman would support Milosevic in the latter's efforts to secure satisfaction in regard to the more heavily Serb-populated areas in Bosnia-Herzegovina. Vance told Tudjman in no uncertain terms that this would be contrary to the principle of no involuntary changes of borders. Tudjman said that Bosnia-Herzegovina could be persuaded—that he, in fact, had already discussed it with Izetbegovic. Vance advised the Croatian President that his idea would not fly and that he "should get off this wicket." Many of Vance's other interlocutors warned him that any land grab by Serbia or Croatia would result in a civil war far worse than what was already in progress.

President Kucan of Slovenia said that the three settlement principles were completely acceptable to Slovenia and Slovenia would cooperate toward their realization in the Hague Conference on Yugoslavia. However, Slovenia wanted no institutionalized association with other republics or with any form of federal authority. Slovenia would help the others to find a new association structure, in the understanding that Slovenia would not be part of it. Kucan strongly objected to the idea that international recognition should be accorded to the new republics only as a package.

Vance found the position of the Yugoslav People's Army disturbing. Given the collapse of the federal government, it was operating without the guidance, control or legitimatization of civilian authority. Non-Serb soldiers were leaving and it was increasingly involved in killing Yugoslav citizens. As his mission progressed, Vance suggested to all his senior interlocutors that a civilian authority more broadly based than the rump four-man presidency be installed on an interim basis to coordinate the steps leading to an overall settlement. Vance found that the EC-led monitor mission was spread very thin and was weak in transportation and communications. Neither organizationally nor operationally were the monitors comparable to a UN peacekeeping operation.

While in Europe, Vance also stopped in Bonn, where he gave Vice-Chancellor Genscher a full account of his discussions in Yugoslavia. Genscher expressed surprise to hear that Slovenia was prepared even to participate in discussions of a new form of Yugoslav presidency. In Genscher's view, Yugoslavia "as we know it" was finished. He acknowledged that in the period after World War I Yugoslavia had stuck together out of fear of Germany and rightly so, he said, recalling the Ustasha regime in Croatia that had been established by Nazi Germany during World War II. But a unitary state was no longer viable. Slovenia and Croatia wanted to be independent. "If we are serious about the right of self-determination," Genscher said, "we should find a way to assist these republics in reaching this outcome." The vice-chancellor was fully persuaded that the EC was prepared to impose economic sanctions against Serbia if the Yugoslav People's Army did not withdraw from Croatia.

While the Vance mission was in progress, the parliament of Bosnia-Herzegovina declared the republic's sovereignty, causing the 72 Serb members to walk out.

In giving me his impressions on returning to New York, Vance stressed that time was running out for Yugoslavia. Serbia and Croatia had both adopted a talk-and-fight strategy, seeking to win ground victories that could be used for tactical advantage at the bargaining table. Bosnia was a powder keg. The arms embargo imposed on Yugoslavia by the Security Council was being widely violated. Among the national leaders, Vance found Gligorov and Izetbegovic to be "solid citizens." Milosevic felt under threat and was primarily interested in getting satisfaction on the human rights of Serbs in Croatia. He had far less interest in the Serbs in Bosnia since they did not form integral communities. Tudjman had his territorial agenda that Milosevic, while denying it, probably shared. The Slovenes were nice people but entirely self-centered and confident that the tide was running in their direction. The strongest recommendation that Cyrus Vance brought back was that the United Nations should remain strictly neutral among the Yugoslav parties. He opposed singling out Serbia for blame and punishment as unjustified and counterproductive in terms of an overall settlement.

I provided a comprehensive report on the situation in Yugoslavia to the Security Council (document S/23169) shortly after Vance's return. In it I expressed strong endorsement of the EC efforts and of the principles for an overall settlement agreed on in The Hague. In describing Vance's findings, I indicated that he had reminded both President Tudjman and President Milosevic that they had committed themselves to the principle of no involuntary changes of border. I reinforced the recommendation that Vance had made to Yugoslav leaders that, without prejudice to the central structure that would ultimately emerge, arrangements be put in place that would provide, on an interim basis, some political direction for certain major functions of state, including the military. I also suggested that Council members should respond appropriately to the violations of the arms embargo.

THE GROWING UN ROLE

Under Resolution 713, my mandate was to assist the EC and CSCE in their efforts to promote peace in Yugoslavia in accordance with Chapter VIII of the UN Charter. The UN role was clearly intended to be secondary to that of the regional organizations. Initially I interpreted my mandate as one of fact-finding and of reporting to the Security Council; fact-finding was the intended purpose of Mr. Vance's first mission to Yugoslavia. As the crisis intensified, however, it became obvious that assistance to the regional organizations must entail more than fact-finding. Cyrus Vance did not hesitate to offer advice to Yugoslav leaders that he knew was supportive of Lord Carrington's search for an acceptable settlement plan. This advice carried with it the weight of Vance's position as UN envoy. It was respected by the Yugoslav parties and, I believe, welcomed by the EC as such. As Vance undertook his second mission at the beginning of November, we agreed that his objectives should be seen in this light. He would see in what way the United Nations could be actively helpful and act accordingly.

The Vance mission and the UN role assumed greater importance, moreover, because the EC was having little success in bringing peace and appeared increasingly ineffective as one after another EC-brokered cease-fires collapsed and repeated EC deadlines and threats were ignored. The EC in the fall of 1991 singled out Serbia as the guilty party and threatened to impose sanctions against it if it continued to refuse to accept the wording of a settlement document proposed by Lord Carrington. Carrington publicly criticized the EC for this policy. Vance shared Carrington's views and discreetly intervened with various EC members to adopt a more objective and less threatening stance. The Rome Declaration issued by the EC on November 8 marked a distinct change in EC policy, suggesting that Vance's influence had been felt. The declaration contained both incentives and disincentives for the various Yugoslav parties to resolve their disputes peacefully. It did not apply the EC's economic sanctions selectively. Referring to the prospect of recognition, the declaration stated that it "can only be envisaged in the framework of an overall settlement." In the declaration the EC called on the Security Council to assist in the peace efforts by taking additional measures to enhance the effectiveness of the arms embargo and to impose an oil embargo. These two measures were beyond the EC's ability to effect.

During a conversation in Belgrade on November 6, General Kadijevic informed Vance that Croatian forces had seized a Yugoslav People's Army garrison and that the Croatian Prime Minister had indicated that army units would not be permitted to leave Croatia with their arms and equipment. He was also informed that Croatian armed forces had launched artillery attacks against two towns in Serbia. Vance, in his UN capacity, wrote immediately to President Tudjman urging him to ensure that the Croatian army abide in full by the cease-fire agreement that Tudjman had signed on October 18. The final sentence of Vance's letter read "I have also urged restraint on General Kadijevic as I now do on you."

As cease-fires continued to be broken, the prospects of reaching agreement in The Hague on a peace settlement for Yugoslavia became ever dimmer. When Vance met with Carrington on November 4 just prior to the opening of another session of the conference, Carrington said that he was inclined to tell the EC ministers that he could not continue if a true cease-fire were not in place and honored in Croatia. Vance felt that Carrington's position made sense, but he advised against giving any indication of an intention to break off the conference. He suggested adjournment as the better course and one that he could support. That is what happened.

In the course of this discussion, Vance gave Lord Carrington a nonpaper he had drafted outlining a number of incentives to encourage the parties, not least the Serbs and the Yugoslav People's Army, to be more forthcoming in the negotiations. Vance also offered other suggestions concerning the substance of the negotiations, all of which Lord Carrington welcomed. Thus, through Cyrus Vance's skillful and tactful initiatives, the United Nations gradually became an active participant in the search for a Yugoslav settlement. At the time I was somewhat concerned that the United Nations might become too closely identified with the European Community's undertakings, since I viewed the United Nations' role as different from that of the regional organization. Moreover, I was not eager for the United Nations to become directly identified with what looked more and more like a failed undertaking. I expressed my reservations to Vance but at the same time made clear that I saw no problem in his extending support to Lord Carrington. Vance fully understood this point. He was especially gifted in bringing his influence to bear within the limits of a vaguely defined mandate, without causing offense or jealousy on the part of the other organizations working for peace. All the Yugoslav parties listened to him with respect. This was due first of all to the fact that he was representing the United Nations. But his authority also derived from his evident objectivity and from his stature as an American statesman whose word would not be ignored in Washington. Although these qualities would not suffice to bring peace to Bosnia (in tandem with the EC), they were effective in finally achieving a durable cease-fire in Croatia.

THE MOVE TOWARD UN PEACEKEEPING

The continued fighting in Croatia, which clearly the EC monitors could not control, prompted renewed calls for the deployment of UN peacekeepers. When

Vance visited the Vatican on November 8, 1991, Cardinal Angelo Sodano expressed the Holy See's support for the introduction of a UN peacekeeping force. The Croatian regime signaled its interest in the deployment of UN peacekeepers. The vice-president of the Federal Yugoslav presidency, Milan Vereus, wrote a letter to the President of the Security Council requesting that UN peacekeeping forces be deployed in the Republic of Croatia "in the border belt between the territories inhabited by a majority Serb population and territories in the which the majority population is Croat." Vereus was a Serb and represented the rump presidency, which the United Nations did not recognize as legitimate. The letter was therefore not circulated as an official document in the Council. Nonetheless, copies were provided informally to Council members so they were aware of the request, which, it could be assumed had Serbian backing. A few days later, on November 14, Lord Carrington stated publicly that all parties to the Yugoslav conflict favored a UN peacekeeping operation.

The French Permanent Representative, Jean-Bernard Merimée, had already told me that France favored exploring various models for a peacekeeping operation but that some EC partners were opposed to the idea. I stated my sympathy with the latter attitude. I did not see how peacekeepers could function when there was no peace to keep. Shortly thereafter I learned that the EC members on the Security Council were preparing a draft resolution that would include both a call for the imposition of an oil embargo and for a study of the feasibility of a peacekeeping operation in Croatia. I invited the British Permanent Representative, Sir David Hannay, to discuss this matter with me. I remained opposed to a peacekeeping operation before the fighting stopped but I recognized the growing sentiment in favor of it and thought that sending a feasibility mission that could provide an authoritative assessment of the conditions in which peacekeeping forces eventually might operate would be useful. I suggested to Sir David that EC members should consider whether it was wise to combine in one resolution a call for an oil embargo, which was bound to be controversial, and a call for me to undertake a peacekeeping feasibility study, a matter of obvious urgency. Sir David saw merit in this suggestion but feared that if the Council adopted a resolution exclusively devoted to the possibility of a peacekeeping force for Croatia, the parties in Yugoslavia would assume that its deployment was a foregone conclusion. The leverage that the possibility of a peacekeeping operation could provide in obtaining satisfactory conditions for deployment would be lost. This view was widely shared among EC members, and there was also disagreement in the Council on the proposed oil embargo. As a result, no resolution was adopted. I therefore took the decision on my own authority to send a mission to Yugoslavia to investigate the conditions for a peacekeeping operation in Croatia. Cyrus Vance again headed the mission together with the Under-Secretary-General in charge of peacekeeping, Marrack Goulding.

THE UNITED NATIONS ASSUMES AN OPERATIONAL ROLE

As the number of displaced persons and refugees rapidly mounted in the autumn of 1991, I requested the UN High Commissioner for Refugees, Sadako Ogata, to assume lead responsibility for humanitarian assistance in Yugoslavia. She did this with notable competence, coordinating to good effect the work of the other humanitarian agencies and mounting a large voluntarily funded UN assistance program. From that time on, the United Nations assumed a major operational role in dealing with the Yugoslav disaster. Many of the United Nations' subsequent military actions were determined by this humanitarian responsibility, which at first related to the protection and assistance of refugees but quickly encompassed assistance to the many thousands who were cut off from food and medical supplies by the continuing conflict.

With the arrival in Yugoslavia of the peacekeeping feasibility mission, the United Nations assumed a further direct role in the conflict. If there was to be a peacekeeping operation, it would be purely a United Nations operation. This was understood and supported by all the Yugoslav parties. The Dutch Foreign Minister, Hans van den Broek, raised with Vance the question of the complementarity of the EC Monitor Mission and an eventual UN peacekeeping operation. He suggested that the mission could be helpful in preparing the ground for the UN peacekeepers. Vance responded that once a peacekeeping force was deployed, that group alone should be responsible for peacekeeping activities.

In meetings with President Milosevic, President Tudjman and General Kadijevic, Vance and Goulding explained in detail the characteristics and conditions of peacekeeping operations, emphasizing that such an operation could take place only after a cease-fire was in place and holding; that the consent of all the parties, including irregular forces and authorities, was required; and that the deployment could not violate the principle of no involuntary change of borders. President Milosevic proposed (as he had earlier to Lord Carrington) that the peacekeeping force should be deployed along a line separating the predominantly Serbian areas from the rest of Croatia. It was explained that this green line approach could lead to new borders within Yugoslavia and therefore was not acceptable. Instead, the UN team proposed to carry out what Vance termed an "ink blot" deployment, which would scatter the UN troops and police in the areas of greatest tension.

The requirement that the parties consent to a peacekeeping operation posed a special problem. Who were the parties whose consent should be sought or, indeed, accepted? The rump Federal Presidency was perfectly willing to give its consent, but this could not be accepted as authoritative or legitimate. The Yugoslav People's Army was operating as an independent party in Croatia; therefore, the consent of its head, General Kadijevic, was needed. More complicated was the question of who could speak for Krajina and eastern Slavonia, the Serbian-dominated areas in Croatia. When asked whether the authorities there would comply with his decisions, Milosevic replied that in each case a local authority had been established over which he had no legal control. He thought, however, that his political influence was sufficient to ensure that they would follow his lead.

Following individual exploratory conversations with Tudjman, Kadejevic and Milosevic, Mr. Vance convened a meeting with the three in Geneva to pursue the feasibility of establishing a peacekeeping operation. A principal objective was to obtain the commitment of the three Yugoslavs, who already had stated their support for the deployment of UN peacekeepers, to take those actions required to make the deployment feasible. Lord Carrington attended the meeting but Cyrus Vance, representing the United Nations, occupied the chair.

The meeting proved constructive.[2] The Presidents of Croatia and Serbia and the secretary of defense of the Yugoslav Federation reconfirmed their support for a UN peacekeeping operation and signed a document stating that:

- Croatia would immediately lift its blockade of all JNA barracks and installations in Croatia.
- The JNA would immediately begin the withdrawal from Croatia of the personnel and equipment in those barracks and installations.
- The three would immediately instruct all units under their command to observe an unconditional cease-fire as of the next day, November 24. They would further make sure that any paramilitary or irregular units not formally under their command, control or political influence also observe the cease-fire.
- They would facilitate the delivery of humanitarian assistance.

Lord Carrington undertook to ensure that the International Monitoring Mission did everything within its power and mandate to ensure that the cease-fire held.

The three Yugoslavs had made practically these same commitments before at the instigation of the EC only to abandon them before the ink was dry. This time the commitment was to the United Nations and was the necessary price for the peacekeeping operation that they wanted. Cyrus Vance made very clear during the meeting that the deployment of a UN peacekeeping force could not be envisaged without a lasting and effective cease-fire. The Security Council officially endorsed this position on November 27 in Resolution 721.

The cease-fire was slow in coming despite the firm commitment of the three Yugoslav parties and would not be achieved during my term in office. While JNA personnel were allowed gradually to leave installations that had been blockaded, Croatian elements initiated a new blockade of a JNA technical installation, which was ended only through the skillful intervention of Ambassador Herbert Okun, the Special Advisor to Mr. Vance. Serb artillery again shelled Dubrovnik. I reported to the Security Council on December 11 (document S/23280), that conditions for a peacekeeping operation still did not exist. I stressed that the most urgent need was for the three Yugoslav signatories to comply with the terms of the Geneva Agreement of November 23 and warned again, as I had the previous day in a letter to the Netherlands foreign minister, that selective, uncoordinated recognition of the newly independent republics could hold very serious dangers.

Pressure mounted nonetheless, especially from the West Europeans, to send some form of UN force to Croatia. President Izetbegovic requested the deployment of UN troops to Bosnia as a preventive measure. The representatives of the 12 EC countries met with Cyrus Vance in New York on December 12. They informed him that they hoped to have a resolution adopted by the Security Council within the next days that would invite the Secretary-General to send an advance party to Yugoslavia, including a group of military observers, to carry forward the preparation for the possible deployment of a peacekeeping operation and to assess whether the commitments contained in the Geneva Agreement were being complied with and implemented by the parties, "thus assisting the Secretary-General to reach a decision on whether the conditions for a PKO in Yugoslavia exist."

The British and French Representatives, who carried on an intense campaign for this move, stated that the intention was to fill a vacuum now existing on the ground; if nothing was done, Yugoslav parties could be expected to continue fighting. In a separate conversation with the two ambassadors, Cyrus Vance told them that their idea of an immediate deployment of military observers was not a good one. He could not see what function the military observers could carry out. For them to go into the areas of conflict in the absence of a respected cease-fire would undermine the conditionality that the Secretary-General and the Security Council had imposed on the deployment of a peacekeeping force. Moreover, it would expose the observers to great danger. If, on the other hand, they were to avoid entering the conflict areas, they would become a laughingstock. Vance emphasized very strongly to the two ambassadors that my strategy was to make the deployment of a peacekeeping force dependent on sustained observance of the cease-fire and on assurances, especially from President Milosevic, that irregular forces would cooperate with such a force. Vance stated his conviction that an embryonic deployment as proposed in the EC draft would persuade the Yugoslav parties that full deployment would inevitably follow, requiring no sacrifice on their part. Before meeting with the two ambassadors, Vance had called the U.S. Deputy Secretary of State, Larry Eagleberger, who termed the Anglo-French initiative asinine and said the U.S. mission would be instructed to vote against it.

I felt that it was very important to have the Security Council adopt without further delay a resolution that would reinforce the arms embargo and the views I had expressed in my December 11 report. I therefore suggested a compromise under which the Council would reaffirm that conditions for establishing a peacekeeping operation in Yugoslavia still did not exist. In these circumstances and in the context of providing assistance to the Yugoslav people, I would send a small group of personnel, including military personnel, as part of the continuing mission of my Personal Envoy, to carry forward preparations for possible deployment of a peacekeeping operation. This was accepted and incorporated in Security Council Resolution 724, which was adopted unanimously on December 15 with the strong support of the United States and with reservations in the case of France.

Four days after the adoption of Resolution 724, Ambassador Okun led the preparatory group of 20 military, police and civilian personnel to Yugoslavia. The mission found that while the unblocking of the JNA barracks and facilities in Croatia and the withdrawal of the blockaded JNA units had been successfully completed, the commitment to an unconditional cease-fire remained unimplemented. Significant fighting continued in western Slavonia, and there were sporadic exchanges in eastern Slavonia. Assurances of cooperation from leaders in the areas where UN peacekeeping personnel would be deployed were not yet forthcoming. Accordingly I informed the Security Council on December 27, in my last statement on Yugoslavia to that body, that, in my view, the conditions for establishing a peacekeeping operation there still did not exist.

I stated to the Council my concern not only over the increased fighting in parts of Croatia but also over the heightened tension in Bosnia-Herzegovina "that followed certain decisions taken recently outside the country," by which I was referring to the decision by the EC to extend recognition to Croatia and Slovenia and the other republics that requested it. I told the Council that the heightened tension had led the President of Bosnia-Herzegovina to request the deployment of United Nations peacekeeping forces in his republic. While I understood the deep anxiety that underlay this request, I felt compelled to repeat that such deployment "could effectively be made only with support from all those concerned on the ground—something that at the moment is clearly lacking."

After consulting with my successor, Dr. Boutros-Ghali, I requested Cyrus Vance to undertake a further visit to Yugoslavia to see if the outstanding obstacles to a peacekeeping operation could be removed. In so informing the Security Council, I added that both my successor and I attached great importance to the role of the European Community "and especially to the Conference on Yugoslavia, which is the only forum in which all of the Yugoslav republics have agreed to participate in peacefully seeking a long-term solution to their differences."

RECOGNITION OF THE NEW REPUBLICS

As soon as Croatia and Slovenia declared their independence, Germany began to push for their recognition. I felt that recognition of individual republics before a settlement was reached that would provide for a loose Yugoslav federation along the lines being sought in The Hague Conference on Yugoslavia would be a serious mistake. It would reduce the incentive of Croatia and Slovenia to join in such a settlement and would seriously alienate Serbia and prejudice the likelihood of its cooperation. Further, it would almost certainly increase tension in Bosnia-Herzegovina where the predominantly Moslem government would be faced with a choice between remaining part of a Serbian-dominated rump Yugoslavia or declaring its independence against the will of its Serbian minority. This view was shared by Lord Carrington and by most Security Council members. Cyrus Vance was quickly convinced during his first mission to Yugoslavia that premature recognition of Croatia and Slovenia would be a serious mistake, a view that, as I have already mentioned, he communicated directly to German Foreign Minister Genscher.

In my first report to the Security Council on Yugoslavia, on October 25, 1991, after reporting that my Personal Envoy had found serious differences among the leaders in Yugoslavia on recognition, I warned that "wisdom and prudence are . . . required in connection with the seeking of recognition of unilateral declarations of independence." On November 8, in Rome, the EC issued a ministerial declaration recalling the EC position that "the prospect of recognition of the independence of those Republics wishing it, can only be envisaged in the framework of an overall settlement that includes adequate guarantees for the protection of human rights and the rights of national and ethnic groups." Thus the issue appeared for the moment to have been settled, since Germany concurred in the declaration. This, however, was far from the case. Reports continued to circulate that Germany was pushing for early recognition of Croatia and the other newly independent republics. On December 10 Cyrus Vance, in reporting to me on his just-concluded visit to Yugoslavia, described widely expressed apprehensions about the possibility of premature recognition of some of the Yugoslav republics and the effect that such a move might have on the remaining republics. The leaders of Bosnia and Macedonia were among the many political and military figures who emphasized their strong fears in this regard to Mr. Vance. More than one of his high-level interlocutors described such a development as a time bomb with possibly explosive consequences. This was also my view.

I wrote immediately to Netherlands Foreign Minister van den Broek, the current chair of the EC Council of Ministers, and gave him the gist of Mr. Vance's report. In view of the anxieties evidenced by many Yugoslav leaders, I believed that the 12 EC members were correct in stating in their November 8 declaration that recognition could be envisaged only in the framework of an overall settlement. I then wrote:

> Let me be clear: I am not in any way calling into question the principle of self-determination. . . . However, I am deeply worried that any early, selective recognition could widen the present conflict and fuel an explosive situation especially in Bosnia-Herzegovina and Macedonia; indeed, serious consequences could ensue for the entire Balkan region.

I requested the foreign minister to bring my concerns to the attention of his partners among the 12.

Two days later, I received an extraordinary letter from Foreign Minister Genscher. With reference to my letter to Minister van den Broek, Herr Genscher wrote that he would like to express to me his deep concern that:

> my statements—and their publication—were apt to encourage those elements in Yugoslavia which all along have vehemently been resisting the successful conclusion of the peace process. As ascertained by the EC and the monitors, the Serbian leadership together with the Yugoslav National Army bear the main responsibility for the non-compliance in Croatia with the cease-fire and for the fact that the conference on Yugoslavia in The Hague has been stalemated for several weeks. . . . To refuse recognition to those republics which desire their independence must lead to a further escalation of the use of force by the National Army which would construe it as a validation of its policy of conquest.

The most surprising aspect of this letter was Genscher's disregard for the EC declaration on recognition in which he had concurred. It was clear that he would continue to push for recognition of Croatia and Slovenia no matter how much opposition this might evoke from the other republics.

In my reply, which was more acerbic than is my usual wont, I recalled that I had at no point suggested that recognition of particular Yugoslav republics should be denied or withheld indefinitely. My concern related to the prospect of early, selective and uncoordinated recognition. My letter continued:

> I cannot but note the omission from your letter of any reference to the common position adopted by you and your colleagues at the Special Ministerial European Political Cooperation Meeting held at Rome on 8 November 1991 . . .
>
> Furthermore, you will no doubt be aware of the letter sent by Lord Carrington on 2 December to Minister van den Broek in which Lord Carrington stated that early and selective recognition "would undoubtedly lead to the break-up of the

conference."

I trust you will have learned of the deep concern that has been expressed by the Presidents of Bosnia-Hercegovina and Macedonia, as well as by many others, that early selective recognitions could result in a widening of the present conflict to those sensitive areas. Such a development . . . would seriously undermine my own efforts and those of my Personal Envoy to secure conditions necessary for the deployment of a peace-keeping operation in Yugoslavia.

I am confident that you will understand that in view of my responsibilities under the Charter, I am duty bound to express such concerns when they are also my own.

In its Resolution 724 the Security Council, on December 15, in approving my December 11 report, also urged "all States and parties to refrain from any action which might contribute to increasing tension, to inhibiting the establishment of an effective cease-fire and to impeding or delaying a peaceful and negotiated outcome to the conflict in Yugoslavia." Thus the Security Council, with the affirmative votes of the EC Council members, also warned, if obliquely, against recognition of Croatia and Slovenia at that time.

Notwithstanding these widespread warnings, Germany had its way. In a remarkable shift of position, for which no explanation was given, the European Community on December 16 issued a new declaration stating that its members agreed to recognize on January 15, 1992, the independence of all Yugoslav republics that requested it, subject only to the acceptance of certain conditions pertaining mainly to respect for human rights, the inviolability of borders, acceptance of relevant disarmament commitments and continued support for the Conference on Yugoslavia and the provisions so far agreed to there.[3] It was clear that Croatia and Slovenia would accept these conditions, at least on paper. In addition to Croatia and Slovenia, Macedonia and Bosnia-Herzegovina requested recognition. The die was cast.

The Netherlands foreign minister sent me the text of the EC declaration under a letter stating that the 12 had carefully weighed my warnings concerning premature recognition. He suggested that my concern about early recognition was taken care of by the provision that recognition would not take place until January 15.

TOWARD THE BOSNIAN DISASTER

The EC decision to grant recognition to those Yugoslav republics requesting it was certainly a contributing factor in the subsequent civil war in Bosnia. President Izetbegovic told Ambassador Okun immediately after the declaration was issued that Bosnia-Herzegovina, unlike Slovenia, had always wished to remain in a greater Yugoslav community. The Bosnian parliament had already voted for independence, but if independence could have been realized after agreement had been reached in The Hague on continuation of Yugoslavia as a loose federation, the disastrous ethnic conflict might have been avoided. But the decision to recognize, coming when it did, undermined the conference. Having gained the promise of early recognition, Croatia no longer had an interest in the kind of agreement that had been sought there. For his part, President Milosevic contended that the EC had disqualified itself as sponsor of the Conference on Yugoslavia, which could only be resumed under the auspices of the United Nations. He insisted that the EC was only a regional organization "which had no authority to abolish another country."

Premature recognition was, of course, only one factor in the outbreak of war in Bosnia. It may be that once they saw the initial success of the Croatian Serbs in gaining control of Serb-populated areas, with no intervention by the United Nations, sooner or later the Bosnian Serbs would have done likewise. This raises the question of whether the United Nations should have moved sooner to deploy a peacekeeping force in Croatia. It was my strongly held position, one shared by all my senior advisors on Yugoslavia, that a peacekeeping operation should not be undertaken until a cease-fire was solidly in place and fighting had stopped. I am still convinced that it would have been a folly—somewhat similar to what subsequently happened in Bosnia—to send UN forces with the standard peacekeeping limitation on the use of arms into Croatia while fighting was still going on. If, at an early stage, a substantial UN or UN-authorized force had been deployed with a mandate to use such arms as necessary to *enforce* an EC-brokered cease-fire, and the operation was successful, theoretically it might have served to prevent the subsequent conflict in Bosnia. I do not believe that the Security Council could have been persuaded to authorize such action at the time, nor would I have recommended it, having been then, as I remain today, doubtful of the wisdom of using peacekeeping troops, whether UN or UN-authorized, for enforcement purposes in internal conflicts.

PART

———————

EPILOGUE

———————

SIX

EIGHTEEN

PERSPECTIVES
ON THE FUTURE

IN THE SIX YEARS SINCE I LEFT the post of Secretary-General it has become ever clearer that societal tensions such as those that lie at the roots of current conflict will bring continuing violence unless remedial measures are taken. The tensions may stem from infringement of human rights, from ethnic hostility, from economic inequity or from a host of other causes. But in most cases the cure will lie in economic development, in the strengthening of democratic institutions of government, in the guarantee of freedom within the rule of law. These are the objectives on which the United Nations must concentrate if it is to maintain peace in the next century. I am even more persuaded now than I was six years ago that the focus of UN attention will need to be on the social and economic fields. I would not suggest that the need for mediation and good offices, for peacekeeping and peace enforcement will disappear; but it should decline as economic and social conditions improve in all geographic regions and as there is a concomitant strengthening of democratic institutions. I would hope that it will be possible in the future to see peacekeeping more as a tool for building peace than as a means of restricting conflict.

In concentrating on the economic and social areas, the United Nations will continue to face two major problems that affect both development and democratization. The first is the likely inadequacy of available resources; the second is the tension between respect for sovereignty and intervention for political, humanitarian or development purposes. A key element in managing both problems—neither is likely to be entirely resolved—is increased involvement of civil society.

The provision from governments of significantly increased resources as needed for economic and social development, including the restoration of economic and political stability in states where governance has failed, will depend heavily on public attitudes. Bringing wide public understanding of the distribution of resources required to discourage social violence poses a major challenge to the leadership of the United Nations and to national elites. The best argument—though whether it will be sufficient is open to doubt—is that there is in the future a real possibility of a world at peace; that nations, while preserving their cultural identity, can, at a globally manageable cost, be brought together in the mutually beneficial enhancement of human well-being. The alternative could be a multiplication of present ills, of civil wars, vast migratory flows, explosive disparities in conditions of life, all of which ultimately can jeopardize the security and prosperity of the wealthy countries as well as the poor.

From my first days as Secretary-General, I stressed the importance of preventative diplomacy in the conviction that this is the best and cheapest way to enhance peace. I took steps to improve the availability of information and analysis as the first requirement in preventing or resolving conflict. Given the importance that social and economic factors have assumed in the maintenance of peace, I believe it would be more accurate to speak of "preventative measures." When warning is received of dangerous tensions within a society, whether it stems from violation of human rights, from economic despair, from a disintegration of governance or from a combination of the three, the United Nations must be in a position to take timely countermeasures.

Countermeasures inevitably entail the expenditure of resources. The resources may be needed in the form of readily available military and civilian personnel to be used in the restoration of essential order, to encourage conciliation between hostile elements within a society, to strengthen the institutions of free government or, if conflict cannot be prevented, to enforce compliance with any settlement agreed to by the parties. Resources also will be needed for the economic development that is an essential antidote to the social ills and a requisite for the strengthening of the democratization process.

The private sector is far and away the largest source of investment capital. This "civil society asset" needs to be seen along with bilateral and multilateral economic assistance as a major "preventative measure" to be factored into UN development planning. This does not imply UN control over private investment flows. But just as civic society is increasingly seen as a necessary participant with intergovernmental organizations in the democratization process, so too should the private sector be given a place at the planning tables and in policy councils as an integral part of the peace-building process.

To gain maximum advantage from available resources, all of my experience indicates that in the future the central UN organization—either the Secretary-General or one of the other principal organs—must have greater coordinating authority. The financial institutions, which have the greatest resources to contribute toward this common goal, must be brought into a closer consultative relationship with the United Nations.

It has become ever more evident since I first faced the problem in Central America that the United Nations will repeatedly confront the question of when and for what purpose UN intervention in the internal affairs of states is justified. It is already clear that the involvement of nongovernmental organizations can alleviate this problem. Their activities, whether in support of democratic institutions or in response to humanitarian emergencies, frequently involve them in the domestic concerns of a state. Because of their private—or civil—status, the activities of these organizations often are seen as posing less of a threat to national sovereignty than activities of intergovernmental organizations. Nongovernmental organizations also are able to invest substantial resources in various forms of humanitarian assistance and social development. The United Nations will need in the future to open its doors even wider to a working relationship with responsible nongovernmental organizations that are engaged in complementary activities.

Another partial response to the need to clarify the basis of UN intervention can, I believe, be found in the further enhancement of the Universal Declaration of Human Rights as binding international law. This could be accomplished by incorporating the declaration directly into the United Nations Charter with appropriate provision for enforcement. A clear basis thus would be provided for the UN Security Council to bring a case of massive human rights abuse before the proposed International Criminal Court, which should be given the mandate to hear such cases and impose sentences. Were the Charter so amended, the potential consequences for any perpetrator of punishable acts would be known and serve as a deterrent.

While something of a skeptic by nature (and perhaps from my years in the United Nations), I am persuaded that there is a greater opportunity to meet the reasonable expectations of the global population in the next century than ever before in history. As Secretary-General I repeatedly said I could afford to be neither optimistic nor pessimistic. Then I had in mind specific crises that we were seeking to resolve. Now I have in mind the broad direction in which the world is moving, and I am prepared to be optimistic. I believe that within a framework of enduring cultural diversity, a core ethic is taking global root that reflects the principles of the UN Charter.

As chair for the last three years of the joint UN/UNESCO World Commission on Culture and Development, I have seen little sign of a forthcoming clash of civilizations. To the contrary, I have found ever-widening acceptance of freedom as the ideology of choice, an ideology that, if called democracy, is admittedly sometimes rejected as Western-imposed. But by far the large majority of the global population wishes to live in freedom and economic security under a representative government that respects the rule of law and will honor cultural diversity. This concept, this emerging global ethic, should be seen as neither of the North or the South nor of the East or the West but as a common human heritage. With strong but sensitive leadership from the United Nations, this growing commonality can be strengthened and can provide the basis in the next millennium of a global society at peace.

It is surely natural that I should add when speaking of leadership my perspective on the role of the Secretary-General. The Secretary-General of the United Nations will need to be a persuasive proponent of these ideals around which the people of the world can unite. He or she will need to be a principal force in mobilizing the support of governments and people that will be required to translate these ideals into reality. The portrait I would paint would be of a person (all too evidently not myself) having the following characteristics:

- A statesperson capable of representing the moral authority of the UN Charter.
- A person open to dialogue with all parties and with a readiness to listen.
- A gifted communicator who can inspire a global audience.
- A skillful and experienced manager.
- An objective negotiator able to maintain the confidence of all parties to a dispute.
- A leader and moderator able and willing to delegate responsibility.
- A person of patience willing to endure in good grace the foibles of persons of greater or lesser power in the world.
- An observer and analyst able to advise governments and civic society on the state of the world and what to do about it.

I would not suggest that a person having all of these qualities can be easily found, but the search should be undertaken and in good time. The new century will deserve nothing less. Should the search—if undertaken—discover no one with quite all of these qualifications, there should be consolation in knowing that past secretaries-general who were deficient in one or more of these qualities nonetheless accomplished quite a bit for the good of the world. This, in my case, was the purpose of undertaking, even while recognizing my inadequacies, a pilgrimage for peace.

NOTES

Chapter 3

1. The three responses are quoted in UN document S/15178, 7 June 1982.
2. UN document S/15408, 20 September 1982.
3. Letter dated 23 December 1983 from Yehuda Z. Blum, Permanent Representative of Israel to the United Nations.
4. One of the innumerable cease-fires--this one more or less imposed by Syria and Saudi Arabia—was in effect. It was extremely fragile and clearly doomed to failure unless monitored by an outside force.
5. UN document S/20789.
6. UN document S/20790.

Chapter 4

1. The text of President Reagan's address is in the *New York Times* 2 September, 1982.
2. Unpublished letter of 2 September, 1982 from George P. Shultz to Javier Pérez de Cuéllar.
3. The text is in George Shultz, *Turmoil and Triumph* (New York: Scribners, 1993), pp. 1028-1029.
4. Edouard Brunner, the Swiss ambassador to Washington, had been appointed in March 1991 to succeed Gunnar Jarring as Special Representative to the Middle East under the terms of Security Council Resolution 242.

Chapter 5

1. At the time of the installation of the second Begin government in August 1981, the Israeli parliament approved foreign policy guidelines that provided that at the end of the transition period set down in the Camp David Accords, Israel "will present its claim, and act to realize its right of sovereignty over Judea, Samaria and the Gaza district."
2. See, for example, General Assembly resolution 38/79D, 15 December 1983.
3. "Declaration of Independence" issued by the 19th Extraordinary Session of the Palestine National Council, Algiers, 12-15 November 1988.
4. See George Shultz, *Turmoil and Triumph,* (New York: Scribners, 1993), pp. 1037-1045.
5. S/19443, 21 January 1988.
6. Israel rejects the applicability of the Fourth Geneva Convention to the occupied territories on the ground that they were not the legal territory of any other country prior to the assumption of Israeli control. This position has not been accepted either by the

International Committee of the Red Cross or the High Contracting Parties to the Fourth Geneva Convention.

7.   Press bulletin of the State of Israel dated 14 October 1990.

8.   Quoted in S/21919.

9.   Ibid.

Chapter 7

1.   Letter no. 396 of 4 October 1982 addressed to Secretary-General Pérez de Cuéllar by Said Rajaie Khorassani, the Permanent Representative of Iran.

2.   Saddam Hussein, prior to invading Iran, abrogated the Algiers Agreement, which he had negotiated with the Shah of Iran in 1975. This agreement constituted a bargain between the two countries according to which Iraq accepted the thalweg in the Shatt-al-Arab rather than, as before, the high-water mark on the Iranian side, as the border between Iran and Iraq; the Shah committed himself to end support of the Kurds in Iraq who were in rebellion against the Iraqi regime. This agreement was incorporated in a formal treaty signed in Baghdad on June 13, 1975, settling all disputes relating to the frontiers between the two countries. Iran continued to occupy three small pieces of territory that were supposed to be returned to Iraq, a circumstance that Saddam Hussein cited to justify his contention that Iran was guilty of starting the war.

3.   UN document S/15834, 20 June 1983.

4.   During a meeting with U.S. Secretary of State Shultz in Washington on January 14, 1983, I described the deep concern that the president and foreign minister of Algeria had expressed to me about the continuing supply of arms to Iran by Israel, which, they felt, could only prolong the war. The mayor of Paris, Jacques Chirac, had expressed the same concern. Secretary Shultz recalled seeing a statement by Ariel Sharon that Israel had sold $390 million worth of arms to Iran. He doubted that Chirac's information on the continuation of the sales was correct, but he would check. Ambassador Jeane Kirkpatrick, who was present, added that Shamir had stated that Israeli aid to Iran had ended. She felt that Chirac's information was "probably wrong." However, it turned out that Mr. Shultz and Mrs. Kirkpatrick were wrong.

5.   UN document S/16213, 12 December 1983.

6.   UN documents A/38/560, S/16120, 1 November 1983.

7.   UN document S/16337, 10 February 1984.

8.   The responses of Iran and Iraq are contained in UN documents S/16340, 14 February 1984, S/16342, 15 February 1984, S/16352, 17 February 1984, and S/16354, 19 February 1984.

9.   UN documents S/16610 and S/16611, 11 June 1984.

10. Letter transmitted under a letter (no. 086) of 5 March 1985 from Iranian Permanent Representative Said Rajaie-Khorassani on file in UN archives.

11. The texts are in UN document S/18480, 26 November 1985.

12. UN press release SG/SM/3956, 13 January 1987.

13. UN press release SG/SM/3961, 26 January 1987.

14. White House press release, 30 June, 1987.

15. *New York Times,* 6 July, 1987.

16. George Shultz, *Turmoil and Triumph,* (New York: Scribners, 1993), p. 932.

17. For a full account of the Security Council meeting see UN document S/pv.2750, 20 July 1987.
18. UN document S/19045, 14 August 1987.
19. Press release no. 6, 29 July l987, of the Permanent Mission of Iran to the United Nations in Geneva.
20. UN document S/20020, 18 July 1988.
21. The saying originated with Count Galeazzo Ciano. See Galeazzo Ciano, *The Ciano Diaries 1939-1943* (New York: Doubleday, 1946).
22. UN document S/20039, 20 July 1988.
23. UN document S/20092, 6 August 1988.
24. Text is in UN press release SC/5042, 28 September 1988.
25. See UN document S/22263, 26 February 1991, for details on the ending of the UNIIMOG mandate.
26. UN document S/23273.

Chapter 8

1. Letter dated March 26, 1987, from Abdul Wakil, minister of foreign affairs of the Democratic Republic of Afghanistan, to Javier Pérez de Cuéllar, United Nations Secretary-General. UN archives.
2. Statement by Najibullah, President of the Republic of Afghanistan, 8 February 1988. UN archives.
3. Letter dated 25 March 1988, from S. Shah Nawaz, Permanent Representative of Pakistan to the United Nations, to Javier Pérez de Cuéllar, United Nations Secretary-General, p. 3. UN archives.
4. Letter dated 13 April 1988; to Secretary-General Javier Pérez de Cuéllar from Mohammad Ja'afar Mahallati, Acting Permanent Representative of the Islamic Republic of Iran. UN archives.
5. See letter dated 14 April 1988 from the Secretary-General addressed to the President of the Security Council, United Nations Document S/19834; letter dated 22 April 1988 from the Secretary-General addressed to the President of the Security Council, United Nations Document S/19835; and letter dated 25 April 1988 from the President of the Security Council addressed to the Secretary-General, United Nations Document S/19836.
6. Text is in "The Geneva Accords, Agreements on the settlement of the Situation Related to Afghanistan" (UNDPI publication 935, 1988), pp. 5-6.
7. United Nations Document A/43/PV.72, p. 21.
8. Nonpaper dated 15 March 1989 handed to the Secretary-General on 16 March 1989 by the Soviet Union. UN archives.
9. Letter from Acting Secretary of State of the United States, Lawrence S. Eagleburger, to the Secretary-General, dated 28 August 1990. UN archives.
10. United Nations Document SG/Conf.3/1, 10 June 1988 and United Nations Press Release SG/SM/4142, 10 June 1988.
11. United Nations Document SG/Conf.3/2, 26 September 1988, p. 4.
12. United Nations Document A/44/661-S/20911, p. 5, para. 19.
13. Letter dated 25 January 1989 from Sadruddin Aga Khan to the Secretary-General.
14. UN archives.

Chapter 10

1. UN document S/PV.2963, 29 November 1990.

Chapter 11

1. Unpublished letter from R. F. Botha to Javier Pérez de Cuéllar dated 12 January 1982. UN archives.
2. Security Council document S/15943, 29 August 1983.
3. Letter of 15 December 1983 from R. F. Botha to Javier Pérez de Cuéllar transmitted under a letter of the same date from Kurt von Schirnding. UN archives.
4. A full account of the plan may be found in the Report of the Secretary-General to the Security Council of January 23, 1989, document S/20412.
5. The Security Council imposed an embargo on the shipment of military equipment to South Africa. Economic sanctions were imposed by various countries, including the United States outside the framework of the United Nations.

Chapter 12

1. A full description of the UNAVEM verification mission may be found in the Report of the Secretary-General on the United Nations Angola Verification Mission (UNAVEM II), document S/23191, 31 October 1991.

Chapter 13

1. Interview at the Press Club of Radio France Internationale, November 25, 1985.

Chapter 14

1. Interview with Nicanor Costa Mendez, October 27, 1990, in UN Oral History Collection, Sterling Memorial Library, Yale University.

Chapter 15

1. The text of the Arias Plan was transmitted to the Secretary-General under a letter dated 17 February 1987 from the Permanent Representative of Costa Rica, Carlos José Gutiérrez.
2. The full text of the request is in Security Council document S/20791.
3. The text is in UN document A/44/872.
4. The FMLN, the insurgent movement in El Salvador, was opposed to the ONUCA operation because it refused to recognize the Esquipulas agreements.
5. UN documents A/44/872 and S/21019, 1989.
6. The text is in *El Salvador Agreements: The Path to Peace,* United Nations (July 1992).
7. A full account of ONUVEH's activities may be found in UN document A/45/870/add.1, 22 February 1991.

8. Letter of March 4, 1991 from James A. Baker, III, to Dr. Javier Pérez de Cuéllar.

Chapter 16

1. Since the Vietnamese-installed government of Cambodia in Phnom Penh was not recognized by the United Nations, UN Representatives, other than those concerned strictly with humanitarian relief, did not visit Cambodia during this period. Contacts with members of the government of Democratic Cambodia, including Prince Sihanouk, were held in locations outside Cambodia.
2. Congressman Solarz introduced a resolution in the House of Representatives in January 1990 in which major UN responsibility for the interim administration of Cambodia was recommended as the last, best chance to achieve a solution of the Cambodian problem.
3. Representatives from Australia, Canada, Indonesia and Japan also were sometimes invited to join informal meetings of the Five.
4. The text of the framework may be found in UN document A/45/472, S/21689, 31 August 1990.
5. The full texts are contained in "Agreements on a Comprehensive Settlement of the Cambodia Conflict, Paris 23 October 1991," published by the UN Department of Public Information (DPI/1180-92077), January 1992-10M.

Chapter 17

1. By this time, Macedonia had also voted for independence but it had not yet been declared.
2. A fuller description of the meeting is contained in UN document S/23239 of 24 November 1991.
3. Text is in UN document A/46/805, 18 December 1991.

INDEX